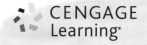
CENGAGE
Learning®

Australia • Brazil • Mexico • Singapore •
United Kingdom • United States

E. Bruce Goldstein
University of Pittsburgh
University of Arizona

Cognitive Psychology

Connecting Mind, Research, and
Everyday Experience

4th Edition

CENGAGE Learning

Cognitive Psychology: Connecting Mind, Research, and Everyday Experience, 4th Edition
E. Bruce Goldstein

Product Director: Jon-David Hague

Product Manager: Joann Kozyrev

Content Developer: Shannon LeMay-Finn

Product Assistant: Nicole Richards

Media Developer: Mary Noel

Marketing Manager: Melissa Larmon

Content Project Manager: Charlene M. Carpentier

Content Development Services Manager:
 Jeremy Judson

Content Development Services Coordinator:
 Joshua Taylor

Art Director: Jennifer Wahi

Manufacturing Planner: Karen Hunt

Production Service: Scratchgravel Publishing
 Services

Photo Researcher: Veerabhagu Nagarajan

Text Researcher: Manjula Subramanian

Copy Editor: Margaret C. Tropp

Art Editor: Lisa Torri, Precision Graphics

Illustrator: Precision Graphics

Cover/Text Designer: Jeff Bane

Cover Image: Peter Rutherhagen/Getty Images

Compositor: Integra Software Services Pvt. Ltd.

For product information and technology assistance, contact us at
Cengage Learning Customer & Sales Support, 1-800-354-9706.
For permission to use material from this text or product,
submit all requests online at **www.cengage.com/permissions.**
Further permissions questions can be e-mailed to
permissionrequest@cengage.com.

Library of Congress Control Number: 2014934186

Student Edition:
ISBN-13: 978-1-285-76388-0
ISBN-10: 1-285-76388-2

Cengage Learning
200 First Stamford Place, 4th Floor
Stamford, CT 06902
USA

Cengage Learning is a leading provider of customized learning solutions with office locations around the globe, including Singapore, the United Kingdom, Australia, Mexico, Brazil, and Japan. Locate your local office at **www.cengage.com/global**.

Cengage Learning products are represented in Canada by Nelson Education, Ltd.

To learn more about Cengage Learning Solutions, visit **www.cengage.com**.

Purchase any of our products at your local college store or at our preferred online store **www.cengagebrain.com**.

Printed in Canada
4 5 6 7 18 17 16 15

To Barbara

About the Author

E. BRUCE GOLDSTEIN is Associate Professor Emeritus of Psychology at the University of Pittsburgh and Adjunct Professor of Psychology at the University of Arizona. He has received the Chancellor's Distinguished Teaching Award from the University of Pittsburgh for his classroom teaching and textbook writing. He received his bachelor's degree in chemical engineering from Tufts University and his PhD in experimental psychology from Brown University. He was a postdoctoral fellow in the Biology Department at Harvard University before joining the faculty at the University of Pittsburgh. Bruce has published papers on a wide variety of topics, including retinal and cortical physiology, visual attention, and the perception of pictures. He is the author of *Sensation and Perception*, 9th edition (Wadsworth/Cengage, 2014) and is the editor of the *Blackwell Handbook of Perception* (Blackwell, 2001) and the two-volume *Sage Encyclopedia of Perception* (Sage, 2010).

Brief Contents

Contents

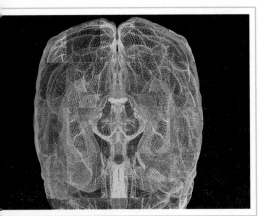

CHAPTER 3

CHAPTER 4

CHAPTER 8

CHAPTER 9

CHAPTER 10

CHAPTER 13

CogLab Experiments

Numbers in parentheses refer to the experiment numbers in CogLab 5.0.

The first experiments in each chapter are "primary experiments." These experiments are directly or closely related to discussion in the text.

Asterisks (*) indicate "related experiments." These experiments are relevant to the topic of the chapter but are not directly related to the discussion in the text.

CHAPTER 1

Simple Detection (2) A simple reaction time task that measures how fast you react to the appearance of a dot.

CHAPTER 2

Brain Asymmetry (15)* How speed of processing for shapes and words may be different in the left and right hemispheres.

CHAPTER 3

Apparent Motion (3) Determining how fast two dots have to be flashed, one after the other, to achieve an illusion of movement.

Statistical Learning (47) How learning can occur in response to exposure to sequences of forms.

Signal Detection (1)* Collecting data that demonstrate the principle behind the theory of signal detection, which explains the processes behind detecting hard-to-detect stimuli.

Garner Interference: Integral Dimensions (4)* Making light/dark judgments for a square. A one-dimensional task.

Garner Interference: Separable Dimensions (5)* Making light/dark judgments for squares of different sizes. A second dimension is added.

Müller-Lyer Illusion (6)* Measuring the size of a visual illusion.

Blind Spot (14)* Mapping the blind spot in your visual field that is caused by the fact that there are no receptors where the optic nerve leaves the eye.

Metacontrast Masking (16)* How presentation of a masking stimulus can impair perception of another stimulus.

Categorical Perception: Discrimination (39)* Demonstration of categorical perception based on the ability to discriminate between sounds.

Categorical Perception: Identification (40)* Demonstration of categorical perception based on the identification of different sound categories.

CHAPTER 4

Visual Search (7) Feature search experiment. Searching for a green circle among blue lines, with different numbers of blue lines.

Change Detection (9) A task involving detecting changes in alternating scenes.

Inhibition of Return (10) How presentation of a target away from fixation can cause a slowing of responding.

Spatial Cueing (12) How cueing attention affects reaction time to the cued area. Evidence for the spotlight model of attention.

Stroop Effect (13) How reaction time to naming font colors is affected by the presence of conflicting information from words.

Attentional Blink (8)* Testing your ability to detect stimuli that are presented in rapid succession.

Simon Effect (11)* How speed and accuracy of responding is affected by the location of the response to a stimulus.

Von Restorff Effect (32)* How the distinctiveness of a stimulus can influence memory.

CHAPTER 5

Partial Report (18) The partial report condition of Sperling's iconic memory experiment.

Brown-Peterson Task (20) How memory for trigrams fades.

Irrelevant Speech Effect (23) How recall for items on a list is affected by the presence of irrelevant speech.

Memory Span (24) Measuring memory span for numbers, letters, and words.

Operation Span (25) Measuring the operation-word span, a measure of working memory.

Phonological Similarity Effect (26) How recall for items on a list is affected by how similar the items sound.

Word Length Effect (27) Measurement of the word length effect.

Modality Effect (17)* How memory for the last one or two items in a list depends on whether the list is heard or read.

Position Error (21)* Memory errors when trying to remember the order of a series of letters.

Sternberg Search (22)* A method to determine how information is retrieved from short-term memory.

Von Restorff Effect (32)* How the distinctiveness of a stimulus can influence memory.

Neighborhood Size Effect (42)* How recall in a short-term memory task is affected by the size of a word's "neighborhood" (how many words can be created by changing a letter or phoneme).

CHAPTER 6

Serial Position (31) How memory for a list depends on an item's position on the list.

Remember-Know (36) Distinguishing between remembered items in which there is memory for learning the item and items that just seem familiar.

Implicit Learning (45) How we can learn something without being aware of the learning.

Suffix Effect (19)* How adding an irrelevant item to the end of a list affects recall for the final items on a list in a serial position experiment.

CHAPTER 7

Encoding Specificity (28) How memory is affected by conditions at both encoding and retrieval, and the relation between them

Levels of Processing (29) How memory is influenced by depth of processing.

Production Effect (30)* How memory depends on whether words are read out loud or silently.

Von Restorff Effect (32)* How the distinctiveness of a stimulus can influence memory.

CHAPTER 8

False Memory (33) How memory for words on a list sometimes occurs for words that were not presented.

Forgot It All Along (34) How it is possible to remember something and also have the experience of having previously forgotten it.

Memory Judgment (35) A test of how accurate people are at predicting their memory performance.

CHAPTER 9

Lexical Decision (41) Demonstration of the lexical decision task, which has been used to provide evidence for the concept of spreading activation.

Prototypes (46) A method for studying the effect of concepts on responding.

Absolute Identification (44)* Remembering levels that have been associated with a stimulus.

CHAPTER 10

Link Word (37) A demonstration of how imagery can be used to help learn foreign vocabulary.

Mental Rotation (38) How a stimulus can be rotated in the mind to determine whether its shape matches another stimulus.

CHAPTER 11

Lexical Decision (41) Demonstration of the lexical decision task.

Word Superiority (43) Comparing speed of identifying a letter when the letter is isolated or in a word.

Categorical Perception: Discrimination (39)* Demonstration of categorical perception based on the ability to discriminate between sounds.

Categorical Perception: Identification (40)* Demonstration of categorical perception based on the identification of different sound categories.

Neighborhood Size Effect (42)* How recall in a short-term memory task is affected by the size of a word's "neighborhood" (how many words can be created by changing a letter or phoneme).

CHAPTER 13

Decision Making (48) How decisions can be affected by the context within which the decision is made.

Risky Decisions (50) How decision making is influenced by framing effects.

Typical Reasoning (51) How the representativeness heuristic can lead to errors of judgment.

Wason Selection (52) Two versions of the Wason four-card problem.

Monty Hall (49)* A simulation of the Monty Hall three-door problem, which involves an understanding of probability.

Demonstrations

Methods

Preface to Instructors

The Evolution of a Cognitive Psychology Textbook

This book is the culmination of a process that began in 2002, when I decided to write the first edition. From a survey of more than 500 instructors and my conversations with colleagues, it became apparent that many teachers were looking for a text that not only covers the field of cognitive psychology but is also accessible to students. From my teaching of cognitive psychology, it also became apparent that many students perceive cognitive psychology as being abstract, too theoretical, and not connected to everyday experience. With this information in hand, I set out to write a book that would tell the story of cognitive psychology in a concrete way that would help students appreciate the connections between empirical research, the principles of cognitive psychology, and everyday experience.

I did a number of things to achieve this result. I started by including numerous **real-life examples** in each chapter, and **neuropsychological case studies** where appropriate. To provide students with firsthand experience with the phenomena of cognitive psychology, I included more than 40 **Demonstrations**—easy-to-do mini-experiments that were contained within the narrative of the text—as well as 20 additional suggestions of things to try, throughout the chapters. The Demonstrations in this edition are listed on page xix.

One thing I avoided was simply presenting the results of experiments. Instead, whenever possible, I described **how experiments were designed** and what the subjects were doing, so students would understand how results were obtained. In addition, most of these descriptions were supported by illustrations such as pictures of stimuli, diagrams of the experimental design, or graphs of the results.

Students with instructors who adopted CogLab also received access to more than 45 online **CogLab experiments** (now more than 50) that they could run themselves and then compare their data to the class average and to the results of the original experiments from the literature.

The first edition (2005) therefore combined many elements designed to achieve the goal of covering the basic principles of cognitive psychology in a way that students would find interesting and easy to understand. My goal was for students to come away feeling excited about the field of cognitive psychology.

The acceptance of the first edition was gratifying, but one thing I've learned from years of teaching and textbook writing is that there are always explanations that can be clarified, new pedagogical techniques to try, and new research and ideas to describe. With this in mind as I began preparing the second edition (2008), I elicited feedback from students in my classes and received more than 1,500 written responses indicating areas in the first edition that could be improved. In addition, I also received feedback from instructors who had used the first edition. This feedback was the starting point for the second edition, and I repeated this process of eliciting student and instructor feedback for the third and fourth editions as well. Thus, in addition to updating the science, I revised many sections that students and instructors had flagged as needing clarification.

Retained Features

All of the features described above were well received by students and instructors, and so are continued in this new fourth edition. Additional pedagogical features that have been retained from previous editions include **Test Yourself** sections, which help students review the material, and end-of-chapter **Think About It** questions, which ask students to consider questions that go beyond the material.

Methods sections, which were introduced in the second edition, highlight the ingenious methods cognitive psychologists have devised to study the mind. The 29 Methods sections, which are integrated into the text, describe methods such as brain imaging, the lexical decision task, and think-aloud protocols. This not only highlights the importance of the method, but makes it easier to return to its description when it is referred to later in the text. See page xx for a list of Methods.

The end-of-chapter **Something to Consider** sections describe cutting-edge research, important issues, or applied research. A few examples of topics covered in this section are *What Neuroscience Tells Us About Cognition* (Chapter 2); *Math Performance and Working Memory* (Chapter 5); and *The Dual Systems Approach to Thinking* (Chapter 13). **Chapter Summaries** provide succinct outlines of the chapters, without serving as a substitute for reading the chapters.

What Is New in the Fourth Edition

As with previous editions of this book, this edition features updates to material throughout, and in a few cases chapters have been rewritten or reorganized to improve clarity and pedagogy.

One indication of changes to this edition is over 80 new key terms, such as the following: attentional capture; Bayesian inference; belief bias; change detection; common ground; conceptual knowledge; corpus; diffusion tensor imaging; dual systems approach to thinking; embodied approach; group brainstorming; hierarchical processing; hub and spoke model; inverse projection problem; meaning dominance; mental model; myside bias; neural mind reading; neural network; personal semantic memory; processing capacity; remember/know procedure; semantic dementia; sensory-functional hypothesis; sparse coding; syntactic coordination; visual world paradigm.

Following is a chapter-by-chapter list that highlights a few of the key changes in this edition. Text in *italics* indicates section headings new to this edition.

CHAPTER 1 Introduction to Cognitive Psychology

- *Modern Research in Cognitive Psychology* includes Beilock's research on "choking under pressure" to illustrate how research progresses from one question to another.
- Treatment of the role of models in cognitive psychology has been expanded.

CHAPTER 2 Cognitive Neuroscience

- *Why Study Cognitive Neuroscience?* introduces the idea of levels of analysis and an expanded discussion of the rationale for the physiological study of the mind.
- The use of fMRI while subjects are viewing movies to determine semantic brain maps (Huth et al., 2012) is described.
- *All Together Now: Neural Networks* includes new methods such as diffusion tensor imaging.
- *Something to Consider: What Neuroscience Tells Us About Cognition* follows up on *Why Study Cognitive Neuroscience?* by providing examples of how neuroscience can contribute to our understanding of mechanisms suggested by behavioral research.

CHAPTER 3 Perception

- Chapter has been rewritten to focus on the idea that although perception appears easy, it is based on invisible underlying processes. It opens with a discussion of why it is so difficult to design robotic vision systems.

- Pain is used to illustrate the effect of top-down processing.
- *Bayesian Inference* has been added to accompany Helmholtz's theory of unconscious inference.
- *Something to Consider: Where Perception Meets Memory* describes how neurons in the hippocampus fire to remembered perceptions (Gelbard-Sagiv et al., 2008).

CHAPTER 4 Attention

- New opening emphasizes the idea that there are a number of different aspects of attention.
- Description of Schneider and Shiffrin's (1977) experiments on automatic processing has been streamlined.
- Treatment of distractions while driving has been updated to include texting and Internet use (Strayer et al., 2013).
- *Something to Consider: Taking Possession by the Brain* is a new discussion of the physiology of attention that reflects William James's idea of attention "taking possession" of the mind (Datta & DeYoe, 2009).

CHAPTER 5 Short-Term and Working Memory

- New opening introduces the different types of memory that will be discussed in Chapters 5–8.
- Discussion of the capacity of short-term memory has been updated to add the idea of defining capacity in terms of the amount of information (Alvarez & Cavanagh, 2004).
- *Method: Change Detection* (Luck & Vogel, 1997) follows up on the Change Detection demonstration in Chapter 4.
- fMRI study showing that the visual cortex is involved in holding information during a delay (Harrison & Tong, 2009) has been added.
- *Something to Consider: Math Performance and Working Memory* describes how writing can prevent choking under pressure (Ramirez & Beilock, 2011). This follows up on the "choking under pressure" discussion in Chapter 1.

CHAPTER 6 Long-Term Memory: Structure

- New opening describes chapter theme, "Division and Interaction," reflecting that there are different types of memory mechanisms that interact with each other.
- *What Happens to Episodic and Semantic Memories as Time Passes?* is an updated discussion of the semanticization of remote memories (Petrican et al., 2010).
- *Method: Remember/Know Procedure* accompanies Petrican et al. research.
- *Imagining the Future* outlines the connection between episodic memory and the ability to imagine the future (Addis et al., 2007; Schacter, 2012).

CHAPTER 7 Long-Term Memory: Encoding and Retrieval

- *Consolidation: The Life History of Memories* is an updated section on memory and the brain with expanded treatment of the physiology of consolidation, including new research on the multiple trace hypothesis (Viskentas et al., 2009) and consolidation and sleep (Wilhelm et al., 2011).
- *Something to Consider: Effective Studying* previously appeared earlier in the text.

CHAPTER 8 Everyday Memory and Memory Errors

- Discussion of memory and emotion has been updated to include how emotion can enhance consolidation (Cahill et al., 2003; Roozendaal & McGaugh, 2011) and how emotion can interfere with memory (Mather & Sutherland, 2011).

- Discussion of flashbulb memory includes the idea that emotion can increase recollection but decrease memory for details (Rimmele et al., 2011).

- *Something to Consider: The Power of Pictures* describes how pictures can create false memories (Nash & Wade, 2009).

CHAPTER 9 Knowledge

- Discussion of connectionist networks has been simplified.

- *The Representation of Concepts in the Brain* includes an expanded discussion of categories in the brain to more accurately reflect the varied approaches proposed to explain how concepts are represented (Hoffman & Lambon Ralph, 2012; Mahon & Caramazza, 2011; Pulvermüller, 2013; Warrington & Shallice, 1985).

- *Something to Consider: The Hub and Spoke Model* has been added (Jeffries, 2013; Pobric et al., 2010; Pulvermüller, 2013).

- *Method: Sentence Verification Technique* has been added. *Method: Transcranial Magnetic Stimulation (TMS)* has been introduced in conjunction with research on the hub and spoke model.

CHAPTER 10 Visual Imagery

- *Something to Consider: Imagery and Food Craving* describes using visual imagery to decrease food cravings (Harvey et al., 2005).

CHAPTER 11 Language

- Treatment of lexical ambiguity has been updated to include a discussion of how accessing a word's meaning is affected by meaning dominance (Rayner & Fraizer, 1989).

- Material on Broca and Wernicke has been moved from Chapter 2 to this chapter.

- In discussion of sentence processing, material has been added on making predictions based on knowledge of the environment (Federmeier & Kustas, 1999) and on knowledge of language constructions (Fine et al., 2013).

- Situation models have been updated with new material on predictions based on knowledge about situations (Metusalem et al., 2012).

- Section on conversations has been revised to include material on common ground (Clark, 1996).

CHAPTER 12 Problem Solving

- Treatment of creative problem solving has been expanded with added examples, a section on practical creativity, and a discussion of problem solving as a process.

- Discussion of how too much knowledge can be a bad thing has been revised (Smith et al., 1993).

- *Something to Consider: Creativity, Mental Illness, and the Open Mind* considers whether there is a link between mental illness and creativity (Carson, 2011; Chi & Snyder, 2012).

CHAPTER 13 Judgment, Decisions, and Reasoning

- Chapter now opens with material on judgment and heuristics. Deductive reasoning, which students find more difficult, has been moved to the end of the chapter.

- Further examples have been added to illustrate how decision making is influenced by the number of alternatives available (Shen et al., 2010) and whether the person making the decision is hungry or tired (Danzinger et al., 2011).

- Discussion of deductive reasoning uses new examples to make syllogisms, and the distinction between validity and truth, easier to understand.

- *Mental Models of Deductive Reasoning* describes a way to determine the validity of a syllogism (Johnson-Laird, 1999).
- *Something to Consider: The Dual Systems Approach to Thinking* describes research based on the idea of two systems for thinking, one fast and the other slow (Evans & Stanovich, 2013; Kahneman, 2011).

Ancillaries to Support Your Teaching

All of these supplements are available online for download. Go to **login.cengage.com** to create an account and log in.

Online Instructor's Manual

The Instructor's Manual contains a variety of resources to aid instructors in preparing and presenting text material in a manner that meets their personal preferences and course needs. It presents chapter-by-chapter suggestions and resources to enhance and facilitate learning.

Online Test Bank

The Test Bank contains multiple-choice and essay questions to challenge your students and assess their learning.

Cengage Learning Testing Powered by Cognero

The Test Bank also is available through Cognero, a flexible online system that allows you to author, edit, and manage test content as well as create multiple test versions in an instant. You can deliver tests from your school's learning management system, your classroom, or wherever you want.

Online PowerPoints

Vibrant Microsoft PowerPoint lecture slides for each chapter assist you with your lecture by providing concept coverage using images, figures, and tables directly from the textbook.

CogLab 5.0

CogLab Online is a series of virtual lab demonstrations designed to help students understand cognition through interactive participation in cognitive experiments. Students with instructors that adopt CogLab 5.0 also receive access to more than 50 online CogLab experiments that they can run themselves, and then compare their data to the class average and to the results of the original experiments from the literature. To view a demo, visit coglab.cengage.com.

CourseMate

Cengage Learning's Psychology CourseMate brings course concepts to life with interactive learning, study, and exam preparation tools that support the printed textbook. CourseMate includes an integrated eBook, glossaries, flashcards, quizzes, videos, and more—as well as EngagementTracker, a first-of-its-kind tool that monitors student engagement in the course. CourseMate can be bundled with the student text. Contact your Cengage sales representative for information on getting access to CourseMate.

As you begin reading this book, you probably have some ideas about how the mind works from things you have read, from other media, and from your own experiences. In this book, you will learn what we actually do and do not know about the mind, as determined from the results of controlled scientific research. Thus, if you think that there is a system called "short-term memory" that can hold information for short periods of time, then you are right; when you read the chapters on memory, you will learn more about this system and how it interacts with other parts of your memory system. If you think that some people can accurately remember things that happened to them as very young infants, you will see that there is a good chance that these reports are inaccurate. In fact, you may be surprised to learn that even more recent memories that seem extremely clear and vivid may not be entirely accurate due to basic characteristics of the way the memory system works.

But what you will learn from this book goes much deeper than simply adding more accurate information to what you already know about the mind. You will learn that there is much more going on in your mind than you are conscious of. You are aware of experiences such as seeing something, remembering a past event, or thinking about how to solve a problem—but behind each of these experiences are a myriad of complex and largely invisible processes. Reading this book will help you appreciate some of the "behind the scenes" activity in your mind that is responsible for everyday experiences such as perceiving, remembering, and thinking.

Another thing you will become aware of as you read this book is that there are many practical connections between the results of cognitive psychology research and everyday life. You will see examples of these connections throughout the book. For now I want to focus on one especially important connection—what research in cognitive psychology can contribute to improving your studying. This discussion appears on pages 202–203 of Chapter 7, but you might want to look at this material now rather than waiting until later in the course. I invite you to also consider the following two principles, which are designed to help you get more out of this book.

Principle 1: It is important to know what you know.

Professors often hear students lament, "I came to the lecture, read the chapters a number of times, and still didn't do well on the exam." Sometimes this statement is followed by "... and when I walked out of the exam, I thought I had done pretty well." If this is something that you have experienced, the problem may be that you didn't have a good awareness of what you knew about the material and what you didn't know. If you think you know the material but actually don't, you might stop studying or might continue studying in an ineffective way, with the net result being a poor understanding of the material and an inability to remember it accurately come exam time. Thus, it is important to test yourself on the material you have read by writing or saying the answers to the Test Yourself questions in the chapter and also by taking advantage of the sample test questions that are available on Psychology CourseMate. To access these questions and other valuable learning aids, go to *www.cengagebrain.com*.

Principle 2: Don't mistake ease and familiarity for knowing.

One of the main reasons that students may think they know the material, even when they don't, is that they mistake familiarity for understanding. Here is how it works: You read the chapter once, perhaps highlighting as you go. Later, you read the chapter again, perhaps focusing on the highlighted material. As you read it over, the material is familiar because you remember it from before, and this familiarity might lead you to think, "Okay, I know that." The problem is that this feeling of familiarity is not necessarily equivalent to knowing the material and may be of no help when you have to come up with an answer on the exam. In fact, familiarity can often lead to errors on multiple-choice exams because you might pick a choice that looks familiar, only to find out later that although it was something you had read, it wasn't really the best answer to the question.

This brings us back again to the idea of testing yourself. One finding of cognitive psychology research is that the very act of *trying* to answer a question increases the chances that you will be able to answer it when you try again later. Another related finding is that testing yourself on the material is a more effective way of learning it than simply rereading the material. The reason testing yourself works is that *generating* material is a more effective way of getting information into memory than simply *reviewing* it. Thus, you may find it effective to test yourself before rereading the chapter or going over your highlighted text.

Whichever study tactic you find works best for you, keep in mind that an effective strategy is to rest (take a break or study something else) before studying more and then retesting yourself. Research has shown that memory is better when studying is spaced out over time, rather than being done all at once. Repeating this process a number of times—testing yourself, checking back to see whether you were right, waiting, testing yourself again, and so on—is a more effective way of learning the material than simply looking at it and getting that warm, fuzzy feeling of familiarity, which may not translate into actually knowing the material when you are faced with questions about it on the exam.

I hope you will find this book to be clear and interesting and that you will sometimes be fascinated or perhaps even surprised by some of the things you read. I also hope that your introduction to cognitive psychology extends beyond just "learning the material." Cognitive psychology is endlessly interesting because it is about one of the most fascinating of all topics—the human mind. Thus, once your course is over, I hope you will take away an appreciation for what cognitive psychologists have discovered about the mind and what still remains to be learned. I also hope that you will become a more critical consumer of information about the mind that you may encounter on the Internet or in movies, magazines, or other media.

Acknowledgments

The starting point for a textbook like this one is an author who has an idea for a book, but other people soon become part of the process. Writing is guided by feedback from editors and reviewers on writing and content. When the manuscript is completed, the production process begins, and a new group of people take over to turn the manuscript into a book. This means that this book has been a group effort and that I had lots of help, both during the process of writing and after submitting the final manuscript. I would therefore like to thank the following people for their extraordinary efforts in support of this book.

- JOANN KOZYREV, product manager, for supporting the production of this book in both print and digital formats, and for all of her "behind the scenes" efforts on its behalf. Thank you for providing the resources I needed to create the best book possible, and for being open to my input during the writing and production process.

- SHANNON LEMAY-FINN, content developer, for focusing her uncanny critical radar on my writing and for letting me know when my writing didn't make sense, didn't parse well, or had left out an essential part of the story. Thanks also for appreciating my writing and for being interested in cognitive psychology. Writing a book is a solitary pursuit, but I was fortunate enough to have Shannon comment on everything I wrote. Working with Shannon is one of the things that makes writing these books worthwhile.

- ANNE DRAUS of Scratchgravel Publishing Services, for once again being there to take care of this book as it progressed through the production process. Producing a book is a complex process that involves close attention to detail and, in the case of this book, dealing with an author who could perhaps be described as being obsessive about detail. Although Anne has handled production since the first edition of this book, I am still amazed by both her patience and her professionalism and thankful that I was able to rest assured that everything would be handled just as it should be during production.

- MARGARET TROPP, for her expert and extremely thorough copy editing that went beyond just "copy editing" to include pointing out places that needed further clarification.

- JENNIFER WAHI, the art director, for directing the team responsible for the look and layout of this book and for being open to suggestions, even from the author!

- JEFF BANE, for the elegant and beautiful cover and for the eye-catching and functional interior design.

- LISA TORRI, art editor, for yet again directing the art program for one of my books. Thanks, Lisa, for putting up with my changes, and also for suggesting improvements in some of the figures.

- CHARLENE CARPENTIER, content project manager, for making sure everything was done correctly and on time during the production process.

- DHARANIVEL BHASKER and VEERABHAGU NAGARAJAN of PreMediaGlobal photo research, for obtaining permissions and for patiently waiting for my answers to their questions.

- MARTHA GHENT, for the essential task of proofreading.

- JAMES MINKIN, for creating the index.

- JESSICA ALDERMAN, assistant content developer, for coordinating the supplements for the book.

- MARY NOEL, media developer, for her work on the media that accompany the book.

In addition to the help I received from the above people on the editorial and production side, I received a great deal of help from teachers and researchers who gave me feedback on what I wrote and made suggestions regarding new work in the field.

First, the experts listed below each read one of the chapters from the third edition and provided suggestions on updating the content for the fourth edition. These reviewers pointed me in the right direction but did not see the revised text. They therefore deserve credit for much of the updating of this edition but no responsibility for the final result.

CHAPTER 5 Short-Term and Working Memory

Stephen Emrich
Brock University

Geoffrey Woodman
Vanderbilt University

CHAPTER 6 Long-Term Memory: Structure

Shayna Rosenbaum
York University

CHAPTER 7 Long-Term Memory: Encoding and Retrieval

Almut Hupbach
Lehigh University

Jeffrey Karpicke
Purdue University

CHAPTER 8 Everyday Memory and Memory Errors

Steve Lindsay
University of Victoria

Karen Mitchell
Yale University

CHAPTER 9 Knowledge

Gregory Murphy
New York University

Timothy Rogers
University of Wisconsin

CHAPTER 10 Visual Imagery

Giorgio Ganis
University of Plymouth

CHAPTER 11 Language

Sarah Brown-Schmidt
University of Illinois

Tessa Warren
University of Pittsburgh

Keith Rayner
University of California at San Diego

CHAPTER 12 Problem Solving

Miriam Bassok
University of Washington

CHAPTER 13 Judgment, Decisions, and Reasoning

Ruth Byrne
University of Dublin

Ken Manktelow
University of Wolverhampton

Keith Holyoak
University of California, Los Angeles

The following reviewers read parts of chapters to check for accuracy in their areas of expertise, or took the time to answer questions that I posed.

Sian Beilock
University of Chicago

Charles Kemp
Carnegie-Mellon University

Deon Benton
Carnegie-Mellon University

Daniel Kersten
University of Minnesota

Jason C. K. Chan
Iowa State University

Brad Mahon
University of Rochester

Marlene Cohen
University of Pittsburgh

Lynn Nadel
University of Arizona

Alex Fine
University of Illinois

Thomas Naselaris
University of California, Berkeley

Jack Gallant
University of California, Berkeley

Tim Nokes
University of Pittsburgh

Daniel Goldreich
McMaster University

Mary Peterson
University of Arizona

Robert Goldstone
University of Indiana

Christopher Schunn
University of Pittsburgh

Alexender Huth
University of California, Berkeley

In addition, the following reviewers provided "teaching reviews" of the third edition:

Karl G.D. Bailey
Andrews University

Trevor Morris
Utah Valley University

Christie Chung
Mills College

Robyn Oliver
Roosevelt University

Christine Feeley
Adelphi University

Evan Raiewski
University of California, San Diego

Stephani Foraker
Buffalo State College, SUNY

Thomas S. Redick
Indiana University–Purdue University Columbus

Ralf Greenwald
Central Washington University

Jennifer K. Roth
Concordia College–New York

Paul G. Helton
Freed-Hardeman University

Stacie Shaw
Presentation College

Pernille Hemmer
Rutgers University

John R. Silvestro
Elms College

Elizabeth A. Hennon
University of Evansville

Madhu Singh
Tougaloo College

Robert J. Hines
University of Arkansas, Little Rock

Scott Sinnett
University of Hawaii at Manoa

Vanesa M. McKinney
SUNY Fredonia

Erin I. Smith
California Baptist University

Katherine Moore
Elmhurst College

I also thank the following people who donated photographs and research records for illustrations that are new to this edition.

Donna Rose Addes
University of Auckland, New Zealand

Alex Huth
University of California, Berkeley

Roberto Cabeza
Duke University

Robert Nash
University of Surry

Fernando Calamante
Florey Institute, Heidelberg, Australia

Friedemann Pulvermüller
University of Berlin

Francesca Carota
University of Cambridge

SR Research Ltd.
Ottawa, Ontario, Canada

Jack Gallant
University of California, Berkeley

Kimberly Wade
University of Warwick

Cognitive Psychology

A hiker steps out of a cave into the sunlight and anticipates his journey through an amazing and varied landscape. Now you, the reader of this book, are about to embark on an intellectual journey that will take you through the remarkable inner workings of the mind. This chapter sets the stage for this journey, by tracing the history of the scientific study of the mind from its beginnings in a few laboratories in Europe in the late 19th century, to today's widespread scientific study of what the mind is and what it does.

Introduction to Cognitive Psychology

▶ How is cognitive psychology
relevant to everyday
experience? (4)

▶ Are there practical applications
of cognitive psychology? (4)

▶ How is it possible to study the
inner workings of the mind
when we can't really see the
mind directly? (7)

▶ How are models used in
cognitive psychology? (17)

As Raphael is walking across campus, talking to Susan on his cell phone about meeting at the student union later this afternoon, he remembers that he left the book she had lent him at home (Figure 1.1). "I can't believe it," he thinks, "I can see it sitting there on my desk, where I left it. I should have put it in my backpack last night when I was thinking about it."

As he finishes his call with Susan and makes a mental note to be on time for their appointment, his thoughts shift to how he is going to survive after Wednesday when his car is scheduled to go into the shop. Renting a car offers the most mobility, but is expensive. Depending on his roommate for rides is cheap, but limiting. "Maybe I'll pick up a bus schedule at the student union," he thinks, as he puts his cell phone in his pocket.

Entering his anthropology class, he remembers that an exam is coming up soon. Unfortunately, he still has a lot of reading to do, so he decides that he won't be able to go to the movies with Susan tonight as they had planned. As the lecture begins, Raphael is anticipating, with some anxiety, his meeting with Susan.

This brief slice of Raphael's life is noteworthy because it is ordinary, while at the same time so much is happening. Within a short span of time, Raphael does the following things that are related to material covered in chapters in this book:

■ *Perceives* his environment—seeing people on campus and hearing Susan talking on the phone (Chapter 3: Perception)

■ *Pays attention* to one thing after another—the person approaching on his left, what Susan is saying, how much time he has to get to his class (Chapter 4: Attention)

■ *Remembers* something from the past—that he had told Susan he was going to return her book today (Chapters 5–8: Memory)

■ *Distinguishes items in a category*, when he thinks about different possible forms of transportation—rental car, roommate's car, bus (Chapter 9: Knowledge)

■ *Visualizes* the book on his desk the night before (Chapter 10: Visual Imagery)

■ *Understands and produces language* as he talks to Susan (Chapter 11: Language)

■ Works to *solve a problem*, as he thinks about how to get places while his car is in the shop (Chapter 12: Problem Solving)

■ *Makes a decision*, when he decides to postpone going to the movies with Susan so he can study (Chapter 13: Judgment, Decisions, and Reasoning)

Figure 1.1 What's happening in Raphael's mind as he walks across campus? Each of the thought bubbles corresponds to something in the story in the text.

The things Raphael is doing not only are covered in this book but also have something very important in common: They all involve the mind. **Cognitive psychology** is *the branch of psychology concerned with the scientific study of the mind.* As you read the story told in this book, about the quest to understand the mind, you will learn what the mind is, how it has been studied, and what researchers have discovered about how the mind works. In this chapter we will first describe the mind in more detail, then consider some of the history behind the field of cognitive psychology, and finally begin considering how modern cognitive psychologists have gone about studying the mind.

Cognitive Psychology: Studying the Mind

You may have noticed that we have been using the term **mind** without precisely defining it. As we will see, mind, like other concepts in psychology, such as intelligence or emotion, can be thought of in a number of different ways.

WHAT IS THE MIND?

One way to approach the question "What is the mind?" is to consider how "mind" is used in everyday conversation. Here are a few examples:

1. "He was able to call to mind what he was doing on the day of the accident." (The mind as involved in memory)

2. "If you put your mind to it, I'm sure you can solve that math problem." (The mind as problem-solver)

3. "I haven't made up my mind yet" or "I'm of two minds about this." (The mind as used to make decisions or consider possibilities)

4. "He is of sound mind and body" or "When he talks about his encounter with aliens, it sounds like he is out of his mind." (A healthy mind being associated with normal functioning, a nonfunctioning mind with abnormal functioning)

5. "A mind is a terrible thing to waste." (The mind as valuable, something that should be used)

6. "He has a brilliant mind." (Used to describe people who are particularly intelligent or creative)

These statements tell us some important things about what the mind is. Statements 1, 2, and 3, which highlight the mind's role in memory, problem solving, and making decisions, are related to the following definition of the mind: *The mind creates and controls mental functions such as perception, attention, memory, emotions, language, deciding, thinking, and reasoning.* This definition reflects the mind's central role in determining our various mental abilities, which are reflected in the titles of the chapters in this book.

Another definition, which focuses on how the mind operates, is: *The mind is a system that creates representations of the world so that we can act within it to achieve our goals.* This definition reflects the mind's importance for functioning and survival, and also provides the beginnings of a description of how the mind achieves these ends. The idea of creating representations is something we will return to throughout this book.

These two definitions of the mind are not incompatible. The first one indicates different types of **cognition**—the mental processes, such as perception, attention, and memory, that are what the mind does. The second definition indicates something about how the mind operates (it creates representations) and its function (it enables us to act and to achieve goals). It is no coincidence that all of the cognitions in the first definition play important roles in acting to achieve goals.

Statements 4, 5, and 6 emphasize the mind's importance for normal functioning, and the amazing abilities of the mind. The mind is something to be used, and the products of some people's minds are considered extraordinary. But one of the messages of this book is that the idea that the mind is amazing is not reserved for "extraordinary" minds, because even the most "routine" things—recognizing a person, having a conversation, or deciding what courses to take next semester—become amazing in themselves when we consider the properties of the mind that enable us to achieve these familiar activities.

What exactly are the properties of the mind? What are its characteristics? How does it operate? Saying that the mind creates cognition and is important for functioning and survival tells us *what the mind does,* but not *how it achieves what it does.* The question of how the mind achieves what it does is what cognitive psychology is about. Our goals in the rest of this chapter are to describe how the field of cognitive psychology evolved from its early beginnings to where it is today, and to begin describing how cognitive psychologists approach the scientific study of the mind.

STUDYING THE MIND: EARLY WORK IN COGNITIVE PSYCHOLOGY

In the 1800s, ideas about the mind were dominated by the belief that it is not possible to study the mind. One reason given was that it is not possible for the mind to study itself, but there were other reasons as well, including the idea that the properties of the mind simply cannot be measured. Nonetheless, some researchers defied the common wisdom and decided to study the mind anyway. One of these people was the Dutch physiologist Franciscus Donders, who in 1868, 11 years before the founding of the first laboratory of scientific psychology, did one of the first experiments that today would be called a cognitive psychology experiment. (It is important to note that the term "cognitive psychology" was not coined until 1967, but the early experiments we are going to describe qualify as cognitive psychology experiments.)

DONDERS'S PIONEERING EXPERIMENT: HOW LONG DOES IT TAKE TO MAKE A DECISION? Donders was interested in determining how long it takes for a person to make a decision. He determined this by measuring **reaction time**—how long it takes to respond to presentation of a stimulus. He used two measures of reaction time. He measured **simple reaction time** by asking his subjects to push a button as rapidly as possible when they saw a light go on (**Figure 1.2a**). He measured **choice reaction time** by using two lights and asking his subjects to push the left button when they saw the left light go on and the right button when they saw the right light go on (**Figure 1.2b**).

The steps that occur in the simple reaction time task are shown in **Figure 1.3a**. Presenting the stimulus (the light) causes a mental response (perceiving the light), which leads to a behavioral response (pushing the button). The reaction time (dashed line) is the time between the presentation of the stimulus and the behavioral response.

But remember that Donders was interested in determining how long it took for a person to make a decision. The choice reaction time task added decisions by requiring subjects to decide whether the left or right light was illuminated and then which button to push. The diagram for this task, in **Figure 1.3b**, adds deciding which light was illuminated and which button to push to the mental response. Donders reasoned that the difference in reaction time between the simple and choice conditions would indicate how long it took to make the decision that led to pushing the correct button. Because the choice reaction time took one-tenth of a second longer than simple reaction time, Donders concluded that the decision-making process took one-tenth of a second.

Donders's experiment is important, both because it was one of the first cognitive psychology experiments and because it illustrates something extremely significant about studying the mind: Mental responses (perceiving the light and deciding which button to push, in this example) cannot be measured directly, but must be *inferred*

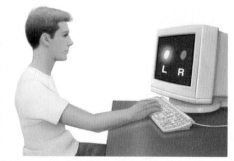

(a) Press J when light goes on.   (b) Press J for left light, K for right.

Figure 1.2 A modern version of Donders's (1868) reaction time experiment: (a) the simple reaction time task and (b) the choice reaction time task. In the simple reaction time task, the subject pushes the J key when the light goes on. In the choice reaction time task, the subject pushes the J key if the left light goes on and the K key if the right light goes on. The purpose of Donders's experiment was to determine how much time it took to decide which key to press in the choice reaction time task. © Cengage Learning

from behavior. We can see why this is so by noting the dashed lines in **Figure 1.3**. These lines indicate that when Donders measured reaction time, he was measuring the relationship between presentation of the stimulus and the subject's response. He did not measure mental responses directly, but *inferred* how long they took from the reaction times. The fact that mental responses cannot be measured directly, but must be inferred from observing behavior, is a principle that holds not only for Donders's experiment but for all research in cognitive psychology.

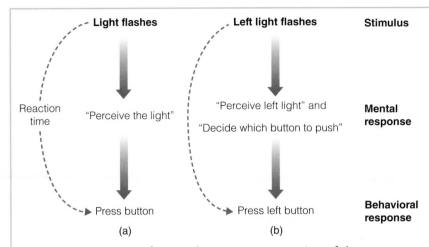

Figure 1.3 Sequence of events between presentation of the stimulus and the behavioral response in Donders's experiments: (a) simple reaction time task and (b) choice reaction time task. The dashed line indicates that Donders measured reaction time— the time between presentation of the light and the participant's response. © Cengage Learning

WUNDT'S PSYCHOLOGY LABORATORY: STRUCTURALISM AND ANALYTIC INTROSPECTION In 1879, 11 years after Donders's reaction time experiment, Wilhelm Wundt founded the first laboratory of scientific psychology at the University of Leipzig in Germany. Wundt's approach, which dominated psychology in the late 1800s and early 1900s, was called **structuralism**. According to structuralism, our overall experience is determined by combining basic elements of experience the structuralists called *sensations*. Thus, just as chemistry developed a periodic table of the elements, which combine to create molecules, Wundt wanted to create a "periodic table of the mind," which would include all of the basic sensations involved in creating experience.

Wundt thought he could achieve this scientific description of the components of experience by using **analytic introspection**, a technique in which trained subjects described their experiences and thought processes in response to stimuli. Analytic introspection required extensive training because the subjects' goal was to describe their experience in terms of elementary mental elements. For example, in one experiment, Wundt asked participants to describe their experience of hearing a five-note chord played on the piano. One of the questions Wundt hoped to answer was whether his subjects were able to hear each of the individual notes that made up the chord. As we will see when we consider perception in Chapter 3, structuralism was not a fruitful approach and so was abandoned in the early 1900s. Nonetheless, Wundt made a substantial contribution to psychology by his commitment to studying behavior and the mind under controlled conditions. In addition, he trained many PhDs who established psychology departments at other universities, including many in the United States.

EBBINGHAUS'S MEMORY EXPERIMENT: WHAT IS THE TIME COURSE OF FORGETTING? Meanwhile, 120 miles from Leipzig, at the University of Berlin, German psychologist Hermann Ebbinghaus (1885/1913) was using another approach to measuring the properties of the mind. Ebbinghaus was interested in determining the nature of memory and forgetting—specifically, how rapidly information that is learned is lost over time. Rather than using Wundt's method of analytic introspection, Ebbinghaus used a quantitative method for measuring memory. Using himself as the subject, he repeated lists of 13 nonsense syllables such as DAX, QEH, LUH, and ZIF to himself one at a time at a constant rate. He used nonsense syllables so that his memory would not be influenced by the meaning of a particular word.

Ebbinghaus determined how long it took to learn a list for the first time. He then waited for a specific amount of time (the *delay*) and then determined how long it took to relearn the list. Because forgetting had occurred during the delay, Ebbinghaus made

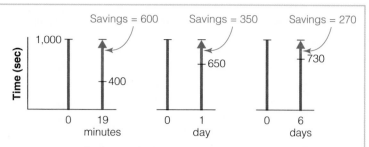

Figure 1.4 Calculating the savings score in Ebbinghaus's experiment. In this example, it took 1,000 seconds to learn the list of nonsense syllables for the first time. This is indicated by the lines at 0. The time needed to relearn the list at delays of (a) 19 minutes, (b) 1 day, and (c) 6 days are indicated by the line to the right of the 0 line. The red line indicates the savings score for each delay. Notice that savings decrease for longer delays. This decrease in savings provides a measure of forgetting. © 2015 Cengage Learning

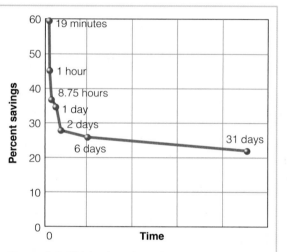

Figure 1.5 Ebbinghaus's savings curve. Ebbinghaus considered the percent savings to be a measure of the amount remembered, so he plotted this versus the time between initial learning and testing. The decrease in savings (remembering) with increasing delays indicates that forgetting occurs rapidly over the first 2 days and then occurs more slowly after that. *(Source: Based on H. Ebbinghaus,* Memory: A contribution to experimental psychology, *H. A. Ruger & C. E. Bussenius, Trans., New York: Teachers College, Columbia University, 1885/1913.)*

errors when he first tried to remember the list. But because he had retained something from his original learning, he relearned the list more rapidly than when he had learned it for the first time.

Ebbinghaus used a measure called **savings**, calculated as follows, to determine how much was forgotten after a particular delay: Savings = (Original time to learn the list) − (Time to relearn the list after the delay). Thus, if it took 1,000 seconds to learn the list the first time and 400 seconds to relearn the list after the delay, the savings would be 1,000 − 400 = 600 seconds. **Figure 1.4**, which represents original learning and relearning after three different delays, shows that longer delays result in smaller savings.

According to Ebbinghaus, this reduction in savings provided a measure of forgetting, with smaller savings meaning more forgetting. Thus, the plot of percent savings versus time in **Figure 1.5**, called a **savings curve**, shows that memory drops rapidly for the first 2 days after the initial learning and then levels off. This curve was important because it demonstrated that memory could be quantified and that functions like the savings curve could be used to describe a property of the mind—in this case, the ability to retain information. Notice that although Ebbinghaus's savings method was very different from Donders's reaction time method, both measured *behavior* to determine a property of the *mind*.

WILLIAM JAMES'S *PRINCIPLES OF PSYCHOLOGY* William James, one of the early American psychologists (although not a student of Wundt's), taught Harvard's first psychology course and made significant observations about the mind in his textbook, *Principles of Psychology* (1890). James's observations were based not on the results of experiments but on observations about the operation of his own mind. One of the best known of James's observations is the following, on the nature of attention:

> Millions of items … are present to my senses which never properly enter my experience. Why? Because they have no interest for me. My experience is what I agree to attend to. … Everyone knows what attention is. It is the taking possession by the mind, in clear and vivid form, of one out of what seem several simultaneously possible objects or trains of thought. … It implies withdrawal from some things in order to deal effectively with others.

The observation that paying attention to one thing involves withdrawing from other things still rings true today and has been the topic of many modern studies of attention. As impressive as the accuracy of James's observations, so too was the range of cognitive topics he considered, which included thinking, consciousness, attention, memory, perception, imagination, and reasoning.

The founding of the first laboratory of psychology by Wundt, the quantitative experiments of Donders and Ebbinghaus, and the perceptive observations of James provided what seemed to be a promising start to the study of the mind (**Table 1.1**). However, research on the mind was soon to be curtailed, largely because of events early in the 20th century that shifted the focus of psychology away from the study of the mind and mental processes. One of the major forces that caused psychology to reject the study of mental processes was a negative reaction to Wundt's technique of analytic introspection.

Table 1.1: Early Pioneers in Cognitive Psychology

PERSON	PROCEDURE	RESULTS AND CONCLUSIONS	CONTRIBUTION
Donders (1868)	Simple reaction time vs. choice reaction time	Choice reaction time takes 1/10 seconds longer; therefore, it takes 1/10 second to make a decision	First cognitive psychology experiment
Wundt (1879)	Analytic introspection	No reliable results	Established the first laboratory of scientific psychology
Ebbinghaus (1885)	Savings method to measure forgetting	Forgetting occurs rapidly in the first 1 to 2 days after original learning	Quantitative measurement of mental processes
James (1890)	No experiments; reported observations of his own experience	Descriptions of a wide range of experiences	First psychology textbook; some of his observations are still valid today

Abandoning the Study of the Mind

Many early departments of psychology conducted research in the tradition of Wundt's laboratory, using analytic introspection to analyze mental processes. This emphasis on studying the mind was to change, however, because of the efforts of John Watson, who received his PhD in psychology in 1904 from the University of Chicago.

WATSON FOUNDS BEHAVIORISM

The story of how John Watson founded an approach to psychology called behaviorism is well known to introductory psychology students. We will briefly review it here because of its importance to the history of cognitive psychology.

As a graduate student at the University of Chicago, Watson became dissatisfied with the method of analytic introspection. His problems with this method were (1) it produced extremely variable results from person to person, and (2) these results were difficult to verify because they were interpreted in terms of invisible inner mental processes. In response to what he perceived to be deficiencies in analytic introspection, Watson proposed a new approach called **behaviorism**. One of Watson's papers, "Psychology As the Behaviorist Views It," set forth the goals of this approach to psychology in this famous quote:

> Psychology as the Behaviorist sees it is a purely objective, experimental branch of natural science. Its theoretical goal is the prediction and control of behavior. *Introspection forms no essential part of its methods,* nor is the scientific value of its data dependent upon the readiness with which they lend themselves to interpretation in terms of consciousness.... What we need to do is start work upon psychology making *behavior, not consciousness,* the objective point of our attack. (Watson, 1913, pp. 158, 176; emphasis added)

This passage makes two key points: (1) Watson rejects introspection as a method, and (2) observable behavior, not consciousness (which would involve unobservable processes such as thinking, emotions, and reasoning), is the main topic of study. In other words, Watson wanted to restrict psychology to behavioral data, such as Donders's reaction times, and rejected the idea of going beyond those data to draw conclusions about unobservable mental events. Watson eliminated the mind as a topic for investigation by proclaiming that "psychology … need no longer delude itself into thinking that it is making mental states the object of observation" (p. 163). Watson's goal was to replace the mind as a topic of study in psychology with the study of directly observable behavior. As behaviorism became the dominant force in American psychology, psychologists' attention shifted from asking "What does behavior tell us about the mind?" to "What is the relation between stimuli in the environment and behavior?"

Watson's most famous experiment was the "Little Albert" experiment, in which Watson and Rosalie Rayner (1920) subjected Albert, a 9-month-old-boy, to a loud noise every time a rat (which Albert had originally liked) came close to the child. After a few pairings of the noise with the rat, Albert reacted to the rat by crawling away as rapidly as possible.

Watson's ideas are associated with **classical conditioning**—how pairing one stimulus (such as the loud noise presented to Albert) with another, previously neutral stimulus (such as the rat) causes changes in the response to the neutral stimulus. Watson's inspiration for his experiment was Ivan Pavlov's research, begun in the 1890s, that demonstrated classical conditioning in dogs. In these experiments (**Figure 1.6**), Pavlov's pairing of food (which made the dog salivate) with a bell (the initially neutral stimulus) caused the dog to salivate to the sound of the bell (Pavlov, 1927).

Figure 1.6 In Pavlov's famous experiment, he paired ringing a bell with presentation of food. Initially, presentation of the food caused the dog to salivate, but after a number of pairings of bell and food, the bell alone caused salivation. This principle of learning by pairing, which came to be called *classical conditioning*, was the basis of Watson's "Little Albert" experiment. © Cengage Learning

Watson used classical conditioning to argue that behavior can be analyzed without any reference to the mind. For Watson, what was going on inside Albert's head (or inside Pavlov's dog's head!), either physiologically or mentally, was irrelevant. He cared only about how pairing one stimulus with another affected behavior.

SKINNER'S OPERANT CONDITIONING

In the midst of behaviorism's dominance of American psychology, B. F. Skinner, who received his PhD from Harvard in 1931, provided another tool for studying the relationship between stimulus and response, which ensured that this approach would dominate psychology for decades to come. Skinner introduced **operant conditioning**, which focused on how behavior is strengthened by the presentation of positive reinforcers, such as food or social approval (or withdrawal of negative reinforcers, such as a shock or social rejection). For example, Skinner showed that reinforcing a rat with food for pressing a bar maintained or increased the rat's rate of bar pressing. Like Watson, Skinner was not interested in what was happening in the mind, but focused solely on determining how behavior was controlled by stimuli (Skinner, 1938).

The idea that behavior can be understood by studying stimulus–response relationships influenced an entire generation of psychologists and dominated psychology in the United States from the 1940s through the 1960s. Psychologists applied the techniques of classical and operant conditioning to classroom teaching, treating psychological disorders, and testing the effects of drugs on animals. **Figure 1.7** is a time line showing the initial studies of the mind and the rise of behaviorism. But even as behaviorism was dominating psychology, events were occurring that eventually led to the rebirth of the study of the mind.

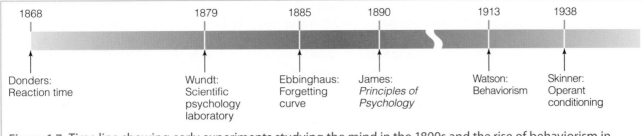

Donders: Reaction time

Wundt: Scientific psychology laboratory

Ebbinghaus: Forgetting curve

James: *Principles of Psychology*

Watson: Behaviorism

Skinner: Operant conditioning

Figure 1.7 Time line showing early experiments studying the mind in the 1800s and the rise of behaviorism in the 1900s. © Cengage Learning

SETTING THE STAGE FOR THE REEMERGENCE OF THE MIND IN PSYCHOLOGY

Although behaviorism dominated American psychology for many decades, some research-ers were not toeing the strict behaviorist line. One of these researchers was Edward Chace Tolman. Tolman, who from 1918 to 1954 was at the University of California at Berkeley, called himself a behaviorist because his focus was on measuring behavior. But in reality he was one of the early cognitive psychologists, because he used behavior to infer mental processes.

In one of his experiments, Tolman (1938) placed a rat in a maze like the one in **Figure 1.8**. Initially, the rat explored the maze, running up and down each of the alleys (**Figure 1.8a**). After this initial period of exploration, the rat was placed at A and food was placed at B, and the rat quickly learned to turn right at the intersection to obtain the food. This is exactly what the behaviorists would predict, because turning right was rewarded with food (**Figure 1.8b**). However, when Tolman (after taking precautions to be sure the rat couldn't determine the location of the food based on smell) placed the rat at C, something interesting happened. The rat turned *left* at the intersection to reach the food at B (**Figure 1.8c**). Tolman's explanation of this result was that when the rat initially experienced the maze it was developing a **cognitive map**—a conception within the rat's mind of the maze's layout (Tolman, 1948). Thus, even though the rat had previously been rewarded for turning right, its mental map indicated that it should turn left to reach the food. Tolman's use of the word *cognitive*, and the idea that some-thing other than stimulus–response connections might be occurring in the rat's mind, placed Tolman outside of mainstream behaviorism.

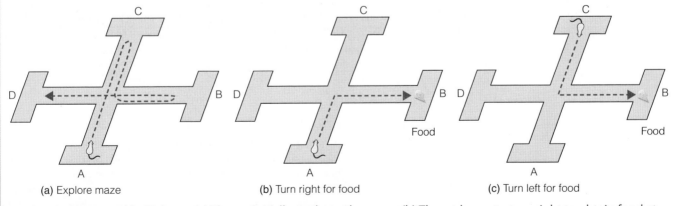

(a) Explore maze   (b) Turn right for food   (c) Turn left for food

Figure 1.8 Maze used by Tolman. (a) The rat initially explores the maze. (b) The rat learns to turn right to obtain food at B when it starts at A. (c) When placed at C, the rat turns left to reach the food at B. In this experiment, precautions are taken to prevent the rat from knowing where the food is based on cues such as smell. © Cengage Learning

Other researchers were aware of Tolman's work, but for most American psychologists in the 1940s, the use of the term *cognitive* was difficult to accept because it violated the behaviorists' idea that internal processes, such as thinking or maps in the head, were not acceptable topics to study. It wasn't until about a decade after Tolman introduced the idea of cognitive maps that developments occurred that led to a resurgence of the mind in psychology. Ironically, one of these developments was the publication, in 1957, of a book by B. F. Skinner titled *Verbal Behavior.*

In his book, Skinner argued that children learn language through operant conditioning. According to this idea, children imitate speech that they hear, and repeat correct speech because it is rewarded. But in 1959, Noam Chomsky, a linguist from the Massachusetts Institute of Technology, published a scathing review of Skinner's book, in which he pointed out that children say many sentences that have never been rewarded by parents ("I hate you, Mommy," for example), and that during the normal course of language development, they go through a stage in which they use incorrect grammar, such as "the boy hitted the ball," even though this incorrect grammar may never have been reinforced.

Chomsky saw language development as being determined not by imitation or reinforcement, but by an inborn biological program that holds across cultures. Chomsky's idea that language is a product of the way the mind is constructed, rather than a result of reinforcement, led psychologists to reconsider the idea that language and other complex behaviors, such as problem solving and reasoning, can be explained by operant conditioning. Instead, they began to realize that to understand complex cognitive behaviors, it is necessary not only to measure observable behavior but also to consider what this behavior tells us about how the mind works.

The Rebirth of the Study of the Mind

The decade of the 1950s is generally recognized as the beginning of the **cognitive revolution**— a shift in psychology from the behaviorist's stimulus–response relationships to an approach whose main thrust was to understand the operation of the mind. Even before Chomsky's critique of Skinner's book, other events were happening that signaled a shift away from focusing only on behavior and toward studying how the mind operates.

Saying that psychologists should go beyond just looking at behavior and look at how the mind operates is one thing. But in order to look beyond behavior, psychologists needed to develop new ways of conceptualizing the mind. Luckily, just as psychologists were questioning behaviorism, a new technology was emerging that suggested a new way of describing the operation of the mind. That new technology was the digital computer.

INTRODUCTION OF THE DIGITAL COMPUTER

The first digital computers, developed in the late 1940s, were huge machines that took up entire buildings, but in 1954 IBM introduced a computer that was available to the general public. These computers were still extremely large compared to the laptops of today, but they found their way into university research laboratories, where they were used both to analyze data and, most important for our purposes, to suggest a new way of thinking about the mind.

FLOW DIAGRAMS FOR COMPUTERS One of the characteristics of computers that captured the attention of psychologists in the 1950s was that they processed information in stages, as illustrated in **Figure 1.9a**. In this diagram, information is first received by an "input processor." It is then stored in a "memory unit" before it is processed by an "arithmetic unit," which then creates the computer's output. Using this stage approach as their inspiration, some psychologists proposed the **information-processing approach** to studying the mind—an approach that traces sequences of mental operations involved in cognition. According to the information-processing approach, the operation of the mind can be described as occurring in a number of stages. Applying this stage approach to the mind led psychologists to ask new questions and to frame their answers to these questions in new ways. One of the first experiments influenced by this new way of thinking about the mind involved studying how well people are able to focus their attention on some information when other information is being presented at the same time.

FLOW DIAGRAMS FOR THE MIND Beginning in the 1950s, a number of researchers became interested in describing how well the mind can deal with incoming information. One question they were interested in answering followed from William James's idea that when we decide to attend to one thing, we must withdraw from other things. Taking this idea as a starting point, British psychologist Colin Cherry (1953) presented subjects with two auditory messages, one to the left ear and one to the right ear, and told them to focus their attention on one of the messages (the *attended message*) and to ignore the other one (the *unattended message*). For example, the subject might be told to attend to the left-ear message that began "As Susan drove down the road in her new car ..." while simultaneously receiving, but not attending to, the right-ear message "Cognitive psychology, which is the study of mental processes ..."

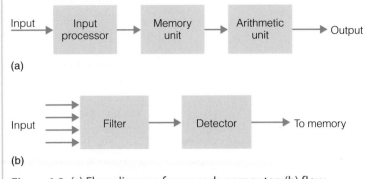

Figure 1.9 (a) Flow diagram for an early computer; (b) flow diagram for Broadbent's filter model of attention. This diagram shows many messages entering a "filter," which selects the message to which the person is attending for further processing by a detector and then storage in memory. We will describe this diagram more fully in Chapter 4. © Cengage Learning

The result of this experiment, which we will describe in detail when we discuss attention in Chapter 4, was that when people focused on the attended message, they could hear the sounds of the unattended message but were unaware of the contents of that message. This result led another British psychologist, Donald Broadbent (1958), to propose the first flow diagram of the mind (**Figure 1.9b**). This diagram represents what happens in a person's mind when directing attention to one stimulus in the environment. Applied to Cherry's attention experiment, "input" would be the sounds of both the attended and unattended messages; the "filter" lets through the attended message and filters out the unattended message; and the "detector" records the information that gets through the filter.

Applied to your experience when talking to a friend at a noisy party, the filter lets in your friend's conversation and filters out all the other conversations and noise. Thus, although you might be aware that there are other people talking, you are not aware of detailed information such as what the other people are talking about.

Broadbent's flow diagram provided a way to analyze the operation of the mind in terms of a sequence of processing stages and proposed a model that could be tested by further experiments. You will see many more flow diagrams like this throughout this book because they have become one of the standard ways of depicting the operation of the mind. But the British psychologists Cherry and Broadbent weren't the only researchers finding new ways of studying the mind. At about the same time in the United States, researchers organized two conferences that, taking their cue from computers, conceived of the mind as a processor of information.

CONFERENCES ON ARTIFICIAL INTELLIGENCE AND INFORMATION THEORY

In the early 1950s, John McCarthy, a young professor of mathematics at Dartmouth College, had an idea. Would it be possible, McCarthy wondered, to program computers to mimic the operation of the human mind? Rather than simply asking the question, McCarthy decided to organize a conference at Dartmouth in the summer of 1956 to provide a forum for researchers to discuss ways that computers could be programmed to carry out intelligent behavior. The title of the conference, *Summer Research Project on Artificial Intelligence,* was the first use of the term **artificial intelligence**. McCarthy defined the artificial intelligence approach as "making a machine behave in ways that would be called intelligent if a human were so behaving" (McCarthy et al., 1955).

Researchers from a number of different disciplines—psychologists, mathematicians, computer scientists, linguists, and experts in information theory—attended the conference, which spanned 10 weeks. A number of people attended most of the conference, others dropped in and out, but perhaps the two most important participants—Herb Simon and Alan Newell from the Carnegie Institute of Technology—were hardly there at all (Boden, 2006). The reason they weren't there is that they were busy back in Pittsburgh trying to create the artificial intelligence machine that McCarthy had envisioned. Simon and Newell's goal was to create a computer program that could create proofs for problems in logic—something that up until then had only been achieved by humans.

Newell and Simon succeeded in creating the program, which they called the **logic theorist**, in time to demonstrate it at the conference. What they demonstrated was revolutionary, because the logic theorist program was able to create proofs of mathematical theorems that involve principles of logic. This program, although primitive compared to modern artificial intelligence programs, was a real "thinking machine" because it did more than simply process numbers—it used humanlike reasoning processes to solve problems.

Shortly after the Dartmouth conference, in September of the same year, another pivotal conference was held, the *Massachusetts Institute of Technology Symposium on Information Theory*. This conference provided another opportunity for Newell and Simon to demonstrate their logic theorist program, and the attendees also heard George Miller, a Harvard psychologist, present a version of a paper "The Magical Number Seven Plus or Minus Two," which had just been published (Miller, 1956). In that paper, Miller presented the idea that there are limits to the human's ability to process information—that the information processing of the human mind is limited to about seven items (for example, the length of a telephone number).

As we will see when we discuss this idea in Chapter 5, there are ways to increase our ability to take in and remember information (for example, we have little trouble adding an area code to the seven digits of many telephone numbers). Nonetheless, Miller's basic principle that there are limits to the amount of information we can take in and remember was an important idea, which, you might notice, was similar to the point being made by Broadbent's filter model at about the same time.

THE COGNITIVE "REVOLUTION" TOOK A WHILE

The events we have described—Cherry's experiment, Broadbent's filter model, and the two conferences in 1956—represented the beginning of a shift in psychology from behaviorism to the study of the mind. Although we have called this shift the *cognitive revolution*, it is worth noting that the shift from Skinner's behaviorism to the cognitive approach, which was indeed revolutionary, occurred over a period of time. The scientists attending the conferences in 1956 had no idea that these conferences would, years later, be seen as historic events in the birth of a new way of thinking about the mind or that scientific historians would someday call 1956 "the birthday of cognitive science" (Bechtel et al., 1998; Miller, 2003; Neisser, 1988). In fact, even years after these meetings, a textbook on the history of psychology made no mention of the cognitive approach (Misiak & Sexton, 1966), and it wasn't until 1967 that Ulrich Neisser published a textbook with the title *Cognitive Psychology* (Neisser, 1967). **Figure 1.10** shows a time line of some of the events that led to the establishment of the field of cognitive psychology.

LOOKING AHEAD

Neisser's textbook, which coined the term *cognitive psychology* and emphasized the information-processing approach to studying the mind, is, in a sense, the grandfather of the book you are now reading. As often happens, each successive generation creates new ways of approaching problems, and cognitive psychology has been no exception. Since the 1956 conferences and the 1967 textbook, many experiments have been carried out, new theories proposed, and new techniques developed; as a result, cognitive psychology, and

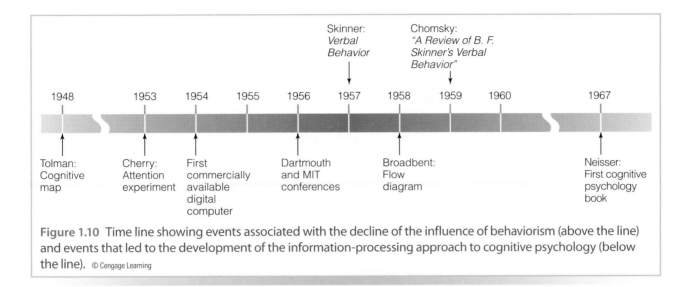

Figure 1.10 Time line showing events associated with the decline of the influence of behaviorism (above the line) and events that led to the development of the information-processing approach to cognitive psychology (below the line). © Cengage Learning

the information-processing approach to studying the mind, has become one of the dominant approaches in psychology.

We have come a long way since Donders measured the relationship between reaction time and making a decision (should I press the left button or the right button?). But modern cognitive psychology experiments still measure relationships. For example, we will see that it is easier to remember the first and last words than those in the middle of a list of 20 words we have just heard (Chapter 5: Memory); that we respond faster to words that appear more frequently in our language (like *house*) than to words that appear less frequently (like *hike*) (Chapter 11: Language); and that people often judge events they have heard about (like tornados) as more likely to cause death than events they haven't heard much about (like asthma), even though the opposite might be true (asthma is 20 times more likely to cause death than tornados) (Chapter 13: Judgment, Decisions, and Reasoning).

The goal of all of the experiments that measure these relationships is to use behavior to reveal how the mind operates. But the goal of modern cognitive psychology research extends beyond measuring single relationships, because the ultimate goal is to understand the mind, and the mind is a complex system.

Modern Research in Cognitive Psychology

How do cognitive psychologists think about the complexity of the mind? How does this influence the questions they ask and the experiments they carry out? The answers to these questions may be different for different researchers and different types of problems, but we will consider two aspects of research that apply to cognitive psychology in general: (1) how research progresses from one question to another; and (2) the role of models in cognitive psychology.

FOLLOWING A TRAIL: HOW RESEARCH PROGRESSES FROM ONE QUESTION TO ANOTHER

Research in cognitive psychology, like research in science in general, begins with what is known about a problem. From that starting point, researchers ask questions, design experiments, and obtain and interpret results. These findings then become the basis for new questions, experiments, and results. We can thus think of the process of research in terms of following a trail in which one thing leads to another. As with many trails, there are places where it is necessary to choose one path or another. In terms of research, the pathway taken is determined by the questions that are asked. The biggest challenge of research is, therefore, not doing the experiments, but picking the right questions.

To illustrate the idea of research as following a trail, we will describe research by Sian Beilock (2010) on the problem of "choking under pressure," where *choking* is performing more poorly than expected given a person's skill level when the person feels pressure to perform at a high level. We pick this research because the topic of choking is relevant to many people's experience, and because the experiments we are going to describe provide a good example of following a trail in which one question leads to another.

Choking is observed in many different contexts. A golfer flubbing an easy putt that would have clinched a championship and a basketball player "going cold" and missing 10 shots in a row in a crucial game are examples of choking in sports. Choking can also occur in an academic setting. Josh studies hard for an important exam and feels he knows the material, but he becomes nervous in the testing situation and does poorly.

In one of Beilock's early papers, written when she was a graduate student in Thomas Carr's laboratory at Michigan State University, she begins by stating that "the phenomenon of choking under pressure remains to be explained" (Beilock & Carr, 2001). The beginning of the research trail, then, was a phenomenon (choking) that needed an explanation. Another starting point was the proposal of a type of memory called *working memory*, which is involved in holding information in memory as it is being manipulated, as occurs when doing a math problem in our head (Baddeley & Hitch, 1974).

To look for a link between working memory and choking, Beilock and Carr (2004) did an experiment in which they presented subjects with math problems and asked them to indicate whether the result had a remainder. For example, for the problem below, answer "yes" if there is a remainder, "no" if there isn't.

$$(32 - 8) \text{ divided by } 4 = ?$$

Think about how you solved the problem (we'll come back to this later), then try this one:

$$(32 - 6) \text{ divided by } 4 = ?$$

The answers are "no" for the first problem and "yes" for the second.

When Beilock presented problems such as these to subjects under low-pressure conditions ("Here's a problem") and high-pressure conditions ("You will be videotaped and need to do well to receive a cash payment"), she found that performance decreased (choking occurred) for problems that were more difficult and so depended more on working memory. The reason for this finding, Beilock hypothesized, was that pressure caused subjects to worry, and this worry used up some of their working memory capacity.

Let's stop for a moment to appreciate what this conclusion means. This research has gone beyond simply describing a phenomenon ("People choke under pressure") or showing when it occurs ("Choking is more likely for hard tasks") to hypothesizing something about *what is going on in the mind* ("Working memory is being disrupted"). Does this sound familiar? This is the Donders technique of measuring behavior and then inferring what is happening in the mind.

But remember that we are following a trail, and another question is required in order to continue. Beilock posed that question in her next paper (Beilock & Carr, 2005) by stating that in order to understand the causal mechanism responsible for choking, "one must identify the characteristics of individuals most likely to fail." Following this idea, Beilock again built on previous research. Twenty-five years earlier, Meredyth Daneman and Patricia Carpenter (1980) had developed a test to measure working memory capacity and found that, based on this test, they could divide their subjects into two groups: low working memory (LWM) subjects and high working memory (HWM) subjects.

With this division of subjects into LWM and HWM in mind, Beilock used the experimental design shown in Figure 1.11, in which LWM and HWM subjects did the math problems under either low-pressure or high-pressure conditions. Based on what you now know, which subjects do you think were more likely to choke under pressure? It makes sense to think that the LWM subjects would be more likely to choke, because worrying could use up their already limited working memory capacity.

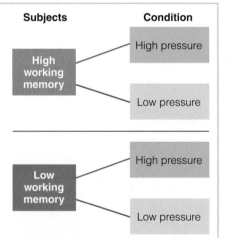

Figure 1.11 Experimental design for Beilock and Carr's (2005) experiment. See text for details. © 2015 Cengage Learning

But remember that research builds upon previous results, and Michael Kane and Randall Engle (2000) had recently published a paper in which they presented a verbal task to LWM and HWM subjects under two conditions: low load (the verbal task was presented alone) and high load (subjects did another task while they were doing the verbal task). In the low load condition, HWM subjects performed better than the LWM subjects, but in the high load condition, the performance of both groups was the same. Thus, the advantage of the HWM subjects vanished under high load conditions.

Kane and Engle's result, and the reasons for it (which we won't go into here), led Beilock to expect that HWM subjects would be more likely to choke under high pressure, and **Figure 1.12** shows that this is exactly what happened. HWM subjects did better than LWM subjects under low-pressure conditions, but the performance of HWM subjects decreased in the high-pressure situation. In other words, subjects with the best working memory reserves were more likely to choke.

In research, one result leads to another question, and the next question was why the HWM subjects were more susceptible to choking. Perhaps, Beilock thought, the answer could be found by considering the strategy that LWM and HWM subjects used to solve the math problems.

How is it possible to determine the strategy a person is using to solve a problem? One way is to ask them! When Beilock and Marci DeCaro (2007) asked their subjects to solve problems and then describe how they had solved them, they found that in low-pressure situations, the HWM subjects were more likely to arrive at their answer by doing the calculation. Thus, in our first example, on page 16, they would subtract 8 from 32 and divide the result by 4. This method always results in the correct answer but places a heavy load on working memory. In contrast, the LWM subjects were more likely to use a "short cut" that states that if all of the numbers are even, the answer is "no." This strategy works for many problems (like the first one), but not for all (like the second one). This short-cut strategy places a low load on working memory, but doesn't always result in the correct answer.

The strategy used by the HWM subjects in the low-pressure condition is clearly better in terms of accuracy, and that's why they score higher in the low-pressure condition. But increasing the pressure increased the likelihood that HWM subjects would shift to the short-cut strategy. When they did this, their performance dropped to the level of the LWM subjects. Meanwhile, the LWM subjects continued using the short-cut strategy, which, because it didn't use much working memory, wasn't affected by the pressure.

There are, of course, further questions that could be asked about choking. One of them is "How can choking be prevented?" which Beilock (2010) investigated in further experiments. Thus, understanding cognitive mechanisms underlying behavior is not just of academic interest. Practical applications such as ways to help people cope with pressure, or how to study more effectively (which we will discuss in Chapter 7), often follow from basic research on cognitive mechanisms.

From this example of starting with a phenomenon and then following a trail created by asking questions, observing experimental results, asking further questions, and so on, we can appreciate the complexities faced by researchers who are studying cognitive processes. One way cognitive psychologists have dealt with this complexity is to create models that represent structures and processes involved in cognition.

THE ROLE OF MODELS IN COGNITIVE PSYCHOLOGY

Models are representations of structures or processes that help us visualize or explain the structure or process. We will consider two kinds of models: *structural models*, which represent structures in the brain that are involved in specific functions; and *process models*, which illustrate how a process operates.

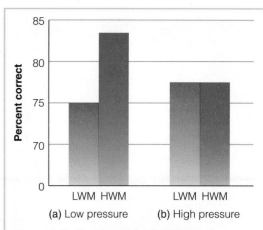

Figure 1.12 Results of the Beilock and Carr (2005) experiment show mathematics problem-solving performance for low working memory (LWM) and high working memory (HWM) subjects under (a) low-pressure and (b) high-pressure conditions. HWM subjects performed better under low-pressure conditions, but lost their advantage under high-pressure conditions. *(Source: Based on S. L. Beilock & T. H. Carr, When high-powered people fail, Psychological Science, 16, 101–105, 2005.)*

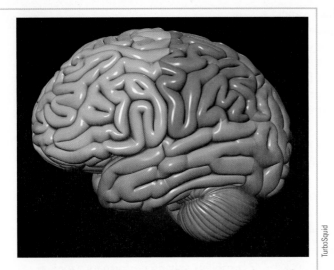

Figure 1.13 A plastic model of the brain can be used to illustrate the locations of different brain structures.

TurboSquid

STRUCTURAL MODELS **Structural models** are representations of a physical structure. A model can mimic the appearance of an object, as a model car or airplane represents the appearance of a real car or airplane. Similarly, plastic models such as the one in **Figure 1.13** have been used to illustrate the locations of different structures of the brain. Structures can also be represented by diagrams that don't resemble the structure but that instead indicate how different areas of the brain are connected. For example, **Figure 1.14** indicates the complexities of the connections between structures in the visual system.

One purpose of models is to simplify. We can appreciate this purpose by considering how we might build a model of the brain. The plastic model in **Figure 1.13** can be taken apart to reveal different structures. Of course, this model isn't anything like a real brain, because besides being made of plastic, it doesn't show what is happening inside each structure and how the structures are connected to each other. We would have to increase the amount of detail in our model to represent this. In fact, if we really wanted our model to be like the brain, we would represent the individual cells, called neurons, that make up the brain (which we will describe in Chapter 2) and how they are connected. But this would be no easy task, because there are

Figure 1.14 A model of the visual system. Each box represents a structure. Lines represent connections between structures. *(Source: D. J. Felleman & D. C. Van Essen, Distributed hierarchical processing in the primate cerebral cortex, Cerebral Cortex, 1, 1–47, 1991).*

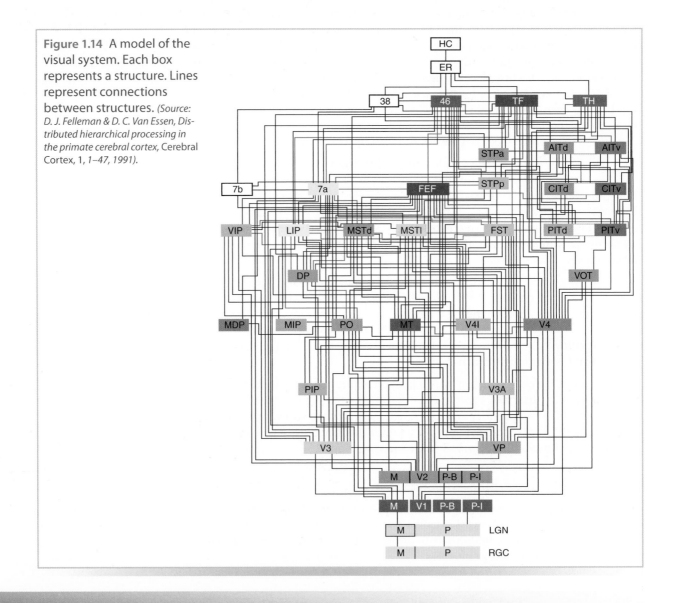

more than 100 billion neurons in the human brain and about 10 trillion connections between them (Horstman, 2012).

Our hypothetical exercise in model building has gotten out of hand, because representing every neuron and every connection takes us far beyond our present knowledge of the brain. Models are not identical replicas of the real thing. They are simplifications that don't contain as much detail, but do contain important information about the structures being represented. Even the complex model of the visual system in **Figure 1.14** is simplified, because each box represents a complex structure. Nonetheless, this model helps us visualize the layout of a system and how different components are connected and might interact. The simplification that is a characteristic of most models is actually an advantage, because it makes it easier to study and understand the system.

It is important to note that most structural models are designed to represent the structures involved in specific functions. Thus, all of the structures in **Figure 1.14** are involved in vision. In Chapter 3, we will describe a model of the system involved in identifying objects. Or consider **Figure 1.15**, which shows a model depicting a group of structures, called the *pain matrix*, that are involved in our perception of pain. This model identifies structures that create different components of the pain experience, which when activated communicate with each other to create the overall experience of pain.

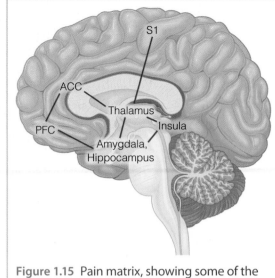

Figure 1.15 Pain matrix, showing some of the structures that are involved in experiencing pain, and their connections. © 2015 Cengage Learning

PROCESS MODELS **Process models** represent the processes that are involved in cognitive mechanisms, with boxes usually representing specific processes and arrows indicating connections between processes. Broadbent's filter model of attention is an example of a process model. In this model, the box representing the "filter" represents the process that separates the attended message from other messages. This process is not necessarily located in one particular place in the brain, so the boxes do not necessarily represent specific structures; rather, they indicate a process that could be carried out by a number of different structures working together.

Figure 1.16 shows a process model that represents the operation of memory. This model of memory, which we will describe in Chapter 5, was proposed in the 1960s and guided memory research for many years. *Sensory memory* holds incoming information for a fraction of a second and then passes most of this information to *short-term memory*, which has limited capacity and holds information for seconds (like an address you are trying to remember until you can write it down). The curved arrow represents the process of rehearsal, which occurs when we repeat something, like a phone number, to keep from forgetting it. The blue arrow indicates that some information in short-term memory can be transferred to *long-term memory*, a high-capacity system that can hold information for long periods of time (like your memory of what you did last weekend, or the names of recent U.S. presidents). The green arrow indicates that some of the information in long-term memory can be returned to short-term memory. The green arrow, which represents what happens when we remember something that was stored in long-term memory, is based on the idea that remembering something involves bringing it back into short-term memory.

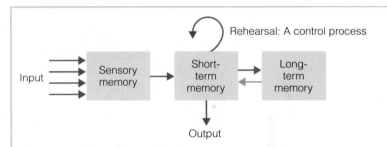

Figure 1.16 An early model of memory. *(Source: Based on R. C. Atkinson & R. M. Shiffrin, Human memory: A proposed system and its control processes, in K. W. Spence & J. T. Spence, Eds., The psychology of learning and motivation, Vol. 2, pp. 89–195, New York: Academic Press, 1968.)*

Process models like this one make complicated systems easier to understand and also provide a starting point for research. For example, research on the long-term component of the memory model in **Figure 1.16** has shown that there are a number of different types of long-term memory, illustrated in **Figure 1.17** (Tulving, 1972, 1985). *Episodic memory* is memory for events in your life (like what you did last weekend). *Semantic memory* is memory for facts (such as the names of recent

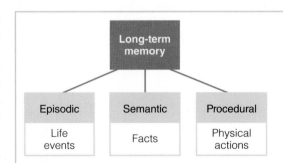

Figure 1.17 A diagram showing three components of long-term memory. *(Source: Based on E. Tulving, How many memory systems are there? American Psychologist, 40, 385–398, 1985.)*

U.S. presidents). *Procedural memory* is memory for physical actions (such as how to ride a bike or play the piano). Realizing that the long-term memory box can be subdivided into types of long-term memory added detail to the model that provided the basis for research into how each of these components operates. As we will see in Chapters 6, 7, and 8, there is evidence that these components are served by different areas of the brain, that their operation is based on different mechanisms, and that they interact with each other to create our total experience of memory. Thus, models simplify complex systems but often become more detailed as researchers study the different components of a model.

We have emphasized behavior in this chapter, because behavior is what cognitive psychologists are trying to explain. But in addition to measuring behavior, cognitive psychologists also measure physiological processes that underlie that behavior. For example, in addition to considering how memory operates behaviorally, cognitive psychologists are also interested in how memory operates in the brain. In fact, for every behavioral question, there is a physiological question, because the brain is the "machinery" responsible for creating the behavior. In Chapter 2: Cognitive Neuroscience, we will introduce principles of brain operation and methods used to uncover the physiological mechanisms of cognition.

Something to Consider

LEARNING FROM THIS BOOK

Congratulations! You now know how some researchers began doing cognitive psychology experiments in the 19th century, how the study of the mind was suppressed in the middle of the 20th century, how the study of the mind made a glorious comeback in the 1950s, and why present-day psychologists create models of the mind. One of the purposes of this chapter—to orient you to the field of cognitive psychology—has been accomplished.

Another purpose of this chapter is to help you get the most out of this book. After all, cognitive psychology is the study of the mind, and there are things that have been discovered about memory that can help you improve your study techniques so you can get as much as possible from this book and from the course you are taking. One way to appreciate how cognitive psychology can be applied to studying is to look at pages 202–203 in Chapter 7. It would make sense to skim this material now, rather than waiting. There will be some terms that you may not be familiar with, but these aren't crucial for what you want to accomplish, which is picking up some hints that will make your studying more efficient and effective. Two terms worth knowing, as you read these pages, are *encoding*—which is what is happening as you are learning the material—and *retrieval*—what is happening when you are remembering the material. The trick is to encode the material during your studying in a way that will make it easier to retrieve it later. (Also see page xxvi in the preface.)

Something else that might help you learn from this book is to be aware of how it is constructed. As you read the book, you will see that often a basic idea or theory is presented and then it is supported by examples or experiments. This way of presenting information breaks the discussion of a particular topic into a series of "mini-stories." Each story begins with an idea or phenomenon and is followed by demonstrations of the phenomenon and usually evidence to support it. Often there is also a connection between one story and the next. The reason topics are presented as mini-stories is that it is easier to remember a number of facts if they are presented as part of a story than if they are presented as separate, unrelated facts. So, as you read this book, keep in mind that your main job is to understand the stories, each of which is a basic premise followed by supporting evidence. Thinking about the material in this way will make it more meaningful and therefore easier to remember.

One more thing: Just as specific topics can be described as a number of small stories that are linked together, the field of cognitive psychology as a whole consists of many themes that are related to each other, even if they appear in different chapters. Perception, attention, memory, and other cognitive processes all involve the same nervous system and therefore share many of the same properties. The principles shared by many cognitive processes are part of the larger story of cognition that will unfold as you progress through this book.

TEST YOURSELF 1.1

1. What are two ways of defining the mind?

2. Why could we say that Donders and Ebbinghaus were cognitive psychologists, even though in the 19th century there was no field called cognitive psychology? Describe Donders's experiment and the rationale behind it, and Ebbinghaus's memory experiments. What do Donders's and Ebbinghaus's experiments have in common?

3. Who founded the first laboratory of scientific psychology? Describe the method of analytic introspection that was used in this laboratory.

4. What method did William James use to study the mind?

5. Describe the rise of behaviorism, especially the influence of Watson and Skinner. How did behaviorism affect research on the mind?

6. Describe the events that helped lead to the decline in importance of behaviorism in psychology and the events that led to the "cognitive revolution." Be sure you understand what the information-processing approach is.

7. Describe the research on choking under pressure. How does this example illustrate how research progresses from one question to another, and how behavior is used to infer what is going on in the mind?

8. Why are models important in cognitive psychology? What are structural models? Process models? Do the boxes in process models correspond to structures in the brain?

9. What are two suggestions for improving your ability to learn from this book?

CHAPTER SUMMARY

1. Cognitive psychology is the branch of psychology concerned with the scientific study of the mind.

2. The mind creates and controls mental capacities such as perception, attention, and memory, and creates representations of the world that enable us to function.

3. The work of Donders (simple vs. choice reaction time) and Ebbinghaus (the forgetting curve for nonsense syllables) are examples of early experimental research on the mind.

4. Because the operation of the mind cannot be observed directly, its operation must be inferred from what we can measure, such as behavior or physiological responding. This is one of the basic principles of cognitive psychology.

5. The first laboratory of scientific psychology, founded by Wundt in 1879, was concerned largely with studying the mind. Structuralism was the dominant theoretical approach of this laboratory, and analytic introspection was one of the major methods used to collect data.

6. William James, in the United States, used observations of his own mind as the basis of his textbook, *Principles of Psychology*.

7. In the first decades of the 20th century, John Watson founded behaviorism, partly in reaction to structuralism and the method of analytic introspection. His procedures were based on classical conditioning. Behaviorism's central tenet was that psychology was properly studied by measuring observable behavior, and that invisible mental processes were not valid topics for the study of psychology.

8. Beginning in the 1930s and 1940s, B. F. Skinner's work on operant conditioning assured that behaviorism would be the dominant force in psychology through the 1950s.

9. In the 1950s, a number of events occurred that led to what has been called the cognitive revolution—a decline in the influence of behaviorism and a reemergence of the study of the mind. These events included the following: (a) Chomsky's

critique of Skinner's book *Verbal Behavior*; (b) the introduction of the digital computer and the idea that the mind processes information in stages, like a computer; (c) Cherry's attention experiments and Broadbent's introduction of flow diagrams to depict the processes involved in attention; and (d) interdisciplinary conferences at Dartmouth and the Massachusetts Institute of Technology.

10. The phenomenon of choking under pressure, as studied by Sian Beilock, illustrates how research progresses from one question to the next, and how the results of behavioral experiments can be used to infer what is happening in the mind.

11. Models play an essential role in cognitive psychology by representing structures or processes. Structural models represent structures in the brain and how they are connected. Process models illustrate how a process operates. Models make complicated systems easier to understand and often provide a starting point for research.

12. Two things that may help in learning the material in this book are to read the study hints in Chapter 7, which are based on some of the things we know about memory research, and to realize that the book is constructed like a story, with basic ideas or principles followed by supporting evidence.

THINK ABOUT IT

1. What do you think the "hot topics" of cognitive psychology are, based on what you have seen or heard in the media? Hint: Look for stories such as the following: "Scientists Race to Find Memory Loss Cure"; "Defendant Says He Can't Remember What Happened."

2. The idea that we have something called "the mind" that is responsible for our thoughts and behavior is reflected in the many ways that the word *mind* can be used. A few examples of the use of *mind* in everyday language were cited at the beginning of the chapter. See how many more examples you can think of that illustrate different uses of the word *mind*, and decide how relevant each is to what you will be studying in cognitive psychology (as indicated by the table of contents of this book).

3. The idea that the operation of the mind can be described as occurring in a number of stages was the central principle of the information-processing approach, which was one of the outcomes of the cognitive revolution that began in the 1950s. How can Donders's reaction time experiment from the 1800s be conceptualized in terms of the information-processing approach?

4. Donders compared the results of his simple and choice reaction time experiments to infer how long it took, when given a choice, to make the decision as to which button to push. But what about other kinds of decisions? Design an experiment to determine the time it takes to make a more complex decision. Then relate this experiment to the diagram in **Figure 1.3**.

KEY TERMS

Analytic introspection, 7

Artificial intelligence, 13

Behaviorism, 9

Choice reaction time, 6

Classical conditioning, 10

Cognition, 5

Cognitive map, 11

Cognitive psychology, 4

Cognitive revolution, 12

Information-processing approach, 12

Logic theorist, 14

Mind, 4

Operant conditioning, 10

Process model, 19

Reaction time, 6

Savings, 8

Savings curve, 8

Simple reaction time, 6

Structuralism, 7

Structural model, 18

COGLAB EXPERIMENT Number in parentheses refers to the experiment number in CogLab.

Simple Detection (2)

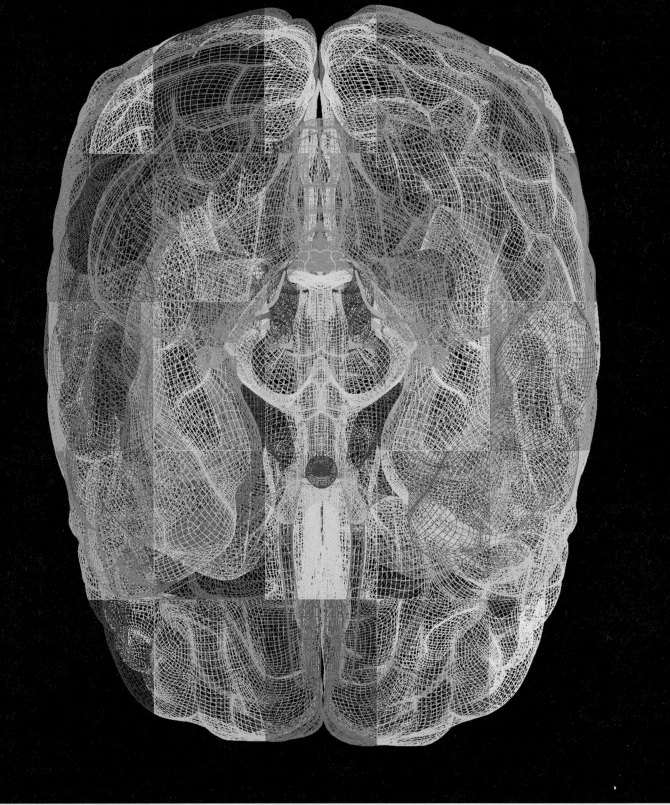

This picture of the brain as seen from the bottom has been artistically embellished with colors and patterns that don't exist in real brains. The beauty of this fanciful image is in the way it symbolizes the mysteries of the brain's operation. Cognitive neuroscience, the study of the physiological mechanisms of cognition, has revealed what is happening in the brain during cognition, and has provided insights that have added to what researchers have learned from purely behavioral experiments. This chapter provides the foundation for understanding the physiological research that you will read about in the chapters that follow.

Cognitive Neuroscience

SOME QUESTIONS WE WILL CONSIDER

▶ What is cognitive neuroscience, and why is it necessary? (27)

▶ How is information transmitted from one place to another in the nervous system? (30)

▶ How are things in the environment, such as faces and trees, represented in the brain? (34)

▶ What does studying the brain tell us about cognition? (46)

At 7:00 AM, in response to hearing the familiar but irritating sound of his alarm clock, Juan swings his arm in a well-practiced arc, feels the contact of his hand with the snooze button, and in the silence he has created, turns over for 10 more minutes of sleep. How can we explain Juan's behavior in terms of physiology? What is happening inside Juan's brain that makes it possible for him to hear the alarm, take appropriate action to turn it off, and know that he can sleep a little longer and still get to his early morning class on time?

We can give a general answer to this question by considering some of the steps involved in Juan's action of turning off the alarm. The first step in hearing the alarm occurs when sound waves from the alarm enter Juan's ears and stimulate receptors that change the sound energy into electrical signals (**Figure 2.1a**). These signals then reach the auditory area of Juan's brain, which causes him to hear the ringing of the bell (**Figure 2.1b**). Then signals are sent from a number of places in the brain to the motor area, which controls movement. The motor area sends signals to the muscles of Juan's hand and arm (**Figure 2.1c**), which carry out the movement that turns off the alarm.

Figure 2.1 Some of the physiological processes that occur as Juan turns off his alarm. (a) Sound waves are changed to electrical signals in the ear and are sent to the brain. (b) Signals reaching the auditory areas of the brain—located inside the brain, under the hatched area—cause Juan to hear the alarm. (c) After Juan hears the alarm, signals are sent to the motor area. The two dashed arrows symbolize the fact that these signals reach the motor area along a number of different pathways. Signals are then sent from the motor area to muscles in Juan's arm and hand so he can turn off the alarm.

© Cengage Learning

(a) Sound to electricity

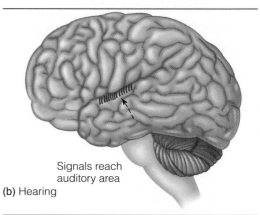

Signals reach auditory area

(b) Hearing

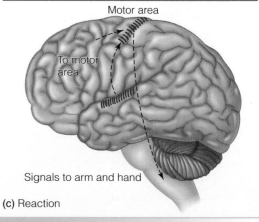

Motor area

To motor area

Signals to arm and hand

(c) Reaction

But there is more to the story than this sequence of events. For one thing, Juan's decision to hit the snooze button of his alarm is based on his knowledge that this will silence the alarm temporarily, and that the alarm will sound again in 10 minutes. He also knows that if he stays in bed for 10 more minutes, he will still have time to get to his class. A more complete picture of what's happening in Juan's brain when the alarm rings would therefore have to include processes involved in retrieving knowledge from memory and making decisions based on that knowledge. Thus, a seemingly simple behavior such as turning off an alarm in the morning involves a complex series of physiological events. The purpose of this chapter is to introduce some of the basic physiological principles of **cognitive neuroscience**—the study of the physiological basis of cognition.

Why Study Cognitive Neuroscience?

Some students taking their first course in cognitive psychology are surprised to find that studying the mind involves both behavioral experiments and physiological experiments. "Why," they ask, "is it necessary to learn about the operation of the brain to understand how people perceive or remember?" But for other students, especially those who have studied the brain in a previous course, it is obvious that taking a physiological approach provides important insights into how the mind works.

The point of view taken in this book is that to understand how the mind works, we need to do both behavioral experiments and physiological experiments. The reasoning behind this conclusion is based on the idea of *levels of analysis*. **Levels of analysis** refers to the idea that a topic can be studied in a number of different ways, with each approach contributing its own dimension to our understanding. To understand what this means, let's consider a topic outside the realm of cognitive psychology: understanding the automobile.

Our starting point for this problem might be to take a car out for a test drive. We could determine its acceleration, its braking, how well it corners, and its gas mileage. When we have measured these things, which come under the heading of "performance," we will know a lot about the particular car we are testing. But to learn more, we can consider another level of analysis: what is going on under the hood. This would involve looking at the mechanisms responsible for the car's performance: the motor and the braking and steering systems. For example, we can describe the car as being powered by a 4-cylinder 250 HP internal combustion engine and having independent suspension and disc brakes.

But we can look even deeper into the operation of the car by considering another level of analysis designed to help us understand how the car's engine works. One approach would be to look at what happens inside a cylinder. When we do this, we see that when vaporized gas enters the cylinder and is ignited by the spark plug, an explosion occurs that pushes the cylinder down and sends power to the crankshaft and then to the wheels. Clearly, considering the automobile from the different levels of driving the car, describing the motor, and observing what happens inside a cylinder provides more information about cars than simply measuring the car's performance.

Applying this idea of levels of analysis to cognition, we can consider measuring behavior to be analogous to measuring the car's performance, and measuring the physiological processes behind the behavior as analogous to what we learned by looking under the hood. And just as we can study what is happening under a car's hood at different levels, we can study the physiology of cognition at levels ranging from the whole brain, to structures within the brain, to chemicals that create electrical signals within these structures.

Consider, for example, a situation in which Gil is talking with Mary in the park (**Figure 2.2a**), and then a few days later he passes the park and remembers what she was

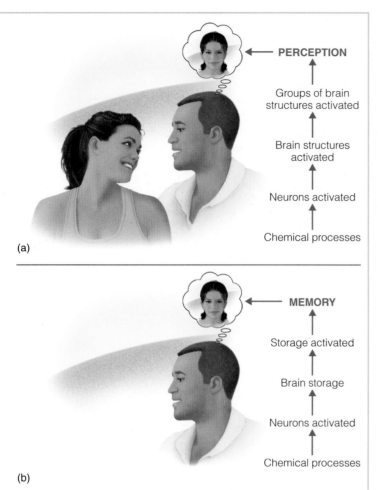

(a)

(b)

Figure 2.2 Physiological levels of analysis. (a) Gil perceives Mary and their surroundings as he talks with her. The physiological processes involved in Gil's perception can be described at levels ranging from chemical reactions to single neurons, to structures in the brain, to groups of structures in the brain. (b) Later, Gil remembers his meeting with Mary. The physiological processes involved in remembering can also be described at different levels of analysis. © 2015 Cengage Learning

wearing and what they talked about (**Figure 2.2b**). This is a simple behavioral description of having an experience and later having a memory of that experience.

But what is going on at the physiological level? During the initial experience, in which Gil perceives Mary as he is talking with her, chemical processes occur in Gil's eyes and ears, which create electrical signals in neurons (which we will describe shortly); individual brain structures are activated, then multiple brain structures are activated, all leading to his perception of Mary and what is happening as they talk (**Figure 2.2a**).

Meanwhile, other things are happening, both during Gil's conversation with Mary and after it is over. The electrical signals generated as Gil was talking with Mary trigger chemical and electrical processes that result in the storage of Gil's experiences in his brain. Then, when Gil passes the park a few days later, another sequence of physiological events is triggered that retrieves the information that was stored earlier, which enables him to remember his conversation with Mary (**Figure 2.2b**).

We have gone a long way to make a point, but it is an important one. To fully understand any phenomenon, whether it is how a car operates or how people remember past experiences, it needs to be studied at different levels of analysis. In this book, we will therefore be describing research in cognition at both the behavioral and physiological levels.

The plan of this chapter is to begin by describing some basic principles of nervous system functioning by first considering the structure and functioning of *neurons*, cells that are the building blocks and transmission lines of the nervous system. We then describe how cognitions are represented by the firing of neurons in the brain, activity in specific areas of the brain, and activity in groups of interconnected areas of the brain. As we do this, we will introduce three methods that have been used to study cognitive neuroscience: recording from single neurons; studying the effects of brain damage in humans; and creating images of the brain.

Neurons: Communication and Representation

How is it possible that the 3.5-pound structure called the brain could be the seat of the mind? The brain appears to be static tissue. It has no moving parts (like the heart). It doesn't expand or contract (like the lungs), and when observed with the naked eye it looks almost solid. As it turns out, to understand the relation between the brain and the mind, and specifically to understand the physiological basis for everything we perceive, remember, and think, it is necessary to look within the brain and observe the small units called **neurons** that create and transmit information about what we experience and know.

THE MICROSTRUCTURE OF THE BRAIN: NEURONS

For many years, the nature of the brain's tissue was a mystery. Looking at the interior of the brain with the unaided eye gave no indication that it is made up of billions of smaller units. The nature of electrical signals in the brain and the pathways over which they traveled were just beginning to be discovered in the 19th century.

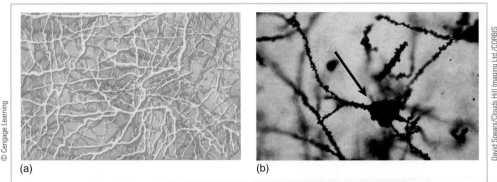

(a)

(b)

Figure 2.3 (a) Nerve net theory proposed that signals could be transmitted throughout the net in all directions. (b) A portion of the brain that has been treated with Golgi stain shows the shapes of a few neurons. The arrow points to a neuron's cell body. The thin lines are dendrites or axons (see **Figure 2.4**).

To observe the structure of the brain, 19th-century anatomists applied special stains to brain tissue, which increased the contrast between different types of tissue within the brain. When they viewed this stained tissue under a microscope, they saw a network they called a **nerve net** (**Figure 2.3a**). This network was believed to be continuous, like a highway system in which one street connects directly to another, but without stop signs or traffic lights. When visualized in this way, the nerve net provided a complex pathway for conducting signals uninterrupted through the network.

One reason for describing the microstructure of the brain as a continuously interconnected network was that the staining techniques and microscopes used during that period could not resolve small details, and without these details, the nerve net appeared to be continuous. However, in the 1870s, the Italian anatomist Camillo Golgi developed a staining technique in which a thin slice of brain tissue was immersed in a solution of silver nitrate. This technique created pictures like the one in **Figure 2.3b**, in which fewer than 1 percent of the cells were stained, so they stood out from the rest of the tissue. (If all of the cells had been stained, it would be difficult to distinguish one cell from another because the cells are so tightly packed). Also, the cells that were stained were stained completely, so it was possible to see their structure.

This brings us to Ramon y Cajal, a Spanish physiologist who was interested in investigating the nature of the nerve net. Cajal cleverly used two techniques to achieve his goal. First, he used the Golgi stain, which stained only some of the cells in a slice of brain tissue. Second, he decided to study tissue from the brains of newborn animals, because the density of cells in the newborn brain is small compared to the density in the adult brain. This property of the newborn brain, combined with the fact that the Golgi stain affects less than 1 percent of the neurons, made it possible for Cajal to clearly see that the nerve net was not continuous, but was instead made up of individual units connected together (Kandel, 2006). Cajal's discovery that individual units called neurons were the basic building blocks of the brain was the centerpiece of **neuron doctrine**—the idea that individual cells transmit signals in the nervous system, and that these cells are not continuous with other cells as proposed by nerve net theory.

Figure 2.4a shows the basic parts of a neuron. The **cell body** is the metabolic center of the neuron; it contains mechanisms to keep the cell alive. The function of **dendrites** that branch out from the cell body is to receive signals from other neurons. **Axons** (also called **nerve fibers**) are usually long processes that transmit signals to other neurons. **Figure 2.4b** shows a neuron with a receptor that receives stimuli from the environment—pressure, in this example. Thus, the neuron has a receiving end and a transmitting end, and its role, as visualized by Cajal, was to transmit signals.

Cajal also came to some other conclusions about neurons: (1) There is a small gap between the end of a neuron's axon and the dendrites or cell body of another neuron. This

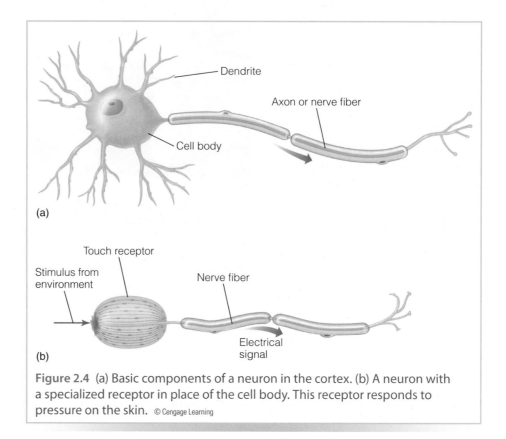

Figure 2.4 (a) Basic components of a neuron in the cortex. (b) A neuron with a specialized receptor in place of the cell body. This receptor responds to pressure on the skin. © Cengage Learning

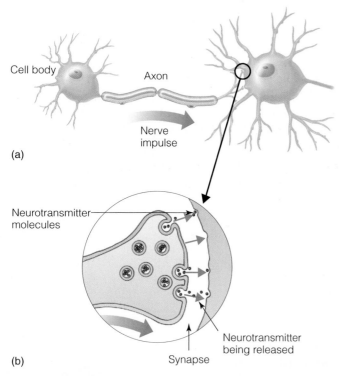

Figure 2.5 (a) Neuron synapsing on cell body of another neuron. (b) Close-up of the synapse showing the space between the end of one neuron and the cell body of the next neuron, and neurotransmitter being released. © Cengage Learning

gap is called a **synapse** (**Figure 2.5**). (2) Neurons are not connected indiscriminately to other neurons, but form connections only to specific neurons. This forms groups of interconnected neurons, which together form **neural circuits**. (3) In addition to neurons in the brain, there are also neurons that are specialized to pick up information from the environment, such as the neurons in the eye, ear, and skin. These neurons, called **receptors** (**Figure 2.4b**), are similar to brain neurons in that they have an axon, but they have specialized receptors that pick up information from the environment.

Cajal's idea of individual neurons that communicate with other neurons to form neural circuits was an enormous leap forward in the understanding of how the nervous system operates. The concepts introduced by Cajal—individual neurons, synapses, and neural circuits—are basic principles that today are used to explain how the brain creates cognitions. These discoveries earned Cajal the Nobel Prize in 1906, and today he is recognized as "the person who made this cellular study of mental life possible" (Kandel, 2006, p. 61).

THE SIGNALS THAT TRAVEL IN NEURONS

Cajal succeeded in describing the structure of individual neurons and how they are related to other neurons, and he knew that these neurons transmitted signals. However, determining the exact nature of these signals had to await the development of electronic amplifiers that were powerful enough to make the extremely small electrical signals generated by the neuron visible. In the 1920s, Edgar Adrian was able to record electrical signals from single sensory neurons, an achievement for which he was awarded the Nobel Prize in 1932 (Adrian, 1928, 1932).

METHOD
RECORDING FROM A NEURON

Adrian recorded electrical signals from single neurons using **microelectrodes**—small shafts of hollow glass filled with a conductive salt solution that can pick up electrical signals at the electrode tip and conduct these signals back to a recording device. Modern physiologists use metal microelectrodes.

Figure 2.6 shows a typical setup used for recording from a single neuron. There are two electrodes: a **recording electrode**, shown with its recording tip inside the neuron,[1] and a **reference electrode**, located some distance away so it is not affected by the electrical signals. The difference in charge between the recording and reference electrodes is fed into a computer and displayed on the computer's screen.

When the axon, or nerve fiber, is at rest, the meter records a difference in potential between the tips of the two electrodes of −70 millivolts (a millivolt is 1/1000 of a volt), as shown on the right in Figure 2.6a. This value, which stays the same as long as there are no signals in the neuron, is called the **resting potential**. In other words, the inside of the

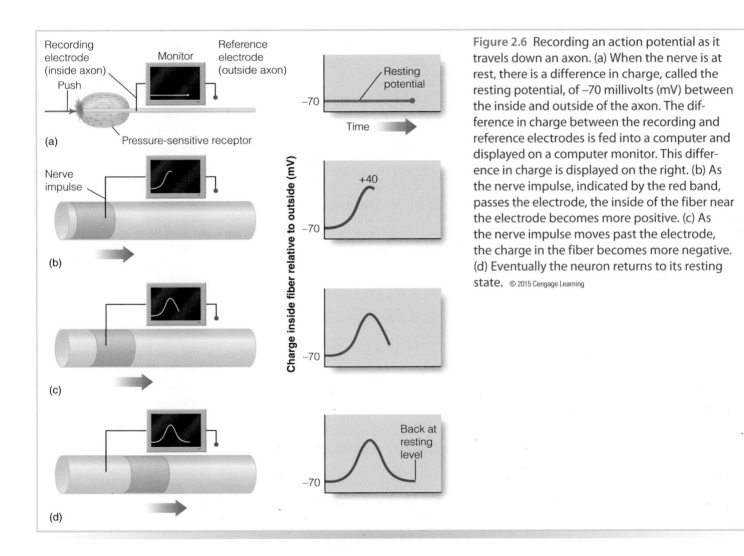

Figure 2.6 Recording an action potential as it travels down an axon. (a) When the nerve is at rest, there is a difference in charge, called the resting potential, of −70 millivolts (mV) between the inside and outside of the axon. The difference in charge between the recording and reference electrodes is fed into a computer and displayed on a computer monitor. This difference in charge is displayed on the right. (b) As the nerve impulse, indicated by the red band, passes the electrode, the inside of the fiber near the electrode becomes more positive. (c) As the nerve impulse moves past the electrode, the charge in the fiber becomes more negative. (d) Eventually the neuron returns to its resting state. © 2015 Cengage Learning

---

[1]In practice, most recordings are achieved with the tip of the electrode positioned just outside the neuron because it is technically difficult to insert electrodes into the neuron, especially if it is small. However, if the electrode tip is close enough to the neuron, the electrode can pick up the signals generated by the neuron.

neuron has a charge that is 70 mV more negative than the outside, and this difference continues as long as the neuron is at rest.

Figure 2.6b shows what happens when the neuron's receptor is stimulated so that a **nerve impulse** is transmitted down the axon. As the impulse passes the recording electrode, the charge inside the axon rises to +40 millivolts compared to the outside. As the impulse continues past the electrode, the charge inside the fiber reverses course and starts becoming negative again (**Figure 2.6c**), until it returns to the resting potential (**Figure 2.6d**). This impulse, which is called the **action potential**, lasts about 1 millisecond (1/1000 second).

Figure 2.7a shows action potentials on a compressed time scale. Each vertical line represents an action potential, and the series of lines indicates that a number of action potentials are traveling past the electrode. **Figure 2.7b** shows one of the action potentials on an expanded time scale, as in **Figure 2.6**. There are other electrical signals in the nervous system, but we will focus here on the action potential, because it is the mechanism by which information is transmitted throughout the nervous system.

In addition to recording action potentials from single neurons, Adrian made other discoveries as well. He found that each action potential travels all the way down the axon without changing its height or shape. This property makes action potentials ideal for sending signals over a distance, because it means that once an action potential is started at one end of an axon, the signal will still be the same size when it reaches the other end.

At about the same time Adrian was recording from single neurons, other researchers were showing that when the signals reach the synapse at the end of the axon, a chemical called a **neurotransmitter** is released. This neurotransmitter makes it possible for the signal to be transmitted across the gap that separates the end of the axon from the dendrite or cell body of another neuron (see **Figure 2.5b**).

Although all of these discoveries about the nature of neurons and the signals that travel in them were extremely important (and garnered a number of Nobel Prizes for their discoverers), our main interest is not in how axons transmit signals, but in how these signals contribute to the operation of the mind. So far our description of how signals are transmitted is analogous to describing how the Internet transmits electrical signals, without describing how the signals are transformed into words and pictures that people can understand. Adrian was acutely aware that it was important to go beyond simply describing nerve signals, so he did a series of experiments to relate nerve signals to stimuli in the environment and therefore to people's experience.

Adrian studied the relation between nerve firing and sensory experience by measuring how the firing of a neuron from a receptor in the skin changed as he applied more pressure to the skin. What he found was that the shape and height of the action potential remained the same as he increased the pressure, but the *rate* of nerve firing—that is, the number of action potentials that traveled down the axon per second—increased (**Figure 2.8**). From this result, Adrian drew a connection between nerve firing and experience. He describes this connection in his book *The Basis of Sensation* (1928) by stating that if nerve impulses "are crowded closely together the sensation is intense, if they are separated by long intervals the sensation is correspondingly feeble" (p. 7).

What Adrian is saying is that electrical signals are *representing* the intensity of the stimulus, so pressure that generates "crowded" electrical signals feels stronger than pressure that generates signals separated by long intervals. Later experiments demonstrated similar results for vision. Presenting high-intensity light generates a high rate of nerve firing and the light appears bright; presenting lower intensity light generates a lower rate of nerve firing and the light appears dimmer. Thus, the rate of neural firing is related to the intensity of stimulation, which, in turn, is related to the magnitude of an experience, such as feeling pressure on the skin or experiencing the brightness of a light.

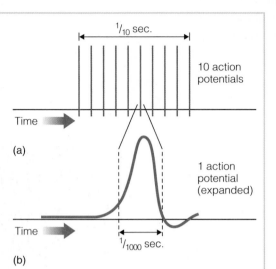

(a)

(b)

Figure 2.7 (a) A series of action potentials displayed on a time scale that makes each action potential appear as a thin line. (b) Changing the time scale reveals the shape of one of the action potentials. © 2015 Cengage Learning

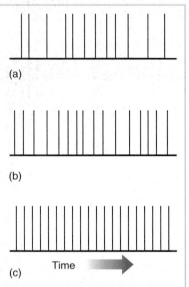

(a)

(b)

(c)

Figure 2.8 Action potentials recorded from an axon in response to three levels of pressure stimulation on the skin: (a) light; (b) medium; (c) strong. Increasing stimulus intensity causes an increase in the rate of nerve firing. © Cengage Learning

We can extend this idea that there is a relationship between nerve firing and perceptual experience by asking how nerve impulses are involved in other aspects of cognition such as memory, language, and thinking. The first step toward doing this is to consider the representational function of nerve impulses.

THE PRINCIPLE OF NEURAL REPRESENTATION

We introduced the idea of representation in Chapter 1, when we defined the mind as *a system that creates representations of the world so that we can act within it to achieve our goals* (page 5). The key word in this definition is *representation*, because what it means is that everything we experience is the result of something that *stands for* that experience. When considering this idea at a neural level, we will study the **principle of neural representation**, which states that everything a person experiences is based not on direct contact with stimuli, but on representations in the person's nervous system.

For example, let's return to Gil's conversation with Mary. Gil sees Mary because light reflected from Mary enters Gil's eyes and Mary's image is focused onto his **retina**, the layer of neurons that lines the back of the eye (**Figure 2.9**). The important word here is *image*, because it is the image created by light reflected by Mary that gets into Gil's eye, not Mary herself. The idea of Mary not getting into the eye may seem silly because it is so obvious, but the point is an important one: What enters the eye is a *representation* of Mary—something that stands for her—and one property of this representation is that although it may look like Mary, it is also different from her. It is not only two-dimensional and smaller, but may be distorted or blurred because of the optics of the eye.

The difference between Mary and her representation on the retina becomes more dramatic a few thousandths of a second later when receptors in the retina transform her image into electrical signals, which then travel through the retina, leave the back of the eye in the optic nerve, and eventually reach the **visual cortex**, the area at the back of the brain that receives signals from the eye. Gil's perception of Mary is therefore based not on direct contact with Mary, but on the way she is represented by action potentials in the brain.

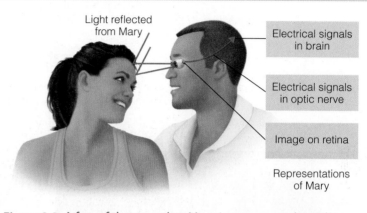

Figure 2.9 A few of the ways that Mary is represented in Gil's visual system. Light reflected from Mary creates an image inside Gil's eye. This image is then transformed into electrical signals that travel out of the eye in the optic nerve and reach the visual area of the brain. © 2015 Cengage Learning

Carrying this idea further, we can consider what happens a few days later when Gil passes the park and remembers what Mary looked like and what they talked about. These memories, which are recreations of Gil's experiences from a few days before, are also created by electrical signals in the brain.

This idea of representation is extremely important in cognitive psychology, because one approach to understanding cognition is to consider how our experiences are represented, both in our mind (measured behaviorally) and in the brain (measured physiologically). Since our focus in this chapter is on physiology, we will now consider how our cognitions are represented physiologically. We start with neurons.

Representation by Neurons

We will use perception as our example to discuss representation by neurons, keeping in mind that the principles that apply to perception also apply to other cognitions such as memory, language, and thinking. Starting with Adrian's idea that the magnitude of experience—our perception of a 100-watt light as brighter than a 40-watt bulb—is related to the rate of nerve firing, we can take the next step and ask, what about the *quality* of experience? For the senses, quality *across the senses* refers to the different experience associated with each of the senses—perceiving light for vision, sound for hearing, smells for olfaction, and so on. We can also ask about quality *within a particular sense*, such as shape, color, or movement for vision, or recognizing different kinds of objects based on their shapes or different people based on their faces.

One way to answer the question of how action potentials determine different qualities is to propose that the action potentials for each quality might look different. However, Adrian ruled out that possibility by determining that all action potentials have basically the same height and shape. If all nerve impulses are basically the same whether they are caused by seeing a red fire engine or remembering what you did last week, how can these impulses stand for different qualities? We begin answering this question by first considering single neurons and then moving on to groups of neurons.

REPRESENTATION BY SINGLE NEURONS

Research on how neural signals represent things followed Adrian's lead and focused on how neurons fire to different sensory stimuli.

FEATURE DETECTORS In the 1960s, David Hubel and Thorsten Wiesel started a series of experiments in which they presented visual stimuli to cats, as shown in **Figure 2.10a**, and determined which stimuli caused specific neurons to fire. They found that each neuron in the visual area of the cortex responded to a specific type of stimulation presented to a small area of the retina. **Figure 2.10b** shows some of the stimuli that caused neurons in and near the visual cortex to fire (Hubel, 1982; Hubel & Wiesel, 1959, 1961, 1965). They called these neurons **feature detectors** because they responded to specific stimulus features such as orientation, movement, and length.

This knowledge that neurons in the visual system fire to specific types of stimuli led to the idea that each of the thousands of neurons that fire when we look at a tree fire to different features of the tree. Some neurons fire to the vertically oriented trunk, others to the variously oriented branches, and some to more complex combinations of a number of features.

The idea that the tree is represented by the combined response of many feature detectors is similar to building objects by combining building blocks like Legos. But these feature detectors are in the visual cortex, which is the first place that electrical signals from the eye reach the brain. Further research in areas beyond the visual cortex revealed neurons that respond to stimuli that are more complex than oriented lines.

NEURONS THAT RESPOND TO COMPLEX STIMULI How are complex stimuli represented by the firing of neurons in the brain? One answer to this question began to emerge in the laboratory of Charles Gross. Gross's experiments, in which he recorded from single neurons in the monkey's temporal lobe, on the side of the brain, required a great deal of endurance by the researchers, because the experiments typically lasted 3 or 4 days. In these experiments, the results of which were reported in now classic papers in 1969 and 1972, Gross's research team presented a variety of different stimuli to anesthetized monkeys. On a projection screen like the one in **Figure 2.10a**, they presented lines, squares, and circles. Some stimuli were light, and some dark.

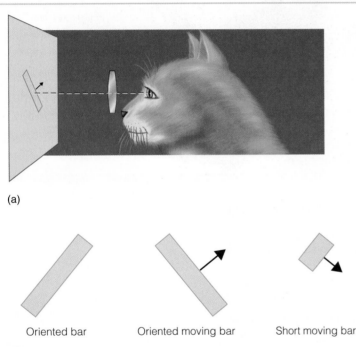

(a)

(b)

Oriented bar   Oriented moving bar   Short moving bar

Figure 2.10 (a) An experiment in which electrical signals are recorded from the visual system of an anesthetized cat that is viewing stimuli presented on the screen. The lens in front of the cat's eye ensures that the images on the screen will be focused on the cat's retina. The recording electrode is not shown. (b) A few of the types of stimuli that cause neurons in the cat's visual cortex to fire. © 2015 Cengage Learning

The discovery that neurons in the temporal lobe respond to complex stimuli came a few days into one of their experiments, when they had found a neuron that refused to respond to any of the standard stimuli like oriented lines or circles or squares. Nothing worked,

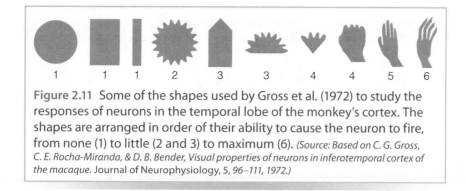

Figure 2.11 Some of the shapes used by Gross et al. (1972) to study the responses of neurons in the temporal lobe of the monkey's cortex. The shapes are arranged in order of their ability to cause the neuron to fire, from none (1) to little (2 and 3) to maximum (6). *(Source: Based on C. G. Gross, C. E. Rocha-Miranda, & D. B. Bender, Visual properties of neurons in inferotemporal cortex of the macaque.* Journal of Neurophysiology, 5, 96–111, 1972.)

until one of the experimenters pointed at something in the room, casting a shadow of his hand on the screen. When this hand shadow caused a burst of firing, the experimenters knew they were onto something and began testing the neuron with a variety of stimuli, including cutouts of a monkey's hand. After a great deal of testing, they determined that this neuron responded to a handlike shape with fingers pointing up (**Figure 2.11**) (Rocha-Miranda, 2011; also see Gross, 2002). After expanding the types of stimuli presented, they also found some neurons that responded best to faces; later researchers extended these results and provided many examples of neurons that respond to faces but don't respond to other types of stimuli (**Figure 2.12**) (Perrett et al., 1982; Rolls, 1981).

Let's stop for a moment and consider the results we have presented so far. We saw that neurons in the visual cortex respond to simple stimuli like oriented bars, neurons in the temporal lobe respond to complex geometrical stimuli, and neurons in another area of the temporal lobe respond to faces. What is happening is that neurons in the visual cortex that respond to relatively simple stimuli send their axons to higher levels of the visual system, where signals from many neurons combine and interact; neurons at this higher level, which respond to more complex stimuli such as geometrical objects, then send signals to higher areas, combining and interacting further and creating neurons that respond to even more complex stimuli such as faces. This progression from lower to higher areas of the brain is called **hierarchical processing**. Does hierarchical processing solve the problem of neural representation? Could it be that higher areas of the visual system contain neurons that are specialized to respond only to a specific object, so that object would be represented by the firing of that one type of specialized neuron? As we will see, the problem of neural representation most likely involves a number of neurons working together.

SENSORY CODING

The problem of neural representation for the senses has been called the *problem of sensory coding*, where the **sensory code** refers to how neurons represent various characteristics of the environment. The idea that an object could be represented by the firing of a specialized neuron that responds only to that object is called **specificity coding**. This is illustrated in **Figure 2.13**, which shows how a number of neurons respond to three different faces. Only neuron #4 responds to Bill's face, only #9 responds to Mary's face, and only #6 responds to Raphael's face. Also note that the neuron specialized to respond only to Bill, which we can call a "Bill neuron," does not respond to Mary or Raphael. In addition, other faces or types of objects would not affect this neuron. It fires only to Bill's face.

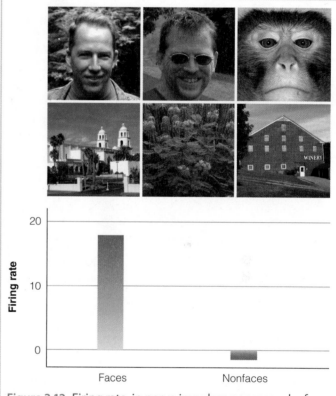

Bruce Goldstein

Figure 2.12 Firing rate, in nerve impulses per second, of a neuron in the monkey's temporal lobe that responds to face stimuli, but not to nonface stimuli. *(Source: Based on E. T. Rolls & M. J. Tovee, Sparseness of the neuronal representation of stimuli in the primate temporal visual cortex,* Journal of Neurophysiology, 73, 713–726, 1995.)

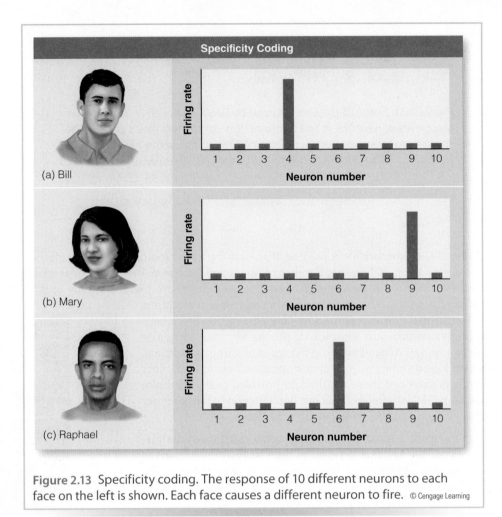

Figure 2.13 Specificity coding. The response of 10 different neurons to each face on the left is shown. Each face causes a different neuron to fire. © Cengage Learning

Although the idea of specificity coding is straightforward, it is unlikely to be correct. Even though there are neurons that respond to faces, these neurons usually respond to a number of different faces (not just Bill's). There are just too many different faces and other objects (and colors, tastes, smells, and sounds) in the world to have a separate neuron dedicated to each object. An alternative to the idea of specificity coding is that a number of neurons are involved in representing an object.

Population coding is the representation of a particular object by the pattern of firing of a large number of neurons. According to this idea, Bill's face might be represented by the pattern of firing shown in **Figure 2.14a**, Mary's face by a different pattern (**Figure 2.14b**), and Raphael's face by another pattern (**Figure 2.14c**). An advantage of population coding is that a large number of stimuli can be represented, because large groups of neurons can create a huge number of different patterns. There is good evidence for population coding in the senses and for other cognitive functions as well. But for some functions, a large number of neurons aren't necessary. *Sparse coding* occurs when small groups of neurons are involved.

Sparse coding occurs when a particular object is represented by a pattern of firing of only a small group of neurons, with the majority of neurons remaining silent. As shown in **Figure 2.15a**, sparse coding would represent Bill's face by the pattern of firing of a few neurons (neurons 2, 3, 4, and 7). Mary's face would be signaled by the pattern of firing of a few different neurons (neurons 4, 6, and 7; **Figure 2.15b**), but possibly with some overlap with the neurons representing Bill, and Raphael's face would have yet another pattern (neurons 1, 2, and 4; **Figure 2.15c**). Notice that a particular neuron can respond to more

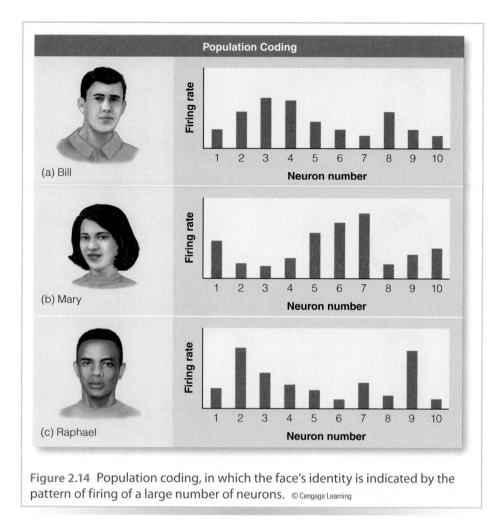

Figure 2.14 Population coding, in which the face's identity is indicated by the pattern of firing of a large number of neurons. © Cengage Learning

than one stimulus. For example, neuron #4 responds to all three faces, although most strongly to Mary's.

Recently, neurons were discovered when recording from the temporal lobe of patients undergoing brain surgery for epilepsy. (We should point out that stimulating and recording from neurons is a common procedure before and during brain surgery, because it makes it possible to determine the exact layout of a particular person's brain.) These neurons responded to very specific stimuli. **Figure 2.16** shows the records for a neuron that responded to pictures of the actor Steve Carell and not to other people's faces (Quiroga et al., 2007). However, the researchers who discovered this neuron (as well as other neurons that responded to other people) point out that they had only 30 minutes to record from these neurons and that if more time were available, it is likely that they would have found other faces that would cause this neuron to fire. Given the likelihood that even these special neurons are likely to fire to more than one stimulus, Quiroga and coworkers (2008) suggested that their neurons are probably an example of sparse coding.

There is also other evidence that the code for representing objects in the visual system, tones in the auditory system, and odors in the olfactory system may involve the pattern of activity across a relatively small number of neurons, as sparse coding suggests (Olshausen & Field, 2004).

Memories are also represented by the firing of neurons, but there is a difference between representation of perceptions and representation of memories. The neural firing associated with experiencing a perception is associated with what is happening as perception is occurring, as in our example in **Figure 2.9** when Gil is looking at Mary. Firing

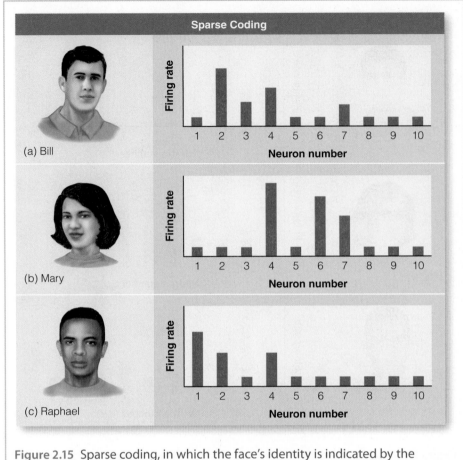

Sparse Coding

(a) Bill

Firing rate / Neuron number

(b) Mary

Firing rate / Neuron number

(c) Raphael

Firing rate / Neuron number

Figure 2.15 Sparse coding, in which the face's identity is indicated by the pattern of firing of a small group of neurons. © Cengage Learning

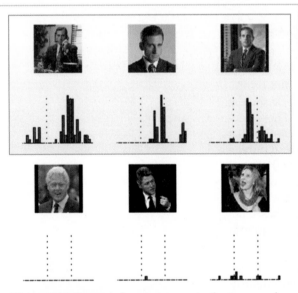

Figure 2.16 Records from a neuron in the temporal lobe that responded to different views of Steve Carell (top records) but did not respond to pictures of other well-known people (bottom records). *(Source: R. Q. Quiroga, L. Reddy, G. Kreiman, C. Koch, & I. Fried, Sparse but not "grandmother-cell" coding in the medial temporal lobe, Trends in Cognitive Sciences, 12, 87–91, 2008. Reproduced by permission.)*

associated with memory is associated with information about the past that has been stored in the brain, as when Gil *remembers* seeing Mary. We know less about the actual form of this stored information for memory, but it is likely that the basic principles of population and sparse coding also operate for memory, with specific memories being represented by particular patterns of stored information that result in a particular pattern of nerve firing when we experience the memory.

Saying that individual neurons and groups of neurons contain information for perception, memory, and other cognitive functions is the first step toward understanding representation. The next step involves looking at organization: how different types of neurons and functions are organized within the brain.

TEST YOURSELF 2.1

1. Describe the idea of levels of analysis. How does this relate to answering the question "Why study cognitive neuroscience?"

2. How did early brain researchers describe the brain in terms of a nerve net? How does the idea of individual neurons differ from the idea of a nerve net?

3. Describe the research that led Cajal to propose the neuron doctrine.

4. Describe the structure of a neuron. Describe the synapse and neural circuits.

5. How are action potentials recorded from a neuron? What do these signals look like, and what is the relation between action potentials and stimulus intensity?

6. How has the question of how different perceptions can be represented by neurons been answered? Consider both research involving recording from single neurons and ideas about sensory coding.

7. How is neural representation for memory different from representation for perception? How is it similar?

Organization: Neuropsychology and Recording From Neurons

One of the basic principles of brain organization is **localization of function**—specific functions are served by specific areas of the brain. Most of the cognitive functions are served by the **cerebral cortex**, which is a layer of tissue about 3 mm thick that covers the brain (Fischl & Dale, 2006). The cortex is the wrinkled covering you see when you look at an intact brain (**Figure 2.17**). Early evidence for localization of function came from **neuropsychology**—the study of the behavior of people with brain damage.

LOCALIZATION DEMONSTRATED BY NEUROPSYCHOLOGY

A great deal of neuropsychological research has involved the study of patients who have suffered brain damage caused by stroke—disruption of the blood supply to the brain, usually by a blood clot. An early report of localization of function based on a stroke patient was Paul Broca's (1861) proposal that an area in the left frontal lobe, now called **Broca's area**, is specialized for speech (**Figure 2.17**). His proposal was based on his study of a patient who had suffered damage to his frontal lobe and was called "Tan" because this was the only word he could say. In 1879, Carl Wernicke studied another group of patients with damage in an area of the temporal lobe, now called **Wernicke's area**, whose speech was fluent and grammatically correct but tended to be incoherent.

Broca and Wernicke thus identified one area for *producing* language (Broca's area) and one area for *comprehending* language (Wernicke's area). Although this straightforward categorization in terms of production and comprehension has been modified by the results of later research (see Novick et al., 2005, and page 308 in Chapter 11), the idea that these two areas of the brain serve different functions is still valid and was a major impetus to accepting the idea of localization of function.

Further evidence for localization of function came from studies of the effect of brain injury in wartime. Studies of Japanese soldiers in the Russo-Japanese war of 1904–1905 and Allied soldiers in World War I showed that damage to the **occipital lobe** of the brain, where the visual cortex is located (**Figure 2.18**), resulted in blindness, and that there was a connection between the area of the occipital lobe that was damaged and the place in visual space where the person was blind (Glickstein & Whitteridge, 1987; Holmes & Lister, 1916; Lanska, 2009). For example, damage to the left part of the occipital lobe caused an area of blindness in the upper right part of visual space.

As noted earlier, other areas of the brain have also been associated with specific functions. The auditory cortex, which receives signals from the ears, is in the upper **temporal lobe** and is responsible for hearing. The somatosensory cortex, which receives signals from the

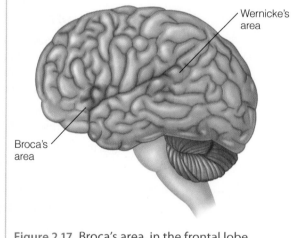

Figure 2.17 Broca's area, in the frontal lobe, and Wernicke's area, in the temporal lobe, were identified in early research as being specialized for language production and comprehension, respectively. © Cengage Learning

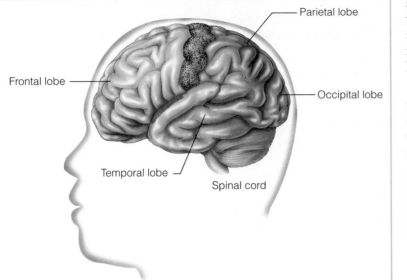

Figure 2.18 The human brain, showing the locations of the primary receiving areas for the senses: vision = occipital lobe; skin senses = parietal lobe (dotted blue area); hearing = temporal lobe (located within the temporal lobe, approximately under the dark shaded area). Areas for taste and smell are not visible. The frontal lobe responds to all of the senses and is involved in higher cognitive functioning. © Cengage Learning

skin, is in the **parietal lobe** and is responsible for perceptions of touch, pressure, and pain. The **frontal lobe** receives signals from all of the senses and is responsible for coordination of the senses, as well as higher cognitive functions like thinking and problem solving.

Another effect of brain damage on visual functioning, reported in patients who have damage to the temporal lobe on the lower right side of the brain, is **prosopagnosia**—an inability to recognize faces. People with prosopagnosia can tell that a face is a face, but can't recognize whose face it is, even for people they know well such as friends and family members. In some cases, people with prosopagnosia look into a mirror and, seeing their own image, wonder who the stranger is looking back at them (Burton et al., 1991; Hecaen & Angelergues, 1962; Parkin, 1996).

One of the goals of neuropsychology research is to determine whether a particular area of the brain is specialized to serve a particular cognitive function. Though it might be tempting to conclude, based on a single case of prosopagnosia, that the damaged brain area in the lower temporal lobe is responsible for recognizing faces, it is necessary to take further steps before reaching this conclusion. To reach more definite conclusions about the functions of a particular area, researchers usually test a number of different patients with damage to different brain areas, in order to demonstrate a *double dissociation*.

METHOD
DEMONSTRATING A DOUBLE DISSOCIATION

A **double dissociation** occurs if damage to one area of the brain causes function A to be absent while function B is present, and damage to another area causes function B to be absent while function A is present. To demonstrate a double dissociation, it is necessary to find two people with brain damage that satisfy the above conditions.

Double dissociations have been demonstrated for face recognition and object recognition, by finding patients who can't recognize faces (Function A) but who can recognize objects (Function B), and other patients, with damage in a different area, who can't recognize objects (Function B) but who can recognize faces (Function A) (McNeal & Warrington, 1993; Moscovitch et al., 1997). The importance of demonstrating a double dissociation is that it enables us to conclude that functions A and B are served by different mechanisms, which operate independently of one another.

The results of the neuropsychology studies described above indicate that face recognition is served by one area in the temporal lobe and that this function is separate from mechanisms associated with recognizing other types of objects, which is served by another area of the temporal lobe. Neuropsychological research has also identified areas that are important for perceiving motion and, as we will see later in this book, for different functions of memory, thinking, and language. In addition to neuropsychology, another tool for demonstrating localization of function is recording from single neurons.

LOCALIZATION DEMONSTRATED BY RECORDING FROM NEURONS

We previously discussed how visual stimuli can be represented by the firing of groups of neurons. We can also use single-neuron recording to demonstrate localization of function.

Most of this research has been done on animals. For example, Doris Tsao and coworkers (2006) found that 97 percent of neurons within a small area in the lower part of a monkey's temporal lobe responded to pictures of faces but not to pictures of other types of objects. This "face area," as it turns out, is located near the area in humans that is associated with prosopagnosia. The idea that our perception of faces is associated with a specific area of the brain is also supported by research using a technique called **brain imaging**, which makes it possible to determine which areas of the brains of humans are activated by different cognitions.

Organization: Brain Imaging

In the 1980s, a technique called **magnetic resonance imaging (MRI)**, which made it possible to create images of structures within the brain, was introduced for clinical practice; since then, it has become a standard technique for detecting tumors and other brain abnormalities. This technique is excellent for revealing brain structures, but it doesn't indicate neural activity. Another technique, **functional magnetic resonance imaging (fMRI)**, has enabled researchers to determine how various types of cognition activate different areas of the brain.

METHOD
BRAIN IMAGING

Functional magnetic resonance imaging takes advantage of the fact that blood flow increases in areas of the brain activated by a cognitive task. The measurement of blood flow is based on the fact that hemoglobin, which carries oxygen in the blood, contains a ferrous (iron) molecule and therefore has magnetic properties. If a magnetic field is presented to the brain, the hemoglobin molecules line up like tiny magnets. fMRI indicates the presence of brain activity because the hemoglobin molecules in areas of high brain activity lose some of the oxygen they are transporting. This makes the hemoglobin more magnetic, so these molecules respond more strongly to the magnetic field. The fMRI apparatus determines the relative activity of various areas of the brain by detecting changes in the magnetic response of the hemoglobin.

The setup for an fMRI experiment is shown in **Figure 2.19a**, with the person's head in the scanner. As a person engages in a cognitive task such as perceiving an image, the activity of

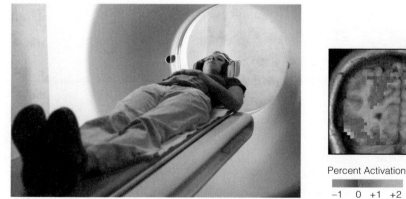

Percent Activation

−1 0 +1 +2

(a)   (b)

Figure 2.19 (a) Person in a brain scanner. (b) fMRI record. Colors indicate locations of increases and decreases in brain activity. Red and yellow indicate increases in brain activity; blue and green indicate decreases. *(Source: Part b from Alumit Ishai, Leslie G. Ungerleider, Alex Martin, & James V. Haxby, The representation of objects in the human occipital and temporal cortex, Journal of Cognitive Neuroscience, 12: 2, 35–51. © 2000 by the Massachusetts Institute of Technology.)*

the brain is determined. Activity is recorded in **voxels**, which are small cube-shaped areas of the brain about 2 or 3 mm on a side. Voxels are not brain structures but are simply small units of analysis created by the fMRI scanner. One way to think about voxels is that they are like the small square pixels that make up digital photographs or the image on your computer screen, but since the brain is three-dimensional, voxels are small cubes rather than small squares. Figure 2.19b shows the result of an fMRI scan. Increases or decreases in brain activity associated with cognitive activity are indicated by colors, with specific colors indicating the amount of activation.

It bears emphasizing that these colored areas do not appear as the brain is being scanned. They are determined by a calculation in which brain activity that occurred during the cognitive task is compared to baseline activity that was recorded prior to the task. The results of this calculation, which indicate increases or decreases in activity in specific areas of the brain, are then converted into colored displays like those in Figure 2.19b.

BRAIN IMAGING EVIDENCE FOR LOCALIZATION OF FUNCTION

Most of the brain imaging experiments that have provided evidence for localization of function have involved determining which brain areas were activated when people observed pictures of different objects.

LOOKING AT PICTURES As shown in Figures 2.20a and 2.20b, faces activate a specific area in the brain (Kanwisher et al., 1997; Kanwisher & Dilks, 2013). This area, called the **fusiform face area (FFA)** because it is in the fusiform gyrus on the underside of the temporal lobe (Kanwisher et al., 1997), is the same part of the brain that is damaged in cases of prosopagnosia.

Further evidence for localization of function comes from fMRI experiments that have shown that perceiving pictures representing indoor and outdoor scenes like those shown in Figure 2.21a activates the **parahippocampal place area (PPA)** (Aguirre et al., 1998; R. Epstein et al., 1999). Apparently, what is important for this area is information about spatial layout, because increased activation occurs when viewing pictures both of empty rooms and of rooms that are completely furnished (Kanwisher, 2003). The other specialized area, the **extrastriate body area (EBA)**, is activated by pictures of bodies and parts of bodies (but not by faces), as shown in Figure 2.21b (Downing et al., 2001).

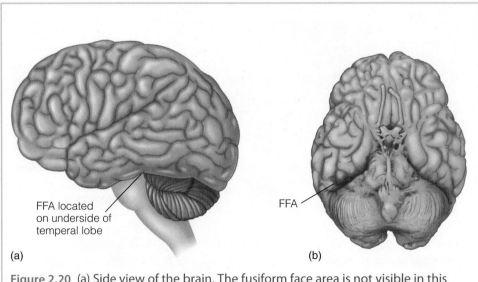

FFA located
on underside of
temporal lobe

FFA

(a)

(b)

Figure 2.20 (a) Side view of the brain. The fusiform face area is not visible in this view because it is located on the underside of the brain. (b) Underside of the brain, showing the location of the FFA. © Cengage Learning

LOOKING AT MOVIES In everyday life, our usual experience involves seeing scenes that contain many different objects, some of which are moving. Therefore, Alex Huth and coworkers (2012) conducted an fMRI experiment using stimuli similar to what we see in the environment, by having subjects view film clips. Huth's subjects viewed 2 hours of film clips while in a brain scanner. To analyze how the voxels in these subjects' brains responded to different objects and actions in the films, Huth created a list of 1,705 different objects and action categories and determined which categories were present in each film scene.

Figure 2.22 shows four scenes and the categories (labels) associated with them. By determining how each voxel responded to each scene and then analyzing his results using a complex statistical procedure, Huth was able to determine what kinds of stimuli each voxel responded to. For example, one voxel responded well when streets, buildings, roads, interiors, and vehicles were present.

Figure 2.23 shows the types of stimuli that cause voxels across the surface of the brain to respond. Objects and actions similar to each other are located near each other in the brain. The reason there are two areas for humans and two for animals is that each area represents different features related to humans or animals. For example, the area labeled "human" at the bottom of the brain (which is actually on the underside of the brain) corresponds to the fusiform face area (**Figure 2.20b**), which responds to all aspects of faces. The human area higher on the brain responds specifically to facial expressions. The areas labeled "talking" correspond to Broca's and Wernicke's areas.

The results in **Figure 2.23** present an interesting paradox. On one hand, the results confirm the earlier research that identified specific areas of the brain responsible for the perception of specific types of stimuli like faces, places, and bodies. On the other hand,

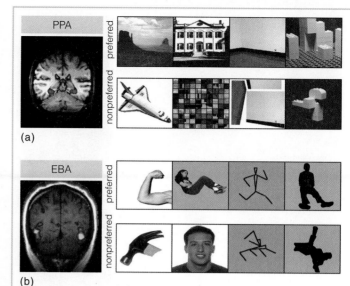

Figure 2.21 (a) The parahippocampal place area (PPA) is activated by places (top row) but not by other stimuli (bottom row). (b) The extrastriate body area (EBA) is activated by bodies (top), but not by other stimuli (bottom). *(Source: From L. M. Chalupa & J. S. Werner, eds., The Visual Neurosciences, 2-vol. set, figure from pp. 1179–1189, © 2003 Massachusetts Institute of Technology, by permission of The MIT Press.)*

Movie Clip	Labels	Movie Clip	Labels
	butte.n desert.n sky.n cloud.n brush.n		city.n expressway.n skyscraper.n traffic.n sky.n
	woman.n talk.v gesticulate.v book.n		bison.n walk.v grass.n stream.n

Figure 2.22 Four frames from the movies viewed by subjects in Huth et al.'s (2012) experiment. The words on the right indicate categories that appear in the frames (n = noun, v = verb). *(Source: From A. G. Huth et al., A continuous semantic space describes the representation of thousands of object and action categories across the human brain, Neuron, 76, 1210–1224, Figure S1, Supplemental materials, 2012.)*

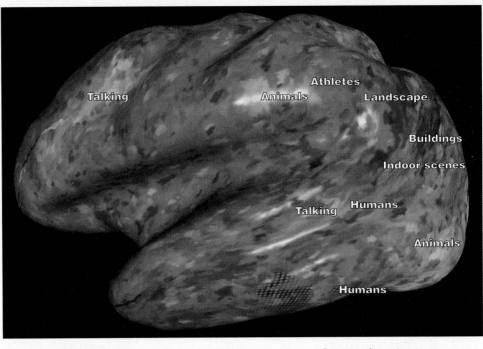

Figure 2.23 The results of Huth et al.'s (2012) experiment, showing locations on the brain where the indicated categories are most likely to activate the brain.

these new results reveal a map that stretches over a large area of the cortex. As we will now see, even though there is a great deal of evidence for localization of function, we need to consider the brain as a whole in order to understand the physiological basis of cognition.

DISTRIBUTED REPRESENTATION ACROSS THE BRAIN

We have seen that brain imaging research has made it possible to zero in on specific areas in the brain that are specialized to serve specific functions. We will now describe research in which brain imaging has been used to show that specific cognitions can affect many structures in the brain. The idea that specific cognitive functions activate many areas of the brain is called **distributed representation**. Although the idea of distributed representation might at first seem to contradict the idea of localization of function described above, we will see that these two ideas actually complement each other.

Consider, for example, the localization of face perception in the brain. We saw that brain imaging experiments have identified an area called the FFA that is strongly activated by faces and responds more weakly to other types of stimuli. But just because there is an area that is specialized to respond to faces doesn't mean that faces activate *only* that area. Faces strongly activate the FFA, *plus* other areas as well.

While a number of areas of the brain participate in *perception* of a face, other areas also respond to various *reactions* to a face. For example, when you see someone walking down the street, looking at the person's face activates many neurons in your FFA, plus neurons in other areas that are responding to the face's form. But your response to that person's face may go beyond simply "That's a person's face." You may also be affected by whether the person is looking at you, how attractive you think the person is, any emotions the face may elicit, and your reactions to the person's facial expression. As it turns out, different areas in the brain are activated by each of these responses to a face (see **Figure 2.24**). Looking at a face thus activates a number of areas involved in perceiving the face, plus other areas associated with reactions elicited by the face.

But what about an encounter with a much simpler stimulus—one that doesn't look at you, have emotional expressions, or elicit emotional responses? How about perceiving a rolling red ball, as the person is doing in **Figure 2.25**? Even this simple, neutral stimulus causes a wide distribution of activity in the brain, because each of the ball's qualities—color (red), movement (to the right), shape (round), depth, location—is processed in a different area of the brain.

What is remarkable about the rolling red ball is that even though it causes activity in a number of separated areas in the brain, our experience contains little or no evidence of this widely distributed activity. We just see the ball! The importance of this observation extends beyond perceiving a rolling red ball to other cognitive functions, such as memory, language, making decisions, and solving problems, all of which involve distributed activity in the brain.

For example, research on the physiology of memory, which we will consider in detail in Chapters 5 and 7, has revealed that multiple areas in every lobe of the brain are involved in storing memories for facts and events and then remembering them later. Recalling a fact or remembering an event not only elicits associations with other facts or events but can also elicit visual, auditory, smell, or taste perceptions associated with the memory; emotions elicited by the memory; and other thought processes as well. Additionally, there are different types of memory—short-term memory, long-term memory, memories about events in a person's life, memories for facts, and so on— all of which activate different, although sometimes partially overlapping, areas of the brain.

The idea that the principle of distributed representation holds for perception, memory, and other cognitive processes reflects the generality of the mechanisms responsible for cognition. Even though this book contains separate chapters on various types of cognitions, this separation does not always occur in the mind or the brain. The mind is, after all, not a textbook; it does not necessarily subdivide our experiences or cognitions into neat categories. Instead, the mind creates cognitive processes that can involve a number of different functions. Just as a symphony is created by many different instruments, all working together in an orchestra to create the harmonies and melodies of a particular composition, cognitive processes are created by many specialized brain areas, all working together to create a distributed pattern of activity that creates all of the different components of that particular cognition.

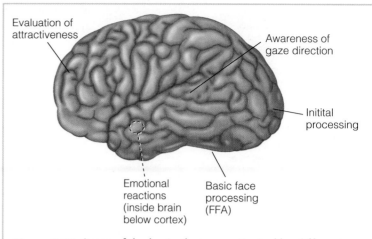

Figure 2.24 Areas of the brain that are activated by different aspects of faces. *(Source: Adapted from Ishai, 2008; based on data from Calder et al., 2007; Gobbini & Haxby, 2007; Grill-Spector et al., 2004; Haxby et al., 2000; Ishai et al., 2004.)* © Cengage Learning

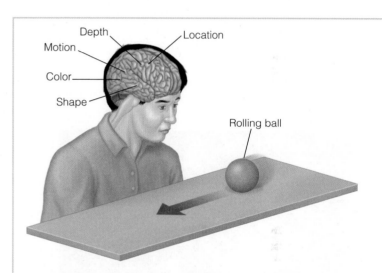

Figure 2.25 As this person watches the red ball roll by, different properties of the ball activate different areas of his cortex. These areas are in separate locations, although there is communication between them. © Cengage Learning

All Together Now: Neural Networks

The idea that the brain is like a symphony in which many different brain areas work together to create various cognitions is suggested not only by the discovery of different brain areas that relate to different aspects of cognition, but also by research on **neural networks**—groups of neurons or structures that are connected together.

Figure 2.26 shows the network we introduced in Chapter 1 to illustrate structural models (see **Figure 1.15**, page 19). This network, called the pain matrix, consists of a number of connected structures that are involved in the perception of pain. In this figure, we have replaced the names of structures with some of the functions these structures serve. Thus, one area is involved in determining the location of pain and its sensory aspects (described by words like *throbbing, prickly,* and *intense*); some areas are involved in emotional aspects

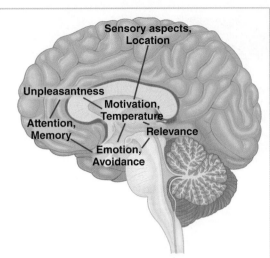

Figure 2.26 The perception of pain is caused by the activation of a network called the pain matrix, consisting of a number of different connected structures. Many structures have multiple functions. Some of the functions associated with structures in the pain matrix are indicated here. © 2015 Cengage Learning

of pain (described by words such as *unpleasant, torturing,* and *frightful*); other areas are involved in evaluating the significance of a pain stimulus for ongoing behavior, directing attention to or away from a painful stimulus, and recording memories of the stimulus. All of the structures in this network, working together, determine the nature of the overall experience of pain.

The network in **Figure 2.26** is just one example of many networks that have been proposed based on research involving all of the methods we have described in this chapter: recording from single neurons, neuropsychology, and brain imaging. In addition, a new generation of anatomical techniques has been developed to trace the pathways of the nerve fibers that create communication between different structures. One technique, called **diffusion tensor imaging (DTI)**, is based on detection of how water diffuses along the length of nerve fibers. **Figure 2.27** shows nerve tracts determined by this technique (Calamante, 2013). New techniques like this are constantly being developed, in order to determine more precisely how areas of the brain communicate with each other.

Earlier in this chapter, we introduced the ideas of *levels of analysis*—studying a topic at different levels—and *neural representation*—how experience is determined by representations in the nervous system. The way various structures in the brain communicate and interact with each other illustrates both of these ideas. To understand the neural basis of cognition, we need to consider levels ranging from individual neurons to structures created from these neurons to groups of structures working together. We also need to realize that all of this activity taken together is what creates representations of our cognitions in the nervous system.

In the next chapter, on perception, we will encounter evidence for these interactions when we see how knowledge we bring to a situation can combine with information provided by signals received from our sensory receptors to create our perception of the environment.

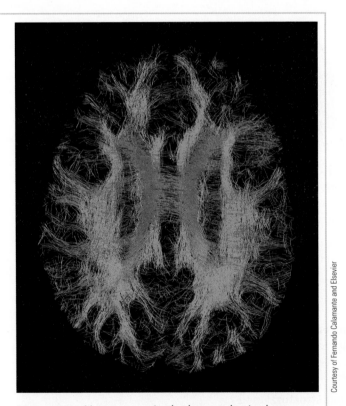

Courtesy of Fernando Calamante and Elsevier

Figure 2.27 Nerve tracts in the human brain determined by diffusion tensor imaging. *(Source: From F. Calamante, et al., Track-weighted functional connectivity [TW-FC]: A tool for characterizing the structural-functional connections in the brain, NeuroImage 70, 199–210, Figure 2a, page 202, 2013.)*

Something to Consider

WHAT NEUROSCIENCE TELLS US ABOUT COGNITION

We have seen that one of the contributions of neuroscience has been to determine where different capacities occur in the brain—a continuing research project that we could call the study of the *geography of the brain*. But the contribution of neuroscience extends beyond just determining where different functions are located. Much neuroscience research has focused on dynamic processes that are happening within the brain, and on determining the mechanisms responsible for cognitive behaviors. In Chapter 4, Attention, we will describe an impressive demonstration of a dynamic process when we revisit the cortical map shown in **Figure 2.23**. As it turns out, this map is not static but can expand or contract. Thus, when you are looking for a cat, aspects of the map relevant to cats expand and aspects distant from cats contract. In other words, the geography of the brain becomes tuned to enable you to more effectively find cats (Çukur, 2013)!

We will also encounter experiments in which proposals based on behavioral observations are supported by the results of physiological research. Consider, for example, Endel Tulving's (1985) distinction, which we introduced in Chapter 1 (page 19) and will consider in detail in Chapter 7, between two types of long-term memory, *episodic memory* and *semantic memory*. Episodic memory, according to Tulving, is memory for personal experiences. Your memory for your trip to New York City and the things you did there would be episodic memories. Semantic memories are stored knowledge and memory for facts. Your knowledge that New York City is in New York State, that throngs of people converge on Times Square every New Year's Eve, and the layout of the New York City subway map are examples of semantic memories.

But although we can distinguish between these two types of memory based on the types of things we remember, can we say that they are served by different mechanisms? One answer to this question is provided by neuropsychological research that has demonstrated a double dissociation between episodic and semantic memory (see Method: Demonstrating a Double Dissociation, page 40). As we will describe in Chapter 7, there are people with brain damage who have lost the ability to remember personal experiences (episodic memory) but still retain memory for facts about the world (semantic memory). There are also people with the opposite problem: Their brain damage has taken away their ability to access their knowledge for facts, but they can still remember personal experiences. These two types of people, taken together, create a double dissociation and enable us to conclude that episodic and semantic memories are served by independent mechanisms. This is just one example of how a proposal based on behavioral observations has been supported and expanded by the results of physiological experiments.

Our description of cognitive neuroscience in this chapter has taken us from the firing of single neurons to maps covering the brain, from linking brain areas to specific cognitions to linking many brain areas together to create more complex cognitions. But let's not lose sight of the purpose of these physiological mechanisms, which is to determine cognitions ranging from recognizing your friend to having a conversation. Although it may be nice to know how neurons work or where brain structures are located, we are not really interested in studying just the properties of neurons or brain structures. We are interested in determining how neurons and brain structures determine cognition. In other words, our main focus is on explaining behaviors related to cognition, and the approach in this book is based on the idea that the best way to explain these behaviors is by conducting both behavioral and physiological experiments. As you read this book, you will encounter many examples of the results of behavioral and physiological experiments combining to provide a richer understanding of the mind than would be provided by either alone.

TEST YOURSELF 2.2

1. What is localization of function? Describe how localization has been demonstrated by neuropsychology and recording from neurons. Be sure you understand the principle of double dissociations.

2. Describe the basic principles behind functional magnetic resonance imaging.

3. Describe brain imaging evidence for localization of function. Describe experiments that involved looking at still pictures and that involved looking at movies. What does each type of experiment tell us about localization of function?

4. What is distributed representation? How is distributed processing illustrated by how the brain responds to faces? By how it responds to a rolling red ball?

5. What is a neural network? What is the connection between the network called the pain matrix and our perception of pain?

6. Describe two things that neuroscience can tell us about cognition.

CHAPTER SUMMARY

1. Cognitive neuroscience is the study of the physiological basis of cognition. Taking a levels-of-analysis approach to the study of the mind involves research at both behavioral and physiological levels.

2. Ramon y Cajal's research resulted in the abandonment of the neural net theory in favor of the neuron doctrine, which states that individual cells called neurons transmit signals in the nervous system.

3. Signals can be recorded from neurons using microelectrodes. Adrian, who recorded the first signals from single neurons, determined that action potentials remain the same size as they travel down an axon and that increasing stimulus intensity increases the rate of nerve firing.

4. The principle of neural representation states that everything that a person experiences is based not on direct contact with stimuli, but on representations in the person's nervous system.

5. Representation by neurons can be explained by considering feature detectors, neurons that respond to complex stimuli, and how neurons are involved in specificity coding, population coding, and sparse coding.

6. The idea of localization of function in perception is supported by the existence of a separate primary receiving area for each sense, by the effects of brain damage on perception (for example, prospoganosia), by recording from single neurons, and from the results of brain imaging experiments.

7. Brain imaging measures brain activation by measuring blood flow in the brain. Functional magnetic resonance imaging (fMRI) is widely used to determine brain activation during cognitive functioning. Brain imaging experiments have measured the response to still pictures to identify areas in the human brain that respond best to faces, places, and bodies, and the response to movies to create a brain map indicating the kinds of stimuli that activate different areas of the brain.

8. The idea of distributed processing is that specific functions are processed by many different areas in the brain. This principle is illustrated by the finding that faces activate many areas of the brain and by the simpler example of the rolling red ball, which also activates a number of areas.

9. Distributed processing also occurs for other cognitive functions, such as memory, decision making, and problem solving. A basic principle of cognition is that different cognitive functions often involve similar mechanisms.

10. Neural networks are groups of neurons or structures that are connected together. The structures that create the pain matrix are, together, an example of a neural network.

11. One of the contributions of neuroscience to the understanding of the mind is determining where different capacities occur in the brain. In addition, proposals based on behavioral research can be supported by the results of physiological research. One example is how the proposal of different types of long-term memory, based on behavior, has been supported by neuropsychological research, studying patients with different types of brain damage.

THINK ABOUT IT

1. Some cognitive psychologists have called the brain the mind's computer. What are computers good at that the brain is not? How do you think the brain and computers compare in terms of complexity? What advantage does the brain have over a computer?

2. People generally feel that they are experiencing their environment directly, especially when it comes to sensory experiences such as seeing, hearing, or feeling the texture of a surface. However, our knowledge of how the nervous system operates indicates that this is not the case. Why would a physiologist say that all of our experiences are indirect?

3. When brain activity is being measured in an fMRI scanner, the person's head is surrounded by an array of magnets and must be kept perfectly still. In addition, the operation of the machine is very noisy. How do these characteristics of brain scanners limit the types of behaviors that can be studied using brain scanning?

4. It has been argued that we will never be able to fully understand how the brain operates because doing this involves using the brain to study itself. What do you think of this argument?

KEY TERMS

Action potential, 32

Axon, 29

Brain imaging, 41

Broca's area, 39

Cell body, 29

Cerebral cortex, 39

Cognitive neuroscience, 27

Dendrites, 29

Diffusion tensor imaging (DTI), 46

Distributed representation, 44

Double dissociation, 40

Extrastriate body area (EBA), 42

Feature detectors, 34

Frontal lobe, 40

Functional magnetic resonance imaging (fMRI), 41

Fusiform face area (FFA), 42

Hierarchical processing, 35

Level of analysis, 27

Localization of function, 39

Magnetic resonance imaging (MRI), 41

Microelectrode, 31

Nerve fiber, 29

Nerve impulse, 32

Nerve net, 29

Neural circuit, 30

Neural network, 45

Neural representation, principle of, 33

Neuron, 28

Neuron doctrine, 29

Neuropsychology, 39

Neurotransmitter, 32

Occipital lobe, 39

Parahippocampal place area (PPA), 42

Parietal lobe, 40

Population coding, 36

Prosopagnosia, 40

Receptors, 30

Recording electrode, 31

Reference electrode, 31

Resting potential, 31

Retina, 33

Sensory code, 35

Sparse coding, 36

Specificity coding, 35

Synapse, 30

Temporal lobe, 39

Visual cortex, 33

Voxel, 42

Wernicke's area, 39

COGLAB EXPERIMENT Number in parentheses refers to the experiment number in CogLab.

Brain Asymmetry (15)

What do you see when you look at the colored pattern in the top panel? Most people find it difficult to tell exactly what object created this image. Only when looking at the lower panel does it become clear that it is the roof of a building. Our perceptual system solves problems like this every time we look at something. Although you might think this would be simple, especially for objects that are less confusing than the top panel in this picture, we will see that there is nothing simple about the process of perception. Perception of even "simple" objects involves complex mechanisms, most of which occur without our awareness, and some of which resemble reasoning.

Perception

CHAPTER

3

SOME QUESTIONS WE WILL CONSIDER

▶ Why can two people experience different perceptions in response to the same stimulus? (60)

▶ How does perception depend on a person's knowledge about characteristics of the environment? (67)

▶ How does the brain become tuned to respond best to things that are likely to appear in the environment? (73)

▶ How are perception and memory represented in the brain? (79)

Crystal begins her run along the beach just as the sun is rising over the ocean. She loves this time of day, both because it is cool and because the mist rising from the sand creates a mystical effect. As she looks down the beach, she notices something about 100 yards away that wasn't there yesterday. "What an interesting piece of driftwood," she thinks, although it is difficult to see because of the mist and dim lighting (**Figure 3.1a**). As she approaches the object, she begins to doubt her initial perception, and just as she is wondering whether it might not be driftwood, she realizes that it is, in fact, the old beach umbrella that was lying under the lifeguard stand yesterday (**Figure 3.1b**). When she realizes this, she is amazed at what has happened. "Driftwood transformed into an umbrella, right before my eyes," she thinks.

Continuing down the beach, she passes some coiled rope that appears to be abandoned (**Figure 3.1c**). She stops to check it out. Grabbing one end, she flips the rope and sees that, as she suspected, it is one continuous strand. But she needs to keep running, because she is supposed to meet a friend at Beach Java, a coffeehouse far down the beach. Later, sitting in the coffeehouse, she tells her friend about the piece of magic driftwood that was transformed into an umbrella.

The Nature of Perception

We define **perception** as experiences resulting from stimulation of the senses. To appreciate how these experiences are created, let's return to Crystal on the beach.

SOME BASIC CHARACTERISTICS OF PERCEPTION

Crystal's experiences illustrate a number of things about perception. Her experience with the umbrella illustrates how perceptions can change based on added information (Crystal's view became better as she got closer to the umbrella) and how perception can involve a process similar to reasoning or problem solving (Crystal figured out what the object

(a) (b) (c)

Figure 3.1 (a) Initially Crystal thinks she sees a large piece of driftwood far down the beach. (b) Eventually she realizes she is looking at an umbrella. (c) On her way down the beach, she passes some coiled rope. © Cengage Learning

Bruce Goldstein

was based partially on remembering having seen the umbrella the day before). (Another example of an initially erroneous perception followed by a correction is the line "It's a bird. It's a plane. It's Superman!") Crystal's guess that the coiled rope was continuous illustrates how perception can be based on a perceptual rule (*when objects overlap, the one underneath usually continues behind the one on top*), which may be based on the person's past experiences.

Crystal's experience also demonstrates how arriving at a perception can involve a *process*. It took some time for Crystal to realize that what she thought was driftwood was actually an umbrella, so it is possible to describe her perception as involving a "reasoning" process. In most cases, perception occurs so rapidly and effortlessly that it appears to be automatic. But, as we will see in this chapter, perception is far from automatic. It involves complex, and usually invisible, processes that do resemble reasoning, although they occur much more rapidly than Crystal's realization that the driftwood was actually an umbrella.

Finally, Crystal's experience also illustrates how perception occurs in conjunction with action. Crystal is running and perceiving at the same time; later, at the coffee shop, she easily reaches for her cup of coffee, a process that involves coordination between seeing the coffee cup, determining its location, physically reaching for it, and grasping its handle. This aspect of Crystal's experiences is just like what happens in everyday perception. We are usually moving, and even when we are just sitting in one place watching TV, a movie, or a sporting event, our eyes are constantly moving as we shift our attention from one thing to another to perceive what is happening. We also grasp and pick up things many times a day, whether it is a cup of coffee, a pen or pencil, or this book. As we will see in this chapter, perception involves dynamic processes that accompany and support our actions.

Before describing these processes, it is important to note that the role of perception extends beyond identifying objects or helping us take action within our environment. We can appreciate this by remembering that cognitive psychology is about acquiring knowledge, storing this knowledge in memory, and retrieving it later to accomplish various tasks such as remembering events from the past, solving problems, communicating with other people, recognizing someone you met last week, and answering questions on a cognitive psychology exam. Without perception, it is unlikely that these feats of cognition would be possible.

Think about this for a moment. How aware could you be of things that are happening right now, and how well could you accomplish the cognitive skills mentioned above, if you had lost all of your senses and, therefore, your ability to perceive? Considered in this way, perception is the gateway to all the other cognitions we will be describing in other chapters in this book.

The goal of this chapter is to explain the mechanisms responsible for perception. To begin, we move from the beach to a city scene: Pittsburgh as seen from the upper deck of PNC Park, home of the Pittsburgh Pirates.

PERCEIVING A SCENE

Sitting in the upper deck of PNC Park, Roger looks out over the city (**Figure 3.2**). He sees a group of about 10 buildings on the left and can easily tell one building from another. Looking straight ahead, he sees a small building in front of a larger one, and has no trouble telling that they are two separate buildings. Looking down toward the river, he notices a horizontal yellow band above the right field bleachers. It is obvious to him that this is not part of the ballpark but is located across the river.

All of Roger's perceptions come naturally to him and require little effort. But when we look closely at the scene, it becomes apparent that the scene poses many "puzzles." The following demonstration points out a few of them.

Figure 3.2 It is easy to tell that there are a number of different buildings on the left and that straight ahead there is a low rectangular building in front of a taller building. It is also possible to tell that the horizontal yellow band above the bleachers is across the river. These perceptions are easy for humans but would be quite difficult for a computer vision system. The letters on the left indicate areas referred to in the Demonstration.

DEMONSTRATION
PERCEPTUAL PUZZLES IN A SCENE

The following questions refer to the areas labeled in **Figure 3.2**. Your task is to answer each question and indicate the reasoning behind each answer:

- What is the dark area at A?
- Are the surfaces at B and C facing in the same or different directions?
- Are areas B and C on the same building or on different buildings?
- Does the building at D extend behind the one at A?

Although it may have been easy to answer the questions, it was probably somewhat more challenging to indicate what your "reasoning" was. For example, how did you know the dark area at A is a shadow? It could be a dark-colored building that is in front of a light-colored building. On what basis might you have decided that building D extends behind building A? It could, after all, simply end right where A begins. We could ask similar questions about everything in this scene because, as we will see, a particular pattern of shapes can be created by a wide variety of objects.

One of the messages of this demonstration is that to determine what is "out there," it is necessary to go beyond the pattern of light and dark that a scene creates on the retina—the structure that lines the back of the eye and contains the receptors for seeing. One way to appreciate the importance of this "going beyond" process is to consider how difficult it has been to program even the most powerful computers to accomplish perceptual tasks that humans achieve with ease.

Consider, for example, the robotic vehicles that were designed to compete in the Urban Challenge race that took place on November 3, 2007, in Victorville, California. This race, which was sponsored by the Defense Advanced Research Project Agency (DARPA), required that vehicles drive for 55 miles through a course that resembled city streets, with other moving vehicles, traffic signals, and signs. The vehicles had to accomplish this feat on their own, with human involvement limited to entering global positioning coordinates of the course's layout into the vehicle's guidance system. Vehicles had to stay on course and avoid unpredictable traffic without any human intervention, based only on the operation of their onboard computer systems.

The winner of the race, a vehicle from Carnegie Mellon University, succeeded in staying on course and avoiding other cars while maintaining an average speed of 14 miles per hour. Vehicles from Stanford, Virginia Tech, MIT, Cornell, and the University of Pennsylvania also successfully completed the course, out of a total of 11 teams that qualified for the final race.

The ability of driverless cars to navigate through the environment, especially one that contains moving obstacles, is extremely impressive. Continued development of robotic vehicles has resulted in the Google driverless car, which has logged more than 500,000 miles of driving and is being developed as an alternative to today's driver-operated vehicles. While these driverless vehicles are able to sense things to be avoided and can identify some objects such as pedestrians and cars, they aren't designed to be able to recognize the large number of different objects that humans identify with little effort ("That's a Siamese cat," "That's Fred," "Here is the house I live in").

Development of computer vision systems that are able to make fine-grained judgments, such as recognizing specific species of animals and plants, is an area of active research (Yang et al., 2012), but performance is still below what humans routinely achieve. For example, programs have been developed that can tell the difference between cats and dogs with about 90 percent accuracy and can identify different breeds of cats and dogs with about 60 percent accuracy (Parkhi et al., 2012). This is a difficult task for computers, involving complex programs and a great deal of training on thousands of different images. One of the problems facing many of the current computer programs is that even though they may be able to identify some objects, they often make errors that a human would never make, such as calling a camera lens cover or the top of a teapot a tennis ball (Simonyan et al., 2012). (See Figure 3.3.)

One object that has received a tremendous amount of attention from computer vision researchers is the human face. With large amounts of research invested in computer surveillance systems, programs have been developed that can determine, just as well as humans can, whether two faces that are seen straight on, as in Figure 3.4a and Figure 3.4b, are the same or different people (O'Toole, 2007; O'Toole et al., 2007; Simonyan et al., 2013; Yang, 2009). However, when one of the faces is seen at an angle, as in Figure 3.4c, humans outperform computers.

Finally, computer vision systems specifically designed to determine the location of a room's walls and to locate furniture within the room are able to achieve these tasks crudely for some photographs, as in Figure 3.5a, but they often make large errors, as in Figure 3.5b (Del Pero et al., 2011). Although the location and extent of the bed in Figure 3.5b may be obvious to a person, it isn't so obvious to a computer, even though the computer program

Figure 3.3 Even computer vision programs that are able to recognize objects fairly accurately make mistakes, such as confusing objects that share features. In this example, the lens cover and the top of the teapot are erroneously classified as a "tennis ball." *(Source: Based on K. Simonyan, Y. Aytar, A. Vedaldi, & A. Zisserman, Presentation at Image Large Scale Visual Recognition Competition, 2012, ILSVRC2012.)*

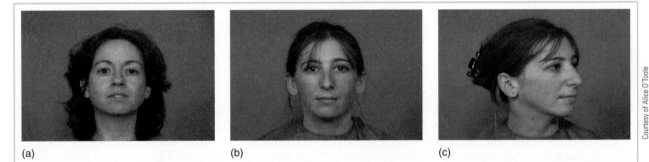

(a)   (b)   (c)

Figure 3.4 A computer or a person can determine whether the two straight-on views in (a) and (b) are the same person, but the person outperforms the computer for faces at an angle, as in (c). *(Source: From A. J. O'Toole, J. Harms, S. L. Snow, D. R. Hurst, M. R. Pappas, & H. Abdi, A video database of moving faces and people, IEEE Transactions on Pattern Analysis and Machine Intelligence, 27, 5, 812–816, 2005.)*

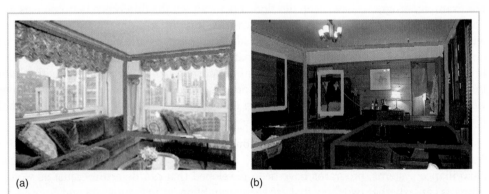

(a)   (b)

Figure 3.5 (a) The red lines represent the attempt of a computer vision program to determine the corners of the room and the places where the wall, ceiling, and floor meet. In this example, the computer does a fairly good job. (b) Another example for the same computer vision program, in which the program's indications of the locations of straight-line contours in the room were inaccurate. *(Source: From L. Del Pero, J. Guan, E. Brau, J. Schlecht, & K. Barnard, Sampling bedrooms, IEEE Computer Society Conference on Computer Vision and Pattern Recognition [CVPR], pp. 2009–2016, 2011. Reproduced by permission.)*

was specifically designed to detect objects like the bed that are defined by straight lines. Even if the program could find the borders of the bed, determining the identity of other objects in the room is far beyond the capabilities of this recently developed program.

Why Is It So Difficult to Design a Perceiving Machine?

We will now describe a few of the difficulties involved in designing a "perceiving machine." Remember that although the problems we describe pose difficulties for computers, humans solve them easily.

THE STIMULUS ON THE RECEPTORS IS AMBIGUOUS

When you look at the page of this book, the image cast by the borders of the page on your retina is ambiguous. It may seem strange to say that, because (1) the rectangular shape of the page is obvious, and (2) once we know the page's shape and its distance from the eye, determining its image on the retina is a simple geometry problem, which, as shown in Figure 3.6, can be solved by extending "rays" from the corners of the page (in red) into the eye.

But the perceptual system is not concerned with determining an object's image on the retina. It *starts* with the image on the retina, and its job is to determine the object "out there" that created the image. The task of determining the object responsible for a particular image on the retina is called the **inverse projection problem**, because it involves starting with the retinal image and extending rays out from the eye. When we do this, as shown by extending the lines in Figure 3.6 out from the eye, we see that the retinal image created by the rectangular page could have also been created by a number of other objects, including a tilted trapezoid, a much larger rectangle, and an infinite number of other objects, located at different distances. When we consider that a particular image on the retina can be created by many different objects in the environment, it is easy to see why we say that the image on the retina is ambiguous. Nonetheless, humans typically solve the inverse projection problem easily, even though it poses serious challenges to computer vision systems.

OBJECTS CAN BE HIDDEN OR BLURRED

Sometimes objects are hidden or blurred. Look for the pencil and eyeglasses in Figure 3.7 before reading further. Although it might take a little searching, people can find the pencil in the foreground and the glasses frame sticking out from behind the computer next to the picture, even though only a small portion of these objects is visible. People also easily

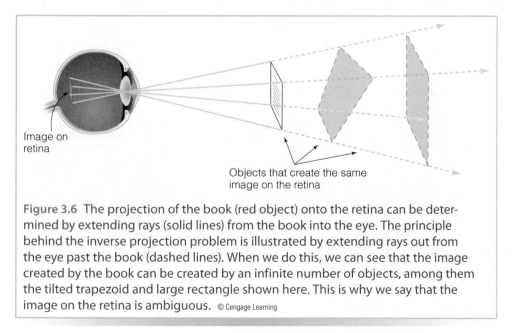

Image on retina

Objects that create the same image on the retina

Figure 3.6 The projection of the book (red object) onto the retina can be determined by extending rays (solid lines) from the book into the eye. The principle behind the inverse projection problem is illustrated by extending rays out from the eye past the book (dashed lines). When we do this, we can see that the image created by the book can be created by an infinite number of objects, among them the tilted trapezoid and large rectangle shown here. This is why we say that the image on the retina is ambiguous. © Cengage Learning

Figure 3.7 A portion of the mess on the author's desk. Can you locate the hidden pencil (easy) and the author's glasses (hard)?

perceive the book, scissors, and paper as whole objects, even though they are partially hidden by other objects.

This problem of hidden objects occurs any time one object obscures part of another object. This occurs frequently in the environment, but people easily understand that the part of an object that is covered continues to exist, and they are able to use their knowledge of the environment to determine what is likely to be present.

People are also able to recognize objects that are not in sharp focus, such as the faces in **Figure 3.8**. See how many of these people you can identify, and then consult the answers on page 83. Despite the degraded nature of these images, people can often identify most of them, whereas computers perform poorly on this task (Sinha, 2002).

OBJECTS LOOK DIFFERENT FROM DIFFERENT VIEWPOINTS

Another problem facing any perceiving machine is that objects are often viewed from different angles. This means that the images of objects are continually changing, depending on the angle from which they are viewed. Thus, although humans continue to perceive the object in **Figure 3.9** as the same chair viewed from

Figure 3.8 Who are these people? See page 83 for the answers. *(Source: Based on P. Sinha, Recognizing complex patterns, Nature Neuroscience, 5, 1093–1097, 2002.)*

(From left to right) © s_bukley/Shutterstock.com; © Featureflash/Shutterstock .com; Soeren Stache/dpa picture alliance archive/Alamy; Peter Muhly/Alamy; © s_bukley/ Shutterstock.com; © Joe Seer/ Shutterstock.com; © DFree/ Shutterstock.com

(a)   (b)   (c)

Figure 3.9 Your ability to recognize each of these views as being of the same chair is an example of viewpoint invariance.

Bruce Goldstein

different angles, this isn't so obvious to a computer. The ability to recognize an object seen from different viewpoints is called **viewpoint invariance**.

The difficulties facing any perceiving machine illustrate that the process of perception is more complex than it seems. Our task, therefore, in describing perception is to explain this process, focusing on how our human perceiving machine operates. We begin by considering two types of information used by the human perceptual system.

Information for Human Perception

Because one purpose of perception is to inform us about what is "out there" in the environment, it makes sense that perception is built on a foundation of information from the environment. Thus, as we described in Chapter 2, Mary is represented in Gil's eye by an image on the retina, by electrical signals that are transmitted through the retina, and by signals transmitted out the back of the eye to the visual receiving area of the brain (**Figure 3.10**).

This information from the light entering the eye and the electrical signals in the brain is crucial for perceiving Mary, because without it, Mary will not be represented in Gil's nervous system. This sequence of events from eye to brain is called **bottom-up processing**, because it starts at the "bottom" or beginning of the system, when environmental energy stimulates the receptors.

But perception involves information in addition to the foundation provided by activation of the receptors and bottom-up processing. Perception also involves factors such as a person's knowledge of the environment, the expectations people bring to the perceptual situation, and their attention to specific stimuli. This additional information is the basis of **top-down processing**—processing that originates in the brain, at the "top" of the perceptual system.

One way to illustrate how top-down processing is involved in perception is to consider examples of situations in which perception is influenced by factors in addition to the bottom-up information from stimulation of the receptors. We will consider three different examples: (1) perceiving objects; (2) hearing words in a sentence; and (3) experiencing pain.

PERCEIVING OBJECTS

An example of how top-down processing is involved in perceiving objects is illustrated in **Figure 3.11**, which is called "the multiple personalities of a blob" (Oliva & Torralba, 2007). Even though the blobs in all of the pictures are identical, they are perceived as different objects depending on their orientation and the context within which they are seen. The blob appears to be an object on a table in (b), a shoe on a person bending down in (c), and a car and a person crossing the street in (d). We perceive it as different objects because of our knowledge of the kinds of objects that are likely to be found in different types of scenes. The human advantage over computers is therefore due, in part, to the additional top-down knowledge available to humans. The idea that knowledge plays a role in perception is also illustrated by the following demonstration.

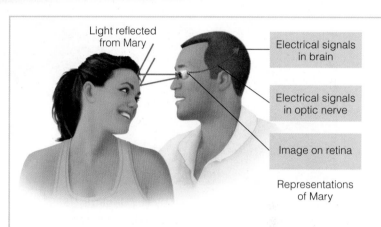

Figure 3.10 Gil looking at Mary, from page 33, showing that Mary is represented in Gil's nervous system by an image on Gil's retina, by electrical signals in Gil's optic nerve, and by electrical signals in Gil's brain. All of this information represents bottom-up processing. © 2015 Cengage Learning

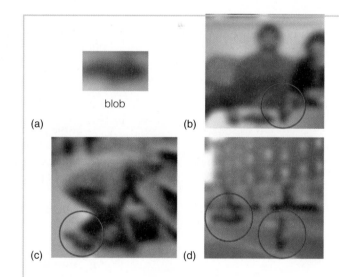

Figure 3.11 "Multiple personalities of a blob." What we expect to see in different contexts influences our interpretation of the identity of the "blob" inside the circles. *(Source: Adapted from A. Oliva & A. Torralba, The role of context in object recognition,* Trends in Cognitive Sciences, 11, *Figure 2, 520–527. Copyright © 2007, with permission from Elsevier. Photographs courtesy of Antonio Torralba.)*

Figure 3.12 *The Forest Has Eyes* by Bev Doolittle (1985). Can you find 13 faces in this picture? (See page 83 for the answers.) *(Source: The Forest Has Eyes © 1984 Bev Doolittle, courtesy of The Greenwich Workshop, Inc.)*

DEMONSTRATION
FINDING FACES IN A LANDSCAPE

Consider the picture in Figure 3.12. At first glance, this scene appears to contain a person and two horses, plus trees, rocks, and water. On closer inspection, however, you can see some faces in the trees in the background, and if you look more closely, you can see that a number of faces are formed by various groups of rocks. See if you can find all 13 faces hidden in this picture.

Some people find it difficult to perceive the faces at first, but then suddenly they succeed. The change in perception from "rocks in a stream" or "trees in a forest" to "faces" occurs because of our familiarity with faces. The remarkable thing about how meaning influences perception in this situation is that once you perceive a particular grouping of rocks as a face, it is often difficult *not* to perceive them in this way—they have become permanently grouped together to create faces within the scene.

HEARING WORDS IN A SENTENCE

An example of how top-down processing influences speech perception is provided by something that happens when I watch Telemundo, a Spanish-language TV channel. Unfortunately, I don't understand anything the people are saying because I don't understand Spanish. In fact, the dialogue sounds to me like an unbroken string of sound, except occasionally when a familiar word like *gracias* pops out. My perception reflects the fact that the sound signal for speech is generally continuous, and when there are breaks in the sound, they do not necessarily occur between words. You can see this in Figure 3.13 by comparing the place where each word in the sentence begins with the pattern of the sound signal.

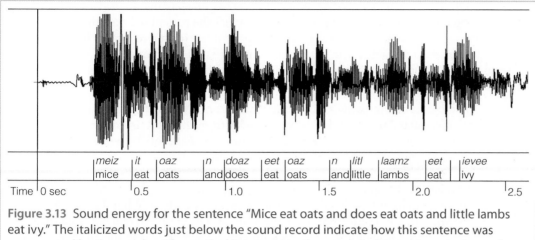

	meiz	it	oaz	n	doaz	eet	oaz	n	litl	laamz	eet	ievee
	mice	eat	oats	and	does	eat	oats	and	little	lambs	eat	ivy

Time   0 sec   0.5   1.0   1.5   2.0   2.5

Figure 3.13 Sound energy for the sentence "Mice eat oats and does eat oats and little lambs eat ivy." The italicized words just below the sound record indicate how this sentence was pronounced by the speaker. The vertical lines next to the words indicate where each word begins. Note that it is difficult or impossible to tell from the sound record where one word ends and the next one begins. *(Speech signal courtesy of Peter Howell.)*

But someone who understands Spanish perceives this unbroken string of sound as individual, meaningful words in a conversation. Because of their knowledge of the language, they are able to tell when one word ends and the next one begins, a phenomenon called **speech segmentation**. The fact that a listener familiar only with English and another listener familiar with Spanish can receive identical sound stimuli but experience different perceptions means that each listener's experience with language (or lack of it!) is influencing his or her perception. The continuous sound signal enters the ears and triggers signals that are sent toward the speech areas of the brain (bottom-up processing); if a listener understands the language, that knowledge (top-down processing) creates the perception of individual words.

EXPERIENCING PAIN

The perception of pain is perhaps the best example of how top-down processing influences perception. We begin our discussion by considering how early researchers thought about pain. In the 1950s and early 1960s, pain was explained by the **direct pathway model**. According to this model, pain occurs when receptors in the skin called *nociceptors* are stimulated and send their signals in a direct pathway from the skin to the brain (Melzack & Wall, 1965). This is a bottom-up process because it depends on stimulation of the receptors. But in the 1960s, some researchers began noting situations in which pain was affected by factors in addition to stimulation of the skin.

An early example was the report by Beecher (1959) that most American soldiers wounded at the World War II Anzio beachhead "entirely denied pain from their extensive wounds or had so little that they did not want any medication to relieve it" (p. 165). One reason for this was that the soldiers' wounds had a positive aspect: They provided escape from a hazardous battlefield to the safety of a behind-the-lines hospital.

Modern research has shown that pain can be influenced by what a person expects, how the person directs his or her attention, and the type of distracting stimuli that are present (Wiech et al., 2008). In a hospital study in which surgical patients were told what to expect and were instructed to relax to alleviate their pain, the patients requested fewer painkillers following surgery and were sent home 2.7 days earlier than patients who were not provided with this information. Studies have also shown that a significant proportion of patients with pathological pain get relief from taking a **placebo**, a pill that they believe contains painkillers but that, in fact, contains no active ingredients (Finniss & Benedetti, 2005; Weisenberg, 1977, 1999).

This decrease in pain from a substance that has no pharmacological effect is called the **placebo effect**. The key to the placebo effect is that the patient believes that the substance is an effective therapy. This belief leads the patient to expect a reduction in pain, and this reduction does, in fact, occur. Although many different mechanisms have been proposed to explain the placebo effect, expectation is one of the more powerful determinants (Colloca & Benedetti, 2005).

The perception of pain can increase if attention is focused on the pain or decrease if the pain is ignored or attention is diverted away from the pain. Examples of this effect of attention on pain were noted in the 1960s (Melzack & Wall, 1965). Here is a recent description of such a situation, as reported by a student in my class:

> I remember being around five or six years old, and I was playing Nintendo when my dog ran by and pulled the wire out of the game system. When I got up to plug the wire back in I stumbled and banged my forehead on the radiator underneath the living room window. I got back up and staggered over to the Nintendo and plugged the controller back into the port, thinking nothing of my little fall.... As I resumed playing the game, all of a sudden I felt liquid rolling down my forehead, and reached my hand up to realize it was blood. I turned and looked into the mirror on the closet door to see a gash running down my forehead with blood pouring from it. All of a sudden I screamed out, and the pain hit me. My mom came running in, and took me to the hospital to get stitches. (Ian Kalinowski)

The important message of this description is that Ian's pain occurred not when he was injured, but when he *realized* he was injured. One conclusion that we might draw from this example is that one way to decrease pain would be to distract a person's attention from the source of the pain. This technique has been used in hospitals using virtual reality techniques as a tool to distract attention from the painful stimulus. Consider, for example, the case of James Pokorny, who had received third-degree burns over 42 percent of his body when the fuel tank of the car he was repairing exploded. While having his bandages changed at the University of Washington Burn Center, he wore a black plastic helmet that contained a computer monitor on which he saw a virtual world of multicolored three-dimensional graphics. This world placed him in a virtual kitchen that contained a virtual spider, and he was able to chase the spider into the sink so he could grind it up with a virtual garbage disposal (Robbins, 2000).

The point of this "game" was to reduce Pokorny's pain by shifting his attention from the bandages to the virtual reality world. Pokorny reported that because he was concentrating on something other than the pain, his pain level went down significantly. Studies of other patients indicate that burn patients using this virtual reality technique while their bandages were being changed experienced much greater pain reduction than did patients in a control group who were distracted by playing video games (Hoffman et al., 2000) or who were not distracted at all (Hoffman et al., 2008; also see Buhle et al., 2012).

All of these examples—how context affects our perception of the blob; how knowledge of speech affects our ability to create words from a continuous speech stream; and how expectation and attention can influence a person's experience of pain—illustrate that perception is created by a combination of bottom-up and top-down processing.

This idea that perception depends on multiple sources of information supports the idea that perception involves a complex process. But identifying different types of information used by the perceptual system is only part of the story. In addition, we can ask how perceivers use this information. After all, both "bottom-up" and "top-down" include the word "processing," which implies that the perceptual system is doing something with this information. Exactly how the perceptual system uses this information has been conceived of in different ways by different people. We will now describe four prominent approaches to perceiving objects, which will take us on a journey that begins in the 1800s and ends with modern conceptions of object perception.

Conceptions of Object Perception

An early idea about how people use information was proposed by 19th-century physicist and physiologist Hermann von Helmholtz (1866/1911).

HELMHOLTZ'S THEORY OF UNCONSCIOUS INFERENCE

Hermann von Helmholtz (1821–1894) was one of the geniuses of the 19th century. He was a physicist who made important contributions to fields as diverse as thermodynamics, nerve physiology, visual perception, and aesthetics. He also invented the ophthalmoscope, versions of which are still used today to enable physicians to examine the blood vessels inside the eye.

One of Helmholtz's contributions to perception was based on his realization that the image on the retina is ambiguous. We have seen that ambiguity means that a particular pattern of stimulation on the retina can be caused by a large number of objects in the environment (see **Figure 3.6**). For example, what does the pattern of stimulation in **Figure 3.14a** represent? For most people, this pattern on the retina results in the perception of a blue rectangle in front of a red rectangle, as shown in **Figure 3.14b**. But as **Figure 3.14c** indicates, this display could also have been caused by a six-sided red shape positioned in front of, behind, or right next to the blue rectangle.

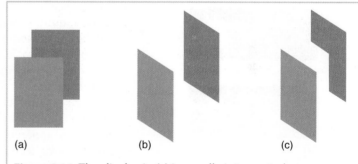

(a) (b) (c)

Figure 3.14 The display in (a) is usually interpreted as being (b) a blue rectangle in front of a red rectangle. It could, however, be (c) a blue rectangle and an appropriately positioned six-sided red figure. © Cengage Learning

Helmholtz's question was, How does the perceptual system "decide" that this pattern on the retina was created by overlapping rectangles? His answer was the **likelihood principle**, which states that we perceive the object that is *most likely* to have caused the pattern of stimuli we have received. This judgment of what is most likely occurs, according to Helmholtz, by a process called **unconscious inference**, in which our perceptions are the result of unconscious assumptions, or inferences, that we make about the environment. Thus, we *infer* that it is likely that **Figure 3.14a** is a rectangle covering another rectangle because of experiences we have had with similar situations in the past.

Helmholtz's description of the process of perception resembles the process involved in solving a problem. For perception, the problem is to determine which object has caused a particular pattern of stimulation, and this problem is solved by a process in which the perceptual system applies the observer's knowledge of the environment in order to infer what the object might be.

Figure 3.15 According to structuralism, a number of sensations (represented by the dots) add up to create our perception of the face. © Cengage Learning

(a) One light flashes

(b) Darkness

(c) The second light flashes

(d) Flash—dark—flash

Figure 3.16 The conditions for creating apparent movement. (a) One light flashes, followed by (b) a short period of darkness, followed by (c) another light flashing at a different position. The resulting perception, symbolized in (d), is a light moving from left to right. Movement is seen between the two lights even though there is only darkness in the space between them. © Cengage Learning

An important feature of Helmholtz's proposal is that this process of perceiving what is most likely to have caused the pattern on the retina happens rapidly and unconsciously. These unconscious assumptions, which are based on the likelihood principle, result in perceptions that seem "automatic," even though they are the outcome of a rapid process. Thus, although you might have been able to "automatically" solve the perceptual puzzles in the scene in **Figure 3.3**, this ability, according to Helmholtz, is the outcome of a rapid process that we are unaware of. (See Rock, 1983, for a more recent version of this idea.)

THE GESTALT PRINCIPLES OF ORGANIZATION

We will now consider an approach to perception proposed by a group called the **Gestalt psychologists** about 30 years after Helmholtz proposed his theory of unconscious inference. The goal of the Gestalt approach was the same as Helmholtz's—to explain how we perceive objects—but they approached the problem in a different way.

The Gestalt approach to perception originated, in part, as a reaction to Wilhelm Wundt's structuralism (see page 7). Remember from Chapter 1 that Wundt proposed that our overall experience could be understood by combining basic elements of experience called *sensations*. According to this idea, our perception of the face in **Figure 3.15** is created by adding up many sensations, represented as dots in this figure.

The Gestalt psychologists rejected the idea that perceptions were formed by "adding up" sensations. One of the origins of the Gestalt idea that perceptions could not be explained by adding up small sensations has been attributed to the experience of psychologist Max Wertheimer, who while on vacation in 1911 took a train ride through Germany (Boring, 1942). When he got off the train to stretch his legs at Frankfurt, he bought a stroboscope from a toy vendor on the train platform. The stroboscope, a mechanical device that created an illusion of movement by rapidly alternating two slightly different pictures, caused Wertheimer to wonder how the structuralist idea that experience is created from sensations could explain the illusion of movement he observed.

Figure 3.16 diagrams the principle behind the illusion of movement created by the stroboscope, which is called **apparent movement** because although movement is perceived, nothing is actually moving. There are three components to stimuli that create apparent movement: (1) One light flashes on and off (**Figure 3.16a**); (2) there is a period of darkness, lasting a fraction of a second (**Figure 3.16b**); and (3) the second light flashes on and off (**Figure 3.16c**). Physically, therefore, there are two lights flashing on and off separated by a period of darkness. But we don't see the darkness because our perceptual system adds something during the period of darkness—the perception of a light moving through the space between the flashing lights (**Figure 3.16d**). Modern examples of apparent movement are electronic signs that display moving advertisements or news headlines, and movies. The perception of movement in these displays is so compelling that it is difficult to imagine that they are made up of stationary lights flashing on and off (for the news headlines) or still images flashed one after the other (for the movies).

Wertheimer drew two conclusions from the phenomenon of apparent movement. His first conclusion was that apparent movement cannot be explained by sensations, because there is nothing in the dark space between the flashing lights. His second conclusion became one of the basic principles of Gestalt psychology: *The whole is different than the sum of its parts.* This conclusion follows from the fact that the perceptual system creates the perception of movement from stationary images. This idea that the whole is different than the sum of its parts led the Gestalt psychologists to propose a number of **principles of perceptual organization** to explain the way elements are grouped together to create larger objects. For example, in **Figure 3.17**, some of the black areas become grouped to form a Dalmatian and others are seen as shadows in the background. We will describe a few of the Gestalt principles, beginning with one that brings us back to Crystal's run along the beach.

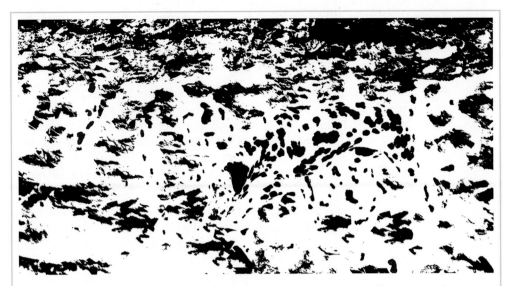

Figure 3.17 Some black and white shapes that become perceptually organized into a Dalmatian. (See page 83 for an outline of the Dalmatian.) © Cengage Learning; © AnetaPics/Shutterstock.com; Scratchgravel Publishing Services

GOOD CONTINUATION The **principle of good continuation** states the following: *Points that, when connected, result in straight or smoothly curving lines are seen as belonging together, and the lines tend to be seen in such a way as to follow the smoothest path. Also, objects that are overlapped by other objects are perceived as continuing behind the overlapping object.* Thus, when Crystal saw the coiled rope in **Figure 3.1c**, she wasn't surprised that when she grabbed one end of the rope and flipped it, it turned out to be one continuous strand (**Figure 3.18**). The reason this didn't surprise her is that even though there were many places where one part of the rope overlapped another part, she didn't perceive the rope as consisting of a number of separate pieces; rather, she perceived the rope as continuous. (Also consider your shoelaces!)

PRAGNANZ *Pragnanz*, roughly translated from the German, means "good figure." The **law of pragnanz**, also called the **principle of good figure** or the **principle of simplicity**, states: *Every stimulus pattern is seen in such a way that the resulting structure is as simple as possible.* The familiar Olympic symbol in **Figure 3.19a** is an example of the law of simplicity at work.

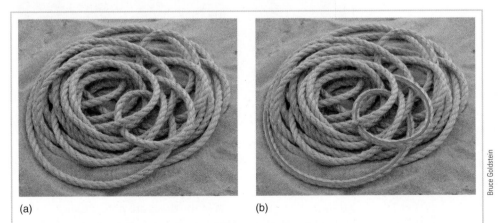

(a) (b)

Bruce Goldstein

Figure 3.18 (a) Rope on the beach. (b) Good continuation helps us perceive the rope as a single strand.

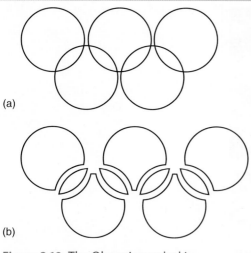

(a)

(b)

Figure 3.19 The Olympic symbol is perceived as five circles (a), not as the nine shapes in (b). © Cengage Learning

We see this display as five circles and not as a larger number of more complicated shapes such as the ones shown in the "exploded" view of the Olympic symbol in **Figure 3.19b**. (The law of good continuation also contributes to perceiving the five circles. Can you see why this is so?)

SIMILARITY Most people perceive **Figure 3.20a** as either horizontal rows of circles, vertical columns of circles, or both. But when we change the color of some of the columns, as in **Figure 3.20b**, most people perceive vertical columns of circles. This perception illustrates the **principle of similarity**: *Similar things appear to be grouped together.* A striking example of grouping by similarity of color is shown in **Figure 3.21**. Grouping can also occur because of similarity of size, shape, or orientation.

There are many other principles of organization, proposed by the original Gestalt psychologists (Helson, 1933) as well as by modern psychologists (Palmer, 1992; Palmer & Rock, 1994), but the main message, for our discussion, is that the Gestalt psychologists realized that perception is based on more than just the pattern of light and dark on the retina. In their conception, perception is determined by specific organizing principles.

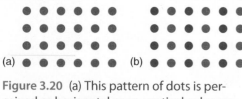

Figure 3.20 (a) This pattern of dots is perceived as horizontal rows, vertical columns, or both. (b) This pattern of dots is perceived as vertical columns. © Cengage Learning

Courtesy of Wilma Hurskainen

Figure 3.21 This photograph, *Waves*, by Wilma Hurskainen, was taken at the exact moment that the front of the white water aligned with the white area on the woman's clothing. Similarity of color causes grouping; differently colored areas of the dress are perceptually grouped with the same colors in the scene. Also notice how the front edge of the water creates grouping by good continuation across the woman's dress.

But where do these organizing principles come from? Max Wertheimer (1912) describes these principles as "intrinsic laws," which implies that they are built into the system. This idea that the principles are "built in" is consistent with the Gestalt psychologists' idea that although a person's experience can *influence* perception, the role of experience is minor compared to the perceptual principles (also see Koffka, 1935). This idea that experience plays only a minor role in perception differs from Helmholtz's likelihood principle, which proposes that our knowledge of the environment enables us to determine what is most likely to have created the pattern on the retina. In agreement with Helmholtz, modern perceptual psychologists also see our experience with the environment as a central component of the process of perception.

TAKING REGULARITIES OF THE ENVIRONMENT INTO ACCOUNT

Modern perceptual psychologists have introduced the idea that perception is influenced by our knowledge of **regularities in the environment**—characteristics of the environment that occur frequently. For example, blue is associated with open sky, landscapes are often green and smooth, and verticals and horizontals are often associated with buildings. We can distinguish two types of regularities: *physical regularities* and *semantic regularities*.

PHYSICAL REGULARITIES **Physical regularities** are regularly occurring physical properties of the environment. For example, there are more vertical and horizontal orientations in the environment than oblique (angled) orientations. This occurs in human-made environments (for example, buildings contain lots of horizontals and verticals) and also in natural environments (trees and plants are more likely to be vertical or horizontal than slanted) (Coppola et al., 1998) (**Figure 3.22**). It is therefore no coincidence that people can perceive horizontals and verticals more easily than other orientations, an effect called the **oblique effect** (Appelle, 1972; Campbell et al., 1966; Orban et al., 1984). Another example of a physical regularity is that when one object partially covers another one, the contour of the partially covered object "comes out the other side," as occurs for the rope in **Figure 3.18**.

Bruce Goldstein

Figure 3.22 In these two scenes from nature, horizontal and vertical orientations are more common than oblique orientations. These scenes are special examples, picked because of the large proportion of verticals. However, randomly selected photos of natural scenes also contain more horizontal and vertical orientations than oblique orientations. This also occurs for human-made buildings and objects.

Another physical regularity is illustrated by **Figure 3.23a**, which shows two textured protrusions jutting out from a wall. But when the picture is turned upside down, as in **Figure 3.23b**, the protrusions appear reversed—now the textured surface appears indented. Our perception in these two situations has been explained by the **light-from-above assumption**: We usually assume that light is coming from above, because light in our environment, including the sun and most artificial light, usually comes from above (Kleffner & Ramachandran, 1992). **Figure 3.23c** shows how light from above would hit the top surface of a protrusion to result in the right-side-up perception. **Figure 3.23d** shows how light from above would hit the lower surface of a recess to result in the upside-down perception.

Another example of how lighting direction can determine perception is shown by the carved wood panel in **Figure 3.24a**, which is the side of a church pew. In this example, light is coming from above and from the right. In this picture, a panel juts out in the center

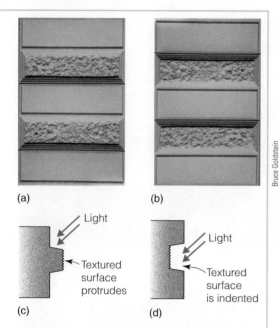

Figure 3.23 (a) A wall with textured surfaces that jut out. (b) The same picture turned upside down. (c) How light coming from above would hit the top of a protrusion, causing the textured surface to appear to be jutting out. (d) How light coming from above hits the bottom of an indentation, causing the textured surface to appear indented. © 2015 Cengage Learning

and is surrounded by two borders containing eight small indentations. Our perception of the panel as jutting out and the eight small areas as indentations is consistent with the light-from-above assumption.

But things become interesting when we invert the photograph, as shown in **Figure 3.24b**. Now our perception depends on where we assume the light is coming from. The usual light-from-above assumption causes the inner panel to appear indented. But if you imagine that light is coming from the bottom, the panel pops out. And then there are the eight small indentations. Do they appear to be "innies" or "outies" in the inverted picture? In this example, turning the picture upside down makes us uncertain of where the light is coming from, creating unstable perceptions. Luckily, when we are normally perceiving overall scenes, the lighting direction is usually obvious, and it is usually from above. Thus, our perceptual system's assumption that light is coming from above results in an accurate perception of three-dimensional objects.

One of the reasons humans are able to perceive and recognize objects and scenes so much better than computer-guided robots is that our system is adapted to respond to the physical characteristics of our environment, such as the orientations of objects and the direction of light. But this adaptation goes beyond physical characteristics. It also occurs because, as we saw when we considered the multiple personalities of a blob (page 59), we have learned about what types of objects typically occur in specific types of scenes.

SEMANTIC REGULARITIES In language, *semantics* refers to the meanings of words or sentences. Applied to perceiving scenes, *semantics* refers to the meaning of a scene. This meaning is often related to what happens within a scene. For example, food preparation, cooking, and perhaps eating occur in a kitchen; waiting around, buying tickets, checking luggage, and going through security checkpoints happen in airports. **Semantic regularities** are the characteristics associated with the functions carried out in different types of scenes.

One way to demonstrate that people are aware of semantic regularities is simply to ask them to imagine a particular type of scene or object, as in the following demonstration.

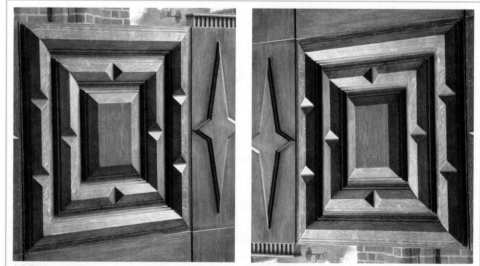

(a) Right side up   (b) Upside down

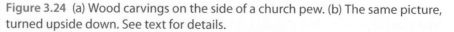

Figure 3.24 (a) Wood carvings on the side of a church pew. (b) The same picture, turned upside down. See text for details.

DEMONSTRATION
VISUALIZING SCENES AND OBJECTS

Your task in this demonstration is simple. Close your eyes and then visualize or simply think about the following scenes and objects:

1. An office
2. The clothing section of a department store
3. A microscope
4. A lion

Most people who have grown up in modern society have little trouble visualizing an office or the clothing section of a department store. What is important about this ability, for our purposes, is that part of this visualization involves details within these scenes. Most people see an office as having a desk with a computer on it, bookshelves, and a chair. The department store scene contains racks of clothes, a changing room, and perhaps a cash register. What did you see when you visualized the microscope or the lion? Many people report seeing not just a single object, but an object within a setting. Perhaps you perceived the microscope sitting on a lab bench or in a laboratory and the lion in a forest, on a savannah, or in a zoo. The point of this demonstration is that our visualizations contain information based on our knowledge of different kinds of scenes. This knowledge of what a given scene typically contains is called a **scene schema**.

Another example of how a scene schema can influence perception is an experiment by Stephen Palmer (1975), which used stimuli like the picture in **Figure 3.25**. Palmer first presented a context scene such as the one on the left and then briefly flashed one of the target pictures on the right. When Palmer asked observers to identify the object in the target picture, they correctly identified an object like the loaf of bread (which is appropriate to the kitchen scene) 80 percent of the time, but correctly identified the mailbox or the drum

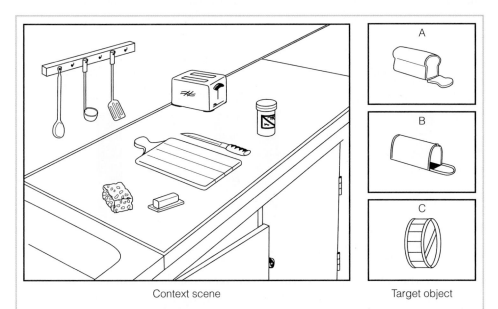

Context scene   Target object

Figure 3.25 Stimuli used in Palmer's (1975) experiment. The scene at the left is presented first, and the observer is then asked to identify one of the objects on the right. *(Source: From S. E. Palmer, The effects of contextual scenes on the identification of objects, Memory and Cognition, 3, 519–526, 1975.)*

(two objects that don't fit into the scene) only 40 percent of the time. Apparently Palmer's observers were using their scene schema for kitchens to help them perceive the briefly flashed loaf of bread.

Although people make use of regularities in the environment to help them perceive, they are often unaware of the specific information they are using. This aspect of perception is similar to what occurs when we use language. Even though people easily string words together to create sentences in conversations, they may not know the rules of grammar that specify how these words are being combined. Similarly, we easily use our knowledge of regularities in the environment to help us perceive, even though we may not be able to identify the specific information we are using.

BAYESIAN INFERENCE

Two of the ideas we have described—(1) Helmholtz's idea that we resolve the ambiguity of the retinal image by inferring what is most likely, given the situation, and (2) the idea that regularities in the environment provide information we can use to resolve ambiguities— are the starting point for our last approach to object perception: *Bayesian inference* (Geisler, 2008, 2011; Kersten et al., 2004; Yuille & Kersten, 2006).

Bayesian inference was named after Thomas Bayes (1701–1761), who proposed that our estimate of the probability of an outcome is determined by two factors: (1) the **prior probability**, or simply the **prior**, which is our initial belief about the probability of an outcome, and (2) the extent to which the available evidence is consistent with the outcome. This second factor is called the **likelihood** of the outcome.

To illustrate Bayesian inference, let's first consider **Figure 3.26a**, which shows Mary's priors for three types of health problems. Mary believes that having a cold or heartburn is likely to occur, but having lung disease is unlikely. With these priors in her head (along with lots of other beliefs about health-related matters), Mary notices that her friend Charles has a bad cough. She guesses that three possible causes could be a cold, heartburn, or lung disease. Looking further into possible causes, she does some research and finds that coughing is often associated with having either a cold or lung disease, but isn't associated with heartburn (**Figure 3.26b**). This additional information, which is the *likelihood*, is combined with Mary's *prior* to produce the conclusion that Charles probably has a cold (**Figure 3.26c**) (Tenenbaum et al., 2011). In practice, Bayesian inference involves a mathematical procedure in which the prior is multiplied by the likelihood to determine the

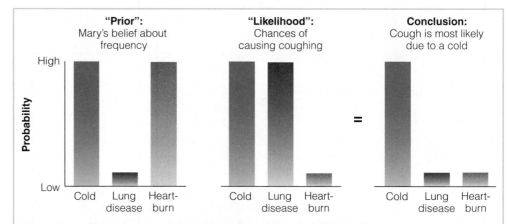

Figure 3.26 These graphs present hypothetical probabilities to illustrate the principle behind Bayesian inference. (a) Mary's beliefs about the relative frequency of having a cold, lung disease, and heartburn. These beliefs are her *priors*. (b) Further data indicate that colds and lung disease are associated with coughing, but heartburn is not. These data contribute to the *likelihood*. (c) Taking the priors and likelihood together results in the conclusion that Charles's cough is probably due to a cold. © 2015 Cengage Learning

probability of the outcome. Thus, people start with a prior, then use additional evidence to update the prior and reach a conclusion (Körding & Wolpert, 2006).

Applying this idea to object perception, let's return to the inverse projection problem from **Figure 3.6**. Remember that the inverse projection problem occurs because a huge number of possible objects could be associated with a particular image on the retina. So the problem is how to determine what is "out there" that is causing a particular retinal image. Luckily, we don't have to rely only on the retinal image, because we come to most perceptual situations with prior probabilities based on our past experiences.

One of the *priors* you have in your head is that books are rectangular. Thus, when you look at a book on your desk, your initial belief is that it is likely that the book is rectangular. The *likelihood* that the book is rectangular is provided by additional evidence such as the book's retinal image, combined with your perception of the book's distance and the angle at which you are viewing the book. If this additional evidence is consistent with your prior that the book is rectangular, the likelihood is high and the perception "rectangular" is strengthened. Further testing by changing your viewing angle and distance can further strengthen the conclusion that the shape is a rectangle. Note that you aren't necessarily conscious of this testing process—it occurs automatically and rapidly. The important point about this process is that while the retinal image is still the starting point for perceiving the shape of the book, adding the person's prior beliefs reduces the possible shapes that could be causing that image.

What Bayesian inference does is to restate Helmholtz's idea—that we perceive what is most likely to have created the stimulation we have received—in terms of probabilities. It isn't always easy to specify these probabilities, particularly when considering complex perceptions. However, because Bayesian inference provides a specific procedure for determining what might be out there, researchers have used it to develop computer vision systems that can apply knowledge about the environment to more accurately translate the pattern of stimulation on their sensors into conclusions about the environment. (Also see Goldreich & Tong, 2013, for an example of how Bayesian inference has been applied to tactile perception.)

COMPARING THE FOUR APPROACHES

Now that we have described four conceptions of object perception (Helmholtz's unconscious inference, the Gestalt laws of organization, regularities in the environment, and Bayesian inference), here's a question: Which one is different from the other three? After you've figured out your answer, look at the bottom of the page.*

The approaches of Helmholtz, regularities, and Bayes all have in common the idea that we use data about the environment, gathered through our past experiences in perceiving, to determine what is out there. Top-down processing is therefore an important part of these approaches.

The Gestalt psychologists, in contrast, emphasized the idea that the principles of organization are built in. They acknowledged that perception is affected by experience, but argued that built-in principles can override experience, thereby assigning bottom-up processing a central role in perception. The Gestalt psychologist Max Wertheimer (1912) provided the following example to illustrate how built-in principles could override experience: Most people recognize **Figure 3.27a** as *W* and *M* based on their past experience with these letters. However, when the letters are arranged as in **Figure 3.27b**, most people see two uprights plus a pattern between them. The uprights, which are created by the principle of good continuation, are the dominant perception and override the effects of past experience we have had with *W*'s and *M*'s.

Although the Gestalt psychologists deemphasized experience, using arguments like the one above, modern psychologists have pointed out that the laws of organization could, in fact, have been created by experience. For example, it is possible that

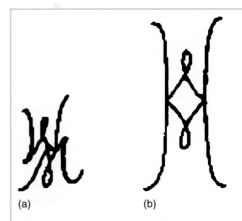

(a)   (b)

Figure 3.27 (a) *W* on top of *M*. (b) When combined, a new pattern emerges, overriding the meaningful letters. *(Source: From M. Wertheimer, Experimentelle Studien über das Sehen von Beuegung, Zeitschrift für Psychologie, 61, 161–265, 1912.)*

*Answer: The Gestalt approach.

Figure 3.28 A usual occurrence in the environment: Objects (the men's legs) are partially hidden by another object (the grey boards). In this example, the men's legs continue in a straight line and are the same color above and below the boards, so it is highly likely that they continue behind the boards.

the principle of good continuation has been determined by experience with the environment. Consider the scene in **Figure 3.28**. From years of experience in seeing objects that are partially covered by other objects, we know that when two visible parts of an object (like the men's legs) have the same color (principle of similarity) and are "lined up" (principle of good continuation), they belong to the same object and extend behind whatever is blocking it. Thus, one way to look at the Gestalt principles is that they describe the operating characteristics of the human perceptual system, *which happen to be determined at least partially by experience.* In fact, there is physiological evidence that experiencing certain stimuli over and over can actually shape the way neurons respond in perceptual systems. We will consider this physiological approach to perception next.

TEST YOURSELF 3.2

1. Describe Helmholtz's theory of unconscious inference. What is the likelihood principle?

2. Describe the Gestalt approach to perception, focusing on the principles of organization. How do these principles originate, according to the Gestalt psychologists?

3. What are regularities of the environment, and how do they influence perception? Distinguish between physical regularities and semantic regularities. What is a scene schema?

4. Describe Bayesian inference in terms of how it would explain the "coughing" example and the inverse projection problem.

5. How does the Gestalt approach differ from the other three? How do modern psychologists explain the relation between experience and the principles of organization?

Neurons and Knowledge About the Environment

We will now follow up on the idea that experience can shape the way neurons respond. Our starting point is the finding that there are more neurons in the animal and human visual cortex that respond to horizontal and vertical orientations than to oblique (slanted) orientations.

NEURONS THAT RESPOND TO HORIZONTALS AND VERTICALS

When we described physical regularities in the environment, we mentioned that horizontals and verticals are common features of the environment (**Figure 3.22**), and behavioral experiments have shown that people are more sensitive to these orientations than to other orientations that are not as common (the *oblique effect*, see page 67). It is not a coincidence, therefore, that when researchers have recorded the activity of single neurons in the visual cortex of monkeys and ferrets, they have found more neurons that respond best to horizontals and verticals than neurons that respond best to oblique orientations (Coppola et al., 1998; DeValois et al., 1982). Evidence from brain scanning experiments suggests that this occurs in humans as well (Furmanski & Engel, 2000).

Why are there more neurons that respond to horizontals and verticals? One possible answer is based on the **theory of natural selection**, which states that characteristics that enhance an animal's ability to survive, and therefore reproduce, will be passed on to future generations. Through the process of evolution, organisms whose visual systems contained neurons that fired to important things in the environment (such as verticals and horizontals, which occur frequently in the forest, for example) would be more likely to survive and pass on an enhanced ability to sense verticals and horizontals than would an organism with a visual system that did not contain these specialized neurons. Through this evolutionary process, the visual system may have been shaped to contain neurons that respond to things that are found frequently in the environment.

While there is no question that perceptual functioning has been shaped by evolution, there is also a great deal of evidence that *learning* can shape the response properties of neurons through a process called *experience-dependent plasticity*.

EXPERIENCE-DEPENDENT PLASTICITY

The brain is changed, or "shaped," by its exposure to the environment so it can perceive the environment more efficiently. The mechanism through which the structure of the brain is changed by experience, called **experience-dependent plasticity**, has been demonstrated in many experiments on animals. These experiments have shown that if an animal is reared in a particular environment, neurons in the animal's brain change so that they become tuned to respond more strongly to specific aspects of that environment. For example, when a kitten is born, its visual cortex contains neurons called feature detectors that respond to oriented bars (see Chapter 2, page 34). Normally, the kitten's brain contains neurons that respond to all orientations, ranging from horizontal to slanted to vertical, and when the kitten grows up into a cat, the cat has neurons that can respond to all orientations.

But what would happen if kittens were reared in an environment consisting only of verticals? Colin Blakemore and Graham Cooper (1970) answered this question by rearing kittens in a space in which they saw only vertical black and white stripes on the walls. Kittens reared in this vertical environment batted at a moving vertical stick but ignored horizontal objects. The basis of this lack of response to horizontals became clear when recording from neurons in the kitten's brain revealed that the visual cortex had been reshaped so it contained neurons that responded mainly to verticals and had no neurons that responded to horizontals. Similarly, kittens reared in an environment consisting only of horizontals ended up with a visual cortex that contained neurons that responded mainly to horizontals. Thus, the kitten's brain had been shaped to respond best to the environment to which it had been exposed.

Experience-dependent plasticity has also been demonstrated in humans, using the brain imaging technique of fMRI (see Method: Brain Imaging, page 41). The starting point for this research is the finding that there is an area in the temporal lobe called the fusiform face area (FFA) that contains many neurons that respond best to faces (see Chapter 2, page 42). Isabel Gauthier and coworkers (1999) showed that experience-dependent plasticity may play a role in determining these neurons' response to faces by measuring the level of activity in the FFA in response to faces and also to objects called Greebles (**Figure 3.29a**). Greebles are families of computer-generated "beings" that all have the same basic configuration but differ in the shapes of their parts (just like faces). The left pair of bars in **Figure 3.29b** show that for "Greeble novices" (people who have had little experience in perceiving Greebles), the faces cause more FFA activity than the Greebles.

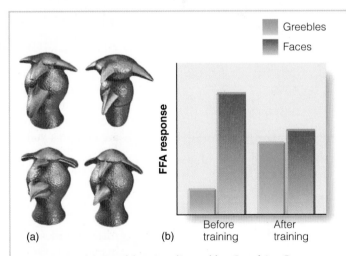

Figure 3.29 (a) Greeble stimuli used by Gauthier. Participants were trained to name each different Greeble. (b) Magnitude of brain responses to faces and Greebles before and after Greeble training. *(Source: Based on I. Gauthier, M. J. Tarr, A. W. Anderson, P. L. Skudlarski, & J. C. Gore, Activation of the middle fusiform "face area" increases with experience in recognizing novel objects, Nature Neuroscience, 2, 568–573, 1999.)*

Gauthier then gave her subjects extensive training over a 4-day period in "Greeble recognition." These training sessions, which required that each Greeble be labeled with a specific name, turned the participants into "Greeble experts." The right bars in **Figure 3.29b** show that after the training, the FFA responded almost as well to Greebles as to faces. Apparently, the FFA contains neurons that respond not just to faces but to other complex objects as well. The particular objects to which the neurons respond best are established by experience with the objects. In fact, Gauthier has also shown that neurons in the FFA of people who are experts in recognizing cars and birds respond well not only to human faces but to cars (for the car experts) and to birds (for the bird experts) (Gauthier et al., 2000). Just as rearing kittens in a vertical environment increased the number of neurons that responded to verticals, training humans to recognize Greebles, cars, or birds causes the FFA to respond more strongly to these objects. These results support the idea that neurons in the FFA respond strongly to faces because we have a lifetime of experience perceiving faces.

These demonstrations of experience-dependent plasticity in kittens and humans show that the brain's functioning can be "tuned" to operate best within a specific environment. Thus, continued exposure to things that occur regularly in the environment can cause neurons to become adapted to respond best to these regularities. Looked at in this way, it is not unreasonable to say that neurons can reflect knowledge about properties of the environment.

We have come a long way from thinking about perception as something that happens automatically in response to activation of sensory receptors. We know that perception is the outcome of an interaction between bottom-up information, which flows from receptors to brain, and top-down information, which usually involves knowledge about the environment or expectations related to the situation.

But the example we described earlier of James Pokorny's pain decreasing when his attention was distracted by a virtual reality game (see page 62) suggests that yet another factor needs to be considered in explaining perception. Consider what James was doing: He was diverting his attention from getting his bandages changed to grinding up a virtual spider in a virtual garbage disposal. This attention is a form of action, as is manipulating the virtual reality game controls. As we will now see, action is something that nearly always accompanies perception and that may also affect it.

The Interaction Between Perceiving and Taking Action

The approach to perception we have described so far could be called the "sitting in a chair" approach to studying perception, because most of the situations we have described could occur as a person sits in a chair viewing various stimuli. In fact, that is probably what you are doing as you read this book—reading words, looking at pictures, doing "demonstrations," all while sitting still. We will now consider how movement helps us perceive, and how action and perception interact.

MOVEMENT FACILITATES PERCEPTION

Although movement adds a complexity to perception that isn't there when we are sitting in one place, movement also helps us perceive objects in the environment more accurately. One reason this occurs is that moving reveals aspects of objects that are not apparent from a single viewpoint. For example, consider the "horse" in **Figure 3.30**. From one viewpoint, this object looks like a metal sculpture of a fairly normal horse (**Figure 3.30a**). However, walking around the horse reveals that it isn't as normal as it first appeared (**Figures 3.30b** and **3.30c**). Thus, seeing an object from different viewpoints provides added information that results in more accurate perception, especially for objects that are out of the ordinary, such as the distorted horse.

(a)   (b)   (c)

Figure 3.30 Three views of a "horse." Moving around an object can reveal its true shape.

THE INTERACTION OF PERCEPTION AND ACTION

Our concern with movement extends beyond noting that it helps us perceive objects by revealing additional information about them. Movement is also important because of the coordination that is continually occurring between perceiving stimuli and taking action toward these stimuli. Consider, for example, what happens when Crystal, resting in the coffee shop after her run, reaches out to pick up her cup of coffee (**Figure 3.31**). She first identifies the coffee cup among the flowers and other objects on the table (**Figure 3.31a**). Once the coffee cup is perceived, she reaches for it, taking into account its location on the table (**Figure 3.31b**). As she reaches, avoiding the flowers, she positions her fingers to grasp the cup, taking into account her perception of the cup's handle (**Figure 3.31c**); then she lifts the cup with just the right amount of force, taking into account her estimate of how heavy it is based on her perception of its fullness. This simple action requires continually perceiving the position of the cup, and of her hand and fingers relative to the cup, while calibrating her actions in order to accurately grasp the cup and then pick it up without spilling any coffee (Goodale, 2010). All this just to pick up a cup of coffee! What's amazing about this sequence is that it happens almost automatically, without much effort at all. But as with everything else about perception, this ease and apparent simplicity are achieved with the aid of complex underlying mechanisms. We will now describe the physiology behind these mechanisms.

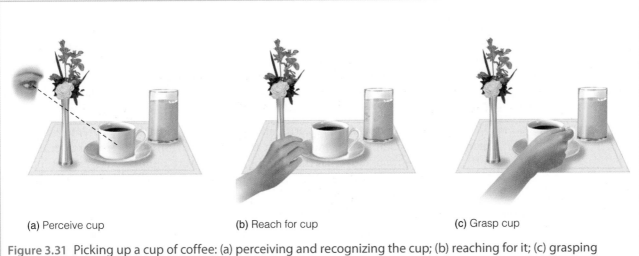

(a) Perceive cup   (b) Reach for cup   (c) Grasp cup

Figure 3.31 Picking up a cup of coffee: (a) perceiving and recognizing the cup; (b) reaching for it; (c) grasping and picking it up. This action involves coordination between perceiving and action that is carried out by two separate streams in the brain, as described in the text. © 2015 Cengage Learning

THE PHYSIOLOGY OF PERCEPTION AND ACTION

Psychologists have long recognized the close connection between perceiving objects and interacting with them, but the details of this link between perception and action have become clearer as a result of physiological research that began in the 1980s. This research has shown that there are two processing streams in the brain—one involved with perceiving objects, and the other involved with locating and taking action toward these objects. This physiological research involves two methods: *brain ablation*—the study of the effect of removing parts of the brain in animals, and *neuropsychology*—the study of the behavior of people with brain damage, which we described in Chapter 2 (see page 39). Both of these methods demonstrate how studying the functioning of animals and humans with brain damage can reveal important principles about the functioning of the normal (intact) brain.

WHAT AND *WHERE* STREAMS   In a classic experiment, Leslie Ungerleider and Mortimer Mishkin (1982) studied how removing part of a monkey's brain affected its ability to identify an object and to determine the object's location. This experiment used a technique called **brain ablation**—removing part of the brain.

METHOD
BRAIN ABLATION

The goal of a brain ablation experiment is to determine the function of a particular area of the brain. This is accomplished by first determining an animal's capacity by testing it behaviorally. Most ablation experiments studying perception have used monkeys because of the similarity of the monkey's visual system to that of humans and because monkeys can be trained to demonstrate perceptual capacities such as acuity, color vision, depth perception, and object perception.

Once the animal's perception has been measured, a particular area of the brain is ablated (removed or destroyed), either by surgery or by injecting a chemical in the area to be removed. Ideally, one particular area is removed and the rest of the brain remains intact. After ablation, the monkey is tested to determine which perceptual capacities remain and which have been affected by the ablation. Ablation is also called *lesioning*.

Ungerleider and Mishkin presented monkeys with two tasks: (1) an object discrimination problem and (2) a landmark discrimination problem. In the **object discrimination problem**, a monkey was shown one object, such as a rectangular solid, and was then presented with a two-choice task like the one shown in **Figure 3.32a**, which included the "target" object (the rectangular solid) and another stimulus, such as the triangular solid. If the monkey pushed aside the target object, it received the food reward that was hidden in a well under the object. The **landmark discrimination problem** is shown in **Figure 3.32b**. Here, the tall cylinder is the landmark, which indicates the food well that contains food. The monkey received food if it removed the food well cover closer to the tall cylinder.

In the ablation part of the experiment, part of the temporal lobe was removed in some monkeys. Behavioral testing showed that the object discrimination problem became very difficult for the monkeys when their temporal lobes were removed. This result indicates that the neural pathway that reaches the temporal lobes is responsible for determining an object's identity. Ungerleider and Mishkin therefore called the pathway leading from the striate cortex to the temporal lobe the *what* pathway (**Figure 3.33**).

Other monkeys, which had their parietal lobes removed, had difficulty solving the landmark discrimination problem. This result indicates that the pathway that leads to the parietal lobe is responsible for determining an object's location. Ungerleider and Mishkin therefore called the pathway leading from the striate cortex to the parietal lobe the *where* pathway (**Figure 3.33**).

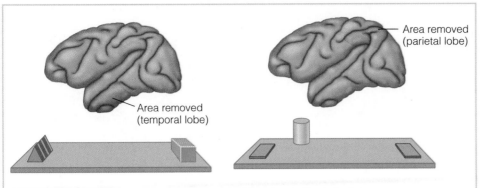

(a) Object discrimination   (b) Landmark discrimination

Figure 3.32 The two types of discrimination tasks used by Ungerleider and Mishkin. (a) Object discrimination: Pick the correct shape. Lesioning the temporal lobe (purple-shaded area) makes this task difficult. (b) Landmark discrimination: Pick the food well closer to the cylinder. Lesioning the parietal lobe makes this task difficult. *(Source: Adapted from M. Mishkin, L. G. Ungerleider, & K. A. Makco, Object vision and spatial vision: Two central pathways, Trends in Neuroscience, 6, 414–417, Figure 2, 1983.)*

Applying this idea of *what* and *where* pathways to our example of a person picking up a cup of coffee, the *what* pathway would be involved in the initial perception of the cup and the *where* pathway in determining its location—important information if we are going to carry out the action of reaching for the cup. In the next section, we consider another physiological approach to studying perception and action by describing how studying the behavior of a person with brain damage provides further insights into what is happening in the brain as a person reaches for an object.

PERCEPTION AND ACTION STREAMS David Milner and Melvyn Goodale (1995) used the neuropsychological approach (studying the behavior of people with brain damage) to reveal two streams, one involving the temporal lobe and the other involving the parietal lobe. The researchers studied D.F., a 34-year-old woman who suffered damage to her temporal lobe from carbon monoxide poisoning caused by a gas leak in her home. One result of the brain damage was revealed when D.F. was asked to rotate a card held in her hand to match different orientations of a slot (**Figure 3.34a**). She was unable to do this, as shown in the left circle in **Figure 3.34b**. Each line in the circle indicates how D.F. adjusted the card's orientation. Perfect matching performance would be indicated by a vertical line for each trial, but D.F.'s responses are widely scattered. The right circle shows the accurate performance of the normal controls.

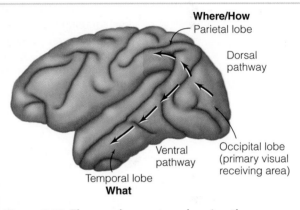

Figure 3.33 The monkey cortex, showing the *what*, or perception, pathway from the occipital lobe to the temporal lobe and the *where*, or action, pathway from the occipital lobe to the parietal lobe. *(Source: Adapted from M. Mishkin, L. G. Ungerleider, & K. A. Makco, Object vision and spatial vision: Two central pathways, Trends in Neuroscience, 6, 414–417, Figure 2, 1983.)*

Because D.F. had trouble rotating a card to match the orientation of the slot, it would seem reasonable that she would also have trouble *placing* the card through the slot because to do this she would have to turn the card so that it was lined up with the slot. But when D.F. was asked to "mail" the card through the slot (**Figure 3.35a**), she could do it, as indicated by the results in **Figure 3.35b**. Even though D.F. could not turn the card to match the slot's orientation, *once she started moving the card toward the slot*, she was able to rotate it to match the orientation of the slot. Thus, D.F. performed poorly in the static orientation matching task but did well as soon as *action* was involved (Murphy, Racicot, & Goodale, 1996). Milner and Goodale interpreted D.F.'s behavior as showing that there is one mechanism for judging orientation and another for coordinating vision and action.

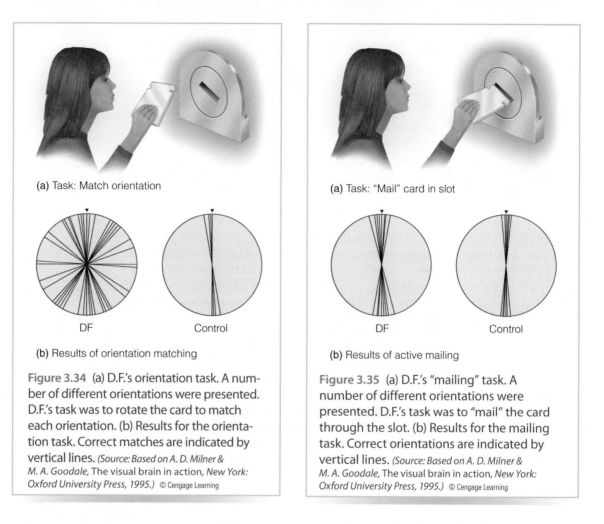

(a) Task: Match orientation

DF   Control

(b) Results of orientation matching

Figure 3.34 (a) D.F.'s orientation task. A number of different orientations were presented. D.F.'s task was to rotate the card to match each orientation. (b) Results for the orientation task. Correct matches are indicated by vertical lines. *(Source: Based on A. D. Milner & M. A. Goodale,* The visual brain in action, *New York: Oxford University Press, 1995.)* © Cengage Learning

(a) Task: "Mail" card in slot

DF   Control

(b) Results of active mailing

Figure 3.35 (a) D.F.'s "mailing" task. A number of different orientations were presented. D.F.'s task was to "mail" the card through the slot. (b) Results for the mailing task. Correct orientations are indicated by vertical lines. *(Source: Based on A. D. Milner & M. A. Goodale,* The visual brain in action, *New York: Oxford University Press, 1995.)* © Cengage Learning

Based on these results, Milner and Goodale suggested that the pathway from the visual cortex to the temporal lobe (which was damaged in D.F.'s brain) be called the **perception pathway** and the pathway from the visual cortex to the parietal lobe (which was intact in D.F.'s brain) be called the **action pathway**. The perception pathway corresponds to the *what* pathway we described in conjunction with the monkey experiments, and the action pathway corresponds to the *where* pathway. Thus, some researchers refer to *what* and *where* pathways and some to *perception* and *action* pathways. Whatever the terminology, the research shows that perception and action are processed in two separate pathways in the brain.

PICKING UP A COFFEE CUP AND OTHER BEHAVIORS

With our knowledge that perception and action involve two separate mechanisms, we can add physiological notations to our description of picking up the coffee cup, as follows: The first step is to identify the coffee cup among the vase of flowers and the glass of orange juice on the table (*perception* or *what pathway*). Once the coffee cup is perceived, we reach for the cup (*action* or *where pathway*), taking into account its location on the table. As we reach, avoiding the flowers and orange juice, we position our fingers to grasp the cup (*action pathway*), taking into account our perception of the cup's handle (*perception pathway*), and we lift the cup with just the right amount of force (*action pathway*), taking into account our estimate of how heavy it is based on our perception of the fullness of the cup (*perception pathway*).

Thus, even a simple action like picking up a coffee cup involves a number of areas of the brain, which coordinate their activity to create perceptions and behaviors. A similar coordination between different areas of the brain also occurs for the sense of hearing.

Thus, hearing someone call your name and then turning to see who it is activates two separate pathways in the auditory system—one that enables you to hear and identify the sound (the auditory *what* pathway) and another that helps you locate where the sound is coming from (the auditory *where* pathway) (Lomber & Malhotra, 2008).

The discovery of different pathways for perceiving, determining location, and taking action illustrates how studying the physiology of perception has helped broaden our conception far beyond the old "sitting in the chair" approach. These physiological findings, combined with behavioral experiments that have focused on active aspects of perception (Gibson, 1979), mean that we can call perception "dynamic" not only because it involves processes such as inference and taking knowledge into account but also because of how closely perception is linked to action.

Something to Consider

WHERE PERCEPTION MEETS MEMORY

Perception provides a window on the world by *creating* sensory experiences. Memory creates our window to the past, by *retrieving* our experiences. Many of our memories—especially recent ones—have strong sensory components, and when we discuss memory we will see that there are close connections between perception and memory.

A question related to this connection between perception and memory is, what happens in the brain when we perceive something and then later have a memory related to that perception? No one experiment can fully answer this question, but Hagar Gelbard-Sagiv and coworkers (2008) have shown that there are neurons in the hippocampus—an area involved in storing memories (see **Figure 5.22**)—that respond both to seeing pictures and to remembering them later. First let's consider how it is possible to record from single neurons in humans.

METHOD
RECORDING FROM SINGLE NEURONS IN HUMANS

The vast majority of single neuron recordings have been carried out on animals. But in a few experiments, single neuron responses have been recorded from humans. In these experiments, the subjects were patients with intractable epilepsy that couldn't be controlled by drugs. For these patients, a possible cure is provided by surgery that removes the small area of the brain called the *epileptic focus*, where the seizures originate.

To determine the location of this focus, electrodes are implanted in these patients' brains and are then monitored over a period of a few days in the hope that spontaneous seizures will help pinpoint the location of the focus (Fried et al., 1999). Because the electrodes are implanted, it is possible, with the patients' consent, to record signals to perceptual stimuli. These experiments make it possible not only to record neural responses to stimuli, as is routinely done in animal experiments, but also to study how these neurons respond when the patients remember these stimuli later.

Gelbard-Sagiv had epilepsy patients view a series of 5- to 10-second video clips a number of times while recording from neurons in their hippocampus. These clips showed famous people, landmarks, and people and animals engaged in various actions. As the person was viewing the clips, some neurons responded better to certain clips. For example, a neuron in one of the patients responded best to a clip from *The Simpsons* TV program.

The patients were then asked to think back to any of the film clips they had seen, while the experimenter continued to record from the hippocampus neurons. One result, shown in **Figure 3.36**, indicates the response of the neuron that fired to the video clip of *The Simpsons*. The patient's description of what he was remembering is shown at the bottom

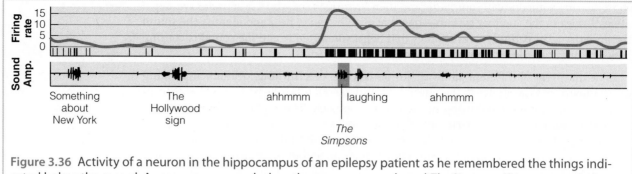

Figure 3.36 Activity of a neuron in the hippocampus of an epilepsy patient as he remembered the things indicated below the record. A response occurred when the person remembered *The Simpsons* TV program. Earlier, this neuron had been shown to respond to viewing a video clip of *The Simpsons*. *(Source: From H. Gelbard-Sagiv, R. Mukamel, M. Harel, R. Malach, & I. Fried, Internally generated reactivation of single neurons in human hippocampus during free recall. Science, 322, 96–101, 2008.)*

of the figure. First the patient remembered "something about New York," then "the Hollywood sign." The neuron responded weakly or not at all to those two memories. However, remembering *The Simpsons* caused a large response, which continued as the person continued remembering the episode (indicated by the laughter).

Results such as this support the idea that these neurons in the hippocampus are involved in storing representations of memories. Note, however, that the fact that the neuron in the hippocampus responded to the visual stimulus indicates it is receiving information as the person is perceiving, but doesn't mean it is *responsible* for perceiving. Some other neurons are taking care of that while the hippocampus neuron is storing information about what is happening. Later, when the person is remembering what happened, it will be the hippocampus's turn to take center stage.

TEST YOURSELF 3.3

1. What is the oblique effect? Describe how this effect could be caused by evolution and by experience.

2. What is experience-dependent plasticity? Describe the kitten-rearing experiment and the Greeble experiment. What is behind the idea that neurons can reflect knowledge about properties of the environment?

3. Describe the interaction between perceiving and taking action, giving a specific example from everyday perception.

4. Describe the Ungerleider and Mishkin experiment. How did they use the procedure of brain ablation to demonstrate *what* and *where* streams in the cortex?

5. Describe how Milner and Goodale's testing of D.F. demonstrated pathways for matching orientation and for combining vision and action. Describe the perception pathway and the action pathway. How do these pathways correspond to Ungerleider and Mishkin's *what* and *where* streams?

6. Describe how the perception and action pathways both play a role in an action such as picking up a cup of coffee.

7. Describe the experiments that recorded from single neurons in people with epilepsy. What do the results of these experiments indicate about the relation between perception and memory?

CHAPTER SUMMARY

1. The example of Crystal running on the beach and having coffee later illustrates how perception can change based on new information, how perception can be based on principles that are related to past experiences, how perception is a process, and how perception and action are connected.

2. We can easily describe the relation between parts of a city scene, but it is often challenging to indicate the reasoning that led to the description. This illustrates the need to go beyond the pattern of light and dark in a scene to describe the process of perception.

3. Attempts to program computers to recognize objects have shown how difficult it is to program computers to perceive at a level comparable to humans. A few of the difficulties facing computers are (1) the stimulus on the receptors is ambiguous, as demonstrated by the inverse projection problem; (2) objects in a scene can be hidden or blurred; and (3) objects look different from different viewpoints.

4. Perception starts with bottom-up processing, which involves stimulation of the receptors, creating electrical signals that reach the visual receiving area of the brain. Perception also involves top-down processing, which originates in the brain.

5. Examples of top-down processing are the multiple personalities of a blob and finding faces in a landscape; how knowledge of a language makes it possible to perceive individual words; and how the perception of pain is influenced by things other than the pain stimulus.

6. The idea that perception depends on knowledge was proposed by Helmholtz's theory of unconscious inference.

7. The Gestalt approach to perception proposed a number of laws of perceptual organization, which were based on how stimuli usually occur in the environment.

8. Regularities of the environment are characteristics of the environment that occur frequently. We take both physical regularities and semantic regularities into account when perceiving.

9. Bayesian inference is a mathematical procedure for determining what is likely to be "out there"; it takes into account a person's prior beliefs about a perceptual outcome and the likelihood of that outcome based on additional evidence.

10. Of the four approaches to object perception—unconscious inference, Gestalt, regularities, and Bayesian—the Gestalt approach relies more on bottom-up processing than the others. Modern psychologists have suggested a connection between the Gestalt principles and past experience.

11. One of the basic operating principles of the brain is that it contains some neurons that respond best to things that occur regularly in the environment.

12. Experience-dependent plasticity is one of the mechanisms responsible for creating neurons that are tuned to respond to specific things in the environment. The experiments in which kittens were reared in vertical or horizontal environments and in which people's brain activity was measured as they learned about Greebles supports this idea.

13. Perceiving and taking action are linked. Movement of an observer relative to an object provides information about the object. Also, there is a constant coordination between perceiving an object (such as a cup) and taking action toward the object (such as picking up the cup).

14. Research involving brain ablation in monkeys and neuropsychological studies of the behavior of people with brain damage have revealed two processing pathways in the cortex—a pathway from the occipital lobe to the temporal lobe responsible for perceiving objects, and a pathway from the occipital lobe to the parietal lobe responsible for controlling actions toward objects. These pathways work together to coordinate perception and action.

15. Recordings from single neurons in the hippocampus of epilepsy patients have discovered neurons that respond both when a visual stimulus is being perceived and when it is being remembered later.

THINK ABOUT IT

1. Describe a situation in which you initially thought you saw or heard something but then realized that your initial perception was in error. (Two examples: misperceiving an object under low-visibility conditions; mishearing song lyrics.) What were the roles of bottom-up and top-down processing in this situation of first having an incorrect perception and then realizing what was actually there?

2. Look at the picture in **Figure 3.37**. Is this a huge giant's hand getting ready to pick up a horse, a normal-size hand picking up a tiny plastic horse, or something else? Explain, based on some of the things we take into account in addition to the image that this scene creates on the retina, why it is unlikely that this picture shows either a giant hand or a tiny horse. How does your answer relate to top-down processing?

3. In the section on experience-dependent plasticity it was stated that neurons can reflect knowledge about properties of the environment. Would it be valid to suggest that the response of these neurons represents top-down processing? Why or why not?

4. Try observing the world as though there were no such thing as top-down processing. For example, without the aid of top-down processing, seeing a restaurant's restroom sign that says "Employees must wash hands" could be taken to mean that we should wait for an employee to wash our hands! If you try this exercise, be warned that it is extremely difficult because top-down processing is so pervasive in our environment that we usually take it for granted.

Figure 3.37 Is a giant hand about to pick up the horse?

Kristin Durr

KEY TERMS

Action pathway, 78

Apparent movement, 64

Bayesian inference, 70

Bottom-up processing, 59

Brain ablation, 76

Direct pathway model, 61

Experience-dependent plasticity, 73

Gestalt psychologists, 64

Inverse projection problem, 57

Law of pragnanz, 65

Landmark discrimination problem, 76

Light-from-above assumption, 67

Likelihood, 70

Likelihood principle, 63

Object discrimination problem, 76

Oblique effect, 67

Perception, 52

Perception pathway, 78

Physical regularities, 67

Placebo, 61

Placebo effect, 62

Principle of good continuation, 65

Principle of good figure, 65

Principle of similarity, 66

Principle of simplicity, 65

Principles of perceptual organization, 64

Prior, 70

Prior probability, 70

Regularities in the environment, 67

Scene schema, 69

Semantic regularities, 68

Speech segmentation, 61

Theory of natural selection, 73

Top-down processing, 59

Unconscious inference, 63

Viewpoint invariance, 59

What pathway, 76

Where pathway, 76

Signal Detection (1)

Apparent Motion (3)

Garner Interference: Integral Dimensions (4)

Garner Interference: Separable Dimensions (5)

Müller-Lyer Illusion (6)

Blind Spot (14)

Metacontrast Masking (16)

Categorical Perception: Discrimination (39)

Categorical Perception: Identification (40)

Statistical Learning (47)

Answers for Figure 3.8

Faces from left to right: Will Smith, Taylor Swift, Barack Obama, Hillary Clinton, Jackie Chan, Ben Affleck, Oprah Winfrey.

Figure 3.38 The faces in **Figure 3.12**, *The Forest Has Eyes* by Bev Doolittle (1985). *(Source:* The Forest Has Eyes © 1984 Bev Doolittle, courtesy of The Greenwich Workshop, Inc.)

Figure 3.39 The Dalmatian in **Figure 3.17**. *© Cengage Learning © AnetaPics/Shutterstock.com; Scratchgravel Publishing Services*

These people are paying rapt attention to something. This focusing of attention on a particular object or event is called *selective attention*. One outcome of selective attention is that whatever is being attended receives enhanced processing. Other things may not receive as much processing and may not even be perceived. This chapter considers selective attention by asking what happens when we focus our attention on one thing. The chapter also considers *divided attention* by asking whether we can attend to more than one thing at a time. The answers to these questions involve considering the nature of the task, the type of stimuli, and the properties of our sensory systems.

Attention

SOME QUESTIONS WE WILL CONSIDER

▶ Is it possible to focus attention on just one thing, even when there are lots of other things going on at the same time? (88)

▶ Under what conditions can we pay attention to more than one thing at a time? (100)

▶ What does attention research tell us about the effect of talking on cell phones while driving a car? (102)

▶ Is it true that we are not paying attention to a large fraction of the things that are happening in our environment? (107)

Roger, sitting in the library, is attempting to do his math homework when some people at the next table start talking. He is annoyed because people aren't supposed to talk in the library, but he is so focused on the math problems that it doesn't distract him (Figure 4.1a). However, a little later, when he decides to take a break from his math homework and play an easy game on his cell phone, he does find their conversation distracting (Figure 4.1b). "Interesting," he thinks. "Their talking didn't bother me when I was doing the math problems."

Deciding to stop resisting the conversation, Roger begins to consciously eavesdrop while continuing to play his cell phone game (Figure 4.1c). But just as he is beginning to figure out what the couple is talking about, his attention is captured by a loud noise and commotion from across the room, where it appears a book cart has overturned, scattering books on the floor. As he notices that one person seems upset and others are gathering up the books, he looks from one person to another and decides he doesn't know any of them (Figure 4.1d).

Roger's experiences illustrate different aspects of **attention**—the ability to focus on specific stimuli or locations. His attempt to focus on his math homework while ignoring

Figure 4.1 Roger's adventures with attention. (a) Selective attention: doing math problems while not being distracted by people talking. (b) Distraction: playing a game but being distracted by the people talking. (c) Divided attention: playing the game while listening in on the conversation. (d) Attentional capture and scanning: a noise attracts his attention, and he scans the scene to figure out what is happening. © Cengage Learning

the people talking is an example of **selective attention**—attending to one thing while ignoring others. The way the conversation in the library interfered with his cell phone game is an example of **distraction**—one stimulus interfering with the processing of another stimulus. When Roger decides to listen in on the conversation while simultaneously playing the game, he is displaying **divided attention**—paying attention to more than one thing at a time. Later, the interruption of his eavesdropping by the noise of the overturned book cart provides an example of **attentional capture**—a rapid shifting of attention usually caused by a stimulus such as a loud noise, bright light, or sudden movement. Finally, Roger's attempt to identify the people across the room, looking from one person's face to another, is an example of **visual scanning**—movements of the eyes from one location or object to another.

With all of these different aspects of attention in mind, let's return to William James's (1890) definition of attention, which we introduced in Chapter 1:

> Millions of items ... are present to my senses which never properly enter my experience. Why? Because they have no interest for me. My experience is what I agree to attend to. . . . Everyone knows what attention is. It is the taking possession by the mind, in clear and vivid form, of one out of what seem several simultaneously possible objects or trains of thought. . . . It implies withdrawal from some things in order to deal effectively with others.

Although this definition is considered a classic, and certainly does capture a central characteristic of attention—withdrawal from some things in order to deal effectively with others—we can now see that it doesn't capture the diversity of phenomena that are associated with attention. Attention, as it turns out, is not one thing. There are many different aspects of attention, which have been studied using different approaches.

This chapter, therefore, consists of a number of sections, each of which is about a different aspect of attention. We begin with a little history, because early research on attention helped establish the information processing approach to cognition, which became the central focus of the new field of cognitive psychology (see Chapter 1, page 12).

Attention as Information Processing

As we saw in Chapter 1, the history of the study of the mind has had its ups and downs. Early research, in the late 1800s and early 1900s, attempted to study the mind by introspection. An example of how introspection might be applied to attention would be to show a person a display consisting of different patches of color and instructing him or her to "pay attention as strongly as you can to the patch in the middle and describe how paying attention affects the clarity of the patch's color." Unfortunately, this task is difficult and would yield results that varied from person to person. Because of such problems, the advent of behaviorism caused research on attention to essentially disappear beginning about 1920 (Moray, 1959). However, as we noted in Chapter 1, a new approach to studying attention, which ushered in the information processing approach to cognition, was introduced by Donald Broadbent in the 1950s. It is here that we begin.

BROADBENT'S FILTER MODEL OF ATTENTION

Attention became an important topic of research in the 1950s, partially for a practical reason: Technology developed during World War II had placed humans in situations in which they were bombarded with information. For example, a pilot in an airplane cockpit is confronted with numerous dials, lights, and controls. How is he or she to know what to attend to, and how to switch from one thing to another, while at the same time listening to instructions from the control tower? These questions, posed by technology, were studied by researchers who made use of a new technological development—the tape recorder—to run experiments that tested people's ability to take in information under different conditions (Moray, 1959).

This is where Broadbent entered the scene and proposed, based on the results of experiments studying selective attention, his **filter model of attention**, which we introduced in Chapter 1 (page 13). You can appreciate what the model was trying to explain by doing the following demonstration.

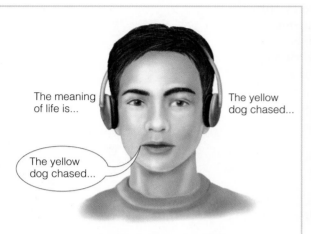

Figure 4.2 In the shadowing procedure, a person repeats out loud the words that have just been heard. This ensures that subjects are focusing their attention on the attended message. © Cengage Learning

DEMONSTRATION
FOCUSING ON ONE MESSAGE

You will need two music players, such as a computer and a portable music player, for this demonstration. Connect separate earbud-style headphones to each player, and find two audio files with two different people talking. If that isn't possible, find two different songs with lyrics, preferably ones that you aren't that familiar with. Insert an earbud from one player in your left ear and an earbud from the other player in your right ear, and play both audio tracks simultaneously. Adjust the volume so the two tracks are equally easy to hear. When you are receiving messages in each ear, you are ready to do an experiment involving **dichotic listening**, where *dichotic* refers to presenting different stimuli to the left and right ears.

Your task is simple: Focus your attention on the words in one ear, which we will call the *attended ear*, and as you hear the words, repeat them out loud. This procedure of repeating what you are hearing is called **shadowing** (Figure 4.2). The second part of the task is to notice, *without shifting your attention from the attended ear*, what you can take in from the other, unattended, ear. Can you tell if it is a male or female voice? Can you tell what is being said?

In an early dichotic listening experiment, Colin Cherry (1953) found that although his subjects could easily shadow a spoken message presented to the attended ear, and they could report whether the unattended message was spoken by a male or female, they couldn't report what was being said in the unattended ear. Other dichotic listening experiments confirmed that subjects are not aware of most of the information being presented to the unattended ear. For example, Neville Moray (1959) showed that subjects were unaware of a word that had been repeated 35 times in the unattended ear. The ability to focus on one stimulus while filtering out other stimuli has been called the **cocktail party effect**, because at noisy parties people are able to focus on what one person is saying even if there are many conversations happening at the same time.

Based on results such as these, Donald Broadbent (1958) created a model of attention designed to explain how it is possible to focus on one message and why information isn't taken in from the other message. This model, which introduced the flow diagram to cognitive psychology (see page 13), proposed that information passes through the following stages (Figure 4.3):

1. *Sensory memory* holds all of the incoming information for a fraction of a second and then transfers all of it to the filter. We will discuss sensory memory in more detail in Chapter 5.

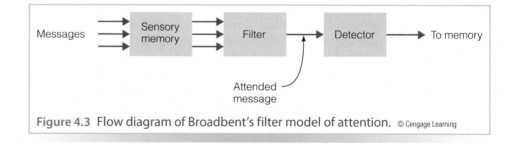

Figure 4.3 Flow diagram of Broadbent's filter model of attention. © Cengage Learning

2. The *filter* identifies the message that is being attended to based on its physical characteristics—things like the speaker's tone of voice, pitch, speed of talking, and accent—and lets only this attended message pass through to the detector in the next stage. All of the other messages are filtered out.

3. The *detector* processes the information from the attended message to determine higher-level characteristics of the message, such as its meaning. Because only the important, attended information has been let through the filter, the detector processes all of the information that enters it.

4. The output of the detector is sent to *short-term memory*, which holds information for 10–15 seconds and also transfers information into *long-term memory*, which can hold information indefinitely. We will describe short- and long-term memory in Chapters 5–8.

Broadbent's model has been called a **bottleneck model** because the filter restricts information flow much as the neck of a bottle restricts the flow of liquid, so the liquid escapes only slowly even though there is a large amount in the bottle. However, an important difference between the neck of a bottle and Broadbent's filter is that the filter doesn't just slow down the flow of information. It keeps a large portion of the information from getting through. Also, unlike the neck of a bottle, which lets through the liquid closest to the neck, Broadbent's filter lets information through based on specific physical characteristics of the information, such as the rate of speaking or the pitch of the speaker's voice. For example, in our dichotic listening experiment, if one voice is male and the other female, the filter could let through only the male voice based on its lower pitch. Broadbent's model is called an **early selection model** because the filter eliminates the unattended information right at the beginning of the flow of information.

MODIFYING BROADBENT'S MODEL: MORE EARLY SELECTION MODELS

The beauty of Broadbent's filter model of attention was that it provided testable predictions about selective attention, which stimulated further research. For example, according to Broadbent's model, since all of the unattended messages are filtered out, we should not be conscious of information in the unattended messages. To test this idea, Neville Moray (1959) did a dichotic listening experiment in which his subjects were instructed to shadow the message presented to one ear and to ignore the message presented to the other ear (as you did in the Demonstration). But when Moray presented the listener's name to the unattended ear, about a third of the subjects detected it (also see Wood & Cowan, 1995).

Moray's subjects had recognized their names even though, according to Broadbent's theory, the filter is supposed to let through only one message, based on its physical characteristics. Clearly, the person's name had not been filtered out and, most important, it had been analyzed enough to determine its meaning. You may have had an experience similar to Moray's laboratory demonstration if, as you were talking to someone in a noisy room, you suddenly heard someone else say your name.

Following Moray's lead, other experimenters showed that information presented to the unattended ear is processed enough to provide the listener with some awareness of its meaning. For example, J. A. Gray and A. I. Wedderburn (1960), while undergraduates at the University of Oxford, did the following experiment, sometimes called the "Dear Aunt Jane" experiment. As in Cherry's dichotic listening experiment, the subjects were told to shadow the message presented to one ear. As you can see in **Figure 4.4**, the attended (shadowed) ear received the message "Dear 7 Jane," and the unattended ear received the message "9 Aunt 6." However, rather than reporting the "Dear 7 Jane" message that was presented to the attended ear, subjects reported hearing "Dear Aunt Jane."

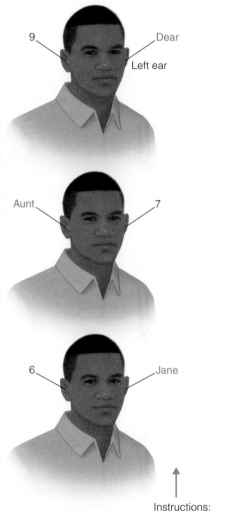

Figure 4.4 In Gray and Wedderburn's (1960) "Dear Aunt Jane" experiment, participants were told to shadow the message presented to the left ear. But they reported hearing the message "Dear Aunt Jane," which starts in the left ear, jumps to the right ear, and then goes back to the left ear. © Cengage Learning

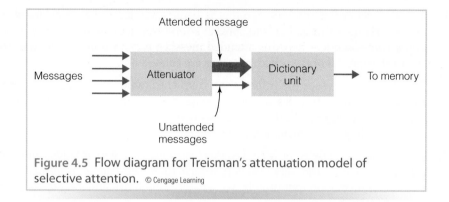

Figure 4.5 Flow diagram for Treisman's attenuation model of selective attention. © Cengage Learning

Switching to the unattended channel to say "Aunt" means that the subject's attention had jumped from one ear to the other and then back again. This occurred because they were taking the *meaning* of the words into account. (An example of top-down processing! See page 59.) Because of results such as these, Anne Treisman (1964) proposed a modification of Broadbent's model.

Treisman proposed that selection occurs in two stages, and she replaced Broadbent's filter with an *attenuator* (**Figure 4.5**). The **attenuator** analyzes the incoming message in terms of (1) its physical characteristics—whether it is high-pitched or low-pitched, fast or slow; (2) its language—how the message groups into syllables or words; and (3) its meaning—how sequences of words create meaningful phrases. Note that the attenuator represents a *process* and is not identified with a specific brain structure.

Treisman's idea that the information in the channel is *selected* is similar to what Broadbent proposed, but in Treisman's **attenuation model of attention**, language and meaning can also be used to separate the messages. However, Treisman proposed that the analysis of the message proceeds only as far as is necessary to identify the attended message. For example, if there are two messages, one in a male voice and one in a female voice, then analysis at the physical level (which Broadbent emphasized) is adequate to separate the low-pitched male voice from the higher-pitched female voice. If, however, the voices are similar, then it might be necessary to use meaning to separate the two messages.

According to Treisman's model, once the attended and unattended messages have been identified, both messages pass through the attenuator, but the attended message emerges at full strength and the unattended messages are attenuated—they are still present, but are weaker than the attended message. Because at least some of the unattended message gets through the attenuator, Treisman's model has been called a "leaky filter" model.

The final output of the system is determined in the second stage, when the message is analyzed by the **dictionary unit**. The dictionary unit contains words, stored in memory, each of which has a threshold for being activated (**Figure 4.6**). A threshold is the smallest signal strength that can barely be detected. Thus, a word with a low threshold might be detected even when it is presented softly or is obscured by other words.

According to Treisman, words that are common or especially important, such as the listener's name, have low thresholds, so even a weak signal in the unattended channel can activate that word, and we hear our name from across the room. Uncommon words or words that are unimportant to the listener have higher thresholds, so it takes the strong signal of the attended message to activate these words. Thus, according to Treisman, the attended message gets through, *plus* some parts of the weaker, unattended messages.

The research we have been describing so far was extremely important, not only because it defined some of the basic phenomena of attention but also because

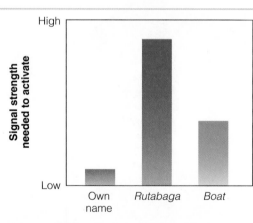

Figure 4.6 The dictionary unit of Treisman's attenuation model of selective attention contains words, each of which has a threshold for being detected. This graph shows the thresholds that might exist for three words. The person's name has a low threshold, so it will be easily detected. The thresholds for the words *rutabaga* and *boat* are higher, because they are used less or are less important to this particular listener. © Cengage Learning

it demonstrated how an aspect of cognition could be conceptualized as a problem of information processing, in which information from the environment passes through various stages of processing. Like Broadbent's model, Treisman's is called an early selection model because it proposes a filter that operates at an early stage in the flow of information. Other models propose that selection can occur later.

A LATE SELECTION MODEL

Other theories were proposed to take into account the results of experiments showing that messages can be selected at a later stage of processing, based primarily on their meaning. For example, in an experiment by Donald MacKay (1973), a subject listened to an ambiguous sentence, such as "They were throwing stones at the bank," that could be interpreted in more than one way. (In this example, "bank" can refer to a riverbank or to a financial institution.) These ambiguous sentences were presented to the attended ear while biasing words were presented to the other, unattended ear. For example, as the subject was shadowing "They were throwing stones at the bank," either the word "river" or the word "money" was presented to the unattended ear.

After hearing a number of ambiguous sentences, the subjects were presented with pairs of sentences, such as "They threw stones toward the side of the river yesterday" and "They threw stones at the savings and loan association yesterday," and asked to indicate which of these two sentences was closest in meaning to one of the sentences they had heard previously. MacKay found that the meaning of the biasing word affected the subjects' choice. For example, if the biasing word was "money," subjects were more likely to pick the second sentence. This occurred even though subjects reported that they were unaware of the biasing words that had been presented to the unattended ear.

MacKay proposed that because the meaning of the word *river* or *money* was affecting the subjects' judgments, the word must have been processed to the level of meaning even though it was unattended. Results such as this led MacKay and other theorists to develop **late selection models of attention**, which proposed that most of the incoming information is processed to the level of meaning before the message to be further processed is selected (Deutsch & Deutsch, 1963; Norman, 1968).

The attention research we have been describing, based on the information processing approach introduced by Broadbent and followed by others such as Moray, Treisman, and MacKay, has focused on when selective attention occurs (early or late) and what types of information are used for the selection (physical characteristics or meaning). But as research in selective attention progressed, researchers realized that there is no one answer to what has been called the "early–late" controversy. Early selection can be demonstrated under some conditions and later selection under others, depending on the observer's task and the type of stimuli presented. Thus, researchers began focusing instead on understanding the many different factors that control attention.

This brings us back to Roger's experience in the library. Remember that he was able to ignore the people talking when he was doing his math homework but became distracted by the talking when he was playing the easy cell phone game. The idea that the ability to selectively attend to a task can depend both on the distracting stimulus and on the nature of the task has been studied by Nilli Lavie, who introduced the concepts of *processing capacity* and *perceptual load.*

Processing Capacity and Perceptual Load

How do people ignore distracting stimuli when they are trying to focus their attention on a task? Lavie answers this question by considering two factors: (1) **processing capacity**, which refers to the amount of information people can handle and sets a limit on their ability to process incoming information; and (2) **perceptual load**, which is related to the difficulty of a task. Some tasks, especially easy, well-practiced ones, have low perceptual

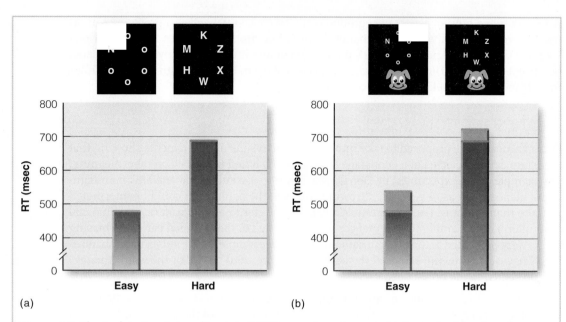

Figure 4.7 The task in Forster and Lavie's (2008) experiment was to indicate the identity of a target (X or N) as quickly as possible in displays like the ones shown here. (a) The reaction time for the easy condition like the display on the left, in which the target is accompanied by small o's, is faster than the reaction time for the hard condition, in which the target is accompanied by other letters. (b) Flashing a distracting cartoon character near the display increases the reaction time for the easy task more than it does for the hard task. The increase for each task is indicated by the gray extensions of the bars. *(Source: Adapted from S. Forster & N. Lavie, Failures to ignore entirely irrelevant distractors: The role of load,* Journal of Experimental Psychology: Applied, 14, 73–83, 2008.)

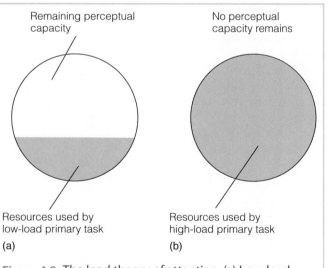

Figure 4.8 The load theory of attention: (a) Low-load tasks that use few cognitive resources may leave resources available for processing unattended task-irrelevant stimuli, whereas (b) high-load tasks that use all of a person's cognitive resources don't leave any resources to process unattended task-irrelevant stimuli. © Cengage Learning

loads; these **low-load tasks** use up only a small amount of the person's processing capacity. Tasks that are difficult and perhaps not as well practiced are **high-load tasks** and use more of a person's processing capacity.

Sophie Forster and Lavie (2008) studied the role of processing capacity and perceptual load in determining distraction by presenting displays like the one in **Figure 4.7a**. The subjects' task was to respond as quickly as possible when they identified a target, either X or N. Subjects pressed one key if they saw the X and another key if they saw the N. This task is easy for displays like the one on the left in **Figure 4.7a**, in which the target is surrounded by just one type of letter, like the small o's. However, the task becomes harder when the target is surrounded by different letters, as in the display on the right. This difference is reflected in the reaction times, with the hard task resulting in longer reaction times than the easy task. However, when a *task-irrelevant stimulus*—like the unrelated cartoon character shown in **Figure 4.7b**—is flashed next to the display, responding slows for the easy task more than for the hard task.

Lavie explains results such as the ones in **Figure 4.7b** in terms of her **load theory of attention**, as diagrammed in **Figure 4.8**, in which the circle represents the person's processing capacity and the shading represents the portion that is used up by a task. **Figure 4.8a** shows that with the low-load task, there is still processing capacity left. This means that resources are available to process the task-irrelevant stimulus, and even though the person was told not to pay attention to the task-irrelevant stimulus, it gets processed and slows down responding.

Figure 4.8b shows a situation in which all of a person's processing capacity is being used for a high-load task, such as the hard task in the experiment. When this occurs, no resources remain to process other stimuli, so irrelevant stimuli can't be processed and they have little effect on performance of the task. Thus, if you are carrying out a hard, high-load task, no processing capacity remains, and you are less likely to be distracted (as Roger found when he was focusing on the hard math problems). However, if you are carrying out an easy, low-load task, the processing capacity that remains is available to process task-irrelevant stimuli (as Roger found out when he was distracted from his easy cell phone game).

The ability to ignore task-irrelevant stimuli is a function not only of the load of the task you are trying to do, but also of how powerful the task-irrelevant stimulus is. For example, while Roger was able to ignore the conversation in the library while he was focused on the difficult math problems, a loud siren, indicating fire, would probably attract his attention. An example of a situation in which task-irrelevant stimuli are difficult to ignore is provided by the *Stroop effect*, described in the following demonstration.

DEMONSTRATION
THE STROOP EFFECT

Look at Figure 4.9. Your task is to name, as quickly as possible, the *color of ink* used to print each of the shapes. For example, starting in the upper left corner and going across, you would say, "red, blue, …" and so on. Time yourself (or a friend you have enlisted to do this task), and determine how many seconds it takes to report the colors of all the shapes. Then repeat the same task for Figure 4.10, remembering that your task is to specify the color of the *ink*, not the color name that is spelled out.

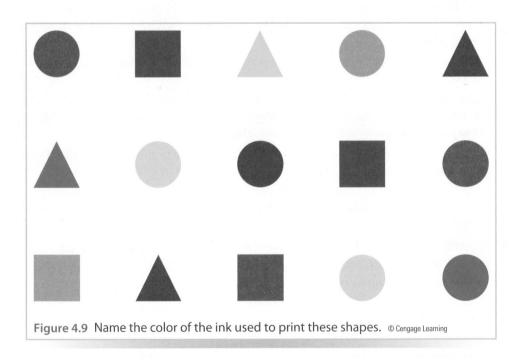

Figure 4.9 Name the color of the ink used to print these shapes. © Cengage Learning

If you found it harder to name the colors of the words than the colors of the shapes, then you were experiencing the **Stroop effect**, which was first described by J. R. Stroop in 1935. This effect occurs because the names of the words cause a competing response and therefore slow responding to the target—the color of the ink. In the Stroop effect, the task-irrelevant stimuli are extremely powerful, because reading words is highly practiced and has become so automatic that it is difficult *not* to read them (Stroop, 1935).

YELLOW	RED	BLUE	PURPLE	GREEN
ORANGE	YELLOW	GREEN	BLUE	RED
GREEN	PURPLE	ORANGE	RED	BLUE

Figure 4.10 Name the color of the ink used to print these words. © Cengage Learning

The approaches to attention we have described so far—early information processing models and Lavie's load approach—are concerned with the ability to focus attention on a particular image or task. But in everyday experience you often shift your attention from place to place, either by moving your eyes or by shifting attention "in your mind" without moving your eyes.

TEST YOURSELF 4.1

1. Give examples of situations that illustrate the following: selective attention, distraction, divided attention, attentional capture, and scanning.

2. How was the dichotic listening procedure used to determine how well people can focus on the attended message and how much information can be taken in from the unattended message? What is the cocktail party effect, and what does it demonstrate?

3. Describe Broadbent's model of selective attention. Why is it called an early selection model?

4. What were the results of experiments by Moray (words in the unattended ear) and Gray and Wedderburn ("Dear Aunt Jane")? Why are the results of these experiments difficult to explain based on Broadbent's filter model of attention?

5. Describe Treisman's attenuation model. First indicate why she proposed the theory, then how she modified Broadbent's model to explain some results that Broadbent's model couldn't explain.

6. Describe MacKay's "bank" experiment. Why does his result provide evidence for late selection?

7. Describe the Forster and Lavie experiment on how processing capacity and perceptual load determine distraction. What is the load theory of attention?

8. What is the Stroop effect? What does it illustrate about task-irrelevant stimuli?

Attention as Selection: Overt and Covert Attention

Roger's curiosity about what was happening in the library when the book cart tipped over led him to scan the scene by moving his eyes. Shifting attention from one place to another by moving the eyes is called **overt attention**. In contrast, shifting attention from one place to another while keeping the eyes stationary is called *covert* attention. We first consider a number of examples of overt attention.

OVERT ATTENTION: SCANNING A SCENE WITH EYE MOVEMENTS

The link between eye movements, attention, and perception is illustrated by the following demonstration.

DEMONSTRATION
LOOKING FOR A FACE IN A CROWD

Your task in this demonstration is to find Jennifer Hudson's face in the group of people in Figure 4.11. Notice how long it takes to accomplish this task.

Figure 4.11 Where is Jennifer Hudson? (Extra credit: Where is Miley Cyrus? Robin Thicke?)

Kevin Mazur/WireImage/Getty Images

Unless you were lucky and just happened to look at Jennifer Hudson immediately, you probably had to scan the scene, checking each face in turn, before finding her. Scanning is necessary because good detail vision occurs only for things you are looking at directly. This is illustrated by the following demonstration.

DEMONSTRATION
LOOKING OFF TO THE SIDE

D I H C N R L A Z I F W N S M Q P Z K D **X**

Look at the X on the right and, without moving your eyes, see how many letters you can identify to the left. If you do this without cheating (resist the urge to look to the left!), you will find that although you can read the letters right next to the X, you can read only a few of the letters that are farther off to the side.

First fixation

Figure 4.12 Scan path of a person viewing a fountain in Bordeaux, France. (Eye movement records by John Henderson.)

Courtesy of John M. Henderson

Charles Feil

Figure 4.13 The tree is highly salient because it is the only tree in the scene and it contrasts with its surroundings.

This demonstration illustrates the difference between central vision and peripheral vision. *Central vision* is the area you are looking at. *Peripheral vision* is everything off to the side. Because of the way the retina is constructed, objects in central vision fall on a small area called the *fovea*, which has much better detail vision than the peripheral retina, on which the rest of the scene falls. Thus, as you scanned the scene in **Figure 4.11**, you were aiming your fovea at one face after another. Each time you briefly paused on one face, you were making a **fixation**. When you moved your eye to observe another face, you were making a **saccadic eye movement**—a rapid, jerky movement from one fixation to the next.

It isn't surprising that you were moving your eyes from one place to another, because you were consciously looking for a particular target (Jennifer Hudson). But it may surprise you to know that even when you are freely viewing an object or scene without searching for a target, you move your eyes about three times per second. This rapid scanning is shown in **Figure 4.12**, which is a pattern of fixations (dots) separated by saccadic eye movements (lines) that occurred as a subject viewed the picture of the fountain.

We will now consider two factors that determine how people shift their attention by moving their eyes: *bottom-up*, based primarily on physical characteristics of the stimulus; and *top-down*, based on cognitive factors such as the observer's knowledge about scenes and past experiences with specific stimuli.

SCANNING BASED ON STIMULUS SALIENCE Attention can be influenced by **stimulus salience**—the physical properties of the stimulus, such as color, contrast, or movement. Capturing attention by stimulus salience is a bottom-up process because it depends solely on the pattern of light and dark, color and contrast in a stimulus. For example, the task of finding the people with blonde hair in **Figure 4.11** would involve bottom-up processing because it involves responding to the physical property of color, without considering the meaning of the image (Parkhurst et al., 2002). When attention due to stimulus salience causes an involuntary shift of attention, as happened when the loud noise in the library caused Roger to shift his attention, this shift is called *attentional capture* (Anderson et al., 2011). This capturing of attention could be important if it serves as a warning of something dangerous, such as an explosion, a dangerous animal, or an object moving rapidly toward us.

Determining how saliency influences the way we scan a scene typically involves analyzing characteristics such as color, orientation, and intensity at each location in the scene and then combining these values to create a **saliency map** of the scene (Itti & Koch, 2000; Parkhurst et al., 2002; Torralba et al., 2006). For example, the highly salient tree in **Figure 4.13** would be indicated by a light area on a saliency map.

Figure 4.14 shows a scene and its saliency map as determined by Derrick Parkhurst and coworkers (2002). When Parkhurst calculated saliency maps for a number of pictures and then measured observers' fixations as they observed the pictures, he found that the first few fixations were closely associated with the light areas on the saliency map, with fixations being more likely on high-saliency areas. But after the first few fixations, scanning begins to be influenced by top-down, or cognitive, processes that depend on things such as the observers' goals and expectations determined by their past experiences in observing the environment.

SCANNING BASED ON COGNITIVE FACTORS One way to show that where we look isn't determined only by saliency is by checking the eye movements of the subject looking at the fountain in **Figure 4.12**. Notice that the person never looks at the fence in the foreground, even though it is very salient because of its high contrast and its position near the front of the scene. Instead, the person focuses on aspects of the fountain that might be more interesting, such as the horses. It is likely that the *meaning* of the horses has attracted this particular person's attention.

It is important to note, however, that just because this person looked at the horses doesn't mean everyone would. Just as there are large variations between people, there are variations in how people scan scenes (Castelhano & Henderson, 2008; Noton & Stark, 1971). Thus, another person, who might be interested in wrought iron fences, might look less at the horses and more at the fence.

Such top-down processing is also associated with scene schemas—an observer's knowledge about what is contained in typical scenes (see Chapter 3, page 69). Thus, when Melissa Võ and John Henderson (2009) showed pictures like the ones in Figure 4.15, observers looked longer at the printer in Figure 4.15b than the pot in Figure 4.15a because a printer is less likely to be found in a kitchen. The fact that people look longer at things that seem out of place in a scene means that attention is being affected by their knowledge of what is usually found in the scene.

You can probably think of other situations in which your knowledge about specific types of scenes might influence where you look. You probably know a lot, for example, about kitchens, college campuses, automobile instrument panels, and shopping malls, and your knowledge about where things are usually found in these scenes can help guide your attention through each scene (Bar, 2004).

Another example of how cognitive factors based on knowledge of the environment influences scanning is an experiment by Hiroyuki Shinoda and coworkers (2001) in which they measured observers' fixations and tested their ability to detect traffic signs as they drove through a computer-generated environment in a driving simulator. They found that the observers were more likely to detect stop signs positioned at intersections than those positioned in the middle of a block, and that 45 percent of the observers' fixations occurred close to intersections. In this example, the observers are using learning about regularities in the environment (stop signs are usually at corners) to determine when and where to look for stop signs.

(a) Visual scene

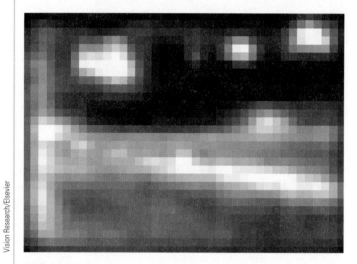

(b) Saliency map

Vision Research/Elsevier

Figure 4.14 (a) A visual scene. (b) Saliency map of the scene determined by analyzing the color, contrast, and orientations in the scene. Lighter areas indicate greater salience. *(Source: Adapted from D. Parkhurst, K. Law, & E. Niebur, Modeling the role of salience in the allocation of overt visual attention, Vision Research, 42, 107–123, 2002.)*

SCANNING BASED ON TASK DEMANDS The examples in the last section demonstrate that knowledge of various characteristics of the environment can influence how people direct their attention. However, the last example, in which subjects drove through a computer-generated environment, was different from the rest. The difference is that instead of looking at pictures of stationary scenes, subjects were interacting with the environment. This kind of situation, in which people are shifting their attention from one place to another as they are doing things, occurs when people are moving through the environment, as in the driving example, and when people are carrying out specific tasks.

Some researchers have focused on determining where people look as they are carrying out tasks. Since most tasks require attention to different places as the task unfolds, it isn't surprising that the timing of when people look at specific places is determined by the

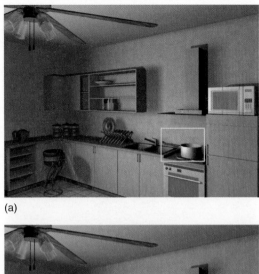

(a)

(b)

Figure 4.15 Stimuli used by Vō and Henderson (2009). Observers spent more time looking at the printer in (b) than at the pot in (a), shown inside the yellow rectangles (which were not visible to the observers). *(Source: M. L.-H. Vō, & J. M. Henderson, Does gravity matter? Effects of semantic and syntactic inconsistencies on the allocation of attention during scene perception, Journal of Vision, 9, 3:24, 1–15, Figure 1, 2009, http:// journalofvision.org/9/3/24/, doi:10.1167/9.3.24.)*

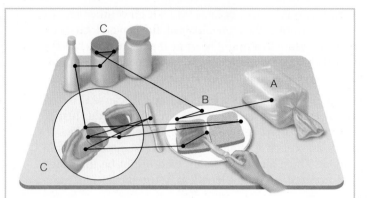

Figure 4.16 Sequence of fixations of a person making a peanut butter sandwich. The first fixation is on the loaf of bread. *(Source: Adapted from M. F. Land, N. Mennie, & J. Rusted, The roles of vision and eye movements in the control of activities of daily living, Perception, 28, 11, 1311–1328. Copyright © 1999 by Pion Ltd, London. Reproduced by permission. www.pion.co.uk and www.envplan.com.)*

sequence of actions involved in the task. Consider, for example, the pattern of eye movements in **Figure 4.16**, which were measured as a person was making a peanut butter sandwich. The process of making the sandwich begins with the movement of a slice of bread from the bag (A) to the plate (B). Notice that this operation is accompanied by an eye movement from the bag to the plate. The observer then looks at the peanut butter jar just before it is lifted and looks at the top just before it is removed (C). Attention then shifts to the knife, which is picked up and used to scoop the peanut butter and spread it on the bread (Land & Hayhoe, 2001).

The key finding of these measurements, and also of another experiment in which eye movements were measured as a person prepared tea (Land et al., 1999), is that the person's eye movements were determined primarily by the task. The person fixated on few objects or areas that were irrelevant to the task, and eye movements and fixations were closely linked to the action the person was about to take. Furthermore, the eye movement usually preceded a motor action by a fraction of a second, as when the person first fixated on the peanut butter jar and then reached over to pick it up. This is an example of the "just in time" strategy—eye movements occur just before we need the information they will provide (Hayhoe & Ballard, 2005; Tatler et al., 2011).

COVERT ATTENTION: DIRECTING ATTENTION WITHOUT EYE MOVEMENTS

In addition to directing attention by moving our eyes, we can also direct our attention while keeping our eyes stationary, a process called **covert attention**. Covert attention is an important part of many sports. Consider, for example, the basketball player in **Figure 4.17**, who looks to the right but then suddenly throws a dead-on pass to a teammate he was covertly attending to off to the left. We will now consider an experiment that used a covert attention task to determine what happens when a person directs his or her attention to a specific location.

ATTENTION TO A LOCATION In a classic series of studies, Michael Posner and coworkers (1978) asked whether paying attention to a location improves a person's ability to respond to stimuli presented there. To answer this question, Posner used the **precueing** procedure shown in **Figure 4.18**.

Figure 4.17 When Steve Nash looks to the right while paying attention to a teammate off to the left, he is covertly attending to the teammate.

Kamil Krzaczynski/epa/Corbis

METHOD
PRECUEING

The general principle behind a precueing experiment is to determine whether presenting a cue indicating where a test stimulus will appear enhances the processing of the target stimulus. The subjects in Posner and coworkers' (1978) experiment kept their eyes stationary throughout the experiment, always looking at the + in the display in **Figure 4.18**. They first saw an arrow cue (as shown in the left panel) indicating on which side of the display they should focus their attention. In **Figure 4.18a**, the arrow cue indicates that they should focus their attention to the right. (Remember, they do this without moving their eyes, so this is an example of covert attention.)

The subject's task was to press a key as rapidly as possible when a target square was presented off to the side (as shown in the right panel). The trial shown in **Figure 4.18a** is a *valid trial* because the target square appears on the side indicated by the cue arrow. On 80 percent of the trials, the cue arrow directed subjects' attention to the side where the target square appeared. However, on 20 percent of the trials, the arrow directed the subject's attention away from where the target was to appear. These were the *invalid trials*. On both the valid and invalid trials, the subject's task was the same—to press the key as quickly as possible when the target square appeared.

The results of this experiment, shown in **Figure 4.18c**, indicate that subjects reacted to the square more rapidly when their attention was focused on the location where the signal was to appear. Posner interpreted this result as showing that information processing is more effective *at the place where attention is directed*. This result and others like it gave rise to the idea that attention is like a spotlight or zoom lens that improves processing when directed toward a particular location (Marino & Scholl, 2005).

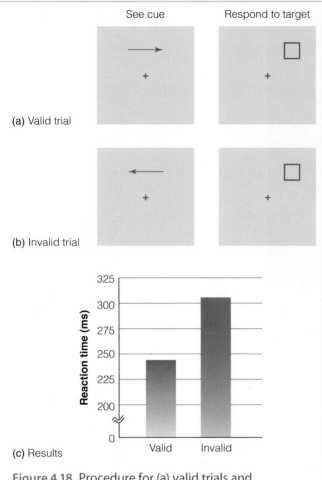

(a) Valid trial

(b) Invalid trial

(c) Results

Figure 4.18 Procedure for (a) valid trials and (b) invalid trials in Posner et al.'s (1978) precueing experiment; (c) the results of the experiment. The average reaction time was 245 ms for valid trials but 305 ms for invalid trials. *(Source: M. I. Posner, M. J. Nissen, & W. C. Ogden, Modes of perceiving and processing information. Copyright © 1978 by Taylor & Francis Group LLC–Books.)*

ATTENTION TO OBJECTS In addition to attending to locations, as in Posner's experiment, we can also covertly attend to specific objects. We will now consider some experiments that show that (1) attention can enhance our response to objects and (2) when attention is directed to one place on an object, the enhancing effect of that attention spreads to other places on the object.

Consider, for example, the experiment diagrammed in **Figure 4.19** (Egly et al., 1994). As subjects kept their eyes on the +, one end of the rectangle was briefly highlighted (**Figure 4.19a**). This was the cue signal that indicated where a target, a dark square (**Figure 4.19b**), would probably appear. In this example, the cue indicates that the target is likely to appear in position A, at the upper part of the right rectangle, and the target is, in fact, presented at A. (The letters used to illustrate positions in our description did not appear in the actual experiment.)

The subjects' task was to press a button when the target was presented anywhere on the display. The numbers indicate the reaction times, in milliseconds, for three target locations when the cue signal had been presented at A. Not surprisingly, subjects responded most rapidly when the target was presented at A, where the cue had been presented. However, the most interesting result is that subjects responded more rapidly when the target was presented at B (reaction time = 358 ms) than when the target was presented at C (reaction time = 374 ms). Why does this occur? It can't be because B is closer to A than C, because B and C are exactly the same distance from A. Rather, B's advantage occurs because it is located *within the object* that was receiving the subject's attention. Attending at A, where the cue was presented, causes the maximum effect at A, but the effect of this attention spreads throughout the object so some enhancement occurs at B as well. The faster responding that occurs when enhancement spreads within an object is called the **same-object advantage** (Marino & Scholl, 2005; also see Baylis & Driver, 1993; Driver & Baylis, 1989, 1998; Katzner et al., 2009; and Lavie & Driver, 1996, for more demonstrations of how attention spreads throughout objects).

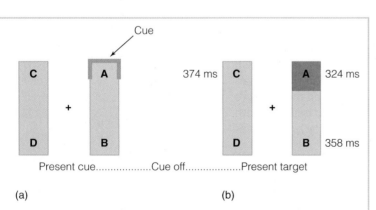

(a)   (b)

Figure 4.19 In Egly and coworkers' (1994) experiment, (a) a cue signal appears at one place on the display, then the cue is turned off and (b) a target is flashed at one of four possible locations, A, B, C, or D. Numbers are reaction times in ms for positions A, B, and C when the cue appeared at position A. © 2015 Cengage Learning

Divided Attention: Can We Attend to More Than One Thing at a Time?

Our emphasis so far has been on attention as a mechanism for focusing on one thing at a time. We have seen that sometimes we take in information from a task-irrelevant stimulus, even when we are trying to focus on one task, as in Forster and Lavie's experiment and the Stroop task. But what if you want to purposely distribute your attention among a few tasks? Is it possible to pay attention to more than one thing at a time? Although you might be tempted to answer "no," based on the difficulty of listening to two conversations at once, there are many situations in which *divided attention—* the distribution of attention among two or more tasks—can occur, as when Roger was able to play his cell phone game and listen in on the nearby conversation. Also, people can simultaneously drive, have conversations, listen to music, and think about what they're going to be doing later that day.

As we will see, the ability to divide attention depends on a number of factors, including practice and the difficulty of the task.

DIVIDED ATTENTION CAN BE ACHIEVED WITH PRACTICE: AUTOMATIC PROCESSING

We are going to describe some experiments by Walter Schneider and Richard Shiffrin (1977) that involve divided attention because they require the subject to carry out two tasks simultaneously: (1) holding information about target stimuli in memory and (2) paying attention to a series of "distractor" stimuli and determining whether one of the target stimuli is present among these distractor stimuli. **Figure 4.20** illustrates the procedure. The subject was shown a *memory set* like the one in **Figure 4.20a**, consisting of one to four characters called *target stimuli*. The memory set was followed by rapid presentation of 20 "test frames," each of which contained *distractors*. On half of the trials, one of the frames contained a target stimulus from the memory set. A new memory set was presented on each trial, so the targets changed from trial to trial, followed by new test frames. In this example, there is one target stimulus in the memory set, there are four stimuli in each frame, and the target stimulus 3 appears in one of the frames.

At the beginning of the experiment, the subjects' performance was only 55 percent correct; it took 900 trials for performance to reach 90 percent (**Figure 4.21**). Subjects reported that for the first 600 trials, they had to keep repeating the target items in each memory set in order to remember them. (Although targets were always numbers and distractors letters, remember that the actual targets and distractors changed from trial to trial.) However, subjects reported that after about 600 trials, the task had become automatic: The frames

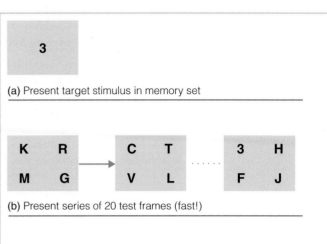

(a) Present target stimulus in memory set

(b) Present series of 20 test frames (fast!)

(c) Was target from memory set present in a frame?

Figure 4.20 Sample stimuli for Schneider and Shiffrin's (1977) experiment. In this experiment, there is one target stimulus in the memory set (the 3) and four stimuli in each frame. The target appears in the last frame in this example. *(Source: R. M. Shiffrin & W. Schneider, Controlled and automatic human information processing: Perceptual learning, automatic attending, and a general theory, Psychological Review, 84, 127–190, 1977.)*

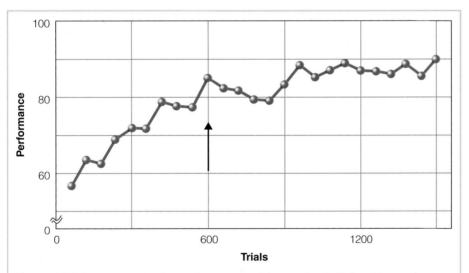

Figure 4.21 Improvement in performance with practice in Schneider and Schiffrin's (1977) experiment. The arrow indicates the point at which participants reported that the task had become automatic. This is the result of experiments in which there were four target stimuli in the memory set and two stimuli in each frame. *(Source: R. M. Shiffrin & W. Schneider, Controlled and automatic human information processing: Perceptual learning, automatic attending, and a general theory, Psychological Review, 84, 127–190, 1977.)*

appeared and subjects responded without consciously thinking about it. They would do this even when as many as four targets had been presented.

What this means, according to Schneider and Shiffrin, is that practice made it possible for subjects to divide their attention to deal with all of the target and test items simultaneously. Furthermore, the many trials of practice resulted in **automatic processing**, a type of processing that occurs (1) without intention (it happens automatically without the person intending to do it) and (2) at a cost of only some of a person's cognitive resources.

Real-life experiences are filled with examples of automatic processing because there are many things that we have been practicing for years. For example, have you ever wondered, after leaving home, whether you had locked the door and then returned to find that you had? Locking the door has, for many people, become such an automatic response that they do it without paying attention. Another example of automatic processing (which is sometimes scary) occurs when you have driven somewhere and can't remember the trip once you get to your destination. In many cases, this involves being "lost in thought" about something else, yet driving has become so automatic that it seems to take care of itself (at least until a traffic "situation" occurs, such as road construction or another car cutting in front of you). Finally, you may carry out many motor skills, such as touch-typing or texting, automatically, without attention. Try paying attention to what your fingers are doing while typing and notice what happens to your performance. Concert pianists have reported that if they start paying attention to their fingers while they are playing, their performance falls apart.

DIVIDED ATTENTION BECOMES MORE DIFFICULT WHEN TASKS ARE HARDER

What Schneider and Shiffrin's experiment shows is that divided attention is possible for some well-practiced tasks. However, in other experiments, they found that if task difficulty is increased—by using letters for both targets and distractors and by changing targets and distractors on each trial so a target on one trial can be a distractor on another—then automatic processing is not possible even with practice (also see Schneider & Chein, 2003).

An example of divided attention becoming difficult when the task is made too hard is provided by driving. You may find it easy to drive and talk at the same time if traffic is light on a familiar road. But if traffic increases, you see a flashing "Construction Ahead" sign, and the road suddenly becomes rutted, you might have to stop your conversation to devote all of your cognitive resources to driving. Because of the importance of driving in our society and the recent phenomenon of people talking on cell phones and texting while driving, researchers have begun to investigate the consequences of attempting to divide attention between driving and distracting activities.

DISTRACTIONS WHILE DRIVING

Driving is one of those tasks that demand constant attention. Not paying attention because of drowsiness or involvement in other tasks can have disastrous consequences. The seriousness of driver inattention was verified by a research project called the 100-Car Naturalistic Driving Study (Dingus et al., 2006). In this study, video recorders in 100 vehicles created records of both what the drivers were doing and the view out the front and rear windows.

These recordings documented 82 crashes and 771 near crashes in more than 2 million miles of driving. In 80 percent of the crashes and 67 percent of the near crashes, the driver was inattentive in some way 3 seconds beforehand. One man kept glancing down and to the right, apparently sorting through papers in a stop-and-go driving situation, until he slammed into an SUV. A woman eating a hamburger dropped her head below the dashboard just before she hit the car in front of her. One of the most distracting activities was pushing buttons on a cell phone or similar device. More than 22 percent of near crashes involved that kind of distraction.

This naturalistic research confirms earlier findings that demonstrated a connection between cell phone use and traffic accidents. A survey of accidents and cell phone use in Toronto showed that the risk of a collision was four times higher when the driver was using a cell phone than when a cell phone was not being used (Redelmeier & Tibshirani, 1997). Perhaps the most significant result of the Toronto study is that hands-free cell phone units offered no safety advantage.

In a laboratory experiment on the effects of cell phones, David Strayer and William Johnston (2001) gave subjects a simulated driving task that required them to apply the brakes as quickly as possible in response to a red light. Doing this task while talking on a cell phone caused subjects to miss twice as many of the red lights as when they weren't talking on the phone (Figure 4.22a) and also increased the time it took them to apply the brakes (Figure 4.22b). As in the Toronto study, the same decrease in performance occurred regardless of whether subjects used a hands-free cell phone device or a handheld model. Strayer and Johnston concluded from this result that talking on the phone uses cognitive resources that would otherwise be used for driving the car (also see Haigney & Westerman, 2001; Lamble et al., 1999; Spence & Read, 2003; Strayer et al., 2013; Violanti, 1998). This idea that the problem posed by cell phone use during driving is related to the use of cognitive resources is an important one. The problem isn't driving with one hand. It is driving with fewer cognitive resources available to focus attention on driving.

Students often react to results such as this by asking what the difference is between talking on a hands-free cell phone and having a conversation with a passenger in the car. There is, in fact, some evidence that having a conversation with a passenger can have an adverse effect on driving, especially if the passenger isn't paying attention to current driving conditions (Strayer et al., 2013). But one way to appreciate the difference between talking on a cell phone and what often happens when talking to a passenger is to imagine the situation in which you are sitting down (not in a car) and you place a call to your friend's cell phone. Your friend answers and you start talking. As far as you are concerned, you are just having a phone conversation. But unbeknownst to you, the person you called is in the process of negotiating his way through heavy traffic, or is perhaps reacting to a car that has just cut in front of him, traveling 70 miles per hour on the highway. The question to ask yourself is, would you be having the same conversation if you were a passenger sitting next to the driver? As a passenger, you would be aware of the traffic situation and would be able to react by pausing the conversation or perhaps

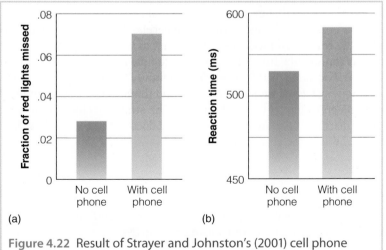

(a) (b)

Figure 4.22 Result of Strayer and Johnston's (2001) cell phone experiment. When participants were talking on a cell phone, they (a) missed more red lights and (b) took longer to apply the brakes. © Cengage Learning

warn the driver of upcoming hazards (sometimes called "backseat driving"!). It is also relevant to consider the social demands of phone conversations. Because it is generally considered poor form to suddenly stop talking or to pause for long periods on the phone, the person talking on the phone while driving might continue talking even when driving is becoming challenging.

An interesting phenomenon related to cell phone use is revealed by the results of a 2008 survey by Nationwide Mutual Insurance, which found that even though an overwhelming majority of people who talk on cell phones while driving consider themselves safe drivers, 45 percent of them reported that they had been hit or nearly hit by another driver talking on a cell phone. Thus, people identify talking on cell phones while driving as risky, but they think others are dangerous, not themselves (Nationwide Insurance, 2008).

Along these lines, some people feel that even though research clearly shows that driving while talking on a cell phone is dangerous, it doesn't apply to them. For example, in response to a class assignment, one of my students wrote, "I do not believe my driving is affected by talking on the phone. . . . My generation learned to drive when cell phones were already out. I had one before driving, so while learning to drive, I also simultaneously learned to talk and drive." Whatever your reaction to this response, the important thing is that this person believes it, and this keeps him talking on his cell phone as he is driving.

Or consider another student's response: "If I have the cognitive resources for driving and have some left over for a cell phone, what's wrong with doing both?" The answer to this question is that no matter how many years a person has been driving without any incidents while talking on the phone, talking on the phone (and certainly texting!) may be using more of their cognitive resources than they realize. Also, and perhaps most important, sometimes things happen suddenly while driving that require all of a person's cognitive resources *immediately*. With more people beginning to send text messages while driving, a study by the Virginia Tech Transportation Institute found that truck drivers who send text messages while driving are 23 times more likely to cause a crash or near crash than truckers who are not texting (Hanowski et al., 2009). Because of results such as these, most states now have laws against text-messaging while driving.

The main message here is that anything that distracts attention can degrade driving performance. And cell phones aren't the only attention-grabbing device found in cars. A 2004 article in the *New York Times* titled "Hi, I'm Your Car. Don't Let Me Distract You" notes that many cars have distraction-producing devices such as GPS systems and menu screens for computer controls (Peters, 2004). In the decade since that article appeared, the number of distracting devices available for cars has greatly increased. For example, voice-activated apps are available that enable drivers to make movie or dinner reservations, send and receive text or emails, and make postings on Facebook. One app, called Joyride, claims to "bring all of the social fun pieces of the Internet to you while you are driving" (Grant, 2013). While this sounds like fun, it is important to note that a recent study from the AAA Foundation for Traffic Safety titled *Measuring Cognitive Distraction in the Automobile* found voice-activated activities to be more distracting, and therefore potentially more dangerous, than either hands-on or hands-free cell phones. The study concludes that "just because a new technology does not take the eyes off the road does not make it safe to be used while the vehicle is in motion" (Strayer et al., 2013).

TEST YOURSELF 4.2

1. What is the difference between central vision and peripheral vision? How is this difference related to overt attention, fixations, and eye movements?

2. What is stimulus salience? How is it related to attention?

3. Describe some examples of how attention is determined by cognitive factors. What is the role of scene schemas?

4. Describe the peanut butter experiment. What does the result tell us about the relation between task demands and attention?

5. What is covert attention? Location-based attention? Describe the precueing procedure used by Posner. What does the result of Posner's experiment indicate about the effect of attention on information processing?

6. Describe the Egly precueing experiment. What is the same-object advantage, and how was it demonstrated by Egly's experiment?

7. Describe Schneider and Shiffrin's experiment that demonstrated automatic processing. What are some real-life examples of automatic processing? When is automatic processing not possible?

8. What conclusions can be reached from the results of experiments testing the ability to drive while talking on a cell phone? What are some of the differences between a driver talking to a passenger and a driver talking on a cell phone?

What Happens When We Don't Attend?

We have seen that paying attention affects how we respond to stimuli. But what happens when we don't pay attention? One idea is that you don't perceive things you aren't attending to. After all, if you're looking at something over to the left, you're not going to see something else that is far off to the right. But research has shown not only that we miss things that are out of our field of view, but that not attending can cause us to miss things even if we are looking directly at them.

INATTENTIONAL BLINDNESS

One example of not attending to something that is clearly visible is called **inattentional blindness**. In 1998, Arien Mack and Irvin Rock published a book titled *Inattentional Blindness*, in which they described experiments that showed that subjects can be unaware of clearly visible stimuli if they aren't directing their attention to them. In an experiment based on one of Mack and Rock's experiments, Ula Cartwright-Finch and Nilli Lavie (2007) presented the cross stimulus shown in **Figure 4.23**. The cross was presented for five trials, and the observer's task was to indicate which arm of the briefly flashed cross was longer, the horizontal or the vertical. This is a difficult task because the arms were just slightly different in length, the cross was flashed rapidly, and the arm that was longer changed from trial to trial. On the sixth trial, a small outline of a square was added to the display (**Figure 4.23b**). Immediately after the sixth trial, subjects were asked whether they noticed if anything had appeared on the screen that they had not seen before. Out of 20 subjects, only 2 (10 percent) reported that they had seen the square. In other words, most of the subjects were "blind" to the small square, even though it was located right next to the cross.

This demonstration of inattentional blindness used a rapidly flashed geometric test stimulus. But similar effects occur for more naturalistic stimuli that are visible for longer periods of time. For example, imagine looking at a display in a department store window. When you focus your attention on the display, you probably fail to notice the reflections on the surface of the window. Shift your attention to the reflections, and you become less aware of the display inside the window.

The idea that attention can affect perception within a dynamic scene was tested in an experiment by Daniel Simons and Christopher Chabris

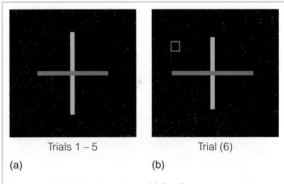

Trials 1 – 5 (a) Trial (6) (b)

Figure 4.23 Inattentional blindness experiment. (a) The cross display is presented for five trials. On each trial, one arm of the cross is slightly longer than the other. The subject's task is to indicate which arm (horizontal or vertical) is longer. (b) On the sixth trial, the subjects carry out the same task, but a small square or other geometric object is included in the display. After the sixth trial, subjects are asked whether they saw anything different than before. *(Source: Adapted from N. Lavie, Attention, distraction, and cognitive control under load, Current Directions in Psychological Science, 19, 143–148, 2010.)*

Figure 4.24 Frame from the film shown by Simons and Chabris in which a person in a gorilla suit walked through the basket-ball game. *(Source: D. J. Simons & C. F. Chabris, Gorillas in our midst: Sustained inattentional blindness for dynamic events, Perception, 28, 1059–1074, 1999. Pion Limited, London. Figure provided by Daniel Simons.)*

(1999), who created a 75-second film that showed two "teams" of three players each. One team, dressed in white, was passing a basketball around, and the other was "guarding" that team by following them around and putting their arms up as in a basketball game (Figure 4.24). Observers were told to count the number of passes, a task that focused their attention on the team wearing white. After about 45 seconds, one of two events occurred: Either a woman carrying an umbrella or a person in a gorilla suit walked through the "game," an event that took 5 seconds.

After seeing the video, observers were asked whether they saw anything unusual happen or whether they saw anything other than the six players. Nearly half of the observers—46 percent—failed to report that they saw the woman or the gorilla. This experiment demonstrated that when observers are attending to one sequence of events, they can fail to notice another event, even when it is right in front of them (also see Goldstein & Fink, 1981; Neisser & Becklen, 1975).

CHANGE DETECTION

Researchers have also demonstrated how a lack of attention can affect perception by first presenting one picture and then presenting another, slightly different picture. To appreciate how this works, try the following demonstration.

Figure 4.25 Stimulus for the change detection demonstration.

Bruce Goldstein

DEMONSTRATION
CHANGE DETECTION

When you are finished reading these instructions, look at the picture in **Figure 4.25** for just a moment; then turn the page and see whether you can determine what is different in **Figure 4.28**. Do this now.

Were you able to see what was different in the second picture? People often have trouble detecting the change even though it is obvious when you know where to look. (Try again, paying attention to the sign near the lower left portion of the picture.) Ronald Rensink and coworkers (1997) did a similar experiment in which they presented one picture, followed by a blank field, followed by the same picture but with an item missing, followed by a blank field, and so on. The pictures were alternated in this way until observers were able to determine what was different about the two pictures. Rensink found that the pictures had to be alternated back and forth a number of times before the difference was detected.

This difficulty in detecting changes in scenes is called **change blindness** (Rensink, 2002). The importance of attention (or lack of it) in determining change blindness is demonstrated by the fact that when Rensink added a cue indicating which part of a scene had been changed, subjects detected the changes much more quickly (also see Henderson & Hollingworth, 2003).

The change blindness effect also occurs when the scene changes in different shots of a film. **Figure 4.26** shows successive frames from a video of a brief conversation between two women. The noteworthy aspect of this video is that changes take place in each new shot. In (b), the woman's scarf has disappeared; in (c), the other woman's hand is on her chin, although seconds later, in (d), both arms are on the table. Also, the plates change color from red in the initial views to white in (d).

Although subjects who viewed this video were told to pay close attention, only 1 of 10 subjects claimed to notice any changes. Even when the subjects were shown the video again and were warned that there would be changes in "objects, body position, or cloth-

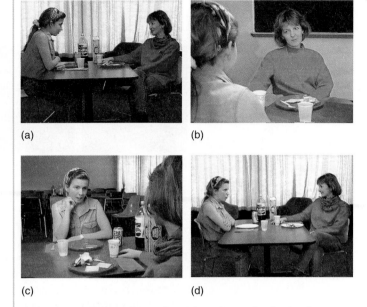

(a)   (b)

(c)   (d)

Figure 4.26 Frames from the video shown in the Levin and Simons (1997) experiment. Note that the woman on the right is wearing a scarf around her neck in shots A, C, and D, but not in shot B. Also, the color of the plates changes from red in the first three frames to white in frame D, and the hand position of the woman on the left changes between shots C and D. *(Source: From D. T. Levin & D. J. Simons, Failure to detect changes to attended objects in motion pictures, Psychonomic Bulletin and Review, 4, 501–506, 1997.)*

ing," they noticed fewer than a quarter of the changes that occurred (Levin & Simons, 1997).

This blindness to change in films is not just a laboratory phenomenon. It occurs regularly in popular films, in which some aspect of a scene that should remain the same changes from one shot to the next, just as objects changed in the film shots in **Figure 4.26**. These changes in films, called *continuity errors*, are spotted by viewers who are looking for them, usually by viewing the film multiple times, but are usually missed by viewers in theaters who are not looking for these errors. For example, in the film *Oceans 11* (2001), Rusty, the character played by Brad Pitt, is talking to Linus, the character played by Matt Damon. In one shot, Rusty is holding a cocktail glass full of shrimp in his hand, but in the next shot, which moves in closer and is from a slightly different angle, the glass has turned into a plate of fruit, and then in the next shot the plate changes back to the cocktail glass full of shrimp! If you are interested in exploring continuity errors further, you can find websites devoted to them by searching for "continuity errors in movies."

WHAT ABOUT EVERYDAY EXPERIENCE?

All of the experiments we have described—both the inattentional blindness experiments, in which a distracting task kept people from noticing a test stimulus, and the change blindness experiments, in which small but easily visible changes in pictures are not perceived—demonstrate that attention is sometimes necessary for perception. This has implications for perception in our everyday experience, because there are a large number of stimuli present in the environment, and we are able to pay attention to only a small fraction of these stimuli at any moment. This means that we are constantly missing things in the environment.

Before you decide that our perceptual system is hopelessly flawed by its inability to detect large portions of our environment, consider the fact that we (and other animals) have somehow survived, so clearly our perceptual system is doing its job well enough to

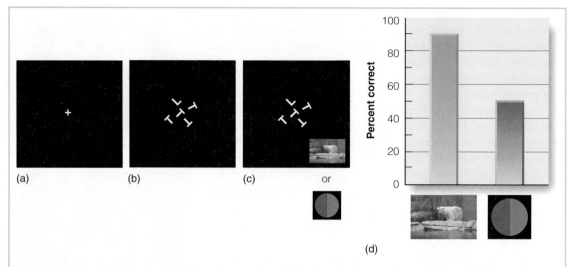

Figure 4.27 (a–c) Procedure for Li and coworkers' (2002) experiment. See text for details. (d) Results of the experiment. Performance is the percent correct when carrying out the central task compared to the percent correct when not carrying out the central task. Performance drops only slightly for the scene task but drops to near chance for the colored-disc task. *(Source: Adapted from F. Li, R. VanRullen, C. Koch, & P. Perona, Rapid natural scene categorization in the near absence of attention, Proceedings of the National Academy of Sciences, 99, 9596–9601, 2002. Photo of polar bear: Barbara Goldstein.)*

take care of most of the perceptual requirements posed by everyday life. In fact, it has been argued that the fact that our perceptual system focuses on only a small portion of the environment is one of its most adaptive features, because by focusing on what is important, our perceptual system is making optimal use of our limited processing resources.

But even as we are focusing on what is important at the moment, our perceptual system has a warning system that causes us to rapidly shift our attention to things that might signal danger, such as a charging animal, a pedestrian on a collision course with us, a bright flash of light, or a loud noise. Once our attention has shifted, we can then evaluate what is happening at our new center of attention and decide whether we need to take action.

It is also important to realize that we don't need to be aware of all the details of what is happening around us. As you walk down a crowded sidewalk, you need to know where the other people are so you can avoid colliding, but you don't need to know that a particular person is wearing glasses or that another is wearing a blue shirt. You also don't need to be continually checking the details of what is happening around you because, from your past experience, you have *scene schemas* for city streets, country roads, or the aisles of supermarkets that enable you to "fill in" what is around you without paying close attention (see Chapter 3, page 69). Finally, some things in the environment are easier to see than others without close attention. This is demonstrated in an experiment by Fei Fei Li and coworkers (2002) that considers what information we can take in about unattended stimuli.

Li's subjects looked at the + on the fixation screen (Figure 4.27a) and then saw the *central stimulus*—an array of five letters (Figure 4.27b). On some trials, all of the letters were the same; on other trials, one of the letters was different from the other four. The letters were followed immediately by the *peripheral stimulus*—either a disc that was half green and half red or a picture of a scene—which flashed for 27 ms at a random position on the edge of the screen (Figure 4.27c).

Figure 4.28 Stimulus for the change detection demonstration.

The subjects' *central task* was to indicate if all of the letters in the central stimulus were the same, and their *peripheral task* was to indicate whether the scene contained an animal (for the picture) or whether the colored discs were red-green or green-red (for the discs). Even though subjects had to keep their attention focused on the letters in the middle in order to carry out the letter task, their performance was 90 percent on the peripheral picture task, but it was only 50 percent on the peripheral colored disc task (**Figure 4.27d**). This means that it is possible to take in information about some objects but not others in scenes even when attention is focused elsewhere. Another experiment, by Lila Reddy and coworkers (2004), demonstrated the same thing when the peripheral task was indicating whether a picture of a face showed a male or a female.

What all of this means is that our perceptual systems are generally well adapted to take in the information we need to survive, even though we can only take in a small proportion of the information that is out there. But before you decide that the combination of focused attention, warning signals on the side, and filling in by schemas enables you to achieve feats of divided attention like driving and texting, remember that driving, texting, and cell phones are recent additions to the environment that weren't present when your perceptual system evolved. Thus, as adaptive as our perceptual system might be, our modern world often puts us in situations that we are not designed to deal with and that, as we saw earlier, can lead to a dented fender, or worse.

Attention and Experiencing a Coherent World

We have seen that attention is an important determinant of what we perceive. Attention brings things to our awareness and can enhance our ability to perceive and to respond. We now consider yet another function of attention, one that is not obvious from our everyday experience. This function of attention is to help create **binding**—the process by which features such as color, form, motion, and location are combined to create our perception of a coherent object.

WHY IS BINDING NECESSARY?

We can appreciate why binding is necessary by remembering our discussion of localization of function in Chapter 2, when we saw that separated areas of the brain are specialized for the perception of different qualities. Thus, when the person in **Figure 4.29** observes a red ball roll by, cells sensitive to the ball's shape fire in his temporal cortex (see page 76), cells sensitive to movement fire in an area specialized for motion, and cells sensitive to depth and color fire in other areas. But even though the ball's shape, movement, depth, and color cause firing in different areas of the person's cortex, he doesn't perceive the ball as separated shape, movement, depth, and color perceptions. He experiences an integrated perception of a ball, with all of the ball's features being bound together to create a coherent perception of a "rolling red ball." The question of how an object's individual features become bound together, which is called the **binding problem**, has been addressed by Anne Treisman's (1986, 1988, 1999) *feature integration theory*.

FEATURE INTEGRATION THEORY

Treisman's **feature integration theory** tackles the question of how we perceive individual features as part of the same object by proposing a two-stage process, shown in **Figure 4.30**. As we will see, attention becomes important in the second stage.

PREATTENTIVE STAGE According to Treisman, the first step in processing an image of an object is the **preattentive stage**. In the

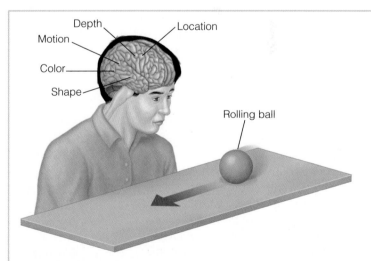

Figure 4.29 Any stimulus, even one as simple as a rolling ball, activates a number of different areas of the cortex. Binding is the process by which these separated signals are combined to create a unified percept. © Cengage Learning

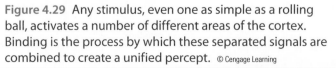

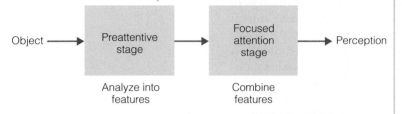

Figure 4.30 Steps in Treisman's feature integration. Objects are analyzed into their features in the preattentive stage, and the features are later combined with the aid of attention. © Cengage Learning

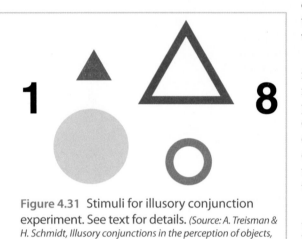

Figure 4.31 Stimuli for illusory conjunction experiment. See text for details. *(Source: A. Treisman & H. Schmidt, Illusory conjunctions in the perception of objects, Cognitive Psychology, 14, 107–141, 1982.)*

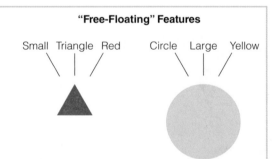

Figure 4.32 Illustration of the idea that in the preattentive stage an object's features are "free floating." Because they are not attached to a particular object, they can potentially become associated with any object in a display. When this happens, an illusory conjunction is created. *(Source: A. Treisman & H. Schmidt, Illusory conjunctions in the perception of objects, Cognitive Psychology, 14, 107–141, 1982.)*

preattentive stage, objects are analyzed into separate features. For example, the rolling red ball would be analyzed into features such as color (red), shape (round), and movement (rolling to the right). Because each of these features is processed in a separate area of the brain, they exist independently of one another at this stage of processing.

The idea that an object is automatically broken into features may seem counterintuitive because when we look at an object, we see the whole object, not an object that has been divided into its individual features. The reason we aren't aware of this process of feature analysis is that it occurs early in the perceptual process, before we have become conscious of the object. Thus, when you see this book, you are conscious of its rectangular shape, but you are not aware that before you saw this rectangular shape, your perceptual system analyzed the book into individual features such as lines with different orientations.

To provide some perceptual evidence that objects are, in fact, analyzed into features, Anne Treisman and Hilary Schmidt (1982) did an ingenious experiment to show that early in the perceptual process, features may exist independently of one another. Treisman and Schmidt's display consisted of four objects flanked by two black numbers (Figure 4.31). They flashed this display onto a screen for one-fifth of a second, followed by a random-dot masking field designed to eliminate any residual perception that might remain after the stimuli were turned off. Subjects were told to report the black numbers first and then to report what they saw at each of the four locations where the shapes had been.

In 18 percent of the trials, subjects reported seeing objects that were made up of a combination of features from two different stimuli. For example, after being presented with the display in Figure 4.31, in which the small triangle is red and the small circle is green, they might report seeing a small red circle and a small green triangle. These combinations of features from different stimuli are called **illusory conjunctions**. Illusory conjunctions can occur even if the stimuli differ greatly in shape and size. For example, a small blue circle and a large green square might be seen as a large blue square and a small green circle.

Although illusory conjunctions are usually demonstrated in laboratory experiments, they can occur in other situations as well. Recently, I ran a class demonstration to illustrate that observers sometimes make errors in eyewitness testimony. In the demonstration, a male wearing a green shirt burst into the class, grabbed a yellow purse that was sitting on a desk (the owner of the purse was in on the demonstration), and left the room. This event happened very rapidly and was a surprise to students in the class. Their task was to describe what had happened as eyewitnesses to a "crime." Interestingly enough, one of the students reported that a male wearing a yellow shirt grabbed a green purse from the desk! Interchanging the colors of these objects is an example of illusory conjunctions (Treisman, 2005).

According to Treisman, illusory conjunctions occur because in the preattentive stage, each feature exists independently of the others. That is, features such as "redness," "curvature," or "tilted line" are, at this early stage of processing, not associated with a specific object. They are, in Treisman's (1986) words, "free floating," as shown in Figure 4.32, and can therefore be incorrectly combined if there is more than one object, especially in laboratory situations when briefly flashed stimuli are followed by a masking field.

You can think of these features as components of a visual "alphabet." At the very beginning of the process, perceptions of each of these components exist independently of one another, just as the letter tiles in a game of Scrabble exist as individual units when the tiles are scattered at the beginning of the game. However, just as the individual Scrabble tiles are combined to form words, the individual features combine to form perceptions of whole objects.

FOCUSED ATTENTION STAGE According to Treisman's model, these "free-floating" features are combined in the second stage, called the **focused attention stage** (Figure 4.30). Once the features have been combined in this stage, we perceive the object.

During the focused attention stage, the observer's attention plays an important role in combining the features to create the perception of whole objects. To illustrate the importance of attention for combining the features, Treisman repeated the illusory conjunction experiment using the stimuli in **Figure 4.31**, but this time she instructed her subjects to ignore the black numbers and to focus all their attention on the four target items. This focusing of attention eliminated illusory conjunctions so that all the shapes were paired with their correct colors.

When I describe this process in class, some students aren't convinced. One student said, "I think that when people look at an object, they don't break it into parts. They just see what they see." To convince such students (and the many others who, at the beginning of the course, are not comfortable with the idea that perception sometimes involves rapid processes we aren't aware of), I describe the case of R.M., a patient who had parietal lobe damage that resulted in a condition called **Balint's syndrome**. A crucial characteristic of Balint's syndrome is an inability to focus attention on individual objects.

According to feature integration theory, lack of focused attention would make it difficult for R.M. to combine features correctly, and this is exactly what happened. When R.M. was presented with two different letters of different colors, such as a red T and a blue O, he reported illusory conjunctions such as "blue T" on 23 percent of the trials, even when he was able to view the letters for as long as 10 seconds (Friedman-Hill et al., 1995; Robertson et al., 1997). The case of R.M. illustrates how a breakdown in the brain can reveal processes that are not obvious when the brain is functioning normally.

The feature analysis approach involves mostly bottom-up processing because knowledge is usually not involved. In some situations, however, top-down processing can come into play. For example, when Treisman and Schmidt (1982) did an illusory conjunction experiment using stimuli such as the ones in **Figure 4.33** and asked subjects to identify the objects, the usual illusory conjunctions occurred; the orange triangle, for example, would sometimes be perceived to be black. However, when she told subjects that they were being shown a carrot, a lake, and a tire, illusory conjunctions were less likely to occur, and subjects were more likely to perceive the triangular "carrot" as being orange. In this situation, the subjects' knowledge of the usual colors of objects influenced their ability to correctly combine the features of each object. In our everyday experience, in which we often perceive familiar objects, top-down processing combines with feature analysis to help us perceive things accurately.

Figure 4.33 Stimuli used to show that top-down processing can reduce illusory conjunctions. *(Source: A. Treisman & H. Schmidt, Illusory conjunctions in the perception of objects, Cognitive Psychology, 14, 107–141, 1982.)*

Another approach to studying the role of attention in binding has used a task called visual search. **Visual search** is something we do anytime we look for an object among a number of other objects, such as you did when you looked for Jennifer Hudson in the group of musicians in **Figure 4.11**, or when you try to find Waldo in a "Where's Waldo?" picture (Handford, 1997). A type of visual search called a *conjunction search* has been particularly useful in studying binding.

DEMONSTRATION
SEARCHING FOR CONJUNCTIONS

We can understand what a conjunction search is by first describing another type of search called a **feature search**. Before reading further, find the horizontal line in **Figure 4.34a**. This is a feature search because you could find the target by looking for a single feature—"horizontal."

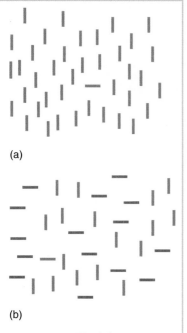

(a)

(b)

Figure 4.34 Find the horizontal line in (a) and then the green horizontal line in (b). Which task took longer? © Cengage Learning

Now find the green horizontal line in **Figure 4.34b**. This is a **conjunction search** because you had to search for a combination (or conjunction) of two or more features in the same stimulus—"horizontal" and "green." In **Figure 4.34b**, you couldn't focus just on green because there are vertical green lines, and you couldn't focus just on horizontal because there are horizontal red lines. You had to look for the *conjunction* of horizontal and green.

Conjunction searches are useful for studying binding because finding the target in a conjunction search involves scanning a display in order to focus attention at a specific location. To test the idea that attention to a location is required for a conjunction search, a number of researchers have tested R.M., the Balint's patient, and have found that he cannot find the target when a conjunction search is required (Robertson et al., 1997). This is what we would expect because of R.M's difficulty in focusing attention. R.M. can, however, find targets when only a feature search is required, as in **Figure 4.34a**, because attention-at-a-location is not required for this kind of search. Feature integration theory therefore considers attention to be an essential component of the mechanism that creates our perception of objects from a number of different features.

Something to Consider

TAKING POSSESSION BY THE BRAIN

Attention, according to the William James quote at the beginning of the chapter, is "taking possession by the mind" of an object or thought. But what's behind this "taking possession"? A large amount of research shows that paying attention enhances brain activity. We will describe two experiments that show how brain activity is affected by shifting attention from one place to another or from one object to another.

The first experiment is based on a basic finding from perception research, which indicates that there is a spatial map of visual stimuli on the visual cortex. This map is called a **topographic map**, because each point on a visual stimulus causes activity at a specific location on the visual cortex, and points next to each other on the stimulus cause activity at points next to each other on the visual cortex.

We can understand the principle of topographic mapping by considering the observer in **Figure 4.35**, who is looking at the center of a patterned disc. Light from location A on the disc creates an image at A on the observer's retina, which causes activity at A on the observer's visual cortex. Similarly, light from locations B and C on the disc creates images at B and C on the retina, which causes activity at B and C on the visual cortex. When this electrical activity is transmitted to higher visual areas in the brain, the observer *perceives* the patterns at locations A, B, and C on the disc.

But what if, instead of just passively looking at the center of the disc, the observer decides to *pay attention* to different locations on the disc? Without moving his eyes from the center, the subject first pays attention to the pattern at A and then shifts his attention to the pattern at B, and then to C. (These are covert shifts of attention, because the observer is not moving his eyes.) Roberto Datta and Edgar DeYoe (2009) determined how these shifts of attention affect the activity of the brain by having an observer covertly shift his attention to different locations on a display while they measured the activity of his brain in an fMRI scanner (**Figure 4.36a**).

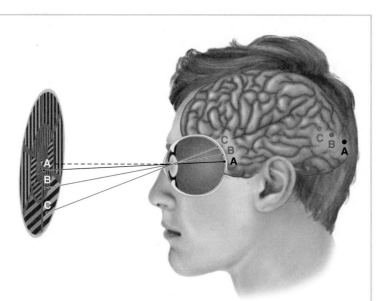

Figure 4.35 A person looking at a patterned disc. The patterns at A, B, and C on the disc create images at A, B, and C on the person's retina and cause activation at A, B, and C on the visual cortex. © Cengage Learning

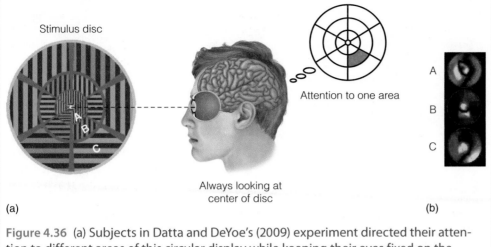

Figure 4.36 (a) Subjects in Datta and DeYoe's (2009) experiment directed their attention to different areas of this circular display while keeping their eyes fixed on the center of the display. (b) Activation of the brain that occurred when subject attended to the areas indicated by the letters on the stimulus disc. The center of each circle is the place on the brain that corresponds to the center of the stimulus. The yellow "hot spot" is the area of the brain that is maximally activated by attention. *(Source: From R. Datta & E. A. DeYoe, I know where you are secretly attending! The topography of human visual attention revealed with fMRI, Vision Research, 49, 1037–1044, 2009.)*

The colors in the circles in **Figure 4.36b** indicate the area of the brain where activity increased when the subject directed his attention to the locations indicated by the letters on the stimulus in **Figure 4.36a**. Notice that the yellow "hot spot," which is the place of greatest increase, is near the center when the subject is paying attention to area A, near where he is looking. But as he shifts his attention to areas B and C, which are farther from where he is looking, the increase in brain activity moves out from the center. Attention, therefore, enhances activity at the locations on the brain's topographic map that represent where the subject is directing his attention. This is the brain's way of "taking possession" of the location where the subject is directing his attention.

By collecting brain activation data for all of the locations on the stimulus, Datta and DeYoe created "attention maps" that show how directing attention to a specific area of space activates a specific area of the brain. What makes this experiment even more interesting is that after attention maps were determined for a particular subject, that subject was told to direct his or her attention to a "secret" place, which was unknown to the experimenters. Based on the location of the resulting yellow "hot spot," the experimenters were able to predict, with 100 percent accuracy, the "secret" place where the subject was attending.

Let's take this idea of attention enhancing brain activity one step further by considering how areas that are specialized to respond to specific types of stimuli are affected by attention. We can ask, for example, what happens when a person focuses his or her attention on one of two superimposed stimuli. This experiment, by Kathleen O'Craven and coworkers (1999), presented subjects with displays like the one in **Figure 4.37a** in which a face and a house were superimposed. Subjects were asked to direct their attention to one stimulus or the other. In each pair, one of the stimuli was stationary and the other was moving slightly back and forth. When looking at a pair, subjects were told to attend to either the moving or stationary house or the moving or stationary face. As they were doing this, O'Craven measured activity in their fusiform face area (FFA) and parahippocampal place area (PPA) (see **Figures 2.20** and **2.21**).

When subjects attended to the moving or stationary face, activity increased in the FFA (**Figure 4.37b**); when they attended to the moving or stationary house, activity increased

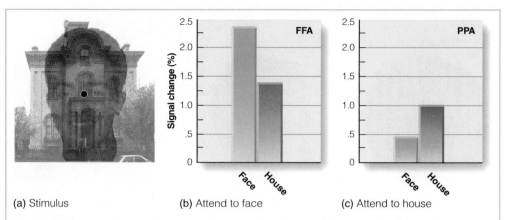

(a) Stimulus (b) Attend to face (c) Attend to house

Figure 4.37 Superimposed face and house stimulus used in the O'Craven et al. (1999) experiment. (b) FFA activation when subject attended to the face or the house. (c) PPA activation for attention to the face or the house. *(Source: Based on data from K. M. O'Craven, P. E. Downing, & N. Kanwisher, fMRI evidence for objects as the units of attentional selection, Nature, 401, 584–587, 1999.)*

in the PPA (Figure 4.37c). Thus, attention caused the brain to *take possession* of the object being attended to by increasing activity in the area specialized to perceive that object.

The story we have told so far has been about interacting with things in the environment. We *perceive* objects visually, hear sounds, experience smells or someone touching us, and in some cases we *pay attention* to some of these things more than others. Both perception and attention support our ability to know about our environment and to act within it. But to take us beyond having immediate experiences, we need to be able to store some of what is happening to us so we can remember it later. This function is achieved by the process of *memory*, which not only helps us survive but also determines our identity as a person. This is so important that we will spend the next four chapters discussing the process of memory. As you will see, many of the things we have introduced in our discussion of perception and attention—the principle of representation, the importance of knowledge gained from experience, our active interaction with both ideas and things—are central to our understanding of memory.

TEST YOURSELF 4.3

1. Describe the following evidence that attention is sometimes necessary for perception: inattentional blindness experiment; "basketball" experiment; change detection experiments.

2. Why can we say that we don't need to be aware of all of the details of what is happening around us?

3. Describe Li's experiment that considers what information we can take in about unattended stimuli.

4. What is binding, and why is it necessary? What is the binding problem?

5. Describe Treisman's feature integration theory. What does the theory seek to explain about perceiving objects? What are the stages of the theory, and at what point does attention become involved?

6. What are illusory conjunctions, and what do they demonstrate about feature analysis? How have illusory conjunction experiments supported the role of attention in feature analysis? How do experiments with Balint's syndrome patients support feature integration theory?

7. What is a feature search? A conjunction search? Which type of search did the Balint's patient find difficult? What does that tell us about the role of attention in feature integration?

8. Describe the following physiological research that demonstrates how attention is "taking possession by the brain": Datta and DeYoe experiment; O'Craven and coworkers experiment.

CHAPTER SUMMARY

1. Selective attention, the ability to focus on one message while ignoring all others, has been demonstrated using the dichotic listening procedure.

2. A number of models have been proposed to explain the process of selective attention. Broadbent's filter model proposes that the attended message is separated from the incoming signal early in the analysis of the signal. Treisman's model proposes later separation and adds a dictionary unit to explain how the unattended message can sometimes get through. Late selection models propose that selection doesn't occur until messages are processed enough to determine their meaning.

3. Lavie proposes that our ability to ignore distracting stimuli can be explained by considering processing capacity and perceptual load. Her load theory of attention states that distraction is less likely for high-load tasks because no capacity remains to process potential distracting stimuli.

4. The Stroop effect demonstrates how a powerful task-irrelevant stimulus, such as meaningful words that result in a response that competes with the observer's task, can capture attention.

5. Overt attention is shifting attention by making eye movements. Overt attention is determined by bottom-up processes such as stimulus salience and by top-down processes such as scene schemas and task demands, which influence how eye movements are directed to parts of a scene.

6. Covert attention is shifting attention without making eye movements. Visual attention can be directed to different places in a scene even without eye movements. The effect of covert attention has been demonstrated by precueing experiments, which have shown that covert attention to a location enhances processing at that location. This is called location-based attention.

7. Object-based attention occurs when attention is directed toward specific objects. The enhancing effects of attention spread throughout an object—an effect called the same-object advantage.

8. Divided attention is possible for easy tasks or for highly practiced difficult tasks. Automatic processing is possible in these situations but is not possible for very difficult tasks.

9. Driver inattention is one of the major causes of automobile accidents. There is evidence that using cell phones while driving is associated with increases in traffic accidents and decreases in performance of driving-related tasks. Hands-free and voice-activated devices are just as distracting as handheld devices.

10. Inattentional blindness and change blindness experiments provide evidence that without attention we may fail to perceive things that are clearly visible in the field of view.

11. Although inattentional blindness and change blindness indicate that we don't notice everything that is happening, our perceptual system is well adapted for survival. We can be warned about possible danger by movement, and the perceptual system makes optimal use of limited processing resources by focusing on what is being attended. In addition, there is evidence that we can detect important stimuli in the absence of full attention.

12. Binding is the process by which object features are combined to create perception of a coherent object. Feature integration theory explains how binding occurs by proposing two stages of processing, preattentive processing and focused attention. The basic idea is that objects are analyzed into their features and that attention is necessary to combine these features to create perception of an object. Illusory conjunction, visual search, and neuropsychology experiments support feature integration theory.

13. Evidence that attention "takes possession" of the brain is provided by experiments showing that covert attention to an object or location enhances brain activity associated with the object or location.

THINK ABOUT IT

1. Pick two items from the following list, and decide how difficult it would be to do both at the same time. Some things are difficult to do simultaneously because of physical limitations. For example, it is extremely dangerous to type on your computer and drive at the same time. Others things are difficult to do simultaneously because of cognitive limitations. For each pair of activities that you pick, decide why it would be easy or difficult to do them simultaneously. Be sure to take the idea of cognitive load into account.

Driving a car	Talking on a cell phone
Reading a book for pleasure	Flying a kite
Doing math problems	Walking in the woods
Talking to a friend	Listening to a story
Thinking about tomorrow	Writing a paper for class
Rock climbing	Dancing

2. Find someone who is willing to participate in a brief "observation exercise." Cover a picture (preferably one that contains a number of objects or details) with a piece of paper, and tell the person that you are going to uncover the picture and that their task is to report everything that they see. Then uncover the picture very briefly (less than a second), and have the person write down, or tell you, what they saw. Then repeat this procedure, increasing the exposure of the picture to a few seconds, so the person can direct his or her attention to different parts of the picture. Perhaps try this a third time, allowing even more time to observe the picture. From the person's responses, what can you conclude about the role of attention in determining what people are aware of in their environment?

3. Art composition books often state that it is possible to arrange elements in a painting in a way that controls both *what* a person looks at in a picture and the *order* in which a person looks at things. What would the results of research on visual attention have to say about this idea?

4. How does the attention involved in carrying out actions in the environment differ from the attention involved in scanning a picture for details, as in the previous "observation exercise"?

5. As you sit in a stadium watching a football game, there is a lot going on in the game, in the stands, and on the sidelines. Which things that you might look at would involve object-based attention, and which would involve location-based attention?

6. As the quarterback steps back to pass, the offensive line blocks the defense, so the quarterback has plenty of time to check out what is happening downfield and hits an open receiver. Later in the game, two 300-pound linemen get through to the quarterback. While he scrambles for safety, he fails to see the open receiver downfield and instead throws a pass toward another receiver that is almost intercepted. How can these two situations be related to the way selective attention is affected by task load?

7. Given the mounting evidence that talking on cell phones (even hands-free) while driving increases the chances of having an accident, it could be argued that laws should be passed making all cell phone use illegal while driving. (The majority of states currently have laws against texting while driving.) What would be your reaction if this occurred? Why?

KEY TERMS

Attention, 86

Attentional capture, 87

Attenuation model of attention, 90

Attenuator, 90

Automatic processing, 102

Balint's syndrome, 111

Binding, 109

Binding problem, 109

Bottleneck model, 89

Change blindness, 107

Cocktail party effect, 88

Conjunction search, 112

Covert attention, 98

Dichotic listening, 88

Dictionary unit, 90

Distraction, 87

Divided attention, 87

Early selection model, 89

Feature integration theory, 109

Feature search, 111

COGLAB EXPERIMENTS Numbers in parentheses refer to the experiment number in CogLab.

If you were to look at this rack of pool balls for about 15 seconds, how well could you recall the numbers in each row? The number of the front ball is easy, but things become more difficult when trying to remember longer rows. Or consider how well you would be able to remember the numbers and locations of the balls right after they were scattered across the pool table. Tasks like these, which involve short-term memory, are difficult because of the short duration and small capacity of short-term memory. Despite this short duration and limited capacity, short-term memory and a related process called working memory are essential for our moment-to-moment interactions with the environment.

Short-Term and Working Memory

SOME QUESTIONS WE WILL CONSIDER

▶ Why can we remember a telephone number long enough to place a call, but then we forget it almost immediately? (127)

▶ How is memory involved in processes such as doing a math problem? (133)

▶ Do we use the same memory system to remember things we have seen and things we have heard? (134)

So much has been written about memory—the advantages of having a good memory, the pitfalls of forgetting, or in the worst case losing one's ability to remember—that it may hardly seem necessary to read a cognitive psychology textbook to understand what memory is. But as you will see over the next four chapters, "memory" is not just one thing. Memory, like attention, comes in many forms. One of the purposes of this chapter and the next is to introduce the different types of memory, describing the properties of each type and the mechanisms responsible for them. Let's begin with two definitions of memory:

■ **Memory** is the process involved in retaining, retrieving, and using information about stimuli, images, events, ideas, and skills after the original information is no longer present.

■ Memory is active any time some past experience has an effect on the way you think or behave now or in the future (Joordens, 2011).

From these definitions, it is clear that memory has to do with the past affecting the present, and possibly the future. But while these definitions are correct, we need to consider the various ways in which the past can affect the present to really understand what memory is. When we do this, we will see that there are many different kinds of memory. With apologies to the English poet Elizabeth Barrett Browning, whose famous poem to her husband begins "How do I love thee, let me count the ways," let's consider Christine as she describes incidents from her life that illustrate a related question: "How do I remember thee, let me count the ways." (See **Figure 5.1**.)

> My first memory of you was brief and dramatic. It was the Fourth of July, and everyone was looking up at the sky to see the fireworks. But what I saw was your face—illuminated for just a moment by a flash, and then there was darkness. But even in the darkness I held your image in my mind for a moment.

When something is presented briefly, such as a face illuminated by a flash, your perception continues for a fraction of a second in the dark. This brief persistence of the image, which is one of the things that makes it possible to perceive movies, is called *sensory memory*.

> Luckily I had the presence of mind to "accidentally" meet you later so we could exchange phone numbers. Unfortunately, I didn't have my cell phone with me or anything to write with, so I had to keep repeating your number over and over until I could write it down.

Information that stays in our memory for brief periods, about 10 to 15 seconds if we don't repeat it over and over as Christine did, is *short-term memory* or *working memory*.

> And the rest is history, because I have countless memories of all the things we have done. I especially remember that crisp fall day when we went bike riding to that place in the woods where we had a picnic.

Long-term memory is responsible for storing information for long periods of time—which can extend from minutes to a lifetime. Long-term memories of *experiences* from the past, like the picnic, are *episodic memories*. The ability to ride a bicycle, or do any of the other things that involve muscle coordination, is a type of long-term memory called *procedural memory*.

> I must admit, however, that as much as I remember many of the things we have done, I have a hard time remembering the address of the first apartment we lived in, although, luckily for me, I do remember your birthday.

Another type of long-term memory is *semantic memory*—memories of facts such as an address or a birthday or the names of different objects ("that's a bicycle").

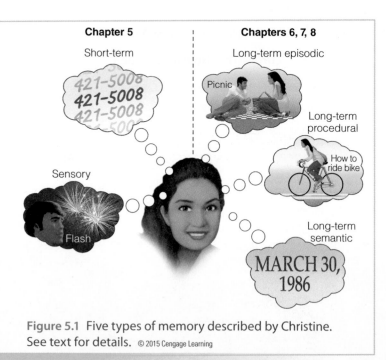

Figure 5.1 Five types of memory described by Christine. See text for details. © 2015 Cengage Learning

We will describe sensory memory and short-term memory in this chapter, we will compare short-term and long-term memory at the beginning of Chapter 6, and we will then spend the rest of Chapter 6 plus Chapters 7 and 8 on long-term memory. We will see that although people often mistakenly use the term "short-term memory" to refer to memory for events that happened minutes, hours, or even days ago, it is actually much briefer. In Chapter 6 we will note that this misconception about the length of short-term memory is reflected in how memory loss is described in movies. People also often underestimate the importance of short-term memory. When I ask my students to create a "top 10" list of what they use memory for, most of the items come under the heading of long-term memory. The top five items on their list are the following:

1. Material for exams
2. Their daily schedule
3. Names
4. Phone numbers
5. Directions to places

Your list may be different, but items from short-term memory rarely make the list, especially since the Internet and cell phones make it less necessary to repeat phone numbers over and over to keep them alive in memory. So what is the purpose of sensory and short-term memory?

Sensory memory is important when we go to the movies (more on that soon), but the main reason for discussing sensory memory is to demonstrate an ingenious procedure for measuring how much information we can take in immediately, and how much of that information remains half a second later.

The purpose of short-term memory will become clearer as we describe its characteristics, but stop for a moment and answer this question: What are you aware of right now? Some material you are reading about memory? Your surroundings? Noise in the background? Whatever your answer, you are describing what is in short-term memory. Everything you know or think about at each moment in time is in short-term memory. Thirty seconds from now your "old" short-term memories may have faded, but new ones will have taken over. Your "to do" list in long-term memory may be important, but as you are doing each of the things on your list, you are constantly using your short-term memory. As you will see in this chapter, short-term memory may be short in duration, but it looms large in importance.

We begin our description of sensory and short-term memory by describing an early and influential model of memory called the *modal model*, which places sensory and short-term memory at the beginning of the process of memory.

The Modal Model of Memory

Models of how the mind works are central to a great deal of research in cognitive psychology. We can appreciate this by remembering Donald Broadbent's (1958) filter model of attention, which introduced the flow chart that helped usher in the information processing approach to cognition (Chapter 1, page 13; Chapter 4, page 87).

Ten years after Broadbent introduced his flow diagram for attention, Richard Atkinson and Richard Shiffrin (1968) introduced the **modal model of memory** shown in **Figure 5.2**. This model proposed three types of memory:

1. *Sensory memory* is an initial stage that holds all incoming information for seconds or fractions of a second.
2. *Short-term memory (STM)* holds five to seven items for about 15 to 20 seconds. We will describe the characteristics of short-term memory in this chapter.
3. *Long-term memory (LTM)* can hold a large amount of information for years or even decades. We will describe long-term memory in Chapters 6, 7, and 8.

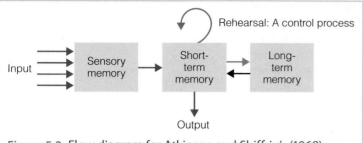

Figure 5.2 Flow diagram for Atkinson and Shiffrin's (1968) modal model of memory. This model, which is described in the text, is called the modal model because it contained features of many of the memory models that were being proposed in the 1960s. © Cengage Learning

The types of memory listed above, each of which is indicated by a box in the model, are called the **structural features** of the model. As we will see, the short-term memory and long-term memory boxes in this diagram were expanded by later researchers, who modified the model to distinguish between the different types of short- and long-term memories. But for now, we take this simpler modal model as our starting point because it illustrates important principles about how different types of memory operate and interact.

Atkinson and Shiffrin also proposed **control processes**, which are dynamic processes associated with the structural features that can be controlled by the person and may differ from one task to another. An example of a control process that operates on short-term memory is **rehearsal**—repeating a stimulus over and over, as you might repeat a telephone number in order to hold it in your mind after looking it up in the phone book or on the Internet. Rehearsal is symbolized by the blue arrow in **Figure 5.2**. Other examples of control processes are (1) strategies you might use to help make a stimulus more memorable, such as relating the digits in a phone number to a familiar date in history, and (2) strategies of attention that help you focus on information that is particularly important or interesting.

To illustrate how the structural features and control processes operate, let's consider what happens as Rachel looks up the number for Mineo's Pizza on the Internet (**Figure 5.3**). When she first looks at the screen, all of the information that enters her eyes is registered in sensory memory (**Figure 5.3a**). Rachel uses the control process of selective attention to focus on the number for Mineo's, so the number enters her short-term memory (**Figure 5.3b**), and she uses the control process of rehearsal to keep it there (**Figure 5.3c**).

Rachel knows she will want to use the number again later, so she decides that in addition to storing the number in her cell phone, she is going to memorize the number so it will also be stored in her mind. The process she uses to memorize the number, which involves control processes we will discuss in Chapter 6, transfers the number into long-term memory, where it is stored (**Figure 5.3d**). The process of storing the number in long-term memory is called *encoding*. A few days later, when Rachel's urge for pizza returns, she remembers the number. This process of remembering information that is stored in long-term memory is called *retrieval* (**Figure 5.3e**).

One thing that becomes apparent from our example is that the components of memory do not act in isolation. Thus, the phone number is first stored in Rachel's STM, but because information is easily lost from STM (as when you forget a phone number), Rachel transfers the phone number into LTM (green arrow), where it is held until she needs it later. When she then remembers the phone number later, it is returned to STM (black arrow), and Rachel becomes aware of the phone number. We will now consider each component of the model, beginning with sensory memory.

Sensory Memory

Sensory memory is the retention, for brief periods of time, of the effects of sensory stimulation. We can demonstrate this brief retention for the effects of visual stimulation with two familiar examples: the trail left by a moving sparkler and the experience of seeing a film.

THE SPARKLER'S TRAIL AND THE PROJECTOR'S SHUTTER

It is dark out on the Fourth of July, and you put a match to the tip of a sparkler. As sparks begin radiating from the tip, you sweep the sparkler through the air, creating a trail of light (**Figure 5.4**). Although it appears that this trail is created by light left by the sparkler as you wave it through the air, there is, in fact, no light along this trail. The lighted trail is a

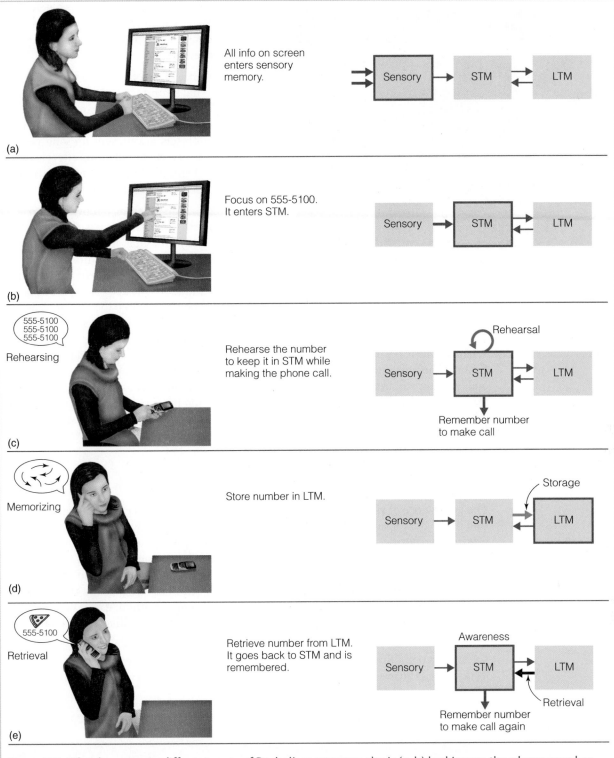

Figure 5.3 What happens in different parts of Rachel's memory as she is (a, b) looking up the phone number, (c) calling the pizza shop, and (d) memorizing the number. A few days later, (e) she retrieves the number from long-term memory to order pizza again. The parts of the modal model that are outlined in red indicate which processes are activated for each action that Rachel takes. © Cengage Learning

Figure 5.4 (a) A sparkler can cause a trail of light when it is moved rapidly. (b) This trail occurs because the perception of the light is briefly held in the mind.

Perceptual trail

creation of your mind, which retains a perception of the sparkler's light for a fraction of a second. This retention of the perception of light in your mind is called the *persistence of vision*.

Persistence of vision is the continued perception of a visual stimulus even after it is no longer present. This persistence lasts for only a fraction of a second, so it isn't obvious in everyday experience when objects are present for long periods. However, the persistence of vision effect is noticeable for brief stimuli, like the moving sparkler or rapidly flashed pictures in a movie theater.

While you are watching a movie, you may see actions moving smoothly across the screen, but what is actually projected, for traditional films, is quite different. First, a single film frame is positioned in front of the projector lens, and when the projector's shutter opens and closes, the image on the film frame flashes onto the screen. When the shutter is closed, the film moves on to the next frame and during that time the screen is dark. When the next frame has arrived in front of the lens, the shutter opens and closes again, flashing the next image onto the screen. This process is repeated rapidly, 24 times per second, with 24 still images flashed on the screen every second and each image followed by a brief period of darkness (see **Table 5.1**). A person viewing the film doesn't see the dark intervals between the images because the persistence of vision fills in the darkness by retaining the image of the previous frame.

SPERLING'S EXPERIMENT: MEASURING THE CAPACITY AND DURATION OF THE SENSORY STORE

The persistence of vision effect that adds a trail to our perception of moving sparklers and fills in the dark spaces between frames in a film has been known since the early days of psychology (Boring, 1942). But George Sperling (1960) wondered how much *information* people can take in from briefly presented stimuli. He determined this in a famous experiment in which he flashed an array of letters, like the one in **Figure 5.5a**, on the screen for 50 milliseconds (50/1000 second) and asked his subjects to report as many of the letters as possible. This part of the experiment used the **whole report method**; that is, subjects were asked to report as many letters as possible from the entire 12-letter display. Given this task, they were able to report an average of 4.5 out of the 12 letters.

At this point Sperling could have concluded that because the exposure was brief, subjects saw only an average of 4.5 of the 12 letters. However, some of the subjects in Sperling's

Table 5.1: Persistence of Vision in Film*

WHAT HAPPENS?	WHAT IS ON THE SCREEN?	WHAT DO YOU PERCEIVE?
Film frame 1 is projected.	Picture 1	Picture 1
Shutter closes and film moves to the next frame.	Darkness	Picture 1 (persistence of vision)
Shutter opens and film frame 2 is projected.	Picture 2	Picture 2

*The sequence indicated here is for movies projected using traditional film. Newer digital movie technologies are based on information stored on discs.

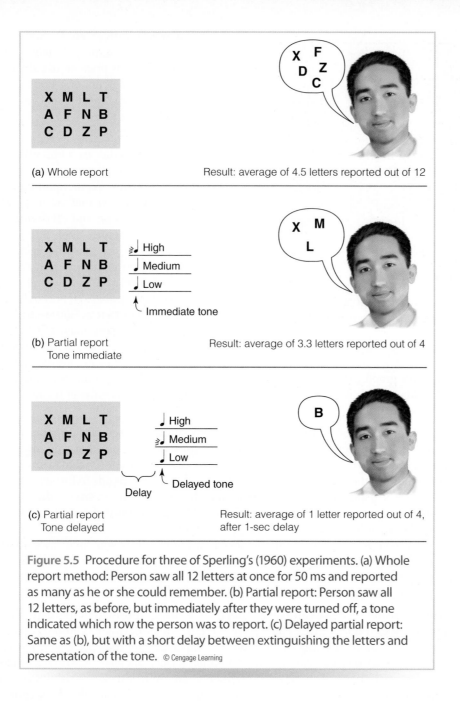

(a) Whole report   Result: average of 4.5 letters reported out of 12

(b) Partial report   Result: average of 3.3 letters reported out of 4
    Tone immediate

(c) Partial report   Result: average of 1 letter reported out of 4,
    Tone delayed   after 1-sec delay

Figure 5.5 Procedure for three of Sperling's (1960) experiments. (a) Whole report method: Person saw all 12 letters at once for 50 ms and reported as many as he or she could remember. (b) Partial report: Person saw all 12 letters, as before, but immediately after they were turned off, a tone indicated which row the person was to report. (c) Delayed partial report: Same as (b), but with a short delay between extinguishing the letters and presentation of the tone. © Cengage Learning

experiment reported that they had seen all of the letters, but that their perception had faded rapidly as they were reporting the letters, so by the time they had reported 4 or 5 letters, they could no longer see or remember the other letters.

Sperling reasoned that if subjects couldn't report the 12-letter display because of fading, perhaps they would do better if they were told to just report the letters in a single 4-letter row. Sperling devised the **partial report method** to test this idea. Subjects saw the 12-letter display for 50 ms, as before, but immediately after it was flashed, they heard a tone that told them which row of the matrix to report. A high-pitched tone indicated the top row; a medium-pitch indicated the middle row; and a low-pitch indicated the bottom row (**Figure 5.5b**).

Because the tones were presented immediately *after* the letters were turned off, the subject's attention was directed not to the actual letters, which were no longer present, but to whatever trace remained in the subject's mind after the letters were turned off. When the subjects focused their attention on one of the rows, they correctly reported an average of about 3.3 of the 4 letters (82 percent) in that row. Because this occurred no

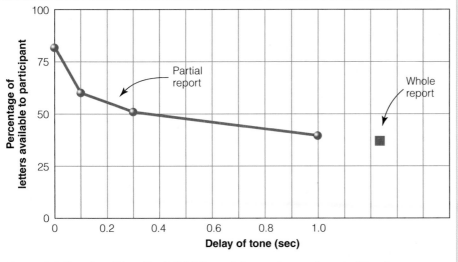

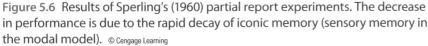

Figure 5.6 Results of Sperling's (1960) partial report experiments. The decrease in performance is due to the rapid decay of iconic memory (sensory memory in the modal model). © Cengage Learning

matter which row they were reporting, Sperling concluded that immediately after the 12-letter display was presented, subjects saw an average of 82 percent of all of the letters but were not able to report all of these letters because they rapidly faded as the initial letters were being reported.

Sperling then did an additional experiment to determine the time course of this fading. For this experiment, Sperling devised a **delayed partial report method** in which the letters were flashed on and off and then the cue tone was presented after a short delay (**Figure 5.5c**). The result of the delayed partial report experiments was that when the cue tones were delayed for 1 second after the flash, subjects were able to report only slightly more than 1 letter in a row. **Figure 5.6** plots this result, showing the percentage of letters available to the subjects from the entire display as a function of time following presentation of the display. This graph indicates that immediately after a stimulus is presented, all or most of the stimulus is available for perception. This is sensory memory. Then, over the next second, sensory memory fades.

Sperling concluded from these results that a short-lived sensory memory registers all or most of the information that hits our visual receptors, but that this information decays within less than a second. This brief sensory memory for visual stimuli, called **iconic memory** or the **visual icon** (icon means "image"), corresponds to the sensory memory stage of Atkinson and Shiffrin's modal model. Other research using auditory stimuli has shown that sounds also persist in the mind. This persistence of sound, called **echoic memory**, lasts for a few seconds after presentation of the original stimulus (Darwin et al., 1972). An example of echoic memory is when you hear someone say something, but you don't understand at first and say "What?" But even before the person can repeat what was said, you "hear" it in your mind. If that has happened to you, you've experienced echoic memory.

Thus, sensory memory can register huge amounts of information (perhaps all of the information that reaches the receptors), but it retains this information for only seconds or fractions of a second. Sperling's experiment is important not only because it reveals the capacity of sensory memory (large) and its duration (brief), but also because it provides yet another demonstration of how clever experimentation can reveal extremely rapid cognitive processes that we are usually unaware of. In the next section we consider the second stage of the modal model, short-term memory, which also holds information briefly, but for much longer than sensory memory.

Short-Term Memory

We saw above that although sensory memory fades rapidly, Sperling's subjects could report some of the letters. These letters are the part of the stimuli that has moved on to short-term memory in the flow diagram in **Figure 5.2**. **Short-term memory (STM)** is the system involved in storing small amounts of information for a brief period of time (Baddeley et al., 2009). Thus, whatever you are thinking about right now, or remember from what you have just read, is in your short-term memory. As we will see below, most of this information is eventually lost, and only some of it reaches the more permanent store of long-term memory (LTM).

Because of the brief duration of STM, it is easy to downplay its importance compared to LTM, but, as we will see, STM is responsible for a great deal of our mental life. Everything we think about or know at a particular moment in time involves STM because short-term memory is our window on the present. (Remember from **Figure 5.3e** that Rachel became aware of the pizzeria's phone number by transferring it from LTM, where it was stored, back into her STM.) We will now describe some early research on STM that focused on answering the following two questions: (1) What is the duration of STM? (2) What is the capacity of STM? These questions were answered in experiments that used the method of *recall* to test memory.

METHOD
RECALL

Most of the experiments we will be describing in this chapter involve **recall**, in which subjects are presented with stimuli and then, after a delay, are asked to report back as many of the stimuli as possible. Memory performance can be measured as a percentage of the stimuli that are remembered. (For example, studying a list of 10 words and later recalling 3 of them is 30 percent recall.) Subjects' responses can also be analyzed to determine whether there is a pattern to the way items are recalled. (For example, if subjects are given a list consisting of types of fruits and models of cars, their recall can be analyzed to determine whether they grouped cars together and fruits together as they were recalling them.) Recall is also involved when a person is asked to recollect life events, such as graduating from high school, or to recall facts they have learned, such as the capital of Nebraska.

WHAT IS THE DURATION OF SHORT-TERM MEMORY?

One of the major misconceptions about short-term memory is that it lasts for a relatively long time. It is not uncommon for people to refer to events they remember from a few days or weeks ago as being remembered from short-term memory. However, short-term memory, as conceived by cognitive psychologists, lasts 15 to 20 seconds or less. This was demonstrated by John Brown (1958) in England and Lloyd Peterson and Margaret Peterson (1959) in the United States, who used the method of recall to determine the duration of STM. In their experiments, subjects were given a task similar to the one in the following demonstration.

DEMONSTRATION
REMEMBERING THREE LETTERS

You will need another person to serve as a subject in this experiment. Read the following instructions to the person:

> I will say some letters and then a number. Your task will be to remember the letters. When you hear the number, repeat it and begin counting backwards by 3s from that number. For example, if I say ABC 309, then you say 309, 306, 303, and so on, until I say "Recall." When I say "Recall," stop counting immediately and say the three letters you heard just before the number.

Start with the letters and number in trial 1 below. It is important that the person count out loud because this prevents the person from rehearsing the letters. Once the person starts counting, time 20 seconds, and say "Recall." Note how accurately the person recalled the three letters and continue to the next trial, noting the person's accuracy for each trial.

Trial 1:   F Z L   45

Trial 2:   B H M   87

Trial 3:   X C G   98

Trial 4:	Y N F	37
Trial 5:	M J T	54
Trial 6:	Q B S	73
Trial 7:	K D P	66
Trial 8:	R X M	44
Trial 9:	B Y N	68
Trial 10:	N T L	39

We will return to your results in a moment. First let's consider what Peterson and Peterson found when they did a similar experiment in which they varied the time between when they said the number and when the subject began recalling the letters. Peterson and Peterson found that their subjects remembered about 80 percent of the three-letter groups if they began their recall after counting for just 3 seconds but remembered only about 12 percent of the three-letter groups after counting for 18 seconds (Figure 5.7a). They interpreted this result as demonstrating that subjects forgot the letters because their memory had decayed during the 18-second passage of time after they heard the letters. That is, their memory trace vanished because of **decay** that occurred during the passage of time after hearing the letters.

But when Geoffrey Keppel and Benton Underwood (1962) looked closely at Peterson and Peterson's results, they found that subjects' memory for the letters on trial 1 was high even when tested after an 18-second delay (Figure 5.7b). However, after a few trials their performance began to drop, so on later trials their performance was poor after the 18-second delay. How does this compare to your results? Did your subjects do well on the first trial but perform poorly on the later trials? Apparently, the finding of poor memory at 18 seconds reported by Peterson and Peterson was a result of poorer performance on later trials.

Why would memory become worse after a few trials? Keppel and Underwood suggested that the drop-off in memory was due not to decay of the memory trace over time, as Peterson and Peterson had proposed, but to **proactive interference**—interference that occurs when information that was learned previously interferes with learning new information.

The effect of proactive interference is illustrated by what might happen when learning a large number of French vocabulary words makes it more difficult to learn a list of Spanish vocabulary words a little later, because the French words you have just learned interfere with the Spanish words. Thus, proactive interference occurs when old learning interferes with new learning. Another kind of interference, **retroactive interference**, occurs when new learning interferes with remembering old learning. For example, retroactive interference occurs when learning Spanish makes it more difficult to remember the French words you had learned earlier.

Keppel and Underwood proposed that, in line with proactive interference, recalling the letters on the first few trials created interference that made it more difficult to remember the letters presented on the later trials. The rapid forgetting that Peterson and Peterson had observed was due, therefore, not to waiting 18 seconds but to interference caused by all of the information the subjects had learned earlier.

What does it mean that the reason for the decrease in short-term memory is proactive interference? From the point of view of our everyday life experience, it is easy to see that interference is happening constantly as one event follows the next and we pay

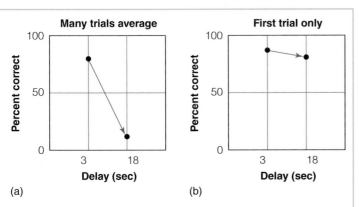

Figure 5.7 Results of Peterson and Peterson's (1959) duration of STM experiment. (a) The result originally presented by Peterson and Peterson, showing a large drop in memory for letters with a delay of 18 seconds between presentation and test. These data are based on the average performance over many trials. (b) Analysis of Peterson and Peterson's results by Keppel and Underwood, showing little decrease in performance if only the first trial is included. © Cengage Learning

attention to one thing after another. The outcome of this constant interference is that the effective duration of STM, when rehearsal is prevented, is about 15 to 20 seconds or less (Zhang & Luck, 2009).

HOW MANY *ITEMS* CAN BE HELD IN SHORT-TERM MEMORY?

Not only is information lost rapidly from STM, but there is a limit to how much information can be held there. As we will see, estimates for how many items can be held in STM range from four to nine.

DIGIT SPAN One measure of the capacity of STM is provided by the **digit span**—the number of digits a person can remember. You can determine your digit span by doing the following demonstration.

DEMONSTRATION
DIGIT SPAN

Using an index card or piece of paper, cover all of the numbers below. Move the card down to uncover the first string of numbers. Read the first set of numbers once, cover it up, and then write the numbers down in the correct order. Then move the card to the next string, and repeat this procedure until you begin making errors. The longest string you are able to reproduce without error is your digit span.

2 1 4 9

3 9 6 7 8

6 4 9 7 8 4

7 3 8 2 0 1 5

8 4 2 6 4 1 3 2

4 8 2 3 9 2 8 0 7

5 8 5 2 9 8 4 6 3 7

If you succeeded in remembering the longest string of digits, you have a digit span of 10 or perhaps more. The typical span is between 5 and 9 digits.

According to measurements of digit span, the average capacity of STM is about five to nine items—about the length of a phone number. This idea that the limit of STM is somewhere between five and nine was suggested by George Miller (1956), who summarized the evidence for this limit in his paper "The Magical Number Seven, Plus or Minus Two," described in Chapter 1 (page 14).

CHANGE DETECTION More recent measures of STM capacity have set the limit at about four items (Cowan, 2001). This conclusion is based on the results of experiments like one by Steven Luck and Edward Vogel (1997), which measured the capacity of STM by using a procedure called **change detection**.

METHOD
CHANGE DETECTION

Following the "Change Detection" demonstration on page 106, we described experiments in which two pictures of a scene were flashed one after the other and the subjects' task was to determine what had changed between the first and second pictures. The conclusion from these experiments was that people often miss changes in a scene.

Change detection has also been used with simpler stimuli to determine how much information a person can retain from a briefly flashed stimulus. An example of change detection is shown in **Figure 5.8**, which shows stimuli like the ones used in Luck and Vogel's experiment. The display on the left was flashed for 100 ms, followed by 900 ms of darkness and then the new display on the right. The subject's task was to indicate if the second display was the same as or different from the first. (Notice that the color of one of the squares is changed in the second display.) This task is easy if the number of items is within the capacity of STM (**Figure 5.8a**) but becomes harder when the number of items becomes greater than the capacity of STM (**Figure 5.8b**).

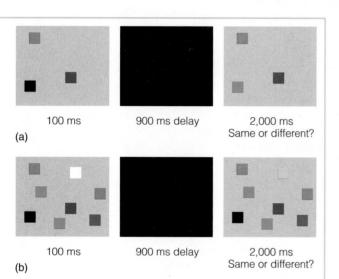

(a)

100 ms   900 ms delay   2,000 ms Same or different?

(b)

100 ms   900 ms delay   2,000 ms Same or different?

Figure 5.8 (a) Stimuli used by Luck and Vogel (1997). The subject sees the first display and then indicates whether the second display is the same or different. In this example, the color of one square is changed in the second display. (b) Luck and Vogel stimuli showing a larger number of items. *(Source: Adapted from E. K. Vogel, A. W. McCollough, & M. G. Machizawa, Neural measures reveal individual differences in controlling access to working memory,* Nature 438, 500–503, 2005.)

The result of Luck and Vogel's experiment, shown in **Figure 5.9**, indicates that performance was almost perfect when there were one to three squares in the arrays, but that performance began decreasing when there were four or more squares. Luck and Vogel concluded from this result that subjects were able to retain about four items in their short-term memory. Other experiments, using verbal materials, have come to the same conclusion (Cowan, 2001).

These estimates of either four items or five to nine items set rather low limits on the capacity of STM. If our ability to hold items in memory is so limited, how is it possible to hold many more items in memory in some situations, as when words are arranged in a sentence? The answer to this question was proposed by Miller, who introduced the idea of *chunking* in his "Seven, Plus or Minus Two" paper.

CHUNKING Miller (1956) introduced the concept of **chunking** to describe the fact that small units (like words) can be combined into larger meaningful units, like phrases, or even larger units, like sentences, paragraphs, or stories. Consider, for example, trying to remember the following words: *monkey, child, wildly, zoo, jumped, city, ringtail, young.* How many units are there in this list? There are eight words, but if we group them differently, they can form the following four pairs: *ringtail monkey, jumped wildly, young child, city zoo.* We can take this one step further by arranging these groups of words into one sentence: The *ringtail monkey jumped wildly* for the *young child* at the *city zoo.*

A **chunk** has been defined as a collection of elements that are strongly associated with one another but are weakly associated with elements in other chunks (Cowan, 2001; Gobet et al., 2001). In our example, the word *ringtail* is strongly associated with the word *monkey* but is not as strongly associated with the other words, such as *child* or *city.*

Thus, chunking in terms of meaning increases our ability to hold information in STM. We can recall a sequence of 5 to 8 unrelated words, but arranging the words to form a meaningful sentence so that the words become more strongly associated with one another increases the memory span to 20 words or more (Butterworth et al., 1990). Chunking of a series of letters is illustrated by the following demonstration.

DEMONSTRATION
REMEMBERING LETTERS

Read the string of letters below at a rate of about one letter every 2 seconds; then cover the letters and write down as many as you can, in the correct order.

    B C I F C N C A S I B B

How did you do? This task isn't easy, because it involves remembering a series of 12 individual letters, which is larger than the usual letter span of 5 to 9.

Now try remembering the following sequence of letters in order:

C I A F B I N B C C B S

How did your performance on this list compare to the one above?

Although the second list has the same letters as the first group, it was easier to remember if you realized that this sequence consists of the names of four familiar organizations. You can therefore create four chunks, each of which is meaningful, and therefore easy to remember.

K. Anders Ericsson and coworkers (1980) demonstrated an effect of chunking by showing how a college student with average memory ability was able to achieve amazing feats of memory. Their subject, S.F., was asked to repeat strings of random digits that were read to him. Although S.F. had a typical memory span of 7 digits, after extensive training (230 one-hour sessions), he was able to repeat sequences of up to 79 digits without error. How did he do it? S.F. used chunking to recode the digits into larger units that formed meaningful sequences. S.F. was a runner, so some of the sequences were running times. For example, 3,492 became "3 minutes and 49 point 2 seconds, near world-record mile time." He also used other ways to create meaning, so 893 became "89 point 3, very old man." This example illustrates an interaction between STM and LTM, because S.F created some of his chunks based on his knowledge of running times that were stored in LTM.

Chunking enables the limited-capacity STM system to deal with the large amount of information involved in many of the tasks we perform every day, such as chunking letters into words as you read this, remembering the first three numbers of familiar telephone exchanges as a unit, and transforming long conversations into smaller units of meaning.

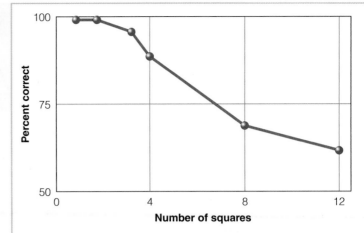

Figure 5.9 Result of Luck and Vogel's (1997) experiment, showing that performance began to decrease once there were four squares in the display. *(Source: Adapted from E. K. Vogel, A. W. McCollough, & M. G. Machizawa, Neural measures reveal individual differences in controlling access to working memory, Nature 438, 500–503, 2005.)*

HOW MUCH *INFORMATION* CAN BE HELD IN SHORT-TERM MEMORY?

The idea that the capacity of short-term memory can be specified as a number of items, as described above, has generated a great deal of research. But some researchers have suggested that rather than describing memory capacity in terms of "number of items," it should be described in terms of "amount of information." When referring to visual objects, information has been defined as visual features or details of the object that are stored in memory (Alvarez & Cavanagh, 2004).

We can understand the reasoning behind the idea that information is important by considering storing pictures on a computer flash drive. The number of pictures that can be stored depends on the size of the drive *and* on the size of the pictures. Fewer large pictures, which have files that contain more detail, can be stored because they take up more space in memory.

With this idea in mind, George Alvarez and Patrick Cavanagh (2004) did an experiment using the change detection procedure used by Luck and Vogel. But in addition to colored squares, they also used more complex objects like the ones in **Figure 5.10a**. For example, for the shaded cubes, which were the most complex stimuli, a subject would see a display containing a number of different cubes, followed by a blank interval, followed by a display that was either the same as the first one or in which one of the cubes was different. The subject's task was to indicate whether the two displays were the same or different.

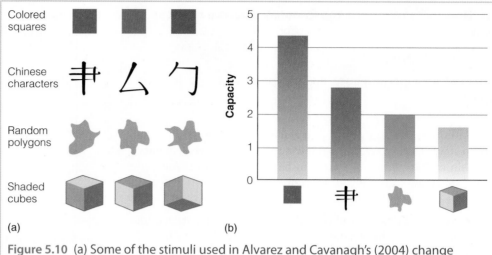

Figure 5.10 (a) Some of the stimuli used in Alvarez and Cavanagh's (2004) change detection experiment. The stimuli range from low information (colored squares) to high information (cubes). In the actual experiments, there were six different objects in each set. (b) Results showing the average number of objects that could be remembered for each type of stimulus. *(Source: Adapted from G. A. Alvarez & P. Cavanagh, The capacity of visual short-term memory is set both by visual information load and by number of objects, Psychological Science, 15, 106–111, 2004.)*

The result, shown in **Figure 5.10b**, was that subjects' ability to make the same/different judgment depended on the complexity of the stimuli. Memory capacity for the colored squares was 4.4, but capacity for the cubes was only 1.6. Based on this result, Alvarez and Cavanagh concluded that the greater the amount of information in an image, the fewer items that can be held in visual short-term memory.

Should short-term memory capacity be measured in terms of "number of items" (Awh et al., 2007; Fukuda et al., 2010; Luck & Vogel, 1997) or "amount of detailed information" (Alvaraz & Cavanagh, 2004; Bays & Husain, 2008; Brady et al., 2011)? There are experiments that argue for both ideas, and the discussion among researchers is continuing. There is, however, agreement that whether considering items or information, the upper limit for short-term memory capacity is about four items.

Our discussion of STM up to this point has focused on two properties: how *long* information is held in STM and how *much* information can be held in STM. Considering STM in this way, we could compare it to a container like a leaky bucket that can hold a certain amount of water for a limited amount of time. But as research on STM progressed, it became apparent that the concept of STM as presented in the modal model was too narrow to explain many research findings. The problem was that STM was described mainly as a short-term storage mechanism. But as we saw in our description of Rachel ordering a pizza, memorizing a phone number involves transferring the number from STM into LTM, and remembering it then involves transferring it from LTM back into STM. Thus, the role of STM extends beyond storage. It is also involved in the transfer of information to and from LTM. This idea that STM is involved with dynamic processes like transferring information led to a rethinking of the nature of STM, and to the proposal that the short-term process be called *working memory*.

TEST YOURSELF 5.1

1. The chapter begins with Christine's descriptions of five different types of memory. What are these? Which are of short duration? Of long duration? Why is short-term memory important?

2. Describe Atkinson and Shiffrin's modal model of memory both in terms of its structure (the boxes connected by arrows) and the control processes. Then describe how each part of the model comes into play when you decide you want to order pizza but can't remember the pizzeria's phone number.

3. Describe sensory memory and Sperling's experiment in which he briefly flashed an array of letters to measure the capacity and duration of sensory memory.

4. Is memory lost from STM by decay or by interference? Be sure you understand the Peterson and Peterson experiment and Keppel and Underwood's interpretation of it. What is the time span of STM?

5. What is the digit span? What does this indicate about the capacity of STM?

6. Describe Luck and Vogel's change detection experiment. What is the capacity of STM according to the results of this experiment?

7. What is chunking? What does it explain?

8. What two proposals have been made about how the capacity of short-term memory should be measured? Describe Alvarez and Cavanagh's experiment and their conclusion.

Working Memory

Working memory, which was introduced in a paper by Baddeley and Hitch (1974), is defined as "a limited-capacity system for temporary storage *and manipulation of information for complex tasks such as comprehension, learning, and reasoning.*" The italicized portion of this definition is what makes working memory different from the old modal model conception of short-term memory.

Short-term memory is concerned mainly with storing information for a brief period of time (for example, remembering a phone number), whereas working memory is concerned with the *manipulation of information* that occurs during complex cognition (for example, remembering numbers while reading a paragraph). We can understand the idea that working memory is involved with the manipulation of information by considering a few examples. First, let's listen in on a conversation Rachel is having with the pizza shop:

Rachel: "I'd like to order a large pizza with broccoli and mushrooms."

Reply: "I'm sorry, but we're out of mushrooms. Would you like to substitute spinach instead?

Rachel was able to understand the pizza shop's reply by holding the first sentence, "I'm sorry, but we're out of mushrooms," in her memory while listening to the second sentence, and then making the connection between the two. If she had remembered only "Would you like to substitute spinach instead?" she wouldn't know whether it was being substituted for the broccoli or for the mushrooms. In this example, Rachel's short-term memory is being used not only for storing information, but also for active processes like understanding conversations.

Another example of an active process occurs when we solve even simple math problems, such as "Multiply 43 times 6 in your head." Stop for a moment and try this while being aware of what you are doing in your head.

One way to solve this problem involves the following steps:

1. Visualize: 43×6.
2. Multiply $3 \times 6 = 18$.
3. Hold 8 in memory, while carrying the 1 over to the 4.
4. Multiply $6 \times 4 = 24$.

5. Add the carried 1 to the 24.

6. Place the result, 25, next to the 8.

7. The answer is 258.

It is easy to see that this calculation involves both storage (holding the 8 in memory, remembering the 6 and 4 for the next multiplication step) and active processes (carrying the 1, multiplying 6 × 4) at the same time. If only storage were involved, the problem could not be solved. There are other ways to carry out this calculation, but whatever method you choose involves both *holding* information in memory and *processing* information.

The fact that STM and the modal model do not consider dynamic processes that unfold over time is what led Baddeley and Hitch to propose that the name *working memory*, rather than *short-term memory*, be used for the short-term memory process. Current researchers often use both terms, short-term memory and working memory, when referring to the short-duration memory process, but the understanding is that the function of this process, whatever it is called, extends beyond just storage.

Returning to Baddeley, one of the things he noticed was that under certain conditions it is possible to carry out two tasks simultaneously, as illustrated in the following demonstration.

DEMONSTRATION
READING TEXT AND REMEMBERING NUMBERS

Keep the numbers 7, 1, 4, and 9 in your mind as you read the following passage:

Baddeley reasoned that if STM had a limited storage capacity of about the length of a telephone number, filling up the storage capacity should make it difficult to do other tasks that depend on STM. But he found that subjects could hold a short string of numbers in their memory while carrying out another task, such as reading or even solving a simple word problem. How are you doing with this task? What are the numbers? What is the gist of what you have just read?

According to Atkinson and Shiffrin's modal model, it should only be possible to perform one of these tasks, which should occupy the entire STM. But when Baddeley did experiments involving tasks similar to those in the previous demonstration, he found that subjects were able to read while simultaneously remembering numbers.

What kind of model can take into account both (1) the dynamic processes involved in cognitions such as understanding language and doing math problems and (2) the fact that people can carry out two tasks simultaneously? Baddeley concluded that working memory must be dynamic and must also consist of a number of components that can function separately. He proposed three components: the *phonological loop*, the *visuospatial sketch pad*, and the *central executive* (**Figure 5.11**).

The **phonological loop** consists of two components: the **phonological store**, which has a limited capacity and holds information for only a few seconds; and the **articulatory rehearsal process**, which is responsible for rehearsal that can keep items in the phonological store from decaying. The phonological loop holds verbal and auditory information. Thus, when you are trying to remember a telephone number or a person's name, or to understand what your cognitive psychology professor is talking about, you are using your phonological loop.

The **visuospatial sketch pad** holds visual and spatial information. When you form a picture in your mind or do tasks like solving a puzzle or finding your way around campus, you are using your visuospatial sketch pad. As you can see from the diagram, the phonological loop and the visuospatial sketch pad are attached to the central executive.

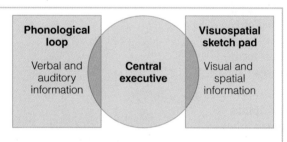

Baddeley's working memory model

Figure 5.11 Diagram of the three main components of Baddeley and Hitch's (1974; Baddeley, 2000a, 2000b) model of working memory: the phonological loop, the visuospatial sketch pad, and the central executive. © Cengage Learning

The **central executive** is where the major work of working memory occurs. The central executive pulls information from long-term memory and coordinates the activity of the phonological loop and visuospatial sketch pad by focusing on specific parts of a task and deciding how to divide attention between different tasks. The central executive is therefore the "traffic cop" of the working memory system.

To understand this "traffic cop" function, imagine you are driving in a strange city, a friend in the passenger seat is reading you directions to a restaurant, and the car radio is broadcasting the news. Your phonological loop is taking in the verbal directions; your sketch pad is helping you visualize a map of the streets leading to the restaurant; and your central executive is coordinating and combining these two kinds of information (**Figure 5.12**). In addition, the central executive might be helping you ignore the messages from the radio so you can focus your attention on the directions.

We will now describe a number of phenomena that illustrate how the phonological loop handles language, how the visuospatial sketch pad holds visual and spatial information, and how the central executive uses attention to coordinate between the two.

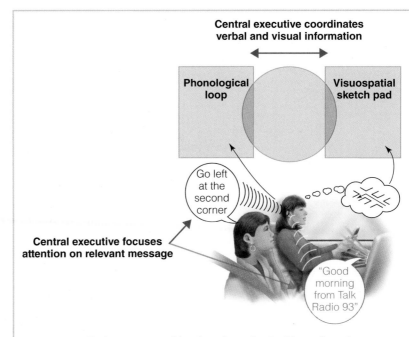

Figure 5.12 Tasks processed by the phonological loop (hearing directions, listening to the radio) and the visuospatial sketch pad (visualizing the route) are being coordinated by the central executive. The central executive also helps the driver ignore the messages from the radio so attention can be focused on hearing the directions. © Cengage Learning

THE PHONOLOGICAL LOOP

We will describe three phenomena that support the idea of a system specialized for language: the phonological similarity effect, the word length effect, and articulatory suppression.

PHONOLOGICAL SIMILARITY EFFECT The **phonological similarity effect** is the confusion of letters or words that sound similar. In an early demonstration of this effect, R. Conrad (1964) flashed a series of target letters on a screen and instructed his subjects to write down the letters in the order they were presented. He found that when subjects made errors, they were most likely to misidentify the target letter as another letter that *sounded like* the target. For example, "F" was most often misidentified as "S" or "X," two letters that sound similar to "F," but was not as likely to be confused with letters like "E," that *looked like* the target. Thus, even though the subjects *saw* the letters, the mistakes they made were based on the letters' *sounds*.

This result fits with our common experience with telephone numbers. Even though our contact with them is often visual, we usually remember them by repeating their sound over and over rather than by visualizing what the numbers looked like on the computer screen (also see Wickelgren, 1965). In present-day terminology, Conrad's result would be described as a demonstration of the phonological similarity effect, which occurs when words are processed in the phonological store part of the phonological loop.

WORD LENGTH EFFECT The **word length effect** occurs when memory for lists of words is better for short words than for long words.

DEMONSTRATION
WORD LENGTH EFFECT

Task 1: Read the following words, look away, and then write down the words you remember.

beast, bronze, wife, golf, inn, limp, dirt, star

Task 2: Now do the same thing for the following list.

> alcohol, property, amplifier, officer, gallery, mosquito, orchestra, bricklayer

Each list in the demonstration contains eight words, but according to the word length effect, the second list will be more difficult to remember because the words are longer. Baddeley and coworkers (1984) demonstrated the word length effect by testing subjects using a procedure similar to the Demonstration; they found that subjects remembered 77 percent of the short words but only 60 percent of the long words. The word length effect occurs because it takes longer to rehearse the long words and to produce them during recall.

In another study of memory for verbal material, Baddeley and coworkers (1975) found that people are able to remember the number of items that they can pronounce in about 1.5–2.0 seconds (also see Schweickert & Boruff, 1986). Try counting out loud, as fast as you can, for 2 seconds. According to Baddeley, the number of words you can say should be close to your digit span. (Note, however, that some researchers have proposed that the word length effect does not occur under some conditions; see Lovatt et al., 2000, 2002.)

ARTICULATORY SUPPRESSION One way that the operation of the phonological loop has been studied is by determining what happens when its operation is disrupted. This occurs when a person is prevented from rehearsing items to be remembered by repeating an irrelevant sound, such as "the, the, the ..." (Baddeley, 2000b; Baddeley et al., 1984; Murray, 1968).

This repetition of an irrelevant sound results in a phenomenon called **articulatory suppression**, which reduces memory because speaking interferes with rehearsal. The following demonstration, which is based on an experiment by Baddeley and coworkers (1984), illustrates this effect of articulatory suppression.

DEMONSTRATION
ARTICULATORY SUPPRESSION

Task 1: Read the following list. Then turn away and recall as many words as you can.

> dishwasher, hummingbird, engineering, hospital, homelessness, reasoning

Task 2: Read the following list while repeating "the, the, the ..." out loud. Then turn away and recall as many words as you can.

> automobile, apartment, basketball, mathematics, gymnasium, Catholicism

Articulatory suppression occurs when remembering the second list becomes harder because repeating "the, the, the ..." overloads the phonological loop.

Baddeley and coworkers (1984) found that repeating "the, the, the ..." not only reduces the ability to remember a list of words, it also eliminates the word length effect (**Figure 5.13a**). According to the word length effect, a list of one-syllable words should be easier to recall than a list of longer words because the shorter words leave more space in the phonological loop for rehearsal. However, eliminating rehearsal by saying "the, the, the ..." eliminates this advantage for short words, so both short and long words are lost from the phonological store (**Figure 5.13b**).

THE VISUOSPATIAL SKETCH PAD

The visuospatial sketch pad handles visual and spatial information and is therefore involved in the process of **visual imagery**—the creation of visual images in the mind in the absence of a physical visual stimulus. The following demonstration illustrates an early visual imagery experiment by Roger Shepard and Jacqueline Metzler (1971).

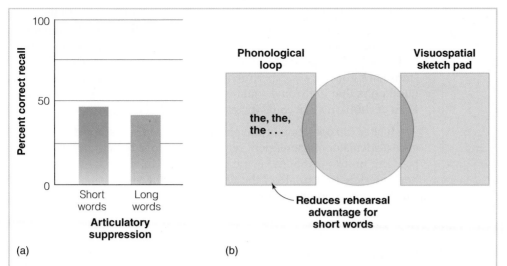

(a)   (b)

Figure 5.13 (a) Saying "the, the, the …" abolishes the word length effect, so there is little difference in performance for short words and long words (Baddeley et al., 1984). (b) Saying "the, the, the …" causes this effect by reducing rehearsal in the phonological loop. © Cengage Learning

DEMONSTRATION
COMPARING OBJECTS

Look at the two pictures in Figure 5.14a and decide, as quickly as possible, whether they represent two different views of the same object ("same") or two different objects ("different"). Also make the same judgment for the two objects in Figure 5.14b.

When Shepard and Metzler measured subjects' reaction time to decide whether pairs of objects were the same or different, they obtained the relationship shown in Figure 5.15 for objects that were the same. From this function, we can see that when one shape was rotated 40 degrees compared to the other shape (as in Figure 5.14a), it took 2 seconds to decide that a pair was the same shape. However, for a greater difference caused by a rotation of 140 degrees (as in Figure 5.14b), it took 4 seconds. Based on this finding that reaction times were longer for greater differences in orientation, Shepard and Metzler inferred that subjects were solving the problem by rotating an image of one of the objects in their mind, a phenomenon called **mental rotation**. This mental rotation is an example of the operation of the visuospatial sketch pad because it involves visual rotation through space.

Another demonstration of the use of visual representation is an experiment by Sergio Della Sala and coworkers (1999) in which subjects were presented with a task like the one in the following demonstration.

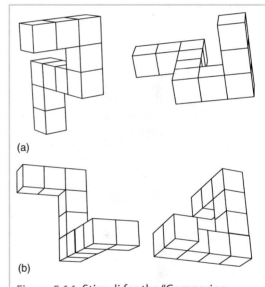

(a)

(b)

Figure 5.14 Stimuli for the "Comparing Objects" demonstration. See text for details. *(Source: Based on R. N. Shepard & J. Metzler, Mental rotation of three-dimensional objects, Science, 171, Figures 1a & b, 701–703, 1971.)*

DEMONSTRATION
RECALLING VISUAL PATTERNS

Look at the pattern in Figure 5.16 for 3 seconds. Then turn the page and indicate which of the squares in Figure 5.18 need to be filled in to duplicate this pattern.

In this demonstration, the patterns are difficult to code verbally, so completing the pattern depends on visual memory. Della Sala presented his subjects with patterns ranging from small (a 2×2 matrix with 2 shaded squares) to large (a 5×6 matrix with 15 shaded squares), with half of the squares being shaded in each pattern. He found that subjects were able to complete patterns consisting of an average of 9 shaded squares before making mistakes.

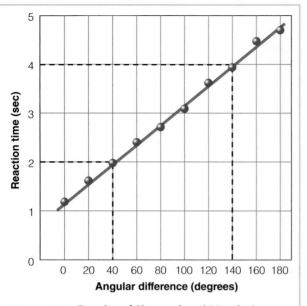

Figure 5.15 Results of Shepard and Metzler's (1971) mental rotation experiment. *(Source: Based on R. N. Shepard & J. Metzler, Mental rotation of three-dimensional objects," Science, 171, Figure 2a, 701–703, 1971.)*

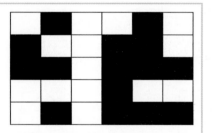

Figure 5.16 Test pattern for visual recall test. After looking at this for 3 seconds, turn the page. © Cengage Learning

The fact that it is possible to remember the patterns in Della Sala's matrix illustrates visual imagery. But how could the subjects remember patterns consisting of an average of 9 squares? This number is at the high end of Miller's range of 5 to 9 and is far above the lower estimate of 4 items from Luck and Vogel's experiment (Figure 5.9). A possible answer to this question is that individual squares can be combined into subpatterns—a form of chunking that could increase the number of squares remembered.

Just as the operation of the phonological loop is disrupted by interference (articulatory suppression, see page 136), so is the visuospatial sketch pad. Lee Brooks (1968) did some experiments in which he demonstrated how interference can affect the operation of the visuospatial sketch pad. The following demonstration is based on one of Brooks's tasks.

DEMONSTRATION
HOLDING A SPATIAL STIMULUS IN THE MIND

This demonstration involves visualizing a large "F" like the one in Figure 5.17a, which has two types of corners, "outside corners" and "inside corners," two of which are labeled.

Task 1: Visualize the F shape in Figure 5.17b. Then cover both F's in Figure 5.17 and while visualizing one F in your mind, start at the upper left corner (the one marked with the * in Figure 5.17b) and, moving around the outline of the F in a clockwise direction in your mind (no looking at the figure!), point to "Out" in Table 5.2 for an outside corner, and "In" for an inside corner. Move your response down one level in Table 5.2 for each new corner.

Task 2: Visualize the F again, but this time, as you move around the outline of the F in a clockwise direction in your mind, say "Out" if the corner is an outside corner or "In" if it is an inside corner.

Which was easier, *pointing* to "Out" or "In" or *saying* "Out" or "In"?

Most people find that the pointing task is more difficult. The reason is that holding the image of the letter and pointing are both visuospatial tasks, so the visuospatial sketch pad becomes overloaded. In contrast, saying "Out" or "In" is an articulatory task that is handled by the phonological loop, so speaking doesn't interfere with visualizing the F.

THE CENTRAL EXECUTIVE

The central executive is the component that makes working memory "work," because it is the control center of the working memory system. Its mission is not to store information but to coordinate how information is used by the phonological loop and visuospatial sketch pad (Baddeley, 1996).

Baddeley describes the central executive as being an *attention controller*. It determines how attention is focused on a specific task, how it is divided between two tasks, and how it is switched between tasks. The central executive is therefore essential in situations such as the ones described in Chapter 4 (page 102), when a person is attempting to simultaneously drive and use a cell phone. In this example, the executive would be controlling phonological loop processes (talking on the phone, understanding the conversation) and sketchpad processes (visualizing landmarks and the layout of the streets, navigating the car).

One of the ways the central executive has been studied is by assessing the behavior of patients with brain damage. As we will see later in the chapter, the frontal lobe plays a central role in working memory. It is not surprising, therefore, that patients with frontal lobe damage have problems controlling their attention. A typical behavior of frontal lobe patients is **perseveration**—repeatedly performing the same action or thought even if it is not achieving the desired goal.

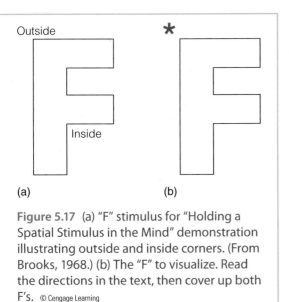

Outside

*

Inside

(a)　　　　(b)

Figure 5.17 (a) "F" stimulus for "Holding a Spatial Stimulus in the Mind" demonstration illustrating outside and inside corners. (From Brooks, 1968.) (b) The "F" to visualize. Read the directions in the text, then cover up both F's. © Cengage Learning

Table 5.2: Use for Demonstration

CORNER	POINT	
1	OUT	IN
2	OUT	IN
3	OUT	IN
4	OUT	IN
5	OUT	IN
6	OUT	IN
7	OUT	IN
8	OUT	IN
9	OUT	IN
10	OUT	IN

Consider, for example, a problem that can be easily solved by following a particular rule ("Pick the red object"). A person with frontal lobe damage might be responding correctly on each trial, as long as the rule stays the same. However, when the rule is switched ("Now pick the blue object"), the person continues following the old rule, even when given feedback that his or her responding is now incorrect. This perseveration represents a breakdown in the central executive's ability to control attention.

But what about subjects without brain damage? Research by Edmund Vogel and coworkers (2005) considered how well the central executive controlled attention in these subjects by first separating them into two groups based on their performance on a test of working memory. Subjects in the *high-capacity group* were able to hold a number of items in working memory; subjects in the *low-capacity group* were able to hold fewer items in working memory. (As you may recall from Chapter 1, page 16, it is possible to classify subjects as having high or low working memory capacity.)

Subjects were tested using the change detection procedure (see Method: Change Detection, page 129). **Figure 5.19a** shows that they first saw a cue indicating whether to direct their attention to the red rectangles on the left side or the red rectangles on the right side of the displays that followed. They then saw a memory display for one-tenth of a second followed by a brief blank screen and then a test display. Their task was to indicate whether the cued red rectangles in the test display had the same or different orientations than the ones in the memory display. While they were making this judgment, a brain response called the *event-related potential* was measured, which indicated how much space was used in working memory as they carried out the task.

METHOD
EVENT-RELATED POTENTIAL

The **event-related potential (ERP)** is recorded with small disc electrodes placed on a person's scalp, as shown in **Figure 5.20a**. Each electrode picks up signals from groups of neurons that fire together. The event-related potential shown in **Figure 5.20b** was recorded as a person was making a judgment in the Vogel experiment. This response had been shown in other experiments to be related to the number of items placed into working memory, so a larger ERP response indicates that more space is used in working memory. We will see later in the book that the ERP has been used to measure the brain's response to other cognitive functions as well.

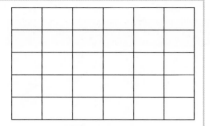

Figure 5.18 Answer matrix for the visual recall test. Put a check in each square that was darkened in the pattern you just looked at. © Cengage Learning

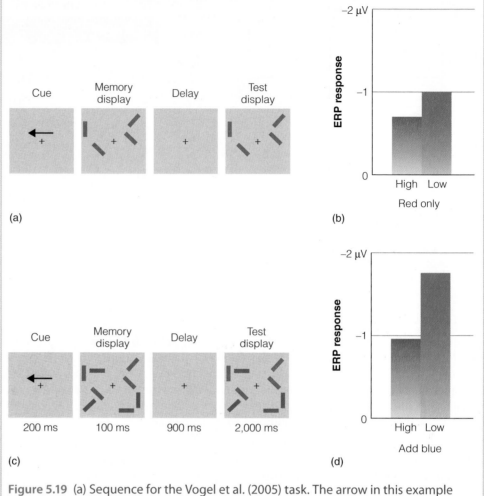

(a)

(b) Red only

(c)

200 ms   100 ms   900 ms   2,000 ms

(d) Add blue

Figure 5.19 (a) Sequence for the Vogel et al. (2005) task. The arrow in this example tells the participant to pay attention to the left side of the memory and test displays. The task is to indicate whether the red rectangles on the attended side are the same or different in the two displays. (b) ERP response for low- and high-capacity subjects for the task in part (a). (c) Display with blue bars added. These bars are added to distract the subjects, who are supposed to be focusing on the red rectangles. (d) ERP response for the task in part (c). (Source: Based on E. K. Vogel, A. W. McCollough, & M. G. Machizawa, Neural measures reveal individual differences in controlling access to working memory, Nature 438, 500–503, 2005.)

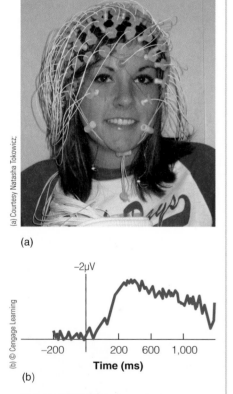

(a)

(b)

Figure 5.20 (a) a person wearing electrodes for recording the event-related potential (ERP). (b) An ERP recorded as a subject is viewing the stimuli.

The results in Figure 5.19b show the size of the ERP for the display in Figure 5.19a, for the high- and low-working memory groups. This isn't a particularly interesting result, because the size of the ERP is nearly the same for both groups. But Vogel also ran another condition in which he added some extra blue bars, as shown in Figure 5.19c. These bars were not relevant to the subject's task; their purpose was to distract the subject's attention. If the central executive is doing its job, these extra bars should have no effect, because attention would remain focused on the red bars. The results in Figure 5.19d show that adding blue bars caused an increase in the response of the high-capacity group, but caused a much larger increase in the response of the low-capacity group.

The fact that adding the blue bars had only a small effect on the response of the high-capacity group means that these subjects were very efficient at ignoring the distractors, so the irrelevant blue stimuli did not take up much space in working memory. Because allocating attention is a function of the central executive, this means that the central executive was functioning well for these subjects.

The fact that adding the two blue bars caused a large increase in the response of the low-capacity group means that these subjects were not able to ignore the irrelevant blue stimuli, so the blue bars were taking up space in working memory. The central executive of these subjects is not operating as efficiently as the central executives of the high-capacity subjects. Vogel and coworkers concluded from these results that some people's central executives are better at allocating attention than others'. The reason this is important is that other experiments have shown that people with more efficient working memories are more likely to perform well on tests of reading and reasoning ability and on tests designed to measure intelligence.

THE EPISODIC BUFFER

We have seen that Baddeley's three-component model can explain a number of results. However, research has shown that there are some things the model can't explain. One of those things is that working memory can hold more than would be expected based on just the phonological loop or visuospatial sketch pad. For example, people can remember long sentences consisting of as many as 15 to 20 words. The ability to do this is related to chunking, in which meaningful units are grouped together (page 130), and it is also related to long-term memory, which is involved in knowing the meanings of words in the sentence and in relating parts of the sentence to each other based on the rules of grammar.

These ideas are nothing new. It had long been known that the capacity of working memory can be increased by chunking and that there is an interchange of information between working memory and long-term memory. But Baddeley decided it was necessary to propose an additional component of working memory to address these abilities. This new component, which he called the **episodic buffer**, is shown in Baddeley's new model of working memory in **Figure 5.21**. The episodic buffer can store information (thereby providing extra capacity) and is connected to LTM (thereby making interchange between working memory and LTM possible). Notice that this model also shows that the visuospatial sketch pad and phonological loop are linked to long-term memory.

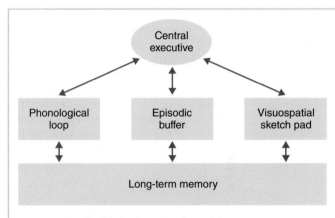

Figure 5.21 Baddeley's revised working memory model, which contains the original three components plus the episodic buffer. © Cengage Learning

The proposal of the episodic buffer represents another step in the evolution of Baddeley's model, which has been stimulating research on working memory for more than 40 years since it was first proposed. If the exact functioning of the episodic buffer seems a little vague, it is because it is a "work in progress." Even Baddeley (Baddeley et al., 2009) states that "the concept of an episodic buffer is still at a very early stage of development" (p. 57). The main "take-home message" about the episodic buffer is that it represents a way of increasing storage capacity and communicating with LTM.

Although we have been focusing on Baddeley's model because of the large amount of research it has generated, his is not the only model of working memory. For example, a model proposed by Nelson Cowan (1988, 1999, 2005) has focused on how working memory is related to attention and suggests that working memory and attention are essentially the same mechanism. Other researchers have provided evidence that supports the close relationship between attention and working memory (Awh et al., 2006; Awh & Jonides, 2001; Chun & Johnson, 2011; Gazzaley & Nobre, 2012; Ikkai & Curtis, 2011).

Working Memory and the Brain

We have seen from previous chapters that cognitive psychologists have a number of tools at their disposal to determine the connection between cognitive functioning and the brain. The major methods are:

1. Analysis of behavior after brain damage, either human or animal (Method: Demonstrating a Double Dissociation, Chapter 2, page 40; Method: Brain Ablation, Chapter 3, page 76)

2. Recording from single neurons in animals (Method: Recording From a Neuron, Chapter 2, page 31)

3. Measuring activity of the human brain (Method: Brain Imaging, Chapter 2, page 41)

4. Recording electrical signals from the human brain (Method: Event-Related Potential, page 139)

What are the researchers who use these methods to study working memory and the brain trying to explain? To answer this question, we have only to look back at this chapter to appreciate that an important characteristic of memory is that it involves *delay* or *waiting*. Something happens, followed by a delay, which is brief for working memory; then, if memory is successful, the person remembers what has happened. Researchers, therefore, have looked for physiological mechanisms that hold information about events after they are over.

We will describe research using the first three methods above to determine where and how this information is held in the brain (**Figure 5.22**): (1) brain damage—how damage to or removal of the prefrontal cortex affects the ability to remember for short periods of time; (2) neurons—how neurons in the monkey prefrontal cortex hold onto information during a brief delay; and (3) brain activity—areas of the brain that are activated by working memory tasks.

THE EFFECT OF DAMAGE TO THE PREFRONTAL CORTEX

We have already seen that damage to the frontal lobe (see **Figure 5.22**) in humans causes problems in controlling attention, which is an important function of the central executive (page 139). Early research on the frontal lobe and memory was carried out in monkeys using a task called the **delayed-response task**, which required a monkey to hold information in working memory during a delay period (Goldman-Rakic, 1992). **Figure 5.23** shows the setup for this task. The monkey sees a food reward in one of two food wells. Both wells are then covered, a screen is lowered, and then there is a delay before the screen is raised again. When the screen is raised, the monkey must remember which well had the food and

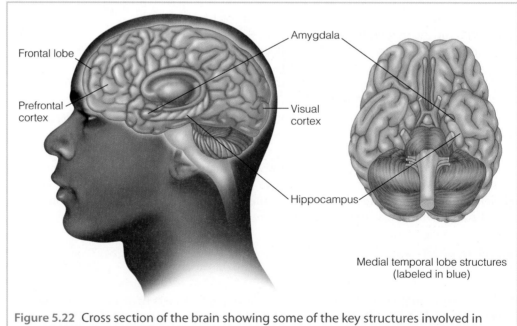

Figure 5.22 Cross section of the brain showing some of the key structures involved in memory. The discussion of working memory focuses on the prefrontal cortex and the visual cortex. The hippocampus, amygdala, and frontal cortex will be discussed in Chapters 6 and 7. © Cengage Learning

| Monkey observes food in tray | Delay | Response |

Figure 5.23 The delayed-response task being administered to a monkey. © 2015 Cengage Learning

uncover the correct food well to obtain a reward. Monkeys can be trained to accomplish this task. However, if their prefrontal cortex is removed, their performance drops to chance level, so they pick the correct food well only about half of the time.

This result supports the idea that the prefrontal (PF) cortex is important for holding information for brief periods of time. In fact, it has been suggested that one reason we can describe the memory behavior of very young infants as "out of sight, out of mind" (when an object that the infant can see is then hidden from view, the infant behaves as if the object no longer exists) is that their frontal and prefrontal cortex does not become adequately developed until about 8 months of age (Goldman-Rakic, 1992).

PREFRONTAL NEURONS THAT HOLD INFORMATION

The idea that the PF cortex is important for working memory is also supported by experiments that have looked at how some neurons in the PF cortex are able to hold information after the original stimulus is no longer present, continuing to respond during a brief delay. Shintaro Funahashi and coworkers (1989) conducted an experiment in which they recorded from neurons in a monkey's PF cortex while the monkey carried out a delayed-response task. The monkey first looked steadily at a fixation point, X, while a square was flashed at one position on the screen (Figure 5.24a). In this example, the square was flashed in the upper left corner (on other trials, the square was flashed at different positions on the screen). This causes a small response in the neuron.

After the square went off, there was a delay of a few seconds. The nerve firing records in Figure 5.24b show that the neuron was firing during this delay. This firing is the neural record of the monkey's working memory for the position of the square. After the delay, the fixation X went off. This was a signal for the monkey to move its eyes to where the square had been flashed (Figure 5.24c). The monkey's ability to do this provides behavioral evidence that it had, in fact, remembered the location of the square.

The key result of this experiment was that Funahashi found neurons that responded only when the square was flashed in a *particular location* and that these neurons *continued responding during the delay*. For example, some neurons responded only when the square was flashed in the upper right corner and then during the delay; other neurons responded only when the square was presented at other positions on the screen and then during the delay. The firing of these neurons indicates that an object was presented at a particular place, and this information about where the object was remains available for as long as these neurons continue firing (also see Funahashi, 2006).

HOLDING INFORMATION IN THE VISUAL CORTEX

For many years, the prefrontal cortex was thought to be the primary brain area for working memory. But one problem with assigning working memory to just the prefrontal

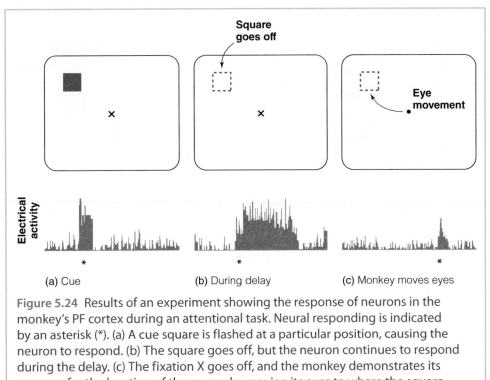

Figure 5.24 Results of an experiment showing the response of neurons in the monkey's PF cortex during an attentional task. Neural responding is indicated by an asterisk (*). (a) A cue square is flashed at a particular position, causing the neuron to respond. (b) The square goes off, but the neuron continues to respond during the delay. (c) The fixation X goes off, and the monkey demonstrates its memory for the location of the square by moving its eyes to where the square was. *(Source: Adapted from S. Funahashi, C. J. Bruce, & P. S. Goldman-Rakic, Mnemonic coding of visual space in the primate dorsolateral prefrontal cortex, Journal of Neurophysiology 61, 331–349, 1989.)*

cortex is that information regarding most of the fine details of objects is found at the beginning of the system, where signals are arriving at the visual area of the cortex (Harrison & Tong, 2009).

To see whether working memory operates in these early visual areas, Stephanie Harrison and Frank Tong (2009) did an experiment in which they flashed two oriented sample gratings (displays of alternating white and black lines) one after another, followed by a cue indicating which of the sample gratings the subjects should remember (**Figure 5.25**). Then, after a delay of 11 seconds, a test grating was presented and the subjects had to indicate whether the lines in the grating were rotated to the left or right compared to the orientation of the sample grating that they had been holding in working memory during the delay. As subjects did this, their brain activity was measured

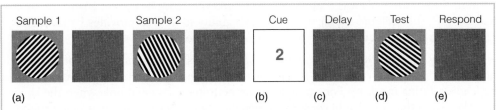

Figure 5.25 Procedure for the Harrison and Tong (2009) experiment. (a) Two sample gratings with different orientations are presented one after another. (b) A cue, in red, indicates which sample grating the subjects should hold in their memory. (c) During an 11-second delay in the dark, the fMRI is measured, and then (d) a test grating is presented. The subjects' task is (e) to indicate whether the test grating was oriented clockwise or counterclockwise relative to the sample grating they were holding in their memory. *(Source: Based on S. A. Harrison & F. Tong, Decoding reveals the contents of visual working memory in early visual areas, Nature, 458, 462–465, 2009.)*

with fMRI. To determine whether information about the orientation of the sample grating was being held in the visual cortex during the 11-second delay, Harrison and Tong used a technique called *neural mind reading*.

METHOD
NEURAL MIND READING

Neural mind reading refers to using a neural response, usually brain activation measured by fMRI, to determine what a person is perceiving or thinking. fMRI measures which voxels in the brain are activated while a subject carries out a task (remember that voxels are small cube-shaped areas of the brain; see Method: Brain Imaging, Chapter 2, page 41). The pattern of voxels activated depends on the task and the nature of the stimulus being perceived or remembered. For example, when a subject observes a slanted black-and-white grating, a particular pattern of voxels is activated (Figure 5.26). When viewing a different orientation, another pattern of voxels is activated.

Figure 5.27 illustrates the basic procedure for neural mind reading. First, the relationship between orientation and the voxel pattern is determined by measuring the brain's response to a number of orientations (Figure 5.27a). Then these data are used to create a "decoder" program that can determine orientation based on the voxel activation pattern (Figure 5.27b). Finally, the decoder is tested by measuring brain activation as a person is looking at different orientations, as before, but this time using the decoder to *predict* the orientation the person is perceiving (Figure 5.27c). If this works, it should be possible to predict what orientation a person is looking at based on his or her brain activation alone.

When Yukiyasu Kamitani and Frank Tong (2005) used the procedure above, they were able to predict with accuracies ranging from 75 to 100 percent (where chance performance is 50 percent) which of two orientations a subject was looking at, with better accuracy for larger differences between the orientations.

Whereas Kamitani and Tong used the mind reading procedure to predict the orientation a person was *looking at*, Harrison and Tong used the mind reading procedure to determine the orientation that subjects were *holding in their mind* during the 11-second delay. Based on fMRI measurements during the delay, they were able to predict the test orientation that subjects were holding in their mind with 83 percent accuracy. What this means is that information about the orientation a person is remembering is being held in the visual cortex during the delay and that the visual cortex is therefore involved in working memory.

Thus, although the PF cortex may be the brain area that is most closely associated with working memory, other areas are also involved (Cabeza & Nyberg, 2000; Curtis & Esposito, 2003). This idea that a number of areas of the brain are involved in working memory is an example of distributed representation, which we introduced in Chapter 2 (page 44).

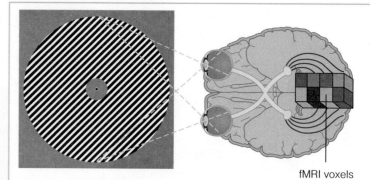

fMRI voxels

Figure 5.26 Observers in Kamitani and Tong's (2005) experiment viewed oriented gratings like the one on the left. The cubes in the brain represent the response of 8 voxels. The activity of 400 voxels was monitored in the experiment. *(Source: Based on Y. Kamitani & F. Tong, Decoding the visual and subjective contents of the human brain, Nature Neuroscience, 8, 679–685, 2005.)*

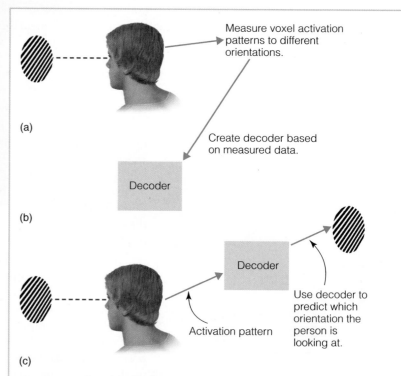

Figure 5.27 Principle behind neural mind reading. (a) As the subject looks at different orientations, fMRI is used to determine voxel activation patterns for each orientation. (b) A decoder is created based on the voxel patterns collected in (a). (c) As a subject looks at an orientation, the decoder analyzes the voxel pattern recorded from the subject's visual cortex. Based on this voxel pattern, the decoder predicts the orientation that the subject is observing. © 2015 Cengage Learning

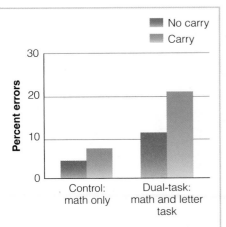

Figure 5.28 Results of Aschraft and Kirk's (2001) experiment. "No carry" refers to simple math problems that don't involve carrying a number. "Carry" refers to more complex problems that involve carrying and would therefore use more working memory. Left pair of bars: Performance when doing just the math problems. Right pair of bars: Performance in the dual-task condition. *(Source: Based on data in M. H. Ashcraft & E. P. Kirk, The relationships among working memory, math anxiety, and performance, Journal of Experimental Psychology: General, 130, 224–237, 2001.)*

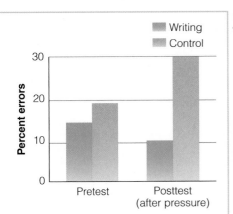

Figure 5.29 Results of Ramirez and Beilock's (2011) experiment. The writing group wrote about their worries before taking the post-test. *(Source: Based on data in G. Ramirez & S. L. Beilock, Writing about testing worries boosts exam performance in the classroom, Science, 331, 211–213, 2011.)*

Something to Consider

MATH PERFORMANCE AND WORKING MEMORY

In order to do well on an exam, you not only need to know the material; you also have to have the resources to function well when you're in the testing situation. It is important, for example, to be well rested so you can focus clearly on the task before you. It is also important, especially for tasks that involve working memory such as solving complex math problems, that all of your working memory resources be available. We will describe two experiments that show what happens when full working memory resources are not available because of competing tasks or worrying. We will then describe an experiment that suggests a way to minimize worrying and therefore maximize working memory.

Recall from our definition of working memory on page 133 that working memory involves the manipulation of information for complex tasks. One task that can be complex and involves manipulation is doing mathematical calculations. Simple math problems, such as 4 + 3, place little load on working memory. However, problems with larger numbers that involve carrying a number, like 25 + 17, require working memory.

Mark Ashcraft and Elizabeth Kirk (2001) investigated how math performance would be affected by having to carry out another task that used some of a person's working memory capacity. Subjects in the *dual-task condition* had to do math problems while simultaneously holding a string of six letters in their memory. Subjects in the *control condition* just did the math problems. The left pair of bars in **Figure 5.28** shows the number of errors for the control condition for simple (no carry) and complex (carry) math problems. Error rates are low for both types of problems when only math problems are involved. The right pair of bars shows the number of errors in the dual-task condition, when subjects were simultaneously holding strings of letters in their memory. Notice that errors increase, especially for the carry group, which requires more working memory. Based on the result of this and other experiments, Ashcraft and Kirk concluded that the large number of errors in the dual-task condition for the carry problems occurred because the letter memory task drained some of the working memory resources required by the math task (Ashcraft & Krause, 2007; Ashcraft & Moore, 2009).

This conclusion is related to our discussion of "choking under pressure" in Chapter 1 (page 16), where we described an experiment by Sian Beilock and Thomas Carr (2005) that showed that when subjects are tested under high-pressure conditions (for example, being told "you will be videotaped and need to do well to receive a cash payment"), performance decreases for difficult problems. Beilock (2008) proposed that one reason for this decrease in performance is that pressure causes subjects to worry about the testing situation and the consequences of poor performance, and that this worrying uses some of the working memory capacity needed to solve the problems.

If worrying uses up working memory capacity, then perhaps, reasoned Ramirez and Beilock (2011), eliminating worrying could decrease the choking under pressure effect. To test this idea, they ran an experiment with two groups of subjects. The *control group* took an initial math pretest, were given instructions calculated to create high pressure, and then sat quietly for 10 minutes before taking a math posttest. The *expressive writing group* took the same pretest and received the same high-pressure instructions, but before taking the posttest were asked to write for 10 minutes about their thoughts and feelings regarding the math problems they were about to perform.

The results, in **Figure 5.29**, show that both the control and writing groups performed similarly on the pretest (left pair of bars), but, when under pressure, errors increased for the control group (right pair of bars). This is similar to the increase in errors that occurred for subjects in Ashcraft and Kirk's dual-task condition (right bars in **Figure 5.28**). Increasing the load on working memory—whether by introducing a second task or creating worry—impairs performance.

But the most important result is the decrease in errors in the writing group. Ramirez and Beilock suggest that subjects worried less while taking the test because they had expressed their worries in writing before taking the test. Supporting this idea is that

writing about something unrelated to the test had no effect—performance was the same as the control group. Thus, one simple procedure—writing about your worries about a test just before you take it—could free up working memory capacity that could possibly be needed to do well on the test, especially if the test involves using your working memory.

TEST YOURSELF 5.2

1. Describe two findings that led Baddeley to begin considering alternatives to the modal model.

2. What are the differences between STM and working memory?

3. Describe Baddeley's three-component model of working memory.

4. Describe the phonological similarity effect, the word length effect, and the effect of articulatory suppression. What do these effects indicate about the phonological loop?

5. Describe the visuospatial sketch pad, the Shepard and Meltzger mental rotation task, Della Sala's visual pattern task, and Brooks's "F" task. Be sure you understand what each task indicates about the visuospatial sketch pad.

6. What is the central executive? What happens when executive function is lost because of damage to the frontal lobe? Describe Vogel's experiment that measured the ERP in high-working-memory-capacity and low-working-memory-capacity subjects as they were carrying out a change detection task. What does the result of this experiment indicate about the central executive in these two types of subjects?

7. What is the episodic buffer? Why was it proposed, and what are its functions?

8. The physiology of working memory has been studied using (1) brain lesions in monkeys, (2) neural recording from monkeys, and (3) brain imaging in humans. What do the results of each of these procedures tell us about working memory and the brain? Be sure you understand the neural mind reading procedure used in the brain imaging experiments.

9. Describe the two experiments that demonstrated ways to decrease the amount of working memory available for a task. Describe the experiment that showed how to decrease worrying and therefore increase available working memory.

CHAPTER SUMMARY

1. Memory is the process involved in retaining, retrieving, and using information about stimuli, images, events, ideas, and skills after the original information is no longer present. Five different types of memory are sensory, short-term, episodic, semantic, and procedural.

2. Atkinson and Shiffrin's modal model of memory consists of three structural features: sensory memory, short-term memory, and long-term memory. Another feature of the model is control process such as rehearsal and attentional strategies.

3. Sperling used two methods, whole report and partial report, to determine the capacity and time course of visual sensory memory. The duration of visual sensory memory (iconic memory) is less than 1 second, and of auditory sensory memory (echoic memory) is about 2–4 seconds.

4. Short-term memory is our window on the present. Brown, and Peterson and Peterson, determined that the duration of STM is about 15–20 seconds. They interpreted the short duration of STM as being caused by decay, but a later reanalysis of their data indicated it was due to proactive interference.

5. Digit span is one measure of the capacity of short-term memory. According to George Miller's classic "Seven, Plus or Minus Two" paper, the capacity of STM is five to nine items. According to more recent experiments, the capacity is about four items. The amount of information held in STM can be expanded by chunking, in which small units are combined into larger, more meaningful units. The memory performance of the runner S.F. provides an example of chunking.

6. It has been suggested that rather than describing short-term memory capacity in terms of number of items, it should be described in terms of amount of information. An experiment by Alvarez and Cavanagh, using stimuli ranging from simple to complex, supports this idea.

7. Baddeley revised the short-term memory component of the modal model in order to deal with dynamic processes that unfold over time and can't be explained by a single short-term process. In this new model, working memory replaces STM.

8. Working memory is a limited-capacity system for storage and manipulation of information in complex tasks. It consists of three components: the phonological loop, which holds auditory or verbal information; the visuospatial sketch pad, which holds visual and spatial information; and the central executive, which coordinates the action of the phonological loop and visuospatial sketch pad.

9. The following effects can be explained in terms of operation of the phonological loop: (a) phonological similarity effect, (b) word-length effect, and (c) articulatory suppression.

10. Shepard and Metzler's mental rotation experiment illustrates visual imagery, which is one of the functions of the visuospatial sketch pad. Della Sala's visual recall task used visual imagery to estimate the capacity of working memory. Brooks's "F" experiment showed that two tasks can be handled simultaneously if one involves the visuospatial sketch pad and the other involves the phonological loop. Performance decreases if one component of working memory is called on to deal with two tasks simultaneously.

11. The central executive coordinates how information is used by the phonological loop and visuospatial sketch pad; it can be thought of as an attention controller. Patients with frontal lobe damage have trouble controlling their attention, as illustrated by the phenomenon of perseveration. Vogel and coworkers used the ERP to demonstrate differences in how the central executive operates for subjects with high and low working memory capacity.

12. The working memory model has been updated to include an additional component called the episodic buffer, which helps connect working memory with LTM and which has a greater capacity and can hold information longer than the phonological loop or the visuospatial sketch pad.

13. Behaviors that depend on working memory can be disrupted by damage to the prefrontal cortex. This has been demonstrated by testing monkeys on the delayed-response task.

14. There are neurons in the prefrontal cortex that fire to presentation of a stimulus and continue firing as this stimulus is held in memory.

15. Brain imaging experiments using the neural mind reading procedure have shown that the visual cortex is involved in working memory.

16. The working memory available for solving math problems can be decreased by introducing a competing task or by using pressure to cause worrying. One way to help decrease worrying is to write about your worries before taking a test.

THINK ABOUT IT

1. Analyze the following in terms of how the various stages of the modal model are activated, using Rachel's pizza-ordering experience in **Figure 5.3** as a guide: (1) listening to a lecture in class, taking notes, and reviewing the notes later as you study for an exam; (2) watching a scene in a James Bond movie in which Bond captures the female enemy agent whom he had slept with the night before.

2. Adam has just tested a woman who has brain damage, and he is having difficulty understanding the results. She can't remember any words from a list when she is tested immediately after hearing the words, but her memory gets better when she is tested after a delay. Interestingly enough, when the woman reads the list herself, she remembers well at first, so in that case the delay is not necessary. Can you explain these observations using the modal model? The working memory model? Can you think of a new model that might explain this result better than those two?

KEY TERMS

COGLAB EXPERIMENTS Numbers in parentheses refer to the experiment number in CogLab.

Think back to your childhood. Which events stand out? A family trip to the beach? Birthday parties? Playing with special friends? Events such as these, as well as routine things that have happened more recently, are part of your long-term memory. After comparing short- and long-term memory, this chapter describes a number of types of long-term memory, including episodic memory—memory for specific experiences; semantic memory—memory for facts; and procedural memory—memory for how to do things. We consider how these different types of memory are represented in the mind and brain, how they interact with each other, and what happens to these memories as time passes.

Long-Term Memory: Structure

SOME QUESTIONS WE WILL CONSIDER

▶ How does damage to the brain affect the ability to remember what has happened in the past and the ability to form new memories of ongoing experiences? (160)

▶ How are memories for personal experiences, like what you did last summer, different from memories for facts, like the capital of your state? (162)

▶ How do the different types of memory interact in our everyday experience? (164)

▶ How has memory loss been depicted in popular films? (172)

At the beginning of Chapter 5, Christine asked, "How do I remember thee, let me count the ways" and provided examples of different types of memory (Figure 5.1, page 120). Some of Christine's memories were short-lived (a briefly flashed face, a rapidly fading phone number), but many were longer-lasting (a memorable picnic, the date of a person's birthday, how to ride a bike). This chapter is the first of three chapters that discuss long-term memories.

The theme of this chapter is "division and interaction." *Division* refers to distinguishing between different types of memory. We introduced this idea in Chapter 5 when we divided Christine's memory into *short-term* and *long-term* and further divided long-term memory into *episodic memory* (memory for specific experiences from the past); *semantic memory* (memory for facts); and *procedural memory* (memory for how to carry out physical actions).

Distinguishing between different types of memory is useful because it divides memory into smaller, easier-to-study components. But this division has to be based on real differences between the components. Thus, one of our goals will be to consider evidence that these different components are based on different mechanisms. We will do this by considering the results of (1) behavioral experiments, (2) neuropsychological studies of the effects of brain damage on memory, and (3) brain imaging experiments.

Interaction refers to the fact that the different types of memory can interact and share mechanisms. We will begin this chapter by revisiting short-term memory. We will then look closely at the episodic, semantic, and procedural components of long-term memory (and at two other kinds of long-term memories as well), with the goal of showing how they differ, what they share in common, and how they interact with one another to create our overall experience of memory.

Comparing Short-Term and Long-Term Memory Processes

Long-term memory (LTM) is the system that is responsible for storing information for long periods of time. One way to describe LTM is as an "archive" of information about past events in our lives and knowledge we have learned. What is particularly amazing about this storage is that it stretches from just a few moments ago to as far back as we can remember.

The long time span of LTM is illustrated in Figure 6.1, which shows what a student who has just taken a seat in class might be remembering about events that have occurred at various times in the past. His first recollection—that he has just sat down—would be in his short-term memory/working memory (STM/WM) because it happened within the last 30 seconds. But everything before that—from his recent memory that 5 minutes ago he was walking to class, to a memory from 10 years earlier of the elementary school he attended in the third grade—is part of long-term memory.

Although all of these memories are contained in LTM, recent memories tend to be more detailed; much of this detail, and often the specific memories themselves, fade with the passage of time and as other experiences accumulate. Thus, on October 1, 2013, this person would probably not remember the details of what happened while walking to class on October 1, 2012, but would remember some of the general experiences from around that time. One of the things we will be concerned with in this chapter and the next is why we retain some information and lose other information.

Our goal in this chapter is to introduce long-term memory by first showing how it can be distinguished from STM/WM in ways that go beyond the basic facts about duration (LTM = long; STM/WM = very short) and capacity (LTM = very large; STM/WM = very limited). After contrasting LTM and STM/WM, the rest of the chapter describes the various types of LTM, including memories for personal experiences (what you did last summer), knowledge or facts (the identity of the third president of the United States), and how to do things (your ability to ride a bike or drive a car).

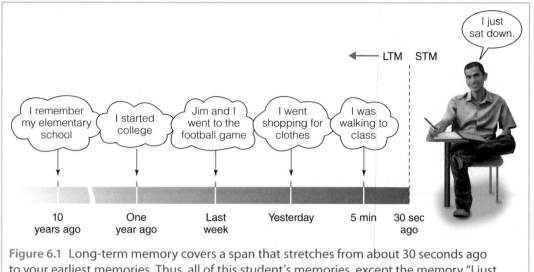

Figure 6.1 Long-term memory covers a span that stretches from about 30 seconds ago to your earliest memories. Thus, all of this student's memories, except the memory "I just sat down" and anything the student was rehearsing, would be classified as long-term memories. © Cengage Learning

Our starting point for comparing LTM and STM/WM takes us back to our discussion of STM, when we noted that one of the problems with STM is that most research emphasized its storage function—how much information it can hold and for how long. This led to the proposal of working memory, with its emphasis on dynamic processes that are needed to explain complex cognitions such as understanding language, solving problems, and making decisions.

A similar situation exists for LTM. While retaining information about the past is an important characteristic of LTM, we also need to understand how this information is used. We can do this by focusing on the dynamic aspects of how LTM operates, including how it interacts with working memory to create our ongoing experience.

Consider, for example, what happens when Tony's friend Cindy says, "Jim and I saw the new James Bond movie last night" (**Figure 6.2**). As Tony's working memory is holding the exact wording of that statement in his mind, it is simultaneously accessing the meaning of words from LTM, which helps him understand the meaning of each of the words that make up the sentence.

Tony's LTM also contains a great deal of additional information about movies, James Bond, and Cindy. Although Tony might not consciously think about all of this information (after all, he has to pay attention to the next thing that Cindy is going to tell him), it is all there in his LTM and adds to his understanding of what he is hearing and his interpretation of what it might mean. LTM therefore provides both an archive that we

Figure 6.2 Tony's working memory, which is dealing with the present, and his LTM, which contains knowledge relevant to what is happening, work together as Cindy tells him something. © Cengage Learning

can refer to when we want to remember events from the past and a wealth of background information that we are constantly consulting as we use working memory to make contact with what is happening at a particular moment.

The interplay between what is happening in the present and information from the past, which we described in the interaction between Tony and Cindy, is based on the distinction between STM/WM and LTM. Beginning in the 1960s, a great deal of research was conducted that was designed to distinguish between short-term and long-term processes. In describing these experiments, we will identify the short-term process as short-term memory (STM) for the early experiments that used that term and as working memory (WM) for more recent experiments that focused on working memory. A classic experiment by B. B. Murdock, Jr. (1962) studied the distinction between STM and LTM using the following method to measure a function called the *serial position curve*.

METHOD
MEASURING A SERIAL POSITION CURVE

A list of words such as the following is presented to a group of subjects at a steady rate.

1.	barricade	11.	phoenix
2.	children	12.	crossbow
3.	diet	13.	doorbell
4.	gourd	14.	muffler
5.	folio	15.	mouse
6.	meter	16.	menu
7.	journey	17.	airplane
8.	mohair	18.	armchair
9.	tomato	19.	dresser
10.	cabin	20.	baseball

At the end of the list, subjects write down all of the words they can remember, in any order. The results are plotted in a curve like the one in Figure 6.3, which indicates the percentage of subjects recalling each word versus its position in the list. For example, *barricade* is in position 1 and *baseball* is in position 20. This is the **serial position curve**.

SERIAL POSITION CURVE

The serial position curve in Figure 6.3 indicates that memory is better for words at the beginning of the list and at the end of the list than for words in the middle (Murdock, 1962). The finding that subjects are more likely to remember words presented at the beginning of a sequence (such as *barricade, children,* and *diet* in our list) is called the **primacy effect**.

A possible explanation of the primacy effect is that subjects had time to rehearse the words at the beginning of the sequence and transfer them to LTM. According to this idea, subjects begin rehearsing the first word right after it is presented; because no other words have been presented, the first word receives 100 percent of the subject's attention. When the second word is presented, attention becomes spread over two words, and so on; as additional words are presented, less rehearsal is possible for later words.

Dewey Rundus (1971) tested this idea that the primacy effect occurs because subjects have more time to rehearse words at the beginning of the list. Rundus first presented a list of 20 words at a rate of 1 word every 5 seconds; after the last word was presented, he asked

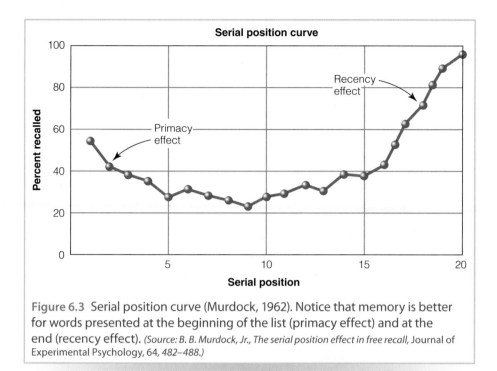

Figure 6.3 Serial position curve (Murdock, 1962). Notice that memory is better for words presented at the beginning of the list (primacy effect) and at the end (recency effect). *(Source: B. B. Murdock, Jr., The serial position effect in free recall, Journal of Experimental Psychology, 64, 482–488.)*

his subjects to write down all the words they could remember. The resulting serial position curve, which is the red curve in **Figure 6.4**, shows the same primacy effect as Murdock's curve in **Figure 6.3**. But Rundus added a twist to his experiment by presenting another list and asking his subjects to repeat the words out loud during the 5-second intervals between words. Subjects were not told which words to repeat—just that they should keep repeating words during the 5-second intervals between words. The dashed blue curve, which indicates how many times each word was repeated, bears a striking resemblance to the first

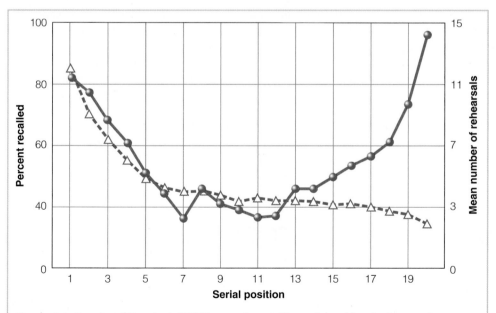

Figure 6.4 Results of Rundus's (1971) experiment. The solid red line is the usual serial position curve. The dashed blue line indicates how many times the subjects rehearsed (said out loud) each word on the list. Note how the rehearsal curve matches the initial part of the serial position curve. *(Source: D. Rundus, Analysis of rehearsal processes in free recall, Journal of Experimental Psychology, 89, 63–77, Figure 1, p. 66, 1971.)*

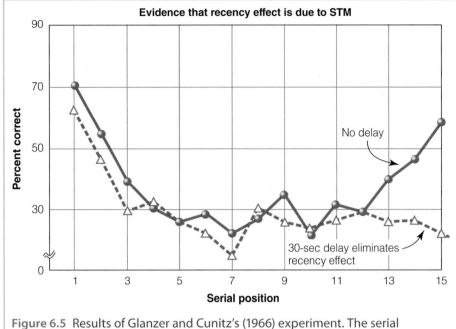

Figure 6.5 Results of Glanzer and Cunitz's (1966) experiment. The serial position curve has a normal recency effect when the memory test is immediate (solid red line), but no recency effect occurs if the memory test is delayed for 30 seconds (dashed blue line). *(Source: M. Glanzer & A. R. Cunitz, Two storage mechanisms in free recall, Journal of Verbal Learning and Verbal Behavior, 5, 351–360, Figures 1 & 2. Copyright © 1966 Elsevier Ltd. Republished with permission.)*

half of the serial position curve. Words presented early in the list were rehearsed more, and were also more likely to be remembered later. This result supports the idea that the primacy effect is related to the longer rehearsal time available for words at the beginning of the list.

The better memory for the stimuli presented at the end of a sequence is called the **recency effect.** The explanation for the recency effect is that the most recently presented words are still in STM and therefore are easy for subjects to remember. To test this idea, Murray Glanzer and Anita Cunitz (1966) first created a serial position curve in the usual way (red curve in **Figure 6.5**). Then, in another experiment, they had subjects recall the words after they had counted backwards for 30 seconds right after hearing the last word of the list. This counting prevented rehearsal and allowed time for information to be lost from STM. The result, shown in the blue dashed curve in **Figure 6.5**, was what we would predict: The delay caused by the counting eliminated the recency effect. Glanzer and Cunitz therefore concluded that the recency effect is due to storage of recently presented items in STM. The serial position results in **Figures 6.3**, **6.4**, and **6.5** are summarized in **Table 6.1**.

Table 6.1: Serial Position Experiments

FIGURE	PROCEDURE	ILLUSTRATES
Figure 6.3	Subject begins recall immediately after hearing the list of words.	Primacy effect and recency effect.
Figure 6.4	List is presented and subject repeats words out loud in 5-second intervals between words.	Words at the beginning of the list are repeated more, so they are more likely to get into LTM.
Figure 6.5	Subject begins recall after counting backwards for 30 seconds.	Recency effect is eliminated because rehearsal is prevented.

CODING IN SHORT-TERM AND LONG-TERM MEMORY

We can also distinguish between STM and LTM by comparing the way information is *coded* by the two systems. **Coding** refers to the form in which stimuli are represented. For example, as we discussed in Chapter 2, a person's face can be represented by the pattern of firing of a number of neurons (see page 36). Determining how a stimulus is represented by the firing of neurons is a *physiological approach to coding*.

In this section we will be taking a *mental approach to coding* by asking how a stimulus or an experience is represented in the mind. To compare the way information is represented in the mind in STM and LTM systems, we describe visual coding (coding in the mind in the form of a visual image), auditory coding (coding in the mind in the form of a sound), and semantic coding (coding in the mind in terms of meaning) in both STM and LTM.

VISUAL CODING IN SHORT-TERM AND LONG-TERM MEMORY You probably used visual coding in the short-term memory demonstration "Recalling Visual Patterns" (Chapter 5, page 137), in which you were asked to remember the visual pattern in **Figure 5.17**. This is visual coding if you remembered the pattern by representing it visually in your mind. You use visual coding in long-term memory when you visualize a person or place from the past. For example, if you are remembering your fifth-grade teacher's face, you are using visual coding.

AUDITORY CODING IN SHORT-TERM AND LONG-TERM MEMORY An example of auditory coding in short-term memory can be found in Conrad's demonstration of the phonological similarity effect (see page 135), which showed that people often misidentify target letters as another letter that sounds like the target (confusing "F" and "S," for example, which don't look alike, but which sound alike). Auditory coding occurs in long-term memory when you "play" a song in your head. Another example of auditory coding sometimes occurs when listening to a CD or playlist that has a short period of silence between tracks. Some people report that for CDs or playlists they have listened to many times, they "hear" the beginning of the next song during the silence, just before it comes on. This happens because an auditory representation from long-term memory is triggered by the end of the previous song.

SEMANTIC CODING IN SHORT-TERM MEMORY: THE WICKENS EXPERIMENT An experiment by Delos Wickens and coworkers (1976) provides an example of semantic coding in short-term memory. **Figure 6.6** shows the experimental design. On each trial, subjects were presented with words related to either (a) fruits (the "Fruits group") or (b) professions (the "Professions group"). Subjects in each group listened to three words (for example, *banana, peach, apple* for the Fruits group), counted backward for 15 seconds, and then attempted to recall the three words. They did this for a total of four trials, with different words presented on each trial. Because subjects recalled the words so soon after hearing them, they were using their short-term memory.

The basic idea behind this experiment was to create *proactive interference*—the decrease in memory that occurs when previously learned information interferes with learning new information (see page 128)—by presenting words from the same *category* on a series of trials. For example, for the Fruits group, *banana, peach*, and *apple* were presented in trial 1 and *plum, apricot*, and *lime* were presented in trial 2. Proactive interference is illustrated by the falloff in performance on each trial, shown by the blue data points in **Figure 6.7a**.

Evidence that this interference for the Fruits group can be attributed to the *meanings* of the words (all of the words were fruits) is provided by the results for the Professions group shown in **Figure 6.7b**. As for the Fruits group, performance is high on trial 1 and then drops on trials 2 and 3 because all of the words are names of professions. But on trial 4, the names of fruits are presented. Because these are from a different category, the proactive interference that built up as the professions were being presented

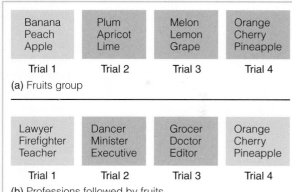

Figure 6.6 Stimuli for the Wickens et al. (1976) experiment. (a) Subjects in the Fruits group are presented with the names of three fruits on each trial. After each presentation, subjects counted backwards for 15 seconds and then recalled the names of the fruits. (b) Subjects in the Professions group were presented with the names of three professions on trials 1, 2, and 3, and with the names of three fruits on trial 4. They also counted backwards for 15 seconds before recalling the names on each trial. *(Source: Based on D. D. Wickens, R. E. Dalezman, & F. T. Eggemeier, Multiple encoding of word attributes in memory,* Memory & Cognition, 4, 307–310, 1976.)

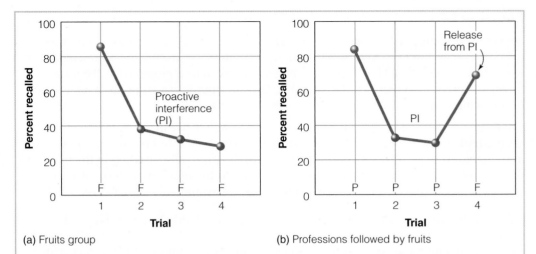

(a) Fruits group

(b) Professions followed by fruits

Figure 6.7 Results of the Wickens et al. (1976) proactive interference experiment. (a) The Fruits group showed reduced performance on trials 2, 3, and 4, caused at least partially by proactive interference (indicated by dark points). (b) The Professions group showed similarly reduced performance on trials 2 and 3. The increase in performance on trial 4 represents a release from proactive interference because the names of fruits, rather than professions, were presented on trial 4. *(Source: Based on D. D. Wickens, R. E. Dalezman, & F. T. Eggemeier, Multiple encoding of word attributes in memory, Memory & Cognition, 4, 307–310, 1976.)*

is absent, and performance increases on trial 4. This increase in performance is called **release from proactive interference.**

What does release from proactive interference tell us about coding in short-term memory? The key to answering this question is to realize that the release from proactive interference that occurs in the Wickens experiment depends on the words' *categories* (fruits and professions). Because placing words into categories involves the *meanings* of the words, and because subjects were recalling the words 15 seconds after they heard them, this represents an effect of semantic coding in short-term memory.

SEMANTIC CODING IN LONG-TERM MEMORY: THE SACHS EXPERIMENT A study by Jacqueline Sachs (1967) demonstrated semantic coding in long-term memory. Sachs had subjects listen to a tape recording of a passage and then measured their *recognition memory* to determine whether they remembered the exact wording of sentences in the passage or just the general meaning of the passage.

METHOD
MEASURING RECOGNITION MEMORY

Recognition memory is the identification of a stimulus that was encountered earlier. The procedure for measuring recognition memory is to present a stimulus during a study period and later to present the same stimulus along with others that were not presented. For example, in the study period, a list of words might be presented that includes the word *house.* Later, in the test, a series of words is presented that includes *house* plus some other words that were not presented, such as *table* and *money.* The subject's task is to answer "Yes" if the word was presented previously (the word *house* in this example) and "No" if it wasn't presented (the words *table* and *money*). Notice that this method is different from testing for *recall* (see Method: Recall, Chapter 5, page 127). In a recall test, the person must *produce* the item to be recalled. An example of a recall test is a fill-in-the-blanks exam question. In contrast, an example of recognition is a multiple-choice exam, in which the task is to pick the correct answer from a number of alternatives. The way Sachs applied recognition to the study of coding in long-term memory is illustrated in the next demonstration.

DEMONSTRATION
READING A PASSAGE

Read the following passage:

> There is an interesting story about the telescope. In Holland, a man named Lippershey was an eyeglass maker. One day his children were playing with some lenses. They discovered that things seemed very close if two lenses were held about a foot apart. Lippershey began experimenting, and his "spyglass" attracted much attention. He sent a letter about it to Galileo, the great Italian scientist. Galileo at once realized the importance of the discovery and set about building an instrument of his own.

Now cover up the passage and indicate which of the following sentences is identical to a sentence in the passage and which sentences are changed.

1. He sent a letter about it to Galileo, the great Italian scientist.

2. Galileo, the great Italian scientist, sent him a letter about it.

3. A letter about it was sent to Galileo, the great Italian scientist.

4. He sent Galileo, the great Italian scientist, a letter about it.

Which sentence did you pick? Sentence (1) is the correct answer because it is the only one that is identical to one in the passage. The task facing Sachs's subjects was more difficult, because they heard a passage two or three times as long, so there was more material to remember and a longer delay between hearing the sentence and being asked to remember it. Many of Sachs's subjects correctly identified sentence (1) as being identical and knew that sentence (2) was changed. However, a number of people identified sentences (3) and (4) as matching one in the passage, even though the wording was different. These subjects apparently remembered the sentence's meaning but not its exact wording. The finding that specific wording is forgotten but the general meaning can be remembered for a long time has been confirmed in many experiments. This description in terms of meaning is an example of semantic coding in LTM.

COMPARING CODING IN SHORT-TERM AND LONG-TERM MEMORY

We have seen that information can be represented in both short-term and long-term memory in terms of vision (visual coding), hearing (auditory coding), and meaning (semantic coding) (Table 6.2). The type of coding that occurs in a particular situation depends largely on the task. Consider, for example, the task of remembering a telephone number that you have just heard. One way of maintaining the number in memory is by repeating it over and over—an example of auditory coding. It is less likely that you would remember the number in terms of either its visual image or the meaning of the phone number. Because

Table 6.2: Examples of Coding in Short-Term and Long-Term Memory

CODE	SHORT-TERM MEMORY	LONG-TERM MEMORY
Visual	Holding an image in the mind to reproduce a visual pattern that was just seen (Della Sala, page 138)	Visualizing what the Lincoln Memorial in Washington, D.C., looked like when you saw it last summer
Auditory	Representing the sounds of letters in the mind just after hearing them (Conrad, page 135)	A song you have heard many times before, repeating over and over in your mind
Semantic	Placing words in an STM task into categories based on their meaning (Wickens, page 157)	Recalling the general plot of a novel you read last week (Sachs, page 159)

© 2015 Cengage Learning

of the nature of many short-term memory tasks, auditory coding is the predominant type of coding in short-term memory.

Now consider another example. You finished reading an adventure story last week and are now remembering what you read. It is unlikely that you remember what the words looked like as you were reading them, but you are more likely to remember what happened in the story. Remembering what happened is semantic coding, which often occurs for long-term memory. If in remembering the story you conjured up images of some of the places you imagined as you read the story (or perhaps saw, if the book included illustrations), this would be an example of visual coding in long-term memory. Generally, semantic coding is the most likely form of coding for long-term memory tasks.

LOCATING MEMORY IN THE BRAIN

At the end of Chapter 5, we saw that the prefrontal cortex and the visual cortex are involved in working memory (Figure 5.22, page 142). Our goal in this section is to describe some experiments that compare where STM and LTM are represented in the brain. We will see that there is evidence that STM and LTM are separated in the brain, but also some evidence for overlap. The strongest evidence for separation is provided by neuropsychological studies.

NEUROPSYCHOLOGY In 1953, Henry Molaison (known as patient H.M. until his death at the age of 82 in 2008) underwent an experimental procedure designed to eliminate his severe epileptic seizures. The procedure, which involved removal of H.M.'s **hippocampus** (see Figure 5.22) on both sides of his brain, succeeded in decreasing his seizures but had the unintended effect of eliminating his ability to form new long-term memories (Corkin, 2002; Scoville & Milner, 1957).

H.M.'s short-term memory remained intact, so he could remember what had just happened, but he was unable to transfer any of this information into long-term memory. One result of this inability to form new long-term memories was that even though psychologist Brenda Milner tested him many times over many decades, H.M. always reacted to her arrival in his room as if he were meeting her for the first time. H.M.'s case, although tragic for him personally, led to an understanding of the role of the hippocampus in forming new long-term memories. Furthermore, the fact that his short-term memory remained intact suggested that short-term and long-term memories are served by separate brain regions.

Another famous case, which led to the same conclusion, is the case of Clive Wearing. Wearing was a highly respected musician and choral director in England who, in his 40s, contracted viral encephalitis, which destroyed parts of his medial temporal lobe, which includes the hippocampus, the amygdala, and other structures in the temporal lobe (Figure 5.22). Because of his brain damage, Wearing lives totally within the most recent 1 or 2 minutes of his life. He remembers what just happened and forgets everything else. If he meets someone and the person leaves the room and returns 3 minutes later, Wearing reacts as if he hadn't met the person earlier. Because of his inability to form new memories, he constantly feels he has just woken up. As with H.M., Wearing's case demonstrates the separation of short-term and long-term memory (Suddendorf et al., 2009; D. Wearing, 2005).

There are also people with a problem opposite to that of H.M. and Clive Wearing—that is, they have normal long-term memory but poor short-term memory. One example is patient K.F., who had suffered damage to his parietal lobe in a motorbike accident. K.F.'s poor STM was indicated by a reduced digit span—the number of digits he could remember (see page 129; Shallice & Warrington, 1970). Whereas the typical span is between five and nine digits, K.F. had a digit span of two; in addition, the recency effect in his serial position curve, which is associated with STM, was reduced. Even though K.F.'s STM was greatly impaired, he had a functioning LTM, as indicated by his ability to form and hold new memories of events in his life.

What's special about these cases together is that because H.M. and Clive Wearing have intact STMs but aren't able to form new long-term memories and K.F. has the opposite problem (intact LTM but a deficient STM), they establish a double dissociation (see Method: Demonstrating a Double Dissociation, page 40) between STM and LTM (Table 6.3).

Table 6.3: A Double Dissociation for STM and LTM

PATIENT	STM	LTM
H.M. and Clive Wearing	OK	Impaired
K.F.	Impaired	OK

© 2015 Cengage Learning

This evidence supports the idea that STM and LTM are caused by different mechanisms, which can act independently.

The combination of the neuropsychological evidence and the results of behavioral experiments such as those measuring the serial position curve, as well as the proposal of the modal model in which STM and LTM are represented by separate boxes, supports the idea of the separation of STM and LTM. However, some recent brain imaging experiments show that this separation is not so straightforward.

BRAIN IMAGING Charan Ranganath and Mark D'Esposito (2001) asked whether the hippocampus, which is crucial for forming new long-term memories, might also play a role in holding information for short periods of time. **Figure 6.8a** shows the sequence of stimuli presented to subjects as they were having their brain scanned. A sample face was presented for 1 second, followed by a 7-second delay period. Then a test face was presented, and the subject's task was to decide whether it matched the sample face. Subjects were run in two conditions. In the "novel face" condition, they were seeing each face for the first time. In the "familiar face" condition, they saw faces that they had seen prior to the experiment.

The results, shown in **Figure 6.8b**, indicate that activity in the hippocampus increases as subjects are holding novel faces in memory during the 7-second delay, but activity changes only slightly for the familiar faces. Based on this result, Ranganath and D'Esposito concluded that the hippocampus is involved in maintaining novel information in memory during short delays. Results such as these, plus the results of many other experiments, show that the hippocampus and other medial temporal lobe structures once thought to be involved only in long-term memory also play some role in short-term memory (Cashdollar et al., 2009; Jonides et al., 2008; Nichols et al., 2006; Ranganath & Blumenfeld, 2005; Rose et al., 2012).

Taking these new results into account, many researchers have concluded that although there is good evidence for the separation of short-term memory and long-term memory, there is also evidence that these functions are not as separated as previously thought, especially for tasks involving novel stimuli. As we now shift our focus to considering only long-term memory, we will focus first on episodic and semantic long-term memory.

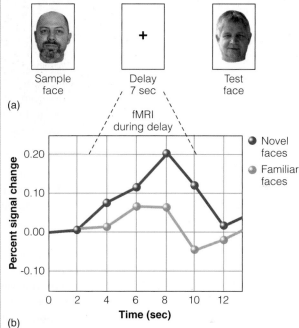

(a)

(b)

Figure 6.8 (a) Stimuli presentation for Ranganath and D'Esposito's (2001) experiment. (b) Hippocampus fMRI response increases during the delay for novel faces but only increases slightly for faces people had seen before. *(Source: Based on C. Ranganath & M. D'Esposito, Medial temporal lobe activity associated with active maintenance of novel information, Neuron, 31, 865–873, 2001. Photos by Bruce Goldstein.)*

TEST YOURSELF 6.1

1. Describe how differences between short-term memory and long-term memory have been determined by measuring serial position curves.

2. What are some examples of visual, auditory, and semantic coding for STM and for LTM?

3. Describe the Wickens and the Sachs semantic memory experiments.

4. What can we conclude about similarities and differences in short-term and long-term memory based on the way coding occurs in both?

5. What conclusions about the separation of short-term and long-term memory followed from neuropsychology studies involving H.M., Clive Wearing, and K.F.?

6. What do more recent experiments, such as the one by Ranganath and D'Esposito, indicate about the separation between brain mechanisms serving short-term and long-term memory?

Episodic and Semantic Memory

Why are episodic memory (memory for experiences) and semantic memory (memory for facts) considered to be two different types of memory? This question has been answered by considering (1) the type of *experience* associated with episodic and semantic memories, (2) how brain damage affects each one, and (3) the fMRI responses to each one.

DISTINCTIONS BETWEEN EPISODIC AND SEMANTIC MEMORY

When we say that episodic memory is memory for experiences and that semantic memory is memory for facts, we are distinguishing between two types of memory based on the types of *information* remembered. Endel Tulving (1985), who first proposed that episodic and semantic memories handled different types of information, also suggested that episodic and semantic memory can be distinguished based on the type of *experience* associated with each (also see Gardiner, 2001; Wheeler et al., 1997).

DIFFERENCES IN EXPERIENCE According to Tulving, the defining property of the experience of episodic memory is that it involves **mental time travel**—the experience of traveling back in time to reconnect with events that happened in the past. For example, I can travel back in my mind to remember cresting the top of a mountain near the California coast and seeing the Pacific Ocean far below, stretching into the distance. I remember sitting in the car, seeing the ocean, saying "Wow!" to my wife who was sitting next to me. I also remember some of the emotions I was experiencing, and other details such as the inside of my car, the sun reflecting off the water, and the expectation of what we were going to see on the way down the mountain. In short, when I remember this incident, I feel as if I am *reliving* it. Tulving describes this experience of mental time travel/episodic memory as *self-knowing* or *remembering*.

In contrast to the mental time travel property of episodic memory, the experience of semantic memory involves accessing knowledge about the world that does not have to be tied to remembering a personal experience. This knowledge can be things like facts, vocabulary, numbers, and concepts. When we *experience* semantic memory, we are not traveling back to a specific event from our past, but we are accessing things we are familiar with and know about. For example, I know many facts about the Pacific Ocean—where it is located, that it is big, that if you travel west from San Francisco you end up in Japan—but I can't remember exactly when I learned these things. The various things I know about the Pacific Ocean are semantic memories. Tulving describes the experience of semantic memory as *knowing*, with the idea that knowing does not involve mental time travel. We will now consider neuropsychological evidence that supports the idea that episodic and semantic memories are served by different mechanisms.

NEUROPSYCHOLOGY Just as neuropsychological evidence was used to distinguish between short-term and long-term memory, it has also been used to distinguish between episodic and semantic memory. We first consider the case of K.C., who at the age of 30 rode his motorcycle off a freeway exit ramp and suffered severe damage to his hippocampus and surrounding structures (Rosenbaum et al., 2005). As a result of this injury, K.C. lost his episodic memory—he can no longer relive any of the events of his past. He does, however, know that certain things happened, which would correspond to semantic memory. He is aware of the fact that his brother died 2 years ago but remembers nothing about personal experiences such as how he heard about his brother's death or what he experienced at the funeral. K.C. also remembers facts like where the eating utensils are located in the kitchen and the difference between a strike and a spare in bowling. Thus, K.C. has lost the episodic part of his memory, but his semantic memory is largely intact.

A person whose brain damage resulted in symptoms opposite to those experienced by K.C. is an Italian woman who was in normal health until she suffered an attack of encephalitis at the age of 44 (DeRenzi et al., 1987). The first signs of a problem were headaches and a fever, which were later followed by hallucinations lasting for 5 days. When she returned home after a 6-week stay in the hospital, she had difficulty recognizing familiar people; she had trouble shopping because she couldn't remember the meaning of words on the shopping list or where things were in the store; and she could no longer recognize famous people or recall facts such as the identity of Beethoven or the fact that Italy was involved in World War II. All of these are semantic memories.

Despite this severe impairment of memory for semantic information, she was still able to remember events in her life. She could remember what she had done during the day and things that had happened weeks or months before. Thus, although she had lost semantic memories, she was still able to form new episodic memories. **Table 6.4** summarizes the two cases we have described. These cases, taken together, demonstrate a double dissociation between episodic and semantic memory, which supports the idea that memory for these two different types of information probably involves different mechanisms.

Table 6.4: A Double Dissociation for Semantic and Episodic Memory

PATIENT	SEMANTIC	EPISODIC
K.C.	OK	Poor
Italian woman	Poor	OK

© 2015 Cengage Learning

Although the double dissociation shown in **Table 6.4** supports the idea of separate mechanisms for semantic and episodic memory, interpretation of the results of studies of brain-damaged patients is often tricky because the extent of brain damage often differs from patient to patient. In addition, the method of testing patients may differ in different studies. It is important, therefore, to supplement the results of neuropsychological research with other kinds of evidence. This additional evidence is provided by brain imaging experiments. (See Squire & Zola-Morgan, 1998, and Tulving & Markowitsch, 1998, for further discussion of the neuropsychology of episodic and semantic memory.)

BRAIN IMAGING Brian Levine and coworkers (2004) did a brain imaging experiment in which they had subjects keep diaries on audiotape describing everyday personal events (example: "It was the last night of our Salsa dance class.... People were dancing all different styles of Salsa....") and facts drawn from their semantic knowledge ("By 1947, there were 5,000 Japanese Canadians living in Toronto"). When the subjects later listened to these audiotaped descriptions while in an fMRI scanner, the recordings of everyday events elicited detailed episodic autobiographical memories (people remembered their experiences), while the other recordings simply reminded people of semantic facts. **Figure 6.9** shows brain activation in a cross section of the brain. The yellow areas represent brain regions associated with episodic memories; the blue areas are brain regions associated with semantic, factual knowledge (personal and nonpersonal). These results and others indicate that while there can be overlap between activation caused by episodic and semantic memories, there are also major differences (also see Cabeza & Nyberg, 2000; Duzel et al., 1999; Nyberg et al., 1996).

The fact that we can draw distinctions between episodic and semantic memory doesn't mean, however, that they operate totally separately from one another. In keeping with this chapter's theme of *division and interaction*, we will now see that there is a great deal of interaction between these two systems.

INTERACTIONS BETWEEN EPISODIC AND SEMANTIC MEMORY

In real life, episodic and semantic memories are often intertwined. Two examples are (1) how knowledge (semantic) affects experience (episodic) and (2) the makeup of autobiographical memory.

KNOWLEDGE AFFECTS EXPERIENCE We bring a vast store of knowledge with us as we are having the experiences we will later remember. For example, I recently was watching a baseball game with a friend who was British and had never been to a baseball game, so his knowledge was limited to the basic principle that the point of the game is to hit the ball, run the bases, and score runs. As we sat watching the game together, I soon realized that I knew many things about the game that I take for granted. At one point in the game, when there was a man on first and one out, I was anticipating the possibility that a ground ball might result in a double play. Thus, when the batter hit a ground ball to the third baseman, I immediately looked to second base, where the third baseman threw the ball for one out, and then to first, where the second baseman threw for the second out. Meanwhile, my British friend's reaction was "What happened?" Clearly, my knowledge of the game influenced how I experienced the game. Our knowledge (semantic memory) guides our experience, and this, in turn, influences the episodic memories that follow from that experience.

AUTOBIOGRAPHICAL MEMORY CONTAINS BOTH SEMANTIC AND EPISODIC COMPONENTS The interplay between episodic and semantic memory also occurs when we consider **autobiographical memory**—memory for specific experiences from our life, which can include both episodic and semantic components. For example, consider the following autobiographical memory: "When I met Gil and Mary at the Le Buzz coffee shop yesterday, we sat at our favorite table, which is located near the window, but which is hard to get in the morning when Le Buzz is busy."

Notice that this description contains episodic components (meeting Gil and Mary yesterday is a specific experience) and semantic components (Le Buzz is a coffee shop; the table near the window is our favorite one; that table is difficult to get in the morning are all facts). The semantic components of this description are called **personal semantic memories** because they are facts associated with personal experiences (Renoult et al., 2012). **Table 6.5** summarizes the characteristics of episodic, semantic, and autobiographical memories.

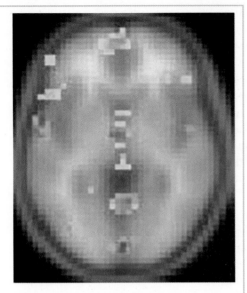

Figure 6.9 Brain showing areas activated by episodic and semantic memories. The yellow areas represent brain regions associated with episodic memories; the blue areas are regions associated with semantic memories. *(Source: B. Levine, G. R. Turner, D. Tisserand, S. J. Hevenor, S. J. Graham, & A. R. McIntosh, The functional neuroanatomy of episodic and semantic autobiographical remembering: A prospective functional MRI study. Journal of Cognitive Neuroscience, 16, 1633–1646, 2004. MIT Press Journals.)*

Table 6.5: Types of Long-Term Memory

TYPE	DEFINITION	EXAMPLE
Episodic	Memory for specific personal experiences, involving mental time travel back in time to achieve a feeling of reliving the experience.	I remember going to get coffee at Le Buzz yesterday morning and talking with Gil and Mary about their bike trip.
Semantic	Memory for facts.	There is a Starbucks down the road from Le Buzz.
Autobiographical	People's memories for experiences from their own lives. These memories have both episodic components (relived specific events) and semantic components (facts related to these events). These semantic components of autobiographical memory are *personal semantic memories*.	I met Gil and Mary at Le Buzz yesterday morning. We sat at our favorite table near the window, which is often difficult to get in the morning when the coffee shop is busy.

© 2015 Cengage Learning

Another interaction between episodic and semantic memory has been demonstrated in an experiment by Robyn Westmacott and Morris Moscovitch (2003), who showed that people's knowledge about public figures, such as actors, singers, and politicians, can include both semantic and episodic components. For example, if you know some facts about Oprah Winfrey and that she had a television program, your knowledge would be mainly semantic. But if you can remember watching some of her television shows, your memory for Oprah Winfrey would have episodic components.

Westmacott and Moscovitch call the memories involving personal episodes *autobiographically significant* semantic memories. When they tested people's ability to remember the names of public figures, they found that recall was better for names of people who had higher autobiographical significance. Thus, you would be more likely to recall the name of a popular singer in a memory test if you had attended one of his or her concerts than if you had just read about the singer in a magazine.

But this intermingling of episodic and semantic memory becomes even more interesting when we ask what happens to long-term memories with the passage of time. Remember that short-term memory lasts only about 15 seconds (unless information is held there by rehearsal), so events we remember from an hour, a day, or a year ago are all remembered from long-term memory. However, as we will now see, all long-term memories are not created equal. We are more likely to remember the details of something that happened yesterday than something that happened a year ago.

WHAT HAPPENS TO EPISODIC AND SEMANTIC MEMORIES AS TIME PASSES?

One procedure for determining what happens to memory as time passes is to present stimuli and then, after some time passes, ask a subject to recall the stimuli (as in the serial position curve experiments on page 154) or to indicate whether they recognize the stimuli (as in the Sachs experiment on page 158). The typical result of these experiments is that subjects forget some of the stimuli, with forgetting increasing at longer time intervals. But when we consider the process of forgetting in more detail, we see that forgetting is not always an "all-or-nothing" process. For example, consider the following situation: A friend introduces you to Roger at the coffee shop on Monday, and you talk briefly. Then later in the week, you see Roger across the street. Some possible reactions to seeing Roger are:

1. That person looks familiar. Where did I meet him?

2. There's Roger. Where did I meet him?

3. There's Roger, who I met at the coffee shop last Monday. We talked about the weather.

From this example, it is clear that there are different degrees of forgetting and remembering. Examples 1 and 2 illustrate *familiarity*—the person seems familiar and you might remember his name, but you can't remember any details about specific experiences involving that person. Example 3 illustrates *recollection*—remembering specific experiences related to the person. Familiarity is associated with semantic memory because it is not associated with the circumstances under which knowledge was acquired. Recollection is associated with episodic memory because it includes details about what was happening when the knowledge was acquired and an awareness of the event as it was experienced in the past. These two ways of remembering have been measured using the **remember/know procedure**.

METHOD
REMEMBER/KNOW PROCEDURE

In the remember/know procedure, subjects are presented with a stimulus they have encountered before and are asked to respond (1) *remember* if the stimulus is familiar and they also remember the circumstances under which they originally encountered it; (2) *know* if the stimulus seems familiar but they don't remember experiencing it earlier; or (3) *don't know* if they don't remember the stimulus at all. This procedure has been used in laboratory experiments in which subjects are asked to remember lists of stimuli, and has also been used to measure people's memory for actual events from the past. This procedure is important because it distinguishes between the episodic components of memory (indicated by a *remember* response) and semantic components (indicated by a *know* response).

Raluca Petrican and coworkers (2010) determined how people's memory for public events changes over time by presenting descriptions of events that had happened over a 50-year period to older adults (average age = 63 years) and asking them to respond *remember* if they had a personal experience associated with the event or recollected seeing details about the event on TV or in the newspaper. They were to respond *know* if they were familiar with the event but couldn't recollect any personal experience or details related to media coverage of the event. If they couldn't remember the event at all, they were to respond *don't know*.

The results of this experiment are shown in **Figure 6.10**, which indicates memory for public events that happened within the most recent 10 years, and memory for events that happened 40 to 50 years earlier. (Intermediate delays were also tested in the experiment. We are focusing on the extremes.) As would be expected, complete forgetting increased over time (red bars). But the interesting result is that *remember* responses decreased much more than *know* responses, meaning that memories for 40- to 50-year-old events had lost much of their episodic character. This result illustrates the **semanticization of remote memories**—loss of episodic detail for memories of long-ago events.

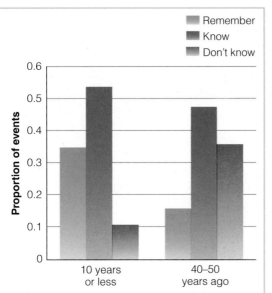

Figure 6.10 Results of the remember/ know experiment that tested older subjects' memory for events over a 50-year period. *(Source: Based on R. Petrican, N. Gopie, L. Leach, T. W. Chow, B. Richards, & M. Moscovitch, Recollection and familiarity for public events in neurologically intact older adults and two brain-damaged patients.* Neuropsychologia, 48, 945–960, 2010.)

This loss of episodic details has been demonstrated both for long-ago events, as in the Petrican experiment, and also for periods as short as 1 week (Addis et al., 2008; D'Argembeau & Van der Linden, 2004; Johnson et al., 1988; Viskontas et al., 2009). This shorter-term semantization makes sense when we consider personal experiences. You probably remember the details of what you did earlier today or yesterday but fewer details about what happened a week ago (unless what happened a week ago was particularly important).

Another way to appreciate the semantization of remote memories is to consider how you have acquired the knowledge that makes up your semantic memories. When you were in the sixth grade, you may have learned that the legislative branch of the U.S. government consists of the Senate and the House of Representatives. Right after learning this, you might have found it easy to remember what was going on in class, including what the classroom looked like, what the teacher was saying, and so on. Remembering all these details about the circumstances of learning comes under the heading of episodic memory. The facts about how the government works is semantic memory.

Many years later, in college, your semantic memory about the structure of the U.S. government remains, but the episodic details about what was happening on the specific day you learned that information are probably gone. Thus, the knowledge that makes up your semantic memories is initially attained through personal experiences that are the basis of episodic memories, but your memory for these experiences often fades, and only semantic memory remains.

Imagining the Future

We usually think of memory in terms of bringing back events or facts from the past. But what about imagining what might happen in the future? Is there a connection between the two? William Shakespeare's line "What's past is prologue," from *The Tempest*, draws a direct connection between the past, the present, and perhaps the future. Steve Jobs, one of the founders of Apple Computer, comments on the connection by noting "You can't connect the dots looking forward; you can only connect them looking backwards; so you have to trust that the dots will somehow connect in your future" (Jobs, 2005).

Extending the dots into the future has become an important topic of memory research. This research doesn't ask how well we can *predict* the future, but asks how well we can create possible scenarios *about* the future. The reason this has become a topic of research is that there is evidence of a connection between the ability to remember the past and the ability to create future scenarios. Evidence for this connection is provided by patients who have lost their episodic memory as a result of brain damage. K.C., the motorcyclist we described earlier as having lost his episodic memory because of a head injury, was unable to use his imagination to describe personal events that might happen in the future (Tulving, 1985). Another patient, D.B., also had difficulty both recalling past events and imagining future events. His inability to imagine future events was restricted to things that might happen to him personally; he could still imagine other future events, such as what might happen in politics or other current events (Addis et al., 2007; Hassabis et al., 2007; Klein et al., 2002).

This behavioral evidence for a link between the ability to remember the past and the ability to imagine what might happen in the future led Donna Rose Addis and coworkers (2007) to look for a physiological link by using fMRI to determine how the brain is activated by remembering the past and imagining the future. When brain activation was measured as neurologically normal subjects silently thought about either events from the past or events that might happen in the future, the results indicated that all the brain regions active during silent description of the past were also active during silent description of the future (Figure 6.11). These results suggest that similar neural mechanisms are involved in remembering the past and predicting the future (Addis et al., 2007, 2009; Schacter & Addis, 2009). Based on these results, Schacter and Addis (2007, 2009) proposed the *constructive episodic simulation hypothesis*, which states that episodic memories are extracted and recombined to construct simulations of future events.

This connection between past and future led Addis and coworkers (2007) to suggest that perhaps the main role of the episodic memory system is not to remember the past, but to enable people to simulate possible future scenarios in order to help anticipate future needs and guide future behavior. This could be useful, for example, in deciding whether to approach or avoid a particular situation (Addis et al., 2007; Schacter, 2012).

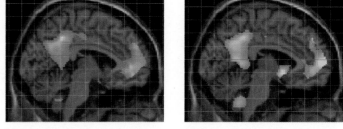

(a) Past events   (a) Future events

Figure 6.11 Brain activation caused by (a) thinking about past events and (b) imagining future events. *(Source: D. R. Addis, A. T. Wong, & D. L. Schacter, Remembering the past and imagining the future: Common and distinct neural substrates during event construction and elaboration, Neuropsychologia, 45, 1363–1377, Figure 2, 2007. With permission from Elsevier.)*

Interestingly, however, some patients with semantic dementia—poor semantic memory but intact episodic memory—also have problems in describing the episodic details of what might happen in the future (Duval et al., 2012; Irish et al., 2012). This result suggests—in keeping with our theme of division and interaction—that both episodic and semantic memory systems need to be functioning in order for us to think about the personal future (Duval et al., 2012; Irish et al., 2012; Irish & Piguet, 2013).

TEST YOURSELF 6.2

1. How have episodic and semantic memory been distinguished from one another? Consider both the definitions and Tulving's idea of mental time travel.

2. Describe neuropsychological evidence for a double dissociation between episodic and semantic memory.

3. Describe Levine's "diary" experiment. What do the brain imaging results indicate about episodic and semantic memory?

4. Describe how schemas for events in semantic memory can influence episodic memory.

5. Describe how personal significance can make semantic memories easier to remember.

6. What is autobiographical memory? How does the definition of autobiographical memory incorporate both episodic and semantic memory?

7. Describe what happens to memory as time passes. What is the semanticization of episodic memory?

8. What is the remember/know procedure? How does it distinguish between episodic and semantic memories? How has it been used to measure how memory changes over time?

9. Describe the following evidence that indicates overlap between episodic memory for the past and the ability to imagine future events: (1) memory of people with amnesia; (2) brain imaging evidence.

10. What is the constructive episodic simulation hypothesis? What role does Addis and coworkers suggest for episodic memory?

11. Describe how semantic dementia affects the ability to describe personal events that might happen in the future. What does this result mean?

Procedural Memory, Priming, and Conditioning

Figure 6.12 is a diagram of the different types of long-term memory. We have been focusing so far on the two types of memory on the left, episodic and semantic, which fall under the heading of *explicit memory*. **Explicit memories** are memories we are aware of. This may seem like a strange statement, because aren't we aware of all of our memories? We tell someone about our vacation or give directions to a lost traveler and not only are we aware of our memories (episodic for describing the vacation; semantic for knowing the directions), but we are making someone else aware of our memories.

But there are, in fact, memories we aren't aware of, called **implicit memories**, shown on the right side of the diagram. Implicit memory occurs when learning from experience is not accompanied by conscious remembering. For example, we do many things without being able to explain how we do them. These abilities come under the heading of *procedural memories*.

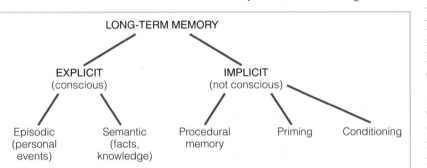

Figure 6.12 Long-term memory can be divided into explicit memory and implicit memory. We can also distinguish between two types of explicit memory, episodic and semantic. There are a number of different types of implicit memory. Three of the main types are procedural memory, priming, and conditioning. © Cengage Learning

PROCEDURAL MEMORY

Procedural memory is also called **skill memory** because it is memory for doing things that usually involve learned skills. Consider, for example, tying your shoes. You might have a hard time explaining to another person how you do it, but when you grab those shoelaces, you just do it! Other examples of skills that people can *do* without being able to explain how they do them are typing, riding a bike, doing a somersault, and playing the piano. As we noted in Chapter 4, concert pianists often report that when they try to become conscious of how they are moving their fingers while playing a difficult passage, they are no longer able to play the passage.

The implicit nature of procedural memory has been demonstrated in amnesiac patients like the musician Clive Wearing, discussed earlier, who lost his ability to form new long-term memories but who could still play the piano. Amnesiac patients can also master new skills even though they don't remember any of the practice that led to this mastery. For example, H.M., whose amnesia was caused by having his hippocampus

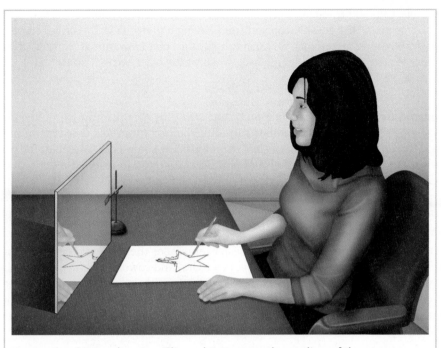

Figure 6.13 Mirror drawing. The task is to trace the outline of the star while looking at its image in the mirror. © Cengage Learning

removed (see page 160), practiced a task called *mirror drawing*, which involves copying a picture that is seen in a mirror (**Figure 6.13**). You can appreciate this task by doing the following demonstration.

DEMONSTRATION
MIRROR DRAWING

Draw a star like the one in **Figure 6.13** on a piece of paper. Place a mirror or some other reflective surface (some cell phone screens work) about an inch or two from the star, so that the reflection of the star is visible. Then, while looking at the reflection, trace the outline of the star on the paper (no fair looking at the actual drawing on the paper!). You will probably find that the task is difficult at first, but becomes easier with practice.

After a number of days of practice, H.M. became quite good at mirror drawing, but since his ability to form long-term memories was impaired, he always thought he was practicing mirror drawing for the first time. H.M.'s ability to trace the star in the mirror, even though he couldn't remember having done it before, illustrates the implicit nature of procedural memory.

K.C. provides another example of a person who can't form new long-term memories but who can still learn new skills. After his motorcycle accident, he learned how to sort and stack books in the library. Even though he doesn't remember learning to do this, he can still do it, and his performance can improve with practice. The fact that people with amnesia can retain skills from the past and learn new ones has led to an approach to rehabilitating patients with amnesia by teaching them tasks, such as sorting mail or performing repetitive computer-based tasks, that they can become expert at, even though they can't remember their training (Bolognani et al., 2000; Clare & Jones, 2008).

The examples so far have been motor skills that involve movement and muscle action. You have also developed many purely cognitive skills that qualify as procedural memory. Consider, for example, your ability to have a conversation. Although you may not be able to describe the rules of grammar, that doesn't stop you from having a grammatically correct conversation. Beginning when we are infants, we learn to apply the rules of grammar, without necessarily being able to state the rules (although later, when we are older, we may study them).

PRIMING

Priming occurs when the presentation of one stimulus (the priming stimulus) changes the way a person responds to another stimulus (the test stimulus). One type of priming, **repetition priming**, occurs when the test stimulus is the same as or resembles the priming stimulus. For example, seeing the word *bird* may cause you to respond more quickly to a later presentation of the word *bird* than to a word you had not seen, even though you may not remember seeing *bird* earlier. Repetition priming is called implicit memory because the priming effect can occur even though subjects may not remember the original presentation of the priming stimuli.

One way to ensure that a person doesn't remember the presentation of the priming stimulus is to test patients with amnesia. Peter Graf and coworkers (1985) did this by testing three groups of subjects: (1) amnesiac patients with a condition called Korsakoff's syndrome, which is associated with alcohol abuse and eliminates the ability to form new long-term memories; (2) patients without amnesia who were under treatment for alcoholism; and (3) patients without amnesia who had no history of alcoholism.

The subjects' task was to read a 10-word list and rate how much they liked each word (1 = like extremely; 5 = dislike extremely). This caused subjects to focus on rating the words rather than on committing the words to memory. Immediately after rating the words, subjects were tested in one of two ways: (1) a test of explicit memory, in which they were asked to recall the words they had read; or (2) a word completion test, which is a test of implicit memory. The word completion test contained the first three letters of the 10 words that the subjects had seen earlier, plus the first three letters of 10 words they had not seen earlier. For example, the three letters *tab_ _* can be completed to create the word *table*. Subjects were presented with three-letter fragments and were asked to add a few letters to create the first word that came into their mind.

The results of the recall experiment, shown in **Figure 6.14a**, show that the amnesiac patients recalled fewer words than the two control groups. This poor recall confirms the poor explicit memory associated with their amnesia. But the results of the word completion test, showing the percentage of primed words that were created (**Figure 6.14b**), indicate that the amnesiac patients performed just as well as the controls. This increase in performance is an example of priming. What is notable about these results is that the Korsakoff amnesiac patients performed as well as the two nonamnesiac groups, even though they had poor memory as measured in the recall test.

Although the poor explicit memory of patients with amnesia means that these patients are not remembering the presentation of the priming stimulus, how can we be sure that a subject with normal memory isn't remembering the priming stimulus when responding to the test stimulus? After all, if we present the word *bird* and then later measure how fast a person reacts to another presentation of the word *bird*, couldn't that happen because the person remembers the first time *bird* was presented? If the person did remember the initial presentation of *bird*, then this would be an example of explicit memory, not implicit memory. Researchers have used a number of methods to reduce the chances that a person in a priming experiment will remember the original presentation of the priming stimulus.

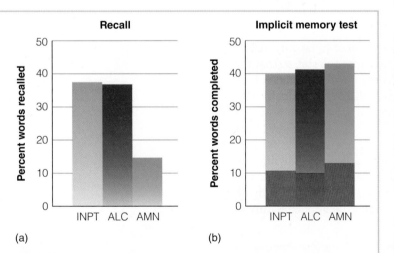

(a)   (b)

Figure 6.14 In the Graf et al. (1985) experiment, (a) amnesiac patients (AMN) did poorly on the recall test compared to the medical inpatients (INPT) and the alcoholic controls (ALC). (b) Amnesiac patients did as well as the other patients on the implicit memory test (completing three-letter word stems). The gray areas on each bar indicate performance on words the subjects hadn't seen earlier. *(Source: P. Graf, A. P. Shimamura, & L. R. Squire, Priming across modalities and priming across category levels: Extending the domain of preserved function in amnesia, Journal of Experimental Psychology: Learning, Memory, and Cognition, 11, 386–396, 1985.)*

METHOD
AVOIDING EXPLICIT REMEMBERING IN A PRIMING EXPERIMENT

One way to minimize the chances that a person with normal memory will remember the presentation of the priming stimulus is to present the priming stimulus in a task that does not appear to be a memory task. For example, if the priming stimuli are the names of animals, subjects could be presented with the names and asked to indicate whether each animal would stand more than 2 feet high. This task causes the subject to focus on the task of estimating height and distracts them from trying to remember the animals' names.

In addition to disguising the purpose of the stimulus during the priming part of the experiment, researchers also use testing procedures that do not refer to memory, as in the word completion task in Graf's experiment. Returning to the results of that experiment, notice that the performance on the word completion task for the nonamnesiac subjects is the same as the performance of the Korsakoff amnesiac patients. We would expect that if the nonamnesiac subjects had remembered the original presentations, their performance would be better than that of the amnesiac patients (Roediger et al.,1994).

Another way of avoiding an obvious memory test is to measure how accurately or quickly the subject responds to a stimulus. For example, subjects could be tested by presenting a list of words and asking them to press a key every time they see a word that has four letters. Priming would be indicated by faster or more accurate responding to four-letter words that corresponded to priming stimuli that subjects had seen earlier. The key characteristic of this test is speed. Requiring a rapid response decreases the chances that the subjects will take the time to consciously recollect whether or not they have previously seen the word.

Using methods such as these, researchers have demonstrated implicit memory not only in amnesiac patients but in normal subjects as well (Graf et al., 1982; Roediger, 1990; Roediger et al., 1994; Schacter, 1987).

As I was discussing repetition priming in class, a student asked whether we are always being primed in everyday life. That's a good question, and the answer is that it is likely that repetition priming does occur in our everyday experience, although we may not be aware of it. An example of a situation in which implicit memory may affect our behavior without our awareness is when we are exposed to advertisements that extol the virtues of a product or perhaps just present the product's name. Although we may believe that we are unaffected by some advertisements, they can have an effect just because we are exposed to them.

This idea is supported by the results of an experiment by T. J. Perfect and C. Askew (1994), who had subjects scan articles in a magazine. Each page of print was faced by an advertisement, but subjects were not told to pay attention to the advertisements. When they were later asked to rate a number of advertisements on various dimensions, such as how appealing, eye-catching, distinctive, and memorable they were, they gave higher ratings to the ones they had been exposed to than to other advertisements that they had never seen. This result qualifies as an effect of implicit memory because when the subjects were asked to indicate which advertisements had been presented at the beginning of the experiment, they recognized only an average of 2.8 of the original 25 advertisements.

This result is related to the **propaganda effect**, in which subjects are more likely to rate statements they have read or heard before as being true, simply because they have been exposed to them before. This effect can occur even when the person is told that the statements are false when they first read or hear them (Begg et al., 1992). The propaganda effect involves implicit memory because it can operate even when people are not aware that they have heard or seen a statement before, and may even have thought it was false when they first heard it.

CLASSICAL CONDITIONING

Classical conditioning occurs when the following two stimuli are paired: (1) a neutral stimulus that initially does not result in a response and (2) a conditioning stimulus that does result in a response (see page 10). An example of classical conditioning from the laboratory is presenting a tone to a person followed by a puff of air to the eye that causes the person to blink. The tone initially does not cause an eyeblink, but after a number of pairings with the puff of air, the person blinks in response to the tone. This is implicit memory because it can occur even if the person has forgotten about the original pairing of the tone and the air puff.

Conditioning in real life is often linked to emotional reactions. I remember, for example, the bad feeling I had when, as I was driving along a country road, I saw the flashing red lights of a police car in my rearview mirror. I wasn't happy about receiving a speeding ticket, but the incident did provide an example of classical conditioning, because when I passed that spot on the road later, I reexperienced the emotions that had been triggered by the police car's flashing lights. This example illustrates the classical conditioning of emotions but doesn't illustrate implicit memory, because I was aware of what was causing my conditioned response.

An example of classical conditioning causing implicit memory is provided by a situation we described earlier (page 165), in which you meet someone who seems familiar but you can't remember how you know him or her. Have you ever had this experience and also felt positively or negatively about the person, without knowing why? If so, your emotional reaction was an example of implicit memory.

Now that we have described how cognitive psychologists have distinguished between different types of memory, we will close this chapter by considering how memory has been described by another group—people who make movies.

Something to Consider

MEMORY LOSS IN THE MOVIES

On September 18, 1993, Kim and Krickett Carpenter, who had been married just 10 weeks earlier, were involved in a car crash. Krickett's head injury erased her memory of her romance with her husband, Kim, and left her thinking he was a complete stranger. The 2012 movie *The Vow*, which is based on the book Kim and Krickett wrote describing their lives after the car crash, accurately describes memory loss because it is based on an actual case. However, this movie is the exception. The accuracy of most movies that describe memory loss ranges from depictions that resemble types of memory loss that actually occur to completely fictional types of memory loss that have never occurred. Sometimes, even when the memory loss in a movie resembles actual cases, it is described using incorrect terminology. We will describe some examples of fact-based memory loss, fictional memory loss, and the use of incorrect terminology in movies.

In some movies, characters lose their memory for everything in their past, including their identity, but are able to form new memories. This is what happened to Jason Bourne, the character played by Matt Damon in *The Bourne Identity* (2002). In this film, the unconscious and badly wounded Bourne is plucked out of the water by a fishing boat. When he regains consciousness, he has no memory of his identity. As he searches for his previous identity, he realizes people are out to kill him, but, because of his memory loss, he doesn't know why. Although Bourne has lost his episodic memories of his past, his semantic memory appears to be intact, and, most interesting of all, he has lost none of his procedural memories from his training as a CIA agent, including ways to outsmart, outrun, and eliminate his adversaries.

Bourne's situation is related to a rare condition called *psychogenic fugue*. Symptoms of this condition include traveling away from where the person lives and a lack of memory for the past, especially personal information such as name, relationships, place of residence, and occupation. In the few cases that have been reported, a person vanishes from his or her normal life situation, often travels far away, and takes on a new identity unrelated to the previous one (Coons & Milstein, 1992; Loewenstein, 1991).

A number of other movies revolve around a central character who loses his or her identity or takes on a new one. In *Who Am I?* (1998), Jackie Chan, a top secret soldier, loses his memory in a helicopter crash, triggering a quest to recover his identity. In *Dead Again* (1991), a mystery woman played by Emma Thompson can't remember anything about her life. In *The Long Kiss Goodnight* (1996), Geena Davis plays a suburban homemaker who begins remembering events from her previous life as a secret agent after suffering a blow to her head.

In other movies, the main character has trouble forming new memories. For example, Lenny, the character played by Guy Pearce in *Memento* (2000), continually forgets what has just happened to him. This situation is based on cases such as those of H.M. and Clive Wearing, who were unable to form new memories and were therefore only able to remember the current 1 or 2 minutes of their lives. Lenny's problem is apparently not as debilitating as in these real-life cases, because he is able to function in the outside world, although with some difficulty. To compensate for his inability to form new memories, Lenny records his experiences with a Polaroid camera and has key facts tattooed on his body (**Figure 6.15**).

Figure 6.15 Guy Pearce's character, Lenny, from the film *Memento*. To deal with his memory problem, he had key facts he wanted to remember tattooed on his body.

The use of terminology in movies that is not the same as that used by psychologists is illustrated in *Memento*, where Lenny's problem is identified as a loss of short-term memory. This reflects a common belief (at least among those who have not taken a cognitive psychology course) that forgetting things that have happened within the last few minutes or hours is a breakdown in short-term memory. Cognitive psychologists, in contrast, identify short-term memory as memory for what has happened in the last 15 to 20 seconds (or longer, if the events are rehearsed). According to that definition, Lenny's short-term memory was fine, because he could remember what had just happened to him. His problem was that he couldn't form new long-term memories, so, like Clive Wearing and H.M., he could remember the immediate present but forgot everything that had happened more than a few minutes previously.

Although some movies, like the ones already mentioned, are based at least loosely on actual memory disorders, some stray farther into fiction. Douglas Quaid, the character played by Arnold Schwarzenegger in *Total Recall* (1990), lives in a future world in which it is possible to implant memories. Quaid makes the mistake of having an artificial memory of a holiday on Mars implanted, which triggers a series of nightmarish events.

The reverse of *creating* specific memories is selectively *forgetting* specific events. This occasionally occurs, as when memories for particularly traumatic events are lost (although sometimes the opposite happens, so traumatic events stand out in memory; Porter & Birt, 2001). But the characters in *The Eternal Sunshine of the Spotless Mind* (2004) take the idea of selective forgetting to an extreme, by purposely undergoing a high-tech procedure to selectively eliminate their memory for a previous relationship. First Clementine, played by Kate Winslet, has her memory for her ex-boyfriend, Joel, played by Jim Carrey, erased. When Joel discovers she has done this, he decides to have Clementine erased from his memory by undergoing the same procedure. The aftermath of this procedure, which I won't reveal in case you want to see the movie, is both thought provoking and entertaining!

The movie *50 First Dates* (2004) is an example of a memory movie based on a condition created by the imagination of the filmmaker. Lucy, played by Drew Barrymore, remembers what is happening to her on a given day (so her short-term and long-term memory are fine during the day), but every morning she contracts a case of retrograde amnesia, which has wiped out her memory for what happened the day before. The fact that her memory "resets" every morning seems not to bother Henry, played by Adam Sandler, who falls in love with her. Henry's problem is that because Lucy wakes up each morning with no memory for the previous day, she doesn't remember him, thus the title *50 First Dates*.

When the film was released in 2004, there were no known cases of anyone with a memory disorder in which their memory from a day vanishes during a night of sleep. However, a recent report documents the case of F.L., a 51-year-old woman who was treated for a head injury from an automobile accident; after she returned home, she reported that every time she awoke she had no memory for the previous day—just like Lucy in *50 First Dates* (Smith et al., 2010)!

But testing in the laboratory revealed something interesting. F.L. performed well on materials she had learned on the same day and exhibited no memory for material she knew had been presented on the previous day. But if, without F.L.'s knowledge, material learned on the previous day was intermixed with new material, she was able to remember the old material. Based on a number of other tests, the researchers concluded that F.L. was not intentionally making believe she had amnesia, but suggested that her symptoms may have been influenced by her knowledge of how amnesia was depicted in *50 First Dates*, which was released 15 months before F.L. reported her symptoms—an interesting example, if true, of life imitating film!

TEST YOURSELF 6.3

1. Distinguish between explicit memory and implicit memory.

2. What is procedural memory? Describe the mirror drawing experiment and other examples from the chapter. Why is procedural memory considered a form of implicit memory?

3. What is priming? Repetition priming? Describe the Graf experiment, including the results and how they support the idea that priming is a form of implicit memory.

4. What precautions are taken to be sure that people with normal memory do not use episodic memory in an experiment that is designed to test implicit memory?

5. Describe the Perfect and Askew advertising experiment. What is the propaganda effect, and why could it be considered a form of priming?

6. What is classical conditioning? Why is it a form of implicit memory?

7. Describe how memory loss is depicted in movies. How accurate are these depictions?

CHAPTER SUMMARY

1. This chapter is about *division*—distinguishing between different types of memory—and *interaction*—how the different types of memory interact.

2. Long-term memory is an "archive" of information about past experiences in our lives and knowledge we have learned. LTM coordinates with working memory to help create our ongoing experience.

3. The primacy and recency effects that occur in the serial position curve have been linked to long-term memory and short-term memory, respectively.

4. Visual and auditory coding can occur in both STM and LTM.

5. Semantic coding has been demonstrated in STM by Wickens, by demonstrating release from proactive inhibition.

6. Semantic coding has been demonstrated in LTM by Sachs, using a recognition memory procedure.

7. Auditory coding is the predominant type of coding in STM. Semantic coding is the predominant type in LTM.

8. Neuropsychological studies have demonstrated a double dissociation between STM and LTM, which supports the idea that STM and LTM are caused by different independent mechanisms.

9. The hippocampus is important for forming new long-term memories. Brain imaging experiments have shown that the hippocampus is also involved in holding novel information over short delays.

10. According to Tulving, the defining property of the experience of episodic memory is that it involves mental time travel (self-knowing or remembering). The experience of semantic memory (knowing) does not involve mental time travel.

11. The following evidence supports the idea that episodic and semantic memory involve different mechanisms: (1) double dissociation of episodic and semantic memory in patients with brain damage; (2) brain imaging, which indicates that overlapping but different areas are activated by episodic and semantic memories.

12. Even though episodic and semantic memories are served by different mechanisms, they are connected in the following ways: (1) Knowledge (semantic memory) can influence the nature of experiences that become episodic memories. (2) Autobiographical memories include both episodic and semantic components.

13. The remember/know procedure is based on the idea that recollection is associated with episodic memory and familiarity is associated with semantic memory.

14. Over time, memories lose their episodic nature. This is called the semanticization of remote memories.

15. There is a link between the ability to remember the past and the ability to imagine the future. This has been demonstrated in both neuropsychological and brain imaging experiments, and has led to the proposal that a function of episodic memory is to help anticipate future needs and guide future behavior.

16. Explicit memories, such as episodic and semantic memories, are memories we are aware of. Implicit memory occurs when learning from experience is not accompanied by conscious remembering. Procedural memory, priming, and classical conditioning involve implicit memory.

17. Procedural memory, also called skill memory, has been studied in amnesiac patients. They are able to learn new skills, although they do not remember learning them. Procedural memory is a common component of many of the skills we have learned.

18. Priming occurs when the presentation of a stimulus affects a person's response to the same or a related stimulus when it is presented later. The implicit nature of priming has been demonstrated in both amnesiac patients and nonamnesiac subjects. Priming is not just a laboratory phenomenon but also occurs in real life. The propaganda effect is one example of real-life implicit memory.

19. Classical conditioning occurs when a neutral stimulus is paired with a stimulus that elicits a response, so that the neutral stimulus than elicits the response. Classically conditioned emotions occur in everyday experience.

20. Memory loss has been depicted in movies in a number of ways, some of which bear at least a resemblance to actual cases of amnesia, and some of which are totally fictional conditions.

THINK ABOUT IT

1. What do you remember about the last 5 minutes? How much of what you are remembering is in your STM while you are remembering it? Were any of these memories ever in LTM?

2. On page 160, we described the case of K.F., who had normal LTM but poor STM. What problem does K.F.'s condition pose for the modal model of memory? Can you think of a way to modify the model that would handle K.F.'s condition?

3. Not all long-term memories are alike. There is a difference between remembering what you did 10 minutes ago, 1 year ago, and 10 years ago, even though all of these memories are called "long-term memories." How would you expand on

the research described in the chapter to demonstrate the properties of these different long-term memories?

4. Rent movies such as *Memento, 50 First Dates*, or others that depict memory loss. (Search the Internet for "Movies amnesia" to find films in addition to those mentioned in the book.) Describe the kinds of memory loss depicted in these movies, and compare the characters' problems with the cases of memory loss described in this chapter. Determine how accurately depictions of memory loss in movies reflect memory loss that occurs in actual cases of trauma or brain damage. You may have to do some additional research on memory loss to answer this question.

KEY TERMS

COGLAB EXPERIMENTS Numbers in parentheses refer to the experiment number in CogLab.

Pool Photograph/Corbis

This famous student is Prince William, studying in the library at St. Andrews University in Scotland, where he received a degree in geography in 2005. No matter who you are, being a student involves taking in information and being able to remember it later. This chapter describes encoding—how to get information into memory—and retrieval—how to get it out later. Encoding and retrieval can be described in terms of both psychological and physiological processes. Research on these processes has resulted in insights about ways to study more effectively.

Long-Term Memory: Encoding, Retrieval, and Consolidation

▶ What is the best way to store
information in long-term
memory? (180)

▶ What are some techniques
we can use to help us get
information out of long-term
memory when we need it? (187)

▶ How is it possible that a lifetime
of experiences and accumulated
knowledge can be stored in
neurons? (193)

▶ How can the results of
memory research be used to
create more effective study
techniques? (202)

In my students' "top 10" list of what they use memory for (Chapter 5, page 121), we saw that remembering material for exams was at the top of the list. Although uses for memory extend far beyond studying for exams, thinking about studying is a good way to begin our discussion of some of the things we need to explain about long-term memory (LTM).

When you study, one of your goals is to get information into LTM. We saw in Chapter 5, when we described Rachel ordering pizza, that the process of acquiring information and transferring it into LTM is called **encoding**. Notice that the term *encoding* is similar to the term *coding* that we discussed in relation to STM and LTM in Chapter 6. Some authors use these terms interchangeably. We have used the term *coding* to refer to the *form* in which information is represented. For example, a word can be coded visually or by its sound or by its meaning. We will use the term *encoding* to refer to the *process* used to get information into LTM. For example, a word can be encoded by repeating it over and over, by thinking of other words that rhyme with it, or by using it in a sentence. One of the main messages in this chapter is that some methods of encoding are more effective than others.

Imagine that you've just finished studying for an exam and are pretty sure that you have encoded the material that is likely to be on the exam into your LTM. But the moment of truth occurs when you are in the exam and you have to remember some of this information to answer a question. This remembering involves accessing some of the information that you've encoded and transferring it from LTM into working memory to become consciously aware of it. This process of transferring information from LTM to working memory is called **retrieval**. It is, of course, essential to your success on the exam, because even if information is in LTM, it doesn't help you answer the exam question if you can't retrieve it. One of the main factors that determines whether you can retrieve information from LTM is the way that information was encoded when you learned it. In the next section, we will focus on how information is encoded into LTM. We will then consider retrieval and how it relates to encoding.

Encoding: Getting Information Into Long-Term Memory

There are a number of ways of getting information into long-term memory, some of which are more effective than others. One example is provided by different ways of rehearsing information. Consider, for example, holding a phone number in your memory by repeating it over and over. If you do this without any consideration of meaning or making connections with other information, you are engaging in **maintenance rehearsal**. Typically, this type of rehearsal results in poor memory, so you don't remember the number when you want to call it again later.

But what if, instead of mindlessly repeating the phone number, you find a way to relate it to something meaningful. As it turns out, the first three numbers are the same as your phone number, and the last four just happen to be the year you were born! Coincidence as this may be, it provides an example of being able to remember the number by considering meaning or making connections to other information. When you do that, you are engaging in **elaborative rehearsal**. Typically, this type of rehearsal results in better memory than maintenance rehearsal.

This contrast between maintenance rehearsal and elaborative rehearsal is one example of how encoding can influence the ability to retrieve memories. We will now consider a number of other examples, many of which show that better memory is associated with encoding that is based on meaning and making connections.

LEVELS OF PROCESSING THEORY

An early idea linking the type of encoding to retrieval, proposed by Fergus Craik and Robert Lockhart (1972), is called **levels of processing theory**. According to levels of processing theory, memory depends on the **depth of processing** that an item receives. Depth of processing distinguishes between *shallow processing* and *deep processing*. **Shallow processing** involves little attention to meaning, as when a phone number is repeated over and over or attention is focused on a word's physical features such as whether it is printed in lowercase or capital letters. **Deep processing** involves close attention, focusing on an item's meaning and relating it to something else. According to levels of processing theory, deep processing results in better memory than shallow processing.

In an experiment testing memory following different levels of processing, Craik and Endel Tulving (1975) presented words to subjects and asked them three different types of questions:

1. A question about the physical features of the word. For example, subjects see the word *bird* and are asked whether it is printed in capital letters (**Figure 7.1a**).

2. A question about rhyming. For example, subjects see the word *train* and are asked if it rhymes with the word *pain*.

3. A fill-in-the-blanks question. For example, subjects see the word *car* and are asked if it fits into the sentence "He saw a _____ on the street."

The three types of questions were designed to create different levels of processing: (1) physical features = shallow processing; (2) rhyming = deeper processing; (3) fill in the blanks = deepest processing. After subjects responded to these three types of questions, they were given a memory test to see how well they recalled the words. The results, shown in **Figure 7.1b**, indicate that deeper processing is associated with better memory.

The idea of levels of processing motivated a great deal of research but became less popular when it became apparent that it was difficult to define exactly what depth of processing is. For example, how do we know that Craik and Tulving's fill-in-the-blanks task results in deeper processing than the rhyming task? You might say that deeper processing for the fill-in-the-blanks task is indicated by Craik and Tulving's finding that this task results in better memory. But this is an example of circular reasoning: Defining a procedure as deeper because it results in better memory and then using that procedure to show that deeper processing results in better memory doesn't really prove anything. What is needed is a way to define depth of processing that is independent of the memory test, but such a definition does not exist.

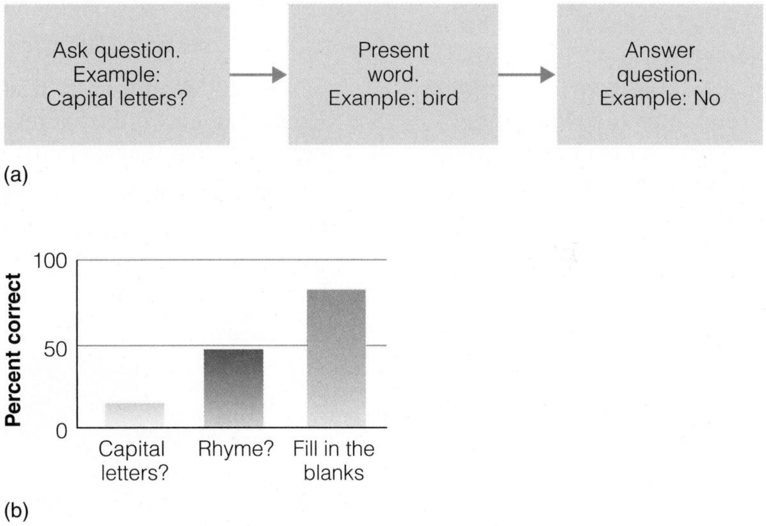

Figure 7.1 (a) Sequence of events in Craik and Tulving's (1975) experiment. (b) Results of this experiment. Deeper processing (fill-in-the-blanks question) is associated with better memory. © Cengage Learning

Even though the term *levels of processing* is rarely used by present-day memory researchers, the basic idea behind levels of processing theory—that memory retrieval is affected by how items are encoded—is still widely accepted, and a great deal of research has demonstrated this relationship. For example, research at about the same time that levels of processing theory was proposed showed that forming images can improve memory for word pairs.

FORMING VISUAL IMAGES

Gordon Bower and David Winzenz (1970) decided to test whether using visual imagery—"images in the head" that connect words visually—can create connections that enhance memory. They used a procedure called **paired-associate learning**, in which a list of word pairs is presented. Later, the first word of each pair is presented, and the subject's task is to remember the word it was paired with.

Bower and Winzenz presented a list of 15 pairs of nouns, such as *boat–tree*, to subjects for 5 seconds each. One group was told to silently repeat the pairs as they were pre-

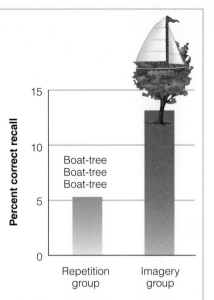

Figure 7.2 Results of the Bower and Winzenz (1970) experiment. Subjects in the repetition group repeated word pairs. Subjects in the imagery group formed images representing the pairs. © Cengage Learning

sented, and another group was told to form a mental picture in which the two items were interacting. When subjects were later given the first word and asked to recall the second one for each pair, the subjects who had created images remembered more than twice as many words as the subjects who had just repeated the word pairs (**Figure 7.2**).

LINKING WORDS TO YOURSELF

Another example of how memory is improved by encoding is the **self-reference effect**: Memory is better if you are asked to relate a word to yourself. T. B. Rogers and coworkers (1977) demonstrated this by using the same procedure Craik and Tulving had used in their depth-of-processing experiment. The design of Rogers's experiment is shown in **Figure 7.3a**. Subjects read a question for 3 seconds and then saw a word. They answered "yes" if the word was the answer to the question and "no" if it wasn't. In the example in **Figure 7.3a**, the question is "Describes you?" Subjects would respond "yes" to the word *shy* if they saw themselves as shy. Here are examples of all four types of questions, along with a sample word:

1. Question: "Printed in small case?" (Physical characteristics of word) Word: *happy*
2. Question: "Rhymes with *happy*?" (Rhyming) Word: *snappy*
3. Question: "Means the same as *happy*?" (Meaning) Word: *upbeat*
4. Question: "Describes you?" (Self-reference) Word: *happy*

When Rogers then tested his subjects' recall, he obtained the results shown in **Figure 7.3b** for words that resulted in a "yes" response. Subjects were more likely to remember words that they had rated as describing themselves.

Why are subjects more likely to remember words they connect to themselves? One possible explanation is that the words become linked to something the subjects know well—themselves. Generally, statements that result in richer, more detailed representations in a person's mind result in better memory.

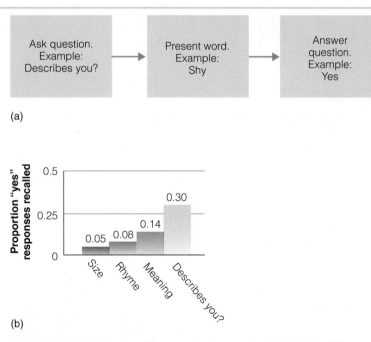

Figure 7.3 (a) Sequence of events in Rogers et al.'s (1977) self-reference experiment. This is the same as the design of Craik and Tulving's (1975) experiment shown in **Figure 7.1**, but the questions refer to the person being tested. (b) Results of the experiment. *(Source: Based on T. B. Rogers, N. A. Kuiper, & W. S. Kirker, Self-reference and the encoding of personal information,* Journal of Personality and Social Psychology, 35, *677–688, 1977.)*

GENERATING INFORMATION

Generating material yourself, rather than passively receiving it, enhances learning and retention. Norman Slameka and Peter Graf (1978) demonstrated this effect, called the **generation effect**, by having subjects study a list of word pairs in two different ways:

1. *Read group*: Read these pairs of related words. king–crown; horse–saddle; lamp–shade; etc.
2. *Generate group*: Fill in the blank with a word that is related to the first word. king–cr _____; horse–sa _____; lamp–sh _____; etc.

After either reading the pairs of words (read group) or generating the list of word pairs based on the word and first two letters of the second word (generate group), subjects were presented with the first word in each pair and were told to indicate the word that went with it. Subjects who had *generated* the second word in each pair were able to reproduce 28 percent more word pairs than subjects who had just *read* the word pairs. You might guess that this finding has some important implications for studying for exams. We will return to this idea later in the chapter.

ORGANIZING INFORMATION

Folders on your computer's desktop, computerized library catalogs, and tabs that separate different subjects in your notebook are all designed to organize information so it can be accessed more efficiently. The memory system also uses organization to access information. This has been shown in a number of ways.

DEMONSTRATION
READING A LIST

Get paper and pen ready. Read the following words, then cover them and write down as many as you can.

apple, desk, shoe, sofa, plum, chair, cherry, coat, lamp, pants, grape, hat, melon, table, gloves

STOP! Cover the words and write down the ones you remember, before reading further.

Look at the list you created and notice whether similar items (for example, *apple, plum, cherry; shoe, coat, pants*) are grouped together. If they are, your result is similar to the result of research that shows that subjects spontaneously organize items as they recall them (Jenkins & Russell, 1952). One reason for this result is that remembering words in a particular category may serve as a **retrieval cue**—a word or other stimulus that helps a person remember information stored in memory. In this case, a word in a particular category, such as fruits, serves as a retrieval cue for other words in that category. So, remembering the word *apple* is a retrieval cue for other fruits, such as *grape* or *plum*, and therefore creates a recall list that is more organized than the original list that you read.

If words presented randomly become organized in the mind, what happens when words are presented in an organized way during encoding? Gordon Bower and coworkers (1969) answered this question by presenting material to be learned in an "organizational tree," which organized a number of words according to categories. For example, one tree organized the names of different minerals by grouping together precious stones, rare metals, and so on (**Figure 7.4**).

One group of subjects studied four separate trees for minerals, animals, clothing, and transportation for 1 minute each and were then asked to recall as many words as they could from all four trees. In the recall test, subjects tended to organize their

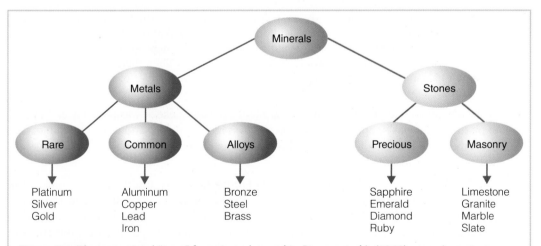

Figure 7.4 The organized "tree" for minerals used in Bower et al.'s (1969) experiment on the effect of organization on memory. *(Source: G. H. Bower et al., Hierarchical retrieval schemes in recall of categorized word lists, Journal of Verbal Learning and Verbal Behavior, 8, 323–343, Figure 1. Copyright © 1969 Elsevier Ltd. Republished with permission.)*

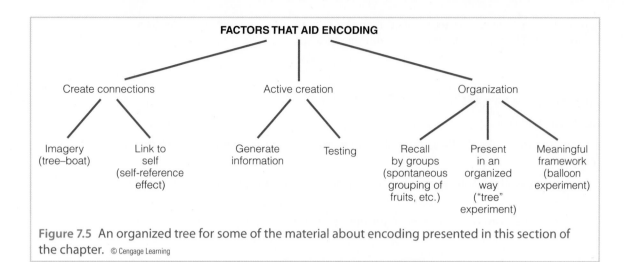

FACTORS THAT AID ENCODING

Create connections
- Imagery (tree–boat)
- Link to self (self-reference effect)

Active creation
- Generate information
- Testing

Organization
- Recall by groups (spontaneous grouping of fruits, etc.)
- Present in an organized way ("tree" experiment)
- Meaningful framework (balloon experiment)

Figure 7.5 An organized tree for some of the material about encoding presented in this section of the chapter. © Cengage Learning

responses in the same way the trees were organized, first saying "minerals," then "metals," then "common," and so on. Subjects in this group recalled an average of 73 words from all four trees.

Another group of subjects also saw four trees, but the words were randomized, so that each tree contained a random assortment of minerals, animals, clothing, and transportation. These subjects were able to remember only 21 words from all four trees. Thus, organizing material to be remembered results in substantially better recall. Perhaps this is something to keep in mind when creating study materials for an exam. You might, for example, find it useful to organize material you are studying for your cognitive psychology exam in trees like the one in **Figure 7.5**.

If presenting material in an organized way improves memory, we might expect that *preventing* organization from happening would *reduce* the ability to remember. This effect was illustrated by John Bransford and Marcia Johnson (1972), who asked their subjects to read the following passage:

> If the balloons popped, the sound wouldn't be able to carry since everything would be too far away from the correct floor. A closed window would also prevent the sound from carrying, since most buildings tend to be well insulated. Since the whole operation depends on the steady flow of electricity, a break in the middle of the wire would also cause problems. Of course, the fellow could shout, but the human voice is not loud enough to carry that far. An additional problem is that the string could break on the instrument. Then there would be no accompaniment to the message. It is clear that the best situation would involve less distance. Then there would be fewer potential problems. With face to face contact, the least number of things could go wrong. (p. 719)

What was that all about? Although each sentence makes sense, it was probably difficult to picture what was happening, based on the passage. Bransford and Johnson's subjects not only found it difficult to picture what was going on, but they also found it extremely difficult to *remember* this passage.

To make sense of this passage, look at **Figure 7.8** on page 187 and then reread the passage. When you do this, the passage makes more sense. Bransford and Johnson's (1972) subjects who saw this picture *before* they read the passage remembered twice as much from the passage as subjects who did not see the picture or subjects who saw the picture *after* they read the passage. The key here is organization. The picture provides a mental framework that helps the reader link one sentence to the next to create a meaningful story. The resulting organization makes this passage easier to comprehend and much easier to remember later. This example illustrates once again that the ability to remember material depends on how that material is programmed into the mind.

RELATING WORDS TO SURVIVAL VALUE

James Nairne (2010) proposes that we can understand how memory works by considering its function, because, through the process of evolution, memory was shaped to increase the ability to survive. The following memory demonstration is based on this idea.

DEMONSTRATION
REMEMBERING LISTS

Part 1. Cover the list below and then uncover each word one by one. Your task is to count the number of vowels in each word and then go right on to the next one. Once you get to the end of the list, cover it and follow the instructions at the end of the list.

chair

mathematics

elephant

lamp

car

elevator

thoughtful

cactus

Instructions: With the list covered, count backward by 3s from 100. When you get to 76, write down the words you remember. Do that now.

Part 2. Cover the list below and uncover each word one by one as you did in the previous part. This time, imagine that you are stranded in the grasslands of a foreign land without any basic survival materials. Rate on a scale of 1 to 5 how relevant each word below would be for finding steady supplies of food and water and protection from predators (1 = totally irrelevant; 5 = extremely relevant). When you get to the end of the list, follow the instructions.

umbrella

exercise

forgiveness

rock

hamburger

sunlight

coffee

bottle

Instructions: With the list covered, count backward by 3s from 99. When you reach 75, write down the words you remember. Do that now.

Which procedure resulted in better memory—counting the number of vowels or rating an item's survival value? When Nairne and coworkers (2007, 2008) ran experiments similar to this (involving longer lists of words), they found that linking words to survival created memory that was not only better than memory created by counting vowels but was also better than memory achieved by the "elaborative" tasks we have described such as forming visual images, linking words to oneself, and generating information. Whether this advantage is due to evolution is debated among memory researchers, but there is no question that relating words to something meaningful and potentially important like survival does enhance memory (also see Klein et al., 2011).

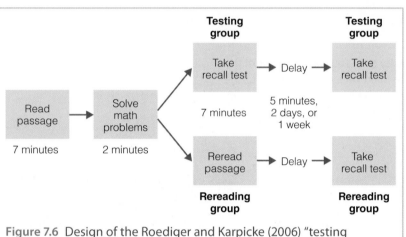

Figure 7.6 Design of the Roediger and Karpicke (2006) "testing effect" experiment. © Cengage Learning

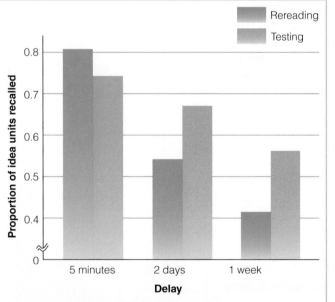

Figure 7.7 Results of the Roediger and Karpicke (2006) experiment. Note that at longer time intervals after learning, the performance of the testing group is better than the performance of the rereading group. *(Source: H. L. Roediger & J. D. Karpicke, Test-enhanced learning: Taking memory tests improves long-term retention, Psychological Science, 17, 249–255, 2006. Reprinted by permission of SAGE Publications.)*

RETRIEVAL PRACTICE

As we will see when we consider study techniques at the end of this chapter, many students prepare for tests by rereading their notes or information they have highlighted in their text (Karpicke et al., 2009). However, recent research shows that practicing retrieval of information by making up and answering practice test questions results in better memory than rereading the information (Karpicke, 2012).

Henry Roediger and Jeffrey Karpicke (2006) demonstrated the advantages of practice testing using the experimental design in **Figure 7.6**. In the first phase of the experiment, college students read prose passages for 7 minutes followed by a 2-minute break during which they solved math problems. Then one group (the testing group) took a 7-minute recall test in which they were asked to write down as much of the passage as they could remember, in no particular order. The other group (the rereading group) were given 7 minutes to reread the material.

In the second phase of the experiment, which occurred after a delay of either 5 minutes, 2 days, or 1 week, all subjects were given the recall test in which they wrote down what they remembered from the passage. The results, in **Figure 7.7**, show that there was little difference between the rereading and testing groups after the 5-minute delay but that after 1 week, the testing group's performance was much better than the rereading group's. This enhanced performance due to retrieval practice is called the **testing effect**. It has been demonstrated in a large number of experiments, both in the laboratory and in classroom settings (Karpicke et al., 2009). For example, testing resulted in better performance than rereading for eighth-grade students' performance on a history test (Carpenter et al., 2009) and for college students' performance on an exam in a brain and behavior course (McDaniel et al., 2007).

Table 7.1 lists all of the examples we have described of encoding methods that increase memory. What do these procedures have in common? Practicing retrieval and generating information both involve actively creating and recreating material. Similarities between the other procedures are not as obvious, but it is probably accurate to say that each, in its own way, increases the richness of representation in memory by providing connections between the material to be remembered and other material in memory. For example, when material is organized, it becomes easier to form links between items (such as *apple, grape,* and *plum*) in a list. What all this means is that there is a close relationship between encoding and retrieval. We will consider further evidence for this connection as we discuss retrieval in the next section.

Table 7.1: Encoding Procedures That Affect Retrieval

CONDITION	EXPERIMENT/RESULT
Forming visual images	Pairs of words are remembered better if images are formed (compared to just reading word pairs).
Linking words to yourself	Words associated with yourself are remembered better (self-reference effect).
Generating information	Memory is better if the second word of a word pair is generated by the person, compared to just being presented with the word (generation effect).
Organizing information	Studying information that is organized, as in a "tree," results in better memory. Presenting information so organization is difficult ("balloon" story) results in poor memory.
Relating words to survival value	Memory is enhanced by relating words to survival value. This works because it helps link words to something meaningful.
Practicing retrieval	Testing following learning results in better memory than rereading material after learning (testing effect).

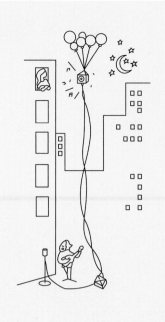

Figure 7.8 Picture used by Bransford and Johnson (1972) to illustrate the effect of organization on memory. *(Source: J. D. Bransford & M. K. Johnson, Contextual prerequisites for understanding: Some investigations of comprehension and recall, Journal of Verbal Learning and Verbal Behavior, 11, 717–726, Figure 1. Copyright © 1972 Elsevier Ltd. Republished with permission.)*

TEST YOURSELF 7.1

1. What is encoding? Retrieval? Why is each necessary for successful memory?

2. What is the difference between elaborative rehearsal and maintenance rehearsal in terms of (a) the procedures associated with each type of rehearsal and (b) their effectiveness for creating long-term memories?

3. What is levels of processing theory? Be sure you understand depth of processing, shallow processing, and deep processing. What would levels of processing theory say about the difference between maintenance rehearsal and elaborative rehearsal?

4. What does it mean to say that levels of processing theory does not define depth of processing independently of memory?

5. Give examples of how memory for a word can be increased by (a) forming visual images, (b) linking words to yourself, (c) generating the word during acquisition, (d) organizing information, (e) rating the word in terms of survival, and (f) practicing retrieval. What do these procedures have in common?

6. What do the results of the procedures in #5 indicate about the relationship between encoding and retrieval?

Retrieval: Getting Information Out of Memory

Before material that has been encoded can be used, it must be retrieved. The process of retrieval is extremely important because many of our failures of memory are failures of retrieval—the information is "in there," but we can't get it out. For example, you've studied hard for an exam but can't come up with an answer when you're taking the exam, only to remember it later after the exam is over. Or you unexpectedly meet someone you have previously met and can't recall the person's name, but it suddenly comes to you as you are talking (or, worse, after the person leaves). In both of these examples, the information you need has been encoded, but you can't retrieve it when you need it.

RETRIEVAL CUES

When we discussed how remembering the word *apple* might serve as a retrieval cue for *grape* (page 183), we defined *retrieval cues* as words or other stimuli that help us remember information stored in our memory. As we now consider these cues in more detail, we will see that they can be provided by a number of different sources.

An experience I had as I was preparing to leave home to go to class illustrates how *location* can serve as a retrieval cue. While I was in my office at home, I made a mental note to be sure to take the DVD on amnesia to school for my cognitive psychology class. A short while later, as I was leaving the house, I had a nagging feeling that I was forgetting something, but I couldn't remember what it was. This wasn't the first time I'd had this problem, so I knew exactly what to do. I returned to my office, and as soon as I got there I remembered that I was supposed to take the DVD. Returning to the place where I had originally thought about taking the disk helped me to retrieve my original thought. My office served as a retrieval cue for remembering what I wanted to take to class.

You may have had similar experiences in which returning to a particular place stimulated memories associated with that place. The following description by one of my students illustrates retrieval of memories of childhood experiences.

> When I was 8 years old, both of my grandparents passed away. Their house was sold, and that chapter of my life was closed. Since then I can remember general things about being there as a child, but not the details. One day I decided to go for a drive. I went to my grandparents' old house and I pulled around to the alley and parked. As I sat there and stared at the house, the most amazing thing happened. I experienced a vivid recollection. All of a sudden, I was 8 years old again. I could see myself in the backyard, learning to ride a bike for the first time. I could see the inside of the house. I remembered exactly what every detail looked like. I could even remember the distinct smell. So many times I tried to remember these things, but never so vividly did I remember such detail. (Angela Paidousis)

My experience in my office and Angela's experience outside her grandparents' house are examples of retrieval cues that are provided by returning to the location where memories were initially formed. Many other things besides location can provide retrieval cues. Hearing a particular song can bring back memories for events you might not have thought about for years. Or consider smell. I once experienced a musty smell like the stairwell of my grandparents' house and was instantly transported back many decades to the experience of climbing those stairs as a child. The operation of retrieval cues has also been demonstrated in the laboratory using a technique called *cued recall*.

METHOD
CUED RECALL

We can distinguish two types of recall procedures. In **free recall**, a subject is simply asked to recall stimuli. These stimuli could be words previously presented by the experimenter or events experienced earlier in the subject's life. We have seen how this has been used in many experiments, such as the retrieval practice experiment described on page 186. In **cued recall**, the subject is presented with retrieval cues to aid in recall of the previously experienced stimuli. These cues are typically words or phrases. For example, Endel Tulving and Zena Pearlstone (1966) did an experiment in which they presented subjects with a list of words to remember. The words were drawn from specific categories such as birds (*pigeon, sparrow*), furniture (*chair, dresser*), and professions (*engineer, lawyer*), although the categories were not specifically indicated in the original list. For the memory test, subjects in the free recall group were asked to write down as many words as they could. Subjects in the cued recall group were also asked to recall the words but were provided with the names of the categories, such as "birds," "furniture," and "professions."

The results of Tulving and Pearlstone's experiment demonstrate that retrieval cues aid memory. Subjects in the free recall group recalled 40 percent of the words, whereas subjects in the cued recall group who had been provided with the names of categories recalled 75 percent of the words.

One of the most impressive demonstrations of the power of retrieval cues was provided by Timo Mantyla (1986), who presented his subjects with a list of 504 nouns, such as *banana, freedom,* and *tree.* During this study phase, subjects were told to write three words they associated with each noun. For example, three words for *banana* might be *yellow, bunches,* and *edible.* In the test phase of the experiment, these subjects were presented with the three words they had generated (self-generated retrieval cues) for half the nouns, or with three words that someone else had generated (other-person-generated retrieval cues) for the other half of the nouns. Their task was to remember the noun they had seen during the study phase.

The results indicated that when the self-generated retrieval cues were presented, subjects remembered 91 percent of the words (top bar in **Figure 7.9**), but when the other-person-generated retrieval cues were presented, subjects remembered only 55 percent of the words (second bar in **Figure 7.9**).

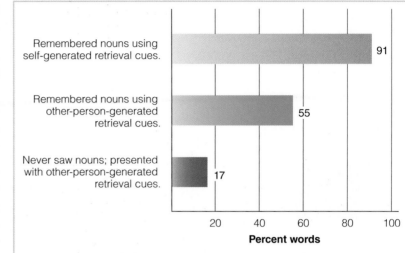

Figure 7.9 Results of Mantyla's (1986) experiment. Memory was best when retrieval cues were created by the person (top bar), and not as good when retrieval cues were created by someone else (middle bar). Control subjects who tried to guess the words based on retrieval cues generated by someone else did poorly (bottom bar). © Cengage Learning

You might think it would be possible to guess *banana* from three properties like *yellow, bunches,* and *edible,* even if you had never been presented with the word *banana.* But when Mantyla ran another control group in which he presented the cue words generated by someone else to subjects who had never seen the 504 nouns, these subjects were able to determine only 17 percent of the nouns. The results of this experiment demonstrate that retrieval cues (the three words) provide extremely effective information for retrieving memories, but that *retrieval cues are significantly more effective when they are created by the person whose memory is being tested.* (Also see Wagenaar, 1986, which describes a study in which Wagenaar was able to remember almost all of 2,400 diary entries he kept over a 6-year period by using retrieval cues.)

MATCHING CONDITIONS OF ENCODING AND RETRIEVAL

The retrieval cues in the two experiments we just described were verbal "hints"—category names like "furniture" in the Tulving and Pearlstone experiment and three-word descriptions created by the subjects in the Mantyla experiment. But we have also seen another kind of "hint" that can help with retrieval: returning to a specific location, such as Angela's grandparents' house or my office.

Let's consider what happened in the office example, in which I needed to return to my office to retrieve my thought about taking a DVD to class. The key to remembering the DVD was that I retrieved the thought "Bring the DVD" by returning to the place where I had originally encoded that thought. This example illustrates the following basic principle: *Retrieval can be increased by matching the conditions at retrieval to the conditions that existed at encoding.*

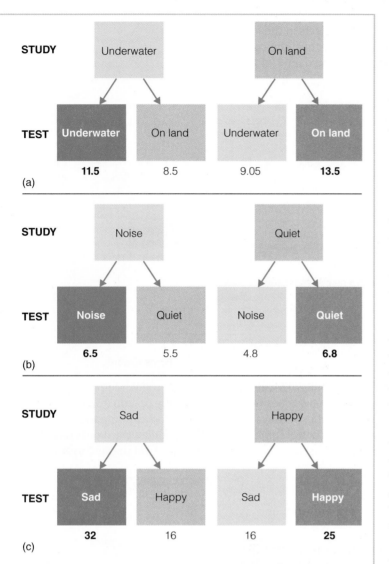

STUDY — Underwater — On land

TEST — **Underwater** 11.5 — On land 8.5 — Underwater 9.05 — **On land** 13.5

(a)

STUDY — Noise — Quiet

TEST — **Noise** 6.5 — Quiet 5.5 — Noise 4.8 — **Quiet** 6.8

(b)

STUDY — Sad — Happy

TEST — **Sad** 32 — Happy 16 — Sad 16 — **Happy** 25

(c)

Figure 7.10 Design and results for (a) Godden and Baddeley's (1975) "diving" experiment; (b) Grant et al.'s (1998) "studying" experiment; (c) Eich and Metcalfe's (1989) "mood" experiment. Results for each test condition are indicated by the number directly under that condition. The matching colors (light green to dark green, and light orange to dark orange) indicate situations in which study and test conditions matched. © 2015 Cengage Learning

We will now describe three specific situations in which retrieval is increased by matching conditions at retrieval to conditions at encoding. These different ways to achieve matching are (1) encoding specificity—matching the *context* in which encoding and retrieval occur; (2) state-dependent learning—matching the *internal mood* present during encoding and retrieval; and (3) transfer-appropriate processing—matching the *task* involved in encoding and retrieval.

ENCODING SPECIFICITY The principle of **encoding specificity** states that we encode information along with its context. For example, Angela encoded many experiences within the context of her grandparents' house. When she reinstated this context by returning to the house many years later, she remembered many of these experiences.

A classic experiment that demonstrates encoding specificity is D. R. Godden and Alan Baddeley's (1975) "diving experiment." In this experiment, one group of subjects put on diving equipment and studied a list of words underwater, and another group studied the words on land (**Figure 7.10a**). These groups were then divided so that half the subjects in the land and water groups were tested for recall on land and half were tested underwater. The results, indicated by the numbers, show that the best recall occurred when encoding and retrieval occurred in the same location.

The results of the diving study, and many others, suggest that a good strategy for test taking would be to study in an environment similar to the environment in which you will be tested. Although this doesn't mean you necessarily have to do all of your studying in the classroom where you will be taking the exam, you might want to duplicate in your study situation some of the conditions that will exist during the exam.

This conclusion about studying is supported by an experiment by Harry Grant and coworkers (1998), using the design in **Figure 7.10b**. Subjects read an article on psychoimmunology while wearing headphones. The subjects in the "quiet" condition heard nothing in the headphones. Subjects in the "noise" condition heard a tape of background noise recorded during lunchtime in a university cafeteria (which they were told to ignore). Half the subjects in each group were then given a short-answer test on the article under the quiet condition, and the other half were tested under the noise condition.

The results indicate that subjects did better when the testing condition matched the study condition. Because your next cognitive psychology exam will take place under quiet conditions, it might make sense to study under quiet conditions. (Interestingly, a number of my students report that having outside stimulation such as music or television present helps them study. This idea clearly violates the principle of encoding specificity. Can you think of some reasons that students might nonetheless say this?)

STATE-DEPENDENT LEARNING Another example of how matching the conditions at encoding and retrieval can influence memory is **state-dependent learning**—learning that is associated with a particular *internal state*, such as mood or state of awareness. According to the principle of state-dependent learning, memory will be better when a person's internal state (mood or awareness) during retrieval matches his or her internal state during encoding. For example, Eric Eich and Janet Metcalfe (1989) demonstrated that memory is better when a person's mood during retrieval matches his or her mood during encoding. They did this by asking subjects to think positive thoughts while listening to "merry" or happy music, or depressing thoughts while listening to "melancholic" or sad music (**Figure 7.10c**). Subjects rated their mood while listening to the music, and the encoding part of the experiment began when their rating reached "very pleasant" or "very unpleasant." Once this occurred, usually within 15 to 20 minutes, subjects studied lists of words while in their positive or negative mood.

After the study session ended, the subjects were told to return in 2 days (although those in the sad group stayed in the lab a little longer, snacking on cookies and chatting with the experimenter while happy music played in the background, so they wouldn't leave the laboratory in a bad mood). Two days later, the subjects returned, and the same procedure was used to put them in a positive or negative mood. When they reached the mood, they were given a memory test for the words they had studied 2 days earlier. The results indicate that they did better when their mood at retrieval matched their mood during encoding (also see Eich, 1995).

The two ways of matching encoding and retrieval that we have described so far have involved matching the physical situation (encoding specificity) or an internal feeling (state-dependent learning). Our next example involves matching the type of *cognitive task* at encoding and retrieval.

MATCHING THE COGNITIVE TASK: TRANSFER-APPROPRIATE PROCESSING Donald Morris and coworkers (1977) did an experiment that showed that retrieval is better if the same cognitive tasks are involved during both encoding and retrieval. The procedure for their experiment was as follows:

Part I. Encoding

Subjects heard a sentence with one word replaced by "blank" and 2 seconds later they heard a target word. There were two encoding conditions. In the *meaning condition*, the task was to answer "yes" or "no" based on the *meaning* of the word when it filled in the blank. In the *rhyming condition*, subjects answered "yes" or "no" based on the *sound* of the word. Here are some examples:

Meaning Condition

1. Sentence: The *blank* had a silver engine.

    Target word: *train*　　　　　　　Correct answer: "yes"

2. Sentence: The *blank* walked down the street.

    Target word: *building*　　　　　　Correct answer: "no"

Rhyming Condition

1. Sentence: *Blank* rhymes with pain.

    Target word: *Train*　　　　　　　Correct answer: "yes"

2. Sentence: *Blank* rhymes with car.

    Target word: *Building*　　　　　　Correct answer: "no"

The important thing about these two groups of subjects is that they were asked to *process* the words differently. In one case, they had to focus on the word's meaning to answer the question, and in the other case they focused on the word's sound.

Part II. Retrieval

The question Morris was interested in was how the subjects' ability to retrieve the target words would be affected by the way they processed the words during the retrieval part of the experiment. There were a number of different conditions in this part of the experiment, but we are going to focus on what happened when subjects were required to process words in terms of their sounds.

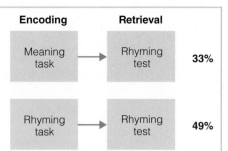

Encoding	Retrieval	
Meaning task	→ Rhyming test	33%
Rhyming task	→ Rhyming test	49%

Figure 7.11 Design and results for the Morris et al. (1977) experiment. Subjects who did a rhyming-based encoding task did better on the rhyming test than subjects who did a meaning-based encoding task. This result would not be predicted by levels of processing theory but is predicted by the principle that better retrieval occurs if the encoding and retrieval tasks are matched. © Cengage Learning

Subjects in both the meaning group and the rhyming group were presented with a series of test words, one by one. Some of the test words rhymed with target words presented during encoding; some did not. Their task was to answer "yes" if the test word rhymed with one of the target words and "no" if it didn't. In the examples below, notice that the test words were always different from the target word.

Test word: *rain*   Answer: "yes" (because it rhymes with the previously presented target word *train*)

Test word: *building*   Answer: "no" (because it doesn't rhyme with any of the target words that were presented during encoding)

The key result of this experiment was that the subjects' retrieval performance depended on whether the retrieval task matched the encoding task. As shown in Figure 7.11, subjects who had focused on rhyming during encoding remembered more words than subjects who had focused on meaning. Thus, subjects who had focused on the word's *sound* during the first part of the experiment did better when the test involved focusing on sound. This result—better performance when the *type of processing* matches in encoding and retrieval—is called **transfer-appropriate processing**.

Transfer-appropriate processing is like encoding specificity and state-dependent learning because it demonstrates that matching conditions during encoding and retrieval improves performance. But, in addition, the result of this experiment has important implications for the levels of processing theory discussed earlier. Remember that the main idea behind levels of processing theory is that deeper processing leads to better encoding and, therefore, better retrieval. Levels of processing theory would predict that subjects who were in the meaning group during encoding would experience "deeper" processing, so they should perform better. Instead, the rhyming group performed better. Thus, in addition to showing that matching the tasks at encoding and retrieval is important, Morris's experiment shows that deeper processing at encoding does not always result in better retrieval, as proposed by levels of processing theory.

Our approach to encoding and retrieval has so far focused on behavioral experiments that consider how conditions of encoding and retrieval affect memory. But there is another approach to studying encoding and retrieval that focuses on physiology. In the rest of this chapter, we will look "under the hood" of memory to consider how physiological changes that occur during encoding influence our ability to retrieve memory for an experience later.

TEST YOURSELF 7.2

1. Retrieval cues are a powerful way to improve the chances that we will remember something. Why can we say that memory performance is better when you use a word in a sentence, create an image, or relate it to yourself, all techniques involving retrieval cues?

2. What is cued recall? Compare it to free recall.

3. Describe the Tulving and Pearlstone cued recall experiment and Mantyla's experiment in which he presented 600 words to his subjects. What was the procedure and what was the result for each experiment, and what does each tell us about retrieval?

4. What is encoding specificity? Describe Baddeley and Godden's "diving" experiment and Grant's studying experiment. What does each one illustrate about encoding specificity? About cued recall?

5. What is state-dependent learning? Describe Eich's experiment.

6. Describe Morris's experiment. What aspect of encoding and retrieval was Morris studying? What implications do the results of this experiment have for matching encoding and retrieval? For levels of processing theory?

Consolidation: The Life History of Memories

Memories have a history. Right after an event or learning has occurred, we remember many details of what happened or what we have learned. But with the passage of time and the accumulation of additional experiences, some of these memories are lost, some change their character, and some might end up being changed from what actually happened.

Another observation about memory is that while every experience creates the potential for a new memory, new memories are fragile and can therefore be disrupted. This was first demonstrated experimentally by German psychologists Georg Müller and Alfons Pilzecker (1900; also see Dewar et al., 2007), who did an experiment in which two groups of subjects learned lists of nonsense syllables. The "immediate" group learned one list and then immediately learned a second list. The "delay" group learned the first list and then waited for 6 minutes before learning the second list (**Figure 7.12**). When recall for the first list was measured, subjects in the delay group remembered 48 percent of the syllables, but subjects in the immediate (no delay) group remembered only 28 percent. Apparently, immediately presenting the second list to the "no delay" group interrupted the forming of a stable memory for the first list. Based on this result, Müller and Pilzecker proposed the term **consolidation**, which is defined as *the process that transforms new memories from a fragile state, in which they can be disrupted, to a more permanent state, in which they are resistant to disruption.*

In the more than 100 years since Müller and Pilzecker's pioneering experiment, researchers have discovered a great deal about the mechanisms responsible for consolidation and have distinguished two types, based on mechanisms that involve both synapses and neural circuits. Remember from Chapter 2 that synapses are the small spaces between the end of one neuron and the cell body or dendrite of another neuron (see **Figure 2.5**, page 30), and that when signals reach the end of a neuron, they cause neurotransmitters to be released onto the next neuron. Neural circuits are interconnected groups of neurons. **Synaptic consolidation**, which takes place over minutes or hours, involves structural changes at synapses. **Systems consolidation**, which takes place over months or even years, involves the gradual reorganization of neural circuits within the brain (Nader & Einarsson, 2010).

The fact that synaptic consolidation is relatively fast and systems consolidation is slower doesn't mean that we should think of them as two stages of a process that occur one after the other, like short-term memory and long-term memory in the modal model of memory (**Figure 5.2**). It is more accurate to think of them as occurring together, as shown in **Figure 7.13**, but at different speeds and at different levels of the nervous system. When something happens, a process is triggered that causes changes at the synapse. Meanwhile, a longer-term process begins that involves reorganization of neural circuits. Thus, synaptic and systems consolidation are processes that occur simultaneously—one that works rapidly, at the level of the synapse, and another that works more slowly, at the level of neural circuits.

SYNAPTIC CONSOLIDATION: EXPERIENCE CAUSES CHANGES AT THE SYNAPSE

According to an idea first proposed by the Canadian psychologist Donald Hebb (1948), learning and memory are represented in the brain by physiological changes that take place at the synapse. Let's assume that a particular experience causes nerve impulses to travel down the axon of neuron A in **Figure 7.14a**, and when these impulses reach the synapse, neurotransmitter is released onto neuron B. Hebb's idea was that

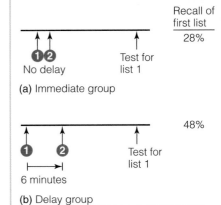

Figure 7.12 Procedure for Müller and Pilzecker's experiment. (a) In the immediate (no delay) condition, subjects used the first list (1) and then immediately learned the second list (2). (b) In the delay condition, the second list was learned after a 6-minute delay. Numbers on the right indicate the percentage of items from the first list recalled when memory for that list was tested later. © Cengage Learning

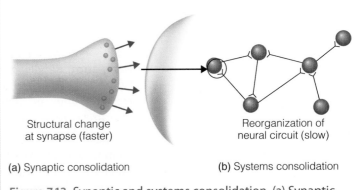

(a) Synaptic consolidation   (b) Systems consolidation

Figure 7.13 Synaptic and systems consolidation. (a) Synaptic consolidation involves changes at the synapses. (a) Systems consolidation involves reorganization of neural connections and takes place over a longer time span. © 2015 Cengage Learning

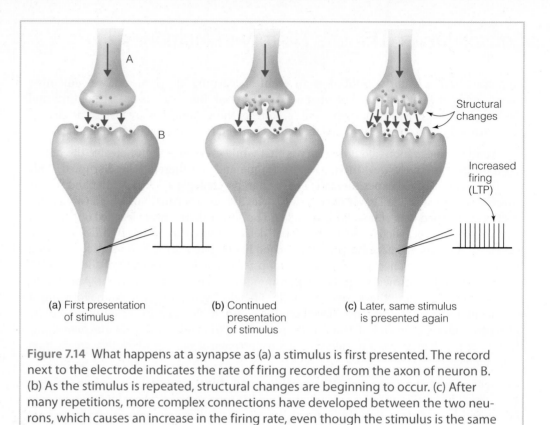

(a) First presentation of stimulus

(b) Continued presentation of stimulus

(c) Later, same stimulus is presented again

Figure 7.14 What happens at a synapse as (a) a stimulus is first presented. The record next to the electrode indicates the rate of firing recorded from the axon of neuron B. (b) As the stimulus is repeated, structural changes are beginning to occur. (c) After many repetitions, more complex connections have developed between the two neurons, which causes an increase in the firing rate, even though the stimulus is the same one that was presented in (a). © Cengage Learning

repeated activity can strengthen the synapse by causing structural changes, greater transmitter release, and increased firing (**Figures 7.14b** and **7.14c**). Hebb also proposed that changes that occur in the hundreds or thousands of synapses that are activated around the same time by a particular experience provide a neural record of the experience. For example, your experience of last New Year's Eve, according to this idea, is represented by the pattern of structural changes that occur at many synapses.

Hebb's proposal that synaptic changes provide a record of experiences became the starting point for modern research on the physiology of memory. Researchers who followed Hebb's lead determined that activity at the synapse causes a sequence of chemical reactions, which result in the synthesis of new proteins that cause structural changes at the synapse like those shown in **Figure 7.14c** (Chklovskii et al., 2004; Kida et al., 2002).

One of the outcomes of structural changes at the synapse is a strengthening of synaptic transmission. This strengthening results in a phenomenon called **long-term potentiation (LTP)**—enhanced firing of neurons after repeated stimulation (Bliss & Lomo, 1973; Bliss et al., 2003; Kandel, 2001). Long-term potentiation is illustrated by the firing records in **Figure 7.14**. The first time neuron A is stimulated, neuron B fires slowly (**Figure 7.14a**). However, after repeated stimulation (**Figure 7.14b**), neuron B fires much more rapidly to the same stimulus (**Figure 7.14c**).

Results such as these indicate how experiences can cause changes at the synapse. Memories for an experience cause changes in many thousands of synapses, and a specific experience is probably represented by the pattern of firing across this group of neurons. This idea of memories being represented by a pattern of firing is similar to the idea of population coding we introduced in Chapter 2 (see page 36).

Early research, inspired by Hebb's pioneering work on the role of the synapse in memory, focused on synaptic consolidation. More recent research has focused on systems consolidation, investigating the role of the hippocampus and cortical areas in the formation of memories.

SYSTEMS CONSOLIDATION: THE HIPPOCAMPUS AND THE CORTEX

The case of H.M., who lost his ability to form new memories after his hippocampus was removed (Chapter 6, page 160), indicates the importance of the hippocampus in forming new memories. Once it became clear that the hippocampus is essential for forming new memories, researchers began determining exactly how the hippocampus responds to stimuli and how it participates in the process of systems consolidation. One outcome of this research was the proposal of the sequence of steps shown in **Figure 7.15**. This picture of the process of consolidation, called the **standard model of consolidation**, proposes that incoming information activates a number of areas in the cortex (**Figure 7.15a**). Activation is distributed across the cortex because memories typically involve many sensory and cognitive areas. For example, your memory for last New Year's Eve could include sights, sounds, and possibly smells, as well as emotions you were feeling and thoughts you were thinking at the stroke of midnight. To deal with the fact that the activity resulting from this experience is distributed across many cortical areas, the cortex communicates with the hippocampus, as indicated by the colored lines in **Figure 7.15a**. The hippocampus coordinates the activity of the different cortical areas, which, at this point, are not yet connected in the cortex.

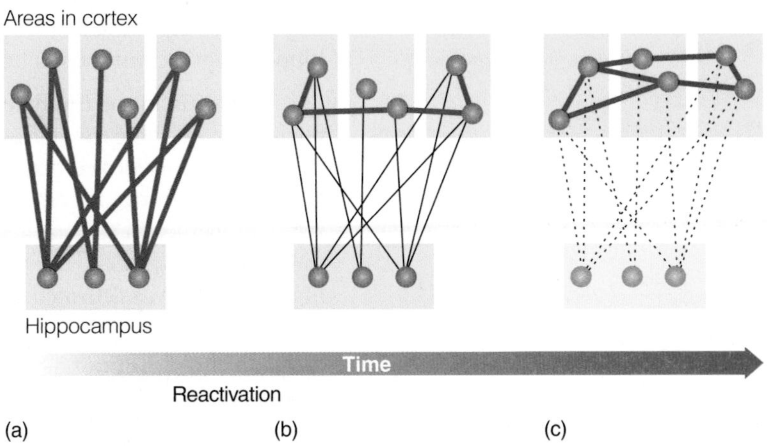

The major mechanism of consolidation is **reactivation**, a process in which the hippocampus replays the neural activity associated with a memory. During reactivation, activity occurs in the network connecting the hippocampus and the cortex (**Figure 7.15b**), and this activity helps form direct connections between the various cortical areas (**Figure 7.15c**). This way of thinking about the interaction between the hippocampus and the cortex pictures the hippocampus as acting like a "glue" that binds together the representations of memory from different cortical areas.

This standard model was based partially on observations of memory loss caused by trauma or injury. It is well known that head trauma, as might be experienced by a football player taking a hard hit as he runs downfield, can cause a loss of memory. Thus, as the player is sitting on the bench after the impact, he might not be aware of what happened during the seconds or minutes before getting hit. This loss of memory for events that occurred before the injury, called **retrograde amnesia**, can extend back minutes, hours, or even years, depending on the nature of the injury.

Figure 7.16 illustrates a characteristic of retrograde amnesia called **graded amnesia**—the amnesia tends to be most severe for events that happened just before the injury and to become less severe for earlier events. This gradual decrease in amnesia corresponds, according to the standard model, to the changes in connections between the hippocampus and cortical areas shown in **Figures 7.15b** and **7.15c**; as time passes after an event, connections between the cortical areas are formed and strengthened, and the connections between the hippocampus and cortex weaken and eventually vanish. Thus, according to the standard model

Figure 7.15 Sequence of events that occur during consolidation, according to the standard model of consolidation. (a) Connections between the cortex and the hippocampus are initially strong. (b) As time passes, activity occurs between the hippocampus and the cortex, a process called reactivation. (c) Over time, connections are formed between cortical areas, and the connections between hippocampus and cortex are weakened and eventually vanish.

(Source: Adapted from P. W. Frankland & B. Bontempi, The organization of recent and remote memories, Neuroscience, 6, 119–130, 2005.)

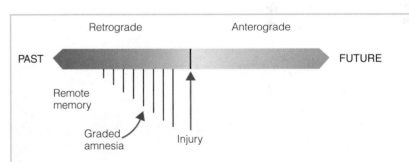

Figure 7.16 Anterograde amnesia is amnesia for events that occur after an injury (the inability to form new memories). Retrograde amnesia is amnesia for events that happened before the injury (the inability to remember information from the past). The vertical lines, which symbolize the amount of retrograde amnesia, indicate that amnesia is more severe for events or learning that was closer in time leading up to the injury. This is the graded nature of retrograde amnesia. © Cengage Learning

of consolidation, the hippocampus is strongly active when memories are first formed and initially recalled but becomes less involved as memories are consolidated, until eventually the connections between cortical areas themselves are sufficient to retrieve *remote memories*—memories for events that occurred long ago.

Most researchers accept that both the hippocampus and the cortex are involved in consolidation. There is, however, some disagreement regarding whether the hippocampus is important only at the beginning of consolidation, as depicted in **Figure 7.15**, or whether the hippocampus continues to be important, even for remote memories.

According to the **multiple trace model of consolidation**, the hippocampus is involved in retrieval of episodic memories, even if they originated long ago (Nadel & Moscovitch, 1997). Evidence for this idea comes from experiments like one by Asaf Gilboa and coworkers (2004), who elicited recent and remote episodic memories by showing subjects photographs of themselves engaging in various activities that were taken at times ranging from very recently to the distant past, when they were 5 years old. The results of this experiment showed that the hippocampus was activated during retrieval of both recent and remote episodic memories.

But this doesn't mean that the hippocampus is involved in all aspects of memory retrieval. Indre Viskontas and coworkers (2009) demonstrated that the response of the hippocampus can change over time. These researchers had subjects view pairs of stimuli, such as the alligator and the candle in **Figure 7.17a**, while undergoing fMRI in a scanner. Subjects were told to imagine the items in each pair interacting with each other. Then 10 minutes later and 1 week later, subjects saw the original pairs plus some others they had not seen and were told to respond to each pair in one of three ways: (1) *remember* (R), meaning "I remember seeing the pair when it was originally presented"; (2) *know* (K), meaning "The pair definitely looks familiar, but I don't remember when I was originally seeing it"; or (3) *don't*, meaning "I don't remember or know the stimuli." As we saw in Chapter 6, when we described the remember/know procedure (see Method, page 165), *remember* responses indicate episodic memory and *know* responses indicate semantic memory.

The behavioral results, shown in **Figure 7.17b**, show that there were more *remember* (episodic) responses than *know* (semantic) responses after 10 minutes, but that only half of the *remember* responses remained after 1 week. This is exactly what we would expect from other research showing that memories lose their episodic character over time, which we described in Chapter 6 (page 166) as the semanticization of remote memories.

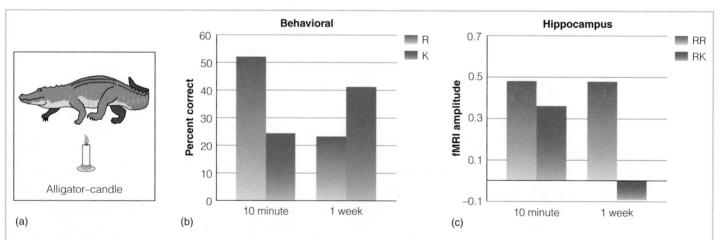

Figure 7.17 Stimulus and results for the Viskontas et al. (2009) experiment. (a) Subjects saw picture pairs like this one while being scanned. (b) When asked to remember the pairs, the *remember* response, which corresponds to episodic memory, was high at 10 minutes, but decreased after 1 week. (c) Activity of the hippocampus remained the same for pictures that were remembered at both 10 minutes and 1 week (RR), but decreased for pictures for which the *remember* response was absent at 1 week (RK). *(Source: Adapted from I. V. Viskontas, V. A. Carr, S. A. Engel, & B. J. Kowlton, The neural correlates of recollection: Hippocampal activation declines as episodic memory fades, Hippocampus, 19, 265–272, Figures 1, 3, & 6, 2009.)*

But what's happening in the brain as the episodic memories are being lost? Viskontas determined the hippocampus's response for pairs to which subjects responded *remember* both at 10 minutes and at 1 week (RR pairs) and for pairs to which subjects responded *remember* at 10 minutes but *know* at 1 week (RK pairs). The results, in **Figure 7.17c**, are striking: The hippocampus response remained high for RR pairs (the ones that remained episodic at 1 week), but dropped to near zero for RK pairs (the ones that had lost their episodic character at 1 week). What this means is that the hippocampus response does change over time, but only for stimuli that have lost their episodic character.

Thus, the response of the hippocampus decreases over time, as proposed by the standard model of consolidation. However, in contrast to the standard model's claim that the hippocampus is not necessary for the retrieval of remote memories, the decrease in response occurs only for memories that have lost their episodic character and are now more semantic in nature. The fact that the hippocampus remains involved in the retrieval of episodic memories is consistent with the multiple trace model of consolidation (Bonnici et al., 2012; Soderlund et al., 2012; Svoboda & Levine, 2009). Research is continuing regarding the physiological basis of consolidation, with some researchers favoring the standard model and others the multiple trace or other models (Hardt et al., 2013; Smith & Squire, 2009; Squire & Bayley, 2007). In addition to research on different models of consolidation, another active area of research is concerned with the relationship between consolidation and sleep.

CONSOLIDATION AND SLEEP: ENHANCING MEMORY

Hamlet says, in his "To be or not to be" soliloquy, "To sleep, perchance to dream." But memory researchers might modify that statement to read "To sleep, perchance to consolidate memory." Not as poetic as Hamlet's statement perhaps, but recent research supports the idea that while the reactivation process associated with consolidation may begin as soon as a memory is formed, it is particularly strong during sleep.

Steffan Gais and coworkers (2006) tested the idea that sleep enhances consolidation by having high school students learn a list of 24 pairs of English–German vocabulary words. The "sleep" group studied the words and then went to sleep within 3 hours. The "awake" group studied the words and remained awake for 10 hours before getting a night's sleep. Both groups were tested within 24 to 36 hours after studying the vocabulary lists. (The actual experiment involved a number of different "sleep" and "awake" groups in order to control for time of day and other factors we aren't going to consider here.) The results of the experiment, shown in **Figure 7.18**, indicate that students in the sleep group forgot much less material than students in the awake group. Why does going to sleep shortly after learning enhance memory? One reason is that going to sleep eliminates environmental stimuli that might interfere with consolidation. Another reason is that consolidation appears to be enhanced during sleep.

Interestingly, not only is there evidence that consolidation is enhanced during sleep, but there is also evidence that some memories are more likely to be consolidated than others. This was demonstrated in an experiment by Ines Wilhelm and coworkers (2011) in which subjects learned a task and were then told either that they would be tested on the task later or that they would be tested on a different task later. After a night's sleep, subjects in both groups were tested on the task to determine if what they *expected* had any effect on consolidation. (In some experiments, some subjects were tested after staying awake. The memory of these groups was worse than the memory of the sleep groups, as was expected from the results of experiments like the one by Gais, described above. We will focus here on what happened for the subjects who went to sleep.)

One of the tasks in Wilhelm's experiment was a card memory task similar to the game Concentration. Subjects would see an array of gray "cards" on the computer screen, with two turned over to reveal one pair of pictures (**Figure 7.19a**). Subjects saw each card pair twice and then learned the locations by practicing. One card would be "turned over" on the screen, and they indicated where they thought the matching card was located. After receiving the correct answer, they continued practicing until they were able to answer correctly

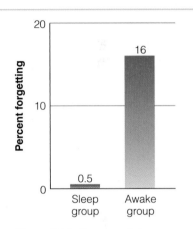

Figure 7.18 Results of the Gais et al. (2007) experiment in which memory for word pairs was tested for two groups. The sleep group went to sleep shortly after learning a list of word pairs. The awake group stayed awake for quite a while after learning the word pairs. Both groups did get to sleep before testing, so they were equally rested before being tested, but the performance of the sleep group was better. © Cengage Learning

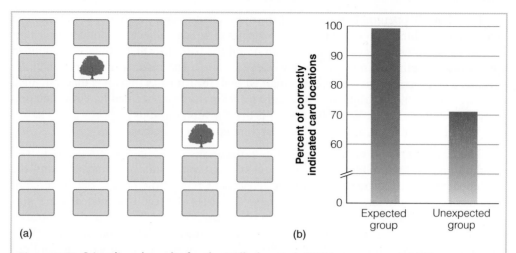

(a)   (b)

Figure 7.19 Stimuli and results for the Wilhelm et al. (2011) experiment. (a) The subjects' task was to remember where each pair of pictures was located. One pair is shown turned over here. (b) After sleeping, the performance of the group that had expected to be tested on the task was better than the performance of the group that did not expect to be tested. This illustrates preferential consolidation for the material that subjects expected would be tested. *(Source: Part b from I. Wilhelm, S. Diekelmann, I. Molzow, A. Ayoub, M. Molle, & J. Born, Sleep selectively enhances memory expected to be of future relevance,* Journal of Neuroscience, 31, *1563–1569, Figure 3a, 2011.)*

60 percent of the time. After their training, they were told either that they would be tested on this task 9 hours later (the *expected group*) or that they would be tested on another task (the *unexpected group*).

Memory performance after a night's sleep, shown in **Figure 7.19b**, indicates that the expected group performed significantly better than the unexpected group. Thus, even though both groups had the same training and received the same amount of sleep, memory for the task was stronger if subjects expected they would be tested. Results such as this suggest that when we sleep after learning, memories that are more important are more likely to be strengthened by consolidation (see also Fischer & Born, 2009; Payne et al., 2008, 2012; Rauchs et al., 2011; Saletin et al., 2011; van Dongen et al., 2012). Thus, we sleep, perchance to selectively consolidate memories for things that might be most useful to remember later!

We have come a long way from Müller and Pilzecker's demonstration of consolidation. But there is one more twist to this story, which involves returning to our original definition of consolidation. Consolidation, according to our definition, is *the process that transforms new memories from a fragile state, in which they can be disrupted, to a more permanent state, in which they are resistant to disruption* (page 193). This definition implies that once memories are consolidated, they become more permanent. As it turns out, this idea of truly permanent memories has been questioned by research that shows that retrieving a memory can cause that memory to become fragile, just as it was when it was first formed.

CONSOLIDATION AND RETRIEVAL: RECONSOLIDATION

Consider the following situation: You are visiting your childhood home. Driving along the roads that lead to your parents' house seems almost automatic, because the route is strongly stamped into your memory. But as you turn onto a street that was part of your old route, you are surprised to find that it is now a dead end. Construction that happened while you were gone has blocked your old route. Eventually, you discover a new route to reach your destination, and—this is the important part—you *update your memory* to form a new map of the route to your parents' home (Bailey & Balsam, 2013).

This example of updating your memory is not unique. It happens all the time. We are constantly learning new things and modifying information stored in memory in order to deal with new circumstances. Thus, although it is useful to be able to remember the past, it is also useful to be able to not let these memories hinder our ability to adapt to new situations.

Recent research, first on rats and then on humans, has suggested a possible mechanism for updating memories. These experiments support the idea that when a memory is retrieved, it becomes fragile, as it was when it was originally formed, and that when it is in this fragile state, it needs to be consolidated again—a process called **reconsolidation**.

The reason this is important is that when the memory has become fragile again, and before it has been reconsolidated, it can be changed or eliminated. According to this idea, retrieving a memory not only puts us in touch with something that happened in the past, but it also opens the door for either modifying or forgetting the memory.

The possibility that retrieved memories can become fragile was demonstrated in an experiment by Karim Nader and coworkers (2000a, 2000b) involving a rat. Nader used classical conditioning (see Chapter 6, page 172) to create a fear response in the rat of "freezing" (not moving) to presentation of a tone. This was achieved by pairing the tone with a shock. Although the tone initially caused no response in the rat, pairing it with the shock caused the tone to take on properties of the shock, so the rat froze in place when the tone was presented alone. Thus, in this experiment, memory for the tone–shock pairing is indicated when the rat freezes to the tone.

The design of the experiment is shown in **Figure 7.20**. In each of the three conditions, the rat receives a tone–shock pairing and is injected with *anisomycin*, an antibiotic that inhibits protein synthesis and so prevents changes at the synapse that are responsible for the formation of new memories. The key to this experiment is *when* the anisomycin is injected. If it is injected before consolidation has occurred, it eliminates memory, but if it is injected after consolidation occurs, it has no effect.

In Condition 1, the rat receives the pairing of the tone and the shock on Day 1, which causes it to freeze. But the anisomycin is injected right away, before consolidation has occurred (**Figure 7.20a**). The fact that the drug has prevented consolidation is indicated by the fact that when the tone is presented on Day 3, the rat doesn't freeze to the tone. That is, it behaves as if it never received the tone–shock pairing.

In Condition 2, the rat receives the pairing of the tone and shock on Day 1, as before, but doesn't receive anisomycin until Day 2, after consolidation has occurred. Thus, when the tone is presented on Day 3, the rat remembers the tone–shock pairing, as indicated by the fact that it freezes to the tone (**Figure 7.20b**).

Condition 3 is the crucial condition, because it creates a situation in which injecting the drug on Day 2 (which had no effect in Condition 2) can eliminate the memory of the tone–shock pairing. This situation is created by presenting the tone on Day 2 to reactivate the rat's memory for the tone–shock pairing. The rat freezes (indicating that memory has occurred) and then the anisomycin is injected. Because the memory was reactivated by presenting the tone, the anisomycin now has an effect. This is indicated by the fact that the rat doesn't freeze when the tone is presented on Day 3.

This result shows that when a memory is reactivated, it becomes fragile, just as it was immediately after it was first formed, and the drug can prevent reconsolidation. Thus, just as the original memory is fragile *until it is consolidated for the first time*, a reactivated memory becomes fragile *until it is reconsolidated*. Looked at in this way, memory becomes susceptible to being changed or disrupted every time it is retrieved. You might think that this is not a good thing. After all, putting your memory at risk of disruption every time you use it doesn't sound particularly useful.

From the driving example at the beginning of this section, however, we can appreciate that being able to update memory can be useful. In fact, updating can be crucial for

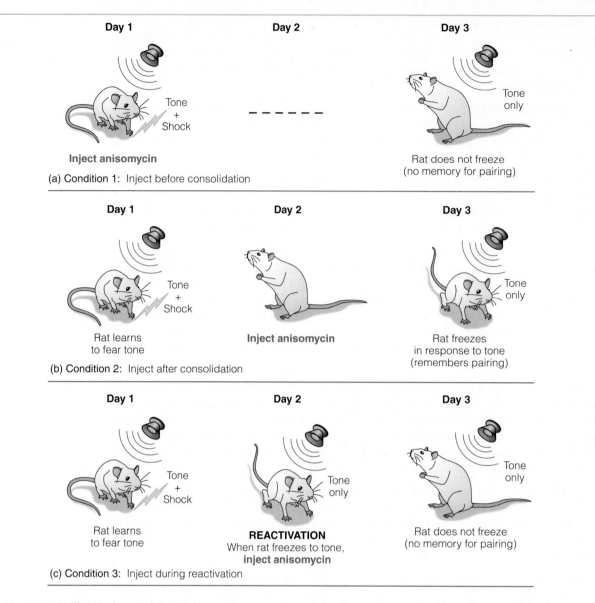

Figure 7.20 The Nader et al. (2000a) experiment on how injecting anisomycin affects fear conditioning. (a) Anisomycin is injected on Day 1, before consolidation, so memory for the tone–shock pairing is not formed. (b) Anisomycin is injected on Day 2, after consolidation, so memory for the tone–shock pairing remains. (c) Anisomycin is injected after reactivation on Day 2, so memory for the tone–shock pairing is eliminated. © Cengage Learning

survival. Consider, for example, an animal version of our driving example: A chipmunk returns to the location of a food source and finds that the food has been moved to a new location nearby. Returning to the original location reactivates the original memory, new information about the change in location updates the memory, and the updated memory is then reconsolidated.

Once Nader demonstrated that reactivated memories become fragile and subject to change, other researchers confirmed this finding, and some researchers looked for evidence of this phenomenon in humans. Almut Hupbach and coworkers (2007) provided evidence for the effect of reactivation in humans using the following procedure: On Day 1, subjects studied a list of words naming everyday objects such as *envelope, teabag,* and *shovel*

(List 1). On Day 2, one group (the reminder group) was reminded of their learning on Day 1 by being asked to remember their training sessions (but without actually recalling the objects). Immediately following this reminder, they learned a new list of objects (List 2). The other group (the no-reminder group) were not reminded of their previous training; they just learned the new list.

To see if having the reminder group think about their learning on Day 1 had any effect, both groups were asked, on Day 3, to remember List 1. The left pair of bars in **Figure 7.21** indicates that the no-reminder group recalled 45 percent of the words from List 1 and mistakenly recalled only 5 percent of the words from List 2. (Remember that their task was to remember only the words from List 1.) The right pair of bars shows that something quite different happened for the reminder group. They recalled 36 percent of the words from List 1, but they also mistakenly recalled 24 percent of the words from List 2.

According to Hupbach, thinking back to the original training session reactivated the memory for List 1, making it vulnerable to being changed. Because subjects immediately learned List 2, some of these new words became integrated into the subjects' memory for List 1. Another way to express this idea is to say that the reminder reactivated memory for List 1 and "opened the door" for changes to occur in the subjects' memory for that list. Thus, in this example, the original memory was not eliminated, but it was changed.

One practical outcome of research on reconsolidation is a possible treatment for posttraumatic stress disorder (PTSD), a condition that occurs when, following a traumatic experience, a person experiences "flashbacks" of the experience, often accompanied by extreme anxiety and physical symptoms. Clinical psychologist Alain Brunet and coworkers (2008) tested the idea that reactivation of a memory followed by reconsolidation can help alleviate these symptoms. The basic method involved is to reactivate the person's memory for the traumatic event and then administer the drug *propranolol*. This drug blocks activation of stress hormone receptors in the amygdala, a part of the brain important for determining the emotional components of memory. This procedure might be equivalent to the administration of anisomycin on Day 2 in Condition 3 of Nader's experiment (**Figure 7.20c**).

Brunet ran two groups. One group of PTSD patients listened to a 30-second recording describing the circumstances of their traumatic experience and received propranolol. Another group listened to the recording describing their experience but received a placebo, which had no active ingredients.

One week later, both groups were told to imagine their traumatic experience while again listening to the 30-second recording. To determine their reaction to imagining their experience, Brunet measured their blood pressure and skin conductance. He found that the propranolol group experienced much smaller increases in heart rate and skin conductance than the placebo group. Apparently, presenting propranolol when the memory was reactivated a week earlier blocked the stress response in the amygdala, and this reduced the emotional reaction associated with remembering the trauma. Brunet has used this procedure to treat patients with PTSD, and many of the patients report significant reductions in their symptoms, even months after the treatment. (See Kindt et al., 2009, and Schiller et al., 2010, for other demonstrations of using reconsolidation to eliminate fear responses in humans.)

Research on reconsolidation and its potential applications is just in its infancy, but from what researchers have learned so far, it appears that our memory is not static or fixed. Rather, it is a "work in progress" that is constantly being constructed and remodeled in response to new learning and changing conditions. We will be describing this aspect of memory in detail in the next chapter, when we consider the creative, constructive properties of memory.

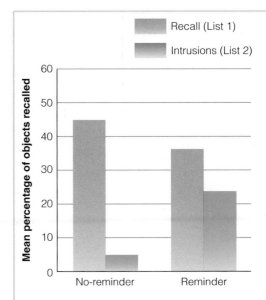

Figure 7.21 Results of Hupbach et al.'s (2007) experiment. The fact that the reminder group had more intrusions supports the idea that reactivation and reconsolidation can affect human memory. *(Source: Based on A. Hupbach, R. Gomez, O. Hardt, & L. Nadel, Reconsolidation of episodic memories: A subtle reminder triggers integration of new information, Learning and Memory, 14, 47–53, 2007.)*

Something to Consider

EFFECTIVE STUDYING

How do you study? Students have developed numerous techniques, which vary depending on the type of material to be studied and what works for a particular student. When students are asked to describe their study techniques, the most popular are highlighting material in text or notes (Bell & Limber, 2010; Gurung et al., 2010) and rereading text or notes (Carrier, 2003; Karpicke et al., 2009; Wissman et al., 2012). Unfortunately, research has generally found that these popular techniques are not very effective (Dunlosky et al., 2013). Apparently, students use highlighting and rereading because they are easy to use, and because they are not aware of more effective methods. We will describe a number of ways of learning material that have been shown to be effective. Even if you think highlighting and rereading work for you, you might want to consider also using one or more of the techniques described below the next time you are studying.

ELABORATE

A process that helps transfer the material you are reading into long-term memory is elaboration—thinking about what you are reading and giving it meaning by relating it to other things that you know. This becomes easier as you learn more because what you have learned creates a structure on which to hang new information.

Techniques based on association, such as creating images that link two things, as in **Figure 7.2**, often prove useful for learning individual words or definitions. For example, when I was first learning the difference between proactive interference (old information interferes with learning new information; see page 128) and retroactive interference (new information interferes with remembering old information; see page 128), I thought of a "pro" football player smashing everything in his path as he runs forward in time, to remind me that proactive interference is the past influencing the present. I no longer need this image to remember what proactive interference is, but it was helpful when I was first learning this concept.

GENERATE AND TEST

The results of research on the generation effect (page 182) and the testing effect (page 186) indicate that devising situations in which you take an active role in creating material is a powerful way to achieve strong encoding and good long-term retrieval.

Testing is actually a form of generation, because it requires active involvement with the material. If you were going to test yourself, where would you get the test questions? One place could be questions that are sometimes provided, such as the Test Yourself questions in this book, or print or electronic study guides. Another way is to make up questions yourself. Because making up the questions involves active engagement with the material, it strengthens encoding of the material. Research has shown that students who read a text with the idea of *making up* questions did as well on an exam as students who read a text with the idea of *answering* questions later, and both groups did better than a group of students who did not create or answer questions (Frase, 1975).

Research has shown that many students believe that reviewing the material is more effective than testing themselves on it; when they do test themselves, it is to determine how they are doing, not as a tool to increase learning (Kornell & Son, 2009). As it turns out, self-testing accomplishes two things. It indicates what you know *and* increases your ability to remember what you know later.

ORGANIZE

The goal of organizing material is to create a framework that helps relate some information to other information to make the material more meaningful and therefore strengthen encoding. Organization can be achieved by making "trees," as in **Figure 7.5**, or outlines or lists that group similar facts or principles together.

Organization also helps reduce the load on your memory. We can illustrate this by looking at a perceptual example. If you see the black and white pattern in **Figure 3.17** (page 65) as unrelated black and white areas, it is extremely difficult to describe what it is. However, once you've seen this pattern as a Dalmatian, it becomes meaningful and therefore much easier to describe and to remember (Wiseman & Neisser, 1974). Organization relates to the phenomenon of chunking that we discussed in Chapter 5. Grouping small elements into larger, more meaningful ones increases memory. Organizing material is one way to achieve this.

TAKE BREAKS

Saying "Take breaks" is another way of saying "Study in a number of shorter study sessions rather than trying to learn everything at once," or "Don't cram." There are good reasons to say these things. Research has shown that memory is better when studying is broken into a number of short sessions, with breaks in between, than when it is concentrated in one long session, even if the total study time is the same. This advantage for short study sessions is called the **spacing effect** (Reder & Anderson, 1982; Smith & Rothkopf, 1984).

Another angle on taking breaks is provided by research that shows that memory performance is enhanced if sleep follows learning (page 197). Although sleeping to avoid studying is probably not a good idea, sleeping soon after studying can improve consolidation, which can result in better memory.

AVOID "ILLUSIONS OF LEARNING"

One of the conclusions of both basic memory research and research on specific study techniques is that some study techniques favored by students may *appear* to be more effective than they actually are. For example, one reason for the popularity of rereading as a study technique is that it can create the illusion that learning is occurring. This happens because reading and rereading material results in greater *fluency*—that is, repetition causes the reading to become easier and easier. But although this enhanced ease of reading creates the illusion that the material is being learned, increased fluency doesn't necessarily translate into better memory for the material.

Another mechanism that creates the illusion of learning is the *familiarity effect*. Rereading causes material to become familiar, so when you encounter it a second or third time, there is a tendency to interpret this familiarity as indicating that you know the material. Unfortunately, recognizing material that is right in front of you doesn't necessarily mean that you will be able to remember it later.

Finally, beware of highlighting. A survey by Sarah Peterson (1992) found that 82 percent of students highlight, and most of them do so while they are reading the material for the first time. The problem with highlighting is that it seems like elaborative processing (you're taking an active role in your reading by highlighting important points), but it often becomes automatic behavior that involves moving the hand, but little deep thinking about the material.

When Peterson compared comprehension for a group of students who highlighted and a group who didn't, she found no difference between the performance of the two groups when they were tested on the material. Highlighting may be a good first step for some people, but it is usually important to go back over what you highlighted using techniques such as elaborative rehearsal or generating questions in order to get that information into your memory.

Looking at all of these techniques, we can see that many of them involve using more effective encoding strategies; elaborating, generating, testing, and organizing all encourage deeper processing of the material you are trying to learn. Making up questions about the material and answering these questions incorporates retrieval into studying. A recent survey of research on many different study techniques concluded that practice testing and distributed practice (taking breaks) are the two most effective study techniques (Dunlosky et al., 2013).

TEST YOURSELF 7.3

1. What is the idea behind the statement "Memories are stored at synapses"? What evidence supports this idea?

2. What is synaptic consolidation? Systems consolidation? How are they related to each other?

3. Describe how the standard model of consolidation explains systems consolidation. What is the multiple trace model of consolidation? Compare it to the standard model.

4. Describe the connection between sleep and consolidation. Be sure you understand the Gais and Wilhelm experiments.

5. What is reconsolidation? What are the implications of the results of experiments that demonstrate reconsolidation?

6. Describe the following five ways of improving the effectiveness of studying: (1) elaborate; (2) generate and test; (3) organize; (4) take breaks; (5) avoid "illusions of learning." How does each technique relate to findings about encoding and retrieval?

CHAPTER SUMMARY

1. Encoding is the process of acquiring information and transferring it into long-term memory (LTM). Retrieval is transferring information from LTM into working memory.

2. Some mechanisms of encoding are more effective than others in transferring information into LTM. Maintenance rehearsal helps maintain information in STM but is not an effective way of transferring information into LTM. Elaborative rehearsal is a better way to establish long-term memories.

3. Levels of processing theory states that memory depends on how information is encoded or programmed into the mind. According to this theory, shallow processing is not as effective as deep processing. An experiment by Craik and Tulving showed that memory was better following deep processing than following shallow processing.

4. The idea of levels of processing, while influential, suffers from the problem of circularity, because it is difficult to define depth of processing independently of memory.

5. Evidence that encoding influences retrieval includes research looking at the effect of (1) forming visual images, (2) linking words to yourself, (3) generating information (the generation effect), (4) organizing information, (5) relating words to survival value, and (6) practicing retrieval (the testing effect).

6. Retrieving long-term memories is aided by retrieval cues. This has been determined by cued recall experiments and experiments in which subjects created retrieval cues that later helped them retrieve memories.

7. Retrieval can be increased by matching conditions at retrieval to conditions that existed at encoding. This is illustrated by encoding specificity, state-dependent learning, and matching type of processing (transfer-appropriate processing).

8. The principle of encoding specificity states that we learn information along with its context. Godden and Baddeley's diving experiment and Grant's studying experiment illustrate the effectiveness of encoding and retrieving information under the same conditions.

9. According to the principle of state-dependent learning, a person's memory will be better when his or her internal state during retrieval matches the state during encoding. Eich's mood experiment supports this idea.

10. Matching types of processing refers to the finding that memory performance is enhanced when the type of coding that occurs during acquisition matches the type of retrieval that occurs during a memory test. The results of an experiment by Morris support this idea, which is called transfer-appropriate processing.

11. Consolidation is the process that transforms new memories from a fragile state into a more permanent state. Müller and Pilzecker carried out an early experiment that illustrated how memory is decreased when consolidation is disrupted.

12. Synaptic consolidation involves structural changes at synapses. Systems consolidation involves the gradual recognition of neural circuits.

13. Hebb introduced the idea that the formation of memories is associated with structural changes at the synapse. These structural changes are then translated into enhanced nerve firing, as indicated by long-term potentiation.

14. The standard model of consolidation proposes that memory retrieval depends on the hippocampus during consolidation but that after consolidation is complete, retrieval involves the cortex, and the hippocampus is no longer involved.

15. The multiple trace model states that the hippocampus is involved both when memories are being established and during the retrieval of remote episodic memories.

16. There is evidence supporting the standard model, but recent research indicates that retrieval of episodic memories can involve the hippocampus.

17. Consolidation is facilitated by sleep. There is also evidence that material people expect they will be asked to remember later is more likely to be consolidated during sleep.

18. Recent research indicates that memories can become susceptible to disruption when they are reactivated by retrieval. After reactivation, these memories must be reconsolidated. There is evidence for reconsolidation in humans and for the usefulness of reconsolidation therapy in treating conditions such as posttraumatic stress disorder.

19. Five memory principles that can be applied to studying are (1) elaborate, (2) generate and test, (3) organize, (4) take breaks, and (5) avoid "illusions of learning."

THINK ABOUT IT

1. Describe an experience in which retrieval cues led you to remember something. Such experiences might include returning to a place where your memory was initially formed, being somewhere that reminds you of an experience you had in the past, having someone else provide a "hint" to help you remember something, or reading about something that triggers a memory.

2. How do you study? Which study techniques that you use should be effective, according to the results of memory research? How could you improve your study techniques by taking into account the results of memory research? (Also see Preface to Students, pages xxvi–xxvii.)

KEY TERMS

Consolidation, 193

Cued recall, 188

Deep processing, 181

Depth of processing, 180

Elaborative rehearsal, 180

Encoding, 180

Encoding specificity, 190

Free recall, 188

Generation effect, 182

Graded amnesia, 195

Levels of processing theory, 180

Long-term potentiation (LTP), 194

Maintenance rehearsal, 180

Multiple trace model of consolidation, 196

Paired-associate learning, 181

Reactivation, 195

Reconsolidation, 199

Retrieval, 180

Retrieval cue, 183

Retrograde amnesia, 195

Self-reference effect, 182

Shallow processing, 181

Spacing effect, 203

Standard model of consolidation, 195

State-dependent learning, 190

Synaptic consolidation, 193

Systems consolidation, 193

Testing effect, 186

Transfer-appropriate processing, 192

COGLAB EXPERIMENTS Number in parentheses refers to the experiment number in CogLab.

Encoding Specificity (28)

Levels of Processing (29)

Production Effect (30)

Von Restorff Effect (32)

These towers of light evoke the memory of the terrorist attack on the World Trade Center on September 11, 2001. This date is etched into the American consciousness, and the events of that day are etched into many people's memories. This chapter considers research on memory for exceptional events such as 9/11, as well as memory for more routine everyday events. This research shows that our memories are not like photographs, accurate and unchanging, but are more like "works in progress," affected not only by the event to be remembered but also by stored knowledge and things that happen after the event.

Everyday Memory and Memory Errors

Three chapters ago, in Chapter 5, we defined memory as *the process involved in retaining, retrieving, and using information about stimuli, images, events, ideas, and skills after the original information is no longer present*. In defining memory as a *process*, we indicated that memory, like perception and attention, is not simple. *Retaining and retrieving information* isn't like writing something on a file card, placing the card in a file box, and then retrieving the card later. There are, instead, *processes* that involve a number of different types of memory, ways of getting information into memory, and strategies for getting that information out. We have seen that only some of the information gets in, some of that information is lost, and only some can be successfully retrieved. Memory is therefore more like storing information on a file card that is written with partially disappearing ink, and, by the way, when you go to retrieve it, there's a chance some of the original information may be changed.

The idea that what we remember may be changed from what actually happened comes as a surprise to many people. In a nationwide poll in which people responded to statements about memory, 63 percent of the respondents agreed with the statement "Human memory works like a video camera, accurately recording the events we see and hear so we can review and interpret them later." In the same survey, 48 percent agreed that "once you have experienced an event and formed a memory of it, that memory does not change" (Simons & Chabris, 2011). Thus, a substantial proportion of people believe memories are recorded accurately, as if by a video camera, and that once recorded, the memory does not change.

As we will see in this chapter, these views are erroneous. Everything that happens is not necessarily recorded accurately in the first place, and what is recorded is subject to change. What is important about this chapter is not only that it demonstrates some limits to our ability to remember, but that it illustrates a basic property of memory. Memories, as we will see, are created by a process of construction, which is based on what actually happened combined with other things that have happened and our general knowledge about how things usually happen.

To illustrate this process of construction, we will be shifting our focus from experiments in which subjects are asked to remember lists of words or short passages to experiments in which subjects are asked to remember descriptions of events that could occur in the environment and events that have occurred in their lives. We begin by considering how we remember events from our lives.

Autobiographical Memory: What Has Happened in My Life

In Chapter 6, we defined autobiographical memory (AM) as *memory for specific experiences from our life, which can include both episodic and semantic components*. As we saw in Chapter 6, experiencing a memory by using mental time travel is episodic memory. However, autobiographical memories can also contain semantic components. For example, an autobiographical memory of a childhood birthday party might include images of the cake, people at the party, and games being played (episodic memory); it might also include knowledge about when the party occurred, where your family was living at the time, and your general knowledge about what usually happens at birthday parties (semantic memory) (Cabeza & St. Jacques, 2007). We now consider two additional characteristics of autobiographical memory: (1) it is multidimensional, and (2) we remember some events in our lives better than others.

THE MULTIDIMENSIONAL NATURE OF AM

Autobiographical memories are usually more complex than memory that might be measured in the laboratory by asking a person to remember a list of words. Autobiographical memories are multidimensional because they consist of spatial, emotional, and sensory components. The memory of patients who have suffered brain damage that causes a loss of visual memory, but without causing blindness, illustrates the importance of the sensory component of AM. Daniel Greenberg and David Rubin (2003) found that patients who had lost their ability to recognize objects or to visualize objects, because of damage to visual areas of the cortex, also experienced a loss of AM. This may have occurred because visual stimuli were not available to serve as retrieval cues for memories. But even memories not based on visual information are lost in these patients. Apparently, visual experience plays an important role in autobiographical memory. (It would seem reasonable that for blind people, auditory experience might take over this role.)

A brain scanning study that illustrates a difference between AM and laboratory memory was done by Roberto Cabeza and coworkers (2004). Cabeza measured the brain activation caused by two sets of stimulus photographs—one set that the subject took and another set that was taken by someone else (**Figure 8.1**). We will call the photos taken by the subject *own-photos*, and the ones taken by someone else *lab-photos*.

The photos were created by giving 12 Duke University students digital cameras and telling them to take pictures of 40 specified campus locations over a 10-day period. After taking the photos, subjects were shown their own-photos and a lab-photo of each location. A few days later they saw the own-photos and the lab-photos they had seen before, along with some new lab-photos they had never seen. As subjects indicated whether each stimulus was an own-photo, a lab-photo they had seen before, or a new lab-photo, their brain activity was measured in an fMRI scanner.

The brain scans showed that own-photos and lab-photos activated many of the same structures in the brain—mainly ones like the medial temporal lobe (MTL) that are associated with episodic memory, as well as an area in the parietal cortex that is involved in processing scenes (**Figure 8.2a**). In addition, the own-photos caused more activation in the prefrontal cortex, which is associated with processing information about the self (**Figure 8.2b**), and in the hippocampus, which is involved in recollection (memory associated with "mental time travel") (**Figure 8.2c**).

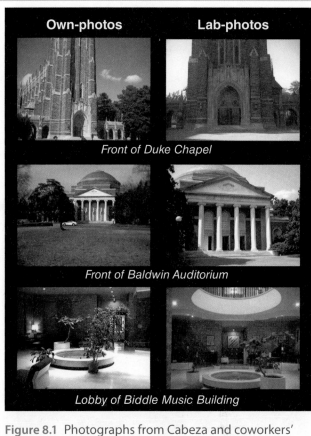

Figure 8.1 Photographs from Cabeza and coworkers' (2004) experiment. Own-photos were taken by the subject; lab-photos were taken by someone else. *(Source: R. Cabeza, S. E. Prince, S. M. Daselaar, D. L. Greenberg, M. Budde, F. Dolcos, et al., Brain activity during episodic retrieval of autobiographical and laboratory events: An fMRI study using novel photo paradigm, Journal of Cognitive Neuroscience, 16, 1583–1594, 2004.)*

Thus, the pictures of a particular location that people took themselves elicited memories presumably associated with taking the picture and, therefore, activated a more extensive network of brain areas than pictures of the same location that were taken by someone else. This activation reflects the richness of experiencing autobiographical memories. Other studies have also found that autobiographical memories can elicit emotions, which activates another area of the brain (which we will describe shortly) called the amygdala (see **Figure 5.22**, page 142).

MEMORY OVER THE LIFE SPAN

What determines which particular life events we will remember years later? Personal milestones such as graduating from college or receiving a marriage proposal stand out, as do highly emotional events such as surviving a car accident (Pillemer, 1998). Events that become significant parts of a person's life tend to be remembered well. For example, going out to dinner with someone for the first time might stand out if you ended up having a long-term relationship with that person, but the same dinner date might be far less memorable if you never saw the person again.

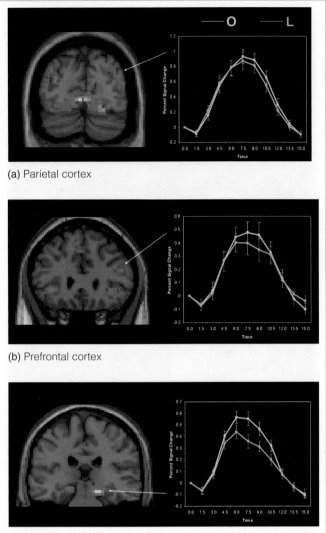

(a) Parietal cortex

(b) Prefrontal cortex

(c) Hippocampus

O photos = more activation

Figure 8.2 (a) fMRI response of an area in the parietal cortex showing time-course and amplitude of response caused by own-photos (yellow) and lab-photos (blue) in the memory test. The graph on the right indicates that activation is the same with the own-photos and lab-photos. The response to own-photos is larger in (b) the prefrontal cortex and (c) the hippocampus. *(Source: R. Cabeza, S. E. Prince, S. M. Daselaar, D. L. Greenberg, M. Budde, F. Dolcos, et al., Brain activity during episodic retrieval of autobiographical and laboratory events: An fMRI study using novel photo paradigm, Journal of Cognitive Neuroscience, 16, 1583–1594, 2004.)*

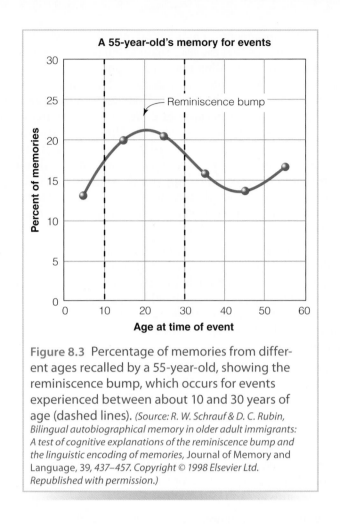

Figure 8.3 Percentage of memories from different ages recalled by a 55-year-old, showing the reminiscence bump, which occurs for events experienced between about 10 and 30 years of age (dashed lines). *(Source: R. W. Schrauf & D. C. Rubin, Bilingual autobiographical memory in older adult immigrants: A test of cognitive explanations of the reminiscence bump and the linguistic encoding of memories, Journal of Memory and Language, 39, 437–457. Copyright © 1998 Elsevier Ltd. Republished with permission.)*

Transition points in people's lives appear to be particularly memorable. This is illustrated by what Wellesley College juniors and seniors said when they were asked to recall the most influential event from their freshman year. Most of the responses to this question were descriptions of events that had occurred in September. When alumni were asked the same question, they remembered more events from September of their freshman year and from the end of their senior year—another transition point (Pillemer et al., 1996).

A particularly interesting result occurs when subjects over 40 are asked to remember events in their lives. As shown in **Figure 8.3** for a 55-year-old, events are remembered for all years between ages 5 and 55, but memory is better for recent events and for events occurring between the ages of about 10 and 30 (Conway, 1996; Rubin et al., 1998). The enhanced memory for adolescence and young adulthood found in people over 40 is called the **reminiscence bump**.

Why are adolescence and young adulthood special times for encoding memories? We will describe three hypotheses, all based on the idea that special life events are happening during adolescence and young adulthood. The **self-image hypothesis**, proposed by Clare Rathbone and coworkers (2008), proposes that memory is enhanced for events that occur as a person's self-image or life identity is being formed. This idea is based on the results of an experiment in which subjects with an average age of 54 created "I am" statements, such as "I am a mother" or "I am a psychologist," that they felt defined them as a person. When they then indicated when each statement had become a significant part of their identity, the average age they assigned to the origin of these statements was 25, which is within the span of the reminiscence bump. When subjects also listed *events* that were connected with each statement (such as "I gave birth to my first child" or "I started graduate school in psychology"), most of the events occurred during the time span associated with the reminiscence bump. Development of the self-image therefore brings with it numerous memorable events, most of which happen during adolescence or young adulthood.

Another explanation for the reminiscence bump, called the **cognitive hypothesis**, proposes that periods of rapid change that are followed by stability cause stronger encoding of memories. Adolescence and young adulthood fit this description because the rapid changes, such as going away to school, getting married, and starting a career, that occur during these periods are followed by the relative stability of adult life. One way this hypothesis has been tested is by finding people who have experienced rapid changes in their lives that occurred at a time later than adolescence or young adulthood. The cognitive hypothesis would predict that the reminiscence bump should occur later for these people. To test this idea, Robert Schrauf and David Rubin (1998) determined the recollections of people who had emigrated to the United States either in their 20s or in their mid-30s. **Figure 8.4**, which shows the memory curves for two groups of immigrants, indicates that the reminiscence bump occurs at the normal age for people who emigrated at age 20–24 but is shifted to later for those who emigrated at age 34–35, just as the cognitive hypothesis would predict.

Notice that the normal reminiscence bump is missing for the people who emigrated later. Schrauf and Rubin explain this by noting that the late emigration eliminates the stable period that usually occurs during early adulthood. Because early adulthood isn't followed by a stable period, no reminiscence bump occurs, as predicted by the cognitive hypothesis.

Finally, the **cultural life script hypothesis** distinguishes between a person's life story, which is all of the events that have occurred in a person's life, and a **cultural life script**, which is the culturally expected events that occur at a particular time in the life span. For example, when Dorthe Berntsen and David Rubin (2004) asked people to list when important events in a typical person's life usually occur, some of the more common responses were falling in love (16 years), college (22 years), marriage (27 years), and having children (28 years). Interestingly, a large number of the most commonly mentioned events occur during the period associated with the reminiscence bump. This doesn't mean that events in a *specific* person's life always occur at those times, but according to the cultural life script hypothesis, events in a person's life story become easier to recall when they fit the cultural life script for that person's culture.

The reminiscence bump is a good example of a phenomenon that has generated a number of explanations, many of them plausible and supported by evidence. It isn't surprising that the crucial factors proposed by each explanation—formation of self-identity, rapid changes followed by stability, and culturally expected events—all occur during the reminiscence bump, because that is what they are trying to explain. It is likely that each of the mechanisms we have described makes some contribution to creating the reminiscence bump. (See Table 8.1.)

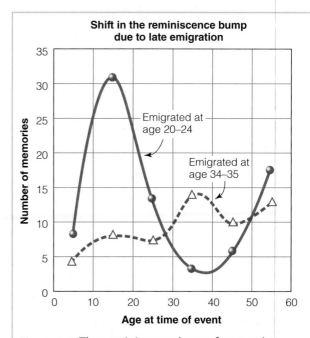

Figure 8.4 The reminiscence bump for people who emigrated at age 34 to 35 is shifted toward older ages, compared to the bump for people who emigrated between the ages of 20 and 24. *(Source: R. W. Schrauf & D. C. Rubin, Bilingual autobiographical memory in older adult immigrants: A test of cognitive explanations of the reminiscence bump and the linguistic encoding of memories, Journal of Memory and Language, 39, 437–457. Copyright © 1998 Elsevier Ltd. Republished with permission.)*

Table 8.1: Explanations for the Reminiscence Bump

EXPLANATION	BASIC CHARACTERISTIC
Self-image	Period of assuming person's self-image.
Cognitive	Encoding is better during periods of rapid change.
Cultural life script	Culturally shared expectations structure recall.

Memory for "Exceptional" Events

It is clear that some events in a person's life are more likely to be remembered than others. A characteristic of most memorable events is that they are significant and important to the person and, in some cases, are associated with emotions. For example, studies of what students remember from their first year of college have found that many of the events that stand out were associated with strong emotions (Pillemer, 1998; Pillemer et al., 1996; Talarico, 2009).

MEMORY AND EMOTION

Emotions and memory are intertwined. Emotions are often associated with "special" events, such as beginning or ending relationships or events experienced by many people simultaneously, like the 9/11 terrorist attacks. The idea that emotions are associated with better memory has some support, although as we will see, this result can depend on the specific situation. In one experiment on the association between emotion and enhanced memory, Kevin LaBar and Elizabeth Phelps (1998) tested subjects' ability to recall arousing words (for example, profanity and sexually explicit words) and neutral words (such as *street* and *store*), and observed better memory for the arousing words (**Figure 8.5a**). In another study, Florin Dolcos and coworkers (2005) tested subjects' ability to recognize emotional and neutral pictures after a 1-year delay and observed better memory for the emotional pictures (**Figure 8.5b**).

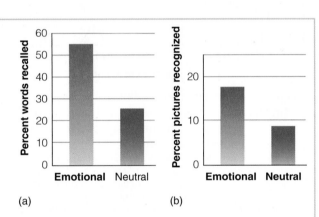

Figure 8.5 (a) Percent of emotional and neutral words recalled immediately after reading a list of words. (b) Percent of emotional and neutral pictures recognized 1 year after viewing the pictures. *(Source: Part a data from K. S. LaBar & E. A. Phelps, Arousal-mediated memory consolidation: Role of the medial temporal lobe in humans,* Psychological Science, 9, 490–493, *Figure 2, 1998. Part b adapted from F. Dolcos, K. S. LaBar, & R. Cabeza, Remembering one year later: Role of the amygdala and the medial temporal lobe memory system in retrieving emotional memories,* Proceedings of the National Academy of Sciences, *102, 2626–2631, Figure 1, 2005.)*

When we look at what is happening physiologically, one structure stands out—the **amygdala** (see **Figure 5.22**, page 142). The importance of the amygdala has been demonstrated in a number of ways. For example, in the experiment by Dolcos and coworkers described above, brain scans using fMRI as people were remembering revealed that amygdala activity was higher for the emotional words (also see Cahill et al., 1996; Hamann et al., 1999).

The link between emotions and the amygdala was also demonstrated by testing a patient, B.P., who had suffered damage to his amygdala. When subjects without brain damage viewed a slide show about a boy and his mother in which the boy is injured halfway through the story, these subjects had enhanced memory for the emotional part of the story (when the boy is injured). B.P.'s memory was the same as that of the non-brain-damaged subjects for the first part of the story, but it was not enhanced for the emotional part (Cahill et al., 1995). It appears, therefore, that emotions may trigger mechanisms in the amygdala that help us remember events that are associated with the emotions.

Emotion has also been linked to improved memory consolidation, the process that strengthens memory for an experience and takes place over minutes or hours after the experience (see Chapter 7, pages 193–198). The link between emotion and consolidation was initially suggested by animal research, mainly in rats, that showed that central nervous system stimulants administered shortly after training on a task can enhance memory for the task. Research then determined that hormones such as the stimulant cortisol are released during and after emotionally arousing stimuli like those used in the testing task. These two findings led to the conclusion that stress hormones released after an emotional experience increase consolidation of memory for that experience (McGaugh, 1983; Roozendaal & McGaugh, 2011)

Larry Cahill and coworkers (2003) carried out an experiment that demonstrated this effect in humans. They showed subjects neutral and emotionally arousing pictures; then they had some subjects (the stress group) immerse their arms in ice water, which causes the release of cortisol, and other subjects (the no-stress group) immerse their arms in warm water, which is a nonstressful situation that doesn't cause cortisol release. When asked to describe the pictures a week later, subjects who had been exposed to stress recalled more of the emotionally arousing pictures than the neutral pictures (**Figure 8.6a**). There was no significant difference between the neutral and emotionally arousing picture for the no-stress group (**Figure 8.6b**).

What is particularly interesting about these results is that the cortisol enhances memory for the emotional pictures but not for the neutral pictures. Results such as these have led to the conclusion that hormone activation that occurs after arousing emotional experiences enhances memory consolidation in humans (also see Phelps & Sharot, 2008). This increased consolidation associated with emotion has also been linked to increased activity in the amygdala (Ritchey et al., 2008).

But although there is evidence linking emotion to better memory, there is also evidence that under certain conditions, emotions can impair memory. For example, emotions can sometimes cause a focusing of attention on objects that are particularly important, drawing attention away from other objects and so decreasing memory for those objects (Mather & Sutherland, 2011). An example of this is a phenomenon called **weapons focus**, the tendency to focus attention on a weapon during the commission of a crime, which is typically a high-emotion situation. Experiments that have studied weapons focus, which we will return to later, have found that the presence of a gun causes decreases in memory for other details of the crime scene (Stanny & Johnson, 2000; Tooley et al., 1987).

As we will see in the next section, there is a link between emotion and memory for highly memorable events, such as the 9/11 terrorist attacks, which cause memories that have been called *flashbulb memories*. But this link is not, as some people might assume, that the high emotion associated with such events leads to better memory. We will first describe research that measures people's memory for these events and then consider how emotions play a special role in flashbulb memories.

FLASHBULB MEMORIES

Many people have memories of the terrorist attacks of September 11, 2001. Research on memories for public events such as this, that have been experienced by large numbers of people, often ask people to remember where they were and how they first learned of the event. I remember walking into the psychology department office and hearing from a secretary that someone had crashed a plane into the World Trade Center. At the time, I pictured a small private plane that had gone off course, but a short while later, when I called my wife, she told me that the first tower of the World Trade Center had just collapsed. Shortly after that, in my cognitive psychology class, my students and I discussed what we knew about the situation and decided to cancel class for the day.

BROWN AND KULIK PROPOSE THE TERM "FLASHBULB MEMORY" The memories I have described about how I heard about the 9/11 attack, and the people and events directly associated with finding out about the attack, are still vivid in my mind more than 12 years later. Is there something special about memories such as this that are associated with unexpected, emotionally charged events? According to Roger Brown and James Kulik (1977), there is. They proposed that memories for the circumstances surrounding learning about events such as 9/11 are special. Their proposal was based on an earlier event, which occurred on November 22, 1963. President John F. Kennedy was sitting high up in his car, waving to people as his motorcade drove down a parade route in Dallas, Texas, that had been reported in the Dallas newspapers several days before the event. As his car was passing the Texas School Book Depository building, three shots rang out. Kennedy slumped over. The motorcade came to a halt, and Kennedy was rushed to the hospital. Shortly afterward, the news spread around the world: John F. Kennedy had been assassinated.

In referring to the day of President Kennedy's assassination, Brown and Kulik stated that "for an instant, the entire nation and perhaps much of the world stopped still to have its picture taken." This description, which likened the process of forming a memory to the

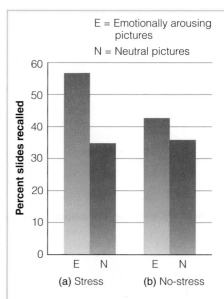

Figure 8.6 (a) Recall for emotional pictures is better than for neutral pictures when subjects are exposed to stress. (b) There is no significant difference between emotional and neutral recall in the no-stress condition. This result has been related to enhanced memory consolidation for the emotional pictures. *(Source: Based on L. Cahill, L. Gorski, & K. Le, Enhanced human memory consolidation with post-learning stress: Interaction with the degree of arousal at encoding, Learning & Memory, 10, 270–274, Figure 2, 2003.)*

taking of a photograph, led them to coin the term **flashbulb memory** to refer to a person's memory for the circumstances surrounding shocking, highly charged events. It is important to emphasize that the term *flashbulb memory* refers to memory for the circumstances surrounding how a person *heard about* an event, not memory for the event itself. Thus, a flashbulb memory for 9/11 would be memory for where a person was and what they were doing when they found out about the terrorist attack.

Brown and Kulik argued that there is something special about the mechanisms responsible for flashbulb memories. Not only do they occur under highly emotional circumstances, but they are remembered for long periods of time and are especially vivid and detailed. Brown and Kulik described the mechanism responsible for these vivid and detailed memories as a "Now Print" mechanism, as if these memories are like a photograph that resists fading.

"FLASHBULB MEMORIES" ARE NOT LIKE PHOTOGRAPHS Brown and Kulik's idea that flashbulb memories are like a photograph was based on their finding that people were able to describe in some detail what they were doing when they heard about highly emotional events like the assassinations of John F. Kennedy and Martin Luther King, Jr. But the procedure Brown and Kulik used was flawed because their subjects weren't asked what they remembered until years after the events had occurred. The problem with this procedure is that there was no way to determine whether the reported memories were accurate. The only way to check for accuracy is to compare the person's memory to what actually happened or to memory reports collected immediately after the event. The technique of comparing later memories to memories collected immediately after the event is called **repeated recall**.

METHOD
REPEATED RECALL

The idea behind repeated recall is to determine whether memory changes over time by testing subjects a number of times after an event. The person's memory is first measured immediately after a stimulus is presented or something happens. Even though there is some possibility for errors or omissions immediately after the event, this report is taken as being the most accurate representation of what happened and is used as a baseline. Days, months, or years later, when subjects are asked to remember what happened, their reports are compared to this baseline. This use of a baseline provides a way to check the accuracy of later reports.

Figure 8.7 Neisser and Harsch (1992) studied people's memories for the day they heard about the explosion of the space shuttle *Challenger*.

Bettmann/Corbis

Over the years since Brown and Kulik's "Now Print" proposal, research using the repeated recall task has shown that flashbulb memories are not like photographs. Unlike photographs, which remain the same for many years, people's memories for how they heard about flashbulb events change over time. In fact, one of the main findings of research on flashbulb memories is that although people report that memories surrounding flashbulb events are especially vivid, they are often inaccurate or lacking in detail. For example, Ulric Neisser and Nicole Harsch (1992) did a study in which they asked subjects how they had heard about the explosion of the space shuttle *Challenger*. Back in 1986 space launches were still considered special and were often highly anticipated. The flight of the *Challenger* was special because one of the astronauts was New Hampshire high school teacher Christa McAuliffe, who was the first member of NASA's Teacher in Space project. The blastoff from Cape Canaveral on January 28, 1986, seemed routine. But 77 seconds after liftoff, *Challenger* broke apart and plummeted into the ocean, killing the crew of seven (**Figure 8.7**).

Subjects in Neisser and Harsch's experiment filled out a questionnaire within a day after the explosion, and then filled out the same questionnaire 2 1/2 to 3 years later. One subject's response, a day after the explosion, indicated that she had heard about it in class:

> I was in my religion class and some people walked in and started talking about [it]. I didn't know any details except that it had exploded and the schoolteacher's students had all been watching, which I thought was so sad. Then after class I went to my room and watched the TV program talking about it, and I got all the details from that.

Two and a half years later, her memory had changed to the following:

> When I first heard about the explosion I was sitting in my freshman dorm room with my roommate, and we were watching TV. It came on a news flash, and we were both totally shocked. I was really upset, and I went upstairs to talk to a friend of mine, and then I called my parents.

Responses like these, in which subjects first reported hearing about the explosion in one place, such as a classroom, and then later remembered that they had first heard about it on TV, were common. Right after the explosion, only 21 percent of the subjects indicated that they had first heard about it on TV, but 2 1/2 years later, 45 percent of the subjects reported that they had first heard about it on TV. Reasons for the increase in TV memories could be that the TV reports become more memorable through repetition and that TV is a major source of news. Thus, memory for hearing about the *Challenger* explosion had a property that is also a characteristic of memory for less dramatic, everyday events: It was affected by people's experiences following the event (people may have seen accounts of the explosion) and their general knowledge (people often first hear about important news on TV).

ARE FLASHBULB MEMORIES DIFFERENT FROM OTHER MEMORIES? The large number of inaccurate responses in the *Challenger* study suggests that perhaps memories that are supposed to be flashbulb memories decay just like regular memories. In fact, many flashbulb memory researchers have expressed doubt that flashbulb memories are much different from regular memories (Schmolck et al., 2000). This conclusion is supported by an experiment in which a group of college students was asked a number of questions on September 12, 2001, the day after the terrorist attacks involving the World Trade Center, the Pentagon, and Flight 93 in Pennsylvania (Talarico & Rubin, 2003). Some of these questions were about the terrorist attacks ("When did you first hear the news?"). Others were similar questions about an everyday event in the person's life that occurred in the days just preceding the attacks. After picking the everyday event, the subject created a two- or three-word description that could serve as a cue for that event in the future. Some subjects were retested 1 week later, some 6 weeks later, and some 32 weeks later by asking them the same questions about the attack and the everyday event.

One result of this experiment was that the subjects remembered fewer details and made more errors at longer intervals after the events, with little difference between the results for the flashbulb and everyday memories (Figure 8.8a). This result supports the idea that there is nothing special about flashbulb memories. However, another result, shown in Figure 8.8b, did indicate a difference between flashbulb and everyday memories: People's *belief* that their memories were accurate stayed high over the entire 32-week period for the flashbulb memories but dropped for the everyday memories. Ratings of vividness and how well they could "relive" the events also stayed high and constant for the flashbulb memories but dropped for the everyday memories. Thus, the idea that flashbulb memories are special appears to be based at least partly on the fact that people *think* the memories are stronger and more accurate; however, this study found that *in reality* there is little or no difference between flashbulb and everyday memories in terms of the amount and *accuracy* of what is remembered.

EMOTIONS AND FLASHBULB MEMORIES The idea that people believe flashbulb memories are stronger and more accurate has led to the conclusion that the special nature of

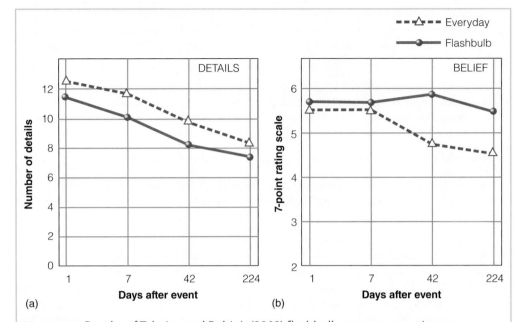

Figure 8.8 Results of Talarico and Rubin's (2003) flashbulb memory experiment. (a) The decrease in the number of details remembered was similar for memories of 9/11 and for memories of an everyday event. (b) Subjects' belief that their memory was accurate remained high for 9/11, but decreased for memories of the everyday event. *(Source: J. M. Talarico & D. C. Rubin, Confidence, not consistency, characterizes flashbulb memories, Psychological Science, 14, 455–461, Figures 1 & 2. Copyright © 2003 American Psychological Society. Reproduced by permission.)*

flashbulb memories can be traced, at least in part, to the emotional nature of flashbulb events. We have seen that emotions have been associated with enhanced memory, but that in some situations emotions can decrease memory. These two effects of emotions are at the heart of proposals by some researchers that emotions enhance the *subjective sense of remembering*—the vividness of the memory, confidence that it is accurate, and the sense of reliving an event—while at the same time causing a decrease in memory for details of a scene.

Ulrike Rimmele and coworkers (2011) did an experiment that demonstrates this dual nature of emotion's effect on memory. Subjects viewed 60 pictures: 30 neutral, such as a landscape, and 30 negative, such as a picture of a car crash. These pictures were framed in one of four different colored borders (**Figure 8.9a**). One hour later, subjects saw the original 60 pictures plus 60 new pictures. For each picture, they (1) made a confidence rating between 1 and 6, where 1 indicated they were sure they had not seen the picture and 6 indicated they were sure they had seen the picture before; (2) made a "remember/know" judgment in which "remember" meant they remembered seeing the picture when it was originally presented, "know" meant that the picture is familiar but they don't remember experiencing it earlier, and "new" meant they had never seen the picture (see Method: Remember/Know Procedure, page 165); and (3) for the pictures they rated as "remember," they indicated the color of the frame that had surrounded the picture.

The results, in **Figure 8.9b**, indicate that subjects were more likely to say they remembered emotional (negative) pictures than neutral pictures (left pair of bars). Another result, not shown on the graph, is that 67 percent of the emotional pictures received a confidence rating of 6 ("I'm sure I saw the picture before"), but only 51 percent of the neutral pictures received a 6. However, despite giving the stronger remember response and higher confidence to the emotional pictures, subjects were less likely to correctly name the color of the frame surrounding the emotional pictures they remembered (right pair of bars). Results such as these have led researchers to conclude that emotions enhance our ability to remember that an event occurred and some of its general characteristics, but do not enhance our memory for details of what happened. Thus, a person may clearly recollect the occurrence of the 9/11 attack or another high-emotion event but may have forgotten the details related to how they first heard about the event (Phelps & Sharot, 2008).

REHEARSAL, MEDIA COVERAGE, AND FLASHBULB MEMORIES Two other factors, in addition to emotion, that can potentially affect memory for flashbulb events are rehearsal and media coverage. Ulric Neisser and coworkers (1996) argue that we may remember events like those that happened on 9/11 not because of a special mechanism but because we rehearse these events after they occur. This idea is called the **narrative rehearsal hypothesis**.

The narrative rehearsal hypothesis makes sense when we consider the events that followed 9/11. Pictures of the planes crashing into the World Trade Center were replayed endlessly on TV, and the event and its aftermath were covered extensively for months afterward in the media. Neisser argues that if rehearsal is the reason for our memories of significant events, then the flashbulb analogy is misleading.

Remember that the memory we are concerned with is the characteristics surrounding how people *first heard about* 9/11, but much of the rehearsal associated with this event is rehearsal for events that occurred *after* hearing about it. Seeing TV replays of the planes crashing into the towers, for example, might result in people's focusing more on those images than on who told them about the event or where they were, and eventually they might come to believe that they originally heard about the event on TV, as occurred in the *Challenger* study.

An indication of the power of TV to "capture" people's memory is provided by the results of a study by James Ost and coworkers (2002), who approached people in an English shopping center and asked if they would be willing to participate in a study examining how well people can remember tragic events. The target event involved Princess Diana and her companion Dodi Fayed, whose deaths in a car crash in Paris on August 31, 1997, were widely covered on British television. Subjects were asked to respond to the following statement: "Have you seen the paparazzi's video-recording of the car crash in which Diana, Princess of Wales, and Dodi Fayed lost their lives?" Of the 45 people who responded to this question, 20 said they had seen the film. This was, however, impossible, because no such film exists. The car crash was reported on TV, but not actually shown. The extensive media coverage of this event apparently caused some people to remember something—seeing the film—that didn't actually occur.

Memory researchers are still discussing the exact mechanism responsible for memory of flashbulb events (Berntsen, 2009; Luminet & Curci, 2009; Talarico & Rubin, 2009). However, whatever mechanism is involved, one important outcome of the flashbulb memory research is that it has revealed that what people believe they remember accurately may not, in fact, be accurate at all. The idea that people's memories for an event can be determined by factors in addition to actually experiencing the event has led many researchers to propose that what people remember is a "construction" that is based on what actually happened plus additional influences. We will discuss this idea in the next section.

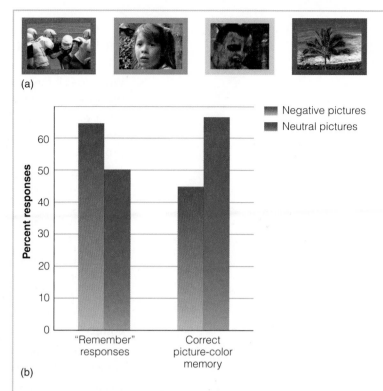

(a)

(b)

Figure 8.9 (a) Pictures with colored frames, like the stimuli used by Rimmele et al., 2011. (b) Results of Rimmele's experiment. "Remember" responses were more likely for the negative pictures (left pair of bars), but memory was better for the frame color that went with the neutral pictures (right bars). *(Source: Based on U. Rimmele, L. Davachi, R. Petrov, S. Dougal, & E. Phelps, Emotion enhances the subjective feeling of remembering, despite lower accuracy for contextual details, Emotion, 11, 553–562, Figure 1, 2011. Photos courtesy of Bruce Goldstein.)*

TEST YOURSELF 8.1

1. What is autobiographical memory? What does it mean to say that it includes both episodic and semantic components?

2. What does it mean to say that autobiographical memories are multidimensional? How did Cabeza's photography experiment provide evidence for this idea?

3. What types of events are often the most memorable? What would a plot of "events remembered" versus "age" look like for a 50-year-old person? What theories have been proposed to explain the peak that occurs in this function?

4. What is the evidence that emotionally charged events are easier to remember than nonemotional events? Describe the role of the amygdala in emotional memory, including brain scan (fMRI) and neuropsychological (patient B.P.) evidence linking the amygdala and memory, and the experiment showing that emotion enhances consolidation.

5. What is the evidence that under some conditions, emotions can decrease the accuracy of memory?

6. Why did Brown and Kulik call memory for public, emotional events, like the assassination of President Kennedy, "flashbulb" memories? Was their use of the term *flashbulb* correct?

7. Compare memory for emotional versus neutral stimuli as studied by Rimmele and coworkers. How is this result related to the role of emotion in flashbulb memories?

8. What is the narrative rehearsal hypothesis? How is the result of the Princess Diana study related to the effect of media coverage on memory?

The Constructive Nature of Memory

We have seen that we remember certain things better than others because of their special significance or because of when they happened in our lives. But we have also seen that what people remember may not match what actually happened. When people report memories for past events, they may not only omit things but also distort or change things that happened, and in some cases even report things that never happened at all.

These characteristics of memory reflect the **constructive nature of memory**—what people report as memories are constructed based on what actually happened plus additional factors, such as the person's knowledge, experiences, and expectations. This approach to memory is called "constructive" because the mind *constructs* memories based on a number of sources of information. One of the first studies to suggest that memory is constructive was the "War of the Ghosts" experiment conducted by British psychologist Fredrick Bartlett before World War I and published in 1932.

BARTLETT'S "WAR OF THE GHOSTS" EXPERIMENT

In this classic study, Bartlett first had his subjects read the following story from Canadian Indian Folklore.

THE WAR OF THE GHOSTS

One night two young men from Egulac went down to the river to hunt seals, and while they were there it became foggy and calm. Then they heard war cries, and they thought: "Maybe this is a war party." They escaped to the shore and hid behind a log. Now canoes came up, and they heard the noise of paddles and saw one canoe coming up to them. There were five men in the canoe, and they said:

"What do you think? We wish to take you along. We are going up the river to make war on the people."

One of the young men said: "I have no arrows." "Arrows are in the canoe," they said. "I will not go along. I might be killed. My relatives do not know where I have gone. But you," he said, turning to the other, "may go with them."

So one of the young men went, but the other returned home. And the warriors went on up the river to a town on the other side of Kalama. The people came down to the water, and they began to fight, and many were killed. But presently the young man heard one of the warriors say: "Quick, let us go home; that Indian has been hit." Now he thought: "Oh, they are ghosts." He did not feel sick, but they said he had been shot.

So the canoes went back to Egulac, and the young man went ashore to his house and made a fire. And he told everybody and said: "Behold I accompanied the ghosts, and we went to fight. Many of our fellows were killed, and many of those who attacked us were killed. They said I was hit, and I did not feel sick."

He told it all, and then he became quiet. When the sun rose, he fell down. Something black came out of his mouth. His face became contorted. The people jumped up and cried. He was dead. (Bartlett, 1932, p. 65)

After his subjects had read this story, Bartlett asked them to recall it as accurately as possible. He then used the technique of **repeated reproduction**, in which the same subjects tried to remember the story at longer and longer intervals after they had first read it. This is similar to the repeated recall technique used in the flashbulb memory experiments (see Method: Repeated Recall, page 214).

One reason Bartlett's experiment is considered important is because it was one of the first to use the repeated reproduction technique. But the main reason the "War of the Ghosts" experiment is considered important is the nature of the errors Bartlett's subjects made. At longer times after reading the story, most subjects' reproductions of the story were shorter than the original and contained many omissions and inaccuracies. But what was most significant about the remembered stories is that they tended to reflect the subject's own culture. The original story, which came from Canadian folklore, was transformed by many of Bartlett's subjects to make it more consistent with the culture of Edwardian England to which they belonged. For example, one subject remembered the two men who were out hunting seals as being involved in a sailing expedition, the "canoes" as "boats," and the man who joined the war party as a fighter that any good Englishman would be proud of—ignoring his wounds, he continued fighting and won the admiration of the natives.

One way to think about what happened in Bartlett's experiment is that his subjects created their memories from two sources. One source was the original story, and the other was what they knew about similar stories in their own culture. As time passed, the subjects used information from both sources, so their reproductions became more like what would happen in Edwardian England. This idea that memories are comprised of details from various sources involves a phenomenon called *source monitoring*, which is at the heart of the constructive approach to memory.

SOURCE MONITORING AND SOURCE MONITORING ERRORS

"Did you hear about the mob scene at the movie theater for the opening of *The Hunger Games: Catching Fire*?"

"Yes, I heard about it on the evening news."

"Really? I heard about it from Bernita, who read the book, or was it Susan? I can't remember."

Source monitoring is the process of determining the origins of our memories, knowledge, or beliefs (Johnson et al., 1993). In the conversation above, one person identified the evening news as his source of information about the movie; the other person seemed unsure of his source, thinking it was either Bernita or Susan. If he thought it was Bernita but it turned out to be Susan, he would be committing a **source monitoring error**—misidentifying the source of a memory. Source monitoring errors are also called **source misattributions** because the memory is attributed to the wrong source. Source monitoring provides an example of the constructive nature of memory because when we remember something, we retrieve the memory ("I heard about the crowd at the *Hunger Games* movie") and then determine where that memory came from ("It was either Bernita or Susan, because I talked to them recently. But it's more likely to be Bernita, because I know that she had just finished reading the book") (Mitchell & Johnson, 2000).

Source monitoring errors are common, and we are often unaware of them (as was probably the case for Bartlett's subjects). Perhaps you have had the experience of remembering that one person told you about something but later realizing you had heard it from someone else—or the experience of claiming you had said something you had only thought ("I'll be home late for dinner") (Henkel, 2004). In the 1984 presidential campaign, President Ronald Reagan, running for reelection, repeatedly related a story about a heroic act by a U.S. pilot, only to have it revealed later that his story was almost identical to a scene from a 1940s war movie, *A Wing and a Prayer* (Johnson, 2006; Rogin, 1987). Apparently the source of the president's memory was the film rather than an actual event.

Some of the more sensational examples of source monitoring errors are cases of **cryptomnesia**, unconscious plagiarism of the work of others. For example, Beatle George Harrison was sued for appropriating the melody from the song "He's So Fine" (originally recorded by the 1960s group The Chiffons) for his song "My Sweet Lord." Although Harrison claimed he had used the tune unconsciously, he was successfully sued by the publisher of the original song. Harrison's problem was that he thought he was the source of the melody, when the actual source was someone else.

Source monitoring errors are important because the mechanisms responsible for them are also involved in creating memories in general. Marcia Johnson (2006) describes memory as a process that makes use of a number of types of information. The primary source of information for memory is information from the actual event, including perceptual experiences, emotions, and thoughts that were occurring at the time. Additional sources of information that influence memory include people's knowledge of the world, and things that happened before or after the event that might become confused with the event.

Later in the chapter we will describe a number of experiments that illustrate how what people know about the world can cause them to misremember material presented earlier. We will also describe experiments in which experimenters provide misleading information after an event that causes subjects to make errors when attempting to remember the event. Source monitoring is a factor in these situations because subjects are using this additional information, rather than information provided by the actual event, as a source for their memory. But first we will describe two experiments that provide examples of how source monitoring errors can influence a person's memory.

THE "BECOMING FAMOUS OVERNIGHT" EXPERIMENT: SOURCE MONITORING AND FAMILIARITY An experiment by Larry Jacoby and coworkers (1989) demonstrated an effect of source monitoring errors by testing subjects' ability to distinguish between famous and nonfamous names. In the acquisition part of the experiment, Jacoby had subjects read a number of made-up nonfamous names like Sebastian Weissdorf and Valerie Marsh (**Figure 8.10**). For the *immediate test group*, subjects were tested immediately after seeing the list of nonfamous names. They were told to pick out the names of famous people from a list containing (1) the nonfamous names they had just seen, (2) new nonfamous names that they had never seen before, and (3) famous names, like Minnie Pearl (a country singer) or Roger Bannister (the first person to run a 4-minute mile), that many people might have recognized in 1988, when the experiment was conducted. Just before this test, subjects were reminded that all of the names they had seen in the first part of the experiment were nonfamous. Because the test was given shortly after the subjects had seen the first list of nonfamous

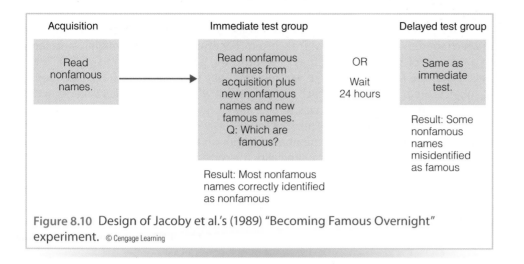

Figure 8.10 Design of Jacoby et al.'s (1989) "Becoming Famous Overnight" experiment. © Cengage Learning

names, they correctly identified most of the old nonfamous names (like Sebastian Weissdorf and Valerie Marsh) as being nonfamous.

The interesting result occurred for subjects in the *delayed test group*, who were tested 24 hours after first seeing the names, after also being told that the names they had seen in the first part of the experiment were nonfamous. When tested after this delay, subjects were more likely to identify the old nonfamous names as being famous. Thus, waiting 24 hours before testing increased the chances that Sebastian Weissdorf would be labeled as famous. Because of this result, Jacoby's paper is titled "Becoming Famous Overnight."

How did Sebastian Weissdorf become famous overnight? To answer this question, put yourself in the place of one of Jacoby's subjects. It is 24 hours since you saw the first list of nonfamous names, and you now have to decide whether Sebastian Weissdorf is famous or nonfamous. How do you make your decision? Sebastian Weissdorf doesn't pop out as someone you know of, but the name is familiar. You ask yourself the question, "Why is this name familiar?" This is a source monitoring problem, because to answer this question you need to determine the source of your familiarity. Are you familiar with the name Sebastian Weissdorf because you saw it 24 hours earlier or because it is the name of a famous person? Apparently, some of Jacoby's subjects decided that the familiarity was caused by fame, so the previously unknown Sebastian Weissdorf became famous!

Later in the chapter, when we consider some of the issues involved in determining the accuracy of eyewitness testimony, we will see that situations that create a sense of familiarity can lead to source monitoring errors, such as identifying the wrong person as having been at the scene of a crime.

REMEMBERING WHO SAID WHAT: SOURCE MONITORING AND GENDER STEREOTYPES
When in doubt about what we remember, we often make use of what we know about the world, and often we do this unconsciously. An example is provided by an experiment by Richard Marsh and coworkers (2006), which showed that people's performance on a source monitoring task can be influenced by gender stereotypes. They used the following method to test for source monitoring.

METHOD
TESTING FOR SOURCE MONITORING

In a typical memory experiment, items such as words, pictures, or statements are presented, and the subject's task in a later test session is to either recall or recognize as many of the previously presented items as possible. In a source monitoring experiment, items are presented that originate from specific sources, and the subject's task in the later test session is to indicate which source was associated with each item. For example, subjects might be presented with a number of statements, such as "'I went to the party today,' John said," or "'I have a feeling that the Mets are going to win tonight,' Sally said." Later, in the source memory test, subjects are presented with each statement, but without the speaker's name, and are asked to indicate who the speaker was. Source monitoring errors occur when the statement is attributed to the wrong person. Thus, the key result in a source memory experiment is not what proportion of items were remembered (although those data may also be collected), but what proportion of items were paired with the correct source.

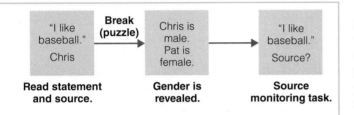

Figure 8.11 Design of Marsh and coworkers' (2006) source monitoring and gender stereotype experiment. © Cengage Learning

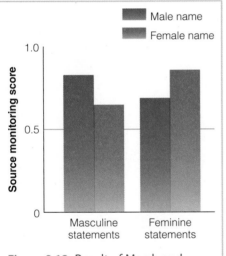

Figure 8.12 Result of Marsh and coworkers' (2006) experiment. © Cengage Learning

The experimental design of Marsh's experiment is shown in **Figure 8.11**. Subjects read a series of statements presented one at a time on a computer screen for 5 seconds each. Some statements were associated with the stereotype for males ("I swore at the guy who insulted me"), some with the stereotype for females ("I made a centerpiece for the dining table"), and some were neutral ("I am very easygoing"). Each statement was presented with a name, either Chris or Pat, and subjects were told to remember the statement and the person who said it.

After seeing all of the statement–name pairs, the subjects did a puzzle for 5 minutes and were then told that Chris was a heterosexual male and Pat was a heterosexual female. It is important to remember that the subjects did not know Chris's or Pat's gender when they first read the statements. Once they knew the genders, they were given the source monitoring task, which was to read the statements they had originally seen and indicate whether they were said by Chris or by Pat.

The results, shown in **Figure 8.12**, indicate that the gender labels affected the subjects' memory judgments. The graph plots the source monitoring score. A score of 1.0 would be perfect source monitoring, with each statement linked to the name it was originally associated with. The left pair of bars indicates that 83 percent of the masculine statements that were associated with the male (Chris) when originally presented were correctly assigned to him, but only 65 percent of the masculine statements associated with the female (Pat) when originally presented were correctly assigned to her. The right pair of bars indicates a similar result for feminine statements, which were more likely to be correctly attributed to the female (Pat) than to the male (Chris).

What this result means, according to Marsh, is that if subjects didn't have a strong memory for who made a particular statement, then their memory was biased by their knowledge of what "typical" males and females would say. The influence of real-world knowledge therefore resulted in source monitoring errors. In the next section we will describe a number of additional experiments that illustrate how real-world knowledge can cause memory errors. As with the experiments we have just described, many of these experiments can be related to source monitoring.

HOW REAL-WORLD KNOWLEDGE AFFECTS MEMORY

The effects of creating familiarity and of gender stereotypes on source monitoring illustrate how factors in addition to what actually happened can affect memory. We will now describe some more examples, focusing on how our knowledge of the world can affect memory.

MAKING INFERENCES Memory reports can be influenced by inferences that people make based on their experiences and knowledge. In this section, we will consider this idea further. But first, do this demonstration.

DEMONSTRATION
READING SENTENCES

For this demonstration, read the following sentences, pausing for a few seconds after each one.

1. The children's snowman vanished when the temperature reached 80.
2. The flimsy shelf weakened under the weight of the books.
3. The absentminded professor didn't have his car keys.
4. The karate champion hit the cinder block.
5. The new baby stayed awake all night.

Now that you have read the sentences, turn to Demonstration: Reading Sentences (Continued) on page 240 and follow the directions.

How do your answers from the fill-in-the-blank exercise on page 240 compare to the words that you originally read above? William Brewer (1977) and Kathleen McDermott and Jason Chan (2006) presented subjects with a similar task, involving many more sentences than you read, and found that errors occurred for about a third of the sentences. For the sentences above, the most common errors were as follows: (1) *vanished* became *melted*; (2) *weakened* became *collapsed*; (3) *didn't have* became *lost*; (4) *hit* became *broke* or *smashed*; and (5) *stayed awake* became *cried*.

These wording changes illustrate a process called **pragmatic inference**, which occurs when reading a sentence leads a person to expect something that is not explicitly stated or implied by the sentence (Brewer, 1977). These inferences are based on knowledge gained through experience. Thus, although reading that a baby stayed awake all night does not include any information about crying, knowledge about babies might lead a person to infer that the baby was crying (Chan & McDermott, 2006).

Here is the scenario used in another memory experiment, which was designed specifically to elicit inferences based on the subjects' past experiences (Arkes & Freedman, 1984):

> In a baseball game, the score is tied 1 to 1. The home team has runners on first and third, with one out. A ground ball is hit to the shortstop. The shortstop throws to second base, attempting a double play. The runner who was on third scores, so it is now 2–1 in favor of the home team.

After hearing a story similar to this one, subjects were asked to indicate whether the sentence "The batter was safe at first" was part of the passage. From looking at the story, you can see that this sentence was never presented, and most of the subjects who didn't know much about baseball answered correctly. However, subjects who knew the rules of baseball were more likely to say that the sentence had been presented. They based this judgment on their knowledge that if the runner on third had scored, then the double play must have failed, which means that the batter safely reached first. Knowledge, in this example, resulted in a correct inference about what probably happened in the ball game, but an incorrect inference about the sentence that was presented in the passage.

SCHEMAS AND SCRIPTS The examples above illustrate how people's memory reports can be influenced by their knowledge. A **schema** is a person's knowledge about some aspect of the environment. For example, a person's schema of a post office might include what a post office building usually looks like from the outside, what is inside the post office, and the services it provides. We develop schemas through our experiences in different situations, such as visiting a post office, going to a ball game, or listening to lectures in a classroom.

Figure 8.13 Office where Brewer and Treyens's (1981) subjects waited before being tested on their memory for what was present in the office. *(Source: W. F. Brewer & J. C. Treyens, Role of schemata in memory for places, Cognitive Psychology, 13, 207–230. Copyright 1981, with permission from Elsevier.)*

In an experiment that studied how memory is influenced by people's schemas, subjects who had come to participate in a psychology experiment were asked to wait in an office (**Figure 8.13**) while the experimenter checked "to make sure that the previous hour's subject had completed the experiment." After 35 seconds, the subjects were called into another room and were told that the purpose of the experiment was to test their memory for the office and that their task was to write down what they had seen while they were sitting in the office (Brewer & Treyens, 1981). The subjects responded by writing down many of the things they remembered seeing, but they also included some things that were not there but that fit into their "office schema." For example, although there were no books in the office, 30 percent of the subjects reported having seen books. Thus, the information in schemas can provide a guide for making inferences about what we remember. In this particular example, the inference turned out to be wrong.

Other examples of how schemas can lead to erroneous decisions in memory experiments have involved a type of schema called a script. A **script** is our conception of the *sequence of actions* that usually occurs during a particular experience. For example, your script for visiting a post office might include waiting in line, filling out forms if you want to send the letter by registered or certified mail, giving your letter to the post office employee, watching the employee weigh the letter and determine the postage, paying for the postage, perhaps buying some stamps for future use, and then leaving the post office.

Scripts can influence our memory by setting up expectations about what usually happens in a particular situation. To test the influence of scripts, Gordon Bower and coworkers (1979) did an experiment in which subjects were asked to remember short passages like the following.

THE DENTIST

Bill had a bad toothache. It seemed like forever before he finally arrived at the dentist's office. Bill looked around at the various dental posters on the wall. Finally the dental hygienist checked and x-rayed his teeth. He wondered what the dentist was doing. The dentist said that Bill had a lot of cavities. As soon as he'd made another appointment, he left the dentist's office. (Bower et al., 1979, p. 190)

The subjects read a number of passages like this one, all of which were about familiar activities such as going to the dentist, going swimming, or going to a party. After a delay period, the subjects were given the titles of the stories they had read and were told to write down what they remembered about each story as accurately as possible. The subjects created stories that included much material that matched the original stories, but they also included material that wasn't presented in the original story but is part of the script for the activity described. For example, for the dentist story, some subjects reported reading that "Bill checked in with the dentist's receptionist." This statement is part of most people's "going to the dentist" script, but it was not included in the original story. Thus, knowledge of the dentist script caused the subjects to add information that wasn't originally presented. Another example of a link between knowledge and memory is provided by the following demonstration.

DEMONSTRATION
MEMORY FOR A LIST

Read the following list at a rate of about one item per second; then cover the list and write down as many of the words as possible. In order for this demonstration to work, it is important that you cover the words and write down the words you remember before reading past the demonstration.

bed, rest, awake, tired, dream

wake, night, blanket, doze, slumber

snore, pillow, peace, yawn, drowsy

FALSE RECALL AND RECOGNITION The demonstration you just did, which is based on experiments by James Deese (1959) and Henry Roediger and Kathleen McDermott (1995), illustrates false recall of items that were not actually presented. Does your list of remembered words include any words that are not on the list above? When I present this list to my class, there are always a substantial number of students who report that they remember the word "sleep." Remembering *sleep* is a false memory because it isn't on the list. This false memory occurs because people associate *sleep* with other words on the list. This is similar to the effect of schemas, in which people create false memories for office furnishings that aren't present because they associate these office furnishings with what is usually found in offices. Again, constructive processes have created an error in memory.

The crucial thing to take away from all of these examples is that false memories arise from the same constructive process that produces true memories. Memory, as we have seen, is not a camera or a tape recorder that creates a perfect, unchanging record of everything that happens. This constructive property of memory may actually serve us well in most situations, as described next, but it may not be such a good thing in situations such as testifying in court, which we will describe later in the chapter.

TAKING STOCK: THE PLUSES AND MINUSES OF CONSTRUCTION

The constructive property of memory reflects the creative nature of our mental processes, which enables us to do things like understand language, solve problems, and make decisions. This creativity also helps us "fill in the blanks" when there is incomplete information. For example, when a person says "we went to the ball game," you have a pretty good idea of many of the things that happened in addition to the game (hot dogs or other ballpark food was likely involved, for example), based on your experience of going to a ball game.

Even though this creativity serves a good purpose, it sometimes results in errors of memory. These errors, plus the fact that we forget many of the things we have experienced, have led many people to wish that their memory were better—an idea that most students would agree with, especially around exam time. However, the case of the Russian memory expert Shereshevskii (S.) shows that perhaps near-perfect memory may not be advantageous after all.

After extensively studying S., Russian psychologist Alexandria Luria (1968) concluded that his memory was "virtually limitless" (though Wilding & Valentine, 1997, point out that he did occasionally make mistakes). Although S.'s impressive memory enabled him to make a living by demonstrating his memory powers on stage, it did not seem to be very helpful in other aspects of his life. Luria described S.'s personal life as "in a haze." When he performed a memory feat, he had trouble forgetting what he had just remembered. His mind was like a blackboard on which everything that happened was written and couldn't be erased. Many things flit through our minds briefly and then we don't need them again; unfortunately for S., these things stayed there even when he wished they would go away. He also was not good at reasoning that involved drawing inferences or "filling in the blanks" based on partial information. We do this so often that we take it for granted, but S.'s ability to record massive amounts of information, and his inability to erase it, may have hindered his ability to do this.

Recently, new cases of impressive memory have been reported; they are described as cases of *highly superior autobiographical memory* (LePort et al., 2012). One, a woman we will call A.J., sent the following email to UCLA memory researcher James McGaugh:

> I am 34 years old and since I was eleven I have had this unbelievable ability to recall my past. . . . I can take a date between 1974 and today, and tell you what day it falls on, what I was doing that day and if anything of great importance . . . occurred on that day I can describe that to you as well. . . . Whenever I see a date flash on the television (or anywhere else for that matter) I automatically go back to that day and remember where I was, what I was doing, what day it fell on and on and on and on and on. It is non-stop, uncontrollable and totally exhausting. . . . I run my entire life through my head every day and it drives me crazy!!! (Parker et al., 2006, p. 35)

A.J. describes her memories as happening automatically and not being under her conscious control. When given a date she would, within seconds, relate personal experiences and also special events that occurred on that day, and these recollections proved to be accurate when checked against a diary of daily events that A.J. had been keeping for 24 years (Parker et al., 2006).

A.J.'s excellent memory for personal experiences differed from S.'s in that the contents that she couldn't erase were not numbers or names from memory performances, but the details of her personal life. This was both positive (recalling happy events) and negative (recalling unhappy or disturbing events). But was her memory *useful* to her in areas other than remembering life events? Apparently, she was not able to apply her powers to help her remember material for exams, as she was an average student. And testing revealed that she had impaired performance on tests that involved organizing material, thinking abstractly, and working with concepts—skills that are important for thinking creatively. Following the discovery of A.J., a study of 10 additional subjects confirmed their amazing powers of autobiographical memory recall, but they also performed at levels similar to normal control subjects on most standard laboratory memory tests. Their skill therefore, seems to be specialized to remembering autobiographical memories (LaPort et al., 2012).

What the cases of S. and A.J. illustrate is that it is not necessarily an advantage to be able to remember everything; in fact, the mechanisms that result in superior powers of memory may work against the constructive processes that are an important characteristic not only of memory but of our ability to think creatively. Moreover, storing everything that is experienced is an inefficient way for a system to operate because storing everything can overload the system. To avoid this "overload," our memory system is designed to selectively remember things that are particularly important to us or that occur often in our environment (Anderson & Schooler, 1991). Although the resulting system does not record everything we experience, it does operate well enough to have enabled humans to survive as a species.

Memory is clearly a highly functional system that serves us well. However, sometimes the requirements of modern life create situations that humans have not been designed to handle. Consider, for example, driving a car. Evolution has not equipped our perceptual and motor systems to deal with weaving in and out of heavy traffic, driving at high rates of speed, or driving while talking on a cell phone. Of course, we do these things anyway, but accidents happen. Similarly, our perceptual and memory systems have not evolved to handle demands such as providing eyewitness testimony in court. In a situation such as this, memory should ideally be perfect. After all, another person's freedom or life might be at stake. But just as car accidents happen, memory accidents happen as well. We will shortly consider what can happen when memory is put to the test in the courtroom, but first we will consider another aspect of memory that can potentially result in memory errors.

TEST YOURSELF 8.2

1. Source monitoring errors provide an example of the constructive nature of memory. Describe what source monitoring and source monitoring errors are and why they are considered "constructive." How does Bartlett's "War of the Ghosts" experiment provide an example of source monitoring errors?

2. Describe the following examples of situations that involved source monitoring errors: (1) familiarity ("Becoming Famous Overnight" experiment); (2) world knowledge (gender stereotype experiment). Be sure you can describe the experiments related to each example.

3. Describe the following examples of how memory errors can occur because of a person's knowledge of the world: (1) making inferences (pragmatic inference; baseball experiment); (2) schemas and scripts (office experiment; dentist experiment); (3) false recall and recognition ("sleep" experiment).

4. What is the evidence from clinical case studies that "super memory" may have some disadvantages? What are some advantages of constructive memory?

5. Why can we say that memory is highly functional but that it may not be perfectly suited to all situations?

Memory Can Be Modified or Created by Suggestion

People are suggestible. Advertisements pitching the virtues of different products influence what people purchase. Arguments put forth by politicians, opinion makers, and friends influence how people vote. Advertisements and political arguments are examples of things that might influence a person's attitudes, beliefs, or behaviors. We will now see that information presented by others can also influence a person's memory for past events. We first consider a phenomenon called the *misinformation effect*, in which a person's memory for an event is modified by things that happen after the event has occurred.

THE MISINFORMATION EFFECT

In a typical memory experiment, a person sees or hears some stimulus, such as words, letters, or sentences, or observes pictures or a film of an event, and is asked to report what he or she experienced. But what if the experimenters were to add additional information as they were asking the person what he or she remembered? This is the question that Elizabeth Loftus and coworkers (1978) asked in a series of pioneering experiments that established the **misinformation effect**—misleading information presented after a person witnesses an event can change how the person describes that event later. This misleading information is referred to as **misleading postevent information**, or **MPI**.

METHOD
PRESENTING MISLEADING POSTEVENT INFORMATION

The usual procedure in an experiment in which misleading postevent information (MPI) is presented is to first present the stimulus to be remembered. For example, this stimulus could be a list of words or a film of an event. The MPI is then presented to one group of subjects before their memory is tested and is not presented to a control group. As you will see below, MPI is often presented in a way that seems natural, so it does not occur to subjects that they are being misled. We will also see, however, that even when subjects are told that postevent information may be incorrect, presenting this information can still affect their memory reports. The effect of MPI is determined by comparing the memory reports of subjects who received this misleading information to the memory reports of subjects who did not receive it.

An experiment by Elizabeth Loftus and coworkers (1978) illustrates a typical MPI procedure. Subjects saw a series of slides in which a car stops at a stop sign and then turns the corner and hits a pedestrian. Some of the subjects then answered a number of questions, including "Did another car pass the red Datsun while it was stopped at the stop sign?" For another group of subjects (the MPI group), the words "yield sign" replaced "stop sign" in the stop sign question. Subjects were then shown pictures from the slide show plus some pictures they had never seen. Those in the MPI group were more likely to say they had seen the picture of the car stopped at the yield sign (which, in actuality, they had never seen) than were subjects who had not been exposed to MPI. This shift in memory caused by MPI demonstrates the misinformation effect.

Presentation of MPI can alter not only what subjects report they saw, but their conclusions about other characteristics of the situation. For example, Loftus and Steven Palmer (1974) showed subjects films of a car crash (**Figure 8.14**) and then asked either (1) "How fast were the cars going when they *smashed* into each other?" or (2) "How fast were the cars going when they *hit* each other?" Although both groups saw the same event, the average speed estimate by subjects who heard the word "smashed" was 41 miles per hour, whereas the estimates for subjects who heard "hit" averaged 34 miles per hour. Even more interesting for the study of memory are the subjects' responses to the question "Did you see any broken glass?" which Loftus asked 1 week after they had seen the film. Although there was no broken glass in the film, 32 percent of the subjects who heard "smashed" before estimating the speed reported seeing broken glass, whereas only 14 percent of the subjects who heard "hit" reported seeing the glass (see Loftus, 1993a, 1998).

Figure 8.14 Subjects in the Loftus and Palmer (1974) experiment saw a film of a car crash, with scenes similar to the picture shown here, and were then asked leading questions about the crash. © Cengage Learning

The misinformation effect shows not only that false memories can be created by suggestion but also provides an example of how different researchers can interpret the same data in different ways. Remember that mental processes must be inferred from the results of behavioral or physiological experiments. The question posed by the misinformation effect is "What is happening that changes the subjects' memory reports?" Different researchers have proposed different answers to this question. We will now describe two explanations, one of which emphasizes the role of interference and another that is based on source monitoring.

MPI AS CAUSING INTERFERENCE One explanation for the MPI effect proposes that the original information is forgotten because of **retroactive interference**, which occurs when more recent learning (the misinformation in this example) interferes with memory for something that happened in the past (the actual event). For example, retroactive interference would be involved if studying for your Spanish exam made it more difficult to remember some of the vocabulary words you had studied for your French exam earlier in the day. Similarly, exposure to MPI could interfere with remembering what happened when you originally viewed a stimulus (Titcomb & Reyna, 1995).

MPI AS CAUSING SOURCE MONITORING ERRORS Another explanation for the misinformation effect is based on the idea of source monitoring, which we discussed earlier. From the source monitoring perspective, a person incorrectly concludes that the source of his or her memory for the incorrect event (yield sign) was the slide show, even though the actual source was the experimenter's statement after the slide show.

The following experiment by Stephen Lindsay (1990) investigated source monitoring and MPI by asking whether subjects who are exposed to MPI really believe they saw something that was only suggested to them. Lindsay's subjects first saw a sequence of slides showing a maintenance man stealing money and a computer (**Figure 8.15**). This slide presentation was narrated by a female speaker, who simply described what was happening as the slides were being shown. The subjects were then divided into two groups.

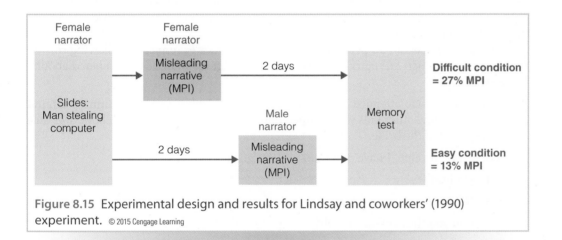

Figure 8.15 Experimental design and results for Lindsay and coworkers' (1990) experiment. © 2015 Cengage Learning

Subjects in the *difficult condition* heard a misleading narrative shortly after seeing the slide presentation. This narrative was read by the same female speaker who had described the slide show. For example, when subjects viewed the slide show, they saw Folgers coffee, but the misleading narrative said the coffee was Maxwell House. Two days later, subjects returned to the lab for a memory test on the slide show. Just before the test, they were told that there were errors in the narrative story that they heard right after the slide show and that they should ignore the information in the story when taking the memory test.

Subjects in the *easy condition* also heard the misleading story, but it was delayed for 2 days, being presented right before they took the memory test. In addition, the story was read by a male speaker. As with the difficult group, these subjects were also told to ignore the information presented in the narrative.

The procedure for the difficult condition made it easy to confuse the misleading narrative and the slide show because they occurred one after the other and were both read by the female. However, in the easy condition, it was easy to separate the misleading narrative from the slide show because they occurred 2 days apart and were read by different speakers. The results indicated that 27 percent of the responses of subjects in the difficult condition corresponded to the incorrect information in the misleading narrative. These responses to the misled items were source monitoring errors because the subjects were confusing information in the misleading narrative story with the information from the slide show. In contrast, only 13 percent of the responses for subjects in the easy condition corresponded to the incorrect information.

Although researchers are still discussing the mechanism or mechanisms that cause the misinformation effect, there is no doubt that the effect is real and that experimenters' suggestions can influence subjects' reports in memory experiments. Some of the most dramatic demonstrations of the effect of experimenter suggestion show that it can cause people to believe that events occurred early in their lives even though these events never happened.

CREATING FALSE MEMORIES FOR EARLY EVENTS IN PEOPLE'S LIVES

Ira Hyman, Jr., and coworkers (1995) created false memories for long ago events in an experiment in which they contacted the parents of their subjects and asked them to provide descriptions of actual events that happened when the subjects were children. The experimenters then also created descriptions of false events, ones that never happened, such as a birthday that included a clown and a pizza, and spilling a bowl of punch at a wedding reception.

Subjects, who as college students were far removed from these childhood experiences, were given some of the information from the parents' descriptions and were told to elaborate on them. They were also given some of the information from the false events and were told to elaborate on them as well. The result was that the subjects "recalled" and described in some detail 20 percent of the false events. For example, the following conversation occurred when an interviewer (I) asked a subject (S) what he remembered about a false event.

I: At age 6 you attended a wedding reception, and while you were running around with some other kids you bumped into a table and turned a punch bowl over on a parent of the bride.

S: I have no clue. I have never heard that one before. Age 6?

I: Uh-huh.

S: No clue.

I: Can you think of any details?

S: Six years old; we would have been in Spokane, um, not at all.

I: OK.

However, in a second interview that occurred 2 days later, the subject responded as follows:

I: The next one was when you were 6 years old and you were attending a wedding.

S: The wedding was my best friend in Spokane, T___. Her brother, older brother, was getting married, and it was over here in P___, Washington, 'cause that's where her family was from, and it was in the summer or the spring because it was really hot outside, and it was right on the water. It was an outdoor wedding, and I think we were running around and knocked something over like the punch bowl or something and um made a big mess and of course got yelled at for it.

I: Do you remember anything else?

S: No.

I: OK.

What is most interesting about this subject's response is that he didn't remember the wedding the first time, but did remember it the second time. Apparently, hearing about the event and then waiting caused the event to emerge as a false memory. This can be explained by familiarity. When questioned about the wedding the second time, the subject's familiarity with the wedding from the first exposure caused him to accept the wedding as having actually happened.

The fact that false memories for early childhood experiences can be created by suggestion has had serious implications for some real-life cases in which false memories may have been created by suggestions made to patients undergoing therapy. For example, consider the case of Gary Romona, whose 19-year-old daughter Holly, while undergoing therapy for an eating disorder, received a suggestion from her therapist that her disorder may have been caused by sexual abuse. After further therapy, and more suggestions from the therapist, Holly became convinced that her father had repeatedly raped her when she was a child. Holly's accusations caused Romona to lose his $400,000-a-year executive job, his reputation, his friends, and contact with his three daughters.

Romona sued Holly's therapists for malpractice, accusing them of implanting memories in his daughter's mind. At the trial, Elizabeth Loftus and other cognitive psychologists described research on the misinformation effect and implanting false memories to demonstrate how suggestion can create false memories for long ago events that never actually happened (Loftus, 1993b). Romona won a $500,000 judgment against the therapists. As a result of this case, highlighting how memory can be influenced by suggestion, a number of criminal convictions based on "recovered memory" evidence have since been reversed.

Why Do People Make Errors in Eyewitness Testimony?

A crime occurs. How is the evidence collected? There are the usual forensic techniques—fingerprinting, determining bullet trajectories, DNA analysis, and a host of other physical measures. But one of the most important sources of evidence, at least in the eyes of jury members, is **eyewitness testimony**—testimony by a person who was present at the crime about what he or she saw during commission of the crime. The acceptance of eyewitness testimony is based on two assumptions: (1) the eyewitness was able to clearly see what happened; and (2) the eyewitness was able to remember his or her observations and translate them into an accurate description of what happened and an accurate identification of the perpetrator(s).

The question for cognitive psychology is, how accurate are witnesses' perceptions and how accurate are their descriptions and identifications, which may be elicited some time after the crime? What do you think the answer to this question is, based on what you know about perception, attention, and memory? As you might imagine, the answer is "not very accurate," unless witness descriptions and identifications are carried out under ideal conditions. Unfortunately, this doesn't always occur, and there is a great deal of evidence that many innocent people have been convicted based on inaccurate eyewitness testimony.

ERRORS OF EYEWITNESS IDENTIFICATION

In the United States, 200 people per day become criminal defendants based on eyewitness testimony (Goldstein et al., 1989). Unfortunately, there are many instances in which errors of eyewitness testimony have resulted in the conviction of innocent people. As of 2012, the use of DNA evidence had exonerated 341 people in the United States who had been wrongly convicted of crimes and served an average of 13 years in prison (Innocence Project, 2012). Seventy-five percent of these convictions involved eyewitness testimony (Quinlivan et al., 2010; Scheck et al., 2000).

To put a human face on the problem of wrongful convictions due to faulty eyewitness testimony, consider the case of David Webb, who was sentenced to up to 50 years in prison for rape, attempted rape, and attempted robbery based on eyewitness testimony. After serving 10 months, he was released after another man confessed to the crimes. Charles Clark went to prison for murder in 1938, based on eyewitness testimony that, 30 years later, was found to be inaccurate. He was released in 1968 (Loftus, 1979). Ronald Cotton was convicted of raping Jennifer Thompson in 1984, based on her testimony that she was extremely positive that he was the man who had raped her. Even after Cotton was exonerated by DNA evidence that implicated another man, Thompson still "remembered" Cotton as being her attacker. Cotton was released after serving 10 years (Wells & Quinlivan, 2009).

The disturbing thing about these examples is not only that they occurred, but that they suggest that many other innocent people are currently serving time for crimes they didn't commit. Many of these miscarriages of justice and others, some of which will undoubtedly never be discovered, are based on the assumption, made by jurors and judges, that people see and report things accurately.

This assumption about the accuracy of testimony is based on the popular conception that memory works like a camera or video recorder, as demonstrated by the results of the nationwide survey described at the beginning of this chapter (page 208). Jurors carry these misconceptions about memory into the courtroom, and many judges and law enforcement officials also share these conceptions of memory (Benton et al., 2006). So, the first problem is that jurors don't understand the basic facts about memory. The second problem is that witnesses' observations and the reporting of their memories are often made under the less than ideal conditions that occur at a crime scene and then afterward, when they are talking with the police. We will now consider a few of the situations in which errors can be created.

ERRORS ASSOCIATED WITH PERCEPTION AND ATTENTION

Witness reports will, of course, be inaccurate if the witness doesn't perceive what happened in the first place. There is ample evidence that identifications are difficult even when subjects in laboratory experiments have been instructed to pay close attention to what is happening. A number of experiments have presented subjects with films of actual crimes or staged crimes and then asked them to pick the perpetrator from a photo spread (photographs of a number of faces, one of which could be the perpetrator). In one study, subjects viewed a security videotape in which a gunman was in view for 8 seconds and then were asked to pick the gunman from photographs. Every subject picked someone they thought was the gunman, even though his picture was not included in the photo spread (Wells & Bradfield, 1998). In another study, using a similar experimental design, 61 percent of the subjects picked someone from a photo spread, even though the perpetrator's picture wasn't included (Kneller et al., 2001).

These studies show how difficult it is to accurately identify someone after viewing a videotape of a crime. But things become even more complicated when we consider some of the things that happen during actual crimes. Emotions often run high during commission of a crime, and this can affect what a person pays attention to and what the person remembers later.

In a study of *weapons focus*, the tendency to focus attention on a weapon that results in a narrowing of attention (see page 213), Claudia Stanny and Thomas Johnson (2000) determined how well subjects remembered details of a filmed simulated crime. They found that subjects were more likely to recall details of the perpetrator, the victim, and the weapon in the "no-shoot" condition (a gun was present but not fired) than in the "shoot" condition (the gun was fired; **Figure 8.16**). Apparently, the presence of a weapon that was fired distracted attention from other things that were happening (also see Tooley et al., 1987).

MISIDENTIFICATIONS DUE TO FAMILIARITY

Crimes not only involve a perpetrator and a victim but often include innocent bystanders (some of whom, as we will see, many not even be near the scene of the crime). These bystanders add yet another dimension to the testimony of eyewitnesses because there is a chance that a bystander could be mistakenly identified as a perpetrator because of familiarity from some other context. In one case of mistaken identification, a ticket agent at a railway station was robbed and subsequently identified a sailor as being the robber. Luckily for the sailor, he was able to show that he was somewhere else at the time of the crime. When asked why he identified the sailor, the ticket agent said that he looked familiar. The sailor

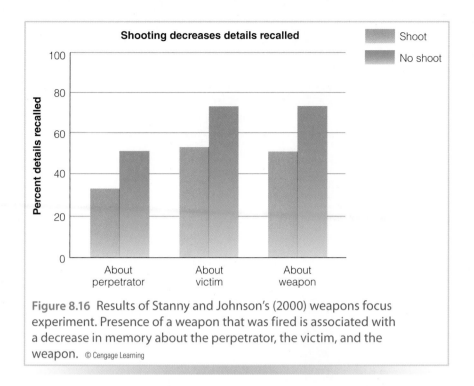

Figure 8.16 Results of Stanny and Johnson's (2000) weapons focus experiment. Presence of a weapon that was fired is associated with a decrease in memory about the perpetrator, the victim, and the weapon. © Cengage Learning

looked familiar not because he was the robber, but because he lived near the train station and had purchased tickets from the agent on a number of occasions. This was an example of a source monitoring error. The ticket agent thought the source of his familiarity with the sailor was seeing him during the holdup; in reality, the source of his familiarity was seeing him when he purchased tickets. The sailor had become transformed from a ticket buyer into a holdup man by a source monitoring error (Ross et al., 1994).

Figure 8.17a shows the design for a laboratory experiment on familiarity and eyewitness testimony (Ross et al., 1994). Subjects in the experimental group saw a film of a male teacher reading to students; subjects in the control group saw a film of a female teacher reading to students. Subjects in both groups then saw a film of the female teacher being robbed and were asked to pick the robber from a photo spread. The photographs did not include the actual robber, but did include the male teacher, who resembled the robber. The results indicate that subjects in the experimental group were three times more likely to pick the male teacher than were subjects in the control group (Figure 8.17b). Even when the actual robber's face was included in the photo spread, 18 percent of subjects in the experimental group picked the teacher, compared to 10 percent in the control group (Figure 8.17c).

ERRORS DUE TO SUGGESTION

From what we know about the misinformation effect, it is obvious that a police officer asking a witness "Did you see the white car?" could influence the witness's later testimony about what he or she saw. But suggestibility can also operate on a more subtle level. Consider the following situation: A witness to a crime is looking through a one-way window at a lineup of six men standing on a stage. The police officer says, "Which one of these men did it?" What is wrong with this question?

The problem with the police officer's question is that it implies that the crime perpetrator is in the lineup. This suggestion increases the chances that the witness will pick someone, perhaps using the following type of reasoning: "Well, the guy with the beard looks more like the robber than any of the other men, so that's probably the one." Of course, looking *like* the robber and actually *being* the robber may be two different things, so the result may be identification of an innocent man. A better way of presenting the task is to let the witness know that the crime suspect may or may not be in the lineup.

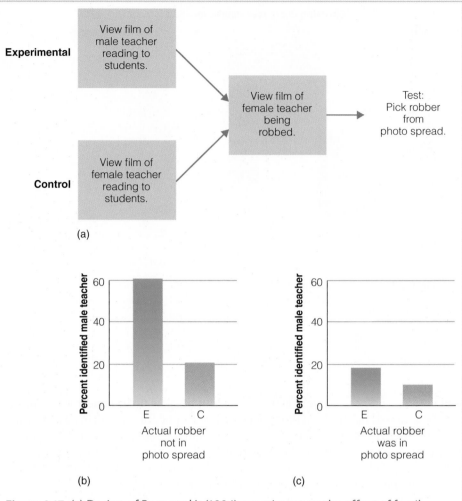

Figure 8.17 (a) Design of Ross et al.'s (1994) experiment on the effect of familiarity on eyewitness testimony. (b) When the actual robber was not in the photo spread, subjects in the experimental group erroneously identified the male teacher as the robber 60 percent of the time. (c) When the actual robber was in the photo spread, the male teacher was identified 18 percent of the time. © Cengage Learning

Here is another situation, taken from a transcript of an actual criminal case, in which suggestion could have played a role.

> Eyewitness to a crime on viewing a lineup: "Oh, my God. . . . I don't know. . . . It's one of those two . . . but I don't know. . . . . Oh, man . . the guy a little bit taller than number two. . . . It's one of those two, but I don't know."
> Eyewitness 30 minutes later, still viewing the lineup and having difficulty making a decision: "I don't know . . . number two?"
> Officer administering lineup: "Okay."
> Months later . . . at trial: "You were positive it was number two? It wasn't a maybe?"
> Answer from eyewitness: "There was no maybe about it. . . . I was absolutely positive."
> (Wells & Bradfield, 1998)

The problem with this scenario is that the police officer's response of "okay" may have influenced the witness to think that he or she had correctly identified the suspect. Thus, the witness's initially uncertain response turns into an "absolutely positive" response. In a paper titled "Good, You Identified the Suspect," Gary Wells and Amy Bradfield (1998) had subjects view a video of an actual crime and then asked them to identify the perpetrator from a photo spread that did not actually contain a picture of the perpetrator (Figure 8.18).

All of the subjects picked one of the photographs, and following their choice, witnesses received either confirming feedback from the experimenter ("Good, you identified the suspect"), no feedback, or disconfirming feedback ("Actually, the suspect was number __"). A short time later, the subjects were asked how confident they were about their identification. The results, shown at the bottom of the figure, indicate that subjects who received the confirming feedback were more confident of their choice.

Wells and Bradfield call this increase in confidence due to confirming feedback after making an identification the **post-identification feedback effect**. This effect creates a serious problem in the criminal justice system, because jurors are strongly influenced by how confident eyewitnesses are about their judgments. Thus, faulty eyewitness judgments can result in picking the wrong person, and the post-identification feedback effect can then increase witnesses' confidence that they made the right judgment (Douglass et al., 2010; Luus & Wells, 1994; Quinlivan et al., 2010; Wells & Quinlivan, 2009).

Paradoxically, the danger of suggestion influencing memory may be increased if it happens when or just after the witness is remembering what happened. This possibility was studied by Jason Chan and coworkers (2009), who showed subjects a 40-minute episode of the television program *24*, in which Jack Bauer, played by Kiefer Sutherland, is trying to thwart a terrorist plot (Figure 8.19). The subjects were then split into two groups. The *test group* took a cued recall test about the video, which contained questions like "What did the terrorist use to knock out the flight attendant?" (correct answers were not provided). The *no-test group* played a computer game. Both groups were then given distraction tasks, such as filling out a questionnaire and completing some tests unrelated to the TV program.

Chan then presented an 8-minute audio that described some of the events in the TV program. Some events were described accurately, but some *misinformation items* differed from what happened in the video. For example, in the video the terrorist knocked out the flight attendant with a hypodermic syringe, but the misinformation item in the audio stated that the terrorist used a chloroform pad. The procedure in this part of

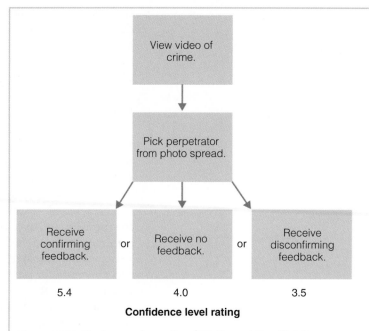

Figure 8.18 Design and results of Wells and Bradfield's (1998) "Good, You Identified the Suspect" experiment. The type of feedback from the experimenter influenced subjects' confidence in their identification, with confirming feedback resulting in the highest confidence. © Cengage Learning

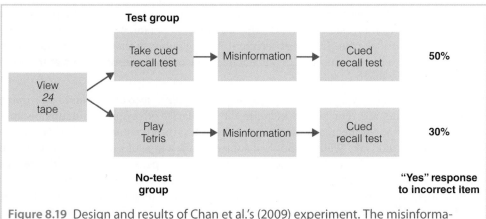

Figure 8.19 Design and results of Chan et al.'s (2009) experiment. The misinformation effect was greater for subjects who had their memory reactivated by the cued recall test. © Cengage Learning

the experiment is therefore similar to the procedure in the misinformation studies we described earlier. Finally, all subjects took the cued recall test (the same one that the test group had taken earlier). The number on the right of **Figure 8.19** indicates the percentage of misinformation items from the 8-minute audio that subjects indicated were in the original TV program. The test group said "yes" incorrectly to 50 percent of these items, compared to 30 percent for the no-test group. Thus, being tested, which brought back memories for the original event, made subjects more likely to be influenced by the misinformation.

Why does being tested increase the misinformation effect? The *attention explanation* proposes that taking the test might draw attention to specific events in the original video, and these events might have stood out more as the misinformation was presented, so were more likely to be changed. Another explanation is based on the *reconsolidation effect* discussed in Chapter 7. We saw that the act of remembering causes *reactivation* of the memory, and once the memory is reactivated, it becomes fragile and subject to change until it is strengthened by the process of reconsolidation (see page 199). According to the *reconsolidation explanation*, having subjects in the test group take the recall test reactivated their memory for the TV program and opened a window during which memory became fragile, so it was more likely that the misinformation would become confused with the original memory. This explanation has been supported in additional experiments (Chan & LaPaglia, 2013).

The fact that memories become more susceptible to suggestion during questioning means that every precaution needs to be taken to avoid making suggestions to the witness. This is often not done, but some steps have been taken to help improve the situation, both in terms of suggestion and other procedures involving witnesses.

WHAT IS BEING DONE?

The first step toward correcting the problem of inaccurate eyewitness testimony was to recognize that the problem exists. This has been achieved, largely through the efforts of memory researchers and attorneys and investigators for unjustly convicted people. The next step is to propose specific solutions. Two problem areas for which cognitive psychologists have made suggestions are lineup procedures and interviewing procedures.

LINEUP PROCEDURES Lineups are notorious for producing mistaken identifications. Here are some of the recommendations that have been made:

Recommendation 1: When asking a witness to pick the perpetrator from a lineup, inform the witness that the perpetrator may not be in the particular lineup he or she is viewing. As we have seen from the results of a number of studies, witnesses will usually pick a person from a lineup even when the perpetrator is not present. When a witness assumes the perpetrator is in the lineup, this increases the chances that an innocent person who looks similar to the perpetrator will be selected. In one experiment, telling subjects that the perpetrator may not be present in a lineup caused a 42 percent decrease in false identifications of innocent people (Malpass & Devine, 1981).

Recommendation 2: When constructing a lineup, use "fillers" who are similar to the suspect. Police investigators are reluctant to increase the similarity of people in lineups because they are afraid this will decrease the chances of identifying the suspect. However, when R. C. L. Lindsay and Gary Wells (1980) had subjects view a tape of a crime scene and then tested them using high-similarity and low-similarity lineups, they obtained the results shown in **Figure 8.20**. When the perpetrator was in the lineup, increasing similarity did decrease identification of the perpetrator, from 0.71 to 0.58 (**Figure 8.20a**). But when the perpetrator was not in the lineup, increasing similarity caused a large decrease in incorrect identification of an innocent person, from 0.70 to 0.31 (**Figure 8.20b**). Thus, increasing similarity does result in missed identification of some guilty suspects, but substantially reduces the erroneous identification of innocent people, especially when the perpetrator is not in the lineup (also see Charman et al., 2011).

Recommendation 3: When presenting a lineup, use sequential rather than simultaneous presentation. The usual depiction of lineups in movies—and the one most often used in police work—is a simultaneous presentation of five or six people standing in a line facing the witness, who is hidden behind a one-way mirror. The problem with the simultaneous presentation is that it increases the chances that the witness will make a relative judgment—comparing people in the lineup to each other, so the question is "Who is most like the person I saw?" However, when each person in the lineup is presented sequentially—one at a time—then the witness compares each person not to the other people, but to the memory of what the witness saw. Lindsay and Wells (1985) found that for lineups in which the perpetrator was not present, an innocent person was falsely identified 43 percent of the time in the simultaneous lineup, but only 17 percent of the time in the sequential lineup. Recent studies of sequential versus simultaneous lineups have confirmed that sequential lineups reduce mistaken identifications from lineups in which the culprit is absent. Although sequential lineups also cause a small decrease in identification of suspects, the identifications that are made are more likely to be accurate (Steblay et al., 2011).

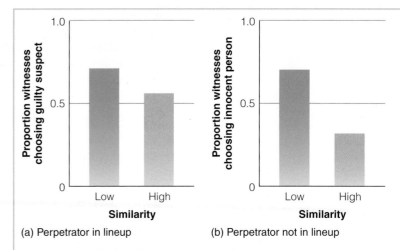

(a) Perpetrator in lineup   (b) Perpetrator not in lineup

Figure 8.20 Results of Lindsay and Wells's (1980) experiment, showing that (a) when the perpetrator was in the lineup, increasing similarity decreased identification of the perpetrator, but (b) when the perpetrator was not in the lineup, increasing similarity caused an even greater decrease in incorrect identification of innocent people. © Cengage Learning

Recommendation 4: Use a "blind" lineup administrator and get an immediate confidence rating. When presenting a lineup, the person administering the lineup should not know who the suspect is. In addition, having witnesses immediately rate their confidence in their choice eliminates the possibility that the postevent feedback effect could increase their confidence.

INTERVIEWING TECHNIQUES We have already seen that making suggestions to the witness ("Good, you identified the suspect") can cause errors. Cognitive psychologists have developed an interview procedure called the **cognitive interview**, which is based on what is known about memory retrieval. This interview procedure, which has been described as "perhaps one of the most successful developments in psychology and law research in the last 25 years" (Memon et al., 2010), involves letting the witness talk with a minimum of interruption and also uses techniques that help witnesses recreate the situation present at the crime scene by having them place themselves back in the scene and recreate things like emotions they were feeling, where they were looking, and how the scene might have appeared when viewed from different perspectives.

An important feature of the cognitive interview technique is that it decreases the likelihood of any suggestive input by the person conducting the interview. Comparisons of the results of cognitive interviews to routine police questioning have shown that the cognitive interview results in a large increase in reports of correct details, as well as a smaller increase in incorrect details. A disadvantage of the cognitive interview is that it takes longer than standard interviewing procedures. To deal with this problem, shorter versions have been developed (Fisher et al., 2013; Geiselman et al., 1986; Memon et al., 2010).

Recommendations like those described above led to the publication in 1999 by the U.S. Justice Department of *Eyewitness Evidence: A Guide for Law Enforcement* (available at www.nij.gov/pubs-sum/178240.htm), which includes many of these suggestions, plus others. Perhaps even more important, some of these recommendations are having a direct effect on actual procedures in the field. In 2011, the New Jersey Supreme Court mandated that judges inform jurors about the scientific findings regarding eyewitness testimony by including instructions to the jury such as "Human memory is not foolproof. Research has shown that human memory is not at all like a video recording that a witness need only replay to remember what happened." Furthermore, many states, including New Jersey, Ohio, California, North Carolina, and Wisconsin, have switched from simultaneous to sequential lineups. Although sometimes the results of psychological research remain in the laboratory, research on eyewitness testimony is an excellent example of research having an impact in real-life situations.

Something to Consider

THE POWER OF PICTURES

Most of the early misinformation experiments used statements like "How fast were the cars going when they smashed into each other?" or "At age 6 you attended a wedding reception . . ." to change people's memories. But pictures have been used as well. For example, Kimberley Wade and coworkers (2002) showed subjects photographs obtained from family members that showed the subject involved in various events like birthday parties or vacations when they were 4 to 8 years old. Subjects also saw a photograph created in Photoshop that showed them in an event that never happened—taking a hot air balloon ride. Subjects were shown the photo and asked to describe what they remembered about the event. If they couldn't remember the event, subjects were told to close their eyes and picture participating in the event.

Subjects easily recalled the real events but initially didn't recall taking the hot air balloon ride. After picturing the event in their minds and further questioning, however, 35 percent of the subjects "remembered" the balloon ride, and after two more interviews, 50 percent of the subjects described their experience while riding in the balloon. This result is similar to the experiment described earlier in which subjects were told that they had turned over a punch bowl at a wedding reception. In another experiment, Robert Nash and Wade (2009) took videos of subjects as they participated in a computerized gambling game. Subjects were told that on a trial in which they won their gamble, a green check would appear on the screen and they should take money from the bank, but when they lost, a red cross would appear and they needed to give money back to the bank. After subjects had played the game, they were shown a doctored video in which the check was replaced by the cross to make them appear to be cheating by taking money when they were supposed to be giving it to the bank (**Figure 8.21**). When confronted with the video "evidence," some subjects expressed surprise, but all confessed to cheating. In another group, who were told there was a video of them cheating (but who didn't see the video), 73 percent of the subjects confessed. Based on this result, we can conclude that if you want people to confess to a crime they didn't commit, show them fake video evidence!

Figure 8.21 Stills from the video used by Nash and Wade (2009). The left panel is from the original video. The right panel is from the doctored video.

© 2008 John Wiley & Sons, Ltd.

These results and others indicate that pictures are a powerful source of misinformation (Frenda et al., 2013; Garry et al., 2007; Nash et al., 2009; Sacchi et al., 2007). One reason is that photographs go beyond describing an event—they provide concrete evidence that it occurred, and do so by providing the perceptual details that people associate with true memories. As a number of subjects said when they were being interviewed in the hot air balloon experiment, "Well, it's a photograph, so it must have happened."

But photographs don't even have to be doctored pictures of supposed events in order to influence memory. Stephen Lindsay and coworkers (2004) presented subjects with descriptions of real childhood experiences supplied by their parents and another experience that never occurred (placing a toy called Slime, a brightly colored gelatinous compound, in their first-grade teacher's desk). Additionally, Lindsay had one group of subjects look at a photograph of their first- or second-grade class, like the one in **Figure 8.22**, as they were being presented with the story about placing Slime in the teacher's desk. The result of this experiment was that subjects who saw the picture experienced more than twice as many false memories as subjects who did not see the picture. Why would this occur? After all, there is no Slime in the class picture. One reason might be that seeing the perceptually detailed picture of their teacher and classmates made it easier for the subjects to mentally travel back to the situation in which the event would have occurred.

Figure 8.22 Photographs of a first- or second-grade class, similar to the one shown here, were shown to subjects in Lindsay et al.'s (2004) experiment.

Ending this chapter by referring to mental time travel is fitting because as we have focused on memory in everyday situations, we have emphasized episodic memory. At the same time we have noted how semantic memory—our storehouse of knowledge and facts about the world—interacts with and influences episodic memory. In the next chapter we will be concerned almost entirely with semantic memory as we consider mechanisms that make it possible for us to gather knowledge about the objects and events that make up our world.

TEST YOURSELF 8.3

1. Experiments showing that memory can be affected by suggestion have led to the proposal of the misinformation effect. How has the misinformation effect been demonstrated, and what mechanisms have been proposed to explain this effect?

2. How has it been shown that suggestion can influence people's memories for early events in their lives?

3. What is the evidence, both from "real life" and from laboratory experiments, that eyewitness testimony is not always accurate? Describe how the following factors have been shown to lead to errors in eyewitness testimony: weapons focus, familiarity, leading questions, feedback from a police officer, and postevent questioning.

4. Describe Chan's experiment that showed that taking a test can influence a person's susceptibility to misinformation. How is this related to how suggestions made by a questioner might influence what a witness remembers?

5. What procedures have cognitive psychologists proposed to increase the accuracy of eyewitness testimony?

6. Describe how pictures have been used to influence memory and why they are effective.

DEMONSTRATION
READING SENTENCES (CONTINUED)

The sentences below are the ones you read in the demonstration on page 223 but with one or two words missing. Without looking back at the original sentences, fill in the blanks with the words that were in the sentence you initially read.

The flimsy shelf _____ under the weight of the books.

The children's snowman _____ when the temperature reached 80.

The absentminded professor _____ his car keys.

The new baby _____ all night.

The karate champion _____ the cinder block.

After doing this, return to page 223 and read the text that follows the demonstration.

CHAPTER SUMMARY

1. A nationwide poll has shown that a substantial proportion of people have erroneous conceptions about the nature of memory.

2. Autobiographical memory (AM) has been defined as memory for specific experiences from our life. It consists of both episodic and semantic components.

3. The multidimensional nature of AM has been studied by showing that people who have lost their visual memory due to brain damage experience a loss of AM. Also supporting the multidimensional nature of AM is Cabeza's experiment, which showed that a person's brain is more extensively activated when viewing photographs taken by the person him- or herself than when viewing photographs taken by someone else.

4. When people are asked to remember events over their lifetime, transition points are particularly memorable. Also, people over 40 tend to have good memory for events they experienced from adolescence to early adulthood. This is called the reminiscence bump.

5. The following hypotheses have been proposed to explain the reminiscence bump: (1) self-image, (2) cognitive, and (3) cultural life script.

6. Emotions are often associated with events that are easily remembered. The amygdala is a key structure for emotional memories, and emotion has been linked to improved memory consolidation. There is also evidence that in some situations emotions can impair memory.

7. Brown and Kulik proposed the term *flashbulb memory* to refer to a person's memory for the circumstances surrounding hearing about shocking, highly charged events. They proposed that these flashbulb memories are vivid and detailed, like photographs.

8. A number of experiments indicate that it is not accurate to equate flashbulb memories with photographs because, as time passes, people make many errors when reporting flashbulb memories. Studies of memories for hearing about the *Challenger* explosion showed that people's responses became more inaccurate with increasing time after the event.

9. Talarico and Rubin's study of people's memory for when they first heard about the 9/11 terrorist attack indicates that memory errors increased with time, just as for other memories, but that people remained more confident of the accuracy of their 9/11 memory.

10. Emotions have been associated with the subjective sense of remembering. An experiment by Rimmele and coworkers demonstrates that emotion can increase general memory while decreasing memory for details.

11. The narrative rehearsal hypothesis proposes that enhanced memory for significant events may be caused by rehearsal. This rehearsal is often linked to TV coverage, as illustrated by the results of the Princess Diana study.

12. According to the constructive approach to memory, originally proposed by Bartlett based on his "War of the Ghosts" experiment, what people report as memories are constructed based on what actually happened plus additional factors such as the person's knowledge, experiences, and expectations.

13. Source monitoring is the process of determining the origins of our memories, knowledge, or beliefs. A source monitoring error occurs when the source of a memory is misidentified. Cryptomnesia (unconscious plagiarism) is an example of a source monitoring error.

14. Familiarity (Jacoby's "Becoming Famous Overnight" experiment) and world knowledge (Marsh's gender stereotype experiment) can result in source monitoring errors.

15. General world knowledge can cause memory errors. Inference is one of the mechanisms of the constructive process of memory. The pragmatic inference experiment and the baseball experiment are examples of the effect of inference on memory.

16. Our knowledge about what is involved in a particular experience is a schema for that experience. The experiment in which participants were asked to remember what was in an office illustrates how schemas can cause errors in memory reports.

17. A script is a type of schema that involves our conception of the sequence of actions that usually occur during a particular experience. The "dentist experiment," in which a participant is asked to remember a paragraph about going to the dentist, illustrates how scripts can result in memory errors.

18. The experiment in which people were asked to recall a list of words related to sleep illustrates how our knowledge about things that belong together (for example, that *sleep* belongs with *bed*) can result in reporting words that were not on the original list.

19. Although people often think that it would be an advantage to have a photographic memory, the cases of S. and A.J. show that it may not be an advantage to be able to remember everything perfectly. The fact that our memory system does not store everything may even add to the survival value of the system.

20. Memory experiments in which misleading postevent information (MPI) is presented to participants indicate that memory can be influenced by suggestion. An example is Loftus's traffic accident experiment. Retroactive interference and source monitoring errors have been proposed to explain the errors caused by misleading postevent information. Lindsay's experiment provides support for the source monitoring explanation.

21. An experiment by Hyman, in which he created false memories for a party, showed that it is possible to create false memories for early events in a person's life. False memories may have been involved in some cases of "recovered memories" of childhood abuse.

22. There is a great deal of evidence that innocent people have been convicted of crimes because of errors of eyewitness testimony. Some of the reasons for errors in eyewitness testimony are (1) not paying attention to all relevant details because of the emotional situation during a crime (weapons focus is one example of such an attentional effect); (2) errors due to familiarity, which can result in misidentification of an innocent person due to source monitoring error; (3) errors due to suggestion during questioning about a crime; and (4) increased confidence due to postevent feedback (the post-identification feedback effect).

23. An experiment by Chan and coworkers shows that taking a test about what a person witnessed can make witnesses more susceptible to misleading information.

24. Cognitive psychologists have suggested a number of ways to decrease errors in eyewitness testimony. These suggestions focus on improving procedures for conducting line-ups and interviewing witnesses.

25. Photographs and videos are a powerful source of misleading information (the hot air balloon and gambling experiments) and may also function to help subjects mentally travel back in time (the Slime experiment).

THINK ABOUT IT

1. What do you remember about how you heard about the terrorist attacks of September 11, 2001 (or some other highly emotional event)? How confident are you that your memory of these events is accurate? Given the results of experiments on flashbulb memories described in this chapter, what do you think the chances are that your memories might be in error? Are there any ways that you could check the accuracy of your memories?

2. What do you remember about what you did on the most recent major holiday (Thanksgiving, Christmas, New Year's, your birthday, etc.)? What do you remember about what you did on the same holiday 1 year earlier? How do these memories differ in terms of (a) how difficult they were to remember, (b) how much detail you can remember, and (c) the accuracy of your memory? (How would you know if your answer to part c is correct?)

3. There have been a large number of reports of people unjustly imprisoned because of errors in eyewitness testimony, with more cases being reported every day, based on DNA evidence. Given this situation, how would you react to the proposal that eyewitness testimony no longer be admitted as evidence in courts of law?

4. Interview people of different ages regarding what they remember about their lives. How do your results fit with the results of AM experiments, especially regarding the idea of a reminiscence bump in older people?

KEY TERMS

COGLAB EXPERIMENTS   Number in parentheses refers to the experiment number in CogLab.

False Memory (33)

Forgot It All Along (34)

Memory Judgment (35)

Saying "That's a car" or "There's my dog" involves using your store of knowledge to place objects into categories ("car" and "dog"). But what is that 40-foot-tall yellow thing in the river near downtown Pittsburgh? People in Pittsburgh call it "The Duck" or "The Rubber Duck," even though it looks nothing like the real ducks swimming nearby and is much larger than a toy rubber duck. It is called a "sculpture" by Dutch artist Florentijn Hofman, who created it, even though it doesn't look like our usual conception of a sculpture. This chapter describes how people place objects in categories like "duck," "toy," or "sculpture" and how information about categories is stored in the brain.

Knowledge

► Why is it difficult to decide if
a particular object belongs
to a particular category, such
as "chair," by looking up its
definition? (247)

► How are the properties of
various objects "filed away" in
the mind? (256)

► How is information about
different categories stored in
the brain? (264)

Imagine that you find yourself in an unfamiliar town, where you have never been before. As you walk down the street, you notice that many things are not exactly the same as what you would encounter if you were in your own town. On the other hand, there are many things that seem familiar. Cars pass by, there are buildings on either side of the street and a gas station on the corner, and a cat dashes across the street and makes it safely to the other side. Luckily, you know a lot about cars, buildings, gas stations, and cats, so you have no trouble understanding what is going on.

This chapter is about the kind of knowledge that enables you to recognize and understand the objects in the street scene and the world. This type of knowledge is called **conceptual knowledge**—knowledge that enables us to recognize objects and events and to make inferences about their properties (Rogers & Cox, in press). This knowledge exists in the form of *concepts*. **Concepts** have been defined in a number of ways, including "the mental representation of a class or individual" (Smith, 1989) and "the meaning of objects, events, and abstract ideas" (Kiefer & Pulvermüller, 2012). To express this in concrete terms, we can say that the concept "cat" is the answer to the question "What is a cat?" If your answer is that a cat is an animal that is furry, meows, moves, and eats mice, you will have described your concept of "cat" (Kiefer & Pulvermüller, 2012).

Because we are interested in our knowledge about the world, we need to go beyond cats! When we start expanding our scope to dogs, automobiles, can openers, radishes, and roses, things start to become both more complicated and more interesting, because the question then becomes "How are all of these things organized in the mind?" One way we organize concepts is in terms of *categories*.

A **category** includes all possible examples of a particular concept. Thus, the category "cats" includes tabbies, Siamese cats, Persian cats, wildcats, leopards, and so on. Looked at in this way, concepts provide the rules for creating categories. Thus, the mental representation for "cat" would affect what animals we place in the "cat" category. Because concepts provide rules for sorting objects into categories, concepts and categories are often discussed together, and a great deal of research has focused on the process of **categorization**—the process by which things are placed in categories.

Categorization is something we do every time we place an object into a category, and once we have assigned an object to a category, we know a lot about it. For example, being able to say that the furry animal across the street is a "cat" provides a great deal of information about it (**Figure 9.1**). Categories have therefore been called "pointers to knowledge" (Yamauchi & Markman, 2000). Once you know that something is in a category, whether "cat," "gas station," or "impressionist painting," you can focus your energy on specifying what's special about this particular object (see Solomon et al., 1999).

Being able to place things in categories can also help us understand behaviors that we might otherwise find baffling. For example, if we see a man with the left side of his face painted black and the right side painted gold, we might wonder what is going on. However, once we note that the person is heading toward the football stadium and it is Sunday afternoon, we can categorize the person as a "Pittsburgh Steelers fan." Placing him in that category explains his painted face and perhaps other strange behaviors that happen to be normal on game day in Pittsburgh (Solomon et al., 1999).

These various uses of categories testify to their importance in everyday life. It is no exaggeration to say that if there were no such thing as categories, we would have a very difficult time dealing with the world. Consider what it would mean if every time you saw a different object, you knew nothing about it other than what you could find out by investigating it individually. Clearly, life would become extremely complicated if we weren't able to rely on the knowledge provided to us by categories. Given the importance of categories, cognitive psychologists have been interested in determining the process involved in categorizing objects.

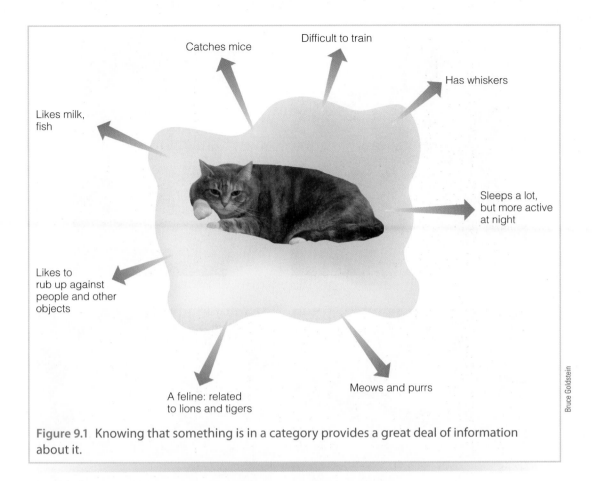

Catches mice

Difficult to train

Has whiskers

Likes milk, fish

Sleeps a lot, but more active at night

Likes to rub up against people and other objects

A feline: related to lions and tigers

Meows and purrs

Bruce Goldstein

Figure 9.1 Knowing that something is in a category provides a great deal of information about it.

How Are Objects Placed Into Categories?

A time-honored approach to determining the characteristics of an object is to look up its definition. We begin by describing how cognitive psychologists have shown that this "definitional approach" to sorting objects into categories doesn't work. We then consider another approach, which is based on determining how similar an object is to other objects in a category.

WHY DEFINITIONS DON'T WORK FOR CATEGORIES

According to the **definitional approach to categorization**, we can decide whether something is a member of a category by determining whether a particular object meets the definition of the category. Definitions work well for some things, such as geometric objects. Thus, defining a square as "a plane figure having four equal sides, with all internal angles the same" works. However, for most natural objects (such as birds, trees, and plants) and many human-made objects (like chairs), definitions do not work well at all.

The problem is that not all of the members of everyday categories have the same features. So, although the dictionary definition of a chair as "a piece of furniture consisting of a seat, legs, back, and often arms, designed to accommodate one person" may sound reasonable, there are objects we call "chairs" that don't meet that definition. For example, although the objects in **Figures 9.2a** and **9.2b** would be classified as chairs by this definition, the ones in **Figures 9.2c** and **9.2d** would not. Most chairs may have legs and a back, as specified in the definition, but most people would still call the

(a)

(b)

(c)

(d)

Bruce Goldstein

Figure 9.2 Different objects, all possible "chairs."

disc-shaped furniture in **Figure 9.2c** a chair, and might go so far as to say that the rock formation in **Figure 9.2d** is being used as a chair.

The philosopher Ludwig Wittgenstein (1953) noted this problem with definitions and offered a solution:

> Consider for example the proceedings we call "games." I mean board-games, card-games, ball-games, Olympic games, and so on. For if you look at them you will not see something in common to all, but similarities, relationships, and a whole series of them at that. I can think of no better expression to characterize these similarities than "family resemblances."

Wittgenstein proposed the idea of **family resemblance** to deal with the problem that definitions often do not include all members of a category. Family resemblance refers to the idea that things in a particular category resemble one another in a number of ways. Thus, instead of setting definite criteria that every member of a category must meet, the family resemblance approach allows for some variation within a category. Chairs may come in many different sizes and shapes and be made of different materials, but every chair does resemble other chairs in some way. Looking at category membership in this way, we can see that the chair in **Figure 9.2a** and the chair in **Figure 9.2c** do have in common that they offer a place to sit, a way to support a person's back, and perhaps a place to rest the arms while sitting.

The idea of family resemblance has led psychologists to propose that categorization is based on determining how similar an object is to some standard representation of a category. We begin considering the idea of comparison to a standard by introducing the prototype approach to categorization.

THE PROTOTYPE APPROACH: FINDING THE AVERAGE CASE

According to the **prototype approach to categorization**, membership in a category is determined by comparing the object to a prototype that represents the category. A **prototype** is a "typical" member of the category.

What is a typical member of a particular category? Eleanor Rosch (1973) proposed that the "typical" prototype is based on an average of members of a category that are commonly experienced. For example, the prototype for the category "birds" might be based on some of the birds you usually see, such as sparrows, robins, and blue jays, but doesn't necessarily look exactly like any one of them. Thus, the prototype is not an actual member of the category but is an "average" representation of the category (**Figure 9.3**).

Figure 9.3 Three real birds—a sparrow, a robin, and a blue jay—and a "prototype" bird that is the average representation of the category "birds."

Of course, not all birds are like robins, blue jays, or sparrows. Owls, buzzards, and penguins are also birds. Rosch describes these variations within categories as representing differences in typicality. High typicality means that a category member closely resembles the category prototype (it is like a "typical" member of the category). Low typicality means that the category member does not closely resemble a typical member of the category.

Rosch (1975a) quantified this idea by presenting subjects with a category title, such as "bird" or "furniture," and a list of about 50 members of the category. The subjects' task was to rate the extent to which each member represented the category title on a 7-point scale, with a rating of 1 meaning that the member is a very good example of what the category is, and a rating of 7 meaning that the member fits poorly within the category or is not a member at all.

Results for some of the objects in two different categories are shown in **Figure 9.4**. The 1.18 rating for sparrow reflects the fact that most people consider a sparrow to be a good example of a bird (**Figure 9.4a**). The 4.53 rating for penguin and 6.15 rating for bat reflect the fact that penguins and bats are not considered good examples of birds. Similarly, chair and sofa (rating = 1.04) are considered very good examples of furniture, but mirror (4.39) and telephone (6.68) are poor examples (**Figure 9.4b**). The idea that a sparrow is a better example of "bird" than a penguin or a bat is not very surprising. But Rosch went beyond this obvious result by doing a series of experiments that demonstrated differences between good and bad examples of a category.

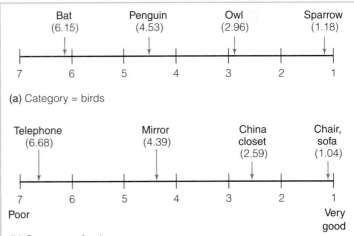

Figure 9.4 Results of Rosch's (1975a) experiment, in which participants judged objects on a scale of 1 (good example of a category) to 7 (poor example): (a) ratings for birds; (b) ratings for furniture. © Cengage Learning

PROTOTYPICAL OBJECTS HAVE HIGH FAMILY RESEMBLANCE How well do good and poor examples of a category compare to other items within the category? The following demonstration is based on an experiment by Rosch and Carolyn Mervis (1975).

DEMONSTRATION
FAMILY RESEMBLANCE

Rosch and Mervis's (1975) instructions were as follows: For each of the following common objects, list as many characteristics and attributes as you can that you feel are common to these objects. For example, common characteristics for bicycles are two wheels, pedals, handlebars, you ride on them, they don't use fuel, and so on. Give yourself about a minute to write down the characteristics for each of the following items:

1. chair

2. sofa

3. mirror

4. telephone

If you responded like Rosch and Mervis's subjects, you assigned many of the same characteristics to chair and sofa. For example, chairs and sofas share the characteristics of having legs, having backs, you sit on them, they can have cushions, and so on. When an item's characteristics have a large amount of overlap with the characteristics of many other items in a category, this means that the family resemblance of these items is high. But when we consider mirror and telephone, we find that there is far less overlap, even though they were both classified by Rosch and Mervis as "furniture" (**Figure 9.4b**). Little overlap with other members of a category means the family resemblance is low.

Rosch and Mervis concluded from their results that there is a strong relationship between family resemblance and prototypicality. Thus, good examples of the category "furniture," such as chair and sofa, share many attributes with other members of this category; poor examples, like mirror and telephone, do not. In addition to the connection between prototypicality and family resemblance, researchers have determined the following connections between prototypicality and behavior.

STATEMENTS ABOUT PROTOTYPICAL OBJECTS ARE VERIFIED RAPIDLY Edward Smith and coworkers (1974) used a procedure called the **sentence verification technique** to determine how rapidly people could answer questions about an object's category.

METHOD
SENTENCE VERIFICATION TECHNIQUE

The procedure for the sentence verification technique is simple. Subjects are presented with statements and are asked to answer "yes" if they think the statement is true and "no" if they think it isn't. Try this yourself for the following two statements:

An apple is a fruit.

A pomegranate is a fruit.

When Smith and coworkers (1974) used this technique, they found that subjects responded faster for objects that are high in prototypicality (like apple for the category "fruit") than they did for objects that are low in prototypicality (like pomegranate; **Figure 9.5**). This ability to judge highly prototypical objects more rapidly is called the **typicality effect**.

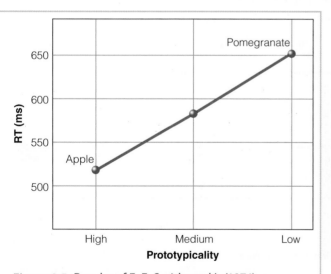

Figure 9.5 Results of E. E. Smith et al.'s (1974) sentence verification experiment. Reaction time (RT) was faster for objects rated higher in prototypicality. © Cengage Learning

PROTOTYPICAL OBJECTS ARE NAMED FIRST When subjects are asked to list as many objects in a category as possible, they tend to list the most prototypical members of the category first (Mervis et al., 1976). Thus, for "birds," sparrow would be named before penguin.

PROTOTYPICAL OBJECTS ARE AFFECTED MORE BY PRIMING Priming occurs when presentation of one stimulus facilitates the response to another stimulus that usually follows closely in time (see Chapter 6, page 170). Rosch (1975b) demonstrated that prototypical members of a category are more affected by a priming stimulus than are nonprototypical members. The procedure for Rosch's experiment is shown in **Figure 9.6**. Subjects first heard the prime, which was the name of a color, such as "green." Two seconds later they saw a pair of colors side by side and indicated, by pressing a key as quickly as possible, whether the two colors were the same or different.

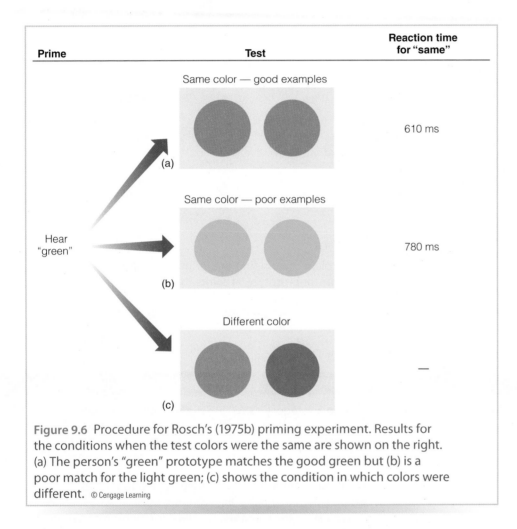

Figure 9.6 Procedure for Rosch's (1975b) priming experiment. Results for the conditions when the test colors were the same are shown on the right. (a) The person's "green" prototype matches the good green but (b) is a poor match for the light green; (c) shows the condition in which colors were different. © Cengage Learning

The side-by-side colors that subjects saw after hearing the prime were paired in three different ways: (1) colors were the same and were good examples of the category (primary reds, blues, greens, etc.; **Figure 9.6a**); (2) colors were the same but were poor examples of the category (less rich versions of the good colors, such as light blue, light green, etc.; **Figure 9.6b**); (3) colors were different, with the two colors coming from different categories (for example, pairing red with blue; **Figure 9.6c**).

The most important result occurred for the two "same" groups. In this condition, priming resulted in faster "same" judgments for the prototypical (good) colors (reaction time, RT = 610 ms) than for the nonprototypical (poor) colors (RT = 780 ms). Thus, when subjects heard the word *green*, they judged two patches of primary green as being the same more rapidly than two patches of light green.

Rosch explains this result as follows: When subjects hear the word *green*, they imagine a "good" (highly prototypical) green (**Figure 9.7a**). The principle behind priming is that the prime will facilitate the subjects' response to a stimulus if it contains some of the information needed to respond to the stimulus. This apparently occurs when the good greens are presented in the test (**Figure 9.7b**), but not when the poor greens are presented (**Figure 9.7c**). Thus, the results of the priming experiments support the idea that subjects create images of prototypes in response to color names. **Table 9.1** summarizes the various ways, previously discussed, that prototypicality affects behavior.

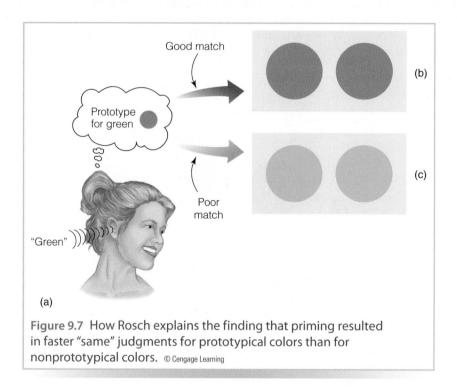

Figure 9.7 How Rosch explains the finding that priming resulted in faster "same" judgments for prototypical colors than for nonprototypical colors. © Cengage Learning

Table 9.1: Some Effects of Prototypicality

EFFECT	DESCRIPTION	EXPERIMENTAL RESULT
Family resemblance	Things in a category resemble each other in a number of ways.	Higher ratings for high-prototypical items when people rate how "good" a member of the category it is (Rosch, 1975a).
Typicality	People react rapidly to members of a category that are "typical" of the category.	Faster reaction time to statements like "A _____ is a bird" for high-prototypical items (like robin) than for low-prototypical items (like ostrich) (Smith et al., 1974).
Naming	People are more likely to list some objects than others when asked to name objects in a category.	High-prototypical items are named first when people list examples of a category (Mervis et al., 1976).
Priming	Presentation of one stimulus affects responses to a stimulus that follows.	Faster same–different color judgments for high-prototypical items (Rosch, 1975b).

© 2015 Cengage Learning

The prototype approach to categorization, and in particular Rosch's pioneering research, represented a great advance over the definitional approach because it provided a wealth of experimental evidence that all items within a category are not the same. Another approach to categorization, called the *exemplar approach*, also takes into account the wide variation among items that belong to a particular category.

THE EXEMPLAR APPROACH: THINKING ABOUT EXAMPLES

The **exemplar approach to categorization**, like the prototype approach, involves determining whether an object is similar to other objects. However, whereas the standard for the prototype approach is a single "average" member of the category, the standard for the exemplar approach involves many examples, each one called an exemplar. **Exemplars** are actual members of the category that a person has encountered in the past. Thus, if a person has encountered sparrows, robins, and blue jays in the past, each of these would be an exemplar for the category "birds."

The exemplar approach can explain many of Rosch's results, which were used to support the prototype approach. For example, the exemplar approach explains the typicality effect (in which reaction times on the sentence verification task are faster for better examples of a category than for poorer examples) by proposing that objects that are like more of the exemplars are classified faster. Thus, a sparrow is similar to many bird exemplars, so it is classified faster than a penguin, which is similar to few bird exemplars. This is basically the same as the idea of family resemblance, described for prototypes, which states that "better" objects will have higher family resemblance.

WHICH APPROACH WORKS BETTER: PROTOTYPES OR EXEMPLARS?

Which approach—prototypes or exemplars—provides a better description of how people use categories? One advantage of the exemplar approach is that by using real examples, it can more easily take into account atypical cases such as flightless birds. Rather than comparing a penguin to an "average" bird, we remember that there are some birds that don't fly. This ability to take into account individual cases means that the exemplar approach doesn't discard information that might be useful later. Thus, penguins, ostriches, and other birds that are not typical can be represented as exemplars, rather than becoming lost in the overall average that creates a prototype. The exemplar approach can also deal more easily with variable categories like games. Although it is difficult to imagine what the prototype might be for a category that contains football, computer games, solitaire, marbles, and golf, the exemplar approach requires only that we remember some of these varying examples.

Based on the results of a number of research studies, some researchers have concluded that people may use both approaches. It has been proposed that as we initially learn about a category, we may average exemplars into a prototype; then, later in learning, some of the exemplar information becomes stronger (Keri et al., 2002; Malt, 1989). Thus, early in learning, we would be poor at taking into account "exceptions" such as ostriches or penguins, but later, exemplars for these cases would be added to the category (Minda & Smith, 2001; Smith & Minda, 2000).

Other research indicates that the exemplar approach may work better for small categories, such as "U.S. presidents" or "mountains taller than 15,000 feet," and the prototype approach may work better for larger categories, such as "birds" or "automobiles." We can describe this blending of prototypes and exemplars in commonsense terms with the following example: We know generally what cats are (the prototype), but we know our own specific cat the best (an exemplar; Minda & Smith, 2001).

Is There a Psychologically "Privileged" Level of Categories?

As we have considered the prototype and exemplar approaches, we have used examples of categories such as "furniture," which contains members such as beds, chairs, and tables. But, as you can see in **Figure 9.8a**, the category "chairs" can contain smaller categories such

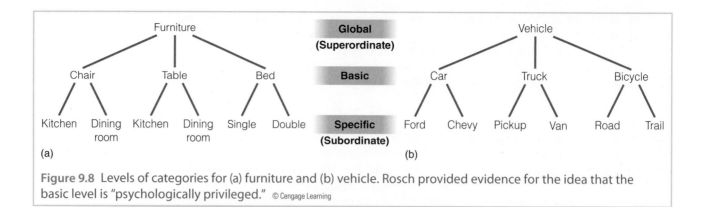

Figure 9.8 Levels of categories for (a) furniture and (b) vehicle. Rosch provided evidence for the idea that the basic level is "psychologically privileged." © Cengage Learning

as kitchen chairs and dining room chairs. This kind of organization, in which larger, more general categories are divided into smaller, more specific categories, creating a number of levels of categories, is called a **hierarchical organization**.

One question cognitive psychologists have asked about this organization is whether there is a "basic" level that is more psychologically important or "privileged" than other levels. The research we will describe indicates that although it is possible to demonstrate that there is a basic level of categories with special psychological properties, the basic level may not be the same for everyone. We begin by describing Rosch's research, in which she introduced the idea of basic level categories.

ROSCH'S APPROACH: WHAT'S SPECIAL ABOUT BASIC LEVEL CATEGORIES?

Rosch's research starts with the observation that there are different levels of categories, ranging from general (like "furniture") to specific (like "kitchen table"), as shown in **Figure 9.8**, and that when people use categories, they tend to focus on one of these levels. She distinguished three levels of categories: the **superordinate level**, which we will call the **global level** (for example, "furniture"); the **basic level** (for example, "table"); and the **subordinate level**, which we will call the **specific level** (for example, "kitchen table"). The following demonstration illustrates some characteristics of the different levels.

DEMONSTRATION
LISTING COMMON FEATURES

This demonstration is a repeat of the task you did in the Family Resemblance demonstration on page 250, but with different categories. For the following categories, list as many features as you can that would be common to all or most of the objects in the category. For example, for "table" you might list "has legs."

1.   furniture
2.   table
3.   kitchen table

If you responded like the subjects in the Rosch and coworkers' (1976) experiment, who were given the same task, you listed only a few features that were common to all furniture, but many features that were shared by all tables and by all kitchen tables. Rosch's subjects listed an average of 3 common features for the global level category "furniture," 9 for basic level categories such as "table," and 10.3 for specific level categories such as "kitchen table" (**Figure 9.9**).

Rosch proposed that the basic level is psychologically special because going above it (to global) results in a large loss of information (9 features at the basic vs. 3 at the global level) and going below it (to specific) results in little gain of information (9 features vs. 10.3). Here is another demonstration that is relevant to the idea of a basic level.

DEMONSTRATION
NAMING THINGS

Look at **Figure 9.10** and, as quickly as possible, write down or say a word that identifies each picture.

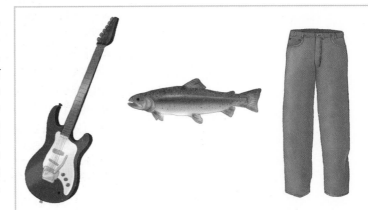

LEVEL	EXAMPLE	NUMBER OF COMMON FEATURES	
Global	Furniture	3	Lose a lot of information.
Basic	Table	9	Gain just a little information.
Specific	Kitchen table	10.3	

Figure 9.9 Category levels, examples of each level, and average number of common features listed by participants in Rosch et al.'s (1976) experiment. © Cengage Learning

What names did you assign to each object? When Rosch and coworkers (1976) did a similar experiment, they found that people tended to pick a basic level name. They said *guitar* (basic level) rather than *musical instrument* (global) or *rock guitar* (specific), *fish* rather than *animal* or *trout*, and *pants* rather than *clothing* or *jeans*.

In another experiment, Rosch and coworkers showed subjects a category label, such as *car* or *vehicle*, and then, after a brief delay, presented a picture. The subjects' task was to indicate, as rapidly as possible, whether the picture was a member of the category. The results showed that they accomplished this task more rapidly for basic level categories (such as car) than for global level categories (such as vehicle). Thus, they would respond "yes" more rapidly when the picture of an automobile was preceded by the word *car* than when the picture was preceded by the word *vehicle*.

HOW KNOWLEDGE CAN AFFECT CATEGORIZATION

Rosch's experiments, which were carried out on college undergraduates, showed that there is a category level, which she called "basic," that reflects college undergraduates' everyday experience. This has been demonstrated by many researchers in addition to Rosch. Thus, when J. D. Coley and coworkers (1997) asked Northwestern University undergraduates to name, as specifically as possible, 44 different plants on a walk around campus, 75 percent of the responses used labels like "tree," rather than more specific labels like "oak."

But instead of asking college undergraduates to name plants, what if Coley had taken a group of horticulturalists around campus? Do you think they would have said "tree" or "oak"? An experiment by James Tanaka and Marjorie Taylor (1991) asked a similar question for birds. They asked bird experts and nonexperts to name pictures of objects. There were objects from many different categories (tools, clothing, flowers, etc.), but Tanaka and Taylor were interested in how the subjects responded to the four bird pictures.

The results (**Figure 9.11**) show that the experts responded by specifying the birds' species (robin, sparrow, jay, or cardinal), but the nonexperts responded by saying "bird." Apparently the experts had learned to pay attention to features of birds that nonexperts were unaware of. Thus, in order to fully understand how people categorize objects, we need to consider not only the properties of the objects but also the learning and experience of the people perceiving those objects (also see Johnson & Mervis, 1997).

Figure 9.10 Stimuli for the Naming Things demonstration. © Cengage Learning

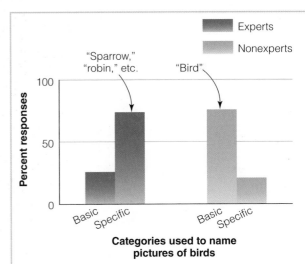

Figure 9.11 Results of Tanaka and Taylor's (1991) "expert" experiment. Experts (left pair of bars) used more specific categories to name birds, whereas nonexperts (right pair of bars) used more basic categories. © Cengage Learning

From the result of Tanaka's bird experiment, we can guess that a horticulturist walking around campus would be likely to label plants more specifically than people who had little specific knowledge about plants. In fact, members of the Guatemalan Itzaj culture, who live in close contact with their natural environment, call an oak tree an "oak," not a "tree" (Coley et al., 1997).

Thus, the level that is "special"—meaning that people tend to focus on it—is not the same for everyone. Generally, people with more expertise and familiarity with a particular category tend to focus on more specific information that Rosch associated with the specific level. This result isn't surprising, because our ability to categorize is learned from experience; it depends on which objects we typically encounter and what characteristics of objects we pay attention to.

TEST YOURSELF 9.1

1. Why is the use of categories so important for our day-to-day functioning?

2. Describe the definitional approach to categories. Why does it initially seem like a good way of thinking about categories, but then become troublesome when we consider the kinds of objects that can make up a category?

3. What is the prototype approach? What experiments did Rosch do that demonstrated connections between prototypicality and behavior?

4. What is the exemplar approach to categorization? How does it differ from the prototype approach, and how might the two approaches work together?

5. What does it mean to say that there are different levels within a category? What arguments did Rosch present to support the idea that one of these levels is "privileged"? How has research on categorization by experts led to modifications of Rosch's ideas about which category is "basic" or "privileged"?

Representing Relationships Between Categories: Semantic Networks

We have seen that categories can be arranged in a hierarchy of levels, from global (at the top) to specific (at the bottom). In this section, our main concern is to explain an approach to categories that focuses on how categories or concepts are organized in the mind. The approach we will be describing, called the semantic network approach, proposes that concepts are arranged in networks.

INTRODUCTION TO SEMANTIC NETWORKS: COLLINS AND QUILLIAN'S HIERARCHICAL MODEL

One of the first semantic network models was based on the pioneering work of Ross Quillian (1967, 1969), whose goal was to develop a computer model of human memory. We will describe Quillian's approach by looking at a simplified version of his model proposed by Allan Collins and Quillian (1969).

Figure 9.12 shows Collins and Quillian's network. The network consists of nodes that are connected by links. Each node represents a category or concept, and concepts are placed in the network so that related concepts are connected. In addition, a number of properties are indicated for each concept.

The links connecting the concepts indicate that they are related to each other in the mind. Thus, the model shown in Figure 9.12 indicates that there is an association in the

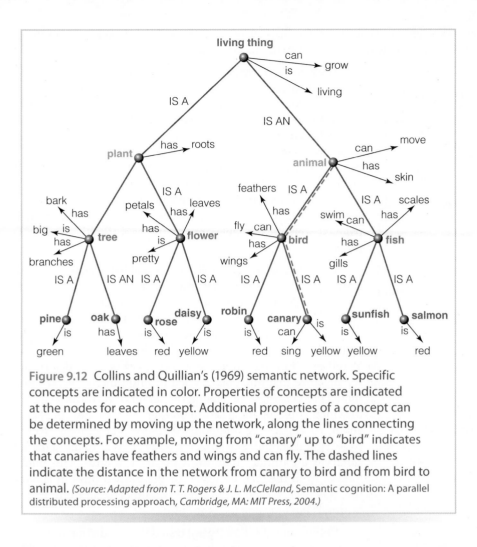

Figure 9.12 Collins and Quillian's (1969) semantic network. Specific concepts are indicated in color. Properties of concepts are indicated at the nodes for each concept. Additional properties of a concept can be determined by moving up the network, along the lines connecting the concepts. For example, moving from "canary" up to "bird" indicates that canaries have feathers and wings and can fly. The dashed lines indicate the distance in the network from canary to bird and from bird to animal. *(Source: Adapted from T. T. Rogers & J. L. McClelland,* Semantic cognition: A parallel distributed processing approach, *Cambridge, MA: MIT Press, 2004.)*

mind between *canary* and *bird*, and between *bird* and *animal* (indicated by the dashes along the links in **Figure 9.12**). It is a **hierarchical model**, because it consists of levels arranged so that more specific concepts, such as "canary" and "salmon," are at the bottom, and more general concepts are at higher levels.

We can illustrate how this network works, and how it proposes that knowledge about concepts is organized in the mind, by considering how we would retrieve the properties of canaries from the network. We start by entering the network at the concept node for "canary." At this node, we obtain the information that a canary can sing and is yellow. To access more information about "canary," we move up the link and learn that a canary is a bird and that a bird has wings, can fly, and has feathers. Moving up another level, we find that a canary is also an animal, which has skin and can move, and finally we reach the level of living things, which tells us it can grow and is living.

You might wonder why we have to travel from "canary" to "bird" to find out that a canary can fly. That information could have been placed at the canary node, and then we would know it right away. But Collins and Quillian proposed that including "can fly" at the node for every bird (canary, robin, vulture, etc.) was inefficient and would use up too much storage space. Thus, instead of indicating the properties "can fly" and "has feathers" for every kind of bird, these properties are placed at the node for "bird" because this property holds for most birds. This way of storing shared properties just once at a higher-level node is called **cognitive economy**.

Although cognitive economy makes the network more efficient, it does create a problem because not all birds fly. To deal with this problem while still achieving the advantages of cognitive economy, Collins and Quillian added exceptions at lower nodes. For example, the node for "ostrich," which is not shown in this network, would indicate the property "can't fly."

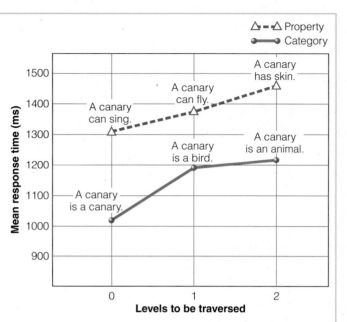

Figure 9.13 Results of Collins and Quillian's (1969) experiment that measured reaction times to statements that involved traversing different distances in the network. Greater distances are associated with longer reaction times, both when verifying statements about properties of canaries (top) and about categories of which the canary is a member (bottom). (Source: A. M. Collins et al., Retrieval time from semantic memory, Journal of Verbal Learning and Verbal Behavior, 8, 240–247, Fig. 2, 1969.)

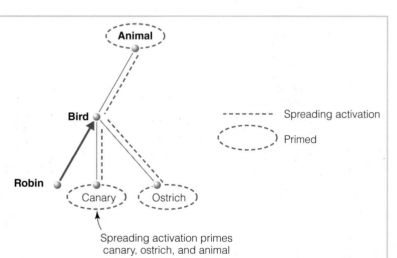

Figure 9.14 How activation can spread through a network as a person searches from "robin" to "bird" (blue arrow). The dashed lines indicate activation that is spreading from the activated bird node. Circled concepts, which have become primed, are easier to retrieve from memory because of the spreading activation. © Cengage Learning

How do the elements in this semantic network correspond to the actual operation of the brain? Remember from our discussion of models in cognitive psychology in Chapter 1 (page 17) that elements of models do not necessarily correspond to specific structures in the brain. Thus, the links and nodes we have been describing do not necessarily correspond to specific nerve fibers or locations in the brain. This model, and other network models we will be describing, are concerned with how concepts and their properties are associated in the mind. In fact, physiological findings relevant to these models, such as neurons that respond best to specific stimuli (see page 35), were not available until many years after these models were proposed.

Putting aside any possible connection between the network and actual physiology, we can ask how accurately Collins and Quillian's model represents how concepts are organized in the mind. The beauty of the network's hierarchical organization, in which general concepts are at the top and specific ones at the bottom, is that it results in the testable prediction that the time it takes for a person to retrieve information about a concept should be determined by the distance that must be traveled through the network. Thus, the model predicts that when using the sentence verification technique, in which subjects are asked to answer "yes" or "no" to statements about concepts (see Method: Sentence Verification Technique, page 250), it should take longer to answer "yes" to the statement "A canary is an animal" than to "A canary is a bird." This prediction follows from the fact, indicated by the dashed lines in Figure 9.12, that it is necessary to travel along two links to get from "canary" to "animal" but only one to get to "bird."

Collins and Quillian (1969) tested this prediction by measuring the reaction time to a number of different statements and obtained the results shown in Figure 9.13. As predicted, statements that required further travel from "canary" resulted in longer reaction times.

Another property of the theory, which leads to further predictions, is spreading activation. **Spreading activation** is activity that spreads out along any link that is connected to an activated node. For example, moving through the network from "robin" to "bird" activates the node at "bird" and the link we use to get from robin to bird, as indicated by the colored arrow in Figure 9.14. But according to the idea of spreading activation, this activation also spreads to other nodes in the network, as indicated by the dashed lines. Thus, activating the canary-to-bird pathway activates additional concepts that are connected to "bird," such as "animal" and other types of birds. The result of this spreading activation is that the additional concepts that receive this activation become "primed" and so can be retrieved more easily from memory.

The idea that spreading activation can influence priming was studied by David Meyer and Roger Schvaneveldt (1971) in a paper published shortly after Collins and Quillian's model was proposed. They used a method called the *lexical decision task*.

METHOD
LEXICAL DECISION TASK

In the **lexical decision task**, subjects read stimuli, some of which are words and some of which are not words. Their task is to indicate as quickly as possible whether each entry is a word or a nonword. For example, the correct responses for *bloog* would be "no" and for *bloat* would be "yes."

Meyer and Schvaneveldt used a variation of the lexical decision task by presenting subjects with pairs of words, one above the other, as shown below:

Pair 1:	Pair 2:	Pair 3:	Pair 4:
Fundt	Bleem	Chair	Bread
Glurb	Dress	Money	Wheat

The subjects' task was to press, as quickly as possible, the "yes" key when both items were words or the "no" key when at least one item in the pair was a nonword. Thus, pairs 1 and 2 would require a "no" response, and pairs 3 and 4 would require a "yes" response.

The key variable in this experiment was the association between the pairs of real words. In some trials, the words were closely associated (like bread and wheat), and in some trials they were weakly associated (chair and money). The result, shown in **Figure 9.15**, was that reaction time was faster when the two words were associated. Meyer and Schvaneveldt proposed that this might have occurred because retrieving one word from memory triggered a spread of activation to other nearby locations in a network. Because more activation would spread to words that were related, the response to the related words was faster than the response to unrelated words.

CRITICISM OF THE COLLINS AND QUILLIAN MODEL

Although Collins and Quillian's model was supported by the results of a number of experiments, such as their reaction time experiment (**Figure 9.13**) and Meyer and Schvaneveldt's priming experiment, it didn't take long for other researchers to call the theory into question. They pointed out that the theory couldn't explain the typicality effect, in which reaction times for statements about an object are faster for more typical members of a category than for less typical members (see page 250; Rips et al., 1973). Thus, the statement "A canary is a bird" is verified more quickly than "An ostrich is a bird," but the model predicts equally fast reaction times because "canary" and "ostrich" are both one node away from "bird."

Researchers also questioned the concept of cognitive economy because of evidence that people may, in fact, store specific properties of concepts (like "has wings" for "canary") right at the node for that concept (Conrad, 1972). In addition, Lance Rips and coworkers (1973) obtained sentence verification results such as the following:

A pig is a mammal.   RT = 1,476 ms

A pig is an animal.   RT = 1,268 ms

"A pig is an animal" is verified more quickly, but as we can see from the network in **Figure 9.16**, the Collins and Quillian model predicts that "A pig is a mammal" should be verified more quickly because a link leads directly from "pig" to "mammal," but we need to travel one link past the "mammal" node to get to "animal." Sentence verification results such as these, plus the other criticisms of the theory, led researchers to look for alternative ways to using networks to describe how concepts are organized (Glass & Holyoak, 1975; Murphy et al., 2012) and eventually, in the 1980s, to the proposal of a new approach to networks, called *connectionism*.

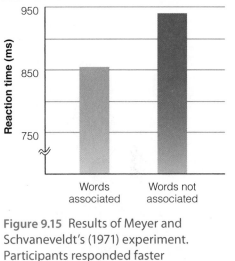

Figure 9.15 Results of Meyer and Schvaneveldt's (1971) experiment. Participants responded faster for words that were more closely associated (left bar). © Cengage Learning

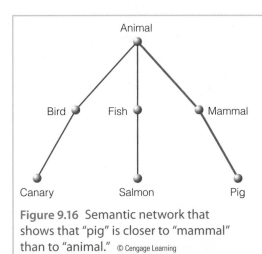

Figure 9.16 Semantic network that shows that "pig" is closer to "mammal" than to "animal." © Cengage Learning

Representing Concepts in Networks: The Connectionist Approach

Criticism of semantic networks, combined with advances in understanding how information is represented in the brain, led to the emergence of a new approach to explaining how knowledge is represented in the mind. In two volumes, both titled *Parallel Distributed Processing: Explorations in the Microstructure of Cognition* (McClelland & Rumelhart, 1986; Rumelhart & McClelland, 1986), James McClelland and David Rumelhart proposed a new approach called *connectionism*. This approach has gained favor among many researchers because (1) it is based on how information is represented in the brain; and (2) it can explain a number of findings, including how concepts are learned and how damage to the brain affects people's knowledge about concepts.

WHAT IS A CONNECTIONIST MODEL?

Connectionism is an approach to creating computer models for representing cognitive processes. We will focus on connectionist models designed to represent concepts. These models are also called **parallel distributed processing (PDP)** models because, as we will see shortly, they propose that concepts are represented by activity that is distributed across a network.

An example of a simple **connectionist network** is shown in **Figure 9.17**. The circles are **units**. These units are inspired by the neurons found in the brain. As we will see, concepts and their properties are represented in the network by the pattern of activity in these units.

The lines are connections that transfer information between units, and are roughly equivalent to axons in the brain. Like neurons, some units can be activated by stimuli from the environment, and some can be activated by signals received from other units. Units activated by stimuli from the environment (or stimuli presented by the experimenter) are **input units**. In the simple network illustrated here, input units send signals to **hidden units**, which send signals to **output units**.

An additional feature of a connectionist network is connection weights. A **connection weight** determines how signals sent from one unit either increase or decrease the activity of the next unit. These weights correspond to what happens at a synapse that transmits signals from one neuron to another (**Figure 2.5**, page 30). In Chapter 7 we saw that some synapses can transmit signals more strongly than others and therefore cause a high firing rate in the next neuron (**Figure 7.14**, page 194). Other synapses can cause a decrease in the firing rate of the next neuron. Connection weights in a connectionist network operate in the same way. High connection weights result in a strong tendency to excite the next unit, lower weights cause less excitation, and negative weights can decrease excitation or inhibit activation of the receiving unit. Activation of units in a network therefore depends on two things: (1) the signal that originates in the input units and (2) the connection weights throughout the network.

In the network of **Figure 9.17**, two of the input units are receiving stimuli. Activation of each of the hidden and output units is indicated by the shading, with darker shading indicating more activation. These differences in activation, and the pattern of activity they create, are responsible for a basic principle of connectionism: A stimulus presented to the input units is represented by the *pattern of activity* that is *distributed across the other units*. If this sounds familiar, it is because it is similar to the distributed representations in the brain we described

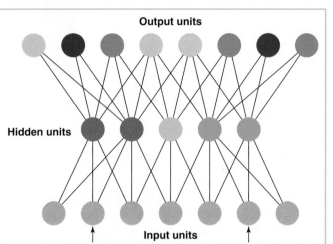

Figure 9.17 A parallel distributed processing (PDP) network showing input units, hidden units, and output units. Incoming stimuli, indicated by the arrows, activate the input units, and signals travel through the network, activating the hidden and output units. Activity of units is indicated by shading, with darker shading indicating more activity. The patterns of activity that occur in the hidden and output units are determined both by the initial activity of the input units and by the connection weights that determine how strongly a unit will be activated by incoming activity. Connection weights are not shown in this figure. © Cengage Learning

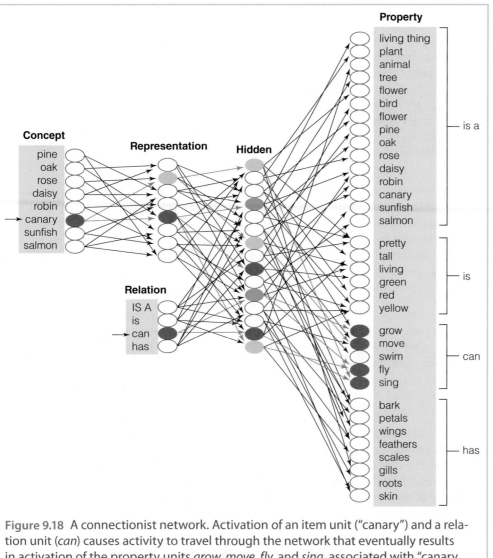

Figure 9.18 A connectionist network. Activation of an item unit ("canary") and a relation unit (*can*) causes activity to travel through the network that eventually results in activation of the property units *grow, move, fly,* and *sing,* associated with "canary can." Shading indicates the activity of the units, with darker shading indicating more activity. Note that only a few of the units and connections that would be activated by "canary" and *can* are shown as being activated. In the actual network, many more units and connections would be activated. *(Source: T. T. Rogers & J. L. McClelland,* Semantic cognition: A parallel distributed processing approach, *p. 56, Figure 2.2. Copyright © 2004 Massachusetts Institute of Technology.)*

in Chapters 2 (page 44), 5 (page 145), and 7 (page 195). Now that we have used the simple network in **Figure 9.17** to introduce the basic principles of connectionist networks, we will consider how some specific concepts are represented in the more complex connectionist network shown in **Figure 9.18**.

HOW ARE CONCEPTS REPRESENTED IN A CONNECTIONIST NETWORK?

The model in **Figure 9.18** was described by James McClelland and Timothy Rogers (2003) to show how different concepts and their properties can be represented in a connectionist network. Although this model is more complex than the one in **Figure 9.17**, it has similar components: units, links, and connection weights (although the connection weights are not shown).

REPRESENTING A CANARY Let's first compare this model to the Collins and Quillian hierarchical model in **Figure 9.12**. The first thing to notice is that both models are dealing with the same concepts. Specific concepts, such as "canary" and "salmon," shown in blue in **Figure 9.12**, are represented on the far left as concept items in **Figure 9.18**. Also notice that the properties of the concepts are indicated in both networks by the following four relation statements: "is a" (A canary is a bird); "is" (A canary is yellow); "can" (A canary can fly); and "has" (A canary has wings). But whereas the hierarchical network in **Figure 9.12** represents these properties at the network's nodes, the connectionist network in **Figure 9.18** indicates these properties by activity in the attribute units on the far right, and also by the pattern of activity in the representation and hidden units in the middle of the network.

Let's consider what happens when we activate the concept "canary" and a relation unit, *can*. As shown in **Figure 9.18**, the activation from "canary" and *can* spreads along the connections so that some of the representation units are activated and some of the hidden units are activated. The connection weights, which are not shown, cause some units to be activated strongly and others more weakly, as indicated by the shading of the units. If the network is working properly, this activation in the hidden units activates the *grow, move, fly,* and *sing* property units. What's important about all of this activity is that the concept "canary" is represented by the pattern of activity in all of the units in the network.

TRAINING A NETWORK According to the above description, the answer to "A canary is a . . ." is represented in the network by activation of the property units plus the pattern of activation of the network's representation and hidden units. But according to connectionism, a connectionist network has to be trained in order for this result to occur. This training involves adjusting the network's connection weights. To understand how this happens, let's consider what would happen if we stimulate the units "canary" and *can* before the network in **Figure 9.18** has been trained to accurately represent "canary."

In our untrained network, stimulating the "canary" and *can* units sends activity to the representation units and to the hidden units. The effect of this activation on each unit depends on the connection weights between the units. Let's assume that in our untrained network, all of the connection weights are 1.0. If all of the connection weights are the same, then many of the units in the network would be activated by "canary" and *can*, including many incorrect property units like *daisy, tall,* and *green*.

For the network to operate properly, the connection weights have to be adjusted so that activating the concept unit "canary" and the relation unit *can* only activates the property units *grow, move, fly,* and *sing*. This adjustment of weights is achieved by a learning process. The learning process occurs when the erroneous responses in the property units cause an **error signal** to be sent back through the network, by a process called **back propagation** (since the signals are being sent *backward* in the network starting from the property units). The error signals that are sent back to the hidden units and the representation units provide information about how the connection weights should be adjusted so that the correct property units will be activated.

To explain the idea behind activation and back propagation, let's consider a behavioral example. A young child is watching a robin sitting on a branch, when suddenly the robin flies away. This simple observation, which strengthens the association between "robin" and *can fly*, would involve activation. But if the child were to see a canary and say "robin," the child's parent might correct her and say "That is a canary" and "Robins have red breasts." The information provided by the parent is similar to the idea of feedback provided by back propagation.

Thus, a child's learning about concepts begins with little information and some incorrect ideas, which are slowly modified in response both to observation of the environment and to feedback from others. Similarly, the connectionist network's learning about concepts begins with incorrect connection weights, which are slowly modified in response to error signals. In this way, the network slowly learns that things that look like birds can fly, things that look like fish can swim, and things that look like trees are places where robins and other birds might perch.

The connectionist network's learning process therefore consists of initially weak and undifferentiated activation of property units, with many errors (for example, the input "canary" causing activation of the property unit *tall*). Error signals are then sent back through the network, which result in changes in connection weights so the next activation of "canary" results in a new activation pattern. Each learning experience causes only a small change in the connection weights, but after many repetitions, the network assigns the correct properties to "canary."

Although this "educated" network might work well for canaries, what happens when a robin flies by and alights on the branch of a pine tree? To be useful, this network needs to be able to represent not just canaries but also robins and pine trees. Thus, to create a network that can represent many different concepts, the network is not trained just on "canary." Instead, presentations of "canary" are interleaved with presentations of "robin," "pine tree," and so on, with small changes in connection weights made after each presentation.

We can appreciate how this learning process occurs over many trials by looking at the results of a computer simulation (McClelland & Rogers, 2003). The network in **Figure 9.18** was presented with a number of different concepts and relation statements, one after another, and the activity of the units and connection weights between units were calculated by the computer. **Figure 9.19** indicates the activation of the eight representation units in response to the concepts "canary," "rose," and "daisy." At the beginning of the process, the experimenter set the connection weights so that activity was about the same in each unit (Learning trials = 0). This corresponds to the initially weak and undifferentiated activation we discussed earlier.

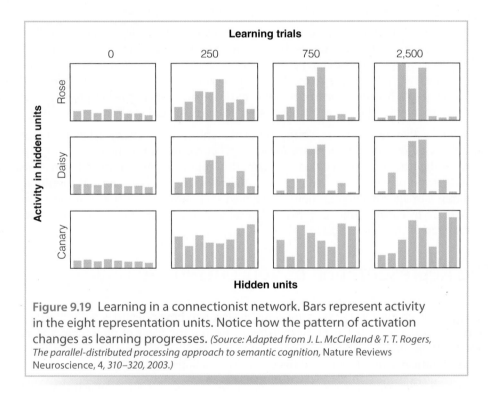

Figure 9.19 Learning in a connectionist network. Bars represent activity in the eight representation units. Notice how the pattern of activation changes as learning progresses. *(Source: Adapted from J. L. McClelland & T. T. Rogers, The parallel-distributed processing approach to semantic cognition, Nature Reviews Neuroscience, 4, 310–320, 2003.)*

As learning progressed, with each concept being presented one after another and the computer changing the weights just slightly after each trial in response to error signals, the patterns became adjusted, so by Trial 250, the patterns for "canary" and "daisy" begin to look different. By Trial 2,500, it is easy to tell the difference between the patterns for "canary" and "daisy," while the two flowers, "daisy" and "rose," have similar but slightly different patterns.

Although our description has been based on one particular connectionist network, most networks have similar properties. Connectionist networks are created by a learning process that shapes the networks so information about each concept is contained in the distributed pattern of activity across a number of units.

Notice how different this operation of the connectionist network is from the operation of Collins and Quillian's hierarchical network, in which concepts and their properties are represented by activation of different nodes. Representation in a connectionist network is far more complex, involving many more units for each concept, but it is also much more like what happens in the brain.

Because of the resemblance between connectionist networks and the brain, and the fact that connectionist networks have been developed that can simulate normal cognitive functioning for processes such as language processing, memory, and cognitive development (Rogers & McClelland, 2004; Seidenberg & Zevin, 2006), many researchers believe that the idea that knowledge is represented by distributed activity holds great promise. The following results also support the idea of connectionism:

1. *The operation of connectionist networks is not totally disrupted by damage.* Because information in the network is distributed across many units, damage to the system does not completely disrupt its operation. This property, in which disruption of performance occurs only gradually as parts of the system are damaged, is called **graceful degradation**. It is similar to what often happens in actual cases of brain damage, in which damage to the brain causes only a partial loss of functioning. Some researchers have suggested that studying the way networks respond to damage may suggest strategies for rehabilitation of human patients (Farah et al., 1993; Hinton & Shallice, 1991; Olson & Humphreys, 1997; Plaut, 1996).

2. *Connectionist networks can explain generalization of learning.* Because similar concepts have similar patterns, training a system to recognize the properties of one concept (such as "canary") also provides information about other, related concepts (such as "robin" or "sparrow"). This is similar to the way we actually learn about concepts because learning about canaries enables us to predict properties of different types of birds we've never seen (see McClelland et al., 1995).

While active research on connectionism continues in many laboratories, some researchers point out that there are limits to what connectionist networks can explain. Whatever the final verdict on connectionism, this approach has stimulated a great deal of research, some of which has added to our understanding of both normal cognition and how brain damage affects cognition. In the next section we will focus even more directly on the brain by considering neuropsychological and brain imaging research on how concepts are represented in the brain.

The Representation of Concepts in the Brain

We began the chapter by considering some ideas about how categories are represented in the mind, focusing on behavioral experiments testing the ideas of prototypes and exemplars. We then considered two approaches based on the idea of networks: Collins and Quillian's semantic network theory and the connectionist approach.

The idea that concepts can be represented by networks is an approach that takes us closer to our description from Chapter 2 of how representations in the brain are based on activity in areas specialized to process information about specific stimuli such as faces, places, and bodies, and also on activity distributed throughout many interconnected structures in the brain.

We will now introduce some ideas about how concepts are represented in the brain by describing studies of brain-damaged patients and brain imaging experiments on normal subjects. In doing so, we will describe four different proposals for how concepts are represented in the brain.

THE SENSORY-FUNCTIONAL HYPOTHESIS

In one of the classic papers in neuropsychology, Elizabeth Warrington and Tim Shallice (1984) reported on four patients who had suffered memory loss from encephalitis. These patients had a **category-specific memory impairment**—an impairment in which they had lost the ability to identify one type of object but retained the ability to identify other types of objects. Specifically, these patients were able to identify nonanimals, like furniture and tools, as well as fruits and vegetables, but had impaired ability to identify living animals (**Figure 9.20**). (As we discuss various cases below, we will use the term *artifacts* to refer to nonliving things, which would include furniture and tools.)

To explain why this selective impairment occurred, Warrington and Shallice considered properties that people use to distinguish between artifacts and living things. They noted that distinguishing living things depends on perceiving their sensory features. For example, distinguishing between a tiger and a leopard depends on perceiving stripes and spots. Artifacts, in contrast, are more likely to be distinguished by their function. For example, a screwdriver, chisel, and hammer are all tools but are used for different purposes (turning screws, scraping, and pounding nails).

The observation that living things are distinguished by sensory properties and artifacts by functions led to the **sensory-functional (S-F) hypothesis**, which states that our ability to differentiate living things and artifacts depends on a semantic memory system that distinguishes sensory attributes and a system that distinguishes function.

While the S-F hypothesis explained the behavior of Warrington and Shallice's patients, plus dozens of others studied by other researchers, cases were reported that couldn't be explained by this hypothesis. For example, the S-F hypothesis predicts that a patient who can't identify living things should have impaired sensory abilities. However, Caramazza and Shelton (1998) reported a patient who couldn't identify living things and had impaired sensory abilities (as the S-F hypothesis would predict), but who also had impaired functional ability (which the S-F hypothesis wouldn't predict.) The S-F hypothesis also predicts that a person who can't identify artifacts should have impaired functional knowledge. However, Matthew Lambon Ralph and coworkers (1998) reported a patient who couldn't recognize artifacts but who had an impaired sensory ability. Because of cases such as these, most researchers concluded that the S-F hypothesis was too simplified, and they began looking for other attributes that distinguished between living things and artifacts.

THE SEMANTIC CATEGORY APPROACH

The **semantic category approach** proposes that there are specific neural circuits in the brain for some specific categories. According to Bradford Mahon and Alfonso Caramazza (2011), there are a limited number of categories that are innately determined because of their importance for survival. This idea is based on research that we described in Chapter 2, which identified areas of the brain that respond to specific types of stimuli such as faces, places, and bodies (page 42). In addition, we described an experiment by Alex Huth and coworkers (2012) based on brain activity measured as people viewed movies, which resulted in the map in **Figure 2.23**, showing how concepts activated different areas of the brain.

Jeremy Wilmer and coworkers (2010) tested the idea that areas of the brain are innately specialized for specific categories of concepts by measuring face recognition ability in monozygotic (identical) and dizygotic (fraternal) twins. Their finding that the correlation of scores between identical twins was more than twice as high as the correlation for fraternal twins (0.70 vs. 0.29) led them to conclude that there is a genetic basis for the mechanisms that support face recognition (also see Zhu et al., 2010).

While the semantic category approach focuses on areas of the brain that are specialized to respond to specific types of stimuli, it also emphasizes that the brain's response

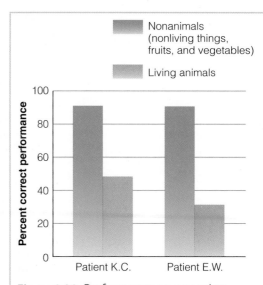

Figure 9.20 Performance on a naming task for patients K.C. and E.W., both of whom had category-specific memory impairment. They were able to correctly name pictures of nonliving things (such as car and table) and fruits and vegetables (such as tomato and pear), but performed poorly when asked to name pictures of animals. *(Source: B. Z. Mahon & A. Caramazza, Concepts and categories: A cognitive neuropsychological perspective, Annual Review of Psychology, 60, 27–51, Figure 1, 2009.)*

to items from a particular category is distributed over a number of different cortical areas (Mahon et al., 2007; Mahon & Caramazza, 2011). Thus, identifying faces may be based on activity in the face area in the temporal lobe (see Chapter 2, page 42), but it also depends on activity in areas that respond to emotions, facial expressions, where the face is looking, and the face's attractiveness (see page 44).

Similarly, the response to a hammer activates visual areas that respond to the hammer's shape and color, but it also causes activity in areas that respond to how a hammer is used and to a hammer's typical motions. It is important to note that the semantic category approach is not suggesting that there is a place in the brain that is specialized for "hammers." It is saying that evolution has resulted in neural circuits that enable us to efficiently interact with some objects by grasping them and carrying out movements such as swinging that would be important for survival.

THE MULTIPLE-FACTOR APPROACH

The idea of distributed representation is a central feature of the **multiple-factor approach**, but this approach focuses not on brain areas or networks that are specialized for specific concepts but on searching for more factors that determine how concepts are divided up within a category.

We can appreciate this approach by posing the following question: Assume that we start with a large number of items selected from lists of different types of animals, plants, and artifacts. If you wanted to arrange them in terms of how similar they are to each other, how would you do it? You could arrange them by shape, but then items like a pencil, a screwdriver, a person's finger, and a breakfast sausage might be grouped together. Or considering just color, you could end up placing fir trees, leprechauns, and Kermit the Frog together. While it is true that members of specific categories do share similar perceptual attributes, it is also clear that we need to use more than just one or two features when grouping objects in terms of similarity.

Taking this idea as their starting point, researchers picked a number of different features and had subjects rate a large number of items with regard to these features. This was the idea behind an experiment by Paul Hoffman and Matthew Lambon Ralph (2013), who used 160 items like the ones shown in **Table 9.2a**. The subjects' task was to rate each item on the features shown in **Table 9.2b**. For example, for the concept "door," the subject would

Table 9.2: Sample Stimuli and Question Used in the Hoffman & Lambon Ralph (2013) Experiment

A. A FEW OF THE 160 ITEMS PRESENTED TO SUBJECTS		
Mammal	Machine	Clothing
Pet	Vehicle	Weapon
Bird	Furniture	Tool
Door	Fish	Fruit

B. QUESTION FOR SUBJECTS	
How much do you associate (insert item from list above) with a particular . . .	
Color	Taste
Visual form	Smell
Motion	Tactile (Touch)
Sound	Performed action (in which you interact with the object)

be asked "How much do you associate door with a particular color (or form, or motion, etc.)?" Subjects assigned a rating of 7 for "very strongly" to 1 for "not at all."

The results, shown in **Figure 9.21**, indicate that animals were more highly associated with motion and color compared to artifacts, and artifacts were more highly associated with performed actions (actions associated with using or interacting with an object). This result conforms to the S-F hypothesis, but Hoffman and Lambon Ralph looked at the groupings more closely, and they found some interesting results. Mechanical devices such as machines, vehicles, and musical instruments overlapped with both artifacts (involving performed actions) and animals (involving sound and motion). For example, musical instruments are associated with specific actions (how you play them), which goes with artifacts, and are also associated with sensory properties (their visual form and the sounds they create), which goes with animals. Thus, mechanical devices have a widely distributed semantic representation that includes regions important for the representation of both living things and artifacts.

Because of the wide distribution of the representation for mechanical devices, sometimes patients are able to identify mechanical devices even if they perform poorly for other types of artifacts. For example, Hoffman and Lambon Ralph note that there are patients who have poor comprehension of smaller objects but better knowledge of larger artifacts, such as vehicles (Cappa et al., 1998; Hillis et al., 1990; Warrington & McCarthy, 1987).

Another factor that researchers have proposed to differentiate between animals and artifacts is **crowding**, which refers to the fact that animals tend to share many properties (like eyes, legs, and the ability to move). In contrast, artifacts like cars and boats share fewer properties, other than that they are both vehicles (**Figure 9.22**) (Rogers & Cox, in press). This has led some researches to propose that patients who appear to have category-specific impairments, such as difficulty recognizing living things but not artifacts, don't really have a category-specific impairment at all. They propose that these patients have difficulty recognizing living things because they have difficulty distinguishing between items that share similar features. According to this idea, because animals tend to be more similar then artifacts, these patients find animals harder to recognize (Cree & McRae, 2003; Lambon Ralph et al., 2007).

Our final approach also proposes that a number of factors are involved in telling the difference between different objects but proposes that the way we interact with objects is especially important.

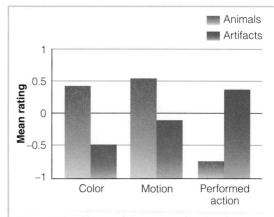

Figure 9.21 How subjects rated animals and artifacts on color, motion, and performed actions. Animals are rated higher on color and motion; artifacts are rated higher on performed actions. *(Source: Based on data in P. Hoffman & M. A. Lambon Ralph, Shapes, scenes and sounds: Quantifying the full multi-sensory basis of conceptual knowledge, Neuropsychologia, 51, 14–25, 2013.)*

Figure 9.22 Some animals and vehicles. Notice that the animals are more similar to each other than are the vehicles. This higher similarity of animals is called crowding.

THE EMBODIED APPROACH

The **embodied approach** states that our knowledge of concepts is based on reactivation of sensory and motor processes that occur when we interact with the object. According to this idea, when a person uses a hammer, sensory areas are activated in response to the hammer's, size, shape, and color, and, in addition, motor areas are activated that are involved in carrying out actions involved in using a hammer. When we see a hammer or read the word *hammer* later, these sensory and motor areas are reactivated, and it is this information that represents the hammer (Barsalou, 2008).

We can understand the basis of the embodied approach by returning to Chapter 3, where we described how perception and taking action interact, as when Crystal reached across the table to pick up a cup of coffee (page 75). The important message behind that example was that even simple actions involve a back-and-forth interaction between pathways in the brain involved in perception and pathways involved in taking action (see **Figure 3.33**, page 77) (Almeida et al., 2013).

An even more impressive interaction between perception and action occurs when we move higher in the brain to the premotor cortex, where researchers have discovered neurons called **mirror neurons** (Figure 9.23a). Vittorio Gallese and coworkers (1996) were investigating how neurons in the monkey's premotor cortex fired as the monkey performed actions such as picking up a toy or a piece of food. As they were recording from neurons while the monkey carried out specific actions, they observed something they didn't expect: Some neurons in the monkey's premotor cortex fired both when the monkey grasped food on a tray (Figure 9.23b) and when the monkey observed the experimenter grasping food on a tray (Figure 9.23c) (Rizzolatti et al., 1996). These neurons are called mirror neurons because the neuron's response to watching the experimenter grasp an object is similar to the response that occurs when the monkey is performing the action itself (Gallese et al., 1996; Rizzolatti et al., 2000).

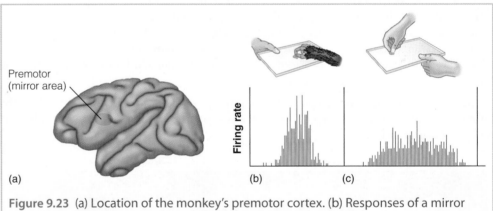

Premotor (mirror area)

Firing rate

(a)   (b)   (c)

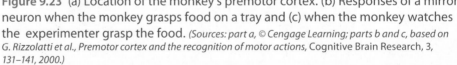

Figure 9.23 (a) Location of the monkey's premotor cortex. (b) Responses of a mirror neuron when the monkey grasps food on a tray and (c) when the monkey watches the experimenter grasp the food. *(Sources: part a, © Cengage Learning; parts b and c, based on G. Rizzolatti et al., Premotor cortex and the recognition of motor actions, Cognitive Brain Research, 3, 131–141, 2000.)*

Most mirror neurons are specialized to respond to only one type of action, such as grasping or placing an object somewhere. Although you might think that the monkey may have been responding to the anticipation of receiving food, the type of object made little difference. The neurons responded just as well when the monkey observed the experimenter pick up an object that was not food. Evidence has been found for similar neurons in humans (Oosterhof et al., 2013), although some researchers have raised questions regarding the function of these neurons in humans (Dinstein et al., 2008; Hickok, 2009).

What do mirror neurons have to do with concepts? The link between perception (a neuron fires when watching the experimenter pick up the food) and motor responses (the same neuron fires when the monkey picks up the food) is central to the embodied approach's proposal that thinking about concepts causes activation of perceptual and motor areas associated with these concepts. Evidence for this link between perceptual and motor responses in the human brain is provided by an experiment by Olaf Hauk and coworkers (2004), who measured subjects' brain activity using fMRI under two conditions: (1) as subjects moved their right or left foot, left or right index finger, or tongue; (2) as subjects read "action words" such as *kick* (foot action), *pick* (finger or hand action), or *lick* (tongue action).

The results show areas of the cortex activated by the actual movements (**Figure 9.24a**) and by reading the action words (**Figure 9.24b**). The activation is more extensive for actual movements, but the activation caused by reading the words occurs in approximately the same areas of the brain. For example, leg words and leg movements elicit activity near the brain's center line, whereas arm words and finger movements elicit activity farther from the center line. This correspondence between words related to specific parts of the body and the location of brain activity, called **semantic somatotopy**, is also illustrated in **Figure 9.25**, which summarizes the results of a number of experiments. Blue symbols represent locations activated by leg/foot words, red by arm/hand words, and green by face/mouth words (Carota et al., 2012; Pulvermüller, 2013).

Although there is convincing evidence linking concepts and activation of motor areas in the brain, some researchers question whether the embodied approach offers a complete explanation of how the brain processes concepts (Almeida et al., 2013; Chatterjee, 2010; Dravida et al., 2013). For example, Frank Garcea and coworkers (2013) tested patient A.A., who had suffered a stroke that affected his ability to produce actions associated with various objects. Thus, when A.A. was asked to use hand motions to indicate how he would use objects such as a hammer, scissors, and a feather duster, he was impaired compared to normal control subjects in producing these actions. According to the embodied approach, a person who has trouble producing actions associated with objects should have trouble recognizing the objects. A.A. was, however, able to identify pictures of the objects. Garcea and coworkers concluded from this result that the ability to represent motor activity associated with actions is not necessary for recognizing objects, as the embodied approach would predict.

Another criticism of the embodied approach is that it isn't well suited to explaining our knowledge of abstract concepts such as "democracy" or "truth." However, proponents of the embodied approach have offered explanations in response to these criticisms (which we won't go into here; see Barsalou, 2005; Chatterjee, 2010).

SORTING OUT THE APPROACHES

In Chapter 1 we described research by Sian Beilock and coworkers on what is responsible for "choking under pressure" (see page 16). One of the messages of that discussion was that research involves following a trail from one result to the next. Beilock's research was described because it provided a good example of how research can progress by asking a series of questions that leads eventually to answers about how a process operates.

Applying this idea to the question of how concepts are represented in the brain, we can take the S-F hypothesis as our starting point. However, determining how concepts are

Movements   **Action Words**

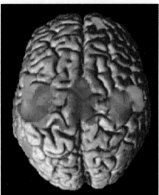 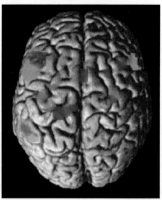

Blue: Foot movements   Blue: Leg words
Red: Finger movements   Red: Arm words
Green: Tongue movements   Green: Face words

(a)   (b)

Figure 9.24 Hauk et al. (2004) results. Colored areas indicate the areas of the brain activated by (a) foot, finger, and tongue movements; (b) leg, arm, and face words. *(Source: O. Hauk, I. Johnsrude, & F. Pulvermuller, Somatotopic representation of action words in human motor and premotor cortex, Neuron, 41, 301–307, 2004, with permission from Elsevier.)*

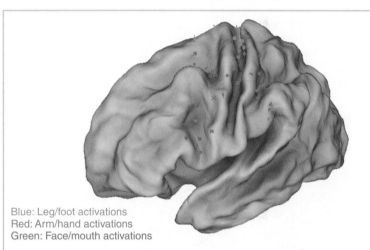

Blue: Leg/foot activations
Red: Arm/hand activations
Green: Face/mouth activations

Figure 9.25 Each symbol represents the results of a different experiment that determined where brain activation occurred in response to action words that were related to different parts of the body. *(From F. Carota, R. Moseley, & F. Pulvermuller, Body-part-specific representations of semantic noun categories, Journal of Cognitive Neuroscience, 24, 1492–1509, Figure 5, 2012. Reprinted by permission of MIT Press.)*

represented in the brain is quite a bit more complicated than understanding choking under pressure because of the large number of concepts and the complexity of the brain. Thus, we found that although many researchers took the S-F hypothesis as their starting point, their research led in different directions and resulted in different hypotheses.

I have found that students in my cognitive psychology class are often frustrated by this situation because they want to know what the *answer* is. Which approach is the correct one? Which most accurately describes concepts in the brain? Although the answer to questions such as these may eventually be known, for now we can only say that this area of research is a work in progress and that each of the approaches we have described provides part of the answer to the overall puzzle of how concepts are represented in the brain.

One thing that all of the approaches agree on is that information about concepts is distributed across many structures in the brain. But the approaches differ in their emphasis on the type of information that is most important. The category-specific approach emphasizes specialized areas of the brain and networks connecting these areas; the multiple-factor approach emphasizes the role of many different features and properties; and the embodied approach emphasizes activity caused by the sensory and motor properties of objects. It is likely that, as research on concepts in the brain continues, the final answer will contain elements of each of these approaches (Goldstone et al., 2012).

Something to Consider

THE HUB AND SPOKE MODEL

The ideas we have been discussing about how concepts are represented in the brain have been based largely on patients with category-specific memory impairments. However, there is another type of problem, called **semantic dementia**, that causes a general loss of knowledge for all concepts. Patients with semantic dementia tend to be equally deficient in identifying living things and artifacts (Patterson et al., 2007).

The generalized nature of the deficits experienced by semantic dementia patients, along with the finding that the **anterior temporal lobe (ATL)** (red area in **Figure 9.26**) is generally damaged in these patients, has led some researchers to propose the **hub and spoke model** of semantic knowledge. According to this model, areas of the brain that are associated with specific functions are connected to the ATL, which serves as a hub that integrates the information from these areas. Evidence supporting this idea is that damage to one of the specialized brain areas (the spokes) can cause specific deficits, such as an inability to identify artifacts, but damage to the ATL (the hub) causes general deficits, as in semantic dementia (Patterson et al., 2007). This difference between hub and spoke functions has also been demonstrated in non-brain-damaged subjects using a technique called **transcranial magnetic stimulation (TMS)**.

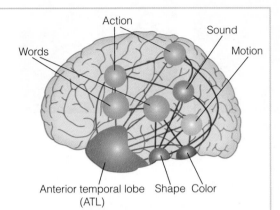

Figure 9.26 The hub and spoke model proposes that areas of the brain specialized for different functions (circles) are linked to the anterior temporal lobe (red), which integrates the information from these areas. *(Source: Adapted from K. Patterson, P. J. Nestor, & T. T. Rogers, Where do you know what you know? The representation of semantic knowledge in the human brain,* Nature Reviews Neuroscience, 8, *976–987, Figure 1, 2007.)*

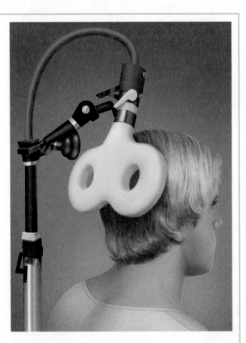

Figure 9.27 TMS coil positioned to present a magnetic field to a person's head. The coil in this position is stimulating the occipital lobe. © 2015 Cengage Learning

METHOD

TRANSCRANIAL MAGNETIC STIMULATION (TMS)

It is possible to temporarily disrupt the functioning of a particular area of the human brain by applying a pulsating magnetic field using a stimulating coil placed over the person's skull (**Figure 9.27**). A series of pulses presented to a particular area of the brain for seconds or minutes interferes with brain functioning in that area for seconds or minutes. If a particular behavior is disrupted by the pulses, researchers conclude that the disrupted area of the brain is involved in that behavior.

Gorana Pobric and coworkers (2010) presented pictures of living things and artifacts to subjects and measured the response time for naming each picture. They then repeated this procedure while TMS was being applied either to the ATL or to an area in the parietal lobe that is normally activated when a person is manipulating an object (**Figure 9.28**). Red bars indicate response time before TMS stimulation; blue bars are response times during stimulation. They found that stimulating the ATL caused a generalized effect: a slowing in responding to both living things and artifacts (left graph). However, stimulating the parietal area caused a more specific effect: a slowing in responding to artifacts but not to living things (right graph). This result—a general effect of stimulating the "hub" (ATL), but a more specific effect of stimulating an area that would be associated with one of the "spokes" (parietal cortex)—supports the idea of a hub with general functions and spokes with more specific functions (Jefferies, 2013).

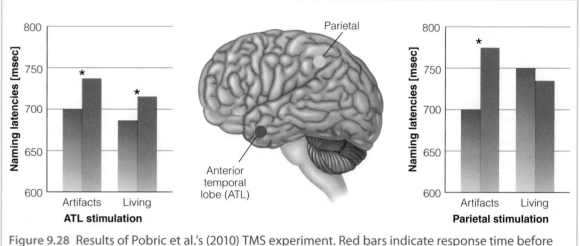

Figure 9.28 Results of Pobric et al.'s (2010) TMS experiment. Red bars indicate response time before TMS stimulation; blue bars are response times during stimulation. Stars above pairs of bars indicate that there is a significant difference between the bars. TMS stimulation of the ATL affected subjects' speed of naming equally for artifacts and living things (left graph). Stimulation of the parietal cortex caused an increase in speed of naming only for artifacts (left pair of bars). *(Source: Adapted from G. Pobric, E. Jefferies, & M. A. Lambon Ralph, Category-specific versus category-general semantic impairment induced by transcranial magnetic stimulation, Current Biology, 20, 964–968, Figure 1B, 2010.)*

Most researchers agree that the ATL plays a role in integrating information from different areas. But it has also been suggested that other structures may be "hubs," or that the most important way concepts are represented is not by "hubs" but by the pattern of connections formed between the "spokes" (Pulvermüller, 2013). Thus, as we noted at the end of the last section, research on how concepts are represented in the brain is still a "work in progress."

TEST YOURSELF 9.2

1. What is the basic idea behind the semantic network approach? What is the goal of this approach, and how did the network created by Collins and Quillian accomplish this goal? What is the evidence for and against the Collins and Quillian model?

2. What is a connectionist network? Describe how a connectionist network learns, considering specifically how connection weights are adjusted. Also consider how the way information is represented in a connectionist network differs from the way it is represented in a semantic network.

3. Describe the four approaches to explaining how concepts are represented in the brain. Indicate the basic idea behind each hypothesis and the evidence for and against each one.

CHAPTER SUMMARY

1. Semantic memory is our memory for facts and knowledge.

2. Categories are "pointers to knowledge." Once you know something is in a category, you know a lot of general things about it and can focus your energy on specifying what is special about this particular object.

3. The definitional approach to categorization doesn't work because most categories contain members that do not conform to the definition. The philosopher Wittgenstein proposed the idea of family resemblances to deal with the fact that definitions do not include all members of a category.

4. The idea behind the prototypical approach to categorization is that we decide whether an object belongs to a category by deciding whether it is similar to a standard representative of the category, called a prototype. A prototype is formed by averaging category members a person has encountered in the past.

5. *Prototypicality* is a term used to describe how well an object resembles the prototype of a particular category.

6. The following is true of high-prototypical objects: (a) They have high family resemblance; (b) statements about them are verified rapidly; (c) they are named first; and (d) they are affected more by priming.

7. The exemplar approach to categorization involves determining whether an object is similar to an exemplar. An exemplar is an actual member of a category that a person has encountered in the past.

8. An advantage to the exemplar approach is that it doesn't discard information about atypical cases within a category, such as penguin in the "bird" category. The exemplar approach can also deal more easily with categories that contain widely varying members, such as games.

9. Researchers have concluded that people use both approaches to categorization. Prototypes may be more important as people initially learn about categories; later, exemplar information may become more important. Exemplars may work best for small categories (such as U.S. presidents), and prototypes may work best for larger categories (such as birds).

10. The kind of organization in which larger, more general categories are divided into smaller, more specific categories is called hierarchical organization. Experiments by Rosch indicate that a basic level of categories (such as guitar, as opposed to musical instrument or rock guitar) is a "privileged" level of categorization that reflects people's everyday experience.

11. Experiments in which experts were tested show that the basic level of categorization can depend on a person's degree of expertise.

12. The semantic network approach proposes that concepts are arranged in networks that represent the way concepts are organized in the mind. Collins and Quillian's model is a network that consists of nodes connected by links. Concepts and properties of concepts are located at the nodes. Properties that hold for most members of a concept are stored at higher-level nodes. This is called cognitive economy.

13. Collins and Quillian's model is supported by the results of experiments using the sentence verification technique. The spreading activation feature of the model is supported by priming experiments.

14. The Collins and Quillian model has been criticized for several reasons: It can't explain the typicality effect, the idea of cognitive economy doesn't always hold, and it can't explain all results of sentence verification experiments.

15. The connectionist approach proposes that concepts are represented in networks that consist of input units, hidden units, and output units, and that information about concepts is represented in these networks by a distributed activation of these units. This approach is also called the parallel distributed processing (PDP) approach.

16. Connectionist networks learn the correct distributed pattern for a particular concept through a gradual learning process that involves adjusting the weights that determine how activation is transferred from one unit to another.

17. Connectionist networks have a number of features that enable them to reproduce many aspects of human concept formation.

18. Four approaches to explaining how concepts are represented in the brain are the sensory-functional hypothesis, the semantic category approach, the multiple-factor approach, and the embodied approach.

19. The hub and spoke model proposes that different functions in the brain are integrated by the anterior temporal lobe (ATL).

THINK ABOUT IT

1. In this chapter we have seen how networks can be constructed that link different levels of concepts. In Chapter 7 we saw how networks can be constructed that organize knowledge about a particular topic (see **Figure 7.5**). Create a network that represents the material in this chapter by linking together things that are related. How is this network similar to or different from the semantic network in **Figure 9.12**? Is your network hierarchical? What information does it contain about each concept?

2. Do a survey to determine people's conception of "typical" members of various categories. For example, ask several people to name, as quickly as possible, three typical "birds" or "vehicles" or "beverages." What do the results of this survey tell you about what level is "basic" for different people? What do the results tell you about the variability of different people's conception of categories?

3. Try asking a number of people to name the objects pictured in **Figure 9.10**. Rosch, who ran her experiment in the early 1970s, found that the most common responses were guitar, fish, and pants. Notice whether the responses you receive are the same as or different from the responses reported by Rosch. If they are different, explain why you think this might have occurred.

KEY TERMS

Anterior temporal lobe (ATL), 270

Back propagation, 262

Basic level, 254

Categorization, 246

Category, 246

Category-specific memory impairment, 265

Cognitive economy, 257

Concept, 246

Conceptual knowledge, 246

Connection weight, 260

Connectionism, 260

Connectionist network, 260

Crowding, 267

Definitional approach to categorization, 247

Embodied approach, 268

Error signal, 262

Exemplar, 253

Exemplar approach to categorization, 253

Family resemblance, 248

Global level, 254

Graceful degradation, 264

Hidden units, 260

Hierarchical model, 257

Hierarchical organization, 254

Hub and spoke model, 270

Input units, 260

Lexical decision task, 259

Mirror neurons, 268

Multiple-factor approach, 266

Output units, 260

Parallel distributed processing (PDP), 260

Prototype, 249

Prototype approach to categorization, 249

Semantic category approach, 265

Semantic dementia, 270

Semantic network approach, 256

Semantic somatotopy, 269

Sensory-functional (S-F) hypothesis, 265

Sentence verification technique, 250

Specific level, 254

Spreading activation, 258

Subordinate (specific) level, 254

Superordinate (global) level, 254

Transcranial magnetic stimulation (TMS), 270

Typicality effect, 250

Unit (in a connectionist network), 260

COGLAB EXPERIMENTS Numbers in parentheses refer to the experiment number in CogLab.

Lexical Decision (41)

Absolute Identification (44)

Prototypes (46)

Bruce Goldstein

"Visual imagery" occurs when a person sees in his or her mind something that isn't physically present. This picture represents the finding that although visual perception and visual imagery share many properties, experiences associated with visual imagery can be less detailed and more fragile than experiences associated with visual perception.

Visual Imagery

Let's return for a moment to Raphael, who, at the beginning of Chapter 1, was walking across campus talking to Susan on his cell phone (see **Figure 1.1**, page 4, for a retrieval cue!). One of Raphael's problems is that he has left Susan's book at home; as he realizes this, he thinks, "I can see it sitting there on my desk, where I left it." Raphael's ability to "see" Susan's book, even though it is not present, is an example of **visual imagery**—seeing in the absence of a visual stimulus.

Another example of visual imagery is my experience of being able to visually remember seeing the Pacific Ocean after cresting a mountain in California (page 162). This example was used to introduce the idea that mental time travel is a characteristic of episodic memory. Although mental time travel does not have to involve visual imagery, it often does, as it did for my "seeing what was on the other side of the mountain" experience. But imagery doesn't have to involve such drama! Consider, for example, the following demonstration.

DEMONSTRATION
EXPERIENCING IMAGERY

Answer the following questions:

- How many windows are there in front of the house or apartment where you live?
- How is the furniture arranged in your bedroom?
- Are an elephant's ears rounded or pointy?
- Is the green of grass darker or lighter than the green of a pine tree?

How did you go about answering these questions? Many people report that they experience visual images when answering questions such as these. On a more practical level, they might create images to help pack suitcases in the trunk of their car or rearrange furniture in the living room (Hegarty, 2010).

Mental imagery, the ability to recreate the sensory world in the absence of physical stimuli, also occurs in senses other than vision. People have the ability to imagine tastes, smells, and tactile experiences. Most people can imagine melodies of familiar songs in their head, so it is not surprising that musicians often report strong auditory imagery and that the ability to imagine melodies has played an important role in musical composition. Paul McCartney says that the song "Yesterday" came to him as a mental image when he woke up with the tune in his head. Another example of auditory imagery is orchestra conductors' using a technique called the "inner audition" to practice without their orchestras by imagining a musical score in their minds. When they do this, they imagine not only the sounds of the various instruments but also their locations relative to the podium.

Just as auditory imagery has played an important role in the creative process of music, visual imagery has resulted in both scientific insights and practical applications. One of the most famous accounts of how visual imagery led to scientific discovery is the story related by the 19th-century German chemist Friedrich August Kekule. Kekule said that the structure of benzene came to him in a dream in which he saw a writhing chain that formed a circle that resembled a snake, with its head swallowing its tail. This visual image gave Kekule the insight that the carbon atoms that make up the benzene molecule are arranged in a ring.

A more recent example of visual imagery leading to scientific discovery is Albert Einstein's description of how he developed the theory of relativity by imagining himself traveling beside a beam of light (Intons-Peterson, 1993). On a more athletic level, many competitors at the Olympics use mental imagery to visualize downhill ski runs, snowboarding moves, bobsled turns, and speedskating races (Clarey, 2014).

One message of these examples is that imagery provides a way of thinking that adds another dimension to the verbal techniques usually associated with thinking. But what is most important about imagery is that it is associated not just with discoveries by famous people but also with most people's everyday experience. In this chapter we will focus on visual imagery, because most of the research on imagery has been on this type of imagery. We will describe the basic characteristics of visual imagery and how it relates to other cognitive processes such as thinking, memory, and perception. This connection between imagery and cognition in general is an important theme in the history of psychology, beginning in the early days of scientific psychology in the 19th century.

Imagery in the History of Psychology

We can trace the history of imagery back to the first laboratory of psychology, founded by Wilhelm Wundt (see Chapter 1, page 7).

EARLY IDEAS ABOUT IMAGERY

Wundt proposed that images were one of the three basic elements of consciousness, along with sensations and feelings. He also proposed that because images accompany thought, studying images was a way of studying thinking. This idea of a link between imagery and thinking gave rise to the **imageless thought debate**, with some psychologists taking up Aristotle's idea that "thought is impossible without an image" and others contending that thinking can occur without images.

Evidence supporting the idea that imagery was not required for thinking was Francis Galton's (1883) observation that people who had great difficulty forming visual images were still quite capable of thinking (also see Richardson, 1994, for more modern accounts of imagery differences between people). Other arguments both for and against the idea that images are necessary for thinking were proposed in the late 1800s and early 1900s, but these arguments and counterarguments ended when behaviorism toppled imagery from its central place in psychology (Watson, 1913; see Chapter 1, page 9). The behaviorists branded the study of imagery as unproductive because visual images are invisible to everyone except the person experiencing them. The founder of behaviorism, John Watson, described images as "unproven" and "mythological" (1928), and therefore not worthy of study. The dominance of behaviorism from the 1920s through the 1950s pushed the study of imagery out of mainstream psychology. However, this situation changed when the study of cognition was reborn in the 1950s.

IMAGERY AND THE COGNITIVE REVOLUTION

The history of cognitive psychology that we described in Chapter 1 recounts events in the 1950s and 1960s that came to be known as the cognitive revolution. One of the keys to the success of this "revolution" was that cognitive psychologists developed ways to measure behavior that could be used to infer cognitive processes. One example of a method that linked behavior and cognition is Alan Paivio's (1963) work on memory. Paivio showed that it was easier to remember concrete nouns, like *truck* or *tree*, that can be imaged, than it is to remember abstract nouns, like *truth* or *justice*, that are difficult to image. One technique Paivio used was *paired-associate learning*.

METHOD
PAIRED-ASSOCIATE LEARNING

In a **paired-associate learning** experiment, subjects are presented with pairs of words, like *boat–hat* or *car–house*, during a study period. They are then presented, during the test period, with the first word from each pair. Their task is to recall the word that was paired with it during the study period. Thus, if they were presented with the word *boat*, the correct response would be *hat*.

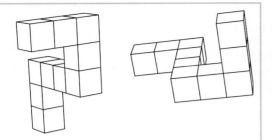

Figure 10.1 Stimuli for Shepard and Metzler's (1971) mental rotation experiment. *(Source: From R. N. Shepard & J. Metzler, Mental rotation of three-dimensional objects, Science, 171, 701–703, Figures 1A & B, 1971.)*

As noted, Paivio (1963, 1965) found that memory for pairs of concrete nouns is much better than memory for pairs of abstract nouns. To explain this result, Paivio proposed the **conceptual peg hypothesis**. According to this hypothesis, concrete nouns create images that other words can "hang onto." For example, if presenting the pair *boat–hat* creates an image of a boat, then presenting the word *boat* later will bring back the boat image, which provides a number of places on which subjects can place the hat in their mind (see Paivio, 2006, for an updating of his ideas about memory).

Whereas Paivio inferred cognitive processes by measuring memory, Roger Shepard and Jacqueline Metzler (1971) inferred cognitive processes by using **mental chronometry**, determining the amount of time needed to carry out various cognitive tasks. In Shepard and Metzler's experiment, which we described in Chapter 5 (see page 137), subjects saw pictures like the ones in **Figure 10.1**. Their task was to indicate, as rapidly as possible, whether the two pictures were of the same object or of different objects. This experiment showed that the time it took to decide that two views were of the same object was directly related to how different the angles were between the two views (see **Figure 5.15**, page 138). This result was interpreted as showing that subjects were mentally rotating one of the views to see whether it matched the other one.

What was important about this experiment was that it was one of the first to apply quantitative methods to the study of imagery and to suggest that imagery and perception may share the same mechanisms. (References to "mechanisms" include both mental mechanisms, such as ways of manipulating perceptual and mental images in the mind, and brain mechanisms, such as which structures are involved in creating perceptual and mental images.)

We will now describe research that illustrates similarities between imagery and perception, and also the possibility that there is a basic difference between how imagery and perception are represented in the mind. As we will see, these comparisons of imagery and perception have involved a large number of behavioral and physiological experiments, which demonstrate both similarities and differences between imagery and perception.

Imagery and Perception: Do They Share the Same Mechanisms?

The idea that imagery and perception may share the same mechanisms is based on the observation that although mental images differ from perception in that they are not as vivid or long lasting, imagery shares many properties with perception. Shepard and Metzler's results showed that mental and perceptual images both involve spatial representation of the stimulus. That is, the spatial experience for both imagery and perception matches the layout of the actual stimulus. This idea, that there is a spatial correspondence between imagery and perception, is supported by a number of experiments by Stephen Kosslyn involving a task called **mental scanning**, in which subjects create mental images and then scan them in their minds.

KOSSLYN'S MENTAL SCANNING EXPERIMENTS

Stephen Kosslyn has done enough research on imagery to fill three books (Kosslyn, 1980, 1994; Kosslyn et al., 2006), and he has proposed some influential theories of imagery based on parallels between imagery and perception. In one of his early experiments, Kosslyn (1973) asked subjects to memorize a picture of an object, such as the boat in **Figure 10.2**, and then to create an image of that object in their mind and to focus on one part of the boat, such as the anchor. They were then asked to look for another part of the boat, such as the motor, and to press the "true" button when they found this part or the "false" button when they couldn't find it.

Kosslyn reasoned that if imagery, like perception, is spatial, then it should take longer for subjects to find parts that are located farther from the initial point of focus because they would be scanning across the image of the object. This is actually what happened, and Kosslyn took this as evidence for the spatial nature of imagery. But, as often happens in science, another researcher proposed a different explanation. Glen Lea (1975) proposed that as subjects scanned, they may have encountered other interesting parts, such as the cabin, and this distraction may have increased their reaction time.

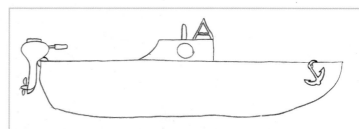

Figure 10.2 Stimulus for Kosslyn's (1973) image-scanning experiment. *(Source: S. M. Kosslyn, Scanning visual images: Some structural Implications, Perception & Psychophysics, 14, 90–94, Figure 1. Copyright © 1973 The Psychonomic Society Publications. Reproduced with permission.)*

To answer this concern, Kosslyn and coworkers (1978) did another scanning experiment, this time asking subjects to scan between two places on a map. Before reading about Kosslyn's experiment, try the following demonstration.

METHOD/DEMONSTRATION
MENTAL SCANNING

Imagine a map of your state that includes three locations: the place where you live, a town that is far away, and another town that is closer but does not fall on a straight line connecting your location and the far town. For example, for my state, I imagine Pittsburgh, the place where I am now; Philadelphia, all the way across the state (contrary to some people's idea, Pittsburgh is not a suburb of Philadelphia!); and Erie, which is closer than Philadelphia but not in the same direction (**Figure 10.3**).

Your task is to create a mental image of your state and, starting at your location, to form an image of a black speck moving along a straight line between your location and the closer town. Be aware of about how long it took to arrive at this town. Then repeat the same procedure for the far town, again noting about how long it took to arrive.

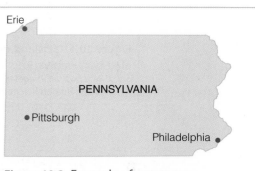

Figure 10.3 Example of a state map for Mental Scanning method/demonstration. Use your own state for this method/demonstration. © Cengage Learning

Kosslyn's subjects used the same procedure as you did for the demonstration but were told to imagine an island, like the one in **Figure 10.4a**, that contained seven different locations. By having subjects scan between every possible pair of locations (a total of 21 trips), Kosslyn determined the relationship between reaction time and distance shown in **Figure 10.4b**. Just as in the boat experiment, it took longer to scan between greater distances on the image, a result that supports the idea that visual imagery is spatial in nature. As convincing as Kosslyn's results were, however, Zenon Pylyshyn (1973) proposed another explanation, which started what has been called the **imagery debate**—a debate about whether imagery is based on spatial mechanisms, such as those involved in perception, or on mechanisms related to language, called *propositional mechanisms*.

THE IMAGERY DEBATE: IS IMAGERY SPATIAL OR PROPOSITIONAL?

Much of the research we have described so far in this book is about determining the nature of the mental representations that lie behind different cognitive experiences. For example, when we considered short-term memory (STM) in Chapter 5, we presented evidence that information in STM is often represented in auditory form, as when you rehearse a telephone number you have just looked up in a phone book or online.

Kosslyn interpreted the results of his research on imagery as supporting the idea that the mechanism responsible for imagery involves a **spatial representation**—a representation in which different parts of an image can be described as corresponding to specific locations in space. But Pylyshyn (1973) disagreed, saying that just because we *experience*

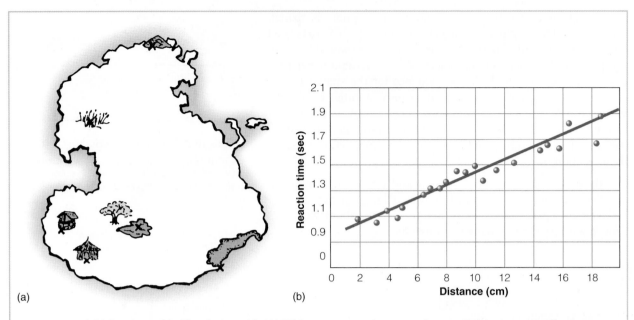

Figure 10.4 (a) Island used in Kosslyn et al.'s (1978) image-scanning experiment. Subjects mentally traveled between various locations on the island. (b) Results of the island experiment. *(Source: S. M. Kosslyn, T. Ball, & B. J. Reiser, Visual images preserve metric spatial information: Evidence from studies of image scanning,* Journal of Experimental Psychology: Human Perception and Performance, 4, *no. 1, 47–60, 1978.)*

imagery as spatial, that doesn't mean that the *underlying representation* is spatial. After all, one thing that is clear from research in cognitive psychology is that we often aren't aware of what is going on in our mind. The spatial experience of mental images, argues Pylyshyn, is an **epiphenomenon**—something that accompanies the real mechanism but is not actually part of the mechanism.

An example of an epiphenomenon is lights flashing as a mainframe computer carries out its calculations. The lights may indicate that *something* is going on inside the computer, but they don't necessarily tell us what is actually happening. In fact, if all of the lightbulbs blew out, the computer would continue operating just as before. Mental images, according to Pylyshyn, are similar—they indicate that *something* is happening in the mind, but don't tell us *how* it is happening.

Pylyshyn proposed that the mechanism underlying imagery is not spatial but propositional. A **propositional representation** is one in which relationships can be represented by abstract symbols, such as an equation, or a statement such as "The cat is under the table." In contrast, a spatial representation would involve a spatial layout showing the cat and the table that could be represented in a picture (**Figure 10.5**). Representations that are like realistic pictures of an object, so that parts of the representation correspond to parts of the object, are called **depictive representations**.

We can understand the propositional approach better by returning to the depictive representation of Kosslyn's boat in **Figure 10.2**. **Figure 10.6** shows how the visual appearance of this boat can be represented propositionally. The words indicate parts of the boat, the length of the lines indicate the distances between the parts, and the words in parentheses indicate the spatial relations between the parts. A representation such as this would predict that when starting at the motor, it should take longer to scan and find the anchor than to find the porthole because it is necessary to travel across three links to get

"The cat is under the table"

Propositional representation

Spatial, or depictive, representation

Figure 10.5 Propositional and spatial, or depictive, representations of "The cat is under the table." © Cengage Learning

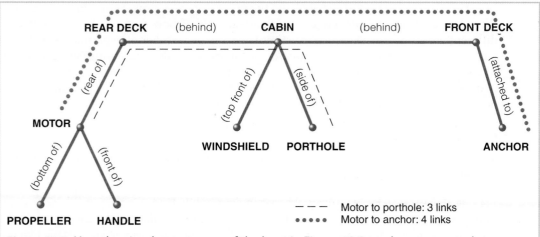

Figure 10.6 How the visual appearance of the boat in Figure 10.2 can be represented propositionally. Paths between motor and porthole (dashed line) and motor and anchor (dotted line) indicate the number of nodes that would be traversed between these parts of the boat. *(Source: Reprinted from S. M. Kosslyn, Mental imagery, in S. M. Kosslyn & D. N. Osherson, An invitation to cognitive science, 2nd ed., vol. 2: Visual cognition, pp. 267–296, Figure 7.6. Copyright © 1995 MIT Press.)*

to the porthole (dashed line) and four links to get to the anchor (dotted line). This kind of explanation proposes that imagery operates in a way similar to the semantic networks we described in Chapter 9 (see page 256).

In addition to suggesting that Kosslyn's results can be explained in terms of propositional representations, Pylyshyn also suggested that one reason that scanning time increases as the distance between two points on an image increases is that subjects are responding to Kosslyn's tasks based on what they know about what usually happens when they are looking at a real scene. According to Pylyshyn (2003), "When asked to imagine something, people ask themselves what it would look like to see it, and they then simulate as many aspects of this staged event as they can" (p. 113). People know that in the real world it takes longer to travel longer distances, just as I know it takes longer to drive from Pittsburgh to Philadelphia than to Erie, so, Pylyshyn suggests, they simulate this result in Kosslyn's experiment. This is called the **tacit knowledge explanation** because it states that subjects unconsciously use knowledge about the world in making their judgments.

Although Pylyshyn was in the minority (most researchers accepted the spatial representation explanation of visual imagery), his criticisms couldn't be ignored, and researchers from the "spatial" camp proceeded to gather more evidence. For example, to counter the tacit knowledge explanation of Kosslyn's mental scanning results, Ronald Finke and Stephen Pinker (1982) briefly presented a four-dot display, like the one in **Figure 10.7a**, and then, after a 2-second delay, presented an arrow, as in **Figure 10.7b**. The subjects' task was to indicate whether the arrow was pointing to any of the dots they had just seen.

Although the subjects were not told to use imagery or to scan outward from the arrow, they took longer to respond for greater distances between the arrow and the dot. In fact, the results look very similar to the results of other scanning experiments. Finke and Pinker argue that because their subjects wouldn't have had time to memorize the distances between the arrow and the dot before making their judgments, it is unlikely that they used tacit knowledge about how long it should take to get from one point to another.

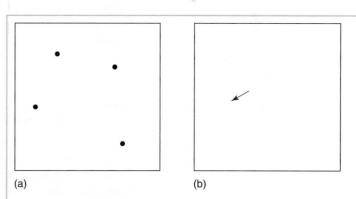

Figure 10.7 Stimuli for Finke and Pinker's (1982) experiment. The display in (a) was presented first, followed, after a 2-second delay, by the arrow in (b). The subjects' task was to determine whether the arrow pointed to any of the dots that had been presented in the first display. *(Source: From R. A. Finke & S. Pinker, Spontaneous imagery scanning in mental extrapolation, Journal of Experimental Psychology: Learning, Memory and Cognition, 8, 2, 142–147, Figure 1, 1982.)*

We've discussed both the spatial and the propositional approaches to imagery because these two explanations provide an excellent example of how data can be interpreted in different ways. Pylyshyn's criticisms stimulated a large number of experiments that have taught us a great deal about the nature of visual imagery (also see Intons-Peterson, 1983). The weight of the evidence supports the idea that imagery is served by a spatial mechanism and that it shares mechanisms with perception. We will now look at additional evidence that supports the idea of spatial representation.

COMPARING IMAGERY AND PERCEPTION

We begin by describing another experiment by Kosslyn. This one looks at how imagery is affected by the size of an object in a person's visual field.

SIZE IN THE VISUAL FIELD If you observe an automobile from far away, it fills only a portion of your visual field, and it is difficult to see small details such as the door handle. As you move closer, it fills more of your visual field, and you can perceive details like the door handle more easily (**Figure 10.8**). With these observations about perception in mind, Kosslyn wondered whether this relationship between viewing distance and the ability to perceive details also occurs for mental images.

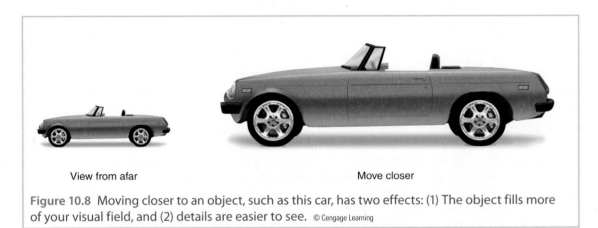

View from afar   Move closer

Figure 10.8 Moving closer to an object, such as this car, has two effects: (1) The object fills more of your visual field, and (2) details are easier to see. © Cengage Learning

To answer this question, Kosslyn (1978) asked subjects to imagine two animals, such as an elephant and a rabbit, next to each other and to imagine that they were standing close enough to the larger animal that it filled most of their visual field (**Figure 10.9a**). He then posed questions such as "Does the rabbit have whiskers?" and asked his subjects to find that part of the animal in their mental image and to answer as quickly as possible. When he repeated this procedure but told subjects to imagine a rabbit and a fly next to each other, subjects created larger images of the rabbit, as shown in **Figure 10.9b**. The result of these experiments, shown alongside the pictures, was that subjects answered questions about the rabbit more rapidly when it filled more of the visual field.

In addition to asking subjects to respond to details in visual images, Kosslyn also asked them to do a **mental walk task**, in which they were to imagine that they were walking toward their mental image of an animal. Their task was to estimate how far away they were from the animal when they began to experience "overflow"—when the image filled the visual field or when its edges started becoming fuzzy. The result was that subjects had to move closer for small animals (less than a foot away for a mouse) than for larger animals (about 11 feet away for an elephant), just as they would have to do if they were walking toward actual animals. This result provides further evidence for the idea that images are spatial, just like perception.

INTERACTIONS OF IMAGERY AND PERCEPTION Another way to demonstrate connections between imagery and perception is to show that they interact with one another. The basic rationale behind this approach is that if imagery affects perception, or perception affects imagery, this means that imagery and perception both have access to the same mechanisms.

The classic demonstration of interaction between perception and imagery dates back to 1910, when Cheves Perky did the experiment pictured in **Figure 10.10**. Perky asked her subjects to "project" visual images of common objects onto a screen, and then to describe these images. Unbeknownst to the subjects, Perky was back-projecting a very dim image of this object onto the screen. Thus, when subjects were asked to create an image of a banana, Perky projected a dim image of a banana onto the screen. Interestingly, the subjects' descriptions of their images matched the images that Perky was projecting. For example, they described the banana as being oriented vertically, just as was the projected image. Even more interesting, not one of Perky's 24 subjects noticed that there was an actual picture on the screen. They had apparently mistaken an actual picture for a mental image.

Modern researchers have replicated Perky's result (see Craver-Lemley & Reeves, 1992; Segal & Fusella, 1970) and have demonstrated interactions between perception and imagery in a number of other ways. Martha Farah (1985) instructed her subjects to imagine either the letter *H* or the letter *T* on a screen (**Figure 10.11a**). Once they had formed a clear image on the screen, they pressed a button that caused two squares to flash, one after the other (**Figure 10.11b**). One of the squares contained a target letter, which was either an *H* or a *T*. The subjects' task was to indicate whether the letter was in the first square or the second one. The results, shown in **Figure 10.11c**, indicate that the target letter was detected more accurately when the subject had been imagining the same letter rather than the different letter. Farah interpreted this result as showing that perception and imagery share mechanisms; later experiments that have also shown that imagery can affect perception have come to the same conclusion (Kosslyn & Thompson, 2000; Pearson et al., 2008).

IS THERE A WAY TO RESOLVE THE IMAGERY DEBATE?

You might think, from the evidence of parallels between imagery and perception and of interactions between them, that the imagery debate would have been settled once and for all in favor of the spatial explanation. But John Anderson (1978) warned that despite this evidence, we still can't rule out the propositional explanation, and Martha Farah (1988) pointed out that it is difficult to rule out Pylyshyn's tacit knowledge explanation just on the basis of the results of behavioral experiments like the ones we have been describing. She argued that it is always possible that subjects can be influenced by their past experiences with perception, so they could unknowingly be simulating perceptual responses in imagery experiments. For example, in the mental walk experiments, in which subjects were supposed to be imagining that they were walking toward their mental image of an animal, subjects could be using their knowledge from prior experience in perceiving animals to conclude that they would have to be closer to a mouse than to an elephant before these animals would fill up their field of view.

But Farah suggested a way out of this problem: Instead of relying solely on behavioral experiments, we should investigate

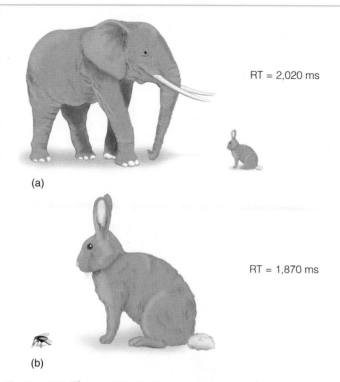

RT = 2,020 ms

RT = 1,870 ms

(a)

(b)

Figure 10.9 These pictures represent images that Kosslyn's (1978) subjects created, which filled different portions of their visual field. (a) Imagine elephant and rabbit, so elephant fills the field. (b) Imagine rabbit and fly, so rabbit fills the field. Reaction times indicate how long it took subjects to answer questions about the rabbit. © Cengage Learning

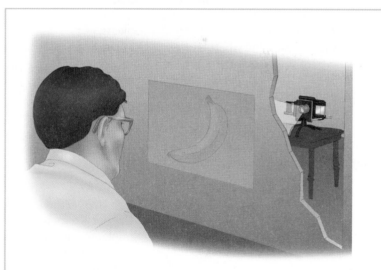

Figure 10.10 Subject in Perky's (1910) experiment. Unbeknownst to the subjects, Perky was projecting dim images onto the screen. © Cengage Learning

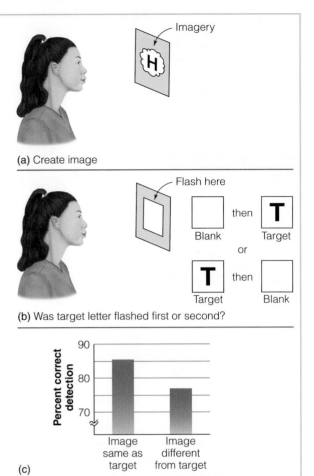

(a) Create image

(b) Was target letter flashed first or second?

(c)

Figure 10.11 Procedure for Farah's (1985) letter visualization experiment. (a) The subject visualizes *H* or *T* on the screen. (b) Then two squares flash, one after the other, on the same screen. As shown on the right, the target letter can be in the first square or in the second one. The subjects' task is to determine whether the test letter was flashed in the first or in the second square. (c) Results showing that accuracy was higher when the letter in (b) was the same as the one that had been imagined in (a). *(Source: Based on M. J. Farah, Psychophysical evidence for a shared representational medium for mental images and percepts,* Journal of Experimental Psychology: General, *114, 91–103, 1985.)*

how the brain responds to visual imagery. The reason Farah was able to make this proposal was that by the 1980s, evidence about the physiology of imagery was becoming available from neuropsychology—the study of patients with brain damage—and from electrophysiological measurements. In addition, beginning in the 1990s, brain imaging experiments provided additional data regarding the physiology of imagery. We will describe measurements of the brain's response to imagery in the next section.

TEST YOURSELF 10.1

1. Is imagery just a "laboratory phenomenon," or does it occur in real life?

2. Make a list of the important events in the history of the study of imagery in psychology, from the imageless thought debate of the 1800s to the studies of imagery that occurred early in the cognitive revolution in the 1960s and 1970s.

3. How did Kosslyn use the technique of mental scanning (in the boat and island experiments) to demonstrate similarities between perception and imagery? Why were Kosslyn's experiments criticized, and how did Kosslyn answer Pylyshyn's criticism with additional experiments?

4. Describe the spatial (or depictive) and propositional explanations of the mechanism underlying imagery. How can the propositional explanation interpret the results of Kosslyn's boat and island image-scanning experiments?

5. What is the tacit knowledge explanation of imagery experiments? What experiment was done to counter this explanation?

6. How have experiments demonstrated interactions between imagery and perception? What additional evidence is needed to help settle the imagery debate, according to Farah?

Imagery and the Brain

As we look at a number of types of physiological experiments, we will see that a great deal of evidence points to a connection between imagery and perception, but the overlap is not perfect. We begin by looking at the results of research that has measured the brain's response to imagery and will then consider how brain damage affects the ability to form visual images.

IMAGERY NEURONS IN THE BRAIN

Studies in which activity is recorded from single neurons in humans are rare (see Method: Recording from Single Neurons in Humans, Chapter 3, page 79). But Gabriel Kreiman and coworkers (2000) were able to study patients who had electrodes implanted in various areas in their medial temporal lobe, which includes the hippocampus and the amygdala (see **Figure 5.22**, page 142), in order to determine the source of severe epileptic seizures that could not be controlled by medication.

In this study, Kreiman and coworkers found neurons that responded to some objects but not to others. For example, the records in **Figure 10.12a** show the response of a neuron that responded to a picture of a baseball but did not respond to a picture of a face. Notice in **Figure 10.12b** that this neuron fired in the same way when the person closed his or her eyes and *imagined* a baseball (good firing) or a face (no firing). Kreiman calls these neurons **imagery neurons.**

Kreiman's discovery of imagery neurons is important, both because it demonstrates a possible physiological mechanism for imagery and because these neurons respond in the same way to *perceiving* an object and to *imagining* it, thereby supporting the idea of a close relation between perception and imagery. However, most research on the physiology of imagery has involved large areas of the brain. Beginning in the early 1990s, researchers began using brain imaging to measure brain activity as subjects were perceiving objects and as they were creating visual images of these objects (see Method: Brain Imaging, Chapter 2, page 41).

BRAIN IMAGING

An early study of imagery using brain imaging was carried out by Samuel Le Bihan and coworkers (1993), who demonstrated that both perception and imagery activate the visual cortex. **Figure 10.13** shows how activity in the striate cortex increased both when a person observed presentations of actual visual stimuli (marked "Perception") *and* when the person was imagining the stimulus ("Imagery"). In another brain imaging experiment, asking subjects to think about questions that involved imagery—for example, "Is the green of the trees darker than the green of the grass?"—generated a greater response in the visual cortex than asking nonimagery questions, such as "Is the intensity of electrical current measured in amperes?" (Goldenberg et al., 1989).

Another imaging experiment, by Stephen Kosslyn (1995), made use of the way the visual cortex is organized as a topographic map, which we described in Chapter 4 (see **Figure 4.35**, page 112). The topographic map refers to the fact that specific locations on a visual stimulus cause activity at specific locations in the visual cortex and that points next to each other on the stimulus cause activity at locations next to each other on the cortex.

Research on the topographic map on the visual cortex indicates that *looking* at a small object causes activity in the back of the visual cortex, as shown by the green area in **Figure 10.14a**, and looking at larger objects causes activity to spread toward the front of the visual cortex, as indicated by the red area. What would happen, Kosslyn wondered, if subjects created mental *images* of different sizes? To answer this question, subjects were instructed to create small, medium, and large visual images while they were in a brain scanner. The result, indicated by the symbols in **Figure 10.14b**, is that when subjects created small visual images, activity was centered near the back of the brain (circles), but as the size of the mental image increased, activation moved toward the front of the visual cortex (squares and triangles), just as it does for perception. (Notice that one of the triangles representing large images is near the back of the visual cortex. Kosslyn suggests that this could have been caused by activation by internal details of the larger image.) Thus, both imagery and perception result in topographically organized brain activation.

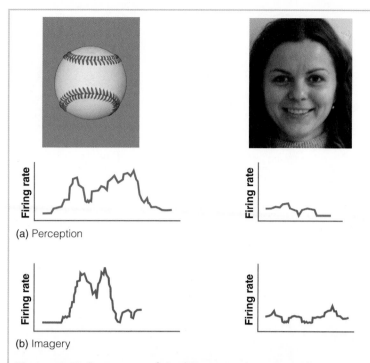

Figure 10.12 Responses of single neurons in a person's medial temporal lobe that (a) respond to perception of a baseball but not of a face, and (b) respond to imagining a baseball but not to imagining a face. *(Source: Based on G. Kreiman, C. Koch, & I. Fried, Imagery neurons in the human brain, Nature 408, 357–361, November 16, 2000. Photos by Bruce Goldstein.)*

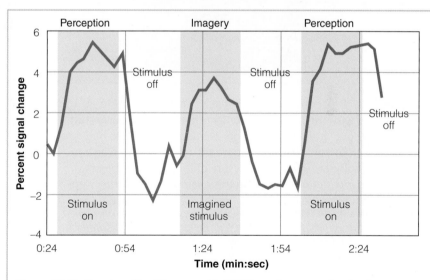

Figure 10.13 Results of Le Bihan et al.'s (1993) study measuring brain activity using fMRI. Activity increases to presentation of a visual stimulus (shaded area marked "Stimulus on") and also increases when subjects are imagining the stimulus (area marked "Imagined stimulus"). In contrast, activity is low when there is no actual or imagined stimulus. *(Source: D. Le Bihan et al., Activation of human primary visual cortex during visual recall: A magnetic resonance imaging study, Proceedings of the National Academy of Sciences, USA, 90, 11802–11805, 1993.)*

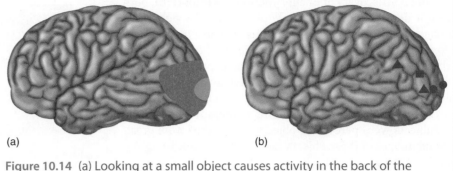

Figure 10.14 (a) Looking at a small object causes activity in the back of the visual cortex (green). Larger objects cause activity to spread forward (red). (b) Results of Kosslyn et al.'s (1995) experiment. The symbols indicate the most activated location caused by imagery: small image (circle); medium image (square); large image (triangle). *(Source: Based on S. M. Kosslyn, Mental imagery, in S. M. Kosslyn & D. N. Osherson (Eds.), An invitation to cognitive science, 2nd ed., Vol 2, pp. 267–296, 1995.)*

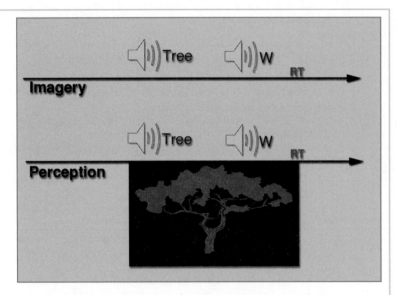

Figure 10.15 Procedure for Ganis et al.'s (2004) experiment. A trial begins with the name of an object that was previously studied, in this case "tree." In the imagery condition, subjects had their eyes closed and had to imagine the tree. In the perception condition, subjects saw a faint picture of the object. Subjects then heard instructions. The *W* in this example means they were to judge whether the object was "wider than tall." *(Source: G. Ganis, W. L. Thompson, & S. M. Kosslyn, Brain areas underlying visual mental imagery and visual perception: An fMRI study, Cognitive Brain Research, 20, 226–241. Copyright © 2004 Elsevier Ltd. Reproduced by permission.)*

Another approach to studying imagery and the brain has been to determine whether there is overlap between brain areas activated by perceiving an object and those activated by creating a mental image of the object. These experiments have demonstrated an overlap between areas activated by perception and by imagery, but have also found differences. For example, Giorgio Ganis and coworkers (2004) used fMRI to measure activation under two conditions, perception and imagery. For the perception condition, subjects observed a drawing of an object, such as the tree in Figure 10.15. For the imagery condition, subjects were told to imagine a picture that they had studied before, when they heard a tone. For both the perception and imagery tasks, subjects had to answer a question such as "Is the object wider than it is tall?"

Results of Ganis's experiment are shown in Figure 10.16, which shows activation at three different locations in the brain. Figure 10.16a shows that perception and imagery both activate the same areas in the frontal lobe. Figure 10.16b shows the same result further back in the brain. However, Figure 10.16c, which shows activation in the visual cortex, in the occipital lobe at the back of the brain, indicates that perception activates much more of this area of the brain than does imagery. This greater activity for perception isn't surprising because the visual cortex is where signals from the retina first reach the cortex. Thus, there is almost complete overlap of the activation caused by perception and imagery in the front of the brain, but some difference near the back of the brain.

Other experiments have also concluded that there are similarities but also some differences between brain activation for perception and for imagery. For example, an fMRI experiment by Amir Amedi and coworkers (2005) showed overlap, but also found that when subjects were using visual imagery, some areas associated with nonvisual stimuli, such as hearing and touch, were *deactivated*. That is, during imagery, their activation was decreased. Amedi suggests that the reason for this might be that visual images are more fragile than real perception and this deactivation helps quiet down irrelevant activity that might interfere with the mental image.

The results of other imaging studies have also found both overlap and differences between activation caused by perception and imagery. For example, Sue-Hynn Lee and coworkers (2012) were able to use brain activation patterns to determine what their subjects were perceiving or imagining (see Method: Neural Mind Reading, Chapter 5, page 145). They found that activity in the visual cortex in the occipital lobe resulted in the best prediction for what their subjects were perceiving, and activity in higher visual areas was the best predictor of what their subjects were imagining. This makes sense when we remember that the visual cortex responds to small details, such as oriented lines, that would be more obvious when perceiving, and higher visual areas respond more to whole objects.

The differences in activation that are observed when comparing perception and imagery are not that surprising. After all, seeing an object is different from imagining it. As we continue describing how the brain responds to perception and imagery, we will encounter more examples of both overlap and differences.

TRANSCRANIAL MAGNETIC STIMULATION

Although the brain imaging experiments we have just described are consistent with the idea that imagery and perception share the same mechanisms, showing that an area of the brain is activated by imagery does not prove that this activity *causes* imagery. Pylyshyn argues that just as the spatial experience of mental images is an epiphenomenon (see page 280), brain activity can also be an epiphenomenon. According to Pylyshyn, brain activity in response to imagery may indicate that *something* is happening but may have nothing to do with causing imagery. To deal with this possibility, Stephen Kosslyn and coworkers (1999) did an experiment using transcranial magnetic stimulation (TMS), which we described in Chapter 9 (see Method: Transcranial Magnetic Stimulation (TMS), page 270).

Kosslyn and coworkers (1999) presented transcranial magnetic stimulation to the visual cortex while subjects were carrying out either a perception task or an imagery task. For the perception task, subjects briefly viewed a display like the one in Figure 10.17 and were asked to make a judgment about the stripes in two of the quadrants. For example, they might be asked to indicate whether the stripes in quadrant 3 were longer than the stripes in quadrant 2. The imagery task was the same, but instead of actually looking at the stripes while answering the questions, the subjects closed their eyes and based their judgments on their mental image of the display.

Kosslyn measured subjects' reaction time to make the judgment, both when transcranial magnetic stimulation was being applied to the visual area of the brain and also during a control condition when the stimulation was directed to another part of the brain. The results indicated that stimulation caused subjects to respond more slowly, and that this slowing effect occurred both for perception and for imagery. Based on these results, Kosslyn concluded that the brain activation that occurs in response to imagery is not an epiphenomenon and that brain activity in the visual cortex plays a causal role in both perception and imagery.

NEUROPSYCHOLOGICAL CASE STUDIES

How can we use studies of people with brain damage to help us understand imagery? One approach is to determine how brain damage affects imagery. Another approach is to determine how brain damage affects both imagery and perception, and to note whether both are affected in the same way.

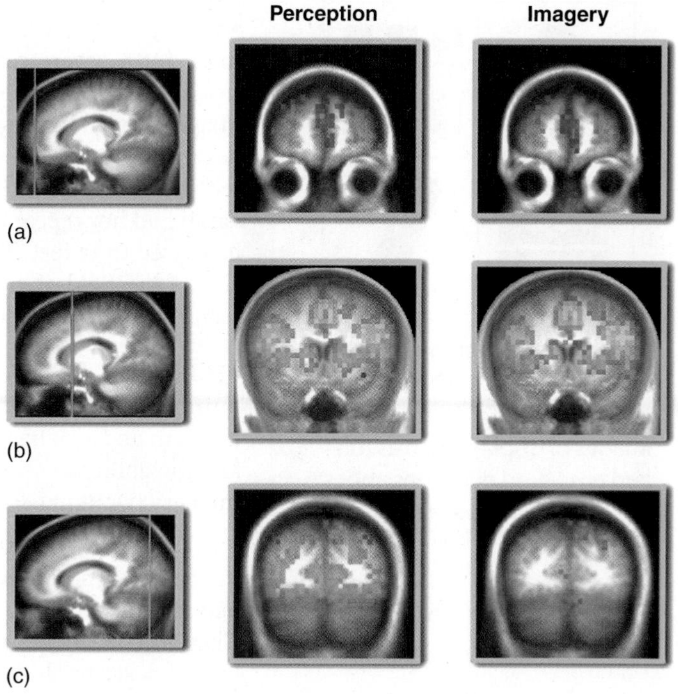

Figure 10.16 Brain scan results from Ganis et al. (2004). The vertical lines through the brains in the far left column indicate where activity was being recorded. The columns labeled "Perception" and "Imagery" indicate responses in the perception and imagery conditions. (a) Responses of areas in the frontal lobe. Perception and imagery cause the same activation. (b) Responses further back in the brain. Activation is the same in this area as well. (c) Responses from the back of the brain, including the primary visual area. There is much more activation in this area in the perception condition. *(Source: G. Ganis, W. L. Thompson, & S. M. Kosslyn, Brain areas underlying visual mental imagery and visual perception: An fMRI study, Cognitive Brain Research, 20, 226–241. Copyright © 2004 Elsevier Ltd. Reproduced by permission.)*

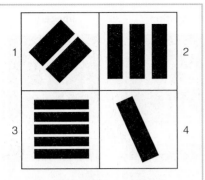

Figure 10.17 Bar stimuli used for Kosslyn et al.'s (1999) experiment. Subjects created visual images of displays such as this and answered questions about the stripes. *(Source: S. M. Kosslyn, A. Pascual-Leone, O. Felician, S. Camposano, J. P. Keenan, W. L. Thompson, et al., The role of area 17 in visual imagery: Convergent evidence form PET and rTMS, Science, 284, 167–170, 1999.)*

"I can get to within 15 feet of the horse in my imagination before it starts to overflow."

"The horse starts to overflow at an imagined distance of about 35 feet."

Figure 10.18 Results of the mental walk task for patient M.G.S. *Left*: Before her operation, she could mentally "walk" to within 15 feet before the image of the horse overflowed her visual field. *Right*: After removal of the right occipital lobe, the size of the visual field was reduced, and she could mentally approach only to within 35 feet of the horse before it overflowed her visual field. *(Source: Based on M. J. Farah, The neural basis of mental imagery, in M. Gazzaniga, ed., The cognitive neurosciences, 2nd ed., Cambridge, MA: MIT Press, pp. 965–974, Figure 66.2, 2000.)*

REMOVING PART OF THE VISUAL CORTEX DECREASES IMAGE SIZE Patient M.G.S. was a young woman who was about to have part of her right occipital lobe removed as treatment for a severe case of epilepsy. Before the operation, Martha Farah and coworkers (1993) had M.G.S. perform the mental walk task that we described earlier, in which she imagined walking toward an animal and estimated how close she was when the image began to overflow her visual field. Figure 10.18 shows that before the operation, M.G.S. felt she was about 15 feet from an imaginary horse before its image overflowed. But when Farah had her repeat this task after her right occipital lobe had been removed, the distance increased to 35 feet. This occurred because removing part of the visual cortex reduced the size of her field of view, so the horse filled up the field when she was farther away. This result supports the idea that the visual cortex is important for imagery.

PERCEPTUAL PROBLEMS ARE ACCOMPANIED BY PROBLEMS WITH IMAGERY A large number of cases have been studied in which a patient with brain damage has a perceptual problem and also has a similar problem in creating images. For example, people who have lost the ability to see color due to brain damage are also unable to create colors through imagery (DeRenzi & Spinnler, 1967; DeVreese, 1991).

Damage to the parietal lobes can cause a condition called **unilateral neglect**, in which the patient ignores objects in one half of the visual field, even to the extent of shaving just one side of his face or eating only the food on one side of her plate. Edoardo Bisiach and Claudio Luzzatti (1978) tested the imagery of a patient with unilateral neglect by asking him to describe things he saw when imagining himself standing at one end of the Piazza del Duomo in Milan, a place with which he had been familiar before his brain was damaged (Figure 10.19).

The patient's responses showed that he neglected the left side of his mental image, just as he neglected the left side of his perceptions. Thus, when he imagined himself standing at A, he neglected the left side and named only objects to his right (small *a*'s). When he imagined himself standing at B, he continued to neglect the left side, again naming only objects on his right (small *b*'s).

The correspondence between the physiology of mental imagery and the physiology of perception, as demonstrated by brain scans in normal subjects and the effects of brain damage in subjects with neglect, supports the idea that mental imagery and perception share physiological mechanisms. However, not all physiological results support a one-to-one correspondence between imagery and perception.

DISSOCIATIONS BETWEEN IMAGERY AND PERCEPTION In Chapter 2 we described dissociations between different types of perception, in which some people with brain damage were unable to recognize faces but could recognize objects and other people had the opposite problem (see Method: Demonstrating a Double Dissociation, Chapter 2, page 40). Cases have also been reported of dissociations between imagery and perception. For example, Cecilia Guariglia and coworkers (1993) studied a patient whose brain damage had little effect on his ability to perceive but caused neglect in his mental images (his mental images were limited to only one side, as in the case of the man imagining the piazza in Milan).

Another case of normal perception but impaired imagery is the case of R.M., who had suffered damage to his occipital and parietal lobes (Farah et al., 1988). R.M. was able to recognize objects and to draw accurate pictures of objects that were placed before him. However, he was unable to draw objects from memory, a task that requires imagery. He also had trouble answering questions that depend on imagery, such as verifying whether the sentence "A grapefruit is larger than an orange" is correct.

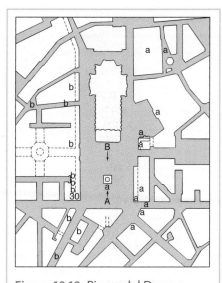

Figure 10.19 Piazza del Duomo in Milan. When Bisiach and Luzzatti's (1978) patient imagined himself standing at A, he could name objects indicated by *a*'s. When he imagined himself at B, he could name objects indicated by *b*'s. *(Source: Based on E. Bisiach & G. Luzzatti, Unilateral neglect of representational space, Cortex, 14, 129–133, 1978.)*

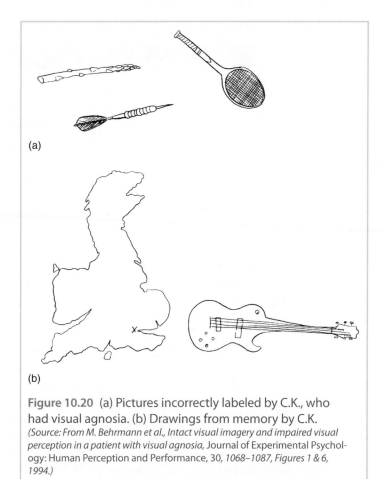

(a)

(b)

Figure 10.20 (a) Pictures incorrectly labeled by C.K., who had visual agnosia. (b) Drawings from memory by C.K. *(Source: From M. Behrmann et al., Intact visual imagery and impaired visual perception in a patient with visual agnosia, Journal of Experimental Psychology: Human Perception and Performance, 30, 1068–1087, Figures 1 & 6, 1994.)*

Dissociations have also been reported with the opposite result, so that perception is impaired but imagery is relatively normal. For example, Marlene Behrmann and coworkers (1994) studied C.K., a 33-year-old graduate student who was struck by a car as he was jogging. C.K. suffered from visual agnosia, the inability to visually recognize objects. Thus, he labeled the pictures in **Figure 10.20a** as a "feather duster" (the dart), a "fencer's mask" (the tennis racquet), and a "rose twig with thorns" (the asparagus). These results show that C.K. could recognize parts of objects but couldn't integrate them into a meaningful whole. But despite his inability to name pictures of objects, C.K. was able to draw objects from memory, a task that depends on imagery (**Figure 10.20b**). Interestingly, when he was shown his own drawings after enough time had passed so he had forgotten the actual drawing experience, he was unable to identify the objects he had drawn.

MAKING SENSE OF THE NEUROPSYCHOLOGICAL RESULTS The neuropsychological cases present a paradox: On one hand, there are many cases that show close parallels between perceptual deficits and deficits in imagery. On the other hand, there are a number of cases in which dissociations occur, so that perception is normal but imagery is poor (Guariglia's patient and R.M.), or perception is poor but imagery is normal (C.K.). The cases in which imagery and perception are affected differently by brain damage provide evidence for a double dissociation between imagery and perception (**Table 10.1**). The presence of a double dissociation is usually interpreted to mean that the two functions (perception and imagery, in this case) are served by different mechanisms (see page 40). However, this conclusion contradicts the other evidence we have presented that shows that imagery and perception share mechanisms.

One way to explain this paradox, according to Behrmann and coworkers (1994), is that the mechanisms of perception and imagery overlap only partially, with the mechanism

Table 10.1: Dissociations Between Perception and Imagery

CASE	PERCEPTION	IMAGERY
Guariglia (1993)	OK.	Neglect (image limited to one side).
Farah et al. (1993) (R.M.)	OK. Recognizes objects and can draw pictures.	Poor. Can't draw from memory or answer questions based on imagery.
Behrmann et al. (1994) (C.K.)	Poor. Visual agnosia, can't recognize objects.	OK. Can draw object from memory.

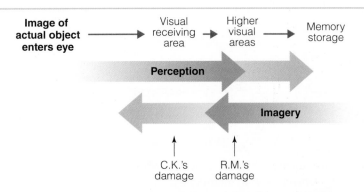

Figure 10.21 Depiction of the idea that mechanisms serving perception, which starts when an image of the actual object enters the eye, are located at both lower and higher visual centers and that mechanisms serving imagery are located mainly at higher levels (Behrmann et al., 1994). The general locations of damage for C.K. and R.M. are indicated by the vertical arrows. These locations can explain why C.K. has a perceptual problem but can still create images, and why R.M. has trouble creating images but can still perceive. © Cengage Learning

for perception being located at both lower and higher visual centers and the mechanism for imagery being located mainly in higher visual centers (Figure 10.21). According to this idea, visual perception necessarily involves *bottom-up processing*, which starts when light enters the eye and an image is focused on the retina, then continues as signals are sent along the visual pathways to the visual cortex and then to higher visual centers.

The visual cortex is crucial for perception because it is here that objects begin being analyzed into components like edges and orientations. This information is then sent to higher visual areas, where perception is "assembled," and top-down processing, which involves a person's prior knowledge, may also be involved (see page 59). In contrast, imagery *originates* as a top-down process, in higher brain areas that are responsible for memory.

Based on this explanation, we can hypothesize that C.K.'s difficulty in perceiving is caused by damage early in the processing stream, but that he can still create images because higher-level areas of his brain are intact. Similarly, we can hypothesize that R.M.'s difficulty in creating mental images is caused by damage to higher-level areas, where mental images originate, but that he can perceive objects because areas earlier in the processing stream are still functioning.

Although this explanation works for C.K. and R.M., it can't explain the case of M.G.S., the woman who had part of her visual cortex removed (see Figure 10.18). Even though M.G.S.'s damage was earlier in the cortex, she experienced changes in both perception and imagery. Cases such as this emphasize the challenge of interpreting the results of neuropsychological research. It is likely that further research will lead to modifications in the explanation shown in Figure 10.21, or perhaps a new explanation altogether.

CONCLUSIONS FROM THE IMAGERY DEBATE

The imagery debate provides an outstanding example of a situation in which a controversy has motivated a large amount of research. Most psychologists, looking at the behavioral and physiological evidence, have concluded that imagery and perception are closely related and share some (but not all) mechanisms (but see Pylyshyn, 2001, 2003, who doesn't agree).

The idea of shared mechanisms follows from all of the parallels and interactions between perception and imagery. The idea that not all mechanisms are shared follows from some of the fMRI results, which show that the overlap between brain activation is not complete; some of the neuropsychological results, which show dissociations between imagery and perception; and also from differences between the experience of imagery and perception. For example, perception occurs automatically when we look at something, but imagery needs to be generated with some effort. Also, perception is stable—it continues as long as you are observing a stimulus—but imagery is fragile—it can vanish without continued effort.

Another example of a difference between imagery and perception is that it is harder to manipulate mental images than images that are created perceptually. This was demonstrated by Deborah Chalmers and Daniel Reisberg (1985), who asked their subjects to create mental images of ambiguous figures such as the one in **Figure 10.22**, which can be seen as a rabbit or a duck. Perceptually, it is fairly easy to "flip" between these two perceptions. However, Chalmers and Reisberg found that subjects who were holding a mental image of this figure were unable to flip from one perception to another.

Later research has shown that people can manipulate simpler mental images. For example, Ronald Finke and coworkers (1989) showed that when subjects followed instructions to imagine a capital letter D, and then rotate it 90 degrees to the left and place a capital letter J at the bottom, they reported seeing an umbrella. Also, Fred Mast and Kosslyn (2002) showed that people who were good at imagery were able to rotate mental images of ambiguous figures if they were provided with extra information such as drawings of parts of the images that are partially rotated. So, the experiments on manipulating images lead to the same conclusion as all of the other experiments we have described: Imagery and perception have many features in common, but there are also differences between them.

Figure 10.22 What is this, a rabbit (facing right) or a duck (facing left)? © Cengage Learning

Using Imagery to Improve Memory

It is clear that imagery can play an important role in memory. But how can you harness the power of imagery to help you remember things better? In Chapter 7 we saw that encoding is aided by forming connections with other information and described an experiment (Bower & Winzenz, 1970) in which subjects who created images based on two paired words (like *boat* and *tree*) remembered more than twice as many words as subjects who just repeated the words (see **Figure 7.2**, page 182). Another principle of memory we described in Chapter 7 was that organization improves encoding. The mind tends to spontaneously organize information that is initially unorganized, and presenting information that is organized improves memory performance. We will now describe a method based on these principles, which involves placing images at locations.

PLACING IMAGES AT LOCATIONS

The power of imagery to improve memory is tied to its ability to create organized locations at which memories for specific items can be placed. An example of the organizational function of imagery from ancient history is provided by a story about the Greek poet Simonides. According to legend, 2,500 years ago Simonides presented an address at a banquet, and just after he left the banquet, the roof of the hall collapsed, killing most of the people inside. To compound this tragedy, many of the bodies were so severely mutilated that they couldn't be identified. But Simonides realized that as he had looked out over the audience during his address, he had created a mental picture of where each person had been seated at the banquet table. Based on this image of people's locations around the table, he was able to determine who had been killed.

What is important about this rather gory example is that Simonides realized that the technique he had used to help him remember who was at the banquet could be used to remember other things as well. He found that he could remember things by imagining a physical space, like the banquet table, and placing, in his mind, items to be remembered in the seats surrounding the table. This feat of mental organization enabled him to later "read out" the items by mentally scanning the locations around the table, just as he had done to identify people's bodies. Simonides had invented what is now called the **method of loci**—a method in which things to be remembered are placed at different locations in a mental image of a spatial layout. The following demonstration illustrates how to use the method of loci to remember something from your own experience.

DEMONSTRATION
METHOD OF LOCI

Pick a place with a spatial layout that is very familiar to you, such as the rooms in your house or apartment, or the buildings on your college campus. Then pick five to seven things that you want to remember—either events from the past or things you need to do later today. Create an image representing each event, and place each image at a location in the house or on campus. If you need to remember the events in a particular order, decide on a path you would take while walking through the house or campus, and place the images representing each event along your walking path so they will be encountered in the correct order. After you have done this, retrace the path in your mind, and see if encountering the images helps you remember the events. To really test this method, try mentally "walking" this path a few hours from now.

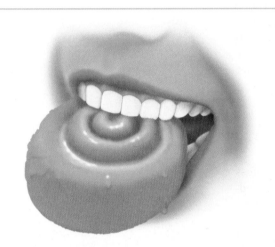

Figure 10.23 An image used by the author to remember a dentist appointment, using the pegword technique. © Cengage Learning

Placing images at locations can help with retrieving memories later. For example, to help me remember a dentist appointment later in the day, I could visually place a huge pair of teeth in my living room. To remind myself to go to the gym and work out, I could imagine an elliptical trainer on the stairs that lead from the living room to the second floor, and to represent the *NCIS* TV show that I want to watch later tonight, I could imagine one of the characters on the show sitting on the landing at the top of the stairs.

ASSOCIATING IMAGES WITH WORDS

The **pegword technique** involves imagery, as in the method of loci, but instead of visualizing items in different locations, you associate them with concrete words. The first step is to create a list of nouns, like the following: one–bun; two–shoe; three–tree; four–door; five–hive; six–sticks; seven–heaven; eight–gate; nine–mine; ten–hen. It's easy to remember these words in order because they were created by rhyming them with the numbers. Also, the rhyming provides a retrieval cue (see page 183) that helps remember each word. The next step is to pair each of the things to be remembered with a pegword by creating a vivid image of your item-to-be-remembered together with the object represented by the word.

Figure 10.23 shows an image I created for the dentist appointment. For the other items I wanted to remember, I might picture an elliptical trainer inside a shoe, and the letters *N, C, I,* and *S* in a tree. The beauty of this system is that it makes it possible to immediately identify an item based on its order on the list. So if I want to identify the third thing I need to do today, I go straight to *tree,* which translates into my image of the letters *N, C, I,* and *S* dangling in a tree, and this reminds me to watch the program *NCIS* on TV.

Imagery techniques like the ones just described are often the basis behind books that claim to provide the key to improving your memory (see Crook & Adderly, 1998; Lorayne & Lucas, 1996; Treadeau, 1997). Although these books do provide imagery-based techniques that work, people who purchase these books in the hope of discovering an easy way to develop "photographic memory" are often disappointed. Although imagery techniques work, they do not provide easy, "magical" improvements in memory, but rather require a great deal of practice and perseverance (Schacter, 2001).

Something to Consider

VISUAL IMAGERY AND FOOD CRAVING

Have you ever had an intense desire to eat a specific food? If so, you have experienced **food craving**, which goes beyond ordinary hunger because of its intensity and specificity (Kemps & Tiggemann, 2013; Weingarten & Elston, 1990). A large proportion of the general population experiences food craving with no problems (Lafay et al., 2001). (The most common food craved in Western societies is, not surprisingly, chocolate; Hetherington & Macdiarmid, 1993.) However, recurrent craving has been associated with problems such as overeating, sabotaging attempts at dieting, and binge eating associated with eating disorders, especially in women (Waters et al., 2001).

Food craving is caused by a number of factors, including nutritional deficiencies, hormonal changes, emotions, and proximity to enticing foods (Kemps & Tiggemann, 2013). But in addition to these biological and psychological factors, food craving is also associated with cognitive factors, including imagery. Thus, people often describe their craving experience with statements such as "I am imagining the taste of it," or "I am visualizing it" (Tiggemann & Kemps, 2005).

Evidence that imagery can cause food craving has been provided by Kirsty Harvey and coworkers (2005), who had female subjects rate their intensity of craving on a 100-point scale and then divided them into two groups. The *food imagery group* were told to imagine their favorite food. The *holiday imagery group* were told to imagine their favorite holiday. Following this imagery, subjects again rated their food craving. The results, shown in **Figure 10.24**, indicate that the food imagery task caused a large increase in craving, but the holiday imagery task had no effect. Interestingly, the effect of imagery was greater in women who were dieting, although the increase in craving occurred in nondieters as well.

While food imagery can increase craving, there is evidence that nonfood imagery can *decrease* craving. Harvey and coworkers demonstrated this by dividing subjects that were in the food imagery group into two groups. Subjects in the *visual imagery group* were asked to close their eyes and create images based on visual cues ("Imagine the appearance of a rainbow"). Subjects in the *auditory imagery group* created images based on auditory cues ("Imagine the sound of a telephone ringing.") Food craving ratings measured before and after these imagery experiences, shown in **Figure 10.25a**, indicate that food craving is reduced following both visual and auditory imagery, but the effect is larger for the visual group.

Harvey explains the larger effect of visual imagery in terms of Baddeley and Hitch's (1974) model of working memory, which we described in Chapter 5 (see page 134). According to this model, shown in **Figure 10.25b**, the phonological loop, which is responsible for processing visual and auditory information, is involved in creating the auditory images, and the visuospatial sketch pad, which is responsible for visual and spatial information, is involved in creating the visual images.

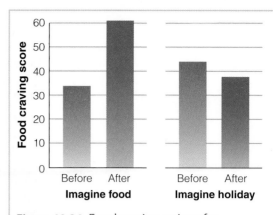

Figure 10.24 Food craving ratings for subjects before and after imagining their favorite food (left pair of bars) or their favorite holiday (right bars). Imagining food increased subjects' rating of the intensity of food craving. These data are for dieters. *(Source: K. Harvey, E. Kemps, & M. Tiggemann, The nature of imagery processes underlying food cravings, British Journal of Health Psychology, 10, 49–56, 2005.)*

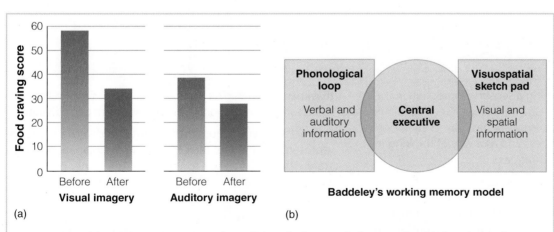

(a) (b)

Figure 10.25 (a) Food craving ratings for subjects before and after nonfood-related visual imagery (left pair of bars) or auditory imagery (right bars). Visual imagery caused a greater decrease in food craving. (b) Baddeley and Hitch's (1974) working memory model, described in Chapter 5. *(Source: part a, based on K. Harvey, E. Kemps, & M. Tiggemann, The nature of imagery processes underlying food cravings, British Journal of Health Psychology, 10, 49–56, Table 2, 2005; part b, © Cengage Learning.)*

Harvey suggests that the nonfood visual imagery uses some of the capacity of the visuospatial sketch pad, so food-related imagery is reduced. The smaller effect of the auditory imagery occurs because auditory images would affect the phonological loop but not the visuospatial sketch pad. It is possible that the small effect observed for the auditory imagery group could be due to unintended visual imagery, as would occur if a person imagines what a telephone looks like as they imagine the telephone's sound.

A number of other laboratory studies have shown that nonfood visual imagery can reduce food cravings and decrease eating associated with craving (Kemps & Tiggemann, 2007). Recently, the effect of nonfood visual imagery on craving has been demonstrated in a 4-week field study. Eva Kemps and Marika Tiggemann (2013) had subjects carry a handheld device that produced a display of dynamic visual noise (randomly moving dots). Subjects were instructed to activate the device and look at the visual noise every time they experienced craving. The idea here, as with the previously described studies, is that the visual noise pattern uses some of the capacity of the phonological loop and reduces the intensity of the food-related imagery that is often associated with craving. As expected, viewing the visual noise decreased food craving and related food consumption. Perhaps, suggest Kemps and Tiggemann, an anticraving app could be developed that would generate visual patterns to look at every time you feel a craving coming on!

TEST YOURSELF 10.2

1. Describe how experiments using the following physiological techniques have provided evidence of parallels between imagery and perception: (a) brain imaging; (b) deactivation of part of the brain; (c) neuropsychology; and (d) recording from single neurons.

2. Some of the neuropsychological results demonstrate parallels between imagery and perception, and some results do not. How has Behrmann explained these contradictory results?

3. What are some differences between imagery and perception? What have most psychologists concluded about the connection between imagery and perception?

4. Under what conditions does imagery improve memory? Describe techniques that use imagery as a tool to improve memory. What is the basic principle that underlies these techniques?

5. What is the relationship between food craving and visual imagery? How has visual imagery been used to reduce food craving?

CHAPTER SUMMARY

1. Mental imagery is experiencing a sensory impression in the absence of sensory input. Visual imagery is "seeing" in the absence of a visual stimulus. Imagery has played an important role in the creative process and as a way of thinking in addition to purely verbal techniques.

2. Early ideas about imagery included the imageless thought debate and Galton's work with visual images, but imagery research stopped during the behaviorist era. Imagery research began again in the 1960s with the advent of the cognitive revolution.

3. Kosslyn's mental scanning experiments suggested that imagery shares the same mechanisms as perception (that is, creates a depictive representation in the person's mind), but these results and others were challenged by Pylyshyn, who stated

that imagery is based on a mechanism related to language (that is, it creates a propositional representation in a person's mind).

4. One of Pylyshyn's arguments against the idea of a depictive representation is the tacit knowledge explanation, which states that when asked to imagine something, people ask themselves what it would look like to see it and then simulate this staged event.

5. Finke and Pinker's "flashed dot" experiment argued against the tacit knowledge explanation. The following experiments also demonstrated parallels between imagery and perception: (a) size in the visual field (visual walk task); (b) interaction between perception and imagery (Perky's 1910 experiment; Farah's experiment in which subjects imagined H or T); and (c) physiological experiments.

6. Parallels between perception and imagery have been demonstrated physiologically by the following methods: (a) recording from single neurons (imagery neurons); (b) brain imaging (demonstrating overlapping activation in the brain); (c) transcranial magnetic stimulation experiments (comparing the effect of brain inactivation on perception and imagery); and (d) neuropsychological case studies (removal of visual cortex affects image size; unilateral neglect).

7. There is also physiological evidence for differences between imagery and perception. This evidence includes (a) differences in areas of the brain activated and (b) brain damage causing dissociations between perception and imagery.

8. Most psychologists, taking all of the above evidence into account, have concluded that imagery is closely related to perception and shares some (but not all) mechanisms.

9. The use of imagery can improve memory in a number of ways: (a) visualizing interacting images; (b) organization using the method of loci; and (c) associating items with nouns using the pegword technique.

10. Food craving has been associated with food-related visual imagery. A reduction in food craving has been associated with nonfood-related visual imagery. It has been suggested that this reduction in food craving occurs because the nonfood-related imagery uses some of the capacity of the visuo-spatial sketch pad.

THINK ABOUT IT

1. Look at an object for a minute; then look away, create a mental image of it, and draw a sketch of the object based on your mental image. Then draw a sketch of the same object while you are looking at it. What kinds of information about the object in the imagery drawing were omitted, compared to the sketch you made while looking at the object?

2. Write a description of an object as you are looking at it. Then compare the written description with the information you can obtain by looking at the object or at a picture of the object. Is it true that "a picture is worth a thousand words"? How does your comparison of written and visual representations relate to the discussion of propositional versus depictive representations in this chapter?

3. Try using one of the techniques described at the end of this chapter to create images that represent things you have to do later today or during the coming week. Then, after some time passes (anywhere from an hour to a few days), check to see whether you can retrieve the memories for these images and if you can remember what they stand for.

KEY TERMS

Conceptual peg hypothesis, 278

Depictive representation, 280

Epiphenomenon, 280

Food craving, 292

Imageless thought debate, 277

Imagery debate, 279

Imagery neuron, 284

Mental chronometry, 278

Mental imagery, 276

Mental scanning, 278

Mental walk task, 282

Method of loci, 291

Paired-associate learning, 277

Pegword technique, 292

Propositional representation, 280

Spatial representation, 279

Tacit knowledge explanation, 281

Unilateral neglect, 288

Visual imagery, 276

COGLAB EXPERIMENTS   Numbers in parentheses refer to the experiment number in CogLab.

Link Word (37)

Mental Rotation (38)

Although this desert scene may be far from your everyday experience, something is happening that is similar to what you experience every day—people are having a conversation. It doesn't matter whether the conversation is in the African desert, in a coffee shop in Cleveland, or on a street corner in Stockholm; language is the primary way people communicate. As we will see, not only is language universal, but the study of how people use and understand language teaches us a great deal about how the mind operates.

Language

One way to appreciate a cognitive ability is to imagine what it would be like if you didn't have it. Clearly, being unable to perceive or remember would threaten your very survival. But what about language? Imagine being stranded on an uninhabited island. If your physical needs were taken care of, you could survive. But imagine the consequences of no conversation with other people or nothing to read. Or how losing the ability to use language would have even more far-reaching consequences—forget about passing the time until the boat comes to rescue you by singing the lyrics to your favorite songs, or keeping a diary, or writing a novel about the shipwreck you just experienced. You get the idea. Not having language might not kill you, but it would have a huge impact on your quality of life.

Our ability to create tens of thousands of meanings with words, to string these words together to create more complex descriptions and thoughts, and to string these descriptions and thoughts together to create a story, a conversation, or even a cognitive psychology book, are some of the things we discuss in this chapter. The plan is to start with small units of language—sounds and words—and to work toward larger units—sentences, stories, and, finally, conversations with other people.

What Is Language?

The following definition of language captures the idea that the ability to string sounds and words together opens the door to a world of communication: **Language** is *a system of communication using sounds or symbols that enables us to express our feelings, thoughts, ideas, and experiences.*

But this definition doesn't go far enough, because it conceivably could include some forms of animal communication. Cats "meow" when their food dish is empty; monkeys have a repertoire of "calls" that stand for things such as "danger" or "greeting"; bees perform a "waggle dance" at the hive to indicate the location of flowers. Although there is some evidence that chimpanzees may be able to use language in a way similar to humans, most animal communication lacks the properties of human language. Let's expand on our definition by considering some of the properties that make human language unique.

THE CREATIVITY OF HUMAN LANGUAGE

Human language goes far beyond a series of fixed signals that transmit a single message such as "feed me," "danger," or "go that way for flowers." Language provides a way of arranging a sequence of signals—sounds for spoken language, letters and written words for written language, and physical signs for sign language—to transmit, from one person to another, things ranging from the simple and commonplace ("My car is over there") to messages that have perhaps never been previously written or uttered in the entire history of the world ("My trip with Zelda, my cousin from California who lost her job in February, was on Groundhog Day").

Language makes it possible to create new and unique sentences because it has a structure that is (1) hierarchical and (2) governed by rules. The hierarchical nature of language means that it consists of a series of small components that can be combined to form larger units. For example, words can be combined to create phrases, which in turn can create sentences, which themselves can become components of a story. The rule-based nature of language means that these components can be arranged in certain ways ("What is my cat saying?" is permissible in English), but not in other ways ("Cat my saying is what?" is not). These two properties—a hierarchical structure and rules—endow humans with the ability to go far beyond the fixed calls and signs of animals to communicate whatever we want to express.

THE UNIVERSAL NEED TO COMMUNICATE WITH LANGUAGE

Although people do "talk" to themselves, as when Hamlet wondered "To be or not to be" or when you daydream in class, language is primarily used for communication, whether it be conversing with another person or reading what someone has written. This need to communicate using language has been called "universal" because it occurs wherever there are people. For example, consider the following:

- People's need to communicate is so powerful that when deaf children find themselves in an environment where nobody speaks or uses sign language, they invent a sign language themselves (Goldin-Meadow, 1982).

- All humans with normal capacities develop a language and learn to follow its complex rules, even though they are usually not aware of these rules. Although many people find the study of grammar to be very difficult, they have no trouble using language.

- Language is universal across cultures. There are more than 5,000 different languages, and there isn't a single culture without language. When European explorers first set foot in New Guinea in the 1500s, the people they discovered, who had been isolated from the rest of the world for eons, had developed more than 750 languages, many of them quite different from one another.

- Language development is similar across cultures. No matter what the culture or the particular language, children generally begin babbling at about 7 months, a few meaningful words appear by their first birthday, and the first multiword utterances occur at about age 2 (Levelt, 2001).

- Even though a large number of languages are very different from one another, we can describe them as being "unique but the same." They are unique in that they use different words and sounds, and they may use different rules for combining these words (although many languages use similar rules). They are the same in that all languages have words that serve the functions of nouns and verbs, and all languages include a system to make things negative, to ask questions, and to refer to the past and present.

STUDYING LANGUAGE

Language has fascinated thinkers for thousands of years, dating back to the ancient Greek philosophers Socrates, Plato, and Aristotle (350–450 BCE), and before. The modern scientific study of language traces its beginnings to the 1800s, when Paul Broca (1861) and Carl Wernicke (1874) identified areas in the frontal and temporal lobes that are involved in different aspects of language (Chapter 2, page 39). We will return to Broca and Wernicke later in the chapter, but our focus for now will be on behavioral and cognitive research, and it is in the 1950s that we take up the story. At that time, behaviorism was still the dominant approach in psychology (see page 9). In 1957, B. F. Skinner, the main proponent of behaviorism, published a book called *Verbal Behavior*, in which he proposed that language is learned through reinforcement. According to this idea, just as children learn appropriate behavior by being rewarded for "good" behavior and punished for "bad" behavior, children learn language by being rewarded for using correct language and punished (or not rewarded) for using incorrect language.

In the same year, linguist Noam Chomsky published a book titled *Syntactic Structures*, in which he proposed that human language is coded in the genes. According to this idea, just as humans are genetically programmed to walk, they are programmed to acquire and use language. Chomsky concluded that despite the wide variations that exist across languages, the underlying basis of all language is similar. Most important for our purposes, Chomsky saw studying language as a way to study the properties of the mind and therefore disagreed with the behaviorist idea that the mind is not a valid topic of study for psychology.

Chomsky's disagreement with behaviorism led him to publish a scathing review of Skinner's *Verbal Behavior* in 1959. In his review, he presented arguments against the behaviorist idea that language can be explained in terms of reinforcements and without reference to the mind. One of Chomsky's most persuasive arguments was that as children learn language, they produce sentences that they have never heard and that have never been reinforced. (A classic example of a sentence that has been created by many children and that is unlikely to have been taught or reinforced by parents is "I hate you, Mommy.")

Chomsky's criticism of behaviorism was an important event in the cognitive revolution and began changing the focus of the young discipline of **psycholinguistics**, the field concerned with the psychological study of language.

The goal of psycholinguistics is to discover the psychological processes by which humans acquire and process language (Clark & Van der Wege, 2002; Gleason & Ratner, 1998; Miller, 1965). The four major concerns of psycholinguistics are as follows:

1. *Comprehension.* How do people understand spoken and written language? This includes how people process language sounds; how they understand words, sentences, and stories expressed in writing, speech, or sign language; and how people have conversations with one another.

2. *Speech production.* How do people produce language? This includes the physical processes of speech production and the mental processes that occur as a person creates speech.

3. *Representation.* How is language represented in the mind and in the brain? This includes how people group words together into phrases and make connections between different parts of a story, as well as how these processes are related to the activation of the brain.

4. *Acquisition.* How do people learn language? This includes not only how children learn language but also how people learn additional languages, either as children or later in life.

Because of the vast scope of psycholinguistics, we are going to restrict our attention to the first three of these concerns, describing research on how we understand language and how we produce it. We begin by considering each of the components of language: small components such as *sounds* and *words*, then combinations of words that form *sentences*, and finally "texts"—*stories* that are created by combining a number of sentences. At the end of the chapter, we describe some of the factors involved in how people participate in and understand conversations. Finally, we look at cross-cultural research that considers how language affects thought, and how thought might affect language.

As we progress from describing the sounds of language to how we understand stories and conversations, we will encounter principles introduced earlier in the book. One of the main principles is the importance of *context*. Whether we are considering letters in a word or the meaning of something being said in a conversation, the context within which letters, words, or sentences appear helps us perceive or understand them. Another principle is *knowledge*. Our ability to understand both written and verbal communication depends not only on what is written or said but also on the knowledge we bring to the situation. As we progress from words to conversations, we will encounter these principles of context and knowledge many times along the way.

Perceiving Phonemes, Words, and Letters

One of the most amazing things about words is how many we know and how rapidly we acquire them. Children produce their first words during their second year (sometimes a little earlier, sometimes later) and, after a slow start, begin adding words rapidly until, by the time they have become adults, they can understand more than 50,000 different words (Altmann, 2001; Dell, 1995). Our knowledge about words is stored in our **lexicon**, which is a person's knowledge of what words mean, how they sound, and how they are used in relation to other words.

COMPONENTS OF WORDS

The words on this page are made up of letters, but the units of language are defined not in terms of letters, but by sounds and meanings. The two smallest units of language are *phonemes*, which refer to sounds, and *morphemes*, which refer to meanings.

PHONEMES When you say words, you produce sounds called phonemes. A **phoneme** is the shortest segment of speech that, if changed, changes the meaning of a word. Thus, the word *bit* contains the phonemes /b/, /i/, and /t/, because we can change *bit* into *pit* by replacing /b/ with /p/, to *bat* by replacing /i/ with /ae/, or to *bid* by replacing /t/ with /d/. (Phonemes are indicated by phonetic symbols that are set off with slashes.)

Note that because phonemes refer to sounds, they are not the same as letters, which can have a number of different sounds (consider the "e" sound in "we" and "wet"), and which can be silent in certain situations (the "e" in "some"). Because different languages use different sounds, the number of phonemes varies in different languages. There are only 11 phonemes in Hawaiian, about 47 in English, and as many as 60 in some African dialects.

MORPHEMES While phonemes refer to sounds, morphemes refer to meanings. **Morphemes** are the smallest units of language that have a definable meaning or a grammatical function. For example, "truck" consists of a number of phonemes, but only one morpheme, because none of the components that create the word truck mean anything. Similarly, even though "table" has two syllables, "tabe" and "ul," it also consists of only a single morpheme, because the syllables alone have no meaning. In contrast "bedroom" has two syllables and two morphemes, because each syllable, "bed" and "room," has a meaning. Although endings such as "s" and "ed," have no meanings in themselves, they are considered morphemes because they change the meaning of a word. Thus "truck," which means "one truck" has one morpheme, and "trucks," which means "more than one truck," has two morphemes.

The reason phonemes and morphemes are important is because they are the building blocks of words. But the idea that printing or writing can represent sounds, and that these sounds can create meanings, is just the beginning of language. Spoken language, in our everyday experience, involves perceiving sounds and assigning meanings to them. As we will now see, there is a close relationship between how we perceive the sounds of a language and the meanings that these sounds create.

HOW PERCEIVING SOUNDS AND LETTERS IS AFFECTED BY MEANING

We begin considering how meaning influences our perception of sounds by describing the *phonemic restoration effect*.

SPEECH: THE PHONEMIC RESTORATION EFFECT The **phonemic restoration effect** occurs when phonemes are perceived in speech when the sound of the phoneme is covered up by an extraneous noise. Richard Warren (1970) demonstrated this effect by having subjects listen to a recording of the sentence "The state governors met with their respective legislatures convening in the capital city." Warren replaced the first /s/ in "legislatures" with the sound of a cough and asked his subjects to indicate where in the sentence the cough occurred (Figure 11.1). No subject identified the correct position of the cough, and, even more significantly, none of them noticed that the /s/ in "legislatures" was missing. This effect was experienced even by students and staff in the psychology department who knew that the /s/ was missing. This "filling in" of the missing phoneme based on the context produced by the sentence and the word containing the phoneme is an example of top-down processing.

Warren also showed that the phonemic restoration effect can be influenced by the meaning of the words that *follow* the missing phoneme. For example, the last word of the phrase "There was time to *ave ..." (where the * indicates the presence of a cough or some other sound) could be *shave, save, wave,* or *rave*, but subjects heard the word *wave* when the remainder of the sentence had to do with saying good-bye to a departing friend. This example of how our knowledge of the meanings of words and the likely meanings of sentences affects speech perception is another example of top-down processing. We will now consider how our knowledge of the meanings of words helps us to perceive them.

Figure 11.1 Phonemic restoration effect. In the sound stimulus presented to the listener, the first /s/ sound in "legislatures" is masked by a cough sound. What the person hears is indicated below. Although the person hears the cough, he also hears the first /s/. © Cengage Learning

SPEECH: PERCEIVING INDIVIDUAL WORDS IN SENTENCES One of the challenges posed by the problem of perceiving words is that not everyone says words in the same way. People talk with different accents and at different speeds, and, most important, people often take a relaxed approach to pronouncing words when they are speaking naturally. For example, if you were talking to a friend, how would you say "Did you go to class today?" Would you say "Did you" or "Dijoo"? You have your own ways of producing various words and phonemes, and other people have theirs. For example, analysis of how people actually speak has determined that there are 50 different ways to pronounce the word *the* (Waldrop, 1988).

When taken out of context and presented alone, words become much more difficult to understand, because of people's often sloppy pronunciation in conversational speech. Irwin Pollack and J. M. Pickett (1964) demonstrated this by recording the conversations of subjects who sat in a room waiting for the experiment to begin. When the subjects were then presented with recordings of single words taken out of their own conversations, they could identify only half the words, even though they were listening to their own voices! The fact that the people in this experiment were able to identify words as they were talking to each other, but couldn't identify the same words when the words were isolated, illustrates that their ability to perceive words in conversations is aided by the context provided by the words and sentences that make up the conversation.

The fact that the sounds of speech are easier to understand when we hear them spoken in a sentence is particularly amazing when we consider that words spoken in a sentence are usually not separated by spaces. This is not what we might expect, because when we listen to someone speak we usually hear the individual words, and sometimes it may seem as if there are spaces that separate one word from another. However, remember our discussion in Chapter 3 in which we noted that a record of the physical energy produced by conversational speech reveals that there are often no physical breaks between words in the speech signal or that breaks can occur in the middle of words (see **Figure 3.13**).

Our ability to perceive individual words even though there are often no pauses between words in the sound signal is called **speech segmentation**. Speech segmentation is aided by a number of factors. In Chapter 3 we pointed out that when we listen to an unfamiliar foreign language, it is often difficult to distinguish one word from the next, but if we know a language, individual words stand out (see page 61). This observation illustrates that knowing the meanings of words helps us perceive them. Perhaps you have had the experience of hearing individual words that you happen to know in a foreign language seem to "pop out" from what appears to be an otherwise continuous stream of speech.

Another example of how meaning is responsible for organizing sounds into words is provided by these two sentences:

Jamie's mother said, "Be a *big girl* and eat your vegetables."

The thing *Big Earl* loved most in the world was his car.

"Big girl" and "Big Earl" are both pronounced the same way, so hearing them differently depends on the overall meaning of the sentence in which these words appear. This example is similar to the familiar "I scream, you scream, we all scream for ice cream" that many people learn as children. The sound stimuli for "I scream" and "ice cream" are identical, so the different organizations must be achieved by the meaning of the sentence in which these words appear.

Although segmentation is aided by knowing the meanings of words and being aware of the context in which these words occur, listeners also use other information to achieve segmentation. As we learn a language, we learn that certain sounds are more likely to follow one another within a word, and some sounds are more likely to be separated by the space between two words. For example, consider the words *pretty baby*. In English it is likely that *pre* and *ty* will follow each other in the same word (**pre-ty**) and that *ty* and *ba* will be separated by a space so will be in two different words (pret*ty ba*by). Thus, the space in the phrase *prettybaby* is most likely to be between *pretty* and *baby*. There is evidence that young children learn these rules about what sounds go together in words and what sounds are more likely to be separated into two different words (Gomez & Gerkin, 1999, 2000; Saffran et al., 1999).

READING: THE WORD SUPERIORITY EFFECT We have been discussing how context helps us perceive the sounds of spoken language. Context also plays a role in perceiving written letters. The **word superiority effect** refers to the finding that letters are easier to recognize when they are contained in a word than when they appear alone or are contained in a nonword. Gerald Reicher first demonstrated this effect in 1969 using the following procedure.

METHOD
THE WORD SUPERIORITY EFFECT

Figure 11.2 shows the procedure for an experiment that demonstrates the word superiority effect. A stimulus that is either a word, such as *FORK* (**Figure 11.2a**); a single letter, such as *K* (**Figure 11.2b**); or a nonword, such as *RFOK* (**Figure 11.2c**) is flashed briefly and is followed immediately by a random pattern located where the stimulus was. This pattern is a mask designed to stop perception of the stimulus. Two letters are presented simultaneously with the mask, one that appeared in the original stimulus (*K* in this example) and another that did not (*M*). The mask and letters are flashed rapidly, and the subject's task is to pick the flashed letter that was presented in the original stimulus. In the example in **Figure 11.2**, *K* would be the correct answer in all three conditions.

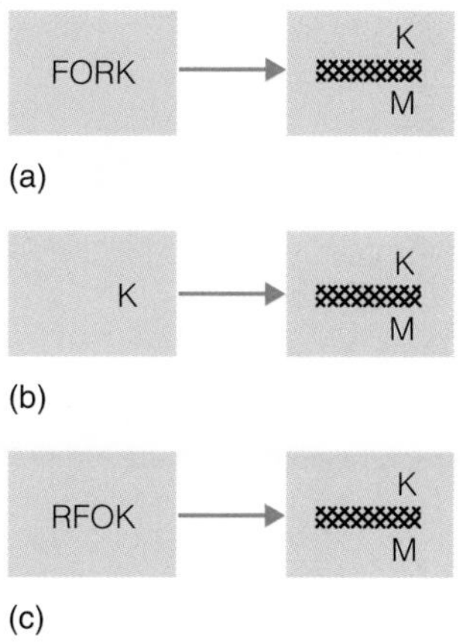

(a)

(b)

(c)

Figure 11.2 Procedure for an experiment that demonstrates the word superiority effect. First the stimulus is presented, then a random pattern and two letters. Three types of stimuli are shown: (a) word condition; (b) letter condition; and (c) nonword condition. © Cengage Learning

When Reicher's subjects were asked to choose which of the two letters they had seen in the original stimulus, they did so more quickly and accurately when the letter had been part of a word, as in **Figure 11.2a**, than when the letter had been presented alone, as in **Figure 11.2b**, or as part of a nonword, as in **Figure 11.2c**. This more rapid processing of letters within a word is the word superiority effect. The word superiority effect shows that letters in words are not processed one by one but that each letter is affected by the context within which it appears. Just as context affects how we *hear* phonemes and words in spoken sentences, context affects how we *see* letters in printed words. **Table 11.1** summarizes the effects of context on perceiving phonemes, words, and letters.

Understanding Words

In the last section, we focused on perception—our ability to sense and identify sounds or see letters. We will now describe some of the factors that influence how we *understand* the meanings of words. We have noted that people have *lexicons*—words they know the

Table 11.1: Perceiving Phonemes, Words, and Letters

EFFECT	DESCRIPTION	CONCLUSION
Phonemic restoration	A phoneme in a spoken word in a sentence can be perceived even if it is obscured by noise.	Knowledge of meaning helps "fill in the blanks" (see **Figure 11.1**).
Words isolated from conversational speech	It is difficult to perceive the isolated words.	The context provided by the surrounding words aids in the perception of a word.
Speech segmentation	Individual words are perceived in spoken sentences even though there are usually no breaks between words in the speech stimulus.	Knowledge of the meanings of words in a language and knowledge of other characteristics of speech, such as sounds that usually go together in a word, help create speech segmentation.
Word superiority	Letters presented visually are easier to recognize when in a word.	Letters are affected by their surroundings (see **Figure 11.2**).

© 2015 Cengage Learning

meaning of—of about 50,000 words. While this number is impressive, we need to go beyond counting how many words we know. The first step in doing this is to determine how words are used in a particular language. This is done by collecting a large representative sample of utterances or written text from a particular language. This sample, which is called a **corpus** of a language, indicates the frequency with which different words are used and the frequency of different meanings and grammatical constructions in that language (Roland et al., 2007). Basically, a corpus reflects how people typically use their language.

The corpus is interesting to language researchers because, as we will see, a lot of what goes on during language comprehension can be traced to *prediction*. That is, we often predict what words, sentences, or passages mean based on what we know about the properties of our language. Does this sound familiar? If it does, you may be thinking back to Chapter 3, in which we discussed how things that occur regularly in our environment (regularities of the environment) influence our perception, or Chapter 8, in which we discussed how our memories are influenced by our knowledge of the world. Continuing with this idea that our experience with the environment influences cognition, we will now show how our ability to perceive written words depends on how frequently they appear in our lexicon.

THE WORD FREQUENCY EFFECT

Some words occur more frequently than others in a particular language. For example, in English, *home* occurs 547 times per million words, and *hike* occurs only 4 times per million words. The frequency with which a word appears in a language is called **word frequency**, and the **word frequency effect** refers to the fact that we respond more rapidly to high-frequency words like *home* than to low-frequency words like *hike*. One way this has been demonstrated is through the *lexical decision task*, introduced in Chapter 9 (see page 259). In this task, subjects are asked to read stimuli and decide whether they are words or nonwords, as illustrated in the following demonstration.

DEMONSTRATION
THE LEXICAL DECISION TASK

The **lexical decision task** involves reading a list that consists of words and nonwords. Your task is to indicate as quickly as possible whether each entry in the two lists below is a word. Try this yourself by silently reading List 1 and saying "yes" each time you encounter a word. Either time yourself to determine how long it takes you to get through the list or just notice how difficult the task is.

> *List 1*
>
> Gambastya, revery, voitle, chard, wefe, cratily, decoy, puldow, faflot, oriole, voluble, boovle, chalt, awry, signet, trave, crock, cryptic, ewe, himpola

Now try the same thing for List 2.

> *List 2*
>
> Mulvow, governor, bless, tuglety, gare, relief, ruftily, history, pindle, develop, grdot, norve, busy, effort, garvola, match, sard, pleasant, coin, maisle

The task you have just completed (taken from D. W. Carroll, 2004; also see Hirsh-Pasek et al., 1993) is called a lexical decision task because you had to decide whether each group of letters was a word in your lexicon.

You may have noticed that you were able to carry out the lexical decision task more rapidly for List 2, which contains high-frequency words such as *history* and *busy*, than for List 1, which contains low-frequency words such as *decoy* and *voluble*. This slower response for less frequent words has also been demonstrated by measuring people's eye movements as they are reading.

METHOD
EYE MOVEMENTS IN READING

In Chapter 4, we considered how people move their eyes from one place to another when looking at a scene (see **Figure 4.12**). These eye movements, called **saccadic eye movements**, and the places where the eye briefly stops to look at a particular place in a scene, called *fixations*, are measured by eye-tracking devices like the one in **Figure 11.3**. We now consider eye movements in relation to language because measurement of eye movements is an important tool in the study of reading. By measuring where people are looking as they read, it is possible to determine which words they look at (fixate), for how long. This provides important information, because tracking a person's eye movements provides a way to track the mental processes that are occurring as the person is reading. For example, if a person pauses for a long time on a particular word, we can infer that he or she is taking longer to perceive that word or to process its meaning (Brown-Schmidt & Hanna, 2011; Rayner & Duffy, 1986).

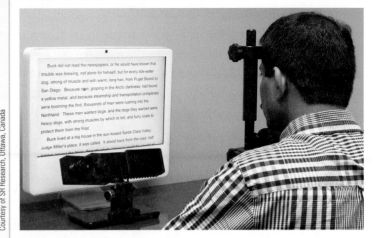

Courtesy of SR Research, Ottawa, Canada

Figure 11.3 Eye tracker. As the subject views words on the screen, the eye tracker on the table uses an infrared beam to determine the position of the subject's eyes. When the system is calibrated, the tracker can determine which words the subject is looking at, and how long the subject is fixating each word.

Keith Rayner and coworkers (2003) measured subjects' eye movements as they read sentences that contained either a high- or a low-frequency target word. For example, the sentence "Sam wore the horrid coat though his pretty girlfriend complained" contains the high-frequency target word *pretty*. The other version of the sentence was exactly the same, but with the high-frequency word *pretty* replaced by the low-frequency word *demure*. The results, shown in **Figure 11.4**, indicate that readers looked at low-frequency words (such as *demure*) about 40 ms longer than high-frequency words (such as *pretty*). One reason could be that the readers needed more time to access the meaning of the low-frequency words. The word frequency effect, therefore, demonstrates how our past experience with words influences our ability to access their meaning.

LEXICAL AMBIGUITY

We just saw that words occur with different frequencies and this affects our ability to access their meaning. We will now consider the fact that some words have more than one meaning, and how this can affect our ability to access the correct meaning of the word. The existence of multiple word meanings is called **lexical ambiguity**. For example, the word *bug* can refer to an insect, a hidden listening device, or being annoying. Or consider the word *bank*. A few of the meanings of *bank* are illustrated by the following: "River bank"; "First National Bank"; "You can bank on it"; "See if you can make a bank shot." Just as words occur with different frequencies in a language, some meanings of a word are more likely than others in a particular language. As Matthew Traxler (2012) puts it, "Many words have multiple meanings, but these meanings are not all created equal."

The fact that some meanings of words occur more frequently than others is known as **meaning dominance**. For example, *tin* (a type of metal) is high dominance because it occurs more frequently than *tin* (small metal container of food), which has low dominance. When words have two or more meanings with different dominances, as in the case of *tin*, these words have **biased dominance**.

In other cases, a word has more than one meaning but the meanings are equally likely. For example, *cast* (members of a play) and *cast* (plaster cast) are equally likely. When a word has more than one meaning but the meanings have about the same dominance, these words have **balanced dominance**.

This difference between biased and balanced dominance influences the way people access the meanings of words as they read them. This has been demonstrated in

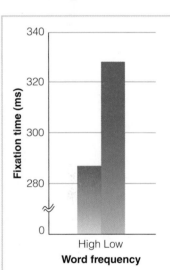

Figure 11.4 Results of Rayner et al.'s (2003) experiment. The bars indicate how long subjects looked at target words such as *pretty* and *demure*. These results show that subjects fixated low-frequency words longer than high-frequency words. *(Source: Based on K. Rayner et al., Reading disappearing text: Cognitive control of eye movements, Psychological Science, 14, 385–388, 2003.)*

experiments in which researchers measure eye movements as subjects read sentences and note the fixation time for an ambiguous word and also for a control word with just one meaning that replaces the ambiguous word in the sentence. Consider the following sentence, in which the ambiguous word *cast* has balanced dominance.

1. The *cast* worked into the night. (control word: *cook*)

As a person reads the word *cast*, both meanings of *cast* are activated, because *cast* (member of a play) and *cast* (plaster cast) are equally likely. Because two meanings are activated, the person looks longer at *cast* than at the control word *cook*, which has only one meaning as a noun. Eventually, when the reader reaches the end of the sentence, the meaning becomes clear (Duffy et al., 1988; Rayner & Frazier, 1989; Traxler, 2012) (Figure 11.5a).

But consider the following, in which the ambiguous word *tin* is biased:

2. The *tin* was bright and shiny. (control word: *gold*)

In this case, people read the biased ambiguous word *tin* just as quickly as the control word, because only the dominant meaning of *tin* is activated, and the meaning of *tin* as a metal is accessed quickly (Figure 11.5b).

But meaning frequency isn't the only factor that determines the accessibility of the meaning of a word. Context can play a role as well. Consider, for example, sentences [3] and [4], in which context is added before the biased ambiguous word *tin*.

In the following sentence added information indicates the less frequent meaning of *tin*:

3. The miners went to the store and saw that they had beans in a *tin*. (control word: *cup*)

In this case, the context indicates the less frequent meaning of *tin* (food container), which strengthens the activation for this meaning. When the person reaches the word *tin*, the less frequent meaning is activated at increased strength because of the prior context, and the more frequent meaning of *tin* is activated as well. Thus, in this example, as with sentence [1], two meanings are activated, so the person looks longer at *tin* (Figure 11.5c).

Finally, consider the following sentence in which the context indicates the more frequent meaning of *tin*:

4. The miners went under the mountain to look for *tin*. (control word: *gold*)

In this example, only the dominant meaning of *tin* is activated, so *tin* is read rapidly (Figure 11.5d).

What these results mean is that the process of accessing the meaning of a word is complicated and is influenced by multiple factors. First, the frequency of a word determines how long it takes to process its meaning. Second, the context of the sentence determines which meaning we access, if a word has more than one meaning. Finally, our ability to access the correct meaning of a word depends on both the word's frequency and, for words with more than one meaning, a combination of meaning dominance and context. (See Table 11.2.)

Table 11.2: Understanding Words

EFFECT	DESCRIPTION	CONCLUSION
Word frequency	Words vary in the frequency with which they are used in a particular language (examples: *pretty*, *demure*), and this affects ease of understanding.	High-frequency words are read faster than low-frequency words (see Figure 11.4).
Lexical ambiguity	Many words have more than one meaning (examples: *cast, tin*). For words with biased dominance, one meaning is more likely. For words with balanced dominance, meanings are equally likely.	A word's meaning dominance and the context in which it appears determine which meanings of the word are activated and how rapidly (see Figure 11.5).

© 2015 Cengage Learning

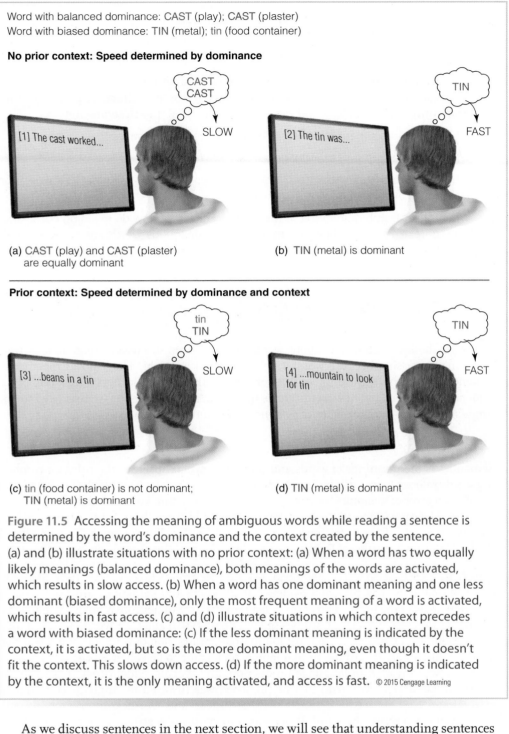

Word with balanced dominance: CAST (play); CAST (plaster)
Word with biased dominance: TIN (metal); tin (food container)

No prior context: Speed determined by dominance

CAST
CAST

SLOW

[1] The cast worked...

TIN

FAST

[2] The tin was...

(a) CAST (play) and CAST (plaster) are equally dominant

(b) TIN (metal) is dominant

Prior context: Speed determined by dominance and context

tin
TIN

SLOW

[3] ...beans in a tin

TIN

FAST

[4] ...mountain to look for tin

(c) tin (food container) is not dominant; TIN (metal) is dominant

(d) TIN (metal) is dominant

Figure 11.5 Accessing the meaning of ambiguous words while reading a sentence is determined by the word's dominance and the context created by the sentence. (a) and (b) illustrate situations with no prior context: (a) When a word has two equally likely meanings (balanced dominance), both meanings of the words are activated, which results in slow access. (b) When a word has one dominant meaning and one less dominant (biased dominance), only the most frequent meaning of a word is activated, which results in fast access. (c) and (d) illustrate situations in which context precedes a word with biased dominance: (c) If the less dominant meaning is indicated by the context, it is activated, but so is the more dominant meaning, even though it doesn't fit the context. This slows down access. (d) If the more dominant meaning is indicated by the context, it is the only meaning activated, and access is fast. © 2015 Cengage Learning

As we discuss sentences in the next section, we will see that understanding sentences involves more than just putting together the meanings of words. Sentences, like words, can have more than one meaning, and this meaning is determined both by the context in which the sentence occurs and by our previous experience with our language.

TEST YOURSELF 11.1

1. What is special about human language? Consider why human language is unique and what it is used for.

2. What events are associated with the beginning of the modern study of language in the 1950s?

3. What is psycholinguistics? What are its concerns, and what part of psycholinguistics does this chapter focus on?

4. What are the two components of words?

5. Describe the following demonstrations of how context helps with the perception of words and components of words: (1) phonemic restoration effect; (2) isolating words from conversations (Pollack and Pickett experiment); (3) speech segmentation.

6. What is the word superiority effect? How has it been demonstrated?

7. What does the corpus of a language tell us?

8. What is the word frequency effect? How has it been studied (a) using the lexical decision task and (b) by measuring eye movements?

9. What is lexical ambiguity? What is meaning dominance? How do meaning dominance and context determine how the meanings of ambiguous words are accessed while reading a sentence?

Understanding Sentences

Although the last section was about words, we ended up discussing sentences as well. This isn't surprising because words rarely appear in isolation. They appear together in sentences in which the meaning of the words plus other factors create the meaning of the sentence. To understand how words create the meaning of a sentence, we first need to distinguish between two properties of sentences: semantics and syntax.

SEMANTICS AND SYNTAX

Semantics is the meanings of words and sentences; **syntax** specifies the rules for combining words into sentences. Changing the sentence "The cats won't eat" into "The cats won't bake" is an error of *semantics* because the meaning doesn't make sense; changing the sentence to "The cats won't eating" is an error of *syntax* because the grammar is not correct. Another example of the operation of syntax is word order: The sentence "The cat chased the bird" follows the rules of English syntax, but "Cat bird the chased" does not.

BRAIN AREAS FOR SYNTAX AND SEMANTICS Neuropsychology, the study of brain-damaged patients, has provided evidence that syntax and semantics are processed in different areas of the brain. Two of the most famous uses of neuropsychology to elucidate brain function were the classic studies of Paul Broca (1861) and Carl Wernicke (1879) that we introduced in Chapter 2 (page 39) to illustrate localization of function. We noted that Broca identified an area in the frontal lobe (which came to be called *Broca's area*) that he proposed was involved in language production, and Wernicke identified an area in the temporal lobe (*Wernicke's area*) that he proposed was involved in language comprehension (**Figure 2.17**). As we look more closely at Broca's and Wernicke's research, we will see that modern researchers link Broca's area to syntax (the structure of sentences) and Wernicke's area to semantics (understanding meaning).

When Broca tested patients who had suffered strokes that damaged their frontal lobe, he found that their speech was slow and labored and often had jumbled sentence structure. Here is an example of the speech of a modern patient, who is attempting to describe when he had his stroke, which occurred when he was in a hot tub.

> Alright.... Uh ... stroke and un.... I ... huh tawanna guy.... H ... h ... hot tub and.... And the.... Two days when uh.... Hos ... uh.... Huh hospital and uh ... amet ... am ... ambulance. (Dick et al., 2001, p. 760)

Patients with this problem—slow, labored, ungrammatical speech caused by damage to Broca's area—are diagnosed as having **Broca's aphasia**. Later research showed that patients with Broca's aphasia not only have difficulty forming complete sentences, they also have difficulty understanding some types of sentences. Consider, for example, the following two sentences:

5. The apple was eaten by the girl.

6. The boy was pushed by the girl.

Patients with Broca's aphasia have no trouble understanding sentence [5] but have difficulty with sentence [6]. The problem they have with sentence [6] is deciding whether the girl pushed the boy or the boy pushed the girl. While you may think it is obvious that the girl pushed the boy, patients with Broca's aphasia have difficulty processing connecting words such as "was" and "by," and this makes it difficult to determine who was pushed. (Notice what happens to the sentence when these two words are omitted). You can see, however, that the first sentence cannot be interpreted in two ways. It is clear that the girl ate the apple, because it is not possible, outside of an unlikely science fiction scenario, for the apple to eat the girl (Dick et al., 2001; Novick et al., 2005). Taking into account problems in both production and understanding experienced by Broca's patients, modern researchers have concluded that damage to Broca's area in the frontal lobe causes problems in syntax—creating meaning based on word order.

The patients studied by Wernicke, who had damage to their temporal lobe, produced speech that was fluent and grammatically correct but tended to be incoherent. Here is a modern example of the speech of a patient with **Wernicke's aphasia**.

> It just suddenly had a feffort and all the feffort had gone with it. It even stepped my horn. They took them from earth you know. They make my favorite nine to severed and now I'm a been habed by the uh stam of fortment of my annulment which is now forever. (Dick et al., 2001, p. 761)

Patients such as this not only produce meaningless speech but are unable to understand speech and writing. While patients with Broca's aphasia have trouble understanding sentences in which meaning depends on word order, as in sentence [6] above, Wernicke's patients have more widespread difficulties in understanding and would be unable to understand sentence [5] as well. Wernicke's area in the temporal lobe is thus involved in semantics—understanding meaning.

ELECTRICAL SIGNALS FOR SYNTAX AND SEMANTICS Syntax and semantics can also be distinguished by measuring the *event-related potential (ERP)*, the rapid electrical response recorded with small disc electrodes placed on a person's scalp. The ERP was introduced in Chapter 5 as a way to measure the number of items placed in working memory (see Method: Event-Related Potential, page 139). We now consider how the ERP has been used to study language.

METHOD
THE EVENT-RELATED POTENTIAL AND LANGUAGE

As we saw in Chapter 5, the event-related potential (ERP) is recorded with small disc electrodes placed on a person's scalp (see **Figure 5.20**). The ERP is a rapid response, occurring on a time scale of fractions of a second, as shown in the responses of **Figure 11.6**. This makes the ERP ideal for investigating a process such as understanding a conversation, in which speakers say three words per second on the average (Levelt, 1999).

In addition to being rapid, the ERP consists of a number of waves that occur at different delays after a stimulus is presented, and which can be linked to different functions. Two components that respond to different aspects of language are the N400 component and the P600 component, where N stands for "negative" (note that negative is up in ERP records) and P for "positive." The numbers 400 and 600 stand for the time at which the response peaks, in milliseconds. The ability of the ERP to provide a nearly continuous record of what is happening in the brain from moment to moment makes it particularly well suited for studying dynamic processes such as language (Kim & Osterhout, 2005; Osterhout et al., 1997).

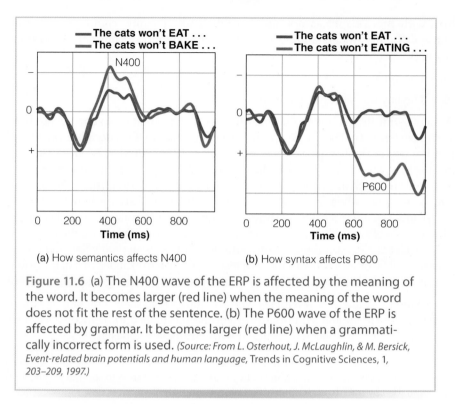

(a) How semantics affects N400   (b) How syntax affects P600

Figure 11.6 (a) The N400 wave of the ERP is affected by the meaning of the word. It becomes larger (red line) when the meaning of the word does not fit the rest of the sentence. (b) The P600 wave of the ERP is affected by grammar. It becomes larger (red line) when a grammatically incorrect form is used. *(Source: From L. Osterhout, J. McLaughlin, & M. Bersick, Event-related brain potentials and human language,* Trends in Cognitive Sciences, 1, *203–209, 1997.)*

Figure 11.6 shows the ERP response to "The cats won't eat" plus the response to two modified versions of this sentence. In **Figure 11.6a**, the sentence "The cats won't bake" results in a larger N400 response. This component of the response is sensitive to the *meaning* of words in a sentence; it is larger when words don't fit the sentence. In **Figure 11.6b**, the sentence "The cats won't eating" results in a larger P600 response. This response is sensitive to the *form* of a sentence; it is larger when the form is incorrect.

What is important about these results is that they illustrate different physiological responses to syntax and semantics. Other experiments have shown that the N400 response is associated with structures in the temporal lobe. For example, damage to areas in the temporal lobes reduces the larger N400 response that occurs when meanings don't fit in a sentence. The P600 response is associated with structures in the frontal lobe, more toward the front of the brain. Damage to areas in the frontal lobe reduces the larger P600 response that occurs when the form of a sentence is incorrect (Van Petten & Luca, 2006).

With the difference between semantics and syntax in mind, we now turn to research that considers how we understand sentences as they unfold in time. We will see that some researchers have focused on the role of syntax in determining a sentence's meaning and others have proposed that semantics and other factors need to be considered as well.

UNDERSTANDING SENTENCES: PARSING

As we read or listen to a sentence, we encounter a series of words, one following another. As this happens, the meaning of a sentence unfolds, derived from both the meanings of the words and how the words are grouped together in phrases. The grouping of words into phrases, called **parsing**, is a central process for determining the meaning of a sentence. We can understand parsing by looking at some sentences. Consider, for example, the beginning of a sentence:

7.   After the musician played the piano ...

What do you think comes next? Some possibilities are:

a. ... she left the stage.

b. ... she bowed to the audience.

c. ... the crowd cheered wildly.

All of these possibilities create sentences that are easy to understand and that make sense. But what if the sentence continued by stating

d. ... was wheeled off of the stage.

Reading sentence [7d] as a whole, "After the musician played the piano was wheeled off of the stage," might take you by surprise. Many people, after getting to "was wheeled," have to stop and rearrange the sentence in their mind so it reads "After the musician played, the piano was wheeled off the stage." Adding the comma makes the correct parsing for sentence [7d] clear.

Sentences like this one, which begin appearing to mean one thing but then end up meaning something else, are called **garden path sentences** (from the phrase "leading a person down the garden path," which means misleading the person.) Garden path sentences illustrate **temporary ambiguity**, because the initial words of the sentence are ambiguous—they can lead to more than one meaning—but the meaning is made clear by the end of the sentence.

THE SYNTAX-FIRST APPROACH TO PARSING

Language researchers have used sentences with temporary ambiguity to help understand the mechanisms that operate during parsing. One of the early proposals to explain parsing, and garden path sentences in particular, is called the **syntax-first approach to parsing**. This approach, proposed by Lynn Frazier (1979, 1987), states that as people read a sentence, their grouping of words into phrases is governed by a number of rules that are based on syntax. If, along the way, readers realize there is something wrong with their parsing, as occurs with sentence [7d], then they take other information into account in order to reinterpret the sentence.

What are the rules the parser uses to group words? The syntax-first approach proposes a number of principles, all based on syntax. We will focus on one principle, called *late closure*. The principle of **late closure** states that when a person encounters a new word, the person's parsing mechanism assumes that this word is part of the current phrase, so each new word is added to the current phrase for as long as possible (Frazier, 1987).

Let's return to sentence [7d] to see how this works. The person begins reading the sentence:

After the musician played ...

So far all the words are in the same phrase. But what happens when we reach the words *the piano*? According to late closure, the parsing mechanism assumes that *the piano* is part of the current phrase, so the phrase now becomes

After the musician played the piano ...

So far, so good. But when we reach *was*, late closure adds this to the phrase to create

After the musician played the piano was ...

And then, when *wheeled* is added to create an even longer phrase, it becomes obvious that something is wrong. Late closure has led us astray (down the garden path!). We need to reconsider, taking the meaning of the sentence into account, and reparse the sentence so "the piano" is not added to the first phrase. Instead, it becomes part of the second phrase to create the grouping

8. [After the musician played] [the piano was wheeled off the stage].

Although it may seem strange that the language system would use a rule that leads to errors, it turns out that late closure is useful because it often leads to the correct parsing. However, other researchers have questioned the proposal that syntactic rules like late closure operate alone to determine parsing until it becomes obvious that a correction is needed. These researchers have provided evidence to show that factors in addition to syntax may be influencing parsing right from the beginning, rather than waiting until halfway through the sentence.

THE INTERACTIONIST APPROACH TO PARSING

The idea that information provided by both syntax and semantics is taken into account simultaneously as we read or listen to a sentence is called the **interactionist approach to parsing**. We will now consider a number of examples that show how parsing can be influenced by factors in addition to syntax.

MEANING OF WORDS IN A SENTENCE One way to demonstrate a role for semantics is to show how the meaning of words in a sentence can influence parsing right from the beginning. We will look at some sentences that have the same structure but that, depending on the meanings of the words, can be either ambiguous or not ambiguous. Consider, for example, the following sentence:

9. The spy saw the man with the binoculars.

This sentence has two meanings, which represent different relationships between the words in the sentence. The relation between the phrases is indicated by the arrows.

Grouping 1: [The spy saw the man] [with the binoculars].

Meaning: The spy with the binoculars is looking at a man (**Figure 11.7a**).

Grouping 2: [The spy saw] [the man with the binoculars].

Meaning: The spy is looking at a man who has a pair of binoculars (**Figure 11.7b**).

But if we change just one word, as in the following sentence, only one meaning becomes reasonable.

10. The bird saw the man with the binoculars.

Because organizing the sentence as in Grouping 1, above, would require birds to look through binoculars, this interpretation isn't even considered, and Grouping 2 is automatically applied to sentence [10]. The important point here is that the structure of the bird sentence is the same as that of the spy sentence, but our knowledge of the properties of spies and of birds influences the way we interpret the relationships between the words in the sentence.

INFORMATION IN A VISUAL SCENE Our interpretation of a sentence is influenced not only by the meaning of the words in the sentence but also by the meaning of a scene we may be observing. To investigate how observing particular objects in a scene can influence how we interpret a sentence, Michael Tanenhaus and coworkers (1995) developed a technique called the **visual world paradigm**, which involves determining how subjects process information as they are observing a visual scene. In Tanenhaus's experiment, subjects' eye movements were measured as they saw objects on a table, as in **Figure 11.8a** (the two-apple condition) or **11.9a** (the one-apple condition). As subjects looked at this display, they were told to carry out the following instructions:

Place the apple on the towel in the box.

The beginning of this sentence, "Place the apple on the towel," can be initially interpreted in either of two ways:

Interpretation 1: The relevant apple is the one on the towel.

Interpretation 2: Move the apple onto the towel.

The interactionist approach to parsing predicts that when there are two apples in the scene (**Figure 11.8a**) and listeners hear "Put the apple," they'll expect the speaker to immediately include information to let them know which apple he or she is talking about and so will pick

(a)

(b)

Figure 11.7 Two possible interpretations of "The spy saw the man with the binoculars." © Cengage Learning

Interpretation 1. To determine if this occurred, Tanenhaus measured subjects' eye movements as they were listening to the instructions.

Figure 11.8b shows the result. Many subjects looked first at the apple on the napkin in response to "Put the apple" (eye movement 1), and then moved to the apple that is on the towel in response to "on the towel" (eye movement 2). This means the subject is

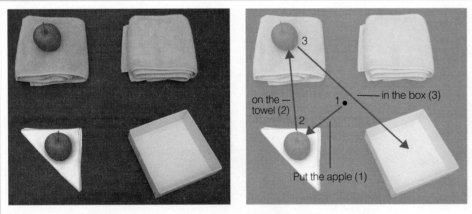

(a) Two-apple condition   (b) Eye movements

Figure 11.8 (a) Two-apple scene similar to the one viewed by Tanenhaus et al.'s (1995) subjects; (b) eye movements while comprehending the task. © Cengage Learning

interpreting the beginning of the sentence as identifying which apple is to be moved, as predicted by the interactionist approach. Then, upon hearing "in the box" the eyes moved to the box (eye movement 3).

The interactionist approach predicts a different result if there is only one apple (**Figure 11.9a**). In this case, subjects will know which apple to move immediately upon hearing "Put the apple," so they'll be more likely to adopt Interpretation 2, above. The eye movement records for this condition, in **Figure 11.9b**, show that upon hearing "Put the apple on the towel," the person immediately looks at the apple (eye movement 1) and then at the other towel (eye movement 2), indicating that this person did adopt the second interpretation, that the apple should be moved to the other towel. However, upon hearing "in the box," the person quickly makes a correction and looks back at the apple (eye movement 3) and then at the box (eye movement 4), indicating the new interpretation that the apple should be placed in the box.

The important result of this experiment is that the way subjects interpret the sentence, as indicated by their eye movements, is determined by the scene they are observing. This result is different from the prediction of the syntax-first approach: If parsing is always based on the structure of the sentence, then changing the scene should have no effect on the eye movements. (Also see Chambers et al., 2004, for another example of a visual world paradigm experiment.)

MAKING PREDICTIONS BASED ON KNOWLEDGE ABOUT THE ENVIRONMENT One of the contributions of the visual world paradigm to our understanding of language is its acknowledgment that we often use language as we interact with the environment. But even when we aren't actively interacting with the environment, we are, according to the results of a number of recent experiments, continually using our knowledge of the environment to make predictions about what we are about to read or hear. According to this idea, we take the "statistics" of the environment—our knowledge of what is most likely to occur—into account to determine meaning. This is similar to the idea, in our discussion of how words affect our interpretation of a sentence, of using the knowledge that birds don't look through binoculars to interpret sentence [10] (page 312). However, the idea that knowledge of the environment affects sentence understanding goes beyond just individual words. Consider, for example, the following:

> "Getting himself and his car to work on the neighboring island was time consuming. Every morning he drove for a few minutes, and then boarded the...."

Although there are a number of ways to complete this sentence, most people respond "ferry" (Federmeier & Kutas, 1999). They do this by going beyond syntax and

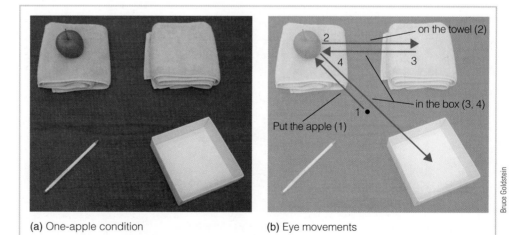

(a) One-apple condition   (b) Eye movements

Bruce Goldstein

Figure 11.9 (a) One-apple scene similar to the one viewed by Tanenhaus et al.'s (1995) subjects; (b) eye movements made while comprehending the task. © Cengage Learning

semantics, or even the meanings of individual words in the sentence. The expectation that the person would be boarding a ferry is created by people's knowledge that getting from one island to another in a car is likely to involve boarding a ferry (not a bridge), and the word *ferry* is a more likely choice than *boat* because a ferry is a type of boat designed to transport cars.

MAKING PREDICTIONS BASED ON KNOWLEDGE OF LANGUAGE CONSTRUCTIONS In addition to making predictions based on knowledge about the environment, readers also make predictions based on their knowledge of how their language is constructed. Consider, for example, the following two sentences:

11. The experienced soldiers <u>warned</u> about the dangers before the midnight raid.

12. The experienced soldiers <u>warned</u> about the dangers conducted the midnight raid.

You probably noticed that sentence [12] is a garden path sentence, because after reading *dangers*, you realized that the correct grouping for this sentence is

[The experienced soldiers warned about the dangers] [conducted the midnight raid].

The reason you didn't predict that the words would be grouped in that way is that a verb like *warned* can occur either as a main verb (MV) in a sentence, as in [11], or be contained in a relative clause (RC), as in [12] (**Figure 11.10**).

According to corpora of the English language (*corpora* is the plural of *corpus*; see page 304), the MV construction in [11] is more likely. Thus, according to the idea that our experience with language leads us to predict the most likely construction, we become "garden pathed" when our experience leads us to predict the MV construction when reading sentence [12].

This idea, that our experience with certain sentence constructions can influence how we predict a sentence will be organized, caused Alex Fine and coworkers (2013) to ask whether readers can learn to change their predictions based on experience with new constructions. They answered this question by having subjects read sentences in a moving window display in which the subject saw one word at a time on a computer

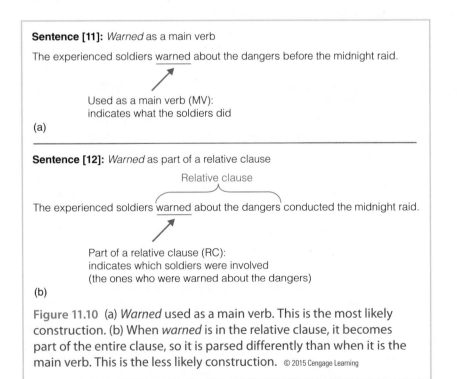

Sentence [11]: *Warned* as a main verb

The experienced soldiers <u>warned</u> about the dangers before the midnight raid.

Used as a main verb (MV):
indicates what the soldiers did

(a)

Sentence [12]: *Warned* as part of a relative clause

Relative clause

The experienced soldiers <u>warned</u> about the dangers conducted the midnight raid.

Part of a relative clause (RC):
indicates which soldiers were involved
(the ones who were warned about the dangers)

(b)

Figure 11.10 (a) *Warned* used as a main verb. This is the most likely construction. (b) When *warned* is in the relative clause, it becomes part of the entire clause, so it is parsed differently than when it is the main verb. This is the less likely construction. © 2015 Cengage Learning

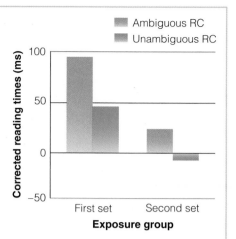

Figure 11.11 Results of the Fine and Jaeger (2013) experiment, showing how repeated exposures can cause reading times to decrease for RC ambiguous sentences. Reading times have been scaled to take into account differences between subjects and the fact that reading becomes faster for all conditions with practice. This is why reading times for the RC ambiguous condition are negative. The difference between the RC ambiguous and RC unambiguous conditions for the second set is not statistically significant, which indicates that there is no ambiguity effect. *(Source: Based on A. B. Fine, T. F. Jaeger, T. A. Farmer, & T. Qian, Rapid expectation adaptation during syntactic comprehension, PLoS One, 8, e77661, Figure 1, 2013.)*

screen and pushed a space bar to view the next word in the sentence. Fine and Jaeger presented both ambiguous and unambiguous relative clause (RC) sentences like the ones below:

12. The experienced soldiers warned about the dangers **conducted the midnight** raid. (This repeats sentence [12] above.)

13. The experienced soldiers who were warned about the dangers **conducted the midnight** raid. (This is the unambiguous version of sentence [12]. Notice that adding the word *who* indicates that *warned* is part of a relative clause and makes the sentence unambiguous.)

The reading times for the boldfaced words in the first 10 sentences (5 ambiguous, like [12], and 5 unambiguous, like [13]), indicted by the left pair of bars in **Figure 11.11**, show that these words in the ambiguous sentences took longer to read than the same words in the unambiguous sentences. This is what we would expect based on our experience that sentences like [12] that use the RC construction for the verb are garden path sentences. The longer time for the RC ambiguous sentences, compared to the unambiguous RC sentences, is the *ambiguity effect*.

However, by the second set of 10 trials, the ambiguity effect vanished, as indicated by the right pair of bars in **Figure 11.11**, in which the difference between the ambiguous and unambiguous reaction times is not statistically significant. Apparently, as subjects gained experience in reading verbs in the RC construction, they adapted to the new sentence statistics, in which RC constructions are common. These results illustrate the role of experience in language processing by showing that the subjects adjusted their expectations about the RC sentences so that these structures eventually became easier to process. This experience-based explanation of sentence understanding supports the interactionist approach to parsing because it shows that a person's predictions about the structure of language can influence processing as the person is reading a sentence. (See **Table 11.3** for a summary of the results of the demonstrations and experiments discussed in this section.)

We are now ready to move from how we understand sentences to how we understand texts and stories. As we will see, most research on understanding texts and stories is concerned with how readers' understanding of a story is determined by information provided by many sentences taken together.

Table 11.3: Understanding Sentences

EFFECT	DESCRIPTION	CONCLUSION
Semantics and syntax are affected by damage to different brain areas.	Broca: Frontal lobe damage affects syntax. Wernicke: Temporal lobe damage affects semantics.	Semantics and syntax are processed by different brain areas (see **Figure 2.17**).
Errors of semantics and syntax generate ERP responses.	Semantic and syntactic errors cause increases in N400 (semantics) and P600 (syntax) components of the ERP.	Semantics and syntax are processed differently in the brain (see **Figure 11.6**).
Words in a sentence can affect processing of an ambiguous sentence.	"The spy saw the man with the binoculars" vs. "The bird saw the man with the binoculars."	Semantics can affect sentence processing (see **Figure 11.7**).
Information in a visual scene can affect processing of an ambiguous sentence.	Different scenes cause different processing of the same sentence.	Content of a scene can affect sentence processing (see **Figures 11.8** and **11.9**).
Temporary ambiguity can be caused by expectations and can be changed by experience.	Less likely sentence construction creates more ambiguity, but effect decreases with experience.	Past experience with statistics of a language plus ongoing experience affects sentence processing (see **Figures 11.10** and **11.11**).

TEST YOURSELF 11.2

1. What is semantics? Syntax? Describe how these two aspects of language have been studied using (a) neuropsychology and (b) the event-related potential.

2. What is parsing? What are garden path sentences?

3. Describe the syntax-first approach to parsing. Be sure you understand the principle of late closure.

4. Describe the interactionist approach to parsing. How does it differ from the syntax-first approach?

5. Describe the following lines of evidence that support the interactionist approach to parsing:
   a. How meanings of words in a sentence affect parsing
   b. How information in a visual scene affects parsing (the visual world paradigm)
   c. How predictions based on world knowledge affect parsing
   d. How predictions based on knowledge of language structure affect parsing

Understanding Text and Stories

Just as sentences are more than the sum of the meanings of individual words, stories are more than the sum of the meanings of individual sentences. In a well-written story, sentences in one part of the story are related to sentences in other parts of the story. The reader's task is to use these relationships between sentences to create a coherent, understandable story.

An important part of the process of creating a coherent story is making **inferences**—determining what the text means by using our knowledge to go beyond the information provided by the text. We have seen how unconscious inference is involved in perception (Chapter 3, page 63), and when we described the constructive nature of memory in Chapter 8, we saw that we often make inferences, often without realizing it, as we retrieve memories of what has happened in the past (page 222).

MAKING INFERENCES

An early demonstration of inference in language was an experiment by John Bransford and Marcia Johnson (1973) in which they had subjects read passages and then tested them to determine what they remembered. One of the passages Bransford and Johnson's subjects read was

> John was trying to fix the birdhouse. He was pounding the nail when his father came out to watch him and help him do the work.

After reading that passage, subjects were likely to indicate that they had previously seen the following passage: "John was using a hammer to fix the birdhouse when his father came out to watch him and help him do the work." They reported seeing this passage, even though they had never read that John was using a hammer, because they *inferred* that John was using a hammer from the information that he was pounding the nail. People use a similar creative process to make a number of different types of inferences as they are reading a text.

One role of inference is to create connections between parts of a story. This process is typically illustrated with excerpts from narrative texts. *Narrative* refers to texts in which there is a story that progresses from one event to another, although stories can also include flashbacks of events that happened earlier. An important property of any narrative is **coherence**—the representation of the text in a person's mind so that information in one part of the text is related to information in another part of the text. Coherence can be created by a number of different types of inference.

ANAPHORIC INFERENCE Inferences that connect an object or person in one sentence to an object or person in another sentence are called **anaphoric inferences**. For example, consider the following:

> Riffifi, the famous poodle, won the dog show. She has now won the last three shows she has entered.

Anaphoric inference occurs when we infer that *She* at the beginning of the second sentence and the other *she* near the end both refer to Riffifi. In the previous "John and the birdhouse" example, knowing that *He* in the second sentence refers to John is another example of anaphoric inference.

We usually have little trouble making anaphoric inferences because of the way information is presented in sentences and our ability to make use of knowledge we bring to the situation. But the following quote from a *New York Times* interview with former heavyweight champion George Foreman (also known for lending his name to a popular line of grills) puts our ability to create anaphoric inference to the test.

> … we really love to … go down to our ranch….I take the kids out and we fish. And then, of course, we grill them. (Stevens, 2002)

From just the structure of the sentences, we might conclude that the kids were grilled, but we know the chances are pretty good that the fish were grilled, not George Foreman's children! Readers are capable of creating anaphoric inferences even under adverse conditions because they add information from their knowledge of the world to the information provided in the text.

INSTRUMENT INFERENCE Inferences about tools or methods are **instrument inferences**. For example, when we read the sentence "William Shakespeare wrote *Hamlet* while he was sitting at his desk," we infer from what we know about the time Shakespeare lived that he was probably using a quill pen (not a laptop computer!) and that his desk was made of wood. Similarly, inferring from the passage about John and the birdhouse that he is using a hammer to pound the nails would be an instrument inference.

CAUSAL INFERENCE Inferences that the events described in one clause or sentence were caused by events that occurred in a previous sentence are **causal inferences** (Goldman et al., 1999; Graesser et al., 1994; van den Broek, 1994). For example, when we read the sentences

> Sharon took an aspirin. Her headache went away.

we make an anaphoric inference that "Her" refers to Sharon, and we make a causal inference that taking the aspirin caused the headache to go away (Singer et al., 1992). This is an example of a fairly obvious inference that most people in our culture would make based on their knowledge about headaches and aspirin. Other causal inferences are not so obvious and may be more difficult to figure out. For example, what do you conclude from reading the following sentences?

> Sharon took a shower. Her headache went away.

You might conclude, from the fact that the headache sentence directly follows the shower sentence, that the shower had something to do with eliminating Sharon's headache. However, the causal connection between the shower and the headache is weaker than the connection between the aspirin and the headache in the first pair of sentences. Making the shower–headache connection requires more work from the reader. You might infer that the shower relaxed Sharon, or perhaps her habit of singing in the shower was therapeutic. Or you might decide there actually isn't much connection between the two sentences.

Inferences create connections that are essential for creating coherence in texts, and making these inferences can involve creativity by the reader. Thus, reading a text involves more than just understanding words or sentences. It is a dynamic process that involves transformation of the words, sentences, and sequences of sentences into a meaningful story. Sometimes this is easy, sometimes harder, depending on the skill and intention of both the reader and the writer (Goldman et al., 1999; Graesser et al., 1994; van den Broek, 1994).

We have been describing the process of text comprehension so far in terms of how people bring their knowledge to bear to infer connections between different parts of a story. Another approach to understanding how people understand stories is to consider the nature of the mental representation that people form as they read a story. This is called the *situation model* approach to text comprehension.

SITUATION MODELS

A **situation model** is a mental representation of what a text is about (Johnson-Laird, 1983). This approach proposes that the mental representation people form as they read a story does not consist of information about phrases, sentences, or paragraphs; instead, it is a representation of the *situation* in terms of the people, objects, locations, and events being described in the story (Barsalou, 2008, 2009; Graesser & Wiemer-Hastings, 1999; Zwaan, 1999).

MENTAL REPRESENTATIONS AS SIMULATIONS What exactly is "a mental representation of what a text is about"? One way this question has been answered is to suggest that a person *simulates* the perceptual and motor (movement) characteristics of the objects and actions in a story. This idea has been tested by having subjects read a sentence that describes a situation involving an object and then indicate as quickly as possible whether a picture shows the object mentioned in the sentence. For example, consider the following two sentences.

1. He hammered the nail into the wall.
2. He hammered the nail into the floor.

In **Figure 11.12a**, the horizontal nail matches the orientation that would be expected for sentence [1], and the vertical nail matches the orientation for sentence [2]. Robert Stan-field and Rolf Zwaan (2001) presented these sentences, followed by either a matching picture or a nonmatching picture. Because the pictures both show nails and the task was to indicate whether the picture shows the object mentioned in the sentence, the correct answer was "yes" no matter which nail was presented. However, subjects responded "yes" more rapidly when the picture's orientation matched the situation described in the picture (**Figure 11.13a**).

The pictures for another experiment, involving object shape, are shown in **Figure 11.12b**. The sentences for these pictures are

1. The ranger saw the eagle in the sky.
2. The ranger saw the eagle in its nest.

In this experiment, by Zwaan and coworkers (2002), the picture of an eagle with wings outstretched elicited a faster response when it followed sentence [1] than when it followed sentence [2]. Again, reaction times were faster when the picture matched the situation described in the sentence. This result, shown in **Figure 11.13b**, matches the result for the orientation experiment, and both experiments support the idea that the subjects created perceptions that matched the situation as they were reading the sentences.

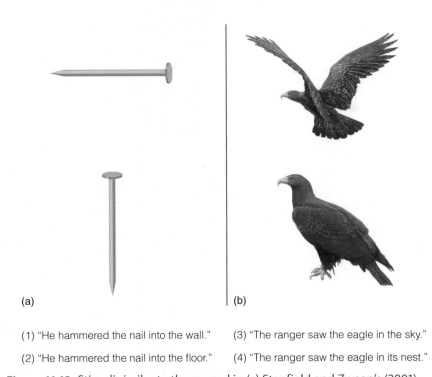

(a)　　　　　　　　　　　　　　(b)

(1) "He hammered the nail into the wall."　(3) "The ranger saw the eagle in the sky."

(2) "He hammered the nail into the floor."　(4) "The ranger saw the eagle in its nest."

Figure 11.12 Stimuli similar to those used in (a) Stanfield and Zwaan's (2001) "orientation" experiment and (b) Zwaan et al.'s (2002) "shape" experiment. Subjects heard sentences and were then asked to indicate whether the picture was the object mentioned in the sentence. © Cengage Learning

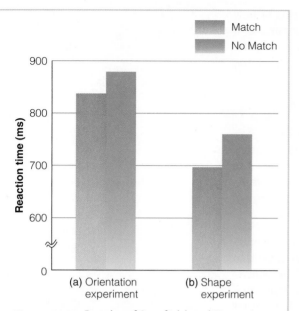

Figure 11.13 Results of Stanfield and Zwaan's (2001) and Zwaan et al.'s (2002) experiments. Subjects responded "yes" more rapidly for the orientation (in a) and the shape (in b) that was more consistent with the sentence. *(Source: Based on R. A. Stanfield & R. A. Zwaan, The effect of implied orientation derived from verbal content on picture recognition, Psychological Science, 12, 153–156, 2001.)*

The experiments we have described so far have emphasized perception. But the situation model approach also includes the idea that a reader or listener simulates the motor characteristics of the objects in a story. According to this idea, a story that involves movement will result in simulation of this movement as the person is comprehending the story. For example, reading a story about a bicycle elicits not only the perception of what a bicycle looks like, but also properties associated with movement, such as how a bicycle is propelled (by peddling) and the physical exertion involved in riding the bicycle under different conditions (climbing hills, racing, coasting). This corresponds to the idea introduced in Chapter 9 that knowledge about a category goes beyond simply identifying a typical object in that category: It also includes various properties of the object, such as how the object is used, what it does, and sometimes even emotional responses it elicits. This way of looking at the reader's response adds a richness to events in a story that extends beyond simply understanding what is going on (Barsalou, 2008; Fischer & Zwaan, 2008).

We saw in Chapter 9 (page 269) how Olaf Hauk and coworkers (2004) determined the link between movement, action words, and brain activation by measuring brain activity using fMRI under two conditions: (1) as subjects moved their right or left foot, left or right index finger, or tongue; (2) as subjects read "action words" such as kick (foot action), pick (finger or hand action), or lick (tongue action).

Hauk's results show areas of the cortex activated by the actual movements (**Figure 9.24a**, page 269) and by reading the action words (**Figure 9.24b**). The activation is more extensive for actual movements, but the activation caused by reading the words occurs in approximately the same areas of the brain. For example, leg words and leg movements elicit activity near the brain's center line, whereas arm words and finger movements elicit activity further from the center line. This link between action words and activation of action areas in the brain suggests a physiological mechanism that may be related to creating situation models as a person reads a story.

PREDICTIONS BASED ON KNOWLEDGE ABOUT SITUATIONS To continue our discussion of situation models, we will consider the idea that we are constantly accessing information about situations as we read, and this helps us make predictions about what we are going to read next.

The role of accessing information in understanding stories has been studied by measuring the event-related potential (ERP) as people are reading short passages. Remember that the N400 response of the ERP is generated in response to errors in word meaning. Thus, as shown in **Figure 11.6**, the N400 response occurs in response to the sentence "the cats won't bake" because the meaning of "bake" doesn't fit with what we know about cats.

Ross Metusalem and coworkers (2012) recorded subjects' ERPs as they read scenarios such as the following:

CONCERT SCENARIO

The band was very popular and Joe was sure the concert would be sold out. Amazingly, he was able to get a seat down in front. He couldn't believe how close he was when he saw the group walk out onto the (*stage/guitar/barn*) and start playing.

Three different versions of each scenario were created, using each of the words shown in parentheses. Each subject read one version of each scenario.

If you were reading this scenario, which word would you predict to follow "he saw the group walk out onto the ..."? *Stage* is the obvious choice, so it was called the "expected" condition. *Guitar* doesn't fit the passage, but since it is related to concerts and bands, it is called the "event-related" word. *Barn* doesn't fit the passage and is also not related to the topic, so it is called the "event-unrelated" word.

Figure 11.14 shows the average ERPs recorded as subjects read the target words. The idea behind this experiment was to note the amplitude of the N400 response. Because *stage* was the expected word, there is only a small N400 response to this word. The interesting result is the response to the other two words. *Barn* causes a large N400, because it isn't related to the passage. *Guitar*, which doesn't fit the passage either but is related to "concerts," generates a smaller N400 than *barn*.

We would expect *stage* to be activated, and to generate little or no N400 response, because it fits the meaning of the sentence. However, the fact that *guitar* generates a smaller N400 than *barn* means that this word is at least slightly activated by the concert scenario. According to Metusalem, our knowledge about different situations is continually being accessed as we read a story, and if *guitar* is activated, it is also likely that other words related to concerts, such as *drums, vocalist, crowds,* and *beer* (depending on your experience with concerts), would also be activated.

The idea that many things associated with a particular scenario are activated is connected with the idea that we create a situation model while we are reading. What the ERP results show is that as we read, models of the situation are activated that include lots of details based on what we know about particular situations (also see Kuperberg, 2013; Paczynski & Kuperberg, 2012).

In addition to suggesting that we are constantly accessing our world knowledge as we read or listen to a story, results like these also indicate that we access this knowledge rapidly, within fractions of a second after reading a particular word. This online monitoring of meaning is consistent with the interactionist approach to sentence processing, because it shows that our knowledge of events influences our understanding of a sentence with little delay.

The overall conclusion from research on how people comprehend stories is that understanding a text or story is a creative and dynamic process. Understanding stories involves understanding sentences by determining how words are organized into phrases; then determining the relationships between sentences, often using inference to link sentences in one part of a story to sentences in another part; and finally, creating mental representations or simulations that involve both perceptual and motor properties of objects and events in the story. **Table 11.4** summarizes the factors associated with understanding text and stories that have been described in this section. As we will now see, a creative and dynamic process also occurs when two or more people are having a conversation.

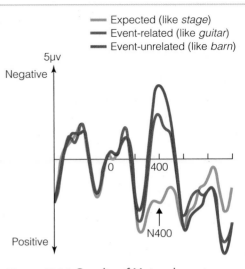

Figure 11.14 Results of Metusalem et al.'s (2012) experiment for the concert scenario. The key result is that the N400 response to an event-related word like *guitar* (red curve) is smaller than the response to an event-unrelated word like *barn* (blue curve). This suggests that even though *guitar* doesn't fit in the sentence, the person's knowledge that guitars are associated with concerts is activated. *(Source: Based on R. Metusalem, M. Kutas, T. P. Urbach, M. Hare, K. McRae, & J. Elman, Generalized event knowledge activation during online sentence comprehension, Journal of Memory and Language, 66, 545–567, Figure 3, 2012.)*

Table 11.4: Understanding Text and Stories

EFFECT	DESCRIPTION	CONCLUSION
Making inferences	Subjects infer meaning that extends beyond the wording of a sentence.	Creative process based on past experience adds meaning.
	There are a number of ways to create coherence in a text (anaphoric, instrument, causal).	Creative processes help create coherence.
Creating situation models	Listeners simulate perceptual and motor characteristics of objects and actions in a story.	Readers create perceptions that match the situations described in sentences (see **Figures 11.12** and **11.13**).
Link between action words and brain activity	Motor areas of cortex are activated by action words.	Readers' responses to words include simulation of actions (see **Figure 9.24**).
Prediction based on knowledge of a situation	Readers access most likely word to fit story, and also related words.	Readers' experiences with situations lead to predictions (see **Figure 11.14**).

Producing Language: Conversations

Although language can be produced by a single person talking alone, as when a person recites a monologue or gives a speech, the most common form of language production is conversation—two or more people talking with one another. Conversation, or dialogue, provides another example of a cognitive skill that seems easy but contains underlying complexities.

TAKING THE OTHER PERSON INTO ACCOUNT

Two or more people are typically involved in a conversation, and each person needs to take into account not only what other people are saying, but also what the other person or people know about the topic that is being discussed (Pickering & Garrod, 2004). When people are talking about a topic, each person brings his or her own knowledge to the conversation. Conversations go more smoothly when the participants bring *shared* knowledge. Thus, when people are talking about current events, it helps if everyone has been keeping up with the news; it is more difficult when one person has just returned from 6 months of meditation in an isolated monastery.

Even when everyone brings similar knowledge to a conversation, it helps if speakers take steps to guide their listeners through the conversation. One way of achieving this is by following the *given–new contract*. The **given–new contract** states that a speaker should construct sentences so that they include two kinds of information: (1) *given information*—information that the listener already knows; and (2) *new information*—information that the listener is hearing for the first time (Haviland & Clark, 1974). For example, consider the following two sentences.

> Sentence 1. Ed was given an alligator for his birthday.
>
> *Given information (from previous conversation)*: Ed had a birthday.
>
> *New information*: He got an alligator.

> Sentence 2. The alligator was his favorite present.
>
> *Given information (from sentence [1])*: Ed got an alligator.
>
> *New information*: It was his favorite present.

Notice how the new information in the first sentence becomes the given information in the second sentence.

Susan Haviland and Herbert Clark (1974) demonstrated the consequences of not following the given–new contract by presenting pairs of sentences and asking subjects to press a button when they thought they understood the second sentence in each pair. They found that it took longer for subjects to comprehend the second sentence in pairs like this one:

> We checked the picnic supplies.
>
> The beer was warm.

than it took to comprehend the second sentence in pairs like this one:

> We got some beer out of the trunk.
>
> The beer was warm.

The reason comprehending the second sentence in the first pair takes longer is that the given information (that there were picnic supplies) does not mention beer. Thus, the reader or listener needs to make an inference that beer was among the picnic supplies. This inference is not required in the second pair because the first sentence includes the information that there is beer in the trunk.

The idea of *given* and *new* captures the collaborative nature of conversations. Herbert Clark (1996) sees collaboration as being central to the understanding of language.

Describing language as "a form of joint action," Clark proposes that understanding this joint action involves considering both the content of a conversation, in terms of given and new information, and the process by which people share information.

Another aspect of this sharing process is the idea of **common ground**—the speakers' mutual knowledge, beliefs, and assumptions (Isaacs & Clark, 1987). The key word in this definition of common ground is *mutual*, because for a conversation to be successful, each person needs to understand the knowledge that the other person brings to the conversation. Ellen Isaacs and Clark (1987) illustrate this idea with the example of how doctors usually assume that their patients have limited knowledge of physiology and medical terminology. Taking this into account, doctors use lay terminology, such as *heart attack* rather than *myocardial infarction*. However, if the doctor realizes that the patient is also a doctor, he or she knows that it is permissible to use medical terminology.

How do people having a conversation establish common ground? In the example above, the patient could announce, "I'm a doctor," or when told he is in danger of having a heart attack could respond by saying, "Oh, you mean a myocardial infarction." Thus, one way to establish common ground is through the back-and-forth exchanges during the conversation. Isaacs and Clark (1987) studied this idea in an experiment in which they paired up subjects and gave each subject the same set of 16 postcards of New York City scenes. Subject 1's postcards were arranged in a 4-by-4 grid. This subject's task was to describe the pictures so that Subject 2 could arrange his or her pictures in the same order.

When Subject 1 was a New Yorker and Subject 2 was not, it was sometimes easy to establish the location for pictures of well-known buildings, as indicated by the following exchange:

Subject 1: Sixth is the Empire State Building.

Subject 2: Yeah.

"Yeah" indicates common ground, and that it is OK to move on. But for a building that wasn't as familiar, a longer exchange was necessary:

Subject 1: Tenth is the ... Citicorp building.

Subject 2: Is that with the slanted top?

Subject 1: Yes.

Subject 2: OK.

Once all 16 cards were correctly arranged, they were scrambled into a new order, and the process started again. One result of this experiment, shown in **Figure 11.15a**, is that on each successive trial subjects needed fewer words to sort the pictures. Thus, 37 words per picture were needed on Trial 1, but only 8 by Trial 5. This illustrates the establishment of common ground by showing that communication becomes more efficient as the conversation progresses.

Another result, shown in **Figure 11.15b**, indicates the percentage of name references such as "Empire State Building." The left pair of bars indicates that a high percentage of name references were used when Subject 1 and Subject 2 were both New York City residents, and that the percentage increased on later trials. The right pair of bars shows that fewer names were used when Subject 2 wasn't a resident, but the percentage also increased on later trials. Thus, common ground is determined both by people's expertise and by the exchange of information during the conversation.

Although the postcard sorting task was part of an experiment, this taking into account what the other person knows and establishing more common ground as the conversation proceeds occurs routinely in everyday conversation (also see Clark, 1996; Wilkes-Gibbs & Clark, 1992).

Our discussion of the given–new contract and common ground has focused on how people take into account what other people know and how they share content with each other. But the coordination between speakers also includes using similar grammatical

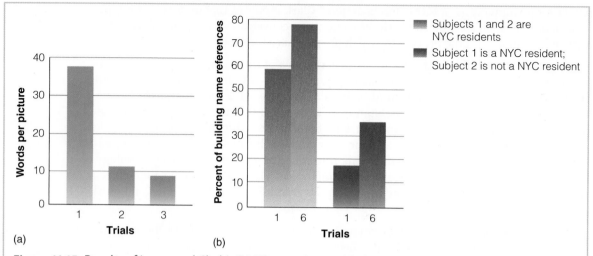

Figure 11.15 Results of Isaacs and Clark's (1987) experiment. (a) The number of words needed to identify a New York City building decreases as a resident talks to a nonresident. (b) From Trials 1 to 6, the percentage of name references to buildings increases when both subjects are New York City residents (left pair of bars) and when subject 2 is a nonresident (right pair of bars). *(Source: Based on E. A. Isaacs & H. H. Clark, References in conversation between experts and novices, Journal of Experimental Psychology: General, 116, 26–37, Figure 1 & Table 1, 1987.)*

constructions. The process by which people use similar grammatical constructions is called **syntactic coordination**.

SYNTACTIC COORDINATION

When two people exchange statements in a conversation, it is common for them to use similar grammatical constructions. Kathryn Bock (1990) provides the following example, taken from a recorded conversation between a bank robber and his lookout, which was intercepted by a ham radio operator as the robber was removing the equivalent of $1 million from a bank vault in England.

Robber: "... *you've got to hear* and witness it *to realize how bad it is.*"

Lookout: "You *have got to experience exactly* the same position as me, mate, *to understand how I feel.*" (from Schenkein, 1980, p. 22)

Bock has added italics to illustrate how the lookout copied the form of the robber's statement. This copying of form reflects a phenomenon called **syntactic priming**—hearing a statement with a particular syntactic construction increases the chances that a sentence will be produced with the same construction. Syntactic priming is important because it can lead people to coordinate the grammatical form of their statements during a conversation. Holly Branigan and coworkers (2000) illustrated syntactic priming by using the following procedure to set up a give-and-take between two people.

METHOD
SYNTACTIC PRIMING

In a syntactic priming experiment, two people engage in a conversation, and the experimenter determines whether a specific grammatical construction used by one person causes the other person to use the same construction. In Branigan's experiment, subjects were told that the experiment was about how people communicate when they can't see each other. They thought they were working with another subject who was on the other side of a screen (the person on the left in Figure 11.16a). In reality, the person on the left was a confederate who was working with the experimenter.

(continued on page 326)

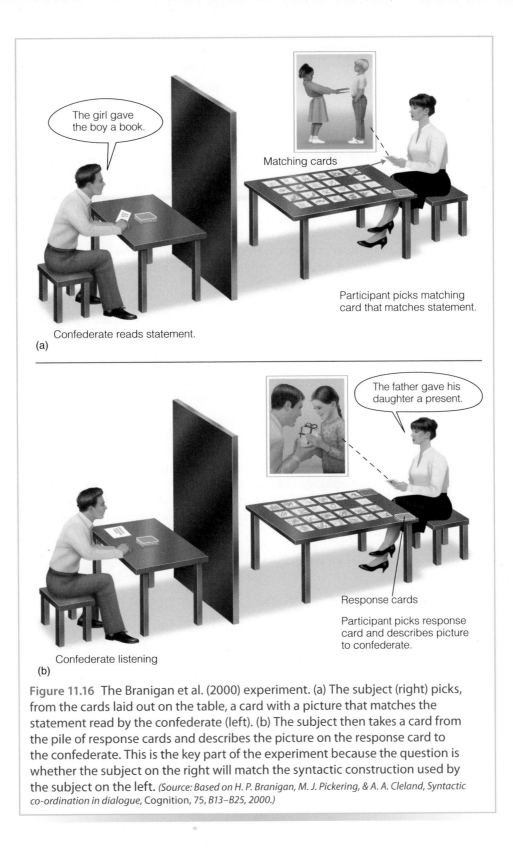

Figure 11.16 The Branigan et al. (2000) experiment. (a) The subject (right) picks, from the cards laid out on the table, a card with a picture that matches the statement read by the confederate (left). (b) The subject then takes a card from the pile of response cards and describes the picture on the response card to the confederate. This is the key part of the experiment because the question is whether the subject on the right will match the syntactic construction used by the subject on the left. *(Source: Based on H. P. Branigan, M. J. Pickering, & A. A. Cleland, Syntactic co-ordination in dialogue, Cognition, 75, B13–B25, 2000.)*

The confederate began the experiment by making a *priming statement*, as shown on the left of Figure 11.16a. This statement was in one of the following two forms:

The girl gave the book to the boy.

or

The girl gave the boy the book.

The subject responded by locating, among the cards laid out on the table, the *matching card* that corresponded to the confederate's statement, as shown on the right in Figure 11.16a. The subject then picked the top card from the response pile on the corner of the table, looked at the picture on the card, and described it to the confederate. The question is: How does the subject phrase his or her description? Saying "The father gave his daughter a present" to describe the picture in Figure 11.16b matches the confederate's syntax in this example. Saying "The father gave a present to his daughter" would not match the syntax. If the syntax does match, as in the example in Figure 11.17b, we can conclude that syntactic priming has occurred.

Branigan found that on 78 percent of the trials, the form of the subject's description matched the form of the confederate's priming statement. This supports the idea that speakers are sensitive to the linguistic behavior of other speakers and adjust their behaviors to match. This coordination of syntactic form between speakers reduces the computational load involved in creating a conversation because it is easier to copy the form of someone else's sentence than it is to create your own form from scratch.

Let's summarize what we have said about conversations: Conversations are dynamic and rapid, but a number of processes make them easier. On the semantic side, people take other people's knowledge into account and help establish common ground if necessary. On the syntactic side, people coordinate or align the syntactic form of their statements. This makes speaking easier and frees up resources to deal with the task of alternating between understanding and producing messages that is the hallmark of successful conversations. (See Table 11.5 for a summary of the factors involved in conversations.)

Something to Consider

CULTURE, LANGUAGE, AND COGNITION

How do you say *blue* in Russian? The answer to that question depends on the shade of blue. Light blues, like the ones on the left of Figure 11.17, are called *goluboy*, and darker blues, like the ones on the right, are called *siniy*. Thus, the Russian language defines *goluboy* and *siniy* as different colors, and Russian children learn these labels for the two blues as they are

Table 11.5: Conversations

EFFECT	DESCRIPTION	CONCLUSION
Given–new contract	Speaker should provide both given and new information in a sentence.	Providing given information facilitates comprehension.
Common ground	Mutually recognized common knowledge.	Speakers tailor information to the listener's level of knowledge. People work together to achieve common ground in a conversation (see Figure 11.15).
Syntactic coordination	Similar grammatical constructions in sentences during conversation.	A person's speech patterns are influenced by the grammatical constructions used by the other person in a conversation (see Figure 11.16).

© 2015 Cengage Learning

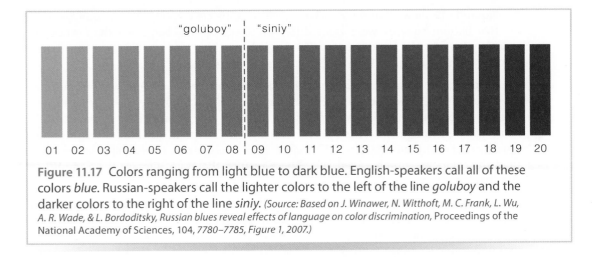

Figure 11.17 Colors ranging from light blue to dark blue. English-speakers call all of these colors *blue*. Russian-speakers call the lighter colors to the left of the line *goluboy* and the darker colors to the right of the line *siniy*. *(Source: Based on J. Winawer, N. Witthoft, M. C. Frank, L. Wu, A. R. Wade, & L. Bordoditsky, Russian blues reveal effects of language on color discrimination, Proceedings of the National Academy of Sciences, 104, 7780–7785, Figure 1, 2007.)*

learning the names of other colors. This contrasts with English, in which all of the colors in **Figure 11.17** are called *blue*.

Do these differences in the way colors are labeled in Russian and English lead to differences in the way these colors are perceived? According to the **Sapir-Whorf hypothesis**, which was proposed by anthropologist Edward Sapir and linguist Benjamin Whorf, the nature of a culture's language can affect the way people think (Whorf, 1956). Although there was little evidence to support this when Whorf made his proposal, recent experiments have provided evidence that favors the idea that language can influence cognition (Davidoff, 2001; Gentner & Goldin-Meadow, 2003; Roberson et al., 2000).

One of these experiments, by Jonathan Winawer and coworkers (2007), compared the way Russian-speaking and English-speaking subjects discriminated between different shades of blue. **Figure 11.18** shows the stimuli. Subjects saw three blue squares and were instructed to pick, as quickly and accurately as possible, which of the squares on the bottom matched the color of the square on the top. On some trials, the two squares on the bottom were from the same Russian category. This is shown in **Figure 11.18a**, in which both bottom squares would both be called *siniy*. On other trials, the two squares on the bottom were from different Russian categories. This is shown in **Figure 11.18b**, in which the left square is *siniy* and the right one is *goluboy*.

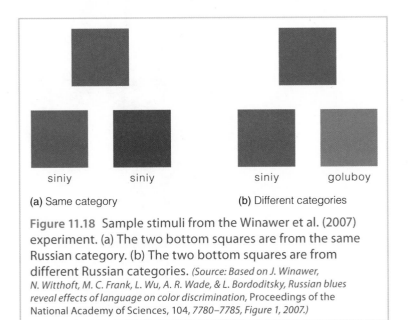

Figure 11.18 Sample stimuli from the Winawer et al. (2007) experiment. (a) The two bottom squares are from the same Russian category. (b) The two bottom squares are from different Russian categories. *(Source: Based on J. Winawer, N. Witthoft, M. C. Frank, L. Wu, A. R. Wade, & L. Bordoditsky, Russian blues reveal effects of language on color discrimination, Proceedings of the National Academy of Sciences, 104, 7780–7785, Figure 1, 2007.)*

Figure 11.19 shows that the Russian-speaking subjects responded more quickly when the two bottom squares were from different categories (*goluboy/siniy*) than when the squares were from the same category. The English-speaking subjects did not respond more quickly when the colors were in different Russian categories.

According to Winawer, the Russians' faster response when stimuli were from different categories occurred because their language distinguishes between *goluboy* and *siniy*. One way of looking at this is that learning the different labels makes it more likely that the colors will be perceived as different, and this makes it easier to quickly determine which square matches the one on the top. This effect does not occur for English-speakers because all of the colors are simply called *blue*. These results, therefore, support the Sapir-Whorf idea that language can affect cognition.

Taking a different approach to studying the relation between color perception and language, Aubrey Gilbert and coworkers (2006) looked for a difference between how colors are processed in the left and right hemispheres of the brain. The basic idea behind this approach is that language is processed in the left hemisphere. Thus, if language does affect color perception, it would be more likely to do so when colors are viewed in the right visual field (which projects to the left hemisphere) than in the left visual field (**Figure 11.20**).

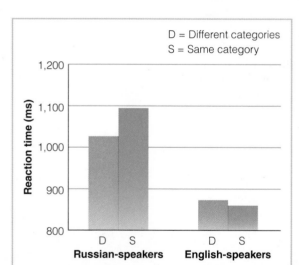

Figure 11.19 Results of the Winawer et al. (2007) experiment. The Russian-speaking subjects responded faster when the bottom stimuli were from different categories than when they were from the same category (left pair of bars). This difference did not occur for English-speaking subjects (right pair of bars). *(Source: Based on J. Winawer, N. Witthoft, M. C. Frank, L. Wu, A. R. Wade, & L. Bordoditsky, Russian blues reveal effects of language on color discrimination, Proceedings of the National Academy of Sciences, 104, 7780–7785, Figure 2, 2007.)*

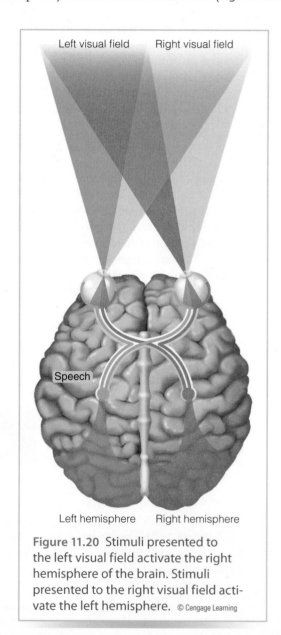

Figure 11.20 Stimuli presented to the left visual field activate the right hemisphere of the brain. Stimuli presented to the right visual field activate the left hemisphere. © Cengage Learning

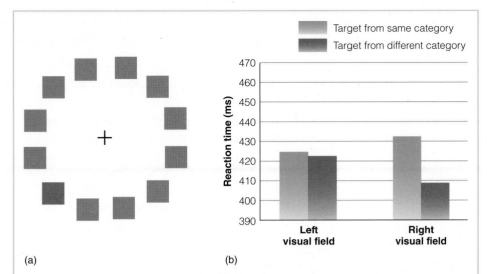

(a)   (b)

Figure 11.21 (a) Color wheel used in Gilbert et al.'s (2006) experiment. The subjects' task was to indicate, as quickly as possible, which side contained the "odd" color. (b) Result of the experiment. The left pair of bars shows that when the color wheel was in the left (nonlanguage) visual field, reaction times were the same whether the odd color was in the same or different category as the other colors. The right pair of bars shows that when the wheel was presented in the right (language) visual field, reaction times were faster when the odd color was from a different category (for example, blue vs. green). *(Source: Based on A. L. Gilbert, T. Regier, P. Kay, & R. B. Ivry, Whorf hypothesis is supported in the right visual field but not the left, Proceedings of the National Academy of Sciences, 103, 489–494, Figure 1, 2006.)*

To test this idea, Gilbert and coworkers presented subjects with a display like the one in **Figure 11.21a**, in which all the squares in the wheel were the same (green in this example) except for a target square (blue). On some trials the target was from a different category than the other squares, as in **Figure 11.21a**. On other trials, the target was from the same category as the other squares (the target was a different shade of green than the other green squares). The subjects' task was to push a button indicating whether the target was on the left or right side of the wheel.

The results, shown in **Figure 11.21b**, indicate that when the display was viewed in the right (language) visual field, the reaction times to identify the target were faster when the target was from a different category (left pair of bars). If the category labels *blue* and *green* are determined by language, this is what we would expect. In contrast, when the display was viewed in the left (nonlanguage) visual field, reaction times were the same whether the target was from the same category or from a different category (right pair of bars). Thus, when the language hemisphere is activated, a category effect does occur, but when the nonlanguage hemisphere is activated, no category effect occurs. So, does language affect perception? From the results of this experiment, the answer would seem to be that it depends on which part of the brain is involved.

TEST YOURSELF 11.3

1. What does the "fixing the birdhouse" experiment indicate about inference?

2. What is coherence? Describe the different types of inference that help achieve coherence.

3. What is the assumption behind a situation model? Describe what the following evidence tells us about this approach to understanding stories: (a) reaction times for pictures that

match or don't match the orientations or shapes of objects in a story; (b) brain activation for action words compared to actual action; (c) predictions based on the situation.

4. What is the given–new contract?

5. What is common ground? How is it established in a conversation? Describe the "New York City" experiment.

6. What is syntactic coordination? What is syntactic priming? Describe how the Branigan experiment used syntactic priming to demonstrate syntactic coordination.

7. What is the Sapir-Whorf hypothesis? Describe the experiment on color perception that supports this hypothesis. Also describe the evidence that indicates that the hypothesis may hold for only one side of the visual field.

CHAPTER SUMMARY

1. Language is a system of communication that uses sounds or symbols that enable us to express our feelings, thoughts, ideas, and experiences. Human language can be distinguished from animal communication by its creativity, hierarchical structure, governing rules, and universality.

2. Modern research in the psychology of language blossomed in the 1950s and 1960s, with the advent of the cognitive revolution. One of the central events in the cognitive revolution was Chomsky's critique of Skinner's behavioristic analysis of language.

3. All the words a person knows are his or her lexicon. Phonemes and morphemes are two basic units of words.

4. The effect of meaning on the perception of phonemes is illustrated by the phonemic restoration effect. Meaning, as well as a person's experience with other aspects of language, are important for achieving speech segmentation.

5. The word superiority effect occurs when letters are easier to recognize when they are in words.

6. The ability to understand words in a sentence is influenced by word frequency. This has been demonstrated using the lexical decision task and by measuring eye movements.

7. Lexical ambiguity refers to the fact that a word can have more than one meaning. The time needed to access a word's meaning from memory is influenced by multiple factors.

8. Semantics (the meanings of words) and syntax (rules for using words in sentences) have been distinguished by the neuropsychology studies of Broca and Wernicke and by how errors of semantics and syntax influence the amplitudes of components of the ERP.

9. Parsing is the process by which words in a sentence are grouped into phrases. Grouping into phrases is a major determinant of the meaning of a sentence. This process has been studied by using garden path sentences that illustrate the effect of temporary ambiguity.

10. Two mechanisms proposed to explain parsing are (1) the syntax-first approach and (2) the interactionist approach. The syntax-first approach emphasizes how syntactic principles such as late closure determine how a sentence is parsed. The interactionist approach states that semantics, syntax, and other factors operate simultaneously to determine parsing. The interactionist approach is supported by (a) the way words with different meanings affect the interpretation of a sentence, (b) eye movement studies in the visual world paradigm, (c) predictions based on a person's knowledge of the environment, and (d) predictions based on a person's knowledge of language constructions.

11. Coherence enables us to understand stories. Coherence is largely determined by inference. Three major types of inference are anaphoric, instrumental, and causal.

12. The situation model approach to text comprehension states that people represent the situation in a story in terms of the people, objects, locations, and events that are being described in the story.

13. Measurements of brain activity have demonstrated how similar areas of the cortex are activated by reading action words and by actual movements.

14. Experiments that measure the ERP response to passages show that many things associated with the passage are activated as the passage is being read.

15. Conversations, which involve give-and-take between two or more people, are made easier by procedures that involve cooperation between participants in a conversation. These procedures include the given–new contract, establishing common ground, and syntactic coordination.

16. There is evidence that a culture's language can influence the way people perceive and think. Experiments comparing color discrimination in Russian-speaking and

English-speaking participants have revealed differences in color perception related to language. Other experiments show that these differences may occur mainly when colors are presented to the right hemisphere, so the left (language) hemisphere is activated.

THINK ABOUT IT

1. How do the ideas of coherence and connection apply to some of the movies you have seen lately? Have you found that some movies are easy to understand whereas others are more difficult? In the movies that are easy to understand, does one thing appear to follow from another, whereas in the more difficult ones, some things seem to be left out? What is the difference in the "mental work" needed to determine what is going on in these two kinds of movies? (You can also apply this kind of analysis to books you have read.)

2. Next time you are able to eavesdrop on a conversation, notice how the give-and-take among participants follows (or does not follow) the given–new contract. Also, notice how people change topics and how that affects the flow of the conversation. Finally, see if you can find any evidence of syntactic priming. One way to "eavesdrop" is to be part of a conversation that includes at least two other people. But don't forget to say something every so often!

3. One of the interesting things about languages is the use of "figures of speech," which people who know the language understand but nonnative speakers often find baffling. One example is the sentence "He brought everything but the kitchen sink." Can you think of other examples? If you speak a language other than English, can you identify figures of speech in that language that might be baffling to English-speakers?

4. Newspaper headlines are often good sources of ambiguous phrases. For example, consider the following actual headlines: "Milk Drinkers Are Turning To Powder," "Iraqi Head Seeks Arms," "Farm Bill Dies In House," and "Squad Helps Dog Bite Victim." See if you can find examples of ambiguous headlines in the newspaper, and try to figure out what it is that makes the headlines ambiguous.

5. People often say things in an indirect way, but listeners can often still understand what they mean. See if you can detect these indirect statements in normal conversation. (Examples: "Do you want to turn left here?" to mean "I think you should turn left here"; "Is it cold in here?" to mean "Please close the window.")

6. It is a common observation that people are more irritated by nearby cell phone conversations than by conversations between two people who are physically present. Why do you think this occurs? (See Emberson et al., 2010, for one answer.)

KEY TERMS

COGLAB EXPERIMENTS Numbers in parentheses refer to the experiment number in CogLab.

Categorical Perception: Discrimination (39)

Categorical Perception: Identification (40)

Lexical Decision (41)

Neighborhood Size Effect (42)

Word Superiority (43)

A problem occurs when there is an obstacle between a present state and a goal, and it is not immediately obvious how to get around the obstacle. The maze shown here is the obstacle to reaching the shelter in the middle. Research in problem solving has focused on determining the mental processes that occur as a person is solving a problem and on finding ways to make it easier to solve problems.

Problem Solving

The following is a story about physicist Richard Feynman, who received the Nobel Prize in Physics for his work in nuclear fission and quantum dynamics and who had a reputation as a scientific genius.

> A physicist working at the California Institute of Technology in the 1950s is having trouble deciphering some of Feynman's notes. He asks Murray Gell-Mann, a Nobel Laureate and occasional collaborator of Feynman, "What are Feynman's methods?" Gell-Mann leans coyly against the blackboard and says—"Dick's method is this. You write down the problem. You think very hard." [Gell-Mann shuts his eyes and presses his knuckles periodically to his forehead.] "Then you write down the answer." (adapted from Gleick, 1992, p. 315)

This is an amusing way of describing Feynman's genius, but it leaves unanswered the question of what was really going on inside his head while he was thinking "very hard." Although we may not know the answer to this question for Feynman, research on problem solving has provided some answers for people in general. In this chapter, we will explore some of the ways cognitive psychologists have described the mental processes that occur as people work toward determining the solution to a problem.

What Is a Problem?

What problems have you had to solve lately? When I ask students in my cognitive psychology class this question, I get answers such as the following: problems for math, chemistry, or physics courses; getting writing assignments in on time; dealing with roommates, friends, and relationships in general; deciding what courses to take, what career to go into; whether to go to graduate school or look for a job; how to pay for a new car. Many of these things fit the following definition: A **problem** occurs when there is an obstacle between a present state and a goal and it is not immediately obvious how to get around the obstacle (Duncker, 1945; Lovett, 2002). Thus, a problem, as defined by psychologists, is difficult, and the solution is not immediately obvious.

We begin by considering the approach of the Gestalt psychologists, who introduced the study of problem solving to psychology in the 1920s.

The Gestalt Approach: Problem Solving as Representation and Restructuring

We introduced the Gestalt psychologists in Chapter 3 by describing their laws of perceptual organization. The Gestalt psychologists were interested not only in perception but also in learning, problem solving, and even attitudes and beliefs (Koffka, 1935). But even as they considered other areas of psychology, they still took a perceptual approach. Problem solving, for the Gestalt psychologists, was about (1) how people represent a problem in their mind and (2) how solving a problem involves a reorganization or restructuring of this representation.

REPRESENTING A PROBLEM IN THE MIND

What does it mean to say that a problem is "represented" in the mind? One way to answer this question is to begin with how problems are presented. Consider, for example, a crossword puzzle (Figure 12.1). This type of problem is represented on the page by a diagram and clues about how to fill in the open squares. How this problem is represented in the mind is probably different for different people, but it is likely to differ from how it is represented on the page. For example, as people try to solve this problem, they may choose to represent only a small part of the puzzle at a time. Some people might

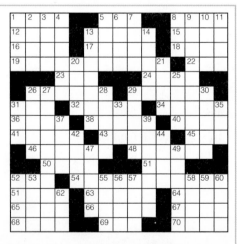

Figure 12.1 This is a picture of how a crossword puzzle is represented on the page. In addition, there are clues for filling in the horizontal and vertical words. © Cengage Learning

focus on filling in horizontal words and then use these words to help determine the vertical words. Others might pick one corner of the puzzle and search in their mind for both verticals and horizontals that fit together. Each of these ways of going about solving the problem involves a different way of representing it in the mind.

One of the central ideas of the Gestalt approach is that success in solving a problem is influenced by how it is represented in the person's mind. This idea—that the solution to a problem depends on how it is represented—is illustrated by the problem in **Figure 12.2**. This problem, which was posed by Gestalt psychologist Wolfgang Kohler (1929), asks us to determine the length of the segment marked *x* if the radius of the circle has a length *r*. (A number of problems will be posed in this chapter. The answers all appear on page 367. Don't turn to page 367 until you try the problems on the next two pages. The answer to the circle problem is also stated in the next paragraph, so don't read any further if you want to try to solve it.)

One way to describe how this problem is represented on the page is "a circle with thin vertical and horizontal lines that divide the circle into quarters, and darker lines that create a small triangle in the upper left quadrant." The key to solving this problem is to change the last part of the representation to "a small rectangle in the upper left quadrant, with *x* being the diagonal between the corners." Once *x* is recognized as the diagonal of the rectangle, the representation can be reorganized by creating the rectangle's other diagonal (**Figure 12.26**). Once we realize that this diagonal is the radius of the circle, and that both diagonals of a rectangle are the same length, we can conclude that the length of *x* equals the length of the radius, *r*.

What is important about this solution is that it doesn't require mathematical equations. Instead, the solution is obtained by first perceiving the object and then representing it in a different way. The Gestalt psychologists called the process of changing the problem's representation **restructuring**.

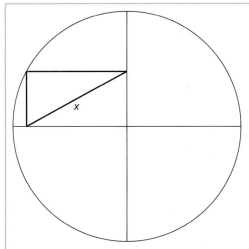

Problem: If the length of the circle's radius is *r*, what is the length of line *x*?

Figure 12.2 Circle problem. See Figure 12.26, page 367, for the solution.
© Cengage Learning

RESTRUCTURING AND INSIGHT

The Gestalt psychologists also introduced the idea that restructuring is associated with **insight**—the sudden realization of a problem's solution. Reflecting this emphasis on insight, the solution to most of the problems posed by Gestalt psychologists involves suddenly discovering a crucial element that leads to the solution (Dunbar, 1998).

The Gestalt psychologists assumed that people solving their problems were experiencing insight because the solutions usually seemed to come to them all of a sudden. Modern researchers have debated whether the process involved in insight and noninsight problems is the same or different. Some point out that people often experience problem solving as an "Aha!" experience—at one point they don't have the answer, and the next minute they have solved the problem—which is one of the characteristics associated with insight problems (Bowden et al., 2005; Kounios et al., 2008). Other researchers have emphasized the lack of evidence, other than anecdotal reports, to support the specialness of the insight experience (Weisberg, 1995; Weisberg & Alba, 1981, 1982).

Janet Metcalfe and David Wiebe (1987) did an experiment designed to distinguish between insight problems and noninsight problems. They hypothesized that there should be a difference in how subjects feel they are progressing toward a solution in insight problems versus noninsight problems. They predicted that subjects working on an insight problem, in which the answer appears suddenly, should not be very good at predicting how near they are to a solution. Subjects working on a noninsight problem, which involves a more methodical process, would be more likely to know when they are getting closer to the solution.

To test this hypothesis, Metcalfe and Wiebe gave subjects insight problems, as in the demonstration below, and noninsight problems and asked them to make "warmth" judgments every 15 seconds as they were working on the problems. Ratings closer to "hot" (7 on a 7-point scale) indicated that they believed they were getting close to a solution; ratings closer to "cold" (1 on the scale) indicated that they felt that they were far from a solution. Here are two examples of insight problems that Metcalfe and Wiebe used.

DEMONSTRATION
TWO INSIGHT PROBLEMS

Triangle Problem The triangle shown in **Figure 12.3a** points to the top of the page. Show how you can move three of the blue dots to get the triangle to point to the bottom of the page. (For the answer, see **Figure 12.27** on page 367.)

As you work on this problem, see whether you can monitor your progress. Do you feel as though you are making steady progress toward a solution until eventually it all adds up to the answer, or as though you are not really making much progress but then suddenly experience the solution as an "Aha!" experience? Once you have tried the triangle problem, try the following problem and monitor your progress in the same way.

Chain Problem A woman has four pieces of chain. Each piece is made up of three links, as shown in **Figure 12.3b**. She wants to join the pieces into a single closed loop of chain. To open a link costs 2 cents and to close a link costs 3 cents. She only has 15 cents. How does she do it? (For the answer, see **Figure 12.28** on page 367.)

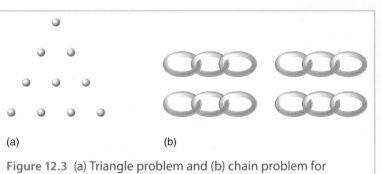

(a)   (b)

Figure 12.3 (a) Triangle problem and (b) chain problem for "Two Insight Problems" demonstration. See page 367 for solutions. © Cengage Learning

For noninsight problems, Metcalfe and Wiebe used algebra problems like the following, which were taken from a high school mathematics text:

$$\text{Solve for } x : (1/5)x + 10 = 25$$

$$\text{Factor } 16y^2 - 40yz + 25z^2$$

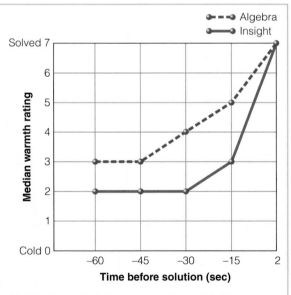

Figure 12.4 Results of Metcalfe and Wiebe's (1987) experiment showing subjects' judgments of how close they were to solving insight problems and algebra problems during the minute just before solving the problem. *(Source: Based on J. Metcalfe & D. Wiebe, Intuition in insight and noninsight problem solving, Memory and Cognition, 15, 238–246, 1987.)*

The results of their experiment are shown in **Figure 12.4**, which indicates the warmth ratings for all of the subjects during the minute just before they solved the two kinds of problems.

For the insight problems (solid line), warmth ratings began at 2 and then didn't change much, until all of a sudden they jumped from 3 to 7 at the end. Thus, 15 seconds before the solution, the median rating was a relatively cold 3 for the insight problems, meaning at this point subjects didn't feel they were close to a solution. In contrast, for the algebra problems (dashed line), the ratings began at 3 and then gradually increased until the problem was solved. Thus, Metcalfe and Wiebe demonstrated that solutions for problems that have been called insight problems do, in fact, occur suddenly, as measured by people's reports of how close they feel they are to a solution.

The Gestalt psychologists believed that restructuring was usually involved in solving insight problems, so they focused on these types of problems. Their research strategy was to devise problems and situations that made it difficult for people to achieve the restructuring needed to solve the problem. They hoped to learn about the processes involved in problem solving by studying obstacles to problem solving.

OBSTACLES TO PROBLEM SOLVING

One of the major obstacles to problem solving, according to the Gestalt psychologists, is **fixation**—people's tendency to focus on a specific characteristic of the problem that keeps them from arriving at a solution. One type of fixation that can work against solving a problem, focusing on familiar functions or uses of an object, is called **functional fixedness** (Jansson & Smith, 1991).

An example of functional fixedness is provided by the **candle problem**, which was first described by Karl Duncker (1945). In his experiment, he asked subjects to use various objects to complete a task. The following demonstration asks you to try to solve Duncker's problem by imagining that you have the specified objects.

DEMONSTRATION
THE CANDLE PROBLEM

You are in a room with a vertical corkboard mounted on the wall. You are given the materials shown in Figure 12.5—some candles, matches in a matchbox, and some tacks. Your task is to mount a candle on the corkboard so it will burn without dripping wax on the floor. Try to figure out how you would solve this problem before reading further; then check your answer in Figure 12.29 (page 367) at the end of the chapter.

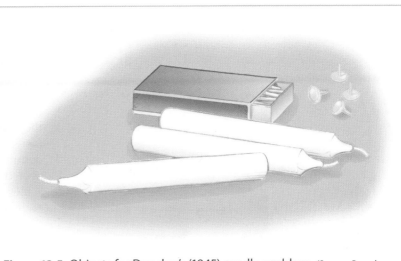

Figure 12.5 Objects for Duncker's (1945) candle problem. *(Source: Based on K. Duncker, On problem solving,* Psychological Monographs 58, 5, Whole No. 270, 1945.*)*

The solution to the problem occurs when the person realizes that the matchbox can be used as a support rather than as a container. When Duncker did this experiment, he presented one group of subjects with small cardboard boxes containing the materials (candles, tacks, and matches) and presented another group with the same materials, but outside the boxes, so the boxes were empty. When he compared the performance of the two groups, he found that the group that had been presented with the boxes as containers found the problem more difficult than did the group presented with empty boxes. Robert Adamson (1952) repeated Duncker's experiment and obtained the same result: Subjects who were presented with empty boxes were twice as likely to solve the problem as subjects who were presented with boxes that were being used as containers (Figure 12.6).

The fact that seeing the boxes as containers inhibited using them as supports is an example of functional fixedness. Another demonstration of functional fixedness is provided by Maier's (1931) **two-string problem**, in which the subjects' task was to tie together two strings that were hanging from the ceiling. This was difficult because the strings were so far apart that it was impossible to reach one of them while holding the other (Figure 12.7). Other objects available for solving this problem were a chair and a pair of pliers.

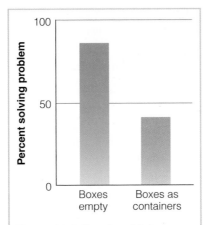

Figure 12.6 Results of Adamson's (1952) replication of Duncker's candle problem. *(Source: Based on R. E. Adamson, Functional fixedness as related to problem solving,* Journal of Experimental Psychology, 44, *288–291, 1952.)*

Figure 12.7 Maier's (1931) two-string problem. As hard as the subject tries, he can't grab the second string. How can he tie the two strings together? (Note: Just using the chair doesn't work!) *(Source: Based on N. R. F. Maier, Reasoning in humans: II. The solution of a problem and its appearance in consciousness,* Journal of Comparative Psychology, 12, *181–194, 1931.)*

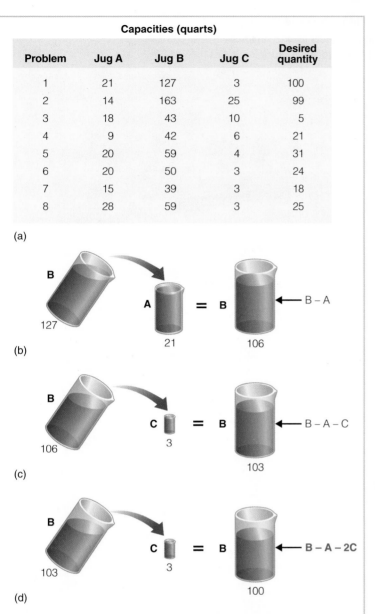

Capacities (quarts)

Problem	Jug A	Jug B	Jug C	Desired quantity
1	21	127	3	100
2	14	163	25	99
3	18	43	10	5
4	9	42	6	21
5	20	59	4	31
6	20	50	3	24
7	15	39	3	18
8	28	59	3	25

(a)

(b)

(c)

(d)

Figure 12.8 (a) The Luchins (1942) water jug problem. Each problem specifies the capacities of jugs A, B, and C and a final desired quantity. The task is to figure out how to use the jugs with these capacities to measure out the desired quantity. (b) The first step in solving Problem 1; (c) the second step; (d) the third step. All of the other problems can be solved using the same pattern of pourings, indicated by the equation Desired quantity = B – A – 2C, but there are more efficient ways to solve Problems 7 and 8. *(Source: Based on A. S. Luchins, Mechanization in problem solving—the effect of einstellung, Psychological Monographs, 54, 6, 195, 1942.)*

To solve this problem, subjects needed to tie the pliers to one of the strings to create a pendulum, which could then be swung to within the person's reach. This is an example of functional fixedness because people usually think of using pliers as a tool, not as a weight at the end of a pendulum. Thus, 37 of the 60 subjects did not solve the problem because they focused on the usual function of pliers.

When the majority of the subjects were unable to solve the problem within 10 minutes, Maier provided a "hint" by setting the string in motion by "accidentally" brushing against it. Once the subjects saw the string moving, 23 of the 37 who hadn't solved the problem solved it within 60 seconds. Seeing the string swinging from side to side apparently triggered the insight that the pliers could be used as a weight to create a pendulum. In Gestalt terms, the solution to the problem occurred once the subjects restructured their representation of how to achieve the solution (get the strings to swing from side to side) and their representation of the function of the pliers (they can be used as a weight to create a pendulum).

Both the candle problem and the two-string problem were difficult because of people's preconceptions about the uses of objects. These preconceptions are a type of **mental set**, a preconceived notion about how to approach a problem, which is determined by a person's experience or what has worked in the past. In these experiments, mental set was created by people's knowledge about the usual uses of objects.

The Gestalt psychologists also showed how mental set can arise out of the situation created as a person solves a problem. An example is provided by the Luchins **water jug problem**, in which subjects were told that their task was to figure out on paper how to obtain a required volume of water, given three empty jars for measures. Luchins (1942) presented the first example to his subjects, in which the three jugs had the following capacities: A = 21 quarts, B = 127 quarts, C = 3 quarts, and the desired volume was 100 quarts. This is Problem 1 in **Figure 12.8a**. After giving his subjects some time to solve the problem, Luchins provided the following solution:

1. Fill jug B with 127 quarts, and pour from B to fill A, so 21 quarts are subtracted from B. This leaves 106 quarts in B (**Figure 12.8b**).

2. Pour from jug B to fill jug C, so 3 quarts are subtracted from B, leaving 103 quarts (**Figure 12.8c**).

3. Pour from jug B again into C, so 3 more quarts are subtracted, leaving 100 quarts (**Figure 12.8d**).

The solution for Problem 1 can be stated as Desired amount = B – A – 2C. After demonstrating how to solve Problem 1 (but without mentioning this formula), Luchins had his subjects solve Problems 2–8, all of which could be solved by applying the same formula. (Some textbook descriptions of the Luchins experiment state that subjects were given water jugs of different capacities and were asked to measure out the specified amounts. If this were the case, subjects would have had to be very strong, since jug A, with 127 quarts of water, would weigh more than 250 pounds! Luckily for the subjects, they were just required to solve the problem on paper.)

Luchins was interested in how his subjects solved Problems 7 and 8, which could be solved by the B – A – 2C formula, but which also could be solved more simply as follows:

Problem 7: Desired quantity = A + C (Fill A and C and pour into B.)

Problem 8: Desired quantity = A – C (Fill A and pour into C.)

The question Luchins asked was: How will subjects solve Problems 7 and 8 with and without mental set? He determined this by running two groups:

Mental set group: Using the procedure described above, he presented Problem 1 first as a demonstration, then had subjects solve Problems 2–8, beginning with Problem 2. This established a mental set for using the B – A – 2C procedure.

No mental set group: Subjects just solved Problems 7 and 8, beginning with 7. In this case, subjects weren't exposed to the B – A – 2C procedure.

The result was that only 23 percent of the subjects in the *mental set group* used the simpler solutions for Problems 7 and 8, but all of the subjects in the *no mental set group* used the simpler solutions. Thus, mental set can influence problem solving both because of preconceptions about the functions of an object (candle and two-string problems) and because of preconceptions about the way to solve a problem (water jug problem).

Between about 1920 and 1950, the Gestalt psychologists described numerous problems illustrating how mental set can influence problem solving and how solving a problem often involves creating a new representation. This idea that problem solving depends on how the problem is represented in the mind is one of the enduring contributions of Gestalt psychology. Modern research has taken this idea as a starting point for the information-processing approach to the study of problem solving.

Modern Research on Problem Solving: The Information-Processing Approach

In our description of the history of cognitive psychology in Chapter 1, we noted that in 1956 there were two important conferences, one at the Massachusetts Institute of Technology and one at Dartmouth University, that brought together researchers from many disciplines to discuss new ways to study the mind. At both of these conferences, Alan Newell and Herbert Simon described their "logic theorist" computer program that was designed to simulate human problem solving. This marked the beginning of a research program that described problem solving as a process that involves search. That is, instead of just considering the initial structure of a problem and then the new structure achieved when the problem is solved, Newell and Simon described problem solving as a search that occurs between the posing of the problem and its solution.

The idea of problem solving as a search is part of our language. People commonly talk about problems in terms of "searching for a way to reach a goal," "getting around roadblocks," "hitting a dead end," and "approaching a problem from a different angle" (Lakoff & Turner, 1989). We will introduce Newell and Simon's approach by describing the **Tower of Hanoi problem**.

NEWELL AND SIMON'S APPROACH

Newell and Simon (1972) saw problems in terms of an **initial state**—conditions at the beginning of the problem—and a **goal state**—the solution of the problem. **Figure 12.9a** shows the initial state of the Tower of Hanoi problem as three discs stacked on the left peg, and the goal state as these discs stacked on the right peg. In addition to specifying initial and goal states of a problem, Newell and Simon also introduced the idea of **operators**—actions that take the problem from one state to another. For the Tower of Hanoi problem, the operators are moving the disc to another peg. The rules in the demonstration specify which actions

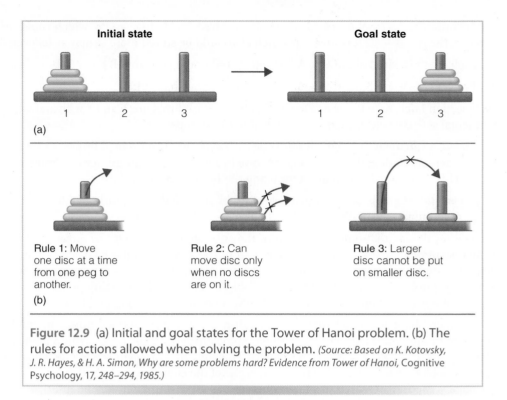

Figure 12.9 (a) Initial and goal states for the Tower of Hanoi problem. (b) The rules for actions allowed when solving the problem. *(Source: Based on K. Kotovsky, J. R. Hayes, & H. A. Simon, Why are some problems hard? Evidence from Tower of Hanoi, Cognitive Psychology, 17, 248–294, 1985.)*

are allowed and which are not (see **Figure 12.9b**). Try solving this problem by following the instructions in the demonstration.

DEMONSTRATION
TOWER OF HANOI PROBLEM

Move the discs from the left peg to the right peg, as shown in **Figure 12.9a**, following these rules:

1. Discs are moved one at a time from one peg to another.
2. A disc can be moved only when there are no discs on top of it.
3. A larger disc can never be placed on top of a smaller disc.

As you try solving this problem, count the number of moves it takes to get from the initial to the goal state.

This problem is called the Tower of Hanoi problem because of a legend that there are monks in a monastery near Hanoi who are working on this problem. Their version of it, however, is vastly more complex than ours, with 64 discs on peg 1. According to the legend, the world will end when the problem is solved. Luckily, this will take close to a trillion years to accomplish even if the monks make one move every second and every move is correct (Raphael, 1976).

As you tried solving the problem, you may have realized that there were a number of possible ways to move the discs as you tried to reach the goal state. Newell and Simon conceived of problem solving as involving a sequence of choices of steps, with each action creating an **intermediate state**. Thus, a problem starts with an initial state, continues through a number of intermediate states, and finally reaches the goal state. The initial state, goal

Table 12.1: Key Terms for Newell-Simon Approach to Problem Solving

TERM	DESCRIPTION	EXAMPLE FROM TOWER OF HANOI
Initial state	Conditions at the beginning of a problem.	All three discs are on the left peg.
Goal state	Solution to the problem.	All three discs are on the right peg.
Intermediate state	Conditions after each step is made toward solving a problem.	After the smallest disc is moved to the right peg, the two larger discs are on the left peg and the smallest one is on the right.
Operators	Actions that take the problem from one state to another. Operators are usually governed by rules.	Rule: A larger disc can't be placed on a smaller one.
Problem space	All possible states that could occur when solving a problem.	See **Figure 12.10**.
Means–end analysis	A way of solving a problem in which the goal is to reduce the difference between the initial and goal states.	Establishing subgoals, each of which moves the solution closer to the goal state.
Subgoals	Small goals that help create intermediate states that are closer to the goal. Occasionally, a subgoal may appear to increase the distance to the goal state but in the long run can result in the shortest path to the goal.	Subgoal 4: To free up the medium-sized disc, need to move the small disc from the middle peg back to the peg on the left.

© Cengage Learning

state, and all the possible intermediate states for a particular problem make up the **problem space**. (See **Table 12.1** for a summary of the terms used by Newell and Simon.)

The problem space for the Tower of Hanoi problem is shown in **Figure 12.10**. The initial state is marked 1 and the goal state is marked 8. All of the other possible configurations of discs on pegs are intermediate states. There are a number of ways to get from the initial state to the goal state. One possibility, indicated by the red lines, involves making 14 moves. The best solution, indicated by the green lines, requires only 7 moves.

Given all of the possible ways to reach the goal, how can we decide which moves to make, especially when starting out? It is important to realize that the problem-solver does not have a picture of the problem space, like the one in **Figure 12.10**, when trying to solve the problem. According to Newell and Simon, the person has to search the problem space to find a solution, and they proposed that one way to direct the search is to use a strategy called **means–end analysis**. The primary goal of means–end analysis is to reduce the difference between the initial and goal states. This is achieved by creating **subgoals**—intermediate states that are closer to the goal.

Our overall goal in applying means–end analysis to the Tower of Hanoi problem is to reduce the size of the difference between initial and goal states. An initial goal would be to move the large disc that is on the left over to the peg on the right. However, if we are to obey the rules, we can't accomplish this in just one step, because we can move only one disc at a

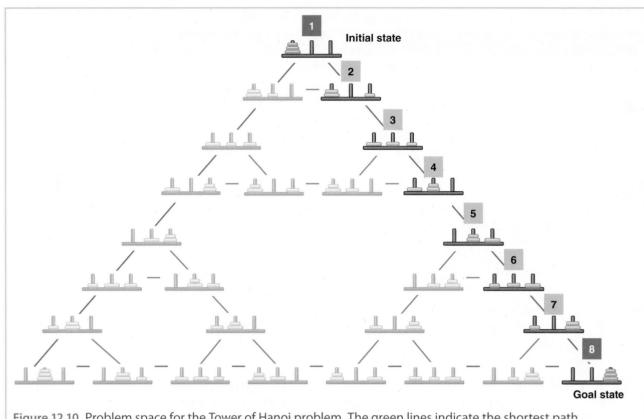

Figure 12.10 Problem space for the Tower of Hanoi problem. The green lines indicate the shortest path between the initial state (1) and the goal state (8). The red lines indicate a longer path. *(Source: Based on K. Dunbar, Problem solving, in W. Bechtel & G. Graham, Eds., A companion to cognitive science, pp. 289–298, London: Blackwell, 1998.)*

time and can't move a disc if another disc is on top of it. To solve the problem we therefore set a series of subgoals, some of which may involve a few moves:

Subgoal 1: Free up the large disc so we can move it onto peg 3. Do this by (a) removing the small disc and placing it on the third peg (**Figure 12.11a**; this is state 2 in the problem space in **Figure 12.10**). (b) Remove the medium disc and place it on the second peg (**Figure 12.11b**; state 3 in the problem space). This completes the subgoal of freeing up the large disc.

Subgoal 2: Free up the third peg so we can move the large disc onto it. Do this by moving the small disc onto the medium one (**Figure 12.11c**; state 4 in the problem space).

Subgoal 3: Move the large disc onto peg 3 (**Figure 12.11d**; state 5 in the problem space).

Subgoal 4: Free up the medium disc.

Now that we have reached state 5 in the problem space, let's stop and decide how to achieve subgoal 4, freeing up the medium disc. We can move the small disc either onto peg 3 or onto peg 1. These two possible choices illustrate that to find the shortest path to the goal, we need to look slightly ahead. When we do this, we can see that we should not move the small disc to peg 3, even though it appears to reduce the difference between the initial and goal states. Moving to peg 3 is the wrong move, because that would block moving the medium disc there, which would be our next subgoal. Thus, we move the disc back to peg 1 (state 6), which makes it possible to move the medium disc to peg 3 (state 7), and we have almost solved the problem! This procedure of setting subgoals and looking slightly ahead often results in an efficient solution to a problem.

Why is the Tower of Hanoi problem important? One reason is that it illustrates means–end analysis, with its setting of subgoals, and this approach can be applied to real-life situations. For example, I recently had to plan a trip from Pittsburgh to Copenhagen. Remember

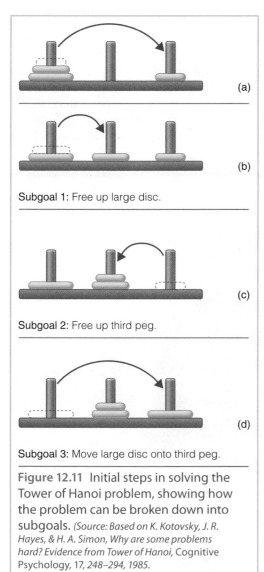

(a)

(b)

Subgoal 1: Free up large disc.

(c)

Subgoal 2: Free up third peg.

(d)

Subgoal 3: Move large disc onto third peg.

Figure 12.11 Initial steps in solving the Tower of Hanoi problem, showing how the problem can be broken down into subgoals. *(Source: Based on K. Kotovsky, J. R. Hayes, & H. A. Simon, Why are some problems hard? Evidence from Tower of Hanoi,* Cognitive Psychology, *17, 248–294, 1985.)*

Figure 12.12 Two possible routes from Pittsburgh to Copenhagen. The route through Paris (black line) immediately reduces the distance to Copenhagen, but doesn't satisfy the rules of the problem. The route through Atlanta (dashed red line) involves some backtracking but works because it satisfies the rules. © Cengage Learning

that in Newell and Simon's terminology, an operator is the action to get from one state to another. The operator for getting from Pittsburgh to Copenhagen is to take a plane, and there are two rules governing this operator:

1. If there isn't a direct flight (there isn't!), it is important to have enough time between flights to ensure that passengers and baggage can get from the first flight to the second one.

2. The cost of the flights have to be within my budget.

My first subgoal was to try to reduce the distance between myself and Copenhagen. One way to achieve this was to take a flight from Pittsburgh to Paris, and then transfer to a flight to Copenhagen (**Figure 12.12**). But the plane schedule showed that there was only 70 minutes between flights, which violated rule 1, and waiting for a later flight to Copenhagen increased the fare, which violated rule 2. The failure of the Pittsburgh to Paris idea led me to create a new subgoal: Find a flight to a city with a number of low-cost connecting flights to Copenhagen. I eventually determined that flying from Pittsburgh to Atlanta satisfied this subgoal. So the problem was solved. Notice that the solution involved setting a subgoal that involved initially traveling away from Copenhagen. Just as for subgoal 4 in the Tower of Hanoi example, in which we had to move a disc away from the right peg to eventually get it there, I had to first fly away from Copenhagen to position myself to achieve my goal.

One of the main contributions of Newell and Simon's approach to problem solving is that it provided a way to specify the possible pathways from the initial to goal states. But research has shown that there is more to problem solving than specifying the problem space. As we will see in the next section, this research has shown that two problems with the same problem space can vary greatly in difficulty.

THE IMPORTANCE OF HOW A PROBLEM IS STATED

How a problem is stated can affect its difficulty. We can appreciate this by considering the *mutilated checkerboard problem*, described on the next page.

DEMONSTRATION
THE MUTILATED CHECKERBOARD PROBLEM

A checkerboard consists of 64 squares, which can be completely covered by placing 32 dominos on the board so that each domino covers two squares. The **mutilated checkerboard problem** asks the following question: If we eliminate two corners of the checkerboard, as shown in **Figure 12.13**, can we now cover the remaining squares with 31 dominos? See whether you can solve this problem before reading further. A solution would be either a "yes" or "no" answer plus a statement of the rationale behind your answer.

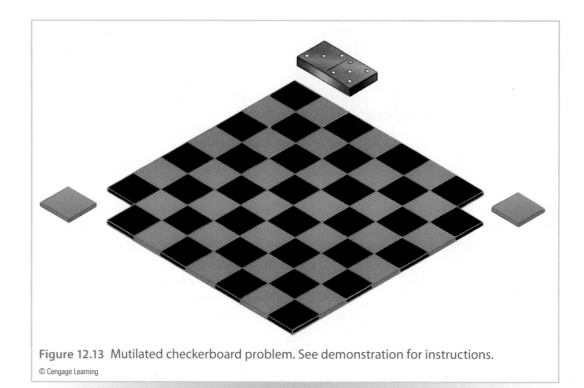

Figure 12.13 Mutilated checkerboard problem. See demonstration for instructions.

© Cengage Learning

Remember the Gestalt idea that adopting the correct problem representation is a key to successful problem solving. The key to solving the mutilated checkerboard problem is understanding the principle that each domino covers two squares and that these squares must be of different colors, so removing the two corner squares with the same color makes it impossible to solve the problem. Starting with this idea, Craig Kaplan and Herbert Simon (1990) hypothesized that versions of the mutilated checkerboard problem that were more likely to lead subjects to become aware of this principle would be easier to solve. To test this idea, they created the following four version of the checkerboard, shown in **Figure 12.14**:

1. Blank: a board with all blank squares

2. Color: alternating black and pink squares as might appear on a regular checkerboard

3. The words *black* and *pink* on the board

4. The words *bread* and *butter* on the board

All four versions of the checkerboard problem have the same board layout and the same solution. What is different is the information on the boards (or lack of information on the blank board) that can be used to provide subjects with the insight that a domino covers two squares and that these squares must be of different colors. Not surprisingly, subjects who were presented boards that emphasized the difference between adjoining squares found the problem easier to solve. The bread-and-butter condition emphasized the difference the most, because bread and butter are very different but are also associated with each other. The blank board had no information about the difference, because all the squares were the same.

Subjects in the bread-and-butter group solved the problem twice as fast as those in the blank group and required fewer hints, which the experimenter provided when subjects appeared to be at a "dead end." The bread-and-butter group required an average of 1 hint; the blank group required an average of 3.14 hints. The performance of the color and the black-and-pink groups fell between these two. This result shows that solving a problem becomes easier when information is provided that helps point people toward the correct representation of the problem.

To achieve a better understanding of subjects' thought processes as they were solving the problem, Kaplan and Simon used a technique introduced by Simon called the *think-aloud protocol*.

METHOD
THINK-ALOUD PROTOCOL

In the **think-aloud protocol** procedure, subjects are asked to say out loud what they are thinking while solving a problem. They are instructed not to describe what they are doing, but to verbalize new thoughts as they occur. One goal of a think-aloud protocol is to determine what information the person is attending to while solving a problem. The following is an example of the instructions given to a subject:

> In this experiment we are interested in what you say to yourself as you perform some tasks that we give you. In order to do this we will ask you to talk aloud as you work on the problems. What I mean by talk aloud is that I want you to say out loud everything that you say to yourself silently. Just act as if you are alone in the room speaking to yourself. If you are silent for any length of time, I will remind you to keep talking aloud.... Any questions? Please talk aloud while you solve the following problem. (Ericsson & Simon, 1993)

The four conditions:

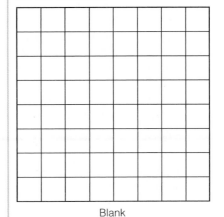

Blank

Color

Black and pink

Bread and butter

Figure 12.14 Conditions in Kaplan and Simon's (1990) study of the mutilated checkerboard problem. *(Source: C. A. Kaplan & H. A. Simon, In search of insight, Cognitive Psychology, 22, 374–419, Figure 2. Copyright © 1990 Elsevier Ltd. Reproduced with permission.)*

Here is an example of the verbalizations from Kaplan and Simon's experiment. This subject was in the bread-and-butter condition.

Subject: Just by trial and error I can only find 30 places.... I dunno, maybe someone else would have counted the spaces and just said that you could fit 31, but if you try it out on the paper, you can only fit 30. (Pause)

Experimenter: Keep trying.

Subject: Maybe it has to do with the words on the page? I haven't tried anything with that. Maybe that's it. OK, dominos, umm, the dominos can only fit ... alright, the dominos can fit over two squares, and no matter which way you put it because it cannot go diagonally, it has to fit over a butter and a bread. And because you crossed out two breads, it has to leave two butters left over so it doesn't ... only 30, so it won't fit. Is that the answer?

Notice that the person was stuck at first and then suddenly got the answer after realizing that the words *bread* and *butter* were important. By recording people's thought processes as they are solving a problem, the think-aloud protocol reveals a shift in how a person perceives elements of the problem. This is very similar to the Gestalt psychologists' idea of restructuring. For example, remember the circle problem in Figure 12.2. The key to solving that problem was realizing that the line x was the same length as the radius of the circle. Similarly, the key to solving the mutilated checkerboard problem is realizing that adjoining squares are paired, because a domino always covers two different-colored squares on a normal checkerboard. Thus, in Gestalt terms, we could say that the person creates a representation of the problem that makes it easier to solve.

Kaplan and Simon used different colors and different names to help their subjects realize that pairing of adjacent squares is important. But this has also been achieved in another way—by telling the following story, which has parallels to the checkerboard problem.

THE RUSSIAN MARRIAGE PROBLEM

In a small Russian village, there were 32 bachelors and 32 unmarried women. Through tireless efforts, the village matchmaker succeeded in arranging 32 highly satisfactory marriages. The village was proud and happy. Then one drunken night, two bachelors, in a test of strength, stuffed each other with pierogies and died. Can the matchmaker, through some quick arrangements, come up with 31 heterosexual marriages among the 62 survivors? (adapted from Hayes, 1978, p. 180)

The answer to this problem is obvious. Losing two males leaves 30 men and 32 women, making it impossible to arrange 31 heterosexual marriages. Of course, this is exactly the situation in the mutilated checkerboard problem, except instead of males and females being paired up, light and dark squares are. People who read this story are usually able to solve the mutilated checkerboard problem if they realize the connection between the couples in the story and the alternating squares on the checkerboard. This process of noticing connections between similar problems and applying the solution for one problem to other problems is called the method of *analogy*. In the next section, we will look more closely at how analogy has been used in problem solving.

TEST YOURSELF 12.1

1. What is the psychological definition of a problem?

2. What is the basic principle behind the Gestalt approach to problem solving? Describe how the following problems illustrate this principle, and also what else these problems demonstrate about problem solving: the circle (radius) problem; the candle problem; the two-string problem; the water jug problem. Be sure you understand functional fixedness.

3. What is insight, and what is the evidence that insight does, in fact, occur as people are solving a problem?

4. Describe Newell and Simon's approach to problem solving, in which "search" plays a central role. How does means–end analysis as applied to the Tower of Hanoi problem illustrate this approach? What is the think-aloud protocol?

5. How does the mutilated checkerboard experiment illustrate that the way a problem is stated can affect a person's ability to solve the problem? What are the implications of this research for Newell and Simon's "problem space" approach?

Using Analogies to Solve Problems

A person is faced with a problem and wonders how to proceed. Questions such as "What move should I make?" or "How should I begin thinking about this problem?" arise. One tactic that is sometimes helpful is to consider whether another problem that the person has solved before is similar to the new problem and ask "Can I apply the same methods to solving this problem?" This technique of using an **analogy**—that is, using the solution to a similar problem to guide solution of a new problem—is called **analogical problem solving**.

Using the Russian marriage problem to help solve the mutilated checkerboard problem is an example of an effective use of analogy to solve a problem. Research on analogical problem solving has considered some of the conditions in which using analogies to solve problems is effective or ineffective.

ANALOGICAL TRANSFER

The starting point for much of the research on analogical problem solving has been to first determine how well people can transfer their experience from solving one problem to solving another, similar problem. This transfer from one problem to another is called **analogical transfer**. Two key terms that are used in research on analogical transfer are **target problem**, which is the problem the subject is trying to solve, and **source problem**, which is another problem that shares some similarities with the target problem and that illustrates a way to solve the target problem.

For the mutilated checkerboard problem, the checkerboard problem is the target problem, and the Russian marriage problem is the source problem. Evidence that analogical transfer has occurred is provided when presentation of the Russian marriage problem enhances the ability to solve the mutilated checkerboard problem. We saw that analogical transfer occurs in this example, because subjects readily see that the principle governing the solution of the Russian marriage problem is similar to the principle that needs to be applied to solve the checkerboard problem. However, as we will now see, good analogical transfer does not always occur.

ANALOGICAL PROBLEM SOLVING AND THE DUNCKER RADIATION PROBLEM

A problem that has been widely used in research on analogical problem solving is Karl Duncker's **radiation problem**.

DEMONSTRATION
DUNCKER'S RADIATION PROBLEM

Try solving the following problem: Suppose you are a doctor faced with a patient who has a malignant tumor in his stomach. It is impossible to operate on the patient, but unless the tumor is destroyed the patient will die. There is a kind of ray that can be used to destroy the tumor. If the ray reaches the tumor at a sufficiently high intensity, the tumor will be destroyed. Unfortunately, at this intensity the healthy tissue that the ray passes through on the way to the tumor will also be destroyed. At lower intensities the ray is harmless to healthy tissue, but it will not affect the tumor either. What type of procedure might be used to destroy the tumor and at the same time avoid destroying the healthy tissue (Gick & Holyoak, 1980)?

If after thinking about this problem for a while, you haven't come up with a suitable answer, you are not alone. When Duncker (1945) originally posed this problem, most of his subjects could not solve it, and Mary Gick and Keith Holyoak (1980, 1983) found that only 10 percent of their subjects arrived at the correct solution, shown in Figure 12.15a. The solution is to bombard the tumor with a number of low-intensity rays from different directions, which destroys the tumor without damaging the tissue the rays are passing through. The solution to this problem is actually the procedure used in modern radiosurgery, in which a tumor is bombarded with 201 gamma ray beams that intersect at the tumor (Tarkan, 2003; Figure 12.15b).

Notice how the radiation problem and its solution fit with the Gestalt idea of representation and restructuring. The initial representation of the problem is a single ray that

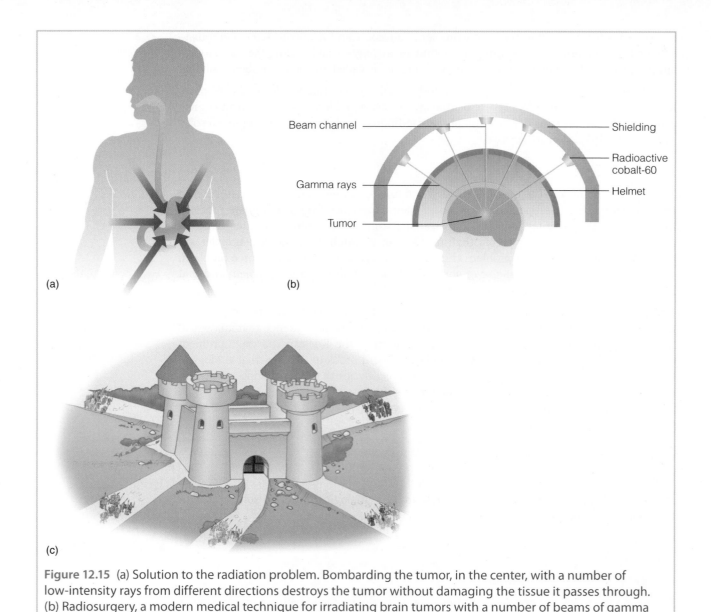

(a)

(b)

Beam channel ———— Shielding

———— Radioactive cobalt-60

Gamma rays ———— Helmet

Tumor ————

(c)

Figure 12.15 (a) Solution to the radiation problem. Bombarding the tumor, in the center, with a number of low-intensity rays from different directions destroys the tumor without damaging the tissue it passes through. (b) Radiosurgery, a modern medical technique for irradiating brain tumors with a number of beams of gamma rays, uses the same principle. The actual technique uses 201 gamma ray beams. (c) How the general solved the fortress problem. © Cengage Learning

destroys the tumor but also destroys healthy tissue. The restructured solution involves dividing the single ray into many smaller rays.

After confirming Duncker's finding that the radiation problem is extremely difficult, Gick and Holyoak (1980, 1983) had another group of subjects read and memorize the fortress story below, giving them the impression that the purpose was to test their memory for the story.

FORTRESS STORY

A small country was ruled from a strong fortress by a dictator. The fortress was situated in the middle of the country, surrounded by farms and villages. Many roads led to the fortress through the countryside. A rebel general vowed to capture the fortress. The general knew that an attack by his entire army would capture the fortress. He gathered his army at the head of one of the roads, ready to launch a full-scale direct attack. However, the general then learned that the dictator had planted mines on each of the roads. The mines were set so that small bodies of men could pass over them safely, since the dictator needed to move his troops and workers to and from the fortress. However, any large force would detonate the mines. Not only would this blow up the road, but it would also destroy many neighboring villages. It therefore seemed impossible to capture the fortress.

However, the general devised a simple plan. He divided his army into small groups and dispatched each group to the head of a different road. When all was ready he gave the signal and each group marched down a different road. Each group continued down its road to the fortress so that the entire army arrived together at the fortress at the same time. In this way, the general captured the fortress and overthrew the dictator. (See **Figure 12.15c**.)

The fortress story is analogous to the radiation problem: The dictator's fortress corresponds to the tumor, and the small groups of soldiers sent down different roads correspond to the low-intensity rays that can be directed at the tumor. After Gick and Holyoak's subjects read the story, they were told to begin work on the radiation problem. Thirty percent of the people in this group were able to solve the radiation problem, an improvement over the 10 percent who solved the problem when it was presented alone. However, what is significant about this experiment is that 70 percent of the subjects were still unable to solve the problem, even after reading an analogous source story. This result highlights one of the major findings of research on using analogies as an aid to problem solving: Even when exposed to analogous source problems, most people do not make the connection between the source problem and the target problem.

However, when Gick and Holyoak's subjects were told to think about the story they had read, their success rate more than doubled, to 75 percent. Since no new information was given about the story, apparently the information needed to recognize the analogy was available in people's memories but had simply not been retrieved (Gentner & Colhoun, 2010). These results led Gick and Holyoak to propose that the process of analogical problem solving involves the following three steps:

1. *Noticing* that there is an analogous relationship between the source problem and the target problem. This step is obviously crucial in order for analogical problem solving to work. However, as we have seen, most subjects need some prompting before they notice the connection between the source problem and the target problem. Gick and Holyoak consider this noticing step to be the most difficult of the three steps. A number of experiments have shown that the most effective source stories are those that are most similar to the target problem (Catrambone & Holyoak, 1989; Holyoak & Thagard, 1995). This similarity could make it easier to notice the analogical relationship between the source story and the target problem, and could also help achieve the next step—mapping.

2. *Mapping* the correspondence between the source story and the target problem. To use the story to solve the problem, the subject has to map corresponding parts of the story onto the test problem by connecting elements of the source problem (for example, the dictator's fortress) to elements of the target problem (the tumor).

3. *Applying* the mapping to generate a parallel solution to the target problem. This would involve, for example, generalizing from the many small groups of soldiers approaching the fortress from different directions to the idea of using many weaker rays that would approach the tumor from different directions.

Once they determined that analogies can help with problem solving but that hints are required to help subjects notice the presence of the source problem, Gick and Holyoak (1983) proceeded to look for factors that might facilitate the noticing and mapping steps. One thing that makes noticing difficult is that people often focus on **surface features**, specific elements of the problem such as the rays and the tumor. Surface features of the source problem and the target problem can be very different. For example, there is a big difference between a tumor and a fortress, and between rays and marching soldiers.

To test the idea that making the surface features more similar might help subjects notice the relationship between the source problem and the target problem, Holyoak and Kyunghee Koh (1987) created a problem that had surface features similar to the radiation problem.

EFFECT OF MAKING SURFACE FEATURES MORE SIMILAR The lightbulb problem is a problem with surface features similar to the radiation problem. The following is a shortened version of this problem.

LIGHTBULB PROBLEM

In a physics lab at a major university, a very expensive lightbulb, which would emit precisely controlled quantities of light, was being used in some experiments. One morning Ruth, the research assistant, came into the lab and found that the lightbulb no longer worked. She noticed that the filament inside the bulb had broken into two parts. The surrounding glass bulb was completely sealed, so there was no way to open it. Ruth knew that the lightbulb could be repaired if a brief, high-intensity laser beam could be used to fuse the two parts of the filament into one.

However, a high-intensity laser beam would also break the fragile glass surrounding the filament. At lower intensities the laser would not break the glass, but neither would it fuse the filament. What type of procedure might be used to fuse the filament with the laser and at the same time avoid breaking the glass? (adapted from Holyoak & Koh, 1987)

Holyoak and Koh (1987) used the radiation problem as the source problem (note that this is different from our previous discussion, in which the radiation problem was the target problem) and the lightbulb problem as the target problem. Subjects in one group were taught about the radiation problem and its solution in an introductory psychology class, just prior to being given the lightbulb problem. Subjects in the control group did not know about the radiation problem. The result was that 81 percent of subjects who knew about the radiation problem solved the lightbulb problem, but only 10 percent of the subjects in the control group solved it. Holyoak and Koh hypothesized that this excellent analogical transfer from the radiation problem to the lightbulb problem occurred because of the high surface similarity between rays (radiation problem) and lasers (lightbulb problem).

EFFECT OF VARYING THE STRUCTURAL FEATURES Having determined that similar surface features enhanced analogical transfer, Holyoak and Koh did another experiment in which they investigated the effect of varying the structural features of the problem. **Structural features** are the underlying principle that governs the solution. In the radiation and lightbulb problem, the structural features are *strong ray destroys tissue* for the radiation problem, and *strong laser breaks lightbulb* for the lightbulb problem.

Holyoak and Koh kept the surface features constant by using the lightbulb problem as the source problem and the radiation problem as the target problem; they varied the structural features by presenting two versions of the lightbulb problem. Both versions began with the story about the broken filament surrounded by glass and the information that the filament could be repaired by fusing it with a high-intensity laser beam. But the problem that needed to be solved in order to fix the filament was different in the two versions. The first version, called the fragile-glass version, was essentially the same as the original lightbulb problem. In this version, the structural features of the lightbulb and radiation problems were similar.

SOURCE PROBLEM 1: FRAGILE-GLASS VERSION

(Source and target problems have similar structural features.)

Problem: A high-intensity laser beam would break the fragile glass surrounding the filament. At lower intensities the laser would not break the glass, but neither would it fuse the filament.

Ruth's Solution: Ruth placed several lasers in a circle around the lightbulb and administered low-intensity laser beams from several directions at once. The beams all converged on the filament, where their combined effect was enough to fuse it. Because each spot on the surrounding glass received only a low-intensity beam from each laser, the glass was left intact.

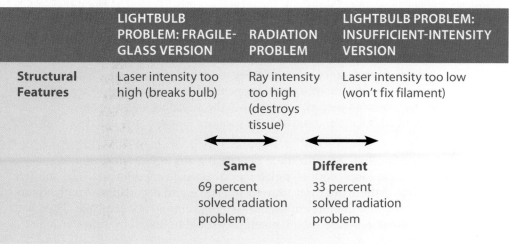

	LIGHTBULB PROBLEM: FRAGILE-GLASS VERSION	RADIATION PROBLEM	LIGHTBULB PROBLEM: INSUFFICIENT-INTENSITY VERSION
Structural Features	Laser intensity too high (breaks bulb)	Ray intensity too high (destroys tissue)	Laser intensity too low (won't fix filament)
		Same 69 percent solved radiation problem	**Different** 33 percent solved radiation problem

© 2015 Cengage Learning

The structural features of this problem and the radiation problem are similar: The intensities of the beams that would fix the tumor or the filament are too high, as indicated in the first two columns of columns of **Table 12.2**. Sixty-nine percent of the subjects who read this solution were able to solve the radiation problem.

In the second version of the problem, called the insufficient-intensity version, the structural features of the lightbulb and radiation problems are different.

SOURCE PROBLEM 2: INSUFFICIENT-INTENSITY VERSION

(Source and target problems have different structural features.)

Problem: The laser generated only low-intensity beams that were not strong enough to fuse the filament. A much more intense laser beam was needed.

Ruth's Solution: Ruth placed several lasers in a circle around the lightbulb and administered low-intensity laser beams from several directions at once. The beams all converged on the filament, where their combined effect was enough to fuse it.

The structural features of this problem are different from the structural features of the radiation problem, as indicated in the far right column of **Table 12.2**. Only 33 percent of the subjects who read this solution were able to solve the radiation problem. The conclusion from comparing the results from these two versions of the lightbulb problem is that analogical transfer is improved by making the structural features of the source and target problems more similar.

All of these experiments taken together show that transfer is aided by making surface features more similar and by making structural features more similar. But the fact remains that it is often difficult for people to apply analogies to solving problems, especially in situations in which surface and structural similarities are not as obvious as in the lightbulb and radiation problems. One way to help people notice structural similarities is through a training procedure called *analogical encoding*.

ANALOGICAL ENCODING

Analogical encoding is the process by which two problems are compared and similarities between them are determined. An experiment by Dedre Gentner and Susan Goldin-Meadow (2003) illustrated analogical encoding by showing that it is possible to get subjects to discover similar structural features by having them compare two cases that illustrate a principle. Their experiment involved a problem in negotiation. In the first part of the experiment, subjects were taught about the negotiation strategies of *trade-off* and *contingency*. Trade-off refers to a negotiating strategy in which one person says to another, "I'll

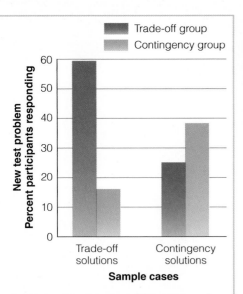

Figure 12.16 Results of Gentner and Goldin-Meadow's (2003) study of negotiating strategies. In the test case, subjects who had compared trade-off examples were more apt to find trade-off solutions, whereas those who had compared contingency examples were more apt to find contingency solutions. *(Source: Based on D. Gentner & S. Goldin-Meadow, Eds., Language in mind, Cambridge, MA: MIT Press, 2003.)*

give you A, if you'll give me B." This is illustrated by two sisters who are quarreling over who should get an orange. Eventually, they reach a trade-off solution when they realize that one wants the juice and the other wants just the peel, so one takes the juice and the other takes the peel. (This example is attributed to management consultant Mary Parker Follet in Gentner & Goldin-Meadow, 2003.)

The strategy of *contingency* refers to a negotiating strategy in which a person gets what he or she wants if something else happens. This is illustrated by a situation in which an author wants 18 percent royalties, but the publisher wants to pay only 12 percent. The contingent solution would be to tie royalties to sales: "You can have 18 percent if sales are high, but less if sales are low."

After being familiarized with these negotiating strategies, one group of subjects received two sample cases, both of which described trade-off solutions. The subjects' task was to compare these two cases to arrive at a successful negotiation. Another group did the same thing, but their examples involved the contingency principle. Then both groups were given a new case, which potentially could be solved by either negotiating principle.

The results of this experiment are shown in **Figure 12.16**. When presented with the new test problem, subjects tended to use the negotiating strategy that had been emphasized in the sample cases. Gentner concluded from these results that having people compare source stories is an effective way to achieve analogical encoding because it forces them to pay attention to structural features that enhance their ability to solve other problems.

ANALOGY IN THE REAL WORLD

So far, our examples of analogy problems have involved laboratory research. But what about the use of analogy in the real world? Many real-world examples of analogical problem solving illustrate what Kevin Dunbar (2001) has called the **analogical paradox**: While it is difficult to apply analogies in laboratory research, people routinely use analogies in real-world settings. Dunbar studied the use of analogies in real-world settings using a technique called *in vivo research*.

METHOD
IN VIVO PROBLEM-SOLVING RESEARCH

In vivo problem-solving research involves observing people to determine how they solve problems in real-world situations. This method has been used to study the use of analogy in a number of different settings, including laboratory meetings of a university research group and brainstorming sessions in which the goal was to develop a new product. Discussions recorded during these meetings have been analyzed for statements indicating that analogy is being used to help solve a problem. The advantage of the in vivo approach is that it captures thinking in naturalistic settings. A disadvantage is that it is time-consuming, and, as with most observational research, it is difficult to isolate and control specific variables.

When Dunbar and coworkers (Dunbar, 1999; Dunbar & Blanchette, 2001) videotaped molecular biologists and immunologists during their lab meetings, they found that researchers used analogies from 3 to 15 times in a 1-hour laboratory meeting. An example of an analogy from these laboratory meetings is the statement "If *E. coli* works like this, maybe your gene is doing the same thing." Similarly, Bo Christensen and Christian Schunn (2007) recorded meetings of design engineers who were creating new plastic products for medical applications. The engineers were trying to figure out how to create a container that would hold small amounts of liquid for a few minutes before falling apart. Christensen and Schunn found that the engineers proposed an analogy about every 5 minutes. When one engineer suggested that the container could be like a paper envelope, the group took off from this suggestion and eventually proposed a solution based on using paper. Thus, analogies play an important role both in solving scientific problems and in designing new products. When we discuss creativity later in this chapter, we will describe some examples of how analogical thinking has led to the development of useful products.

Although we understand some of the mental processes that occur as a person works toward the solution to a problem, what actually happens is still somewhat mysterious. We do know, however, that one factor that can sometimes make problem solving easier is practice or training. Some people can become very good at solving certain kinds of problems because they become experts in an area. We will now consider what it means to be an expert and how being an expert affects problem solving.

How Experts Solve Problems

Experts are people who, by devoting a large amount of time to learning about a field and practicing and applying that learning, have become acknowledged as being extremely knowledgeable or skilled in that particular field. For example, by spending 10,000–20,000 hours playing and studying chess, some chess players have reached the rank of grand master (Chase & Simon, 1973a, 1973b). Not surprisingly, experts tend to be better than nonexperts at solving problems in their field. Research on the nature of expertise has focused on determining differences between the way experts and nonexperts go about solving problems.

DIFFERENCES BETWEEN HOW EXPERTS AND NOVICES SOLVE PROBLEMS

Experts in a particular field usually solve problems faster with a higher success rate than do novices (people who are beginners or who have not had the extensive training of experts; Chi et al., 1982; Larkin et al., 1980). But what is behind this faster speed and greater success? Are experts smarter than novices? Are they better at reasoning in general? Do they approach problems in a different way? Cognitive psychologists have answered these questions by comparing the performance and methods of experts and novices, and have reached the following conclusions.

EXPERTS POSSESS MORE KNOWLEDGE ABOUT THEIR FIELDS An experiment by William Chase and Herbart Simon (1973a, 1973b) compared how well a chess master with more than 10,000 hours of experience and a beginner with fewer than 100 hours of experience were able to reproduce the positions of pieces on a chessboard after looking at an arrangement for 5 seconds. The results showed that experts excelled at this task when the chess pieces were arranged in actual game positions (**Figure 12.17a**) but were no better than the beginners when the pieces were arranged randomly (**Figure 12.17b**). The reason for the experts' superior performance with actual positions is that the chess masters had stored many of the patterns that occur in real games in their long-term memory, so they saw the layout of chess pieces not in terms of individual pieces but in terms of four to six chunks, each made up of a group of pieces that formed familiar, meaningful patterns. When the pieces were arranged randomly, the familiar patterns were destroyed, and the chess masters' advantage vanished (also see DeGroot, 1965; Gobet et al., 2001). We will now see that in addition to the fact that experts possess more knowledge than novices, experts also organize this knowledge differently.

EXPERTS' KNOWLEDGE IS ORGANIZED DIFFERENTLY THAN NOVICES' The difference in organization between experts and novices is illustrated by an experiment by Michelene Chi and coworkers (1982; also see Chi et al., 1981). They presented 24 physics problems to a group of experts (physics professors) and a group of novices (students with one semester of physics) and asked them to sort the problems into groups based on their similarities. **Figure 12.18** shows diagrams of problems that were grouped together by an expert and

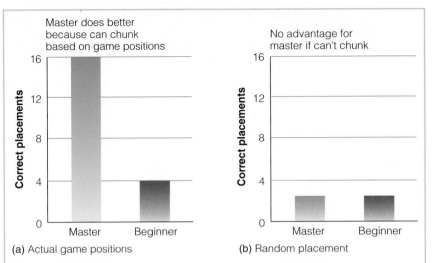

Figure 12.17 Results of Chase and Simon's (1973a, 1973b) chess memory experiment. (a) The chess master is better at reproducing actual game positions. (b) The master's performance drops to the level of the beginner's when the pieces are arranged randomly. *(Source: Based on W. G. Chase & H. A. Simon, Perception in chess, Cognitive Psychology, 4, 55–81, 1973.)*

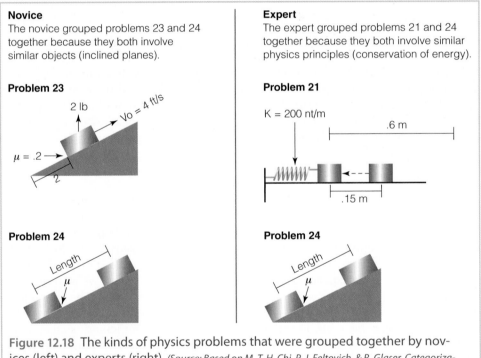

Figure 12.18 The kinds of physics problems that were grouped together by novices (left) and experts (right). *(Source: Based on M. T. H. Chi, P. J. Feltovich, & R. Glaser, Categorization and representation of physics problems by experts and novices, Cognitive Science, 5, 121–152, 1981. Reprinted by permission of Taylor & Francis Group.)*

by a novice. We don't need a statement of the actual problems to see from the diagrams that the novice sorted the problems based on surface characteristics such as how similar the objects in the problem were. Thus, two problems that included inclined planes were grouped together, even though the physical principles involved in the problems were quite different.

The expert, in contrast, sorted problems based on structural features, such as general principles of physics. The expert perceived two problems as similar because they both involved the principle of conservation of energy, even though the diagrams indicate that one problem involved a spring and another an inclined plane. Thus, novices categorized problems based on their surface features (what the objects looked like) and the experts categorized them based on their deep structure (the underlying principles involved). As it turns out, organizing based on principles results in more effective problem solving, and experts' ability to organize knowledge has been found to be important not only for chess masters and physics professors, but for experts in many other fields as well (Egan & Schwartz, 1979; Reitman, 1976).

EXPERTS SPEND MORE TIME ANALYZING PROBLEMS Experts often get off to what appears to be a slow start on a problem, because they spend time trying to understand the problem rather than immediately trying to solve it (Lesgold, 1988). Although this may slow them down at the beginning, this strategy usually pays off in a more effective approach to the problem.

EXPERTISE IS ONLY AN ADVANTAGE IN THE EXPERT'S SPECIALTY

Although there are many differences between experts and novices, it appears that these differences hold only when problems are within an expert's field. When James Voss and coworkers (1983) posed a real-world problem involving Russian agriculture to expert political scientists, expert chemists, and novice political scientists, they found that the expert political scientists performed best and that the expert chemists performed as poorly as the novice political scientists. In general, experts are experts only within their own field and perform like anyone else outside of their field (Bedard & Chi, 1992). This makes sense when we remember that the superior performance of experts occurs largely because they possess a larger and better organized store of knowledge about their specific field.

Before leaving our discussion of expertise, we should note that being an expert is not always an advantage. One disadvantage is that knowing about the established facts and theories in a field may make experts less open to new ways of looking at problems. This may be why younger and less experienced scientists in a field are often the ones responsible for revolutionary discoveries (Kuhn, 1970; Simonton, 1984). Thus, it has been suggested that being an expert may be a disadvantage when confronting a problem that requires flexible thinking—a problem whose solution may involve rejecting the usual procedures in favor of other procedures that might not normally be used (Frensch & Sternberg, 1989).

Creative Problem Solving

There's a story about a physics student who, in answer to the exam question "Describe how the height of a building can be measured using a barometer," wrote "Attach the barometer to a string and lower it from the top of the building. The length of string needed to lower the barometer to the ground indicates the height of the building." The professor was looking for an answer that involved measuring barometric pressure on the ground and on top of the building, using principles learned in class. He therefore gave the student a zero for his answer.

The student protested the grade, so the case was given to another professor, who asked the student to provide an answer that would demonstrate his knowledge of physics. The student's answer was to drop the barometer from the roof and measure how long it took to hit the ground. Using a formula involving the gravitational constant would enable one to determine how far the barometer fell. With further prodding from the appeals professor, the student also suggested another solution: Put the barometer in the sun and measure the length of its shadow and the length of the building's shadow. The height of the building could then be determined using proportions.

Upon hearing these answers, both of which could result in correct solutions, the appeals professor asked the student whether he knew the answer the professor was looking for, which involved the principle of barometric pressure. The student replied that he did, but he was tired of just repeating back information to get a good grade. A footnote to this story is that the student was Niels Bohr, who, after his college career, went on to win a Nobel Prize in Physics (Lubart & Mouchiroud, 2003).

This story illustrates that being too creative can get you into trouble. But it also poses a question. Was the student being creative? The answer is "yes" if we define creativity as producing original answers, or as being able to come up with multiple solutions to a problem. But some creativity researchers have proposed definitions of creativity that go beyond originality.

WHAT IS CREATIVITY?

Creativity is one of those terms, like intelligence, for which many definitions have been proposed. Many examples of creativity focus on **divergent thinking**—thinking that is open-ended, involving a large number of potential "solutions" (although some proposals might work better than others; see Guilford, 1956; Ward et al., 1997). James Kaufman (2009), in his book *Creativity 101*, notes that divergent thinking is the cornerstone of creativity, but it is not all that creativity can be. Kaufman proposes that in addition to being original, a creative response to a problem must be useful. This approach to creativity is captured in the definition of creativity as "anything made by people that is in some way novel and has potential value or utility" (Smith et al., 2009). This definition works well, especially when considering creativity in designing products for people to use. It doesn't do as well in describing the creativity involved in creating visual art, music, or theater. Is a Picasso painting, a Beethoven symphony, or a play by Shakespeare creative? Most people would say yes, without any consideration of "usefulness." But for the purposes of our discussion, we will focus on Smith's definition, in which creativity is applied to creating new things that are useful. We begin by considering some examples of how some practical products were invented.

PRACTICAL CREATIVITY

Many examples of how inventions were created involve analogical thinking, in which observing a phenomenon has led to a new, novel, and useful solution to a practical problem.

EXAMPLES OF CREATIVE ANALOGICAL PROBLEM SOLVING A famous example of an invention that resulted from analogical problem solving is the story of George de Mestral, who in 1948 went for a nature hike with his dog and returned home with burrs covering his pants and the dog's fur. To discover why the burrs were clinging so tenaciously, de Mestral inspected the burrs under a microscope. What he saw were many tiny hook-like structures, which led him to design a fabric fastener with many small hooks on one side and soft loops on the other side. In 1955 he patented his design and called it Velcro!

A more recent example of a creative idea based on analogical thinking is the case of Jorge Odón, an Argentine car mechanic, who designed a device to deal with the life-threatening situation of a baby stuck in the birth canal during delivery. The beginnings of Odón's design can be traced to viewing a YouTube video that demonstrated how to remove a cork that had been pushed inside a wine bottle (see DvorakUncensored, 2007). The procedure involves slipping a plastic bag into the bottle, and blowing up the bag until it pushes the cork to the side of the bottle (**Figure 12.19a**). When the bag is pulled out, the cork comes with it.

The jump from the "removing a cork from a bottle trick" on YouTube to a way to save a baby stuck in the birth canal came to Odón as he slept. He woke at 4 AM with an idea for a device using the same principle: Inflate a bag inside the uterus and pull the bag out, bringing the baby with it. The process of translating this idea into a working model took years. Odón started by building a prototype device in his kitchen, using a glass jar for the womb, a doll for the baby, and a fabric bag as the extraction device. Eventually, after many different prototypes and numerous consultations with obstetricians, the Odón device was born! A plastic bag inside a lubricated sleeve is placed around the baby's head, the bag is inflated, and the bag is pulled out, bringing the baby with it (**Figure 12.19b**; McNeil, 2013; Venema, 2013).

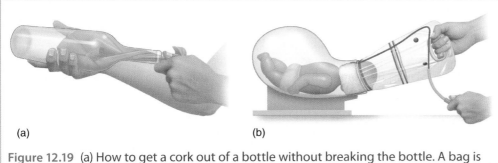

(a)   (b)

Figure 12.19 (a) How to get a cork out of a bottle without breaking the bottle. A bag is pushed into the bottle and inflated; when it is removed, the cork comes with it. (b) The prototype of Odón's device for getting a stuck baby out of the birth canal. For the prototype, Odón used a doll for the baby and a glass container to represent the womb. © 2015 Cengage Learning

The Odón device has been endorsed by the World Health Organization and has the potential for saving babies in poor countries and to reduce cesarean section births in rich ones. It is an example of analogical thinking applied to creative problem solving that resulted in a truly useful product (and also demonstrates that watching YouTube videos can be productive!).

PROBLEM SOLVING AS A PROCESS   The examples of Velcro and the Odón device not only illustrate creative problem solving but also demonstrate that most creative problem solving includes far more than just getting an idea. It also involves a lengthy period of trial-and-error development to turn the idea into a useful device. Odón's device took years to develop, and although de Mestral observed the burrs sticking to his dog in 1948, he didn't patent Velcro until 1955.

Many researchers have proposed the idea that creative problem solving involves a *process*. One proposal, illustrated in **Figure 12.20**, conceives of creative problem solving as a four-stage process that begins with generation of the problem and ends with implementation of the solution (Basadur et al., 2000). If one thinks of problem solving in this way, then one of the most important steps is realizing that there is a problem in the first place, which then leads to ideas, which are evaluated and eventually turned into a product (also see Finke, 1990; Mumford et al., 2012).

Another example of problem solving that involved a long process was the Wright brothers' invention of the airplane (Weisberg, 2009). Their design, which culminated in a successful flight at Kitty Hawk in December 1903, was the culmination of four years of effort in which they had to focus on how to design each component of the airplane, with special emphasis on developing a mechanism to steer the plane.

The Wright brothers example also illustrates that problem solving is not simply about getting an idea in a flash of insight, although that may happen, but about having a base of knowledge that makes the idea possible. The Wright brothers were successful because their knowledge of physics and mechanics, plus their extensive experience with bicycles in their bicycle repair shop, provided a basis for their creative ideas about how to combine a number of components to create an airplane.

Although generating ideas is only one part of the creative process, without ideas the process stops. We will now consider how some principles of cognition have been applied to understanding some of the factors responsible for generating creative ideas.

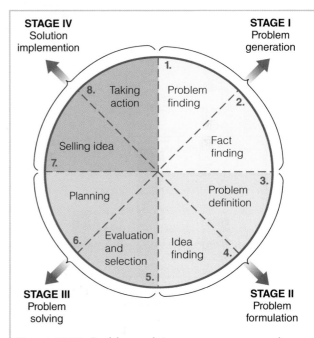

Figure 12.20 Problem solving process proposed by Basadur et al. (2000). Basadur proposes four steps, each of which is divided into two processes. For example, Stage II, problem formulation, consists of two steps: defining the problem and finding ideas. *(Source: Based on M. Basadur, M. Runco, & L. A. Vega, Understanding how creative thinking skills, attitudes and behaviors work together: A causal process model. Journal of Creative Behavior, 34, 77–100, 2000.)*

GENERATING IDEAS

When Linus Pauling, who won the Nobel Prize in Chemistry in 1914, was asked how he got ideas, he replied, "If you want to have good ideas you must have many ideas. Most of them will be wrong, and what you have to learn is which ones to throw away" (Crick, 1995). This answer emphasizes the importance of ideas for scientific discovery, as well as the importance of what occurs after ideas happen.

The question "What leads to ideas?" is difficult to answer because so many different factors are involved. The example of the Wright brothers illustrates that ideas depend on having a base of knowledge. And de Mestral, who was an engineer, knew enough to look at the burrs that his dog brought home under a microscope in order to reveal the hook-like structure that led to the idea for Velcro.

But as important as knowledge is, sometimes too much knowledge can hinder creative problem solving. We noted at the end of the section on expertise that being an expert in a field may be a disadvantage when working on a problem that requires thinking flexibly and rejecting accepted procedures. This is exactly what happened in the case of Odón's invention. Although he had patented a number of inventions, they were for devices related to automobiles, like stabilization bars and car suspensions. It may be no coincidence that an auto mechanic, and not a doctor, developed a device for birthing. As one of the doctors who had worked with Odón said, "Doctors are very structured in their thinking and Jorge is a free mind, he can think of new things" (Venema, 2013). It is perhaps fortunate that Odón didn't have too much knowledge about medicine.

How too much knowledge can be a bad thing was demonstrated in an experiment by Steven Smith and coworkers (1993), who showed that providing examples to people before they solve a problem can influence the nature of their solutions. Smith's subjects were given the task of inventing, sketching, labeling, and describing new and creative toys, or new life forms that might evolve on a planet like Earth. One group of subjects was presented with three examples before they began working on the problem. For the life-form-generation task, all three examples had four legs, an antenna, and a tail.

Compared with the life forms created by a control group that had not seen any examples, the designs generated by the example group incorporated many more of the example features (**Figure 12.21a**). **Figure 12.21b** indicates the proportion of the designs that included example features (antennae, tail, and four legs) for the two groups. The greater use of these features by the example group is related to the idea of functional fixedness, described earlier in the chapter. Sometimes preconceptions can inhibit creativity.

This idea, that preconceptions can inhibit creativity, led Alex Osborn (1953) to propose the technique of **group brainstorming**. The purpose of this technique is to encourage people to freely express ideas that might be useful in solving a particular problem. Instructions given to participants in brainstorming groups emphasize that they should just say whatever ideas come into their mind, without being critical of their own ideas or of the ideas of others in the group. The basis of these instructions is to increase creativity by opening people to "think outside the box."

This proposal has led to the widespread use of brainstorming in organizations. However, research has shown that placing people in groups to share ideas results in fewer ideas than adding up the ideas generated by the same number of

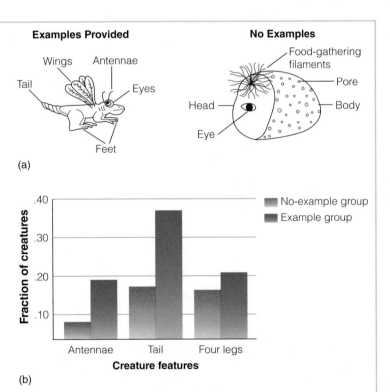

Figure 12.21 Two life forms created by subjects in the Smith et al. (1993) experiment. (a) Subjects who were provided with examples designed life forms that had characteristics that were included in the examples. (b) Proportion of life forms with antennae, tails, and four legs. Subjects in the example group were more likely to include these features. *(Source: Based on S. M. Smith, A. Kerne, E. Koh, & J. Shah, The development and evaluation of tools for creativity, in A. B. Markman & K. L. Wood, Eds., Tools for innovation, pp. 128–152, Figure 8, Oxford, UK: Oxford University Press, 2009.)*

people asked to think of ideas individually (Mullen et al., 1991). This occurs for a number of reasons. In groups, some people may dominate the discussion so others aren't able to participate. Also, despite the instructions to express any idea that comes to mind, being in a group can inhibit some people from expressing their ideas, possibly because they are afraid they will be judged. People also may be paying attention to others in the group, which keeps them from coming up with ideas of their own. Brainstorming in groups therefore turns out not to be a good way to generate ideas. Individual brainstorming to generate ideas, however, can be effective.

One method of individual idea generation that does work has been proposed by Ronald Finke, who developed a technique called **creative cognition** to train people to think creatively. The following demonstration illustrates Finke's technique.

DEMONSTRATION
CREATING AN OBJECT
Figure 12.22 shows 15 object parts and their names. Close your eyes and touch the page three times to randomly pick three of the object parts. After reading these instructions, take 1 minute to construct a new object using these three parts. The object should be interesting-looking and possibly useful, but try to avoid making your object correspond to a familiar object, and don't worry what it might be used for. You can vary the size, position, orientation, and material of the parts, as long as you don't alter the basic shape (except for the wire and the tube, which can be bent). Once you come up with something in your mind, draw a picture of it.

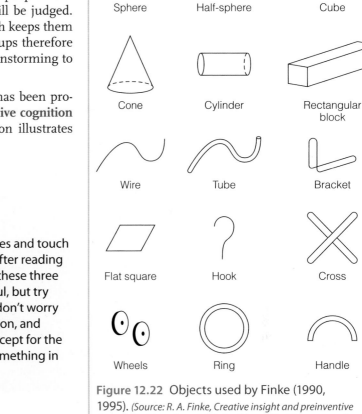

Figure 12.22 Objects used by Finke (1990, 1995). *(Source: R. A. Finke, Creative insight and preinventive forms, in R. J. Sternberg & J. E. Davidson, Eds., The nature of insight, pp. 255–280, Figure 8.1, Cambridge, MA: MIT Press, 1995.)*

This exercise is patterned after one devised by Finke (1990, 1995), who randomly selected three of the object parts from **Figure 12.22** for his subjects. After the subjects had created an object, they were provided with the name of one of the object categories from **Table 12.3** and were given 1 minute to interpret their object. For example, if the category was tools and utensils, the person had to interpret his or her form as

Table 12.3: Object Categories in Preinventive Form Studies

CATEGORIES	EXAMPLES
1. Furniture	Chairs, tables, lamps
2 Personal items	Jewelry, glasses
3. Scientific instruments	Measuring devices
4. Appliances	Washing machines, toasters
5. Transportation	Cars, boats
6. Tools and utensils	Screwdrivers, spoons
7. Toys and games	Baseball bats, dolls
8. Weapons	Guns, missiles

Source: Adapted from R. A. Finke, Creative insight and preinventive forms, in R. J. Sternberg & J. E. Davidson (Eds.), *The nature of insight,* pp. 255–280 (Cambridge, MA: MIT Press, 1995).

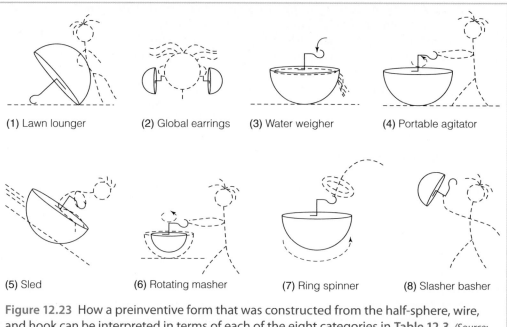

(1) Lawn lounger   (2) Global earrings   (3) Water weigher   (4) Portable agitator

(5) Sled   (6) Rotating masher   (7) Ring spinner   (8) Slasher basher

Figure 12.23 How a preinventive form that was constructed from the half-sphere, wire, and hook can be interpreted in terms of each of the eight categories in **Table 12.3.** *(Source: R. A. Finke, Creative insight and preinventive forms, in R. J. Sternberg & J. E. Davidson, Eds., The nature of insight, pp. 255–280, Figure 8.6, Cambridge, MA: MIT Press, 1995.)*

a screwdriver, a spoon, or some other tool or utensil. To do this for your form, pick a category, and then decide what your object could be used for and describe how it functions. **Figure 12.23** shows how a single form that was constructed from the half-sphere, wire, and hook could be interpreted in terms of each of the eight categories in **Table 12.3.**

Finke called these "inventions" **preinventive forms** because they are ideas that precede the creation of a finished creative product. Just as it took de Mestral years to develop Velcro after his initial insight, preinventive forms need to be developed further before becoming useful "inventions."

In an experiment in which subjects created 360 objects, a panel of judges rated 120 of these objects as being "practical inventions" (the objects received high ratings for "practicality") and rated 65 as "creative inventions" (they received high ratings for both practicality and originality; Finke, 1990, 1995). Remarkably, Finke's subjects had received no training or practice, were not preselected for "creativity," and were not even told they were expected to be creative.

Finke demonstrated not only that you don't have to be an "inventor" to be creative, but also that many of the processes that occur during creative cognition are similar to cognitive process from other areas of cognitive psychology. For example, Finke found that people were more likely to come up with creative uses for preinventive objects that they had created themselves than for objects created by other people. This occurred even though subjects were instructed not to consider uses for the forms as they were creating them. This result is similar to the generation effect we discussed in Chapter 7: People remember material better when they generate it themselves (page 182). This advantage for self-generated material also occurs for retrieval cues (page 189).

The idea behind individual brainstorming and Finke's creative cognition technique—to keep the mind open—is to avoid fixations that limit creativity. Although these basic principles—"Open your mind. Avoid fixation."—are easy to state, they don't come easily to some people. But there are people who are especially creative because they are able to open their minds. Why does this occur? According to some researchers, their ability can be traced to personal characteristics that make them less likely to get stuck in old ideas and more open to new ones.

Something to Consider

CREATIVITY, MENTAL ILLNESS, AND THE OPEN MIND

Do especially creative people have characteristics that distinguish them from other people? One proposal is that highly creative people are more prone to mental illness. Some evidence supports this idea, especially with regard to bipolar disorder and psychotic conditions such as schizophrenia (Carson, 2011). However, a recent study that used health and occupational data from more than a million Swedish citizens concluded that individuals in creative professions, such as researchers and artists, were not more likely than the general population to suffer from psychiatric disorders. (One exception was professional writers, who did have a higher risk of having schizophrenia and bipolar disorder.)

Despite the lack of relationship between creative professions and mental disorders, one particularly interesting result of the Swedish study was that close relatives (parents and siblings) of people with schizophrenia, schizoaffective disorder (a mixture of schizophrenic and mood disorder symptoms), and bipolar disorder, who were not themselves diagnosed with a disorder, had a higher than average chance of being in a creative profession (Kyaga et al., 2013). Other research has also shown that creativity and schizophrenia-like symptoms run in families (Brod, 1997; Prentky, 1989), and close relatives of people with bipolar disorder, who were not themselves diagnosed as having the disorder, scored higher on creativity tests (Richards et al., 1988). This suggests a genetically determined trait that is associated both with mental illness and with creativity.

One trait that seems to be related to both mental illness and creativity is **latent inhibition (LI)**. Latent inhibition is the capacity to screen out stimuli that are considered irrelevant. Everyone has this property; it is one of the mechanisms that keep us from being overwhelmed by the huge number of stimuli that bombard us every day. Think, for example, of all the stimuli that are present as you walk down a city street or across campus. There are people, buildings, perhaps birds, signs, cars, various sounds, and maybe even a few hundred ants whose universe is inside a crack in the sidewalk beneath your feet. Because it would be overwhelming to try to take in all of these stimuli, you focus on what is important at a particular time and shift where you are looking from one place, object, or sound source to another. However, the ability to filter out irrelevant stimuli is impaired in some people with mental illness. Thus, one of the hallmarks of schizophrenia is being bombarded with an overwhelming flow of incoming information.

The link between LI and creativity is that *reduced* LI is associated both with mental illness and with enhanced creativity (Carson, 2011). Reduced LI is associated with being more open to stimuli that would ordinarily be ignored and is often associated with higher levels of the personality trait "openness to experience." This ability to "open the mind," which we mentioned in connection with the techniques of brainstorming and creative cognition, could potentially enhance creativity.

To test the idea of a relationship between LI and creativity in people without mental illness, Shelly Carson and coworkers (2003) had students fill out questionnaires that measured (1) their creative achievement score—their level of producing creative products in art and science, such as exhibiting a painting in a juried art show or being one of the authors of a published scientific paper; and (2) their level of latent inhibition. The results, shown in **Figure 12.24**, indicate that subjects with low LI had higher creative achievement scores. This relationship was especially strong in students with high IQs. So, openness to experience combined with intelligence is associated with high creative output.

Based on results such as these (also see Peterson & Carson, 2000), Carson (2011) concluded that reduced LI enhances creativity by increasing the unfiltered stimuli available to conscious awareness, which increases the possibility of creating useful and novel combinations of stimuli. Carson (2010) concludes that creativity can be enhanced when some of the characteristics of people with mental disorders are present in small doses.

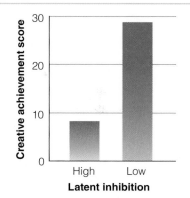

Figure 12.24 Results of Carson et al.'s (2003) experiment showing that students with lower latent inhibition (LI) had greater numbers of creative achievements. This relationship held for students with high IQs. *(Source: Based on S. H. Carson, J. B. Peterson, & D. M. Higgins, Decreased latent inhibition is associated with increased creative achievement in high-functioning individuals, Journal of Personality and Social Psychology, 85, 499–506, 2003.)*

Figure 12.25
Display for the nine-dot problem. See text for instructions.

© 2015 Cengage Learning

The connection between openness to stimuli and mental illness led Alan Snyder (2009) to consider what another type of disorder can tell us about creativity. Snyder considered the **savant syndrome**, in which people with autism or other mental disorders are able to achieve extraordinary feats, such as being able to tell the day of the week for any randomly picked date, or exhibit great artistic talent or mathematical ability. An example of a person with savant syndrome was depicted in the film *Rain Man* (1988), starring Dustin Hoffman.

Snyder proposes that these savant skills reside within everyone but are not normally accessible to conscious awareness. Savants, he suggests, are open to information in the brain that is normally hidden from conscious awareness because of what he calls *top-down inhibition*. Is there a way, wondered Snyder, that this inhibition can be reduced in normally functioning individuals?

Based on the fact that the savant syndrome is often associated with damage to the anterior temporal lobe (ATL; see **Figure 9.26**), Snyder proposed that deactivating the ATL might open people to different ways of perceiving stimuli. To test this idea, Richard Chi and Snyder (2011, 2012) presented normally functioning subjects with the nine-dot problem shown in **Figure 12.25**. The task in this problem is to draw four straight lines that pass through all nine dots, without lifting your pen from the paper or retracing a line. Stop now and try it. Then check the answer in **Figure 12.30** at the end of the chapter.

If you solved the problem, you are in the minority, because most people perceive the nine dots as a square and do not consider the possibility of extending the lines outside the square. None of Chi and Snyder's subjects were able to solve the problem, but when their ATL was deactivated by transcranial magnetic stimulation (see page 270), 40 percent of the subjects were able to solve the problem. This matches the 40 percent who can solve the problem if they are told that the solution involves drawing lines outside the square.

Chi and Snyder concluded that we find the problem difficult because our brains are wired to interpret the world in certain ways, based on past experience. In the nine-dot problem, Gestalt grouping principles (see page 64) cause us to perceive the nine dots as a square. In order to think "outside the box" (or "outside the square" in this case), we need to break free of our normal way of perceiving. This idea is consistent with the research we just described on latent inhibition, which also demonstrates a relationship between mechanisms that open the mind and creativity.

While our discussion of the connection between openness and creativity may be interesting and provide insight into one of the mechanisms underlying creativity, you may wonder whether it is relevant to you. After all, you don't have the option of creating a more open mind by changing your genetic heritage or by having your ATL deactivated. However, there are procedures that have been developed to achieve a more open mind. We described Finke's creative cognition procedure earlier; other techniques are described in Shelly Carson's (2010) book, *Your Creative Brain*.

TEST YOURSELF 12.2

1. What is the basic idea behind analogical problem solving? What is the source problem? The target problem? How effective is it to present a source problem and then the target problem, without indicating that the two are related?

2. Describe Duncker's radiation problem. What is the solution, and how have researchers used this problem to illustrate analogical problem solving?

3. What are the three steps in the process of analogical problem solving? Which of the steps appears to be the most difficult to achieve?

4. How do the surface features and structural features of problems influence a person's ability to make effective use of analogies in problem solving? Describe the lightbulb experiments and what they demonstrated.

5. What is analogical encoding? The analogical paradox? How has analogical problem solving been studied in the real world?

6. What is an expert? What are some differences between the way experts and nonexperts go about solving problems? How good are experts at solving problems outside of their field?

7. Describe attempts to define creativity.

8. Describe analogical problem solving as illustrated by de Mestral's invention of Velcro and Odón's invention of a birthing device.

9. What does it mean to say that problem solving is a process?

10. Discuss the factors involved in generating ideas, including the role of knowledge, the use of brainstorming, and the creative cognition approach.

11. What is the relation between creativity and mental illness? What property is shared by creative people and people with mental illness? Why might this property increase creativity?

12. Describe Chi and Snyder's experiment using the nine-dot problem. What do the results indicate about why creativity is difficult?

CHAPTER SUMMARY

1. A problem occurs when there is an obstacle between a present state and a goal and it is not immediately obvious how to get around the obstacle.

2. The Gestalt psychologists focused on how people represent a problem in their mind. They devised a number of problems to illustrate how solving a problem involves a restructuring of this representation and to demonstrate factors that pose obstacles to problem solving.

3. The Gestalt psychologists introduced the idea that reorganization is associated with insight—a sudden realization of a problem's solution. Insight has been demonstrated experimentally by tracking how close people feel they are to solving insight and noninsight problems.

4. Functional fixedness is an obstacle to problem solving that is illustrated by Duncker's candle problem and Maier's two-string problem. Situationally produced mental set is illustrated by the Luchins water jug problem.

5. Alan Newell and Herbert Simon were early proponents of the information-processing approach to problem solving. They saw problem solving as the searching of a problem space to find the path between the statement of the problem (the initial state) and the solution to the problem (the goal state). This search is governed by operators and is usually accomplished by setting subgoals. The Tower of Hanoi problem has been used to illustrate this process.

6. Research on the mutilated checkerboard problem also illustrates the importance of how a problem is presented.

7. Newell and Simon developed the technique of think-aloud protocols to study subjects' thought process as they are solving a problem.

8. Analogical problem solving occurs when experience with a previously solved source problem or a source story is used to help solve a new target problem. Research involving Duncker's radiation problem has shown that even when people are exposed to analogous source problems or stories, most people do not make the connection between the source problem or story and the target problem.

9. Analogical problem solving is facilitated when hints are given regarding the relevance of the source problem, when the source and target problems have similar surface features, and when structural features are made more obvious. Analogical encoding is a process that helps people discover similar structural features.

10. The analogical paradox is that, while it is difficult to apply analogies in laboratory research, in vivo problem-solving research has shown that analogical problem solving is often used in real-world settings.

11. Experts are better than novices at solving problems in their field of expertise. They have more knowledge of the field, organize this knowledge based more on deep structure than on surface features, and spend more time analyzing a problem when it is first presented.

12. Creative problem solving is associated with divergent thinking. We have only a limited understanding of the

processes involved in creative problem solving and creativity in general. The examples of George de Mestral and Jorge Odón illustrate how analogy has been used to create practical inventions.

13. Creative problem solving has been described as a process that begins with generation of the problem and ends with implementation of the solution, with ideas happening in between.

14. The question of what leads to generation of ideas is a complicated one. Knowledge is often essential for generating ideas, but sometimes too much knowledge can be a bad thing, as illustrated by Smith's experiment showing that providing examples can inhibit creative design.

15. The technique of brainstorming has been proposed as a way to increase creativity, but generating ideas in groups is generally not as effective as generating ideas individually and combining them. The creative cognition technique has been successfully used to create innovative designs.

16. The relationship between mental illness and creativity is complicated. Some studies have demonstrated a relationship and others have not. One particularly interesting result is that close relatives of people with mental disorders tend to be more creative than average. This has led to the idea that there may be a genetically determined characteristic that is associated with both creativity and mental illness.

17. A reduction in latent inhibition has been associated both with mental illness and with creativity. Additionally, it has been demonstrated that deactivation of the anterior temporal cortex, which is damaged in people with the savant syndrome, can increase the ability to solve difficult problems.

THINK ABOUT IT

1. Pick a problem you have had to deal with, and analyze the process of solving it into subgoals, as is done in means–end analysis.

2. Have you ever experienced a situation in which you were trying to solve a problem but stopped working on it because you couldn't come up with the answer? Then, after a while, when you returned to the problem, you got the answer right away? What do you think might be behind this process?

3. On August 14, 2003, a power failure caused millions of people in the northeastern and midwestern United States and eastern Canada to lose their electricity. A few days later, after most people had their electricity restored, experts still did not know why the power failure had occurred and said it would take weeks to determine the cause. Imagine that you are a member of a special commission that has the task of solving this problem, or some other major problem. How could the processes described in this chapter be applied to finding a solution? What would the shortcomings of these processes be for solving this kind of problem?

4. Think of some examples of situations in which you overcame functional fixedness and found a new use for an object.

KEY TERMS

Analogical encoding, 353

Analogical paradox, 354

Analogical problem solving, 349

Analogical transfer, 349

Analogy, 349

Candle problem, 339

Creative cognition, 361

Divergent thinking, 358

Expert, 355

Fixation, 338

Functional fixedness, 338

Goal state, 341

Group brainstorming, 360

In vivo problem-solving research, 354

Initial state, 341

Insight, 337

Intermediate states, 342

Latent inhibition (LI), 363

Means–end analysis, 343

Mental set, 340

Mutilated checkerboard problem, 346

Operators, 341

Preinventive forms, 362

Problem, 336

Solutions to Problems on Pages 337–339

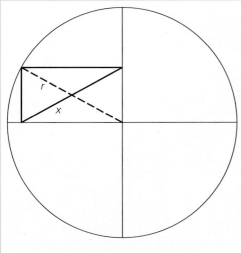

Solution: The length of the line *x* is *r*.

Figure 12.26 Solution to the circle problem. Note that the length of *x* is the same as the radius, *r*, because *x* and *r* are both diagonals of the rectangle. © Cengage Learning

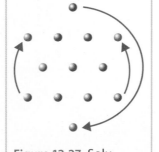

Figure 12.27 Solution to the triangle problem. Arrows indicate movement; colored circles indicate new positions. © Cengage Learning

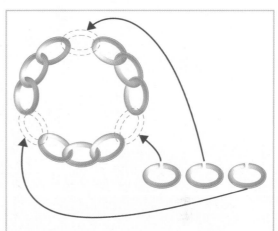

Figure 12.28 Solution to the chain problem. All the links in one chain are cut and separated (3 cuts @ 2 cents = 6 cents). The separated links are then used to connect the other three pieces and then closed (3 closings @ 3 cents = 9 cents). Total = 15 cents. © Cengage Learning

Figure 12.29 Solution to the candle problem. © Cengage Learning

Solution to Problem on Page 364

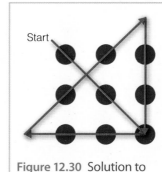

Start

Figure 12.30 Solution to the nine-dot problem.
© 2015 Cengage Learning

(top) Najlah Feanny/Corbis; (bottom) © Darryl Vest/Shutterstock.com

Here's something to think about: One male is selected randomly from the population of the United States. That male, Robert, wears glasses, speaks quietly, and reads a lot. Is it more likely that Robert is a librarian or a farmer? This is one of the questions posed in an experiment we will discuss in this chapter. The way subjects answered this question, plus the results of many other experiments in which people were asked to make judgments, has helped us understand the mental processes involved in making judgments. This chapter also considers the mental processes involved in the closely related topics of decision making and reasoning.

Judgment, Decisions, and Reasoning

SOME QUESTIONS WE
WILL CONSIDER

▶ What kinds of reasoning "traps"
do people get into when making
judgments? (373)

▶ What is the evidence that
people sometimes make
decisions that are not in their
best interests? (378)

▶ How do emotions influence
decision making? (381)

▶ Are there two ways of thinking,
one fast and the other slow?
(396)

The title of this chapter, "Judgment, Decisions, and Reasoning," makes it sound as though it is about three different things. We make judgments all the time: "I met John yesterday. He seems like a nice guy." We make **decisions**—the process of making choices between alternatives: "Whom should I invite to the party? How about John?" It's easy to see how making the decision to invite John may have been based on the judgment that he is a nice guy. The statement "John was wearing a Sierra Club jacket; he must care about the environment" represents **reasoning**—the process of drawing conclusions—because it involves coming to a conclusion based on evidence. Of course, the decision to invite John to the party may have involved reasoning too: "John is talkative. He will fit in well at the party."

We've been devoting a lot of attention to John to make a point: Even though we can distinguish between making judgments, making decisions, and reasoning based on evidence, they are all related. Decisions are based on judgments we make, and applying these judgments can involve various reasoning processes. We could, in fact, have called this chapter "Thinking," although that is too general because it also applies to material in many of the other chapters in this book. Our strategy in this chapter will be to describe judgment, decision making, and reasoning separately, while keeping in mind that they overlap and interact.

Making Judgments

We are constantly making judgments about things in our environment, including people, events, and behaviors. One of the primary mechanisms involved in making judgments is **inductive reasoning**, which is reasoning based on observations, or reaching conclusions from evidence.

THE NATURE OF INDUCTIVE REASONING

Inductive reasoning is the basis of scientific investigations in which observations are made, data are collected, and conclusions are drawn. One of the characteristics of inductive reasoning is that the conclusions we reach are *probably*, but not *definitely*, true. For example, concluding that John cares about the environment based on the observation that he is wearing a Sierra Club jacket makes sense. But it is also possible that he bought the jacket because he liked its style or color, or that he borrowed it from his brother. Thus, the conclusions we reach from inductive reasoning are suggested with various degrees of certainty but do not definitely follow from the observations. This is illustrated by the following two inductive arguments.

> *Observation*: All the crows I've seen in Pittsburgh are totally black. When I visited my brother in Washington, DC, the crows I saw there were black too.
> *Conclusion*: I think it is a pretty good bet that all crows are black.

> *Observation*: Here in Tucson, the sun has risen every morning.
> *Conclusion*: The sun is going to rise in Tucson tomorrow.

Notice there is a certain logic to each argument, but the second argument is more convincing than the first. Remember that inductive arguments lead to what is *probably* true, not what is *definitely* true. Strong inductive arguments result in conclusions that are more likely to be true, and weak arguments result in conclusions that are not as likely to be true. A number of factors can contribute to the strength of an inductive argument. Among them are the following:

- *Representativeness of observations.* How well do the observations about a particular category represent all of the members of that category? Clearly, the crows example suffers from a lack of representativeness because it does not consider crows from other parts of the country or the world.

- *Number of observations.* The argument about the crows is made stronger by adding the Washington, DC, observations to the Pittsburgh observations. However, as it turns out, further research reveals that the hooded crow, found in Europe, is gray with black wings and tail, and the home crow, from Asia, is gray and black. So it turns out that the conclusion "All crows are totally black" is not true. In contrast, the conclusion about the sun rising in Tucson is extremely strong because it is supported by a very large number of observations.

- *Quality of the evidence.* Stronger evidence results in stronger conclusions. For example, although the conclusion "The sun will rise in Tucson" is extremely strong because of the number of observations, it becomes even stronger when we consider scientific descriptions of how the earth rotates on its axis and revolves around the sun. Thus, adding the observation "Scientific measurements of the rotation of the earth indicate that every time the earth rotates the sun will appear to rise" strengthens the conclusion even further.

Although our examples of inductive reasoning have been "academic" in nature, we often use inductive reasoning in everyday life, usually without even realizing it. For example, Sarah observed in a course she took with Professor X that he asked a lot of questions about experimental procedures on his exams. Based on this observation, Sarah concludes that the exam she is about to take in another of Professor X's courses will probably be similar. In another example, Sam has bought merchandise from Internet company Y before and gotten good service, so he places another order based on the prediction that he will continue to get good service. Anytime we make a prediction about what *will happen* based on our observations about what *has happened* in the past, we are using inductive reasoning.

It makes sense that we make predictions and choices based on past experience, especially when predictions are based on familiar situations such as studying for an exam or buying merchandise over the Internet. We make so many assumptions about the world based on past experience that we are using inductive reasoning constantly, often without even realizing it. For example, did you run a stress test on the chair you are sitting in to be sure it wouldn't collapse when you sat down? Probably not. You assumed, based on your past experience with chairs, that it would not collapse. This kind of inductive reasoning is so automatic that you are not aware that any kind of "reasoning" is happening at all. Think about how time-consuming it would be if you had to approach every experience as if you were having it for the first time. Inductive reasoning provides the mechanism for using past experience to guide present behavior.

When people use past experience to guide present behavior, they often use shortcuts to help them reach conclusions rapidly. After all, we don't have the time or energy to stop and gather every bit of information that we need to be 100 percent certain that every conclusion we reach is correct. These shortcuts take the form of **heuristics**—"rules of thumb" that are likely to provide the correct answer to a problem but are not foolproof. People use a number of heuristics in reasoning that often lead to the correct conclusion but sometimes do not. We will now describe two of these heuristics, the *availability heuristic* and the *representative heuristic.*

THE AVAILABILITY HEURISTIC

The following demonstration introduces the availability heuristic.

DEMONSTRATION
WHICH IS MORE PREVALENT?

Answer the following questions:

- Which are more prevalent in English, words that begin with the letter *r* or words in which *r* is the third letter?

■ Some possible causes of death are listed below in pairs. Within each pair, which cause of death do you consider to be more likely for people in the United States? That is, if you randomly picked someone in the United States, would that person be more likely to die next year from cause A or cause B?

Cause A	Cause B
Homicide	Appendicitis
Auto–train collision	Drowning
Botulism	Asthma
Asthma	Tornado
Appendicitis	Pregnancy

When faced with a choice, we are often guided by what we remember from the past. The **availability heuristic** states that events that are more easily remembered are judged as being more probable than events that are less easily remembered (Tversky & Kahneman, 1973). Consider, for example, the problems we posed in the demonstration. When subjects were asked to judge whether there are more words with *r* in the first position or the third, 70 percent responded that more words begin with *r*, even though in reality three times more words have *r* in the third position (Tversky & Kahneman, 1973; but see also Gigerenzer & Todd, 1999).

Table 13.1 shows the results of an experiment in which subjects were asked to judge the relative prevalence of various causes of death (Lichtenstein et al., 1978). For each pair, the more likely cause of death is listed in the left column. The number in parentheses indicates the relative frequency of the more likely cause compared to the less likely cause. For example, 20 times more people die of homicide than die of appendicitis. The number on the right indicates the percentage of subjects who picked the less likely alternative. For example, 9 percent of subjects thought it was more likely that a person would die from appendicitis than as a result of homicide. In this case, therefore, a large majority of people, 91 percent, correctly picked homicide as causing more deaths. However, for the other causes of death, a substantial proportion of subjects misjudged their relative likelihood. In these cases, large numbers of errors were associated with causes that had been publicized by the media. For example, 58 percent thought that more deaths were caused by tornados than by asthma, when in reality, 20 times more people die from asthma than from tornados. Particularly striking is the finding that 41 percent of subjects thought botulism caused more deaths than asthma, even though 920 times more people die of asthma.

The explanation for these misjudgments appears linked to availability. When you try to think of words that begin with *r* or that have *r* in the third position, it is much easier to think

Table 13.1: Causes of Death

MORE LIKELY	LESS LIKELY	PERCENT PICKING LESS LIKELY
Homicide (20)	Appendicitis	9
Drowning (5)	Auto–train collision	34
Asthma (920)	Botulism	41
Asthma (20)	Tornado	58
Appendicitis (2)	Pregnancy	83

Source: Adapted from S. Lichtenstein, P. Slovic, B. Fischoff, M. Layman, & B. Combs, Judged frequency of lethal events, *Journal of Experimental Psychology: Human Learning and Memory, 4,* 551–578 (1978).

of words that begin with *r* (*run, rain, real*) than words that have *r* in their third position (*word, car, arranged*). When people die of botulism or in a tornado, it is front-page news, whereas deaths from asthma go virtually unnoticed by the general public (Lichtenstein et al., 1978).

This example illustrates how the availability heuristic can mislead us into reaching the wrong conclusion when less frequently occurring events stand out in our memory. The availability heuristic doesn't always lead to errors, however, because there are many situations in which we remember events that actually do occur frequently. For example, you might know from past observations that when it is cloudy and there is a certain smell in the air, it is likely to rain later in the day. Or you may have noticed that your boss is more likely to grant your requests when he or she is in a good mood.

Although observing correlations between events can be useful, sometimes people fall into the trap of creating illusory correlations. **Illusory correlations** occur when a correlation between two events appears to exist, but in reality there is no correlation or it is much weaker than it is assumed to be. Illusory correlations can occur when we expect two things to be related, so we fool ourselves into thinking they are related even when they are not. These expectations may take the form of a **stereotype**—an oversimplified generalization about a group or class of people that often focuses on the negative. A stereotype about the characteristics of a particular group may lead people to pay particular attention to behaviors associated with that stereotype, and this attention creates an illusory correlation that reinforces the stereotype. This phenomenon is related to the availability heuristic because selective attention to the stereotypical behaviors makes these behaviors more "available" (Chapman & Chapman, 1969; Hamilton, 1981).

We can appreciate how illusory correlations reinforce stereotypes by considering the stereotype that all gay males are effeminate. A person who believes this stereotype might pay particular attention to gay characters on TV programs or in movies, and to situations in which they see a person who they know is gay acting effeminate. Although these observations support a correlation between being gay and being effeminate, the person has ignored the large number of cases in which gay males are not effeminate. This may be because the person doesn't know about these cases or because the person chooses not to pay attention to them. Whatever the reason, selectively taking into account only the situations that support the person's preconceptions can create the illusion that a correlation exists, when there may be only a weak correlation or none at all.

THE REPRESENTATIVENESS HEURISTIC

While the availability heuristic is related to how *often* we expect events to occur, the representativeness heuristic is related to the idea that people often make judgments based on how much one event *resembles* another event.

MAKING JUDGMENTS BASED ON RESEMBLANCE The **representativeness heuristic** states that the probability that A is a member of class B can be determined by how well the properties of A resembles the properties we usually associate with class B. To put this in more concrete terms, consider the following demonstration.

DEMONSTRATION
JUDGING OCCUPATIONS

We randomly pick one male from the population of the United States. That male, Robert, wears glasses, speaks quietly, and reads a lot. Is it more likely that Robert is a librarian or a farmer?

When Amos Tversky and Daniel Kahneman (1974) presented this question in an experiment, more people guessed that Robert was a librarian. Apparently the description of Robert as wearing glasses, speaking quietly, and reading a lot matched these people's image of a typical librarian (see illusory correlations, above, and the chapter opening illustration on page 368). Thus, they were influenced by the fact that the description of Robert matches their conception of what a librarian is like. However, they were ignoring another important source of information—the base rates of farmers and librarians in the population. The **base rate** is the relative proportion of different classes in the population. In 1972, when this experiment was carried out, there were many more male farmers than male librarians in the United States, so if Robert was randomly chosen from the population, it is much more likely that he was a farmer. (Note that this base rate difference still holds. In 2008, there were more than 10 times as many male farmers as male librarians.)

One reaction to the farmer–librarian problem might be that perhaps the subjects were not aware of the base rates for farmers and librarians, so they didn't have the information they needed to make a correct judgment. The effect of knowing the base rate has been demonstrated by presenting subjects with the following problem:

> In a group of 100 people, there are 70 lawyers and 30 engineers. What is the chance that if we pick one person from the group at random that the person will be an engineer?

Subjects given this problem correctly guessed that there would be a 30 percent chance of picking an engineer. However, for some subjects, the following description of the person who was picked was added to the above statement about base rate information:

> Jack is a 45-year-old man. He is married and has four children. He is generally conservative, careful, and ambitious. He shows no interest in political and social issues and spends most of his free time on his many hobbies, which include home carpentry, sailing, and mathematical puzzles.

Adding this description caused subjects to greatly increase their estimate of the chances that the randomly picked person (Jack, in this case) was an engineer. Apparently, when only base rate information is available, people use that information to make their estimates. However, when any descriptive information is available, people disregard the base rate information, and this can potentially cause errors in reasoning. Note, however, that the right kind of descriptive information can increase the accuracy of a judgment. For example, if the description of Jack also noted that his last job involved determining the structural characteristics of a bridge, then this would greatly increases the chances that he was, in fact, an engineer. Thus, just as it is important to pay attention to base rate information, the information provided by descriptions can also be useful if it is relevant. When such information is available, then applying the representativeness heuristic can lead to correct judgments.

MAKING JUDGMENTS WITHOUT CONSIDERING THE CONJUNCTION RULE The following demonstration illustrates another characteristic of the representativeness heuristic.

DEMONSTRATION
DESCRIPTION OF A PERSON

Linda is 31 years old, single, outspoken, and very bright. She majored in philosophy. As a student, she was deeply concerned with issues of discrimination and social justice, and also participated in antinuclear demonstrations. Which of the following alternatives is more probable?

1. Linda is a bank teller.
2. Linda is a bank teller and is active in the feminist movement.

The correct answer to this problem is that Statement 1 has a greater probability of being true, but when Tversky and Kahneman (1983) posed this problem to their subjects, 85 percent picked Statement 2. It is easy to see why they did this. They were influenced by the representativeness heuristic, because the description of Linda fits people's idea of a typical feminist. However, in doing this they violated the **conjunction rule**, which states that the probability of a conjunction of two events (A and B) cannot be higher than the probability of the single constituents (A alone or B alone). Because there are more bank tellers (A) than feminist bank tellers (B), stating that Linda is a bank teller *includes* the possibility that she is a feminist bank teller (**Figure 13.1**). Similarly, the probability that Anne has a *red* Corvette cannot be greater than the probability that she has a Corvette because the two constituents together (Corvette *and* red) define a smaller number of cars than one constituent (Corvette) alone.

People tend to violate the conjunction rule even when it is clear that they understand it. The culprit is the representativeness heuristic. In the example just cited, the subjects saw Linda's characteristics as more representative of "feminist bank teller" than "bank teller."

INCORRECTLY ASSUMING THAT SMALL SAMPLES ARE REPRESENTATIVE People also make errors in reasoning by ignoring the importance of the size of the sample on which observations are based. The following demonstration illustrates the effect of sample size.

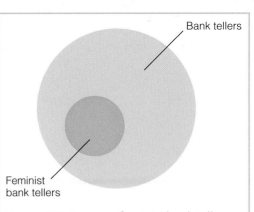

Figure 13.1 Because feminist bank tellers are a subset of bank tellers, it is always more likely that someone is a bank teller than a feminist bank teller. © Cengage Learning

DEMONSTRATION
MALE AND FEMALE BIRTHS

A certain town is served by two hospitals. In the larger hospital about 45 babies are born each day, and in the smaller hospital about 15 babies are born each day. As you know, about 50 percent of all babies are boys. However, the exact percentage varies from day to day. Sometimes it may be higher than 50 percent, sometimes lower. For a period of 1 year, each hospital recorded the days on which more than 60 percent of the babies born were boys. Which hospital do you think recorded more such days?

- The larger hospital?
- The smaller hospital?
- About the same

When subjects were asked this question in an experiment (Tversky & Kahneman, 1974), 22 percent picked the larger hospital, 22 percent picked the smaller hospital, and 56 percent stated that there would be no difference. The group that thought there would be no difference was presumably assuming that the birthrate for males and females in both hospitals would be representative of the overall birthrate for males and females. However, the correct answer is that there would be more days with over 60 percent male births in the small hospital. (And if the question had been about girls, there would also be more days with over 60 percent female births in the small hospital.)

We can understand why this result would occur by considering a statistical rule called the **law of large numbers**, which states that the larger the number of individuals that are randomly drawn from a population, the more representative the resulting group will be of the entire population. Conversely, samples of small numbers of individuals will be less representative of the population. Thus, in the hospital problem it is more likely that the percentage of boys or girls born on any given day will be near 50 percent in the large hospital and farther from 50 percent in the small hospital. To make this conclusion clear, imagine that there is a very small hospital that records only one birth each day. Over a period of a year there will be 365 births, with about 50 percent being boys and 50 percent being girls. However, on any given day, there will be either 100 percent boys or 100 percent girls—clearly percentages that are not representative of the overall population. People often assume that representativeness holds for small samples, and this results in errors in reasoning. (See Gigerenzer & Hoffrage, 1995; Gigerenzer & Todd, 1999, for additional perspectives on how statistical thinking and heuristics operate in reasoning.)

PRECONCEPTIONS, ATTITUDES, AND JUDGMENT

We've seen that the reasoning involved in making judgments may sometimes be in error because we are seduced by various heuristics that lead us to ignore some evidence and reach faulty conclusions. Another influence on judgment is the knowledge, attitudes, and preconceptions that people bring to the situation. Consider, for example, an experiment by Charles Lord and coworkers (1979), who demonstrated how people's attitudes are affected by exposure to evidence that contradicts their attitudes.

By means of a questionnaire, Lord identified one group of subjects in favor of capital punishment and another group against it. Each subject was then presented with descriptions of research studies on capital punishment. Some of the studies provided evidence that capital punishment had a deterrent effect on murder; others provided evidence that capital punishment had no deterrent effect. When the subjects reacted to the studies, their responses reflected the attitudes they had at the beginning of the experiment. For example, an article presenting evidence that supported the deterrence effect of capital punishment was rated as "convincing" by proponents of capital punishment and "unconvincing" by those against capital punishment.

What's going on here? One possibility is that people's prior beliefs may have caused them to focus on information that agreed with their beliefs and to disregard information that didn't. The tendency for people to generate and evaluate evidence and test their hypotheses in a way that is biased toward their own opinions and attitudes is called the **myside bias** (McKenzie, 2004; Stanovich et al., 2013; Taber & Lodge, 2006).

The myside bias is a type of **confirmation bias**. A confirmation bias is broader than the myside bias because it holds for any situation (not just for opinions or attitudes) in which information is favored that confirms a hypothesis. Peter C. Wason (1960) demonstrated how the confirmation bias can affect how people approach solving a problem by presenting subjects with the following instructions:

> You will be given three numbers which conform to a simple rule that I have in mind.... Your aim is to discover this rule by writing down sets of three numbers together with your reasons for your choice of them. After you have written down each set, I shall tell you whether your numbers conform to the rule or not. When you feel highly confident that you have discovered the rule, you are to write it down and tell me what it is. (p. 131)

After Wason presented the first set of numbers, 2, 4, and 6, the subjects began creating their own sets of three numbers, and for each set received feedback from Wason regarding whether their series of three numbers fit his rule. Note that Wason told subjects only whether their numbers fit *his* rule. The subjects did not find out whether *their* rationale for creating the three numbers was correct until they felt confident enough to actually announce their rule. The most common initial hypothesis was "increasing intervals of two." But because the actual rule was "three numbers in increasing order of magnitude," the rule "increasing intervals of two" is incorrect even though it creates sequences that satisfy Wason's rule.

The secret to determining the correct rule is to try to create sequences that *don't* satisfy the person's current hypothesis, but *do* satisfy Wason's rule. Thus, determining that the sequence 2, 4, 5 is correct, allows us to reject our "increasing intervals of two" hypothesis and formulate a new one. The few subjects whose rule was correct on their first guess followed the strategy of testing a number of hypotheses themselves before giving their answer, by creating sequences that were designed to *disconfirm* their current hypothesis. In contrast, subjects who didn't guess the rule correctly on their first try tended to keep creating sequences that confirmed their current hypothesis.

The confirmation bias acts like a pair of blinders—we see the world according to rules we think are correct and are never dissuaded from this view because we seek out only evidence that confirms our rule. As we saw in the Lord experiment, these blinders created by our attitudes can influence our judgment in ways that extend beyond how we go about solving a problem.

Table 13.2: Potential Sources of Errors in Judgments

PAGE	SOURCE	DESCRIPTION	ERROR OCCURS WHEN
371	Availability heuristic	Events that are more easily remembered are judged as more probable.	Easily remembered event is less probable.
373	Illusory correlation	Strong correlation between two events appears to exist but doesn't.	There is no correlation, or it is weaker than it appears to be.
373	Representativeness heuristic	Probability that A is a member of class B is determined by how well properties of A resemble properties usually associated with B.	Presence of similar properties doesn't predict membership in class B.
374	Base rate	Relative proportions of different classes in the population.	Base rate information is not taken into account.
374	Conjunction rule	Probability of conjunction of two events (A and B) cannot be higher than the probability of single constituents.	Higher probability is assigned to the conjunction.
375	Law of large numbers	The larger the number of individuals drawn from a population, the more representative the group will be of the entire population.	It is assumed that a small number of individuals accurately represents the entire population.
376	Myside bias	Tendency for people to generate and evaluate evidence and test their hypotheses in a way that is biased toward their own opinions and attitudes; the myside bias is a type of confirmation bias.	People let their own opinions and attitudes influence how they evaluate evidence needed to make decisions.
376	Confirmation bias	Selectively looking for information that conforms to a hypothesis and overlooking information that argues against it.	There is a narrow focus only on confirming information.

Table 13.2 summarizes the potential sources of errors in judgment that we have discussed. Although you might get the impression from this list that most of our judgments are in error, this isn't actually the case. Judgments are often accurate and useful, but research designed to determine mechanisms involved in making judgments has focused on situations in which errors occur. This isn't surprising when we remember that research in perception, attention, memory, and language has often focused on situations in which people misperceive, miss things that are visible, misremember, and are led to incorrect interpretations of sentences. Interestingly, studying situations in which things go wrong turns out to be a useful way to learn about how the mind operates in general.

TEST YOURSELF 13.1

1. What is inductive reasoning? What factors contribute to the strength of an inductive argument?

2. How is inductive reasoning involved in everyday experience?

3. Describe how the following can cause errors in reasoning: availability heuristic; illusory correlations; representativeness heuristic.

4. How can failure to take into account base rates cause errors in reasoning? Be sure you understand how the judging occupations experiment relates to the representative heuristic and base rates.

5. What is the conjunction rule? Describe the experiment involving Linda the bank teller and indicate how it relates to both the representativeness heuristic and the conjunction rule.

6. Describe the male and female births experiment. How do the results of this experiment relate to the law of large numbers?

7. What is the myside bias? Describe Lord's experiment on attitudes about capital punishment.

8. What is the confirmation bias? Describe Wason's experiment on sequences of numbers.

Decision Making: Choosing Among Alternatives

As we noted at the beginning of the chapter, we make decisions every day, from relatively unimportant ones (what clothes to wear, what movie to see) to those that can have a great impact on our lives (what college to attend, whom to marry, what job to choose). When we discussed the availability and representativeness heuristics, we used examples in which people were asked to make judgments about things like causes of death or people's occupations. As we discuss decision making, our emphasis will be on how people make judgments that involve choices between different *courses of action*. These choices may involve personal decisions, such as what school to attend or whether to fly or drive to a destination, or decisions made in conjunction with a profession, such as "Which advertising campaign should my company run?" We begin by considering one of the basic properties of decision making: Decisions involve both benefits and costs.

THE UTILITY APPROACH TO DECISIONS

Much of the early theorizing on decision making was influenced by **expected utility theory**, which assumes that people are basically rational. According to this theory, if people have all of the relevant information, they will make a decision that results in the maximum expected utility, where **utility** refers to outcomes that achieve a person's goals (Manktelow, 1999; Reber, 1995). The economists who studied decision making thought about utility in terms of monetary value; thus, the goal of good decision making was to make choices that resulted in the maximum monetary payoff.

One of the advantages of the utility approach is that it specifies procedures that make it possible to determine which choice would result in the highest monetary value. For example, if we know the odds of winning when playing a slot machine in a casino and also know the cost of playing and the size of the payoff, it is possible to determine that, in the long run, playing slot machines is a losing proposition. But just because it is possible to predict the optimum strategy doesn't mean that people will follow that strategy. People regularly behave in ways that ignore the optimum way of responding based on probabilities. Even though most people realize that in the long run the casino wins, the huge popularity of gambling indicates that many people have decided to patronize casinos anyway. Observations such as this, as well as the results of many experiments, have led psychologists to conclude that people do not follow the decision-making procedures proposed by expected utility theory.

Here are some additional examples of situations in which people's decisions do not maximize the probability of a good outcome. Veronica Denes-Raj and Seymour Epstein (1994) offered subjects the opportunity to earn up to $7 by receiving $1 every time they drew a red jellybean from a bowl containing red and white jellybeans. When given a choice between drawing from a small bowl containing 1 red and 9 white beans (chances of drawing red = 10 percent; **Figure 13.2a**) or from a larger bowl containing a smaller proportion of red beans (for example, 7 red beans and 93 white beans, chances of drawing red = 7 percent; **Figure 13.2b**), many subjects chose the larger bowl with the less favorable probability. When asked to explain, they reported that even though they knew the probabilities were against them, they somehow felt as if they had a better chance if there were more red beans. Apparently seeing more red beans overpowered their knowledge that the probability was lower (they were told how many red and white beans there were on each trial).

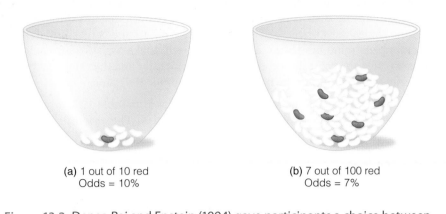

(a) 1 out of 10 red
Odds = 10%

(b) 7 out of 100 red
Odds = 7%

Figure 13.2 Denes-Raj and Epstein (1994) gave participants a choice between randomly picking one jelly bean from (a) a bowl with 1 red bean and 9 white beans or (b) a bowl with 7 red beans and 93 white beans (not all of the white beans are shown in this picture). Participants received money if they picked a red bean. *(Source: Based on V. Denes-Raj & S. Epstein, Conflict between intuitive and rational processing: When people behave against their better judgment,* Journal of Personality and Social Psychology, 66, 819–829, 1994.)

While deciding which bowl to pick jellybeans from is not a particularly important decision, subjects' preference for the lower probability choice shows that they are influenced by considerations other than their knowledge of probabilities. A decision of greater consequence is the real-life decision of whether to travel by car or plane. Although it is well known that the odds are far greater of being killed in a car accident than in a plane crash, a decrease in air travel and an increase in driving occurred following the 9/11 terrorist attacks. According to one calculation, the number of Americans who lost their lives on the road by avoiding the risk of flying was higher than the total number of passengers killed on the four hijacked flights (Gigerenzer, 2004).

The idea that people often ignore probabilities when making decisions is also supported by an analysis of how contestants respond in the TV game show *Deal or No Deal*, which premiered in the United States in 2005. In this show, a contestant is shown a list of 26 amounts of money, ranging from one cent to a million dollars. Each of these amounts is contained in one of 26 briefcases, which are displayed on stage. The game begins when the contestant picks one of these briefcases to be his or her own. The contestant is entitled to whatever amount of money is contained in that briefcase. The problem, however, is that the contestant doesn't know how much is in the briefcase, and the only way to find out is to open the remaining 25 briefcases, one by one, until the contestant's briefcase is the only one left (**Figure 13.3**).

The contestant indicates which of the remaining 25 briefcases to open, one by one. Each time the contestant decides on a briefcase number, the model next to that briefcase opens it and reveals how much money is inside. Each dollar amount that is revealed is taken off the list of 26 dollar amounts or values. Thus, by looking at the list of values, the contestant can tell which values are out of play (the values in briefcases that have been opened) and which values are still in play. One of the values still in play will be in the contestant's briefcase, but the contestant doesn't know which one.

After opening 6 briefcases, the contestant is offered a deal by the bank based on the 20 remaining prizes. At this point, the contestant must choose between taking the guaranteed amount offered by the bank

Patton, Trae/NBC-TV/The Kobal Collection/Picture Desk

Figure 13.3 A decision point early in a game on the television show *Deal or No Deal*. The host, Howie Mandel, on the right, has just asked the contestant whether he wants to accept an offer made by the bank (Deal) or continue the game (No Deal). In the background, models stand next to numbered briefcases that have not yet been opened. Each of these briefcases contains an unknown amount of money. The contestant's briefcase, not shown here, also contains an unknown amount of money.

(Deal) or continuing the game (No Deal). The only information that can help the contestant decide is the amount the bank is offering and the list of values that are still in play, one of which is in the contestant's briefcase. If the contestant rejects the bank's initial offer, then the contestant opens more briefcases, and the bank will make a new offer. Each time the bank makes an offer, the contestant considers the bank's offer and the values that are still in play and decides whether to take the bank's deal or continue the game.

For example, consider the following situation, shown in **Table 13.3**, which occurred in an actual game for a contestant we will call contestant X. The amounts in the left column are the values that were inside the 21 briefcases that contestant X had opened. The amounts in the right column are the values inside the 5 briefcases that had not yet been opened. Four of these briefcases were on stage, and the remaining one belonged to contestant X. Based on these amounts, the bank made an offer of $80,000. In other words, contestant X had a choice between definitely receiving $80,000 or taking a chance at getting a higher amount listed in the right column. The rational choice would seem to be to take the $80,000, because there was only a 1 in 5 chance of winning $300,000 and all of the other amounts were less than $80,000. Unfortunately, contestant X didn't take the deal, and the next briefcase opened contained $300,000, taking it out of play. Contestant X then accepted the bank's new offer of $21,000, ending the game.

Thierry Post and coworkers (2008) analyzed contestants' responses in hundreds of games and concluded that the contestants' choices are determined not just by the amounts of money left in the briefcases but by what has happened leading up to their decision. Post found that if things are going well for the contestant (they have opened a number of small money briefcases) and the bank begins offering more and more, the contestant is likely to be cautious and accept a deal early. In contrast, when contestants are doing poorly (having opened a number of large denomination briefcases, taking those amounts out of play) and the bank's offers go down, they are likely to take more risks and keep playing. Post suggests that one reason for this behavior on the part of contestants who are doing poorly is that they want to avoid the negative feeling of being a loser. They therefore take more risks in the hope of "beating the odds" and coming out ahead in the end. This is probably what happened to contestant X, with unfortunate results. What seems to be happening here is that contestants' decisions are swayed by their emotions. We will now describe a number

Table 13.3: *Deal or No Deal* Payoffs

21 BRIEFCASES OPENED (NO LONGER IN PLAY)		5 BRIEFCASES REMAINING (STILL IN PLAY)
$0.01	$5,000	$100
$1	$10,000	
$5	$25,000	$400
$10	$75,000	
$25	$100,000	$1,000
$50	$200,000	
$75	$400,000	$50,000
$200	$500,000	
$300	$750,000	$300,000
$500	$1,000,000	
$750		

© Cengage Learning

of examples of how decision making is influenced by emotions and also by other factors not considered by utility theory.

HOW EMOTIONS AFFECT DECISIONS

That emotions can play a role in decision making is suggested by the fact that people with damage to an area of their prefrontal cortex, who suffer from flattened emotions and an inability to respond to emotional events, have impaired decision making. One explanation for this effect is that these people find it difficult to evaluate the emotional outcomes that may result from different decisions, although other reasons are likely to be involved as well (Chen et al., 2011).

Personal qualities unrelated to brain damage have also been linked to decision making. Anxious people tend to avoid making decisions that could potentially lead to large negative consequences, a response called *risk avoidance* that we will return to shortly (Maner & Schmidt, 2006; Paulus & Yu, 2012). Another example is the quality of optimism, which is often considered a positive personal quality. However, optimistic people are more likely to ignore negative information and focus on positive information, causing them to base their decisions on incomplete information. Too much optimism can therefore lead to poor decision making (Izuma & Adolphs, 2011; Sharot et al., 2011). We will now consider research that has considered a number of other ways that emotions can affect decisions.

PEOPLE INACCURATELY PREDICT THEIR EMOTIONS One of the most powerful effects of emotion on decision making involves **expected emotions**, emotions that people *predict* they will feel for a particular outcome. For example, a *Deal or No Deal* contestant might think about a choice in terms of how good she will feel about accepting the bank's offer of $125,000 (even though she could potentially win $500,000), how great she will feel if she wins the $500,000, but also how bad she will feel if she doesn't accept the bank's offer and finds out there is only $10 in her briefcase.

Expected emotions are one of the determinants of **risk aversion**—the tendency to avoid taking risks. One of the things that increases the chance of risk aversion is the tendency to believe that a particular loss will have a greater impact than a gain of the same size (Tversky & Kahneman, 1991). For example, if people believe it would be very disturbing to lose $100 but only slightly pleasant to win $100, then this would cause them to decline a bet for which the odds are 50–50, such as flipping a coin (win $100 for heads; lose $100 for tails). In fact, because of this effect, some people are reluctant to take a bet in which there is a 50 percent chance of winning $200 and a 50 percent chance of losing $100, even though in accordance with utility theory, this would be a good bet (Kermer et al., 2006).

Deborah Kermer and coworkers (2006) studied this effect by doing an experiment that compared people's expected emotions with their actual emotions. They gave subjects $5 and told them that based on a coin flip they would either win an additional $5 or lose $3. Subjects rated their happiness before the experiment started and then predicted how their happiness would change if they won the coin toss (gain $5, so they have $10) or lost it (lose $3, so they have $2). The results of these ratings are indicated by the left pair of bars in **Figure 13.4**. Notice that before the experiment, the subjects predicted that the negative effect of losing $3 would be greater than the positive effect of winning $5.

After the coin flip, in which some subjects won and some lost, they carried out a filler task for 10 minutes and then rated their happiness. The bars on the right show that the actual effect of losing was substantially less than predicted, but the positive effect of winning was only a little less than predicted. So, after their gamble, the positive effect of winning and negative effect of losing turned out to be about equal.

Why do people overestimate what their negative feelings will be? One reason is that when making their prediction, they don't take into account the various coping mechanisms they may use to deal with adversity. For example, a person who doesn't get a job he wanted might rationalize the failure by saying "The salary wasn't what

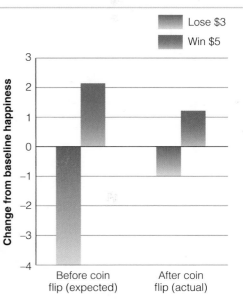

Figure 13.4 The results of Kermer et al.'s (2006) experiments showing that people greatly overestimate the expected negative effect of losing (left red bar), compared to the actual effect of losing (right red bar). The blue bars indicate that people only slightly overestimate the expected positive effect of winning (left blue bar), compared to the actual effect of winning (right blue bar). *(Source: Based on D. A. Kermer, E. Driver-Linn, T. D. Wilson, & D. T. Gilbert, Loss aversion is an affective forecasting error,* Psychological Science, 17, *649–653, 2006.)*

I really wanted" or "I'll find something better." In Kremer's experiment, when subjects predicted how they would feel if they lost, they focused on losing $5, but after the outcome was determined, subjects who actually lost focused on the fact that they still had $2 left.

The results of Kremer's experiment, plus others, show that the inability to correctly predict the emotional outcome of a decision can lead to inefficient decision making (Peters et al., 2006; Wilson & Gilbert, 2003). We will now see how emotions that aren't even related to making the decision can affect the decision.

INCIDENTAL EMOTIONS AFFECT DECISIONS **Incidental emotions** are emotions that are not caused by having to make a decision. Incidental emotions can be related to a person's general disposition (the person is naturally happy, for example), something that happened earlier in the day, or the general environment such as background music being played in a game show or the yells of the game show audience.

How might the fact that you feel happy or sad, or are in an environment that causes positive or negative feelings, affect your decisions? There is evidence that decision making is affected by these incidental emotions, even though they are not directly related to the decision. For example, in a paper titled "Clouds Make Nerds Look Good," Uri Simonsohn (2007) reports an analysis of university admissions decisions in which he found that applicants' academic attributes were more heavily weighted on cloudy days than on sunny days (nonacademic attributes won out on sunny days). In another study, he found that prospective students visiting an academically highly rated university were more likely to enroll if they had visited the campus on a cloudy day (Simonsohn, 2009).

A study by Jennifer Lerner and coworkers (2004) provides an example of how emotions can affect the economic decisions of establishing selling and buying prices. Subjects viewed one of three film clips calculated to elicit emotions: (1) a person dying (sadness); (2) a person using a dirty toilet (disgust); and (3) fish at the Great Barrier Reef (neutral). Subjects in the sadness and disgust groups were also asked to write about how they would feel if they were in the situation shown in the clip.

Lerner and coworkers then gave subjects a set of highlighter pens and determined (1) the price for which subjects would be willing to sell the set (sell condition) and (2) the price at which they would be willing to choose the set instead of accepting the money (choice condition). The choice condition is roughly equivalent to setting the price they would pay for it.

The left bars in **Figure 13.5** show that subjects in the disgust and sadness group were willing to sell the set for less than the neutral group. Lerner suggests that this occurs because disgust is associated with a need to expel things and sad emotions are associated with a need for change. The right bars show that subjects in the sad group were willing to pay more for the set. This also fits with the idea of sadness being associated with a need for change. Lerner's proposed reasons for setting buying and selling prices are hypothetical, but whatever the reasons, this study and others support the idea that a person's mood can influence economic decisions.

DECISIONS CAN DEPEND ON THE CONTEXT WITHIN WHICH THEY ARE MADE

Evidence that decisions can be influenced by context comes from experiments that show that adding alternatives to be considered as possible choices can influence decisions. For example, in a study that asked physicians whether they would prescribe arthritis medication to a hypothetical 67-year-old patient, 72 percent opted to prescribe medication when their choice was to prescribe a specific medication or not to prescribe anything. However, when a second possible medication was added, so the choice became whether to prescribe medication 1, medication 2, or nothing, only 53 percent opted to prescribe medication. Apparently, being faced with a more difficult decision can lead to making no decision at all (Redelmeier & Shafir, 1995).

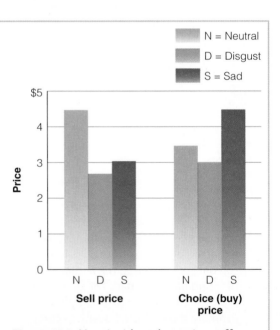

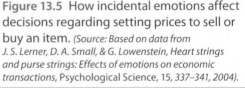

Figure 13.5 How incidental emotions affect decisions regarding setting prices to sell or buy an item. *(Source: Based on data from J. S. Lerner, D. A. Small, & G. Lowenstein, Heart strings and purse strings: Effects of emotions on economic transactions, Psychological Science, 15, 337–341, 2004).*

Another example of how context can affect medical decision making is provided by an experiment in which physicians were presented with a hypothetical test case involving a possible candidate for cesarean section (Shen et al., 2010). The decision whether to opt for cesarean section was made under three different contexts: (1) Control: The test case was presented first. (2) Serious previous cases: The test case was preceded by four other cases in which there were serious complications that would usually call for a cesarean section. (3) Not Serious previous cases: The test case was preceded by four other cases that were fairly routine and usually wouldn't call for a cesarean section. The results, in **Figure 13.6**, show that slightly more than half of the physicians in the control and serious conditions recommended a cesarean delivery. However, 75 percent recommended a cesarean when the test case was preceded by the nonserious cases. Apparently, the test case was perceived to be more serious when preceded by uncomplicated cases that didn't require special actions. What this means, if these results were to translate into an actual medical situation, is that a patient's chances of undergoing a cesarean section can be influenced by the immediately prior experiences of the physician.

If the finding that medical decisions may depend on the doctor's immediately prior experiences is a little unsettling, consider the plight of prisoners applying to Israeli parole boards. Shai Danziger and coworkers (2011) studied more than 1,000 judicial rulings on parole requests and found that the probability of a favorable response (parole granted) was 65 percent when judges heard a case just after taking a meal break, but dropped to near zero when heard just before taking a break. This finding that extraneous variables (whether the judge is hungry or tired) can affect judicial decisions lends credibility to a saying coined by Judge Jerome Frank (1930) that "Justice is what the judge had for breakfast."

DECISIONS CAN DEPEND ON HOW CHOICES ARE PRESENTED

People's judgments are affected by the way choices are stated. For example, take the decision about whether to become a potential organ donor. Although a poll has found that 85 percent of Americans approve of organ donation, only 28 percent have actually granted permission by signing a donor card. This signing of the card is called an **opt-in procedure** because it requires the person to take an active step (Johnson & Goldstein, 2003).

The low American consent rate for organ donation also occurs in other countries, such as Denmark (4 percent), the United Kingdom (27 percent), and Germany (12 percent). One thing that these countries have in common is that they all use an opt-in procedure. However, in France and Belgium the consent rate is more than 99 percent. These countries use an **opt-out procedure**, in which everyone is a potential organ donor unless he or she requests not to be.

Besides having important ramifications for public health (in 1995 more than 45,000 people in the United States died waiting for a suitable donor organ), the difference between opt-in and opt-out procedures has important implications for the theory of decision making. According to the utility approach, people make decisions based on expected utility value; therefore, their decisions shouldn't depend on how the potential choices are stated. However, the opt-in versus opt-out results indicate that the procedure used to identify people's willingness to be organ donors does have an effect.

Related to people's tendency to do nothing when faced with the need to opt in is the **status quo bias**—the tendency to do nothing when faced with making a decision. For example, in some states, drivers have the choice of getting an expensive car insurance policy that protects the driver's right to sue and a cheaper plan that restricts the right to sue. For Pennsylvania drivers, the expensive plan is offered by default, so drivers have to choose the cheaper plan if they want it. However, in New Jersey, the cheaper plan is offered by default, so they have to choose the more expensive plan if they want it. In both cases, most drivers stick with the default option (Johnson et al., 1993). This tendency to stay with the status quo also occurs when people decide to stay with their present electrical service provider, retirement plan, or health plan, even when they are given choices that, in some cases, might be better (Suri et al., 2013).

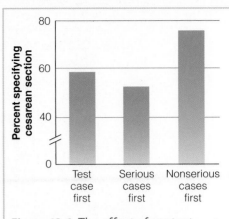

Figure 13.6 The effect of context on decision making. The likelihood that physicians would recommend a cesarean section was the same if the test case was presented first (control condition) or if it was preceded by four serious cases that required a cesarean section. However, the likelihood that physicians would recommend a cesarean section was higher if the same test case was preceded by four nonserious cases that didn't require a cesarean section. *(Source: Based on O. Shen, R. Rabinowitz, R. R. Geist, & E. Shafir, Effect of background case characteristics on decisions in the delivery room, Medical Decision Making, 30, 518–522, Table 2, 2010.)*

The examples involving organ donations and car insurance policies have to do with whether a person chooses to make a decision to change. The way a choice is presented is also important when a person is forced to pick one alternative or another. Paul Slovic and coworkers (2000) showed forensic psychologists and psychiatrists a case history of a mental patient, Mr. Jones, and asked them to judge the likelihood that the patient would commit an act of violence within 6 months of being discharged. The key variable in this experiment was the nature of a statement that presented information about previous cases. When they were told that "20 out of every 100 patients similar to Mr. Jones are estimated to commit an act of violence," 41 percent refused to discharge him. However, when told that "patients similar to Mr. Jones are estimated to have a 20 percent chance of committing an act of violence," only 21 percent refused to discharge him. Why did this difference occur? One possibility is that the first statement conjures up images of 20 people being beaten up, whereas the second is a more abstract probability statement that could be interpreted to mean that there is only a small chance that patients like Mr. Jones will be violent.

Here's another example of choosing between two alternatives, for you to try.

DEMONSTRATION
WHAT WOULD YOU DO?

Imagine that the United States is preparing for the outbreak of an unusual disease that is expected to kill 600 people. Two alternative programs to combat the disease have been proposed. Assume that the exact scientific estimates of the consequences of the programs are as follows:

- If Program A is adopted, 200 people will be saved.

- If Program B is adopted, there is a 1/3 probability that 600 people will be saved, and a 2/3 probability that no people will be saved.

Which of the two programs would you favor?

Now consider the following additional proposals for combating the same disease:

- If Program C is adopted, 400 people will die.

- If Program D is adopted, there is a 1/3 probability that nobody will die, and a 2/3 probability that 600 people will die.

Which of these two programs would you pick?

When offered the first pair of proposals, 72 percent of the students in an experiment by Tversky and Kahneman (1981) chose Program A and the rest picked Program B (**Figure 13.7**). The choice of Program A suggested that subjects were using a **risk aversion strategy**. The idea of saving 200 lives with certainty is more attractive than the 2/3 probability that no one will be saved. However, when Tversky and Kahneman presented the descriptions of Programs C and D to another group of students, 22 percent picked Program C and 78 percent picked Program D. This represents a **risk-taking strategy**, because certain death of 400 people is less acceptable than taking a 2 in 3 risk that 600 people will die.

But if we look at the four programs closely, we can see that they are identical pairs (**Figure 13.7**). Programs A and C both result in 200 people living and 400 people dying. Yet 72 percent of the subjects picked Program A and only 22 percent picked Program C. A similar situation occurs if we compare Programs B and D. Both lead to the same number of deaths, yet one was picked by 28 percent of the subjects and the other by 78 percent. These results illustrate the **framing effect**—decisions are influenced by how the choices are stated, or *framed*. Tversky and Kahneman concluded that, in general, when a choice is framed in terms of gains (as in the first problem, which is stated in terms of saving lives), people use a risk aversion strategy, and when a choice is framed in terms of losses (as in the second problem, which is stated in terms of losing lives), people use a risk-taking strategy.

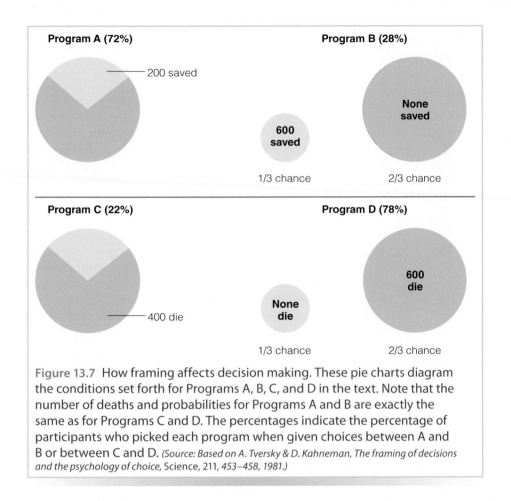

Figure 13.7 How framing affects decision making. These pie charts diagram the conditions set forth for Programs A, B, C, and D in the text. Note that the number of deaths and probabilities for Programs A and B are exactly the same as for Programs C and D. The percentages indicate the percentage of participants who picked each program when given choices between A and B or between C and D. *(Source: Based on A. Tversky & D. Kahneman, The framing of decisions and the psychology of choice, Science, 211, 453–458, 1981.)*

One reason people's decisions are affected by framing is that the way a problem is stated can highlight some features of the situation (for example, that people will die) and deemphasize others (Kahneman, 2003). It should not be a surprise that the way a choice is stated can influence cognitive processes, because this is similar to the results of experiments described in Chapter 12, which showed that the way a problem is stated can influence our ability to solve it (page 345).

NEUROECONOMICS: THE NEURAL BASIS OF DECISION MAKING

A new approach to studying decision making, called **neuroeconomics**, combines research from the fields of psychology, neuroscience, and economics to study how brain activation is related to decisions that involve potential gains or losses (Lee, 2006; Lowenstein et al., 2008; Sanfey et al., 2006). One outcome of this approach has been research that has identified areas of the brain that are activated as people make decisions while playing economic games. This research shows that decisions are often influenced by emotions, and that these emotions are associated with activity in specific areas of the brain.

To illustrate the neuroeconomics approach, we will describe an experiment by Alan Sanfey and coworkers (2003) in which people's brain activity was measured as they played the ultimatum game. The **ultimatum game** involves two players, one designated as the *proposer* and the other as the *responder*. The proposer is given a sum of money, say $10, and makes an offer to the responder as to how this money should be split between them. If the responder accepts the offer, then the money is split according to the proposal. If the responder rejects the offer, neither player receives anything. Either way, the game is over after the responder makes his or her decision.

According to utility theory, the responder should accept the proposer's offer no matter what it is. This is the rational response, because if you accept the offer you get

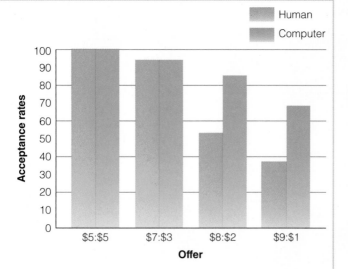

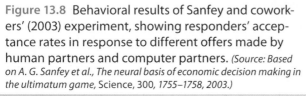

Figure 13.8 Behavioral results of Sanfey and coworkers' (2003) experiment, showing responders' acceptance rates in response to different offers made by human partners and computer partners. *(Source: Based on A. G. Sanfey et al., The neural basis of economic decision making in the ultimatum game, Science, 300, 1755–1758, 2003.)*

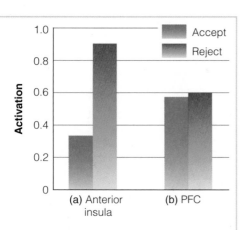

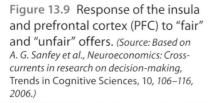

Figure 13.9 Response of the insula and prefrontal cortex (PFC) to "fair" and "unfair" offers. *(Source: Based on A. G. Sanfey et al., Neuroeconomics: Crosscurrents in research on decision-making, Trends in Cognitive Sciences, 10, 106–116, 2006.)*

something, but if you refuse it you get nothing (remember that the game is only one trial long, so there is no second chance).

In Sanfey's experiment, subjects played 20 separate games as responder: 10 with 10 different human partners and 10 with a computer partner. The offers made by both the human and computer partners were determined by the experimenters, with some being "fair" (evenly split, so the responder received $5) and some "unfair" (the responder received $1, $2, or $3). The results of responders' interactions with their human partners (orange bars in **Figure 13.8**) match the results of other research on the ultimatum game: All responders accept an offer of $5, most accept the $3 offer, and half or more reject the $1 or $2 offers.

Why do people reject low offers? When Sanfey and coworkers asked subjects, many explained that they were angry because they felt the offers were unfair. Consistent with this explanation, when subjects received exactly the same offers from their computer partner, more accepted "unfair" proposals (turquoise bars in **Figure 13.8**). Apparently, people are less likely to get angry with an unfair computer than with an unfair person.

In addition to testing people's behavior, Sanfey and coworkers measured brain activity in the responders as they were making their decisions. The results showed that the right anterior insula, an area located deep within the brain between the parietal and temporal lobes, was activated about three times more strongly when responders rejected an offer than when they accepted it (**Figure 13.9a**). Also, subjects with higher activation to unfair offers rejected a higher proportion of the offers. The fact that the insula responded during rejection is not surprising when we consider that this area of the brain is connected with negative emotional states, including pain, distress, hunger, anger, and disgust.

What about the prefrontal cortex (PFC), which plays such a large role in complex cognitive behaviors? The PFC was also activated by the decision task, but this activation was the same for offers that were rejected and offers that were accepted (**Figure 13.9b**). Sanfey hypothesizes that the function of the PFC may be to deal with the cognitive demands of the task, which involves the goal of accumulating as much money as possible. Looked at in this way, each of these brain areas represents a different goal of the ultimatum game—the emotional goal of resenting unfairness is handled by the anterior insula, and the cognitive goal of accumulating money is handled by the PFC.

Sanfey's ultimatum game experiment is just one example of the neuroeconomics approach. A great deal of research has resulted from this approach, and researchers continue to look for links between brain activation, potential payoffs or losses, and other aspects of decision making (Levy & Glimcher, 2013; Lowenstein et al., 2008; Sanfey et al., 2006).

TEST YOURSELF 13.2

1. What is the basic assumption of the expected utility approach to decision making? What are some examples of situations in which people do not behave to maximize the outcome, as the utility approach proposes?

2. Describe what the behavior of contestants on *Deal or No Deal* tells us about what determines their decisions.

3. What is the relation between anxiety, optimism, and decision making?

4. What are expected emotions? Describe how expected emotions are related to risk aversion. Describe the Kermer experiment in which subjects rated their expected happiness before gambling and their actual happiness after the results were known.

5. What is some evidence that incidental emotions affect decisions? Consider the relationship between the weather and university admissions, and Lerner's experiment on the relationship between mood and setting buying and selling prices.

6. How does context affect decisions? Describe the prescribing medication experiment, the cesarean delivery experiment, and the parole board study.

7. How does the way choices are presented affect the decisions people make? Describe the examples of organ donations, car insurance policies, and making judgments about the violence of mental patients.

8. Describe the "What Would You Do?" demonstration. Be sure you understand what determines risk aversion and risk taking, as well as the framing effect.

9. What is neuroeconomics? Describe Sanfey and coworkers' (2003) experiment, and indicate what it adds to our understanding of decision making.

Deductive Reasoning: Syllogisms and Logic

At the beginning of the chapter we considered inductive reasoning, which is reasoning based on observations. We saw that conclusions reached by inductive reasoning can be *probably true*, but not *definitely true*. For example, our initial conclusion about all crows being totally black, which was based on observations made in Pittsburgh and Washington, DC, turned out to be wrong when we expanded our observations to Europe and Asia. We will now consider *deductive reasoning*. In inductive reasoning, we draw conclusions from observations; in **deductive reasoning**, we determine whether a conclusion *logically follows* from statements called **premises**.

The father of deductive reasoning is Aristotle, who introduced the basic form of deductive reasoning called the **syllogism**. A syllogism consists of two premises followed by a third statement called the **conclusion**. We will first consider **categorical syllogisms**, in which the premises and conclusion are statements that begin with *All, No,* or *Some*. An example of a categorical syllogism is the following:

Syllogism 1

Premise 1: All birds are animals. (All A are B)

Premise 2: All animals eat food. (All B are C)

Conclusion: Therefore, all birds eat food. (All A are C)

Notice that the syllogism is stated both in terms of birds, animals, and food, and A, B, and C. We will see that the A, B, C format is a useful way to compare the forms of different syllogisms. Look at this syllogism and decide, before reading further, whether the conclusion follows from the two premises. What was your answer? If it was "yes," you were correct, but what does it mean to say that the conclusion follows from the premises? The answer to this question involves considering the difference between *validity* and *truth* in syllogisms.

VALIDITY AND TRUTH IN SYLLOGISMS

The word *valid* is often used in everyday conversation to mean that something is true or might be true. For example, saying "Susan has a valid point" could mean that what Susan is saying is true, or possibly that her point should be considered further. However, when used in conjunction with categorical syllogisms, the term **validity** has a different meaning: A syllogism is valid when the form of the syllogism indicates that its conclusion follows *logically* from its two premises. Notice that nowhere in this meaning does it say anything about the conclusion being "true." We will return to this in a moment.

Let's now consider another syllogism that has exactly the same form as the first one.

Syllogism 2

All birds are animals. (All A are B)

All animals have four legs. (All B are C)

All birds have four legs. (All A are C)

From the A, B, C notation we can see that this syllogism has the same form as Syllogism 1. Because the syllogism's form is what determines its validity, and we saw that Syllogism 1 is valid, we can therefore conclude that the conclusion of Syllogism 2 follows from the premises, so it is also valid.

At this point you may feel that something is wrong. How can Syllogism 2 be valid when it is obvious that the conclusion is wrong, because birds don't have four legs? This brings us back to the fact that nowhere in our definition of validity does the word "truth" appear. Validity is about whether the conclusion *logically follows* from the premises. If it does, *and* the premises are true, as in Syllogism 1, then the conclusion will be true as well. But if one or both of the premises are not true, the conclusion may not be true, even though the syllogism's reasoning is valid. Returning to Syllogism 2, we see that "All animals have four legs" is not true; that is, it is not consistent with what we know about the world. It is no coincidence, then, that the conclusion, "All birds have four legs," is not true either, even though the syllogism is valid.

The difference between validity and truth can make it difficult to judge whether reasoning is "logical" or not, because not only can valid syllogisms result in false conclusions, as in Syllogism 2, but syllogisms can be invalid even though each of the premises and the conclusion seem reasonable. For example, consider the following syllogism, in which each of the premises could be true and the conclusion could be true.

Syllogism 3

All of the students are tired. (All A are B)

Some tired people are irritable. (Some C are D)

Some of the students are irritable. (Some A are D)

Is the reasoning behind this syllogism valid? Stop and consider this question before reading further. If you tried this one, you may have found that it is more difficult than Syllogisms 1 and 2 because two of the statements start with *Some*. The answer is that this syllogism is not valid—the conclusion does not follow from the two premises.

Students often have a hard time accepting this. After all, they probably know tired and irritable students (maybe including themselves, especially around exam time), and students are people, all of which suggests that it is possible that some students are irritable. One way to appreciate that the conclusion doesn't logically follow from the premises is to consider Syllogism 4, in which the wording is different but the form is the same.

Syllogism 4

All of the students live in Tucson. (All A are B)

Some people who live in Tucson are millionaires. (Some C are D)

Some of the students are millionaires. (Some A are D)

Using this new wording, while keeping the form the same, makes it easier to see that the people in the second premise do not have to include students. I happen to know, from living in Tucson myself, that most students do not live in the same part of town as the millionaires. They are two different groups of people, so it doesn't logically follow that some students are millionaires.

One reason that people think Syllogism 3 is valid can be traced to the **belief bias**—the tendency to think a syllogism is valid if its conclusion is believable. For Syllogism 3, the idea that some students are irritable is believable. But when we change the wording to create Syllogism 4, the new conclusion, "Some of the students are millionaires," isn't as believable. Thus, the belief bias is less likely to operate for Syllogism 4. The belief bias also works the other way, as in valid Syllogism 2, in which an unbelievable conclusion makes it more likely the syllogism will be considered invalid.

Figure 13.10 shows the results of an experiment in which subjects read syllogisms that were valid and had either believable or unbelievable conclusions, and also read syllogisms that were invalid and had either believable or unbelievable conclusions (Evans et al., 1983; Morley et al., 2004). The subjects' task was to indicate whether the conclusion was valid.

The left pair of bars illustrates the belief bias because when the conclusion of a valid syllogism was unbelievable, the acceptance of the syllogism dropped from 80 percent for the believable conclusion to 56 percent. But the most interesting result is on the right, which shows that invalid syllogisms that had believable conclusions were judged as valid 71 percent of the time. The belief bias therefore can cause faulty reasoning to be accepted as valid, especially if the conclusion of an invalid syllogism is believable.

If you've decided at this point that it is not easy to judge the validity of a syllogism, you're right. Unfortunately, there is no easy procedure to determine validity or lack of validity, especially for complex syllogisms. The main message to take away from our discussion is that "good reasoning" and "truth" are not the same thing, and this can have important implications for examples of reasoning that you might encounter. Consider, for example, the following statement:

> Listen to me. I know for a fact that all of the members of Congress from New York are against that new tax law. And I also know that some members of Congress who are against that tax law are taking money from special interest groups. What this means, as far as I can tell, is that some of the members of Congress from New York are taking money from special interest groups.

What is wrong with this argument? You can answer this yourself by putting the argument into syllogism form and then using the A, B, C, D notation. When you do this, you will see that the resulting syllogism has exactly the same form as Syllogism 3, and as with Syllogism 3, it doesn't logically follow that just because all of the members of Congress from New York are against the new tax, and some members of Congress who are against the new tax law are taking money from special interest groups, that some members of Congress from New York are taking money from special interest groups. Thus, even though syllogisms may seem "academic," people often use syllogisms to "prove" their point, often without realizing that their reasoning is sometimes invalid. It is therefore important to realize that it is easy to fall prey to the belief bias, and that even conclusions that might sound true are not necessarily the result of good reasoning.

MENTAL MODELS OF DEDUCTIVE REASONING

We noted that there is no easy method for determining whether a syllogism is valid or invalid. But Phillip Johnson-Laird (1999a, 1999b) has suggested a possible way of approaching this, called the **mental model approach**. To illustrate the use of a mental model, Johnson-Laird (1995) posed a problem similar to this one (try it):

> On a pool table there is a black ball directly above the cue ball. The green ball is on the right side of the cue ball, and there is a red ball between them. If I move so the red ball is between me and the black ball, the cue ball is to the _____ of my line of sight.

How did you go about solving this problem? Johnson-Laird points out that the problem can be solved by applying logical rules, but that most people solve it by imagining the way the balls are arranged on the pool table. The idea that people can imagine situations is the basis of Johnson-Laird's proposal that people use mental models to solve deductive reasoning problems.

A **mental model** is a specific situation represented in a person's mind that can be used to help determine the validity of syllogisms in deductive reasoning. The basic principle

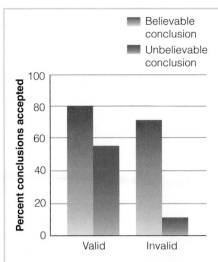

Figure 13.10 The results of the Evans et al. (1983) experiment that demonstrated the effect of belief bias in judging the validity of syllogisms. The left pair of bars indicates that a valid syllogism with an unbelievable conclusion is less likely to be judged as valid than is a valid syllogism with a believable conclusion. The right pair of bars indicates that the tendency to judge an invalid syllogism as valid is high if the conclusion is believable. *(Source: Based on J. St. B. T. Evans, J. Barston, & P. Pollard, On the conflict between logic and belief in syllogistic reasoning, Memory & Cognition, 11, 295–306, 1983.)*

behind mental models is that people create a model, or representation of the situation, for a reasoning problem. They generate a tentative conclusion based on this model and then look for exceptions that might falsify the model. If they do find an exception, they modify the model. Eventually, if they can find no more exceptions and their current model matches the conclusion, they can decide that the syllogism is valid. We can illustrate how this would work for a categorical syllogism by using the following example (from Johnson-Laird, 1999b):

None of the artists are beekeepers.

All of the beekeepers are chemists.

Some of the chemists are not artists.

To help us create a model based on this syllogism, we will imagine that we are visiting a meeting of the Artists, Beekeepers, and Chemists Society (the ABC Society, for short). We know that everyone who is eligible to be a member must be an artist, a beekeeper, or a chemist, and that they must also abide by the following rules, which correspond to the first two premises of the syllogism above:

No artists can be beekeepers.

All of the beekeepers must be chemists.

Our task is made easier because we can tell what professions people have by what hats they are wearing. As shown in **Figure 13.11**, artists are wearing berets, beekeepers are wearing protective beekeepers' veils, and chemists are wearing molecule hats. According to the rules, no artists can be beekeepers, so people wearing berets can never wear beekeepers' veils. Also the fact that all beekeepers must be chemists means that everyone wearing a beekeeper's veil must also be wearing a molecule hat.

When we meet Alice, we know she is an artist because of her beret, and we notice she is following the rule of not being a beekeeper (**Figure 13.12a**). Then we meet Beechem, who is wearing a combination beekeeper-molecule getup, in line with the rule that all beekeepers must be chemists (**Figure 13.12b**). Remember that the conclusion that has been proposed has to do with artists and chemists. Based on what we have seen so far, we can formulate our first model: No artists are chemists.

But we aren't through, because once we have proposed our first model, we need to look for possible exceptions that would falsify this model. We do this by milling around in the crowd until we meet Cyart, who is both an artist and chemist as indicated by his beret and molecule hat (**Figure 13.12c**). We note that he is not violating the rules, so we now know that "No artists are chemists" cannot be true, and, thinking back to Beechem, the beekeeper-chemist, we revise our model to "Some of the chemists are not artists."

We keep looking for an exception to our new model, but find only Clara, who is a chemist, which is also allowed by the membership regulations (**Figure 13.12d**). But this case does not refute our new model, and after more searching, we can't find anyone else in the room whose existence would refute this syllogism's conclusion, so we accept it. This example illustrates the basic principle behind the mental model theory: A conclusion is valid only if it cannot be refuted by any model of the premises.

(a) Artists   (b) Beekeepers   (c) Chemists

Figure 13.11 Types of hats worn by artists, beekeepers, and chemists attending the ABC convention. © 2015 Cengage Learning

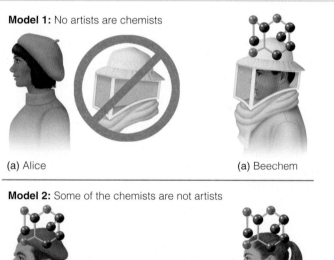

Model 1: No artists are chemists

(a) Alice   (a) Beechem

Model 2: Some of the chemists are not artists

(c) Cyart   (d) Clara

Figure 13.12 Different types of people attending the ABC convention, all wearing hats that obey the rules for the syllogism that has the conclusion "Some of the chemists are not artists." This procedure, which is based on the mental models approach to reasoning, indicates that the syllogism is valid, because case (c) is a chemist who is an artist, but (b) and (d) are chemists who are not artists. © 2015 Cengage Learning

The mental model theory is attractive because it can be applied without training in the rules of logic and because it makes predictions that can be tested. For example, the theory predicts that syllogisms that require more complex models will be more difficult to solve, and this prediction has been confirmed in experiments (Buciarelli & Johnson-Laird, 1999).

There are also other proposals about how people might test syllogisms (see Rips, 1995, 2002), but there isn't agreement among researchers regarding the correct approach. We have presented the mental model theory because it is supported by the results of a number of experiments and because it is one of the models that is easiest to apply and explain. However, a number of challenges face researchers who are trying to determine how people evaluate syllogisms. These problems include the fact that people use a variety of different strategies in reasoning, and that some people are much better at solving syllogisms than others (Buciarelli & Johnson-Laird, 1999). Thus, the question of how people go about solving syllogisms remains to be answered.

But we aren't through with syllogisms yet. In addition to categorical syllogisms, which have premises and conclusions that begin with *All, Some,* or *No,* there is another type of syllogism, called the *conditional syllogism,* in which the first premise has the form "*If ... then.*"

CONDITIONAL SYLLOGISMS

Conditional syllogisms have two premises and a conclusion like categorical syllogisms, but the first premise has the form "If ... then." This kind of deductive reasoning is common in everyday life. For example, let's say that you lent your friend Steve $20, but he has never paid you back. Knowing Steve, you might say to yourself that you knew this would happen. Stated in the form of a syllogism, your reasoning might look like this: *If* I lend Steve $20, *then* I won't get it back. I lent Steve $20. Therefore, I won't get my $20 back.

The four major types of conditional syllogisms are listed in **Table 13.4** in abstract form (using *p* and *q*). Conditional syllogisms typically use the notations *p* and *q* instead of the *A* and *B* used in categorical syllogisms. To make these syllogisms easier to understand, we will replace the *p*'s and *q*'s in the four types of syllogisms in **Table 13.4** with more real-life examples.

Conditional Syllogism 1

If I study, I'll get a good grade.

I studied.

Therefore, I'll get a good grade.

This form of syllogism—called *modus ponens,* which is Latin for (roughly translated) "the way that affirms by affirming"—is valid: The conclusion follows logically

Table 13.4: Four Syllogisms That Begin With the Same First Premise

First premise of all syllogisms: If *p,* then *q*.

SYLLOGISM	SECOND PREMISE	CONCLUSION	IS IT VALID?	JUDGED CORRECTLY?
Syllogism 1: *Modus ponens*	*p*	Therefore, *q*	Yes	97%
Syllogism 2: *Modus tollens*	Not *q*	Therefore, not *p*	Yes	60%
Syllogism 3	*q*	Therefore, *p*	No	40%
Syllogism 4	Not *p*	Therefore, not *q*	No	40%

from the two premises. When subjects are asked to indicate whether the p and q form of this syllogism is valid, about 97 percent of them correctly classify it as valid (see Table 13.4).

Conditional Syllogism 2

If I study, I'll get a good grade.

I didn't get a good grade.

Therefore, I didn't study.

Valid or not valid? The answer is that this type of syllogism, called *modus tollens* (for "the way that denies by denying"), is valid. This form is more difficult to evaluate; only 60 percent get the p and q version of *modus tollens* correct.

Conditional Syllogism 3

If I study, I'll get a good grade.

I got a good grade.

Therefore, I studied.

The conclusion in this syllogism ("I studied") is not valid because even if you didn't study, it is still possible that you could have received a good grade. Perhaps the exam was easy, or maybe you already knew the material. Only 40 percent of subjects correctly classify this syllogism as invalid. But consider the following syllogism, with "study" replaced by "live in Tucson" and "get a good grade" replaced by "live in Arizona."

If I live in Tucson, then I live in Arizona

I live in Arizona.

Therefore, I live in Tucson.

It is much more obvious that the conclusion of this syllogism does not follow from the premises, because if you live in Arizona, there are lots of places other than Tucson that you could live. We have encountered this before: The way a problem or a syllogism is stated can influence how easy it is to solve it.

Finally, let's consider Syllogism 4.

Conditional Syllogism 4

If I study, then I'll get a good grade.

I didn't study.

Therefore, I didn't get a good grade.

The conclusion of this syllogism (I didn't get a good grade) is not valid. As with Syllogism 3, you can probably think of situations that would contradict the conclusion, in which someone got a good grade even though he or she didn't study. Once again, the fact that this syllogism is invalid becomes more obvious when restated in terms of Tucson and Arizona.

If I live in Tucson, then I live in Arizona.

I don't live in Tucson.

Therefore, I don't live in Arizona.

As with Syllogism 3, the fact that the conclusion (I don't live in Arizona) is not valid becomes more obvious when we change the example. Note from Table 13.4 that only 40 percent of subjects correctly evaluate this syllogism as invalid when it is in the p and q format. In the next section we will describe a reasoning problem that supports the idea that the way a syllogism is stated can make it easier to evaluate it correctly.

CONDITIONAL REASONING: THE WASON FOUR-CARD PROBLEM

If reasoning from conditional syllogisms depended only on applying rules of formal logic, then it wouldn't matter whether the syllogism was stated in terms of abstract symbols, such as *p* and *q*, or in terms of real-world examples, such as studying or cities. However, research shows that people are often better at judging the validity of syllogisms when real-world examples are substituted for abstract symbols. As we look at this research, we will see that, as with our syllogism examples, some real-world examples are better than others. Our main goal, however, is not simply to show that stating a problem in real-world terms makes it easier, but to consider how researchers have used various ways of stating a problem to propose mechanisms that explain *why* the real-world problems are easier. Many researchers have used a classic reasoning problem called the **Wason four-card problem**.

If vowel, then even number.

Figure 13.13 The Wason four-card problem (Wason, 1966). Follow the directions in the demonstration and try this problem. *(Source: Based on P. C. Wason, Reasoning, in B. Foss, Ed., New horizons in psychology, pp. 135–151, Harmonsworth, UK: Penguin, 1966.)*

DEMONSTRATION
WASON FOUR-CARD PROBLEM

Four cards are shown in **Figure 13.13**. Each card has a letter on one side and a number on the other side. Your task is to indicate which cards you would need to turn over to test the following rule:

- If there is a vowel on one side, then there is an even number on the other side.

When Wason (1966) posed this task (which we will call the abstract task), 53 percent of his subjects indicated that the E must be turned over. We can see that this is correct from **Figure 13.14a**, which shows the two possibilities that can result from turning over the E: either an odd number or an even number. Outcomes that conform to Wason's rule are outlined in green, those that don't conform are outlined in red, and those that aren't covered by the rule have no color. Thus, turning over the E and revealing an even number conforms to the rule, but revealing an odd number doesn't conform to the rule. Because finding an odd number on the other side of the E would indicate that the rule is not true, it is necessary to turn over the E to test the rule.

However, another card needs to be turned over to fully test the rule. In Wason's experiment, 46 percent of subjects indicated that in addition to the E, the 4 would need to be turned over. But **Figure 13.14b** shows that this tells us nothing, because the rule doesn't mention consonants. Although there's nothing wrong with finding a vowel on the other side of the 4, this provides no information about whether the rule is true other than it works *in this case*. What we're looking for when testing any rule is an example that *doesn't* work. As soon as we find such an example, we can conclude that the rule is false. This is the **falsification principle**: *To test a rule, it is necessary to look for situations that would falsify the rule.*

Returning to **Figure 13.14**, we can see that whatever happens when turning over the K tells us nothing (it's another irrelevant consonant), but finding a vowel on the other side of the 7 falsifies the rule. Only 4 percent of Wason's subjects came up with the correct answer—that the second card that needs to be turned over is the 7.

WHAT REAL-WORLD VERSIONS OF THE WASON TASK TELL US The Wason task has generated a great deal of research, because it is an "If … then" conditional reasoning task. One of the reasons researchers are interested in this problem is

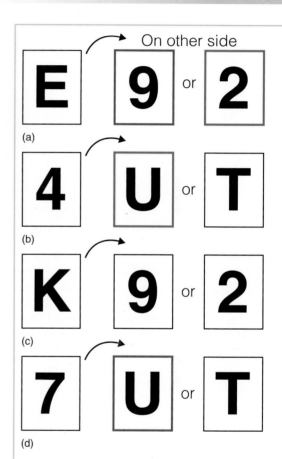

Figure 13.14 Possible outcomes of turning over cards in the Wason four-card problem from **Figure 13.13**. Red borders indicate a situation in which turning over the card falsifies the statement "If there is a vowel on one side, then there is an even number on the other side." Green borders indicate a situation in which turning over the card confirms the statement. No color indicates that the outcome is irrelevant to the statement. To test the statement by applying the falsification principle, it is necessary to turn over the E and 7 cards. © 2015 Cengage Learning

If drinking beer, then over 19 years old.

Figure 13.15 The beer/drinking-age version of the four-card problem. *(Source: Based on R. A. Griggs & J. R. Cox, The elusive thematic-materials effect in Wason's abstract selection task, British Journal of Psychology, 73, 407–420, 1982.)*

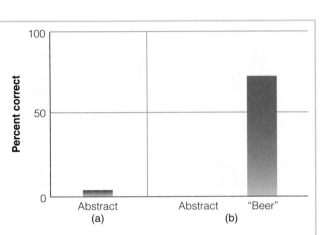

Figure 13.16 Performance on different versions of the four-card problem. (a) Abstract version (Wason, 1966), shown in **Figure 13.14**. (b) Abstract version and beer/drinking-age version (Griggs & Cox, 1982), shown in **Figure 13.15**. *(Sources: Based on P. C. Wason, Reasoning, in B. Foss, Ed., New horizons in psychology, pp. 135–151, Harmondsworth, UK: Penguin, 1966; R. A. Griggs & J. R. Cox, The elusive thematic-materials effect in Wason's abstract selection task, British Journal of Psychology, 73, 407–420, 1982.)*

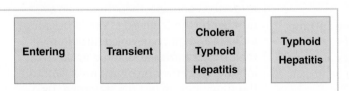

If entering, then cholera is listed.

Figure 13.17 Cholera version of the four-card problem. *(Source: Based on P. W. Cheng & K. J. Holyoak, Pragmatic reasoning schemas, Cognitive Psychology, 17, 391–416, 1985.)*

that when the problem is stated in real-world terms, performance improves. For example, Richard Griggs and James Cox (1982) stated the problem as follows:

Four cards are shown in **Figure 13.15**. Each card has an age on one side and the name of a beverage on the other side. Imagine you are a police officer who is applying the rule "If a person is drinking beer, then he or she must be over 19 years old." (The subjects in this experiment were from Florida, where the drinking age was 19 at the time.) Which of the cards in **Figure 13.15** must be turned over to determine whether the rule is being followed?

This beer/drinking-age version of Wason's problem is identical to the abstract version except that concrete everyday terms (beer and soda; younger and older ages) are substituted for the letters and numbers. Griggs and Cox found that for this version of the problem, 73 percent of their subjects provided the correct response: It is necessary to turn over the "Beer" and the "16 years" cards. In contrast, none of their subjects answered the abstract task correctly (**Figure 13.16**). Why is the concrete task easier than the abstract task? According to Griggs and Cox, the beer/drinking-age version of the task is easier because it involves regulations people are familiar with. Anyone who knows there is a minimum age for drinking knows that if someone looks 16, they need to be checked.

A similar approach was taken by Patricia Cheng and Keith Holyoak (1985), based on the idea that people think in terms of schemas—their knowledge about rules that govern their thoughts and actions. One of these schemas is a **permission schema**, which states that if a person satisfies a specific condition (being of legal drinking age), then he or she gets to carry out an action (being served alcohol). The permission schema "If you are 19, then you get to drink beer" is something that most of the subjects in this experiment had learned, so they were able to apply that schema to the card task.

This idea that people apply a real-life schema like the permission schema to the card task makes it easier to understand the difference between the abstract version of the card task and the beer/drinking-age version. In the abstract task, the goal is to indicate whether an abstract statement about letters and numbers is true. But in the beer/drinking-age task, the goal is to be sure that a person has permission to drink alcohol. Apparently, activating the permission schema helps people focus attention on the card that would test that schema. Subjects' attention is attracted to the "16 years old" card because they know that "Beer" on the other side would be violating the rule that a person must be 19 years old to drink.

To test the idea that a permission schema may be involved in reasoning about the card task, Cheng and Holyoak (1985) ran an experiment with two groups of subjects who both saw the cards in **Figure 13.17**. One of the groups was read the following directions:

You are an immigration officer at the International Airport in Manila, capital of the Philippines. Among the documents you have to check is a sheet called Form H. One side of this form indicates whether the passenger is entering the country or in transit, and the other side of the form lists names of tropical diseases. You have to make sure that if the form says "Entering" on one side, the other side includes cholera among the list of diseases.* Which of the following forms would you have to turn over to check? Indicate only those that you need to check to be sure. [*The asterisk is explained in the text that follows.]

Of the subjects in this group, 62 percent chose the correct cards, "Entering" and "Typhoid, Hepatitis." (If it isn't clear why "Typhoid,

Hepatitis" is the second card, remember that "Entering" on the other side would discon-firm the rule.) Subjects in the other group saw the same cards and heard the same instruc-tions as the first group, but with the following changes: Instead of saying that the form listed tropical diseases, the instructions said that the form listed "inoculations the travelers had received in the past 6 months." In addition, the following sentence was added where indicated by the asterisk (*): "This is to ensure that entering passengers are protected against the disease."

The changes in the instructions were calculated to achieve a very important effect: Instead of checking just to see whether the correct diseases are listed on the form, the immigration officer is checking to see whether the travelers have the inoculations neces-sary to *give them permission* to enter the country. These instructions were intended to acti-vate the subjects' permission schema, and apparently this happened, because 91 percent of the subjects in this condition picked the correct cards.

AN EVOLUTIONARY APPROACH TO THE FOUR-CARD PROBLEM One of the things we have learned from our descriptions of cognitive psychology research is that differ-ent investigators can interpret the same set of data in different ways. We saw this in the case of the misinformation effect in Chapter 8, in which memory errors were caused by presenting misleading postevent information (MPI) after a person witnessed an event (see page 227). We saw that one group of researchers explained these errors as an effect of retroactive interference and another group explained them as source monitoring errors (Lindsay, 1990).

Similarly, different explanations have been offered for the results of various experi-ments involving the Wason four-card problem. One proposed alternative to a permission schema is that performance on the Wason task is governed by a built-in cognitive program for detecting cheating. Let's consider the rationale behind this idea.

Leda Cosmides and John Tooby (1992) are among psychologists who have an **evo-lutionary perspective on cognition**. They argue that we can trace many properties of our minds to the evolutionary principles of natural selection. According to natural selection, adaptive characteristics—characteristics that help organisms survive to pass their genes to the next generation—will, over time, become basic characteristics of the organism.

Applying this idea to cognition, it follows that a highly adaptive feature of the mind would, through the course of evolution, become a basic characteristic of the mind. One such characteristic, according to the evolutionary approach, is related to **social exchange theory**, which states that an important aspect of human behavior is the ability for two people to cooperate in a way that is beneficial to both people. Thus, when caveman Morg lends caveman Eng his carving tool in exchange for some food that Eng has brought back from the hunt, both people benefit from the exchange.

Everything works well in social exchange as long as each person is receiving a benefit for whatever he or she is giving up. However, problems arise when someone cheats. Thus, if Morg gives up his carving tool, but Eng fails to give him the food, this does not bode well for Morg. It is essential, therefore, that people be able to detect cheating behavior so they can avoid it. According to the evolutionary approach, people who can do this will have a bet-ter chance of surviving, so "detecting cheating" has become a part of the brain's cognitive makeup. The evolutionary approach proposes that the Wason problem can be understood in terms of cheating. Thus, people do well in the cholera task (**Figure 13.17**) because they can detect someone who cheats by entering the country without a cholera shot.

To test the idea that cheating (rather than a permission schema) is the important vari-able in the four-card problem, Cosmides and Tooby (1992) devised a number of four-card scenarios involving unfamiliar situations. Remember that one idea behind the permission schema is that people perform well because they are familiar with various rules.

To create unfamiliar situations, Cosmides and Tooby devised a number of experiments that took place in a hypothetical culture called the Kulwane. Subjects in these experiments read a story about this culture, which led to the conditional statement "If a man eats cassava root, then he must have a tattoo on his face." Subjects saw the following four cards: (1) Eats cassava roots; (2) Eats molo nuts; (3) Tattoo; and (4) No tattoo. Their task was to determine which cards they needed to turn over to determine whether the conditional statement above was being adhered to. This is a situation unfamiliar to the subjects, and one in which cheating could occur, because a man who eats cassava roots without a tattoo would be cheating.

Cosmides and Tooby found that subjects' performance was high on this task (correctly indicating it was necessary to turn over the "Eats cassava roots" and the "No tattoo" cards), even though the rule was unfamiliar. They also ran other experiments in which subjects did better for statements that involved cheating than for other statements that could not be interpreted in this way (Cosmides, 1989; also see Gigerenzer & Hug, 1992).

In response to this proposal, however, other researchers have created scenarios involving *permission rules* that are unfamiliar. For example, Ken Manktelow and David Over (1990) tested people by presenting the following rule designed to apply to nurses: "If you clean up spilt blood, you must wear gloves." Note that this is a "permission" statement that most people who aren't nurses or doctors probably haven't heard before. However, stating the problem in this way caused an increase in performance, just as in many of the other examples of the Wason task that we have described.

WHAT HAS THE WASON PROBLEM TAUGHT US?

The controversy continues among those who hold that permission is important, those who focus on cheating, and researchers who have proposed other explanations for the results of the Wason task. Evidence has been presented for and against each of these proposed mechanisms (Johnson-Laird, 1999b; Manktelow, 1999, 2012).

We are left with the important finding that the context within which conditional reasoning occurs makes a big difference. Stating the four-card problem in terms of familiar situations can often generate better reasoning than abstract statements or statements that people cannot relate to. However, familiarity is not always necessary for conditional reasoning (as in the tattoo problem), and situations have also been devised in which people's performance is not improved, even in familiar situations (Evans & Feeney, 2004; Griggs, 1983; Manktelow & Evans, 1979).

Sometimes controversies such as this one are frustrating to read about because, after all, aren't we looking for "answers"? But another way to look at controversies is that they illustrate the complexity of the human mind and the challenge facing cognitive psychologists. Remember that at the beginning of this book we described an experiment by Donders that involved simply indicating when a light was presented or whether the light was presented on the right or on the left (see Chapter 1, page 6). We described this experiment to illustrate the basic principle that cognitive psychologists must infer the workings of the mind from behavioral observations. It is fitting, therefore, that in this, the last chapter of the book, we are now describing a task that involves mental processes far more complex than judging whether a light has flashed, but that illustrates exactly the same principle: The workings of the mind must be inferred from behavioral observations.

We see, in this controversy over how people deal with the Wason task, how a number of different hypotheses about what is happening in the mind can be plausibly inferred from the same behavioral evidence. Perhaps, in the end, the actual mechanism will be something that has yet to be proposed, or perhaps the mind, in its complexity, has a number of different ways of approaching the Wason task, depending on the situation.

Something to Consider

THE DUAL SYSTEMS APPROACH TO THINKING

One of the things that runs through our discussion of judgments, decisions, and reasoning is that people make mistakes. In making judgments, we are misled by heuristics like availability or representativeness. In making decisions, we can be influenced by emotions, context, and how choices are presented, even if these things have nothing to do with the decision. In reasoning by syllogism, we are good at judging the validity of simple syllogisms but are easily misled by the belief bias for more complex ones.

We will see that these errors all have something in common, but first quickly solve the following simple puzzle in your head by using your intuition:

A bat and a ball cost $1.10.

The bat costs one dollar more than the ball.

How much does the ball cost?

Did a number come to your mind? If so, it was probably 10 cents (Frederick, 2005; Kahneman, 2011). This answer, which immediately comes to mind, is wrong, but if that was your answer, you are not alone. More than half of thousands of subjects who tried this problem answered 10 cents (Fredrick, 2005). Further thought indicates that the answer is 5 cents ($1.05 + $0.05 = $1.10), but why does 10 cents jump out for many people?

Daniel Kahneman (2011), in his best-selling book *Thinking Fast and Thinking Slow*, uses the bat and ball example to illustrate the **dual systems approach** to thinking: the idea that there are two mental systems—a fast, automatic, intuitive system, which Kahneman calls System 1, which may have seduced you into the 10 cent answer, and a slower, more deliberative, thoughtful system called System 2, which you would have used if you had thought about the problem more carefully. Other psychologists, including Keith Stanovich and Richard West (2000; also Stanovich, 1999, 2011), who originally proposed the idea of dual systems, favor the terms Type 1 processing and Type 2 processing. We will use System 1 and System 2 for simplicity, but will return to Type 1 and Type 2 processing at the end of our discussion.

This distinction between two systems or types of processing proposes that the two systems have the following properties (Evans & Stanovich, 2013):

System 1	System 2
Intuitive	Reflective
Fast	Slow
Nonconscious	Conscious
Automatic	Controlled

System 1 is linked to many of the errors we have described in this chapter. For example, the belief bias misleads us about the validity of a syllogism when we take into account the believability or lack of believability of the syllogism's conclusion. This influence of believability is the work of System 1. Evidence that System 1 is involved in the belief bias is that evaluating syllogisms under time pressure increases the belief bias effect (Evans & Curtis-Holmes, 2005). Subjects also make more errors in the "Linda the bank teller" problem (page 374) when they are asked to respond quickly (DeNeys, 2006).

But System 2 can intervene. Taking some time to step back and think logically about the situation gives System 2 time to operate. When subjects are given instructions that encourage them to take time to focus on the logic behind a syllogism, System 2 is more likely to operate, and errors go down (Evans & Stanovich, 2013).

But before we condemn System 1 as being completely inept, we need to consider that in our day-to-day lives, System 1 is often running the show. Many of the things we do are automatically controlled by System 1. We perceive things in the environment, react to a loud noise, read emotions in someone's face, or negotiate a curve while driving. All of these things are taken care of by System 1. As we saw when we considered perception and attention, having some things taken care of automatically and without conscious effort is a good thing, because it means we don't have to be monitoring our every thought and move. Kahneman sees System 1 as providing information for System 2—most of which is accurate and is accepted—while System 2 is idling in the background monitoring the information.

However, when the going gets tough, System 2 can take over. Although System 1 may be taking care of routine driving, System 2 takes over when close attention is needed, as when entering a construction zone or passing a large truck at 70 miles an hour. System 2 is also mobilized when a question arises for which System 1 doesn't have an answer. As Kahneman puts it, System 1 automatically calculates 2 + 2 = ? (you couldn't keep yourself from saying 4, right?), but can't deal with 27 × 13. This is a problem for System 2.

Returning to some of the situations discussed in this chapter, we can appreciate that System 1 would use heuristics like availability and representativeness and might not reflect about the law of large numbers. The different versions of the Wason four-card task provide a way to contrast the two systems. The abstract version of the problem, which involves letters and numbers, is out of System 1's league because it involves thoughtful reasoning. However, when the problem involves a more realistic scenario such as beer and drinking age, System 1 can use intuition to solve the problem (Evans & Stanovich, 2013).

This idea of two mental systems is an important one, because it explains many of the mistakes we make in terms of different mental systems or mechanisms. It is important to note, however, that there are many different varieties of dual process theories, which differ in details. Also, some researchers have proposed that two processes aren't necessary and have proposed a single-system approach (Evans & Stanovich, 2013; Gigerenzer, 2011; Keren & Schul, 2009; Kruglanski & Gigerenzer, 2011; Osman, 2004).

To end our discussion of the dual systems approach to thinking, let's return to the issue of terminology. Although we used Kahneman's System 1 and System 2 terminology, there is a reason that many researchers favor using Type 1 processing and Type 2 processing instead. When we talk about two "systems," it almost sounds as though they are two little people in your mind with different characteristics. In fact, in his popular book about dual processing, Kahneman says that you can read about System 1 and System 2 "as a psychodrama with two characters." Although this idea makes for more interesting reading, and may be one of the reasons the book is so popular (in addition to Kahneman's talent for relating psychological theory to everyday life), it is important to realize that these two systems are, in fact, two different types of processing. They are not characters in your head but are the result of complex, interconnected, and distributed processing that is served by many areas of the brain and results in many different behavioral outcomes.

Postscript: Donders Returns

It is perhaps fitting to end this book by again emphasizing the complexity and mystery of the underlying processes that operate to create our cognitions. We've come a long way from the reaction time experiment in which Franciscus Donders (1868/1969) determined how long it takes to make a decision (page 6). But now that you've made it to the end of the book, let's allow ourselves to imagine something magical—Donders is given a chance to visit a 21st-century cognitive psychology laboratory.

When Donders walks into the lab, he is amazed by the technology, especially the computers and the brain scanner. But after noting these new developments, he turns to the lab director and says, "Amazing technology, but what I really want to know is have you figured out a way to measure the operation of the mind directly?" The lab director answers, "Well, no. We measure behavior and physiology and infer what is happening in the mind." "Oh," says Donders, "so the technology has changed, but besides that, nothing's different. Studying the mind still involves measuring indirectly, hypothesizing, and inferring." "That's right," says the lab director, "but let me tell you what we've found out since 1868...."

TEST YOURSELF 13.3

1. What is deductive reasoning? What does it mean to say that the conclusion to a syllogism is "valid"? How can a conclusion be valid but not true? True but not valid?

2. What is a categorical syllogism? What is the difference between validity and truth in categorical syllogisms?

3. What is the belief bias? Be sure you understand the results shown in **Figure 13.10**.

4. What is the mental model approach to determining the validity of reasoning?

5. What is a conditional syllogism? Which of the four types of syllogisms described in the chapter are valid, which are not valid, and how well can people judge the validity of each type? How does changing the wording, while keeping the form the same, influence the ability to determine whether a syllogism is valid?

6. What is the Wason four-card problem? Describe why the 7 card needs to be turned over in order to solve the problem.

7. What do the results of experiments that have used real-life versions of the Wason four-card problem indicate about how knowledge of regulations and permission schemas may be involved in solving this problem?

8. How has the evolutionary approach to cognition been applied to the Wason four-card problem? What can we conclude from all of the experiments on the Wason problem?

9. What is the dual systems approach to thinking? Be sure you understand the properties of System 1 and System 2 and how their operation relates to the various phenomena we have described in this chapter.

10. What would Donders learn if he were to visit a modern cognitive psychology laboratory?

CHAPTER SUMMARY

1. In inductive reasoning, conclusions follow not from logically constructed syllogisms but from evidence. Conclusions are *suggested* with varying degrees of certainty. The strength of an inductive argument depends on the representativeness, number, and quality of observations on which the argument is based.

2. Inductive reasoning plays a major role in everyday life because we often make predictions about what we think will happen based on our observations about what has happened in the past.

3. The availability heuristic states that events that are more easily remembered are judged as being more probable than events that are less easily remembered. This heuristic can sometimes lead to correct judgments, and sometimes not. Errors due to the availability heuristic have been demonstrated by having people estimate the relative prevalence of various causes of death.

4. Illusory correlations and stereotypes, which can lead to incorrect conclusions about relationships between things, are related to the availability heuristic, because they draw attention to specific relationships and therefore make them more "available."

5. The representativeness heuristic is based on the idea that people often make judgments based on how much one event resembles another event. Errors due to this heuristic have been demonstrated by asking subjects to judge a person's occupation based on descriptive information. Errors occur when the representativeness heuristic leads people to ignore base rate information. In other situations, judgment errors occur when people ignore the conjunction rule and the law of large numbers.

6. The myside bias is the tendency for people to generate and evaluate evidence and test their hypotheses in a way that is biased toward their own opinions and attitudes.

7. The confirmation bias is the tendency to selectively look for information that conforms to a hypothesis and to overlook information that argues against it. Operation of this bias was demonstrated by Wason's number sequence task.

8. The utility approach to decision making is based on the idea that people are basically rational, so when they have all of the relevant information, they will make decisions that result in outcomes that are in their best interest. Evidence that people do not always act in accordance with this approach includes gambling behavior, choosing to drive in the face of evidence that it is more dangerous than flying, and the behavior of contestants on quiz shows like *Deal or No Deal*.

9. Emotions can affect decisions. Expected emotions are emotions a person predicts will happen in response to the outcome of a decision. There is evidence that people are not always accurate in predicting their emotions. This can lead to risk aversion. An experiment by Kermer demonstrates the difference between predicted emotions and the emotions actually experienced after making a decision.

10. There is a large amount of evidence that incidental emotions can affect decisions. Examples include the relationship between the weather and college admissions, and Lerner's experiment showing a relationship between emotions like sadness and anger and decisions regarding how to set buying and selling prices.

11. Decisions can depend on the context in which they are made. The number of available choices, the types of decision making that preceded this decision, and hunger or fatigue can all affect decisions.

12. Decisions can depend on how choices are presented, or *framed*. Evidence includes the differences in behavior with opt-in versus opt-out procedures, the results of Slovic's experiment involving decisions about a mental patient, and people's response to the Tversky and Kahneman lethal disease problem. When a choice is framed in terms of gains, people tend to use a risk aversion strategy, but when the choice is framed in terms of losses, people tend to use a risk-taking strategy.

13. Neuroeconomics studies decision making by combining approaches from psychology, neuroscience, and economics. The results of a neuroeconomics experiment using the ultimatum game have shown that people's emotions can interfere with their ability to make rational decisions. Brain imaging indicates that the anterior insula is associated with the emotions that occur during the ultimatum game while the PFC may be involved in the cognitive demands of the task.

14. Reasoning is a cognitive process in which people start with information and come to conclusions that go beyond that information. Deductive reasoning involves syllogisms and can result in definite conclusions.

15. Categorical syllogisms have two premises and a conclusion that describe the relation between two categories by using statements that begin with *All, No*, or *Some*.

16. A syllogism is valid if its conclusion follows logically from its premises. The validity of a syllogism is determined by its form. This is different from *truth*, which is determined by the content of the statements in the syllogism and has to do with how statements correspond to known facts.

17. Conditional syllogisms have two premises and a conclusion like categorical syllogisms, but the first premise has the form "If … then." People do well at judging the validity of the *modus ponens* syllogism but less well at judging the validity of other forms of conditional syllogisms. Changing the wording of syllogisms while keeping the form the same can help people determine validity.

18. The Wason four-card problem has been used to study how people think when evaluating conditional syllogisms. People make errors in the abstract version because they do not apply the falsification principle.

19. Based on experiments using different versions of the Wason problem, such as the beer/drinking-age version, a number of mechanisms have been proposed to explain people's performance. These mechanisms include using permission schemas and the evolutionary approach, which explains performance in terms of social exchange theory. Many experiments have provided evidence for and against these explanations, leaving the controversy about how to explain the Wason problem still unresolved.

20. The dual systems approach to thinking proposes that there are two mental systems. System 1 (or Type 1 processing) is intuitive, fast, nonconscious, and automatic. System 2 (or Type 2 processing) is reflective, slow, conscious, and controlled. Many of the errors of reasoning discussed in this chapter can be linked to System 1, although this system also provides many valuable functions that do not involve error. System 2 takes over when slower, more thoughtful thinking is necessary.

21. If Donders returned today, he would be amazed at the technology but perhaps not surprised that cognitive psychologists still study the mind indirectly, just as he did.

THINK ABOUT IT

1. Astrology is popular with many people because they perceive a close connection between astrological predictions and events in their lives. Explain factors that might lead to this perception even if a close connection does not, in fact, exist.

2. Think about a decision you have made recently. It can be a minor one, such as deciding which restaurant to go to on Saturday evening, or a more important one, such as choosing an apartment or deciding which college to attend. Analyze this decision, taking into account the processes you went through to arrive at it and how you justified it in your mind as being a good decision.

3. Create deductive syllogisms and inductive arguments that apply to the decision you analyzed in the previous question.

4. Johanna has a reputation for being extremely good at justifying her behavior by a process that is often called "rationalization." For example, she justifies the fact that she eats anything she wants by saying "Ten years ago this food was supposed to be bad for you, and now they are saying it may even have some beneficial effects, so what's the point of

listening to the so-called health experts?" or "That movie actor who was really into red meat lived to be 95." Analyze Johanna's arguments by stating them as inductive or deductive arguments; better yet, do the same for one of your own rationalizations.

5. From watching the news or reading the paper, what can you conclude about how the availability heuristic can influence our conceptions of the nature of the lives of different groups of people (for example, movie stars; rich people; various racial, ethnic, or cultural groups) and how accurate these conceptions might actually be?

6. Describe a situation in which you made a poor decision because your judgment was clouded by emotion or some other factor.

KEY TERMS

Availability heuristic, 372

Base rate, 374

Belief bias, 388

Categorical syllogism, 387

Conclusion (of syllogism), 387

Conditional syllogism, 391

Confirmation bias, 376

Conjunction rule, 375

Decisions, 370

Deductive reasoning, 387

Dual systems approach, 397

Evolutionary perspective on cognition, 395

Expected emotion, 381

Expected utility theory, 378

Falsification principle, 393

Framing effect, 384

Heuristics, 371

Illusory correlation, 373

Incidental emotions, 382

Inductive reasoning, 370

Law of large numbers, 375

Mental model, 389

Mental model approach, 389

Myside bias, 376

Neuroeconomics, 385

Opt-in procedure, 383

Opt-out procedure, 383

Permission schema, 394

Premise, 387

Reasoning, 370

Representativeness heuristic, 373

Risk aversion, 381

Risk aversion strategy, 384

Risk-taking strategy, 384

Social exchange theory, 395

Status quo bias, 383

Stereotype, 373

Syllogism, 387

Ultimatum game, 385

Utility, 378

Validity, 387

Wason four-card problem, 393

COGLAB EXPERIMENTS Numbers in parentheses refer to the experiment number in CogLab.

Decision Making (48)

Monty Hall (49)

Risky Decisions (50)

Typical Reasoning (51)

Wason Selection (52)

Glossary

(Number in parentheses is the chapter in which the term first appears.)

Action pathway Neural pathway, extending from the occipital lobe to the parietal lobe, that is associated with neural processing that occurs when people take action. Corresponds to the *where* pathway. *(3)*

Action potential Propagated electrical potential responsible for transmitting neural information and for communication between neurons. Action potentials typically travel down a neuron's axon. *(2)*

Amygdala A subcortical structure that is involved in processing emotional aspects of experience, including memory for emotional events. *(8)*

Analogical encoding A technique in which people compare two problems that illustrate a principle. This technique is designed to help people discover similar structural features of cases or problems. *(12)*

Analogical paradox People find it difficult to apply analogies in laboratory settings, but routinely use them in real-world settings. *(12)*

Analogical problem solving The use of analogies as an aid to solving problems. Typically, a solution to one problem, the source problem, is presented that is analogous to the solution to another problem, the target problem. *(12)*

Analogical transfer Transferring experience in solving one problem to the solution of another, similar problem. *(12)*

Analogy Making a comparison in order to show a similarity between two different things. *(12)*

Analytic introspection A procedure used by early psychologists in which trained participants described their experiences and thought processes in response to stimuli. *(1)*

Anaphoric inference An inference that connects an object or person in one sentence to an object or person in another sentence. See also **Causal inference; Instrument inference**. *(11)*

Anterior temporal lobe (ATL) Area in the temporal lobe. Damage to the ATL has been connected with semantic deficits in dementia patients and with the savant syndrome. *(9)*

Apparent movement An illusion of movement perception that occurs when stimuli in different locations are flashed one after another with the proper timing. *(3)*

Articulatory rehearsal process Rehearsal process involved in working memory that keeps items in the phonological store from decaying. *(5)*

Articulatory suppression Interference with operation of the phonological loop that occurs when a person repeats an irrelevant word such as "the" while carrying out a task that requires the phonological loop. *(5)*

Artificial intelligence The ability of a computer to perform tasks usually associated with human intelligence. *(1)*

Attention Focusing on specific features, objects, or locations or on certain thoughts or activities. *(4)*

Attentional capture A rapid shifting of attention, usually caused by a stimulus such as a loud noise, bright light, or sudden movement. *(4)*

Attenuation model of attention Anne Treisman's model of selective attention that proposes that selection occurs in two stages. In the first stage, an attenuator analyzes the incoming message and lets through the attended message—and also the unattended message, but at a lower (attenuated) strength. *(4)*

Attenuator In Treisman's model of selective attention, the attenuator analyzes the incoming message in terms of physical characteristics, language, and meaning. Attended messages pass through the attenuator at full strength, and unattended messages pass though with reduced strength. *(4)*

Autobiographical memory Memory for specific events from a person's life, which can include both episodic and semantic components. *(6)*

Automatic processing Processing that occurs automatically, without the person's intending to do it, and that also uses few cognitive resources. Automatic processing is associated with easy or well-practiced tasks. *(4)*

Availability heuristic Events that are more easily remembered are judged to be more probable than events that are less easily remembered. *(13)*

Axon Part of the neuron that transmits signals from the cell body to the synapse at the end of the axon. *(2)*

Back propagation A process by which learning can occur in a connectionist network, in which an error signal is transmitted backward through the network. This backward-transmitted error signal provides the information needed to adjust the weights in the network to achieve the correct output signal for a stimulus. *(9)*

Balanced dominance When a word has more than one meaning and all meanings are equally likely. *(11)*

Bayesian inference The idea that our estimate of the probability of an outcome is determined by the prior probability (our initial belief) and the likelihood (the extent to which the available evidence is consistent with the outcome). *(3)*

Balint's syndrome A condition caused by brain damage in which a person has difficulty focusing attention on individual objects. *(4)*

Base rate The relative proportions of different classes in a population. Failure to consider base rates can often lead to errors of reasoning. *(13)*

Basic level In Rosch's categorization scheme, the level below the global (superordinate) level (e.g., "table" or "chair" for the superordinate category "furniture"). According to Rosch, the basic level is psychologically special because it is the level above which much information is lost and below which little is gained. See also **Global level**; **Specific level**. *(9)*

Behaviorism The approach to psychology, founded by John B. Watson, which states that observable behavior provides the only valid data for psychology. A consequence of this idea is that consciousness and unobservable mental processes are not considered worthy of study by psychologists. *(1)*

Belief bias Tendency to think a syllogism is valid if its conclusion is believable or that it is invalid if the conclusion is not believable. *(13)*

Biased dominance When a word has more than one meaning and one meaning is more likely. *(11)*

Binding Process by which features such as color, form, motion, and location are combined to create perception of a coherent object. *(4)*

Binding problem The problem of explaining how an object's individual features become bound together. *(4)*

Bottleneck model Model of attention that proposes that incoming information is restricted at some point in processing, so only a portion of the information gets through to consciousness. Broadbent's model of attention is an example of a bottleneck model. *(4)*

Bottom-up processing Processing that starts with information received by the receptors. This type of processing is also called data-based processing. *(3)*

Brain ablation A procedure in which a specific area is removed from an animal's brain. It is usually done to determine the function of this area by assessing the effect on the animal's behavior. *(3)*

Brain imaging Technique such as functional magnetic resonance imaging (fMRI) that results in images of the brain that represent brain activity. In cognitive psychology, activity is measured in response to specific cognitive tasks. *(2)*

Broca's aphasia A condition associated with damage to Broca's area, in the frontal lobe, characterized by labored ungrammatical speech and difficulty in understanding some types of sentences. *(11)*

Broca's area An area in the frontal lobe associated with the production of language. Damage to this area causes Broca's aphasia. *(2)*

Candle problem A problem, first described by Duncker, in which a person is given a number of objects and is given the task of mounting a candle on a wall so it can burn without dripping wax on the floor. This problem was used to study functional fixedness. *(12)*

Categorical syllogism A syllogism in which the premises and conclusion describe the relationship between two categories by using statements that begin with *All, No,* or *Some.* *(13)*

Categorization The process by which objects are placed in categories. *(9)*

Category Groups of objects that belong together because they belong to the same class of objects, such as "houses," "furniture," or "schools." *(9)*

Category-specific memory impairment A result of brain damage in which the patient has trouble recognizing objects in a specific category. *(9)*

Causal inference An inference that results in the conclusion that the events described in one clause or sentence were caused by events that occurred in a previous clause or sentence. See also **Anaphoric inference; Instrument inference.** *(11)*

Cell body Part of a cell that contains mechanisms that keep the cell alive. In some neurons, the cell body and the dendrites associated with it receive information from other neurons. *(2)*

Central executive The part of working memory that coordinates the activity of the phonological loop and the visuospatial sketch pad. The "traffic cop" of the working memory system. *(5)*

Cerebral cortex The 3-mm-thick outer layer of the brain that contains the mechanisms responsible for higher mental functions such as perception, language, thinking, and problem solving. *(2)*

Change blindness Difficulty in detecting changes in similar, but slightly different, scenes that are presented one after another. The changes are often easy to see once attention is directed to them but are usually undetected in the absence of appropriate attention. *(4)*

Change detection Detecting differences between pictures or displays that are presented one after another. *(5)*

Choice reaction time Time to respond to one of two or more stimuli. For example, in the Donders experiment, subjects had to make one response to one stimulus and a different response to another stimulus. *(1)*

Chunk Used in connection with the idea of chunking in memory. A chunk is a collection of elements that are strongly associated with each other but weakly associated with elements in other chunks. *(5)*

Chunking Combining small units into larger ones, such as when individual words are combined into a meaningful sentence. Chunking can be used to increase the capacity of memory. *(5)*

Classical conditioning A procedure in which pairing a neutral stimulus with a stimulus that elicits a response causes the neutral stimulus to elicit that response. *(1, 6)*

Cocktail party effect The ability to focus on one stimulus while filtering out other stimuli, especially at a party where there are a lot of simultaneous conversations. *(4)*

Coding The form in which stimuli are represented in the mind. For example, information can be represented in visual, semantic, and phonological forms. *(6)*

Cognition The mental processes involved in perception, attention, memory, language, problem solving, reasoning, and decision making. *(1)*

Cognitive economy A feature of some semantic network models in which properties of a category that are shared by many members of a category are stored at a higher-level node in the network. For example, the property "can fly" would be stored at the node for "bird" rather than at the node for "canary." *(9)*

Cognitive hypothesis An explanation for the reminiscence bump, which states that memories are better for adolescence and early adulthood because encoding is better during periods of rapid change that are followed by stability. *(8)*

Cognitive interview A procedure used for interviewing crime scene witnesses that involves letting witnesses talk with a minimum of interruption. It also uses techniques that help witnesses recreate the situation present at the crime scene by having them place themselves back in the scene and recreate emotions they were feeling, where they were looking, and how the scene may have appeared when viewed from different perspectives. *(8)*

Cognitive map Mental conception of a spatial layout. *(1)*

Cognitive neuroscience Field concerned with studying the neural basis of cognition. *(2)*

Cognitive psychology The branch of psychology concerned with the scientific study of the mental processes involved in perception, attention, memory, language, problem solving, reasoning, and decision making. In short, cognitive psychology is concerned with the scientific study of the mind and mental processes. *(1)*

Cognitive revolution A shift in psychology, beginning in the 1950s, from the behaviorist approach to an approach in which the main thrust was to explain behavior in terms of the mind. One of the outcomes of the cognitive revolution was the introduction of the information-processing approach to studying the mind. *(1)*

Coherence The representation of a text or story in a reader's mind so that information in one part of the text or story is related to information in another part. *(11)*

Common ground Knowledge, beliefs, and assumptions shared between two speakers. *(11)*

Concept A mental representation of a class or individual. Also, the meaning of objects, events, and abstract ideas. An example of a concept would be the way a person mentally represents "cat" or "house." *(9)*

Conceptual knowledge Knowledge that enables people to recognize objects and events and to make inferences about their properties. *(9)*

Conceptual peg hypothesis A hypothesis, associated with Paivio's dual coding theory, that states that concrete nouns create images that other words can hang onto, which enhances memory for these words. *(10)*

Conclusion The final statement in a syllogism, which follows from the two premises. *(13)*

Conditional syllogism Syllogism with two premises and a conclusion, like a categorical syllogism, but whose first premise is an "If ... then" statement. *(13)*

Confirmation bias The tendency to selectively look for information that conforms to our hypothesis and to overlook information that argues against it. *(13)*

Conjunction rule The probability of the conjunction of two events (such as feminist and bank teller) cannot be higher than the probability of the single constituents (feminist alone or bank teller alone). *(13)*

Conjunction search Searching among distractors for a target that involves two or more features, such as "horizontal" and "green." *(4)*

Connection weight In connectionist models, a connection weight determines the degree to which signals sent from one unit either increase or decrease the activity of the next unit. *(9)*

Connectionism A network model of mental operation that proposes that concepts are represented in networks that are modeled after neural networks. This approach to describing the mental representation of concepts is also called the parallel distributed processing (PDP) approach. See also **Connectionist network**. *(9)*

Connectionist network The type of network proposed by the connectionist approach to the representation of concepts. Connectionist networks are based on neural networks but are not necessarily identical to them. One of the key properties of a connectionist network is that a specific category is represented by activity that is distributed over many units in the network. This contrasts with semantic networks, in which specific categories are represented at individual nodes. *(9)*

Consolidation The process that transforms new memories into a state in which they are more resistant to disruption. See also **Standard model of consolidation**. *(7)*

Constructive nature of memory The idea that what people report as memories are constructed based on what actually happened plus additional factors, such as expectations, other knowledge, and other life experiences. *(8)*

Control processes In Atkinson and Shiffrin's modal model of memory, active processes that can be controlled by the person and that may differ from one task to another. Rehearsal is an example of a control process. *(5)*

Corpus The frequency with which specific words are used and the frequency of different meanings and grammatical constructions in a particular language. *(11)*

Covert attention Occurs when attention is shifted without moving the eyes, commonly referred to as seeing something "out of the corner of one's eye." Contrasts with **Overt attention**. *(4)*

Creative cognition A technique developed by Finke to train people to think creatively. *(12)*

Crowding Animals tend to share many properties, such as eyes, legs, and the ability to move. This is relevant to the multiple-factor approach to the representation of concepts in the brain. *(9)*

Cryptomnesia Unconscious plagiarism of the work of others. This has been associated with errors in source monitoring. *(8)*

Cued recall A procedure for testing memory in which a participant is presented with cues, such as words or phrases, to aid recall of previously experienced stimuli. See also **Free recall**. *(7)*

Cultural life script Life events that commonly occur in a particular culture. *(8)*

Cultural life script hypothesis The idea that events in a person's life story become easier to recall when they fit the cultural life script for that person's culture. This has been cited to explain the reminiscence bump. *(8)*

Decay Process by which information is lost from memory due to the passage of time. *(5)*

Decisions Making choices between alternatives. *(13)*

Deductive reasoning Reasoning that involves syllogisms in which a conclusion logically follows from premises. See also **Inductive reasoning**. *(13)*

Deep processing Processing that involves attention to meaning and relating an item to something else. Deep processing is usually associated with elaborative rehearsal. See also **Depth of processing; Shallow processing**. *(7)*

Definitional approach to categorization The idea that we can decide whether something is a member of a category by determining whether the object meets the definition of the category. See also **Family resemblance**. *(9)*

Delayed partial report method Procedure used in Sperling's experiment on the properties of the visual icon, in which participants were instructed to report only some of the stimuli in a briefly presented display. A cue tone that was delayed for a fraction of a second after the display was extinguished indicated which part of the display to report. See also **Partial report method; Whole report method**. *(5)*

Delayed-response task A task in which information is provided, a delay is imposed, and then memory is tested. This task has been used to study short-term memory by testing monkeys' ability to hold information about the location of a food reward during a delay. *(5)*

Dendrites Structures that branch out from the cell body to receive electrical signals from other neurons. *(2)*

Depictive representation Corresponds to spatial representation. So called because a spatial representation can be depicted by a picture. *(10)*

Depth of processing The idea that the processing that occurs as an item is being encoded into memory can be deep or shallow. Deep processing involves attention to meaning and is associated with elaborative rehearsal. Shallow processing involves repetition with little attention to meaning and is associated with maintenance rehearsal. See also **Levels of processing theory**. *(7)*

Dichotic listening The procedure of presenting one message to the left ear and a different message to the right ear. *(4)*

Dictionary unit A component of Treisman's attenuation model of attention. This processing unit contains stored words and thresholds for activating the words. The dictionary unit helps explain why we can sometimes hear a familiar word, such as our name, in an unattended message. See also **Attenuation model of attention**. *(4)*

Diffusion tensor imaging (DTI) A technique, based on detection of how water diffuses along the length of nerve fibers, for tracing nerve pathways and determining connections. *(2)*

Digit span The number of digits a person can remember. Digit span is used as a measure of the capacity of short-term memory. *(5)*

Direct pathway model Model of pain perception that proposes that pain signals are sent directly from receptors to the brain. *(3)*

Distraction Occurs when one stimulus interferes with attention to or the processing of another stimulus. *(4)*

Distributed representation Occurs when a specific cognition activates many areas of the brain. *(2)*

Divergent thinking Thinking that is open-ended, involving a large number of potential solutions. *(12)*

Divided attention The ability to pay attention to, or carry out, two or more different tasks simultaneously. *(4)*

Double dissociation A situation in which a single dissociation can be demonstrated in one person and the opposite type of single dissociation can be demonstrated in another person (i.e., Person 1: function A is present, function B is damaged; Person 2: function A is damaged, function B is present). *(2)*

Dual systems approach The idea that there are two mental systems, one fast and the other slower, that have different capabilities and serve different functions. *(13)*

Early selection model Model of attention that explains selective attention by early filtering out of the unattended message. In Broadbent's early selection model, the filtering step occurs before the message is analyzed to determine its meaning. *(4)*

Echoic memory Brief sensory memory for auditory stimuli that lasts for a few seconds after a stimulus is extinguished. *(5)*

Elaborative rehearsal Rehearsal that involves thinking about the meaning of an item to be remembered or making connections between that item and prior knowledge. Compare to Maintenance rehearsal. *(7)*

Embodied approach Proposal that our knowledge of concepts is based on reactivation of sensory and motor processes that occur when we interact with an object. *(9)*

Encoding The process of acquiring information and transferring it into memory. *(7)*

Encoding specificity The principle that we learn information together with its context. This means that presence of the context can lead to enhanced memory for the information. *(7)*

Epiphenomenon A phenomenon that accompanies a mechanism but is not actually part of the mechanism. An example of an epiphenomenon is lights that flash on a mainframe computer as it operates. *(10)*

Episodic buffer A component added to Baddeley's original working memory model that serves as a "backup" store that communicates with both LTM and the components of working memory. It holds information longer and has greater capacity than the phonological loop or visuospatial sketch pad. *(5)*

Error signal During learning in a connectionist network, the difference between the output signal generated by a particular stimulus and the output that actually represents that stimulus. *(9)*

Event-related potential (ERP) An electrical potential, recorded with disc electrodes on a person's scalp, that reflects the response of many thousands of neurons near the electrode that fire together. The ERP consists of a number of waves that occur at different delays after a stimulus is presented and that can be linked to different functions. For example, the N400 wave occurs in response to a sentence that contains a word that doesn't fit the meaning of the sentence. *(5)*

Evolutionary perspective on cognition The idea that many properties of our minds can be traced to the evolutionary principles of natural selection. See also Social exchange theory. *(13)*

Exemplar In categorization, members of a category that a person has experienced in the past. *(9)*

Exemplar approach to categorization The approach to categorization in which members of a category are judged against exemplars—examples of members of the category that the person has encountered in the past. *(9)*

Expected emotion Emotion that a person predicts he or she will feel for a particular outcome of a decision. *(13)*

Expected utility theory The idea that people are basically rational, so if they have all of the relevant information, they will make a decision that results in the most beneficial result. *(13)*

Experience-dependent plasticity A mechanism that causes an organism's neurons to develop so they respond best to the type of stimulation to which the organism has been exposed. *(3)*

Expert Person who, by devoting a large amount of time to learning about a field and practicing and applying that learning, has become acknowledged as being extremely skilled or knowledgeable in that field. *(12)*

Explicit memory Memory that involves conscious recollections of events or facts that we have learned in the past. *(6)*

Extrastriate body area (EBA) An area in the temporal cortex that is activated by pictures of bodies and parts of bodies, but not by faces or other objects. *(2)*

Eyewitness testimony Testimony by eyewitnesses to a crime about what they saw during commission of the crime. *(8)*

Falsification principle The reasoning principle that to test a rule, it is necessary to look for situations that would falsify the rule. *(13)*

Family resemblance In considering the process of categorization, the idea that things in a particular category resemble each other in a number of ways. This approach can be contrasted with the definitional approach, which states that an object belongs to a category only when it meets a definite set of criteria. *(9)*

Feature detectors Neurons that respond to specific visual features, such as orientation, size, or the more complex features that make up environmental stimuli. *(2)*

Feature integration theory An approach to object perception, developed by Anne Treisman, that proposes a sequence of stages in which features are first analyzed and then combined to result in perception of an object. *(4)*

Feature search Searching among distractors for a target item that involves detecting one feature, such as "horizontal." *(4)*

Filter model of attention Model of attention that proposes a filter that lets attended stimuli through and blocks some or all of the unattended stimuli. *(4)*

Fixation In perception and attention, a pausing of the eyes on places of interest while observing a scene. *(4)*

Fixation In problem solving, people's tendency to focus on a specific characteristic of the problem that keeps them from arriving at a solution. See also **Functional fixedness**. *(12)*

Flashbulb memory Memory for the circumstances surrounding hearing about shocking, highly charged events. It has been claimed that such memories are particularly vivid and accurate. See **Narrative rehearsal hypothesis** for another viewpoint. *(8)*

Focused attention stage The second stage of Treisman's feature integration theory. According to the theory, attention causes the combination of features into perception of an object. *(4)*

Food craving An intense desire to eat a specific food. *(10)*

Framing effect Decisions are influenced by how the choices are stated. *(13)*

Free recall A procedure for testing memory in which the participant is asked to remember stimuli that were previously presented. See also **Cued recall**. *(7)*

Frontal lobe The lobe in the front of the brain that serves higher functions such as language, thought, memory, and motor functioning. *(2)*

Functional fixedness An effect that occurs when the ideas a person has about an object's function inhibit the person's ability to use the object for a different function. See also **Fixation** (in problem solving). *(12)*

Functional magnetic resonance imaging (fMRI) A brain imaging technique that measures how blood flow changes in response to cognitive activity. *(2)*

Fusiform face area (FFA) An area in the temporal lobe that contains many neurons that respond selectively to faces. *(2)*

Garden path sentence A sentence in which the meaning that seems to be implied at the beginning of the sentence turns out to be incorrect, based on information that is presented later in the sentence. *(11)*

Generation effect Memory for material is better when a person generates the material him- or herself, rather than passively receiving it. *(7)*

Gestalt psychologists A group of psychologists who proposed principles governing perception, such as laws of organization, and a perceptual approach to problem solving involving restructuring. *(3)*

Given–new contract In a conversation, a speaker should construct sentences so that they contain both given information (information that the listener already knows) and new information (information that the listener is hearing for the first time). *(11)*

Global level The highest level in Rosch's categorization scheme (e.g., "furniture" or "vehicles"). See also **Basic level; Specific level**. *(9)*

Goal state In problem solving, the condition that occurs when a problem has been solved. *(12)*

Good continuation, principle of Law of perceptual organization stating that points that, when connected, result in straight or smoothly curving lines are seen as belonging together. In addition, lines tend to be seen as following the smoothest path. *(3)*

Good figure, principle of See **Pragnanz, law of**. *(3)*

Graceful degradation Disruption of performance due to damage to a system that occurs only gradually as parts of the system are damaged. This occurs in some cases of brain damage and also when parts of a connectionist network are damaged. *(9)*

Graded amnesia When amnesia is most severe for events that occurred just prior to an injury and becomes less severe for earlier, more remote events. *(7)*

Group brainstorming When people in a problem-solving group are encouraged to express whatever ideas come to mind, without censorship. *(12)*

Heuristic A "rule of thumb" that provides a best-guess solution to a problem. *(13)*

Hidden units Units in a connectionist network that are located between input units and output units. See also **Connectionist network; Input units; Output units.** *(9)*

Hierarchical model As applied to knowledge representation, a model that consists of levels arranged so that more specific concepts, such as canary or salmon, are at the bottom and more general concepts, such as bird, fish, or animal, are at higher levels. *(9)*

Hierarchical organization Organization of categories in which larger, more general categories are divided into smaller, more specific categories. These smaller categories can, in turn, be divided into even more specific categories to create a number of levels. *(9)*

Hierarchical processing Processing that occurs in a progression from lower to higher areas of the brain. *(2)*

High-load task A task that uses most or all of a person's resources and so leaves little capacity to handle other tasks. *(4)*

Hippocampus A subcortical structure that is important for forming long-term memories, and that also plays a role in remote episodic memories and in short-term storage of novel information. *(6)*

Hub and spoke model A model of semantic knowledge that proposes that areas of the brain that are associated with different functions are connected to the anterior temporal lobe, which integrates information from these areas. *(9)*

Iconic memory Brief sensory memory for visual stimuli that lasts for a fraction of a second after a stimulus is extinguished. This corresponds to the sensory memory stage of the modal model of memory. *(5)*

Illusory conjunctions A situation, demonstrated in experiments by Anne Treisman, in which features from different objects are inappropriately combined. *(4)*

Illusory correlation A correlation that appears to exist between two events, when in reality there is no correlation or it is weaker than it is assumed to be. *(13)*

Imageless thought debate The debate about whether thought is possible in the absence of images. *(10)*

Imagery debate The debate about whether imagery is based on spatial mechanisms, such as those involved in perception, or on propositional mechanisms that are related to language. *(10)*

Imagery neuron A type of category-specific neuron that is activated by imagery. *(10)*

Implicit memory Memory that occurs when an experience affects a person's behavior, even though the person is not aware that he or she has had the experience. *(6)*

Inattentional blindness Not noticing something even though it is in clear view, usually caused by failure to pay attention to the object or the place where the object is located. See also **Change blindness.** *(4)*

Incidental emotions In a decision-making situation, emotions not directly caused by the act of having to make a decision. *(13)*

Inductive reasoning Reasoning in which a conclusion follows from a consideration of evidence. This conclusion is stated as being probably true rather than definitely true, as can be the case for the conclusions from deductive reasoning. *(13)*

Inference In language, the process by which readers create information that is not explicitly stated in the text. *(11)*

Information-processing approach The approach to psychology, developed beginning in the 1950s, in which the mind is described as processing information through a sequence of stages. *(1)*

Initial state In problem solving, the conditions at the beginning of a problem. *(12)*

Input units Units in a connectionist network that are activated by stimulation from the environment. See also **Connectionist network; Hidden units; Output units.** *(9)*

Insight Sudden realization of a problem's solution. *(12)*

Instrument inference An inference about tools or methods that occurs while reading text or listening to speech. See also **Anaphoric inference; Causal inference.** *(11)*

Interactionist approach to parsing The idea that information provided by both syntax and semantics is taken into account simultaneously as we read or listen to a sentence. Contrasts with the syntax-first approach. *(11)*

Intermediate states In problem solving, the various conditions that exist along the pathways between the initial and goal states. *(12)*

Inverse projection problem Task of determining the object that caused a particular image on the retina. *(3)*

In vivo problem-solving research Observing people to determine how they solve problems in real-world situations. This technique has been used to study the use of analogy in a number of different settings, including laboratory meetings of a university research group and design brainstorming sessions in an industrial research and development department. *(12)*

Landmark discrimination problem Problem in which the task is to remember an object's location and to choose that location after a delay. Associated with research on the *where* processing stream. *(3)*

Language A system of communication using sounds or symbols that enables us to express our feelings, thoughts, ideas, and experiences. *(11)*

Late closure In parsing, when a person encounters a new word, the parser assumes that this word is part of the current phrase. *(11)*

Late selection model of attention A model of selective attention that proposes that selection of stimuli for final processing does not occur until after the information in the message has been analyzed for meaning. *(4)*

Latent inhibition (LI) Mechanism that results in screening out irrelevant stimuli. *(12)*

Law of large numbers The larger the number of individuals that are randomly drawn from a population, the more representative the resulting group will be of the entire population. *(13)*

Law of pragnanz See Pragnanz, law of.

Level of analysis A topic can be understood by studying it at a number of different levels of a system. *(2)*

Levels of processing theory The idea that memory depends on how information is encoded, with better memory being achieved when processing is deep than when processing is shallow. Deep processing involves attention to meaning and is associated with elaborative rehearsal. Shallow processing involves repetition with little attention to meaning and is associated with maintenance rehearsal. *(7)*

Lexical ambiguity When a word can have more than one meaning. For example, *bug* can mean an insect, a listening device, to annoy, or a problem in a computer program. *(11)*

Lexical decision task A procedure in which a person is asked to decide as quickly as possible whether a particular stimulus is a word or a nonword. *(9, 11)*

Lexicon A person's knowledge of what words mean, how they sound, and how they are used in relation to other words. *(11)*

Light-from-above assumption The assumption that light is coming from above. This is a heuristic that can influence how we perceive three-dimensional objects that are illuminated. *(3)*

Likelihood In Bayesian inference, the extent to which the available evidence is consistent with the outcome. *(3)*

Likelihood principle Part of Helmholtz's theory of unconscious inference that states that we perceive the object that is *most likely* to have caused the pattern of stimuli we have received. *(3)*

Load theory of attention Proposal that the ability to ignore task-irrelevant stimuli depends on the load of the task the person is carrying out. High-load tasks result in less distraction. *(4)*

Localization of function Location of specific functions in specific areas of the brain. For example, areas have been identified that are specialized to process information involved in the perception of movement, form, speech, and different aspects of memory. *(2)*

Logic theorist Computer program devised by Alan Newell and Herbert Simon that was able to solve logic problems. *(1)*

Long-term memory (LTM) A memory mechanism that can hold large amounts of information for long periods of time. Long-term memory is one of the stages in the modal model of memory. *(6)*

Long-term potentiation (LTP) The increased firing that occurs in a neuron due to prior activity at the synapse. *(7)*

Low-load task A task that uses few resources, leaving some capacity to handle other tasks. *(4)*

Magnetic resonance imaging (MRI) Brain imaging technique that creates images of structures within the brain. See also **Functional magnetic resonance imaging (fMRI)**. *(2)*

Maintenance rehearsal Rehearsal that involves repetition without any consideration of meaning or making connections to other information. Compare to **Elaborative rehearsal**. *(7)*

Meaning dominance Some meanings of words occur more frequently than others. *(11)*

Means–end analysis A problem-solving strategy that seeks to reduce the difference between the initial and goal states. This is achieved by creating subgoals, intermediate states that are closer to the goal. *(12)*

Memory The processes involved in retaining, retrieving, and using information about stimuli, images, events, ideas, and skills after the original information is no longer present. *(5)*

Mental chronometry Determining the amount of time needed to carry out a cognitive task. *(10)*

Mental imagery Experiencing a sensory impression in the absence of sensory input. *(10)*

Mental model A specific situation that is represented in a person's mind. *(13)*

Mental model approach In deductive reasoning, determining if syllogisms are valid by creating mental models of situations based on the premises of the syllogism. *(13)*

Mental rotation Rotating an image of an object in the mind. *(5)*

Mental scanning A process of mental imagery in which a person scans a mental image in his or her mind. *(10)*

Mental set A preconceived notion about how to approach a problem based on a person's experience or what has worked in the past. *(12)*

Mental time travel According to Tulving, the defining property of the *experience* of episodic memory, in which a person travels back in time in his or her mind to reexperience events that happened in the past. *(6)*

Mental walk task A task used in imagery experiments in which participants are asked to form a mental image of an object and to imagine that they are walking toward this mental image. *(10)*

Method of loci A method for remembering things in which the things to be remembered are placed at different locations in a mental image of a spatial layout. See also **Pegword technique**. *(10)*

Microelectrodes Small wires that are used to record electrical signals from single neurons. *(2)*

Mind System that creates mental representations of the world and controls mental functions such as perception, attention, memory, emotions, language, deciding, thinking, and reasoning. *(1)*

Mirror neurons Neurons in the premotor cortex, originally discovered in the monkey, that respond both when a monkey observes someone else (usually the experimenter) carrying out an action and when the monkey itself carries out the action. There is also evidence for mirror neurons in humans. *(9)*

Misinformation effect Misleading information presented after a person witnesses an event changes how the person describes that event later. *(8)*

Misleading postevent information (MPI) The misleading information that causes the misinformation effect. *(8)*

Modal model of memory The model proposed by Atkinson and Shiffrin that describes memory as a mechanism that involves processing information through a series of stages, including short-term memory and long-term memory. It is called the *modal model* because it contained features of many models that were being proposed in the 1960s. *(5)*

Morpheme The smallest unit of language that has a definable meaning or a grammatical function. For example, *truck* consists of a number of phonemes but only one morpheme, because none of the components that create the word *truck* means anything. *(11)*

Multiple-factor approach Seeking to describe how concepts are represented in the brain by searching for multiple factors that determine how concepts are divided up within a category. *(9)*

Multiple trace model of consolidation The idea that the hippocampus is involved in the retrieval of remote memories, especially episodic memories. This contrasts with the standard model of memory, which proposes that the hippocampus is involved only in the retrieval of recent memories. *(7)*

Mutilated checkerboard problem A problem that has been used to study how the statement of a problem influences a person's ability to reach a solution. *(12)*

Myside bias Type of confirmation bias in which people generate and test hypotheses in a way that is biased toward their own opinions and attitudes. *(13)*

Narrative rehearsal hypothesis The idea that we remember some life events better because we rehearse them. This idea was proposed by Neisser as an explanation for "flashbulb" memories. *(8)*

Nerve fiber See Axon. *(2)*

Nerve impulse An electrical response that is propagated down the length of an axon (nerve fiber). Also called an **Action potential**. *(2)*

Nerve net A network of continuously interconnected nerve fibers (as contrasted with neural networks, in which fibers are connected by synapses). *(2)*

Neural circuit Group of interconnected neurons that are responsible for neural processing. *(2)*

Neural mind reading Using a neural response, usually brain activation measured by fMRI, to determine what a person is perceiving or thinking. *(5)*

Neural network Groups of neurons or structures that are connected together. *(2)*

Neural representation, principle of Everything a person experiences is based on representations in the person's nervous system. *(2)*

Neuroeconomics An approach to studying decision making that combines research from the fields of psychology, neuroscience, and economics. *(13)*

Neuron Cell that is specialized to receive and transmit information in the nervous system. *(2)*

Neuron doctrine The idea that individual cells called neurons transmit signals in the nervous system, and that these cells are not continuous with other cells as proposed by nerve net theory. *(2)*

Neuropsychology The study of the behavioral effects of brain damage in humans. *(2)*

Neurotransmitter Chemical that is released at the synapse in response to incoming action potentials. *(2)*

Object discrimination problem A problem in which the task is to remember an object based on its shape and choose it when presented with another object after a delay. Associated with research on the *what* processing stream. *(3)*

Oblique effect The finding that vertical and horizontal orientations can be perceived more easily than other (slanted) orientations. *(3)*

Occipital lobe The lobe at the back of the brain that is devoted primarily to analyzing incoming visual information. *(2)*

Operant conditioning Type of conditioning championed by B. F. Skinner, which focuses on how behavior is strengthened by presentation of positive reinforcers, such as food or social approval, or withdrawal of negative reinforcers, such as a shock or social rejection. *(1)*

Operators In problem solving, permissible moves that can be made toward a problem's solution. *(12)*

Opt-in procedure Procedure in which a person must take an active step to *choose* a course of action—for example, choosing to be an organ donor. *(13)*

Opt-out procedure Procedure in which a person must take an active step to *avoid* a course of action—for example, choosing not to be an organ donor. *(13)*

Output units Units in a connectionist network that contain the final output of the network. See also **Connectionist network; Hidden units; Input units.** *(9)*

Overt attention Shifting of attention by moving the eyes. Contrasts with **Covert attention.** *(4)*

Paired-associate learning A learning task in which participants are first presented with pairs of words, then one word of each pair is presented and the task is to recall the other word. *(7, 10)*

Parahippocampal place area (PPA) An area in the temporal lobe that contains neurons that are selectively activated by pictures of indoor and outdoor scenes. *(2)*

Parallel distributed processing (PDP) See **Connectionism;** see also **Connectionist network.** *(9)*

Parietal lobe The lobe at the top of the brain that contains mechanisms responsible for sensations caused by stimulation of the skin and also some aspects of visual information. *(2)*

Parsing The mental grouping of words in a sentence into phrases. The way a sentence is parsed determines its meaning. *(11)*

Partial report method Procedure used in Sperling's experiment on the properties of the visual icon, in which participants were instructed to report only some of the stimuli in a briefly presented display. A cue tone immediately after the display was extinguished indicated which part of the display to report. See also **Delayed partial report method; Sensory memory; Whole report method.** *(5)*

Pegword technique A method for remembering things in which the things to be remembered are associated with concrete words. See also **Method of loci.** *(10)*

Perception Conscious experience that results from stimulation of the senses. *(3)*

Perception pathway Neural pathway, extending from the occipital lobe to the temporal lobe, that is associated with perceiving or recognizing objects. Corresponds to the *what* pathway. *(3)*

Perceptual load Related to the difficulty of a task. Low-load tasks use only a small amount of a person's processing capacity. High-load tasks use more of the processing capacity. *(4)*

Perceptual organization, principles of Rules proposed by the Gestalt psychologists to explain how small elements of a scene or a display become perceptually grouped to form larger units. These "laws" are described as "heuristics" in this book. *(3)*

Permission schema A pragmatic reasoning schema that states that if a person satisfies condition A, then they get to carry out action B. The permission schema has been used to explain the results of the Wason four-card problem. *(13)*

Perseveration Difficulty in switching from one behavior to another, which can hinder a person's ability to solve problems that require flexible thinking. Perseveration is observed in cases in which the prefrontal cortex has been damaged. *(5)*

Persistence of vision The continued perception of light for a fraction of a second after the original light stimulus has been extinguished. Perceiving a trail of light from a moving sparkler is caused by the persistence of vision. See also **Iconic memory.** *(5)*

Personal semantic memory Semantic components of autobiographical memories. *(6)*

Phoneme The shortest segment of speech that, if changed, changes the meaning of a word. *(11)*

Phonemic restoration effect When a phoneme in a word is heard even though it is obscured by a noise, such as a cough. This typically occurs when the word is part of a sentence. *(11)*

Phonological loop The part of working memory that holds and processes verbal and auditory information. See also **Central executive; Visuospatial sketch pad; Working memory.** *(5)*

Phonological similarity effect An effect that occurs when letters or words that sound similar are confused. For example, T and P are two similar-sounding letters that could be confused. *(5)*

Phonological store Component of the phonological loop of working memory that holds a limited amount of verbal and auditory information for a few seconds. *(5)*

Physical regularities Regularly occurring physical properties of the environment. For example, there are more vertical and horizontal orientations in the environment than oblique (angled) orientations. *(3)*

Placebo A pill or procedure that patients believe delivers active ingredients (usually pain killers), but which contains no active ingredient. *(3)*

Placebo effect Decrease in pain from a procedure or substance that delivers no active ingredient. *(3)*

Population coding Neural representation of a stimulus by the pattern of firing of a large number of neurons. *(2)*

Post-identification feedback effect An increase in confidence of memory recall due to confirming feedback after making an identification, as in a police lineup. *(8)*

Pragmatic inference Inference that occurs when reading or hearing a statement leads a person to expect something that is not explicitly stated or necessarily implied by the statement. *(8)*

Pragnanz, law of Law of perceptual organization that states that every stimulus pattern is seen in such a way that the resulting structure is as simple as possible. Also called the *law of good figure* and the *law of simplicity.* *(3)*

Preattentive stage The first stage of Treisman's feature integration theory, in which an object is analyzed into its features. *(4)*

Precueing A procedure in which participants are given a cue that will usually help them carry out a subsequent task. This procedure has been used in visual attention experiments in which participants are presented with a cue that tells them where to direct their attention. *(4)*

Preinventive forms Objects created in Finke's "creative cognition" experiment that precede the creation of a finished creative product. *(12)*

Premise The first two statements in a syllogism. The third statement is the conclusion. *(13)*

Primacy effect In a memory experiment in which a list of words is presented, enhanced memory for words presented at the beginning of the list. See also **Recency effect.** *(6)*

Priming A change in response to a stimulus caused by the previous presentation of the same or a similar stimulus. See also **Repetition priming.** *(6)*

Principle(s) of good continuation, good figure, similarity, simplicity See inverted entries (e.g., **Good continuation, principle of**).

Prior A person's initial belief about the probability of an outcome. *(3)*

Prior probability See Prior. *(3)*

Proactive interference When information learned previously interferes with learning new information. See also **Retroactive interference.** *(5)*

Problem A situation in which there is an obstacle between a present state and a goal state and it is not immediately obvious how to get around the obstacle. *(12)*

Problem space The initial state, goal state, and all the possible intermediate states for a particular problem. *(12)*

Procedural memory Memory for how to carry out highly practiced skills. Procedural memory is a type of implicit memory because although people can carry out a skilled behavior, they often cannot explain exactly how they are able to do so. *(6)*

Process model A model that represents the processes involved in cognition. An example is the flow diagram for Broadbent's filter model of attention. *(1)*

Processing capacity The amount of information input that a person can handle. This sets a limit on the person's ability to process information. *(4)*

Propaganda effect People are more likely to rate statements they have read or heard before as being true, just because of prior exposure to the statements. *(6)*

Propositional representation A representation in which relationships are represented by symbols, as when the words of a language represent objects and the relationships between objects. *(10)*

Prosopagnosia Condition caused by damage to the temporal lobe that is characterized by an inability to recognize faces. *(2)*

Prototype A standard used in categorization that is formed by averaging the category members a person has encountered in the past. *(9)*

Prototype approach to categorization The idea that we decide whether something is a member of a category by determining whether it is similar to a standard representation of the category, called a prototype. *(9)*

Psycholinguistics The field concerned with the psychological study of language. *(11)*

Radiation problem A problem posed by Duncker that involves finding a way to destroy a tumor by radiation without damaging other organs in the body. This problem has been widely used to study the role of analogy in problem solving. *(12)*

Reaction time The time it takes to react to a stimulus. This is usually determined by measuring the time between presentation of a stimulus and the response to the stimulus. Examples of responses are pushing a button, saying a word, moving the eyes, and the appearance of a particular brain wave. *(1)*

Reactivation A process that occurs during memory consolidation, in which the hippocampus replays the neural activity associated with a memory. During reactivation, activity occurs in the network connecting the hippocampus and the cortex. This activity results in the formation of connections between the cortical areas. *(7)*

Reasoning Cognitive processes by which people start with information and come to conclusions that go beyond that information. See also **Deductive reasoning; Inductive reasoning.** *(13)*

Recall Subjects are asked to report stimuli they have previously seen or heard. *(5)*

Recency effect In a memory experiment in which a list of words is presented, enhanced memory for words presented at the end of the list. See also **Primacy effect**. *(6)*

Receptors Specialized neural structures that respond to environmental stimuli such as light, mechanical stimulation, or chemical stimuli. *(2)*

Recognition memory Identifying a stimulus that was encountered earlier. Stimuli are presented during a study period; later, the same stimuli plus other, new stimuli are presented. The participants' task is to pick the stimuli that were originally presented. *(6)*

Reconsolidation A process proposed by Nader and others that occurs when a memory is retrieved and so becomes reactivated. Once this occurs, the memory must be consolidated again, as it was during the initial learning. This repeat consolidation is reconsolidation. *(7)*

Recording electrode When used to study neural functioning, a very thin glass or metal probe that can pick up electrical signals from single neurons. *(2)*

Reference electrode Used in conjunction with a recording electrode to measure the difference in charge between the two. Reference electrodes are generally placed where the electrical signal remains constant, so any change in charge between the recording and reference electrodes reflects events happening near the tip of the recording electrode. *(2)*

Regularities in the environment Characteristics of the environment that occur frequently. For example, blue is associated with open sky, landscapes are often green and smooth, and verticals and horizontals are often associated with buildings. *(3)*

Rehearsal The process of repeating a stimulus over and over, usually for the purpose of remembering it, that keeps the stimulus active in short-term memory. *(5)*

Release from proactive interference A situation in which conditions occur that eliminate or reduce the decrease in performance caused by proactive interference. See the Wickens experiment described in Chapter 6. *(6)*

Remember/know procedure A procedure in which subjects are presented with a stimulus they have encountered before and are asked to indicate *remember*, if they remember the circumstances under which they initially encountered it, or *know*, if the stimulus seems familiar but they don't remember experiencing it earlier. *(6)*

Reminiscence bump The empirical finding that people over 40 years old have enhanced memory for events from adolescence and early adulthood, compared to other periods of their lives. *(8)*

Repeated recall Recall that is tested immediately after an event and then retested at various times after the event. *(8)*

Repeated reproduction A method of measuring memory in which a person is asked to reproduce a stimulus on repeated occasions at longer and longer intervals after the original presentation of the material to be remembered. *(8)*

Repetition priming When an initial presentation of a stimulus affects the person's response to the same stimulus when it is presented later. *(6)*

Representativeness heuristic The probability that an event A comes from class B can be determined by how well A resembles the properties of class B. *(13)*

Resting potential Difference in charge between the inside and outside of a nerve fiber when the fiber is at rest (no other electrical signals are present). *(2)*

Restructuring The process of changing a problem's representation. According to the Gestalt psychologists, restructuring is the key mechanism of problem solving. *(12)*

Retina A network of neurons that lines the back of the eye. The transformation of light into electrical signals and the initial processing of visual information occur in the retina. *(2)*

Retrieval The process of remembering information that has been stored in long-term memory. *(7)*

Retrieval cues Cues that help a person remember information that is stored in memory. *(7)*

Retroactive interference When more recent learning interferes with memory for something that happened in the past. See also **Proactive interference**. *(5, 8)*

Retrograde amnesia Loss of memory for something that happened prior to an injury or traumatic event such as a concussion. *(7)*

Risk aversion The tendency to make decisions that avoid risk. *(13)*

Risk aversion strategy A decision-making strategy that is governed by the idea of avoiding risk. Often used when a problem is stated in terms of gains. See also **Risk-taking strategy**. *(13)*

Risk-taking strategy A decision-making strategy that is governed by the idea of taking risks. Often used when a problem is stated in terms of losses. See also **Risk aversion strategy**. *(13)*

Saccadic eye movements Eye movements from one fixation point to another. See also **Fixation** (in perception and attention). *(4, 11)*

Saliency map Map of a scene that indicates the stimulus salience of areas and objects in the scene. *(4)*

Same-object advantage Occurs when the enhancing effect of attention spreads throughout an object, so that attention to one place on an object results in a facilitation of processing at other places on the object. *(4)*

Sapir-Whorf hypothesis The idea that the nature of language in a particular culture can affect the way people in that culture think. *(11)*

Savant syndrome Occurs in people with autism or other mental disorders, who can achieve extraordinary feats of memory or may have great artistic talent or mathematical ability. *(12)*

Savings Measure used by Ebbinghaus to determine the magnitude of memory left from initial learning. Higher savings indicate greater memory. *(1)*

Savings curve Plot of savings versus time after original learning. *(1)*

Scene schema A person's knowledge about what is likely to be contained in a particular scene. This knowledge can help guide attention to different areas of the scene. For example, knowledge of what is usually in an office may cause a person to look toward the desk to see the computer. *(3)*

Schema A person's knowledge about what is involved in a particular experience. See also **Script**. *(8)*

Script A type of schema. The conception of the sequence of actions that describe a particular activity. For example, the sequence of events that are associated with going to class would be a "going to class" script. See also **Schema**. *(8)*

Selective attention The ability to focus on one message and ignore all others. *(4)*

Self-image hypothesis The idea that memory is enhanced for events that occur as a person's self-image or life identity is being formed. This is one of the explanations for the reminiscence bump. *(8)*

Self-reference effect Memory for a word is improved by relating the word to the self. *(7)*

Semantic category approach An approach to describing how semantic information is represented in the brain that proposes that there are specific neural circuits for some specific categories. *(9)*

Semantic dementia Condition in which there is a general loss of knowledge for all concepts. *(9)*

Semantic network approach An approach to understanding how concepts are organized in the mind that proposes that concepts are arranged in networks. *(9)*

Semantic regularities Characteristics associated with the functions carried out in different types of scenes. For example, food preparation, cooking, and perhaps eating occur in a kitchen. *(3)*

Semantic somatotopy Correspondence between words related to specific parts of the body and the location of brain activity associated with that part of the body. *(9)*

Semanticization of remote memory Loss of episodic details for memories of long-ago events. *(6)*

Semantics The meanings of words and sentences. Distinguished from **Syntax**. *(11)*

Sensory code How neural firing represents various characteristics of the environment. *(2)*

Sensory-functional (S-F) hypothesis Explanation of how semantic information is represented in the brain that states that the ability to differentiate living things and artifacts depends on one system that distinguishes sensory attributes and another system that distinguishes function. *(9)*

Sensory memory A brief stage of memory that holds information for seconds or fractions of a second. It is the first stage in the modal model of memory. See also **Iconic memory; Persistence of vision**. *(5)*

Sentence verification technique A technique in which the participant is asked to indicate whether a particular sentence is true or false. For example, sentences like "An apple is a fruit" have been used in studies on categorization. *(9)*

Serial position curve In a memory experiment in which participants are asked to recall a list of words, a plot of the percentage of participants remembering each word against the position of that word in the list. See also **Primacy effect; Recency effect**. *(6)*

Shadowing The procedure of repeating a message out loud as it is heard. Shadowing is commonly used in conjunction with studies of selective attention that use the dichotic listening procedure. *(4)*

Shallow processing Processing that involves repetition with little attention to meaning. Shallow processing is usually associated with maintenance rehearsal. See also **Deep processing; Depth of processing**. *(7)*

Short-term memory (STM) A memory mechanism that can hold a limited amount of information for a brief period of time, usually around 30 seconds, unless there is rehearsal (such as repeating a telephone number) to maintain the information in short-term memory. Short-term memory is one of the stages in the modal model of memory. *(5)*

Similarity, principle of Law of perceptual organization that states that similar things appear to be grouped together. *(3)*

Simple reaction time Reacting to the presence or absence of a single stimulus (as opposed to having to choose between a number of stimuli before making a response). See also **Choice reaction time**. *(1)*

Simplicity, principle of See Pragnanz, law of. *(3)*

Situation model A mental representation of what a text is about. *(11)*

Skill memory Memory for doing things that usually involve learned skills. See **Procedural memory**. *(6)*

Social exchange theory An important aspect of human behavior is the ability for two people to cooperate in a way that is beneficial to both people. According to the evolutionary perspective on cognition, application of this theory can lead to the conclusion that detecting cheating is an important part of the brain's cognitive makeup. This idea has been used to explain the results of the Wason four-card problem. *(13)*

Source misattribution Occurs when the source of a memory is misidentified. See **Source monitoring error**. *(8)*

Source monitoring The process by which people determine the origins of memories, knowledge, or beliefs. Remembering that you heard about something from a particular person would be an example of source monitoring. *(8)*

Source monitoring error Misidentifying the source of a memory. See **Source misattribution**. *(8)*

Source problem A problem or story that is analogous to the target problem and which therefore provides information that can lead to a solution to the target problem. See also **Analogical problem solving; Target problem**. *(12)*

Spacing effect The advantage in performance caused by short study sessions separated by breaks from studying. *(7)*

Sparse coding Neural coding based on the pattern of activity in small groups of neurons. *(2)*

Spatial representation A representation in which different parts of an image can be described as corresponding to specific locations in space. See also **Depictive representation**. *(10)*

Specific level In Rosch's categorization scheme, the level below the basic level (e.g., "kitchen table" for the basic category "table"). See also **Basic level; Global level**. *(9)*

Specificity coding The representation of a specific stimulus by the firing of neurons that respond only to that stimulus. An example would be the signaling of a person's face by the firing of a neuron that responds only to that person's face. *(2)*

Speech segmentation The process of perceiving individual words within the continuous flow of the speech signal. *(3, 11)*

Spreading activation Activity that spreads out along any link in a semantic network that is connected to an activated node. *(9)*

Standard model of consolidation Proposes that memory retrieval depends on the hippocampus during consolidation, but that once consolidation is complete, retrieval no longer depends on the hippocampus. *(7)*

State-dependent learning The principle that memory is best when a person is in the same state for encoding and retrieval. This principle is related to encoding specificity. *(7)*

Status quo bias Tendency to do nothing when faced with making a decision. *(13)*

Stereotype An oversimplified generalization about a group or class of people that often focuses on negative characteristics. See also **Illusory correlation**. *(13)*

Stimulus salience Bottom-up factors that determine attention to elements of a scene. Examples are color, contrast, and orientation. The meaningfulness of the images, which is a top-down factor, does not contribute to stimulus salience. See also **Saliency map**. *(4)*

Stroop effect An effect originally studied by J. R. Stroop, using a task in which a person is instructed to respond to one aspect of a stimulus, such as the color of ink that a word is printed in, and ignore another aspect, such as the color that the word names. The Stroop effect refers to the fact that people find this task difficult when, for example, the word *RED* is printed in blue ink. *(4)*

Structural features (memory models) Types of memory indicated by boxes in models of memory. In the modal model, the types are sensory memory, short-term memory, and long-term memory. *(5)*

Structural features (problem solving) The underlying principle that governs the solution to a problem—for example, in the radiation problem, needing high intensity to fix something surrounded by material that could be damaged by high intensity. Contrast with **Surface features**. *(12)*

Structural model Representation of a physical structure. An example is a model of the brain or structures within the brain and their connections. *(1)*

Structuralism An approach to psychology that explained perception as the adding up of small elementary units called sensations. *(1)*

Subgoals In the means–end analysis approach to problem solving, intermediate states that move the process of solution closer to the goal. *(12)*

Subordinate (specific) level The most specific category level distinguished by Rosch—for example, "kitchen table." *(9)*

Subtraction technique The technique used in brain imaging in which baseline activity is subtracted from the activity generated by a specific task. The result is the activity due only to the task that is being studied. *(2)*

Superordinate (global) level The most general category level distinguished by Rosch—for example, "furniture." *(9)*

Surface features Specific elements that make up a problem. For example, in the radiation problem, the rays and the tumor are surface features. Contrast with **Structural features**. *(12)*

Syllogism A series of three statements: two premises followed by a conclusion. The conclusion can follow from the premises based on the rules of logic. See also **Categorical syllogism**; **Conditional syllogism**. *(13)*

Synapse Space between the end of an axon and the cell body or dendrite of the next axon. *(2)*

Synaptic consolidation A process of consolidation that involves structural changes at synapses that happen rapidly, over a period of minutes. See also **Consolidation**; **Systems consolidation**. *(7)*

Syntactic coordination Process by which people use similar grammatical constructions when having a conversation. *(11)*

Syntactic priming Hearing a statement with a particular syntactic construction increases the chances that a statement that follows will be produced with the same construction. *(11)*

Syntax The rules for combining words into sentences. Distinguished from **Semantics**. *(11)*

Syntax-first approach to parsing The approach to parsing that emphasizes the role of syntax. See also **Interactionist approach to parsing**. *(11)*

Systems consolidation A consolidation process that involves the gradual reorganization of circuits within brain regions and takes place on a long time scale, lasting weeks, months, or even years. See also **Consolidation; Synaptic consolidation.** *(7)*

Tacit knowledge explanation An explanation proposed to account for the results of some imagery experiments that states that participants unconsciously use knowledge about the world in making their judgments. This explanation has been used as one of the arguments against describing imagery as a depictive or spatial representation. *(10)*

Target problem A problem to be solved. In analogical problem solving, solution of this problem can become easier when the problem-solver is exposed to an analogous source problem or story. See also **Source problem.** *(12)*

Temporal lobe The lobe on the side of the brain that contains mechanisms responsible for language, memory, hearing, and vision. *(2)*

Temporary ambiguity A situation in which the meaning of a sentence, based on its initial words, is ambiguous because a number of meanings are possible, depending on how the sentence unfolds. "Cast iron sinks quickly rust" is an example of a sentence that creates temporary ambiguity. *(11)*

Testing effect Enhanced performance on a memory test caused by being tested on the material to be remembered. *(7)*

Theory of natural selection Darwin's theory that characteristics that enhance an animal's ability to survive and reproduce will be passed on to future generations. *(3)*

Think-aloud protocol A procedure in which subjects are asked to say out loud what they are thinking while doing a problem. This procedure is used to help determine people's thought processes as they are solving a problem. *(12)*

Top-down processing Processing that involves a person's knowledge or expectations. This type of processing has also been called knowledge-based processing. *(3)*

Topographic map Each point on a visual stimulus causes activity at a specific location on a brain structure, such as the visual cortex, and points next to each other on the stimulus cause activity at points next to each other on the structure. *(4)*

Tower of Hanoi problem A problem involving moving discs from one set of pegs to another. It has been used to illustrate the process involved in means–end analysis. *(12)*

Transcranial magnetic stimulation (TMS) A procedure in which magnetic pulses are applied to the skull in order to temporarily disrupt the functioning of part of the brain. *(9)*

Transfer-appropriate processing When the type of task that occurs during encoding matches the type of task that occurs during retrieval. This type of processing can result in enhanced memory. *(7)*

Two-string problem A problem first described by Maier in which a person is given the task of attaching two strings together that are too far apart to be reached at the same time. This task was devised to illustrate the operation of functional fixedness. *(12)*

Typicality effect The ability to judge the truth or falsity of sentences involving high-prototypical members of a category more rapidly than sentences involving low-prototypical members of a category. See also **Sentence verification technique.** *(9)*

Ultimatum game A game in which a *proposer* is given a sum of money and makes an offer to a *responder* as to how this money should be split between them. The responder must choose to accept the offer or reject it. This game has been used to study people's decision-making strategies. *(13)*

Unconscious inference Helmholtz's idea that some of our perceptions are the result of unconscious assumptions that we make about the environment. See also Likelihood principle. *(3)*

Unilateral neglect A problem caused by brain damage, usually to the right parietal lobe, in which the patient ignores objects in the left half of his or her visual field. *(10)*

Units "Neuronlike processing units" in a connectionist network. See also Hidden units; Input units; Output units. *(9)*

Utility Outcomes that achieve a person's goals; in economic terms, the maximum monetary payoff. *(13)*

Validity Quality of a syllogism whose conclusion follows logically from its premises. *(13)*

Viewpoint invariance The ability to recognize an object seen from different viewpoints. *(3)*

Visual cortex Area in the occipital lobe that receives signals from the eyes. *(2)*

Visual icon See Iconic memory. *(5)*

Visual imagery A type of mental imagery involving vision, in which an image is experienced in the absence of a visual stimulus. *(5, 10)*

Visual scanning Movement of the eyes from one location or object to another. *(4)*

Visual search Occurs when a person is looking for one stimulus or object among a number of other stimuli or objects. *(4)*

Visual world paradigm In experiments on language processing, determining how subjects are processing information in a scene as they respond to specific instructions related to the scene. *(11)*

Visuospatial sketch pad The part of working memory that holds and processes visual and spatial information. See also Central executive; Phonological loop; Working memory. *(5)*

Voxel Small cube-shaped areas in the brain used in the analysis of data from brain scanning experiments. *(2)*

Wason four-card problem A conditional reasoning task developed by Wason that involves four cards. Various versions of this problem have been used to study the mechanisms that determine the outcomes of conditional reasoning tasks. *(13)*

Water jug problem A problem, first described by Luchins, that illustrates how mental set can influence the strategies that people use to solve a problem. *(12)*

Weapons focus The tendency for eyewitnesses to a crime to focus attention on a weapon, which causes poorer memory for other things that are happening. *(8)*

Wernicke's aphasia A condition, caused by damage to Wernicke's area, that is characterized by difficulty in understanding language, and fluent, grammatically correct, but incoherent speech. *(11)*

Wernicke's area Area in the temporal lobe associated with understanding language. Damage to this area causes Wernicke's aphasia. *(2)*

***What* pathway** Neural pathway, extending from the occipital lobe to the temporal lobe, that is associated with perceiving or recognizing objects. Corresponds to the perception pathway. *(3)*

***Where* pathway** Neural pathway, extending from the occipital lobe to the parietal lobe, that is associated with neural processing that occurs when people locate objects in space. Roughly corresponds to the action pathway. *(3)*

Whole report method Procedure used in Sperling's experiment on the properties of the visual icon, in which participants were instructed to report all of the stimuli they saw in a brief presentation. See also **Partial report method; Sensory memory.** *(5)*

Word frequency The relative usage of words in a particular language. For example, in English, *home* has higher word frequency than *hike*. *(11)*

Word frequency effect The phenomenon of faster reading time for high-frequency words than for low-frequency words. *(11)*

Word length effect The notion that it is more difficult to remember a list of long words than a list of short words. *(5)*

Word superiority effect The idea that letters are easier to identify when they are part of a word than when they are seen in isolation or in a string of letters that do not form a word. *(11)*

Working memory A limited-capacity system for temporary storage and manipulation of information for complex tasks such as comprehension, learning, and reasoning. *(5)*

References

Adamson, R. E. (1952). Functional fixedness as related to problem solving. *Journal of Experimental Psychology, 44*, 288–291.

Addis, D. R., Pan, L., Vu, M.-A., Laiser, N., & Schacter, D. L. (2009). Constructive episodic simulation of the future and the past: Distinct subsystems of a core brain network mediate imagining and remembering. *Neuropsychologia, 47*, 2222–2238.

Addis, D. R., Wong, A. T., & Schacter, D. L. (2007). Remembering the past and imagining the future: Common and distinct neural substrates during event construction and elaboration. *Neuropsychologia, 45*, 1363–1377.

Addis, D. R., Wong, A. T., & Schacter, D. L. (2008). Age-related changes in the episodic simulation of future events. *Psychological Science, 19*, 33–41.

Adrian, E. D. (1928). *The basis of sensation.* New York: Norton.

Adrian, E. D. (1932). *The mechanism of nervous action.* Philadelphia: University of Pennsylvania Press.

Aguirre, G. K., Zarahn, E., & D'Esposito, M. (1998). An area within human ventral cortex sensitive to "building" stimuli: Evidence and implications. *Neuron, 21*, 373–383.

Almeida, J., Fintzi, A. R., & Mahon, B. Z. (2013). Tool manipulation knowledge is retrieved by way of the ventral visual object processing pathway. *Cortex, 49*, 2334–2344.

Altmann, G. T. M. (2001). The language machine: Psycholinguistics in review. *British Journal of Psychology, 92*, 129–170.

Alvarez, G. A., & Cavanagh, P. (2004). The capacity of visual short-term memory is set both by visual information load and by number of objects. *Psychological Science, 15*, 106–111.

Amedi, A., Malach, R., & Pascual-Leone, A. (2005). Negative BOLD differentiates visual imagery and perception. *Neuron, 48*, 859–872.

Anderson, B. A., Laurent, P. A., & Yantis, S. (2011). Value-driven attentional capture. *Proceedings of the National Academy of Sciences, 108*, 10367–10371.

Anderson, J. R. (1978). Arguments concerning representation for mental imagery. *Psychological Review, 85*, 249–277.

Anderson, J. R., & Schooler, L. J. (1991). Reflections of the environment in memory. *Psychological Science, 2*, 396–408.

Appelle, S. (1972). Perception and discrimination as a function of stimulus orientation: The "oblique effect" in man and animals. *Psychological Bulletin, 78*, 266–278.

Arkes, H. R., & Freedman, M. R. (1984). A demonstration of the costs and benefits of expertise in recognition memory. *Memory & Cognition, 12*, 84–89.

Ashcraft, M. H., & Kirk, E. P. (2001). The relationships among working memory, math anxiety, and performance. *Journal of Experimental Psychology: General, 130*, 224–237.

Ashcraft, M. H., & Krause, J. A. (2007). Working memory, math performance, and math anxiety. *Psychonomic Bulletin & Review, 14*, 243–248.

Ashcraft, M. H., & Moore, A. M. (2009). Mathematics anxiety and the affective drop in performance. *Journal of Psychoeducational Assessment, 27*, 197–205.

Atkinson, R. C., & Shiffrin, R. M. (1968). Human memory: A proposed system and its control processes. In K. W. Spence & J. T. Spence (Eds.), *The psychology of learning and motivation* (Vol. 2, pp. 89–195). New York: Academic Press.

Awh, E., Barton, B., & Vogel, E. K. (2007). Visual working memory represents a fixed number of items regardless of complexity. *Psychological Science, 18*, 622–628.

Awh, E., & Jonides, J. (2001). Overlapping mechanisms of attention and spatial working memory. *Trends in Cognitive Sciences, 5*, 119–126.

Awh, E., Vogel, E. K., & Ho, S.-H. (2006). Interactions between attention and working memory. *Neuroscience, 139*, 201–208.

Baddeley, A. D. (1996). Exploring the central executive. *Quarterly Journal of Experimental Psychology, 49A*, 5–28.

Baddeley, A. D. (2000a). The episodic buffer: A new component of working memory? *Trends in Cognitive Sciences, 4*, 417–423.

Baddeley, A. D. (2000b). Short-term and working memory. In E. Tulving & F. I. M. Craik (Eds.), *The Oxford handbook of memory* (pp. 77–92). New York: Oxford University Press.

Baddeley, A. D., Eysenck, M., & Anderson, M. C. (2009). *Memory.* New York: Psychology Press.

Baddeley, A. D., & Hitch, G. J. (1974). Working memory. In G. A. Bower (Ed.), *The psychology of learning and motivation* (pp. 47–89). New York: Academic Press.

Baddeley, A. D., Lewis, V. F. J., & Vallar, G. (1984). Exploring the articulatory loop. *Quarterly Journal of Experimental Psychology, 36*, 233–252.

Baddeley, A. D., Thomson, N., & Buchanan, M. (1975). Word length and the structure of short-term memory. *Journal of Verbal Learning and Verbal Behavior, 14*, 575–589.

Bailey, M. R., & Balsam, P. D. (2013). Memory reconsolidation: Time to change your mind. *Current Biology, 23*, R243–R245.

Bar, M. (2004). Visual objects in context. *Nature Reviews Neuroscience, 5*, 617–629.

Barsalou, L. W. (2005). Continuity of the conceptual system across species. *Trends in Cognitive Sciences, 9*, 309–311.

Barsalou, L. W. (2008). Grounded cognition. *Annual Review of Psychology, 59*, 617–645.

Barsalou, L. W. (2009). Simulation, situated conceptualization and prediction. *Philosophical Transactions of the Royal Society B, 364*, 1281–1289.

Bartlett, F. C. (1932). *Remembering: A study in experimental and social psychology.* Cambridge, UK: Cambridge University Press.

Basadur, M., Runco, M., & Vega, L. A. (2000). Understanding how creative thinking skills, attitudes and behaviors work together: A causal process model. *Journal of Creative Behavior, 34*, 77–100.

Baylis, G. C., & Driver, J. (1993). Visual attention and objects: Evidence for hierarchical coding of location. *Journal of Experimental Psychology: Human Perception and Performance, 19*, 451–470.

Bays, P. M., & Husain, M. (2008). Dynamic shifts of limited working memory resources in human vision. *Science, 321*, 851–854.

Bechtel, W., Abrahamsen, A., & Graham, G. (1998). The life of cognitive science. In W. Bechtel & G. Graham (Eds.), *A companion to cognitive science* (pp. 2–104). Oxford, UK: Blackwell.

Bedard, J., & Chi, M. T. H. (1992). Expertise. *Current Directions in Psychological Science, 1*, 135–139.

Beecher, H. K. (1959) *Measurement of subjective responses.* New York: Oxford University Press.

Begg, I. M., Anas, A., & Farinacci, S. (1992). Dissociation of processes in belief: Source recollection, statement familiarity, and the illusion of truth. *Journal of Experimental Psychology: General, 121*, 446–458.

Behrmann, M., Moscovitch, M., & Winocur, G. (1994). Intact visual imagery and impaired visual perception in a patient with visual agnosia. *Journal of Experimental Psychology: Human Perception and Performance, 30*, 1068–1087.

Beilock, S. L. (2008). Math performance in stressful situations. *Current Directions in Psychological Science, 17*, 339–343.

Beilock, S. L. (2010). *Choke.* New York: Free Press.

Beilock, S. L., & Carr, T. H. (2001). On the fragility of skilled performance: What governs choking under pressure? *Journal of Experimental Psychology: General, 130*, 701–735.

Beilock, S. L., & Carr, T. H. (2004). From novice to expert performance: Attention, memory, and the control of complex sensorimotor skills. In A. M. Williams, N. J. Hodges, M. A. Scott, & M. L. J. Court (Eds.), *Skill acquisition in sport: Research, theory and practice* (pp. 309–328). Routledge.

Beilock, S. L., & Carr, T. H. (2005). When high-powered people fail. *Psychological Science, 16*, 101–105.

Beilock, S. L., & DeCaro, M. S. (2007). From poor performance to success under stress: Working memory, strategy selection, and mathematical problem solving under pressure. *Journal of Experimental Psychology: Learning, Memory, and Cognition, 33*, 983–998.

Bell, K. E., & Limber, J. E. (2010). Reading skill, textbook marking, and course performance. *Literacy Research and Instruction, 49*, 56–67.

Benton, T. R., Ross, D. F., Bradshaw, E., Thomas, W. N., & Bradshaw, G. S. (2006). Eyewitness memory is still not common sense: Comparing jurors, judges and law enforcement to eyewitness experts. *Applied Cognitive Psychology, 20*, 115–129.

Berntsen, D. (2009). Flashbulb memory and social identity. In O. Luminet & A. Curci (Eds.), *Flashbulb memories: New issues and new perspectives* (pp. 187–205). Hove, UK: Psychology Press.

Berntsen, D., & Rubin, C. (2004). Cultural life scripts structure recall from autobiographical memory. *Memory & Cognition, 32*, 427–442.

Bisiach, E., & Luzzatti, C. (1978). Unilateral neglect of representational space. *Cortex, 14*, 129–133.

Blakemore, C., & Cooper, G. G. (1970). Development of the brain depends on the visual environment. *Nature, 228*, 477–478.

Bliss, T. V. P., Collingridge, G. L., & Morris, R. G. M. (2003). Introduction. *Philosophical Transactions of the Royal Society, Series B: Biological Sciences, 358*, 607–611.

Bliss, T. V. P., & Lomo, T. (1973). Long-lasting potentiation of synaptic transmission in the dentate area of the anaesthetized rabbit following stimulation of the perforant path. *Journal of Physiology (London), 232*, 331–336.

Blundo, C., Ricci, M., & Miller, L. (2006). Category-specific knowledge deficit for animals in a patient with herpes simplex encephalitis. *Cognitive Neuropsychology, 23*, 1248–1268.

Bock, K. (1990). Structure in language. *American Psychologist, 45*, 1221–1236.

Boden, M. A. (2006). *Mind as machine: A history of cognitive science.* New York: Oxford University Press.

Bolognani, S. A., Gouvia, P. A., Brucki, S. M., & Bueno, O. F. (2000). Implicit memory and its contribution to the rehabilitation of an amnesic patient: Case study. *Arquiuos de neuro-psiqustria, 58*, 924–930.

Bonnici, H. M., Chadwick, M. J., Lutti, A., Hasabis, D., Weiskopf, N., & Magurie, E. A. (2012). Detecting representations of recent and remote autobiographical memories in vmPFC and hippocampus. *Journal of Neuroscience, 32*, 16982–16991.

Boring, E. G. (1942). *Sensation and perception in the history of experimental psychology.* New York: Appleton-Century-Crofts.

Bowden, E. M., Jung-Beeman, M., Fleck, J., & Kounios, J. (2005). New approaches to demystifying insight. *Trends in Cognitive Sciences, 9*, 322–328.

Bower, G. H., Black, J. B., & Turner, T. J. (1979). Scripts in memory for text. *Cognitive Psychology, 11*, 177–220.

Bower, G. H., Clark, M. C., Lesgold, A. M., & Winzenz, D. (1969). Hierarchical retrieval schemes in recall of categorized word lists. *Journal of Verbal Learning and Verbal Behavior, 8*, 323–343.

Bower, G. H., & Winzenz, D. (1970). Comparison of associative learning strategies. *Psychonomic Science, 20*, 119–120.

Brady, T. F., Konkie, T., & Alvarez, G. A. (2011). A review of visual memory capacity: Beyond individual items and toward structured representations. *Journal of Vision, 11*(5), 1–34.

Branigan, H. P., Pickering, M. J., & Cleland, A. A. (2000). Syntactic co-ordination in dialogue. *Cognition, 75*, B13–B25.

Bransford, J. D., & Johnson, M. K. (1972). Contextual prerequisites for understanding: Some investigations of comprehension and recall. *Journal of Verbal Learning and Verbal Behavior, 11*, 717–726.

Bransford, J. D., & Johnson, M. K. (1973). Consideration of some problems of comprehension. In W. C. Chase (Ed.), *Visual information processing* (pp. 383–438). New York: Academic Press.

Brewer, W. F. (1977). Memory for the pragmatic implication of sentences. *Memory & Cognition, 5*, 673–678.

Brewer, W. F., & Treyens, J. C. (1981). Role of schemata in memory for places. *Cognitive Psychology, 13*, 207–230.

Broadbent, D. E. (1958). *Perception and communication.* London: Pergamon Press.

Broca, P. (1861). Sur le volume et la forme du cerveau suivant les individus et suivant les races. *Bulletin Société d'Anthropologie Paris, 2*, 139–207, 301–321, 441–446.

Brod, J. H. (1997). Creativity and schizotypy. In G. Claridge (Ed.), *Schizotypy: Implications for illness and health* (pp. 274–300). Oxford, UK: Oxford University Press.

Brooks, L. (1968). Spatial and verbal components of the act of recall. *Canadian Journal of Psychology, 22*, 349–368.

Brown, J. (1958). Some tests of the decay theory of immediate memory. *Quarterly Journal of Experimental Psychology, 10,* 12–21.

Brown, R., & Kulik, J. (1977). Flashbulb memories. *Cognition, 5,* 73–99.

Brown-Schmidt, S., & Hanna, J. E. (2011). Talking in another person's shoes: Incremental perspective-taking in language processing. *Dialogue and Discourse, 2,* 11–33.

Brunet, A., Orr, S. P., Tremblay, J., Robertson, K., Nader, K., & Pitman, R. K. (2008). Effect of post-retrieval propranolol on psychophysiologic responding during subsequent script-driven traumatic imagery in post-traumatic stress disorder. *Journal of Psychiatric Research, 42,* 503–506.

Buciarelli, M., & Johnson-Laird, P. N. (1999). Strategies in syllogistic reasoning. *Cognitive Science, 23,* 247–303.

Buhle, J. T., Stevens, B. L., Friedman, J. J., & Wager, T. D. (2012). Distraction and placebo: Two separate routes to pain control. *Psychological Science, 23,* 246–253.

Burton, A. M., Young, A. W., Bruce, V., Johnston, R. A., & Ellis, A. W. (1991). Understanding covert recognition. *Cognition, 39,* 129–166.

Butterworth, B., Shallice, T., & Watson, F. L. (1990). Short-term retention without short-term memory. In G. Vallar & T. Shallice (Eds.), *Neuropsychological impairments of short-term memory* (pp. 187–213). Cambridge, UK: Cambridge University Press.

Cabeza, R., & Nyberg, L. (2000). Imaging cognition II: An empirical review of 275 PET and fMRI studies. *Journal of Cognitive Neuroscience, 12,* 1–47.

Cabeza, R., Prince, S. E., Daselaar, S. M., Greenberg, D. L., Budde, M., Dolcos, F., et al. (2004). Brain activity during episodic retrieval of autobiographical and laboratory events: An fMRI study using novel photo paradigm. *Journal of Cognitive Neuroscience, 16,* 1583–1594.

Cabeza, R., & St. Jacques, P. (2007). Functional neuroimaging of auto biographical memory. *Trends in Cognitive Sciences, 11,* 219–227.

Cahill, L., Babinsky, R., Markowitsch, H. J., & McGaugh, J. L. (1995). The amygdala and emotional memory. *Nature, 377,* 295–296.

Cahill, L., Gorski, L., & Le, K. (2003). Enhanced human memory consolidation with post-learning stress: Interaction with the degree of arousal at encoding. *Learning & Memory, 10,* 270–274.

Cahill, L., Haier, R. J., Fallon, J., Alkire, M. T., Tang, C., Keator, D., et al. (1996). Amygdala activity at encoding correlated with long-term free recall of emotional information. *Proceedings of the National Academy of Sciences, USA, 93,* 8016–8021.

Calamante, F., Masterton, R. A. J., Tournier, J. D., Smith, R. E., Willats, L., Raffelt, D., & Connelly, A. (2013). Track-weighted functional connectivity (TW-FC): A tool for characterizing the structural-functional connections in the brain. *NeuroImage, 70,* 199–210.

Calder, A. J., Beaver, J. D., Winston, J. S., Dolan, R. J., Jenkins, R., Eger, E., et al. (2007). Separate coding of different gaze directions in the superior temporal sulcus and inferior parietal lobule. *Current Biology, 17,* 20–25.

Campbell, F. W., Kulikowski, J. J., & Levinson, J. (1966). The effect of orientation on the visual resolution of gratings. *Journal of Physiology (London), 187,* 427–436.

Cappa, S. F., Frugoni, M., Pasquali, P., Perani, D., & Zorat, F. (1998). Category specific naming impairment for artefacts: A new case. *Neurocase, 4,* 391–397.

Caramazza, A., & Shelton, J. R. (1998). Domain-specific knowledge systems in the brain: The animate–inanimate distinction. *Journal of Cognitive Neuroscience, 10,* 1–34.

Carota, F., Moseley, R., & Pulvermuller, F. (2012). Body-part-specific representations of semantic noun categories. *Journal of Cognitive Neuroscience, 24,* 1492–1509.

Carpenter, S. K., Pashler, H., & Cepeda, N. J. (2009). Using tests to enhance 8th grade students' retention of U.S. history facts. *Applied Cognitive Psychology, 23,* 760–771.

Carrier, L. M. (2003). College students' choices of study strategies. *Perceptual and Motor Skills, 96,* 54–56.

Carroll, D. W. (2004). *Psychology of language* (4th ed.). Belmont, CA: Wadsworth.

Carson, S. H. (2010). *Your creative brain: Seven steps to maximize imagination, productivity, and innovation in your life.* San Francisco: Jossey-Bass.

Carson, S. H. (2011). Creativity and psychoathology: A shared vulnerability model. *Canadian Journal of Psychiatry, 56,* 144–153.

Carson, S. H., Peterson, J. B., & Higgins, D. M. (2003). Decreased latent inhibition is associated with increased creative achievement in high-functioning individuals. *Journal of Personality and Social Psychology, 85,* 499–506.

Cartwright-Finch, U., & Lavie, N. (2007). The role of perceptual load in inattentional blindness. *Cognition, 102,* 321–340.

Cashdollar, N., Malecki, J., Rugg-Gunn, F. J., Duncan, J. S., Lavie, N., & Duzel, E. (2009). Hippocampus-dependent and -independent theta-networks of active maintenance. *Proceedings of the National Academy of Sciences, 106,* 20493–20498.

Castelhano, M. S., & Henderson, J. M. (2008). Stable individual differences across images in human saccadic eye movements. *Canadian Journal of Experimental Psychology, 62,* 1–14.

Catrambone, R., & Holyoak, K. J. (1989). Overcoming contextual limitations on problem-solving transfer. *Journal of Experimental Psychology: Learning, Memory, and Cognition, 15,* 1147–1156.

Chalmers, D., & Reisberg, D. (1985). Can mental images be ambiguous? *Journal of Experimental Psychology: Human Perception and Performance, 11,* 317–328.

Chambers, C. G., Tanenhaus, M. K., & Magnuson, J. S. (2004). Actions and affordances in syntactic ambiguity resolution. *Journal of Experimental Psychology: Learning, Memory, and Cognition, 30,* 687–696.

Chan, J. A., & LaPaglia, J. A. (2013). Impairing existing declarative memory in humans by disrupting reconsolidation. *Proceedings of the National Academy of Sciences, 110,* 9309–9313.

Chan, J. C. K., & McDermott, K. B. (2006). Remembering pragmatic inferences. *Applied Cognitive Psychology, 20,* 633–639.

Chan, J. C. K., Thomas, A. K., & Bulevich, J. B. (2009). Recalling a witnessed event increases eyewitness suggestibility. *Psychological Science, 20,* 66–73.

Chapman, L. J., & Chapman, J. P. (1969). Genesis of popular but erroneous psychodiagnostic observations. *Journal of Abnormal Psychology, 74,* 272–280.

Charman, S. D., Wells, G. L., & Joy, S. W. (2011). The dud effect: Adding highly dissimilar fillers increases confidence in lineup identifications. *Law and Human Behavior, 35,* 479–500.

Chase, W. G., & Simon, H. A. (1973a). The mind's eye in chess. In W. G. Chase (Ed.), *Visual information processing.* New York: Academic Press.

Chase, W. G., & Simon, H. A. (1973b). Perception in chess. *Cognitive Psychology, 4,* 55–81.

Chatterjee, A. (2010). Disembodying cognition. *Language and Cognition, 2,* 79–116.

Chen, V. J., Allen, H., Beb, S., & Humphreys, G. (2011). Role of emotion in shifting choice preference: A neuroscientific perspective. *Frontiers in Psychology, 2*, Article 300, 1–3.

Cheng, P. W., & Holyoak, K. J. (1985). Pragmatic reasoning schemas. *Cognitive Psychology, 17*, 391–416.

Cherry, E. C. (1953). Some experiments on the recognition of speech, with one and with two ears. *Journal of the Acoustical Society of America, 25*, 975–979.

Chi, M. T. H., Feltovich, P. J., & Glaser, R. (1981). Categorization and representation of physics problems by experts and novices. *Cognitive Science, 5*, 121–152.

Chi, M. T. H., Glaser, R., & Rees, E. (1982). Expertise in problem solving. In R. J. Sternberg (Ed.), *Advances in the psychology of human intelligence.* Hillsdale, NJ: Erlbaum.

Chi, R. P., & Snyder, A. W. (2011). Facilitate insight by non-invasive brain stimulation. *PLoS ONE 6*(2), e16655.

Chi, R. P., & Snyder, A. W. (2012). Brain stimulation enables the solution of an inherently difficult problem. *Neuroscience Letters, 515*, 121–124.

Chklovskii, D. B., Mel, B. W., & Svoboda, K. (2004). Cortical rewiring and information storage. *Nature, 431*, 782–788.

Chomsky, N. (1957). *Syntactic structures.* The Hague, Netherlands: Mouton.

Chomsky, N. (1959). A review of Skinner's *Verbal Behavior. Language, 35*, 26–58.

Christensen, B. T., & Schunn, C. D. (2007). The relationship of analogical distance to analogical function and pre-inventive structure: The case of engineering design. *Memory & Cognition, 35*, 29–38.

Chun, M. M., & Johnson, M. K. (2011). Memory: Enduring traces of perceptual and reflective attention. *Neuron, 72*, 520–535.

Clare, L., & Jones, R. S. P. (2008). Errorless learning in the rehabilitation of memory impairment: A critical review. *Neuropsychology Review, 18*, 1–23.

Clarey, C. (2014, February 23). Their minds have seen the glory. *New York Times*, Sports Sunday, p. 1.

Clark, H. H. (1996). *Using language.* Cambridge, UK: Cambridge University Press.

Clark, H. H., & Van der Wege, M. M. (2002). Psycholinguistics. In H. Pashler & S. Yantis (Eds.), *Stevens' handbook of experimental psychology* (3rd ed., pp. 209–259). New York: Wiley.

Coley, J. D., Medin, D. L., & Atran, S. (1997). Does rank have its privilege? Inductive inferences within folkbiological taxonomies. *Cognition, 64*, 73–112.

Collins, A. M., & Quillian, M. R. (1969). Retrieval time from semantic memory. *Journal of Verbal Learning and Verbal Behavior, 8*, 240–247.

Colloca, L., & Benedetti, F. (2005). Placebos and painkillers: Is mind as real as matter? *Nature Reviews Neuroscience, 6*, 545–552.

Conrad, C. (1972). Cognitive economy in semantic memory. *Journal of Experimental Psychology, 92*, 149–154.

Conrad, R. (1964). Acoustic confusion in immediate memory. *British Journal of Psychology, 55*, 75–84.

Conway, M. A. (1996). Autobiographical memory. In E. L. Bjork & R. A. Bjork (Eds.), *Handbook of perception and cognition: Vol. 10. Memory* (2nd ed., pp. 165–194). New York: Academic Press.

Coons, P. M., & Milstein, V. (1992). Psychogenic amnesia: A clinical investigation of 25 cases. *Dissociation, 5*, 73–79.

Coppola, D. M., White, L. E., Fitzpatrick, D., & Purves, D. (1998). Unequal distribution of cardinal and oblique contours in ferret visual cortex. *Proceedings of the National Academy of Sciences, 95*, 2621–2623.

Corkin, S. (2002). What's new with the amnesic patient H.M.? (2002). *Nature Reviews Neuroscience, 3*, 1–8.

Cosmides, L. (1989). The logic of social exchange: Has natural selection shaped how humans reason? Studies with the Wason selection task. *Cognition, 31*, 187–226.

Cosmides, L., & Tooby, J. (1992). Cognitive adaptations for social exchange. In J. H. Barkow, L. Cosmides, & J. Tooby (Eds.), *The adapted mind* (pp. 179–228). Oxford, UK: Oxford University Press.

Cowan, N. (1988). Evolving conceptions of memory storage, selective attention, and their mutual constraints within the human information processing system. *Psychological Bulletin, 104*, 163–191.

Cowan, N. (1999). An embedded-process model of working memory. In A. Miyake & P. Shah (Eds.), *Models of working memory: Mechanisms of active maintenance and executive control* (pp. 62–101). Cambridge, UK: Cambridge University Press.

Cowan, N. (2001). The magical number 4 in short-term memory: A reconsideration of mental storage capacity. *Behavioral Brain Sciences, 24*, 87–185.

Cowan, N. (2005). *Working memory capacity.* New York: Psychology Press.

Craik, F. I. M., & Lockhart, R. S. (1972). Levels of processing: A framework for memory research. *Journal of Verbal Learning and Verbal Behavior, 11*, 671–684.

Craik, F. I. M., & Tulving, E. (1975). Depth of processing and retention of words in episodic memory. *Journal of Experimental Psychology: General, 104*, 268–294.

Craver-Lemley, C., & Reeves, A. (1992). How visual imagery interferes with vision. *Psychological Review, 99*, 633–649.

Cree, G. S., & McRae, K. (2003). Analyzing the factors underlying the structure and computation of the meaning of *chipmunk, cherry, cheese,* and *cello* (and many other such concrete nouns). *Journal of Experimental Psychology: General, 132*, 163–201.

Crick, F. (1995). The impact of Linus Pauling on molecular biology. *The Pauling Symposium.* Corvallis: Oregon State University, The Valley Library, Special Collections.

Crook, T. H., & Adderly, B. (1998). *The memory cure.* New York: Simon & Schuster.

Çukur, T., Nishimoto, S., Huth, A. G., & Gallant, J. L. (2013). Attention during natural vision warps semantic representation across the human brain. *Nature Neuroscience, 16*, 763–770.

Curtis, C. E., & Esposito, M. D. (2003). Persistent activity in the prefrontal cortex during working memory. *Trends in Cognitive Sciences, 7*, 415–423.

D'Argembeau, A., & Van der Linden, M. (2004). Phenomenal characteristics associated with projecting oneself back into the past and forward into the future: Influence of valence and temporal distance. *Consciousness and Cognition, 13*, 844–858.

Daneman, M., & Carpenter, P. A. (1980). Individual differences in working memory and reading. *Journal of Verbal Learning and Verbal Behavior, 19*, 450–466.

Danziger, S., Levav, J., & Avanim-Pesso, L. (2011). Extraneous factors in judicial decisions. *Proceedings of the National Academy of Sciences, 108*, 6889–6892.

Darwin, C. J., Turvey, M. T., & Crowder, R. G. (1972). An auditory analogue of the Sperling partial report procedure: Evidence for brief auditory storage. *Cognitive Psychology, 3*, 255–267.

Datta, R., & DeYoe, E. A. (2009). I know where you are secretly attending! The topography of human visual attention revealed with fMRI. *Vision Research, 49*, 1037–1044.

Davidoff, J. (2001). Language and perceptual categorization. *Trends in Cognitive Sciences, 5,* 382–387.

De Neys, W. (2006). Automatic-heuristic and executive-analytic processing during reasoning: Chronometric and dual-task considerations. *Quarterly Journal of Experimental Psychology, 59,* 1070–1010.

Deese, J. (1959). On the prediction of occurrence of particular verbal intrusions in immediate recall. *Journal of Experimental Psychology, 58,* 17–22.

DeGroot, A. (1965). *Thought and choice in chess.* The Hague, Netherlands: Mouton.

Del Pero, L., Guan, J., Brau, E., Schlecht, J., & Barnard, K. (2011). Sampling bedrooms. *IEEE Computer Society Conference on Computer Vision and Pattern Recognition (CVPR),* pp. 2009–2016.

Dell, G. S. (1995). Speaking and misspeaking. In L. Gleitman & M. Liberman (Eds.), *An invitation to cognitive science* (Vol. 1, pp. 183–208). Cambridge, MA: MIT Press.

Della Sala, S., Gray, C., Baddeley, A., Allamano, N., & Wilson, L. (1999). Attention span: A tool for unwelding visuo-spatial memory. *Neuropsychologia, 37,* 1189–1199.

Denes-Raj, V., & Epstein, S. (1994). Conflict between intuitive and rational processing: When people behave against their better judgment. *Journal of Personality and Social Psychology, 66,* 819–829.

DeRenzi, E., Liotti, M., & Nichelli, P. (1987). Semantic amnesia with preservation of autobiographic memory: A case report. *Cortex, 23,* 575–597.

DeRenzi, E., & Spinnler, H. (1967). Impaired performance on color tasks in patients with hemispheric lesions. *Cortex, 3,* 194–217.

Deutsch, J. A., & Deutsch, D. (1963). Attention: Some theoretical considerations. *Psychological Review, 70,* 80–90.

DeValois, R. L., Yund, E. W., & Hepler, N. (1982). The orientation and direction selectivity of cells in macaque visual cortex. *Vision Research, 22,* 531–544.

DeVreese, L. P. (1991). Two systems for colour-naming defects: Verbal disconnection vs. colour imagery disorder. *Neuropsychologia, 29,* 1–18.

Dewar, M. T., Cowan, N., & Della Sala, S. (2007). Forgetting due to retroactive interference: A fusion of Muller and Pilecker's (1900) early insights into everyday forgetting and recent research on anterograde amnesia. *Cortex, 43,* 616–634.

Dick, F., Bates, E., Wulfeck, B., Utman, J. A., Dronkers, N., & Gernsbacher, M. A. (2001). Language deficits, localization, and grammar: Evidence for a distributive model of language breakdown in aphasic patients and neurologically intact individuals. *Psychological Review, 108,* 759–788.

Dingus, T. A., Klauer, S. G., Neale, V. L., Petersen, A., Lee, S. E., Sudweeks, J., et al. (2006). *The 100-Car Naturalistic Driving Study: Phase II. Results of the 100-car field experiment* (Interim Project Report for DTNH22-00-C-07007, Task Order 6; Report No. DOT HS 810 593). Washington, DC: National Highway Traffic Safety Administration.

Dinstein, I., Thomas, C., Behrmann, M., & Heeger, D. J. (2008). A mirror up to nature. *Current Biology, 18,* R13–R18.

Dolcos, F., LaBar, K. S., & Cabeza, R. (2005). Remembering one year later: Role of the amygdala and the medial temporal lobe memory system in retrieving emotional memories. *Proceedings of the National Academy of Sciences, 102,* 2626–2631.

Donders, F. C. (1969). Over de snelheid van psychische processen [Speed of mental processes]. Onderzoekingen gedann in het Psyciologish Laboratorium der Utrechtsche Hoogeschool (W. G. Koster, Trans.). In W. G. Koster (Ed.), Attention and performance II. *Acta Psychologica, 30,* 412–431. (Original work published 1868)

Douglass, A. B., Neuschatz, J. S., Imrich, J., & Wilkinson, M. (2010). Does post-identification feedback affect evaluations of eyewitness testimony and identification procedures? *Law and Human Behavior, 34,* 282–294.

Downing, P. E., Jiang, Y., Shuman, M., & Kanwisher, N. (2001). Cortical area selective for visual processing of the human body. *Science, 293,* 2470–2473.

Dravida, S., Saxe, R., & Bedny, M. (2013). People can understand descriptions of motion without activating visual motion brain regions. *Frontiers in Psychology, 4,* Article 537, 1–14.

Driver, J., & Baylis, G. C. (1989). Movement and visual attention: The spotlight metaphor breaks down. *Journal of Experimental Psychology: Human Perception and Performance, 15,* 448–456.

Driver, J., & Baylis, G. C. (1998). Attention and visual object segmentation. In R. Parasuraman (Ed.), *The attentive brain* (pp. 299–325). Cambridge, MA: MIT Press.

Duffy, S. A., Morris, R. K., & Rayner, K. (1988). Lexical ambiguity and fixation times in reading. *Journal of Memory and Language, 27,* 429–446.

Dunbar, K. (1998). Problem solving. In W. Bechtel & G. Graham (Eds.), *A companion to cognitive science* (pp. 289–298). London: Blackwell.

Dunbar, K. (1999). How scientists build models: In vivo science as a window on the scientific mind. In L. Magnani, N. Nersessian, & P. Thagard (Eds.), *Model-based reasoning in scientific discovery* (pp. 89–98). New York: Plenum Press.

Dunbar, K. (2001). The analogical paradox: Why analogy is so easy in naturalistic settings yet so difficult in the psychological laboratory. In D. Gentner, K. J. Holyoak, & B. Kokinov (Eds.), *Analogy: Perspectives from cognitive science.* Cambridge, MA: MIT Press.

Dunbar, K., & Blanchette, I. (2001). The *in vivo/in vitro* approach to cognition: The case of analogy. *Trends in Cognitive Sciences, 5,* 334–339.

Duncker, K. (1945). On problem solving. *Psychological Monographs, 58*(5, Whole No. 270).

Dunlosky, J., Rawson, K. A., Marsh, E. J., Nathan, M. J., & Willingham, D. T. (2013). Improving students' learning and comprehension: Promising directions from cognitive and educational psychology. *Psychological Science in the Public Interest, 14,* 4–58.

Duval, C., Desgranges, B., de La Sayettte, V., Beillard, S., Eustache, F., & Piolino, P. (2012). What happens to personal identity when semantic knowledge degrades? A study of the self and autobiographical memory in semantic dementia. *Neuropsychologia, 50,* 254–265.

Duzel, E., Cabeza, R., Picton, T. W., Yonelinas, A. P., Scheich, H., Heinze, H.-J., et al. (1999). Task-related and item-related brain processes of memory retrieval. *Proceedings of the National Academy of Sciences, USA, 96,* 1794–1799.

DvorakUncensored. (2007). Removing a cork from the bottle trick. *YouTube.*

Ebbinghaus, H. (1913). *Memory: A contribution to experimental psychology* (Henry A. Ruger & Clara E. Bussenius, Trans.). New York: Teachers College, Columbia University. (Original work, *Über das Gedächtnis,* published 1885)

Egan, D. E., & Schwartz, B. J. (1979). Chunking in recall of symbolic drawings. *Memory & Cognition, 7,* 149–158.

Egly, R., Driver, J., & Rafal, R. D. (1994). Shifting visual attention between objects and locations: Evidence from normal and parietal lesion subjects. *Journal of Experimental Psychology: General, 123,* 161–177.

Eich, E. (1995). Searching for mood dependent memory. *Psychological Science, 6,* 67–75.

Eich, E., & Metcalfe, J. (1989). Mood dependent memory for internal vs. external events. *Journal of Experimental Psychology: Learning, Memory, and Cognition, 15,* 443–455.

Emberson, L. L., Lupyan, G., Goldstein, M. H., & Spivey, M. J. (2010). Overheard cell-phone conversations: When less speech is more distracting. *Psychological Science, 21,* 1383–1388.

Epstein, R., Harris, A., Stanley, D., & Kanwisher, N. (1999). The parahippocampal place area: Recognition, navigation, or encoding? *Neuron, 23,* 115–125.

Ericsson, K. A., Chase, W. G., & Falloon, F. (1980). Acquisition of a memory skill. *Science, 208,* 1181–1182.

Ericsson, K. A., & Simon, H. A. (1993). *Protocol analysis.* Cambridge, MA: MIT Press.

Evans, J. St. B. T., Barston, J., & Pollard, P. (1983). On the conflict between logic and belief in syllogistic reasoning. *Memory & Cognition, 11,* 295–306.

Evans, J. St. B. T., & Curtis-Holmes, J. (2005). Rapid responding increases belief bias: Evidence for the dual-process theory of reasoning. *Thinking & Reasoning, 11,* 382–389.

Evans, J. St. B. T., & Feeney, A. (2004). In J. P. Leighton & R. J. Steinberg (Eds.), *The nature of reasoning* (pp. 78–102). Cambridge, UK: Cambridge University Press.

Evans, J. St. B. T., & Stanovich, K. E. (2013). Dual-process theories of higher cognition: Advancing the debate. *Perspectives on Psychological Science, 8,* 223–241.

Farah, M. J. (1985). Psychophysical evidence for a shared representational medium for mental images and percepts. *Journal of Experimental Psychology: General, 114,* 91–103.

Farah, M. J. (1988). Is visual imagery really visual? Overlooked evidence from neuropsychology. *Psychological Review, 95,* 307–317.

Farah, M. J. (2000). The neural basis of mental imagery. In M. Gazzaniga (Ed.), *The cognitive neurosciences* (2nd ed., pp. 965–974). Cambridge, MA: MIT Press.

Farah, M. J., Levine, D. N., & Calvanio, R. (1988). A case study of mental imagery deficit. *Brain and Cognition, 8,* 147–164.

Farah, M. J., O'Reilly, R. C., & Vecera, S. P. (1993). Dissociated overt and covert recognition as an emergent property of a lesioned neural network. *Psychological Review, 100,* 571–588.

Federmeier, K. D., & Kutas, M. (1999). A rose by any other name: Long-term memory structure and sentence processing. *Journal of Memory and Language, 41,* 469–495.

Felleman, D. J., & Van Essen, D. C. (1991). Distributed hierarchical processing in the primate cerebral cortex. *Cerebral Cortex, 1,* 1–47.

Fine, A. B., Jaeger, T. F., Farmer, T. A., & Qian, T. (2013). Rapid expectation adaptation during syntactic comprehension. *PLoS One, 8*(10), e77661.

Finke, R. A. (1990). *Creative imagery: Discoveries and inventions in visualization.* Hillsdale, NJ: Erlbaum.

Finke, R. A. (1995). Creative insight and preinventive forms. In R. J. Sternberg & J. E. Davidson (Eds.), *The nature of insight* (pp. 255–280). Cambridge, MA: MIT Press.

Finke, R. A., & Pinker, S. (1982). Spontaneous imagery scanning in mental exploration. *Journal of Experimental Psychology: Learning, Memory, and Cognition, 8,* 142–147.

Finke, R. A., Pinker, S., & Farah, M. J. (1989). Reinterpreting visual patterns in visual imagery. *Cognitive Science, 13,* 51–78.

Finniss, D. G., & Benedetti, F. (2005). Mechanisms of the placebo response and their impact on clinical trials and clinical practice. *Pain, 114,* 3–6.

Fischer, M. H., & Zwaan, R. A. (2008). Embodied language: A review of the role of the motor system in language comprehension. *Quarterly Journal of Experimental Psychology, 61,* 825–850.

Fischer, S., & Born, J. (2009). Anticipated reward enhances offline learning during sleep. *Journal of Experimental Psychology: Learning, Memory, and Cognition, 35,* 1586–1593.

Fischl, B., & Dale, A. M. (2000). Measuring the thickness of the human cerebral cortex from magnetic resonance images. *Proceedings of the National Academy of Sciences, 97,* 11050–11055.

Fisher, R. P., Schreiber, C., Rivard, J., & Hirn, D. (2013). Interviewing witnesses. In T. Perfect & S. Lindsay (Eds.), *The Sage handbook of applied memory.* London: Sage.

Forster, S., & Lavie, N. (2008). Failures to ignore entirely irrelevant distractors: The role of load. *Journal of Experimental Psychology: Applied, 14,* 73–83.

Frank, J. (1930). *Law and the modern mind.* New York: Brentano's.

Frankland, P. W., & Bontempi, B. (2005). The organization of recent and remote memories. *Neuroscience, 6,* 119–130.

Frase, L. T. (1975). Prose processing. In G. H. Bower (Ed.), *The psychology of learning and motivation* (Vol. 9). New York: Academic Press.

Frazier, L. (1979). *On comprehending sentences: Syntactic parsing strategies.* PhD thesis, University of Connecticut.

Frazier, L. (1987). Sentence processing: A tutorial review. In M. Coltheart (Ed.), *Attention and performance: Vol. 12. The psychology of reading* (pp. 559–586). Hove, UK: Erlbaum.

Fredrick, S. (2005). Cognitive reflection and decision making. *Journal of Economic Perspectives, 19*(4), 25–42.

Frenda, S. J., Knowles, E. D., Saletan, W., & Loftus, E. F. (2013). False memories of fabricated political events. *Journal of Experimental Social Psychology, 49,* 280–286.

Frensch, P. A., & Sternberg, R. J. (1989). Expertise and intelligent thinking: When is it worse to know better? In R. J. Sternberg (Ed.), *Advances in the psychology of human intelligence* (Vol. 5). Hillsdale, NJ: Erlbaum.

Fried, T., Wilson, C., Maidment, N. T., Engel, J., Behnke, E., Fields, T. A., et al. (1999). Cerebral microdialysis combined with single-neuron and electroencephalographic recording in neurosurgical patients. *Journal of Neurosurgery, 91,* 697–705.

Friedman-Hill, S. R., Robertson, L. C., & Treisman, A. (1995). Parietal contributions to visual feature binding: Evidence from a patient with bilateral lesions. *Science, 269,* 853–855.

Fukuda, K., Awh, E., & Vogel, E. K. (2010). Discrete capacity limits in visual working memory. *Current Opinion in Neurobiology, 20,* 177–182.

Funahashi, S. (2006). Prefrontal cortex and working memory processes. *Neuroscience, 139,* 251–261.

Funahashi, S., Bruce, C. J., & Goldman-Rakic, P. S. (1989). Mnemonic coding of visual space in the primate dorsolateral prefrontal cortex. *Journal of Neurophysiology, 61,* 331–349.

Furmanski, C. S., & Engel, S. A. (2000). An oblique effect in human primary visual cortex. *Nature Neuroscience, 3*, 535–536.

Gais, S., Lucas, B., & Born, J. (2006). Sleep after learning aids memory recall. *Learning and Memory, 13*, 259–262.

Gallese, V., Fadiga, L., Fogassi, L., & Rizzolatti, G. (1996). Action recognition in the premotor cortex. *Brain, 119*, 593–609.

Galton, F. (1883). *Inquiries into human faculty and its development*. London: Macmillan.

Ganis, G., Thompson, W. L., & Kosslyn, S. M. (2004). Brain areas underlying visual mental imagery and visual perception: An fMRI study. *Cognitive Brain Research, 20*, 226–241.

Garcea, F. E., Dombovy, M., & Mahon, B. Z. (2013). Preserved tool knowledge in the context of impaired action knowledge: Implications for models of semantic memory. *Frontiers in Human Neuroscience, 7*, Article 120, 1–18.

Gardiner, J. M. (2001). Episodic memory and autonoetic consciousness: A first-person approach. *Philosophical Transactions of the Royal Society of London B, 356*, 1351–1361.

Garry, M., Strange, D., Bernstein, D. M., & Kinzett, T. (2007). Photographs can distort memory for the news. *Applied Cognitive Psychology, 21*, 995–1004.

Gauthier, I., Skudlarski, P., Gore, J. C., & Anderson, A. W. (2000). Expertise for cars and birds recruits brain areas involved in face recognition. *Nature Neuroscience, 3*, 191–197.

Gauthier, I., Tarr, M. J., Anderson, A. W., Skudlarski, P., & Gore, J. C. (1999). Activation of the middle fusiform "face area" increases with expertise in recognizing novel objects. *Nature Neuroscience, 2*, 568–573.

Gazzaley, A., & Nobre, A. C. (2012). Top-down modulation: Bridging selective attention and working memory. *Trends in Cognitive Sciences, 16*, 129–135.

Geiselman, R. E., Fisher, R. P., MacKinnon, D. P., & Holland, H. L. (1986). Enhancement of eyewitness memory with the cognitive interview. *American Journal of Psychology, 99*, 385–401.

Geisler, W. S. (2008). Visual perception and statistical properties of natural scenes. *Annual Review of Psychology, 59*, 167–192.

Geisler, W. S. (2011). Contributions of ideal observer theory to vision research. *Vision Research, 51*, 771–781.

Gelbard-Sagiv, H., Mukamel, R., Harel, M., Malach, R., & Fried, I. (2008). Internally generated reactivation of single neurons in human hippocampus during free recall. *Science, 322*, 96–101.

Gentner, D., & Colhoun, J. (2010). Analogical processes in human thinking and learning. In B. Glatzeder, V. Goel, & A. von Maller (Vol. Eds.), *On thinking: Vol. 2. Towards a theory of thinking* (pp. 35–48). Berlin: Springer-Verlag.

Gentner, D., & Goldin-Meadow, S. (Eds.). (2003). *Language in mind*. Cambridge, MA: MIT Press.

Gibson, J. J. (1979). *The ecological approach to visual perception*. Boston: Houghton Mifflin.

Gick, M. L., & Holyoak, K. J. (1980). Analogical problem solving. *Cognitive Psychology, 12*, 306–355.

Gick, M. L., & Holyoak, K. J. (1983). Schema induction and analogical transfer. *Cognitive Psychology, 15*, 1–38.

Gigerenzer, G. (2004). Dread risk, September 11, and fatal traffic accidents. *Psychological Science, 15*, 286–287.

Gigerenzer, G. (2011). Personal reflections on theory and psychology. *Theory and Psychology, 20*, 733–743.

Gigerenzer, G., & Hoffrage, U. (1995). How to improve Bayesian reasoning without instruction: Frequency formats. *Psychological Review, 98*, 506–528.

Gigerenzer, G., & Hug, K. (1992). Domain-specific reasoning: Social contracts, cheating, and perspective change. *Cognition, 43*, 127–171.

Gigerenzer, G., & Todd, P. M. (1999). *Simple heuristics that make us smart*. Oxford, UK: Oxford University Press.

Gilbert, A. L., Regier, T., Kay, P., & Ivry, R. B. (2006). Whorf hypothesis is supported in the right visual field but not the left. *Proceedings of the National Academy of Sciences, 103*, 489–494.

Gilboa, A., Winocur, G., Grady, C. L., Hevenor, S. J., & Moscovitch, M. (2004). Remembering our past: Functional neuroanatomy of recollection of recent and very remote personal events. *Cerebral Cortex, 14*, 1214–1225.

Glanzer, M., & Cunitz, A. R. (1966). Two storage mechanisms in free recall. *Journal of Verbal Learning and Verbal Behavior, 5*, 351–360.

Glass, A. L., & Holyoak, K. J. (1975). Alternative conceptions of semantic memory. *Cognition, 3*, 313–339.

Gleason, J. B., & Ratner, N. B. (1998). Language acquisition. In J. B. Gleason & N. B. Ratner (Eds.), *Psycholinguistics* (2nd ed., pp. 347–407). Fort Worth, TX: Harcourt.

Gleick, J. (1992). *Genius: The life and science of Richard Feynman*. New York: Pantheon.

Glickstein, M., & Whitteridge, D. (1987). Tatsuki Inouye and the mapping of the visual fields in the human cerebral cortex. *Trends in Neuroscience, 10*, 350–353.

Gobbini, M. I., & Haxby, J. V. (2007). Neural systems for recognition of familiar faces. *Neuropsychologia, 45*, 32–41.

Gobet, F., Land, P. C. R., Croker, S., Cheng, P. C.-H., Jones, G., Oliver, I., et al. (2001). Chunking mechanisms in human learning. *Trends in Cognitive Science, 5*, 236–243.

Godden, D. R., & Baddeley, A. D. (1975). Context-dependent memory in two natural environments: On land and underwater. *British Journal of Psychology, 66*, 325–331.

Goldenberg, G., Podreka, I., Steiner, M., Willmes, K., Suess, E., & Deecke, L. (1989). Regional cerebral blood flow patterns in visual imagery. *Neuropsychologia, 27*, 641–664.

Goldin-Meadow, S. (1982). The resilience of recursion: A study of a communication system developed without a conventional language model. In E. Wanner & L. R. Gleitman (Eds.), *Language acquisition: The state of the art* (pp. 51–77). Cambridge, UK: Cambridge University Press.

Goldman, S. R., Graesser, A. C., & Van den Broek, P. (Eds.). (1999). *Narrative comprehension, causality, and coherence*. Mahwah, NJ: Erlbaum.

Goldman-Rakic, P. S. (1992, September). Working memory and the mind. *Scientific American*, pp. 111–117.

Goldreich, D., & Tong, J. (2013). Prediction, postdiction, and perceptual length contraction: A Bayesian low-speed prior captures the cutaneous rabbit and related illusions. *Frontiers in Psychology, 4*, Article 221, 1–26.

Goldstein, A. G., Chance, J. E., & Schneller, G. R. (1989). Frequency of eyewitness identification in criminal cases: A survey of prosecutors. *Bulletin of the Psychonomic Society, 27*, 71–74.

Goldstein, E. B. (2014). *Sensation and perception* (9th ed.). Belmont, CA: Cengage Learning.

Goldstein, E. B., & Fink, S. I. (1981). Selective attention in vision: Recognition memory for superimposed line drawings. *Journal of Experimental Psychology: Human Perception and Performance, 7*, 954–967.

Goldstone, R. L., Kersten, A., & Carvalho, P. F. (2012). Concepts and categorization. In I. B. Weiner (Ed.), *Handbook of psychology* (2nd ed., Vol. 4, pp. 607–630). Hoboken, NJ: Wiley.

Gomez, R. L., & Gerken, L. A. (1999). Artificial grammar learning by one-year-olds leads to specific and abstract knowledge. *Cognition, 70,* 109–135.

Gomez, R. L., & Gerken, L. A. (2000). Infant artificial language learning and language acquisition. *Trends in Cognitive Sciences, 4,* 178–186.

Goodale, M. (2010). Action and vision. In E. B. Goldstein (Ed.), *Sage encyclopedia of perception* (Vol. 1, pp. 6–11). Thousand Oaks, CA: Sage.

Graesser, A. C., Singer, M., & Trabasso, T. (1994). Constructing inferences during narrative text comprehension. *Psychological Review, 101,* 371–395.

Graesser, A. C., & Wiemer-Hastings, K. (1999). Situation models and concepts in story comprehension. In S. R. Goldman, A. C. Graesser, & P. Van den Broek (Eds.), *Narrative comprehension, causality, and coherence* (pp. 77–92). Mahwah, NJ: Erlbaum.

Graf, P., Mandler, G., & Haden, P. E. (1982). Simulating amnesic symptoms in normal subjects. *Science, 218,* 1243–1244.

Graf, P., Shimamura, A. P., & Squire, L. R. (1985). Priming across modalities and priming across category levels: Extending the domain of preserved function in amnesia. *Journal of Experimental Psychology: Learning, Memory, and Cognition, 11,* 386–396.

Grant, H., Bredahl, L. S., Clay, J., Ferrie, J., Goves, J. E., McDorman, T. A., et al. (1998). Context-dependent memory for meaningful material: Information for students. *Applied Cognitive Psychology, 12,* 617–623.

Grant, R. (2013). Joyride's voice-activated mobile apps "turn cars into starships." Venturebeat.com/2013/03/05/joyrides-voice-activated-mobile-apps-turn-cars-into-starships.

Gray, J. A., & Wedderburn, A. I. (1960). Grouping strategies with simultaneous stimuli. *Quarterly Journal of Experimental Psychology, 12,* 180–184.

Greenberg, D. L., & Rubin, D. C. (2003). The neuropsychology of autobiographical memory. *Cortex, 39,* 687–728.

Griggs, R. A. (1983). The role of problem content in the selection task and in the THOG problem. In J. St. B. T. Evans (Ed.), *Thinking and reasoning: Psychological approaches.* London: Routledge & Kegan Paul.

Griggs, R. A., & Cox, J. R. (1982). The elusive thematic-materials effect in Wason's abstract selection task. *British Journal of Psychology, 73,* 407–420.

Grill-Spector, K., Knouf, N., & Kanwisher, N. (2004). The fusiform face area subserves face perception, not generic within-category identification. *Nature Neuroscience, 7,* 555–562.

Gross, C. G. (2002). The genealogy of the "grandmother cell." *The Neuroscientist, 8,* 512–518.

Gross, C. G., Bender, D. B., & Roche-Miranda, C. E. (1969). Visual receptive fields of neurons in inferotemporal cortex of the monkey. *Science, 166,* 1303–1306.

Gross, C. G., Rocha-Miranda, C. E., & Bender, D. B. (1972). Visual properties of neurons in inferotemporal cortex of the macaque. *Journal of Neurophysiology, 5,* 96–111.

Guariglia, C., Padovani, A., Pantano, P., & Pizzamiglio, L. (1993). Unilateral neglect restricted to visual imagery. *Nature, 364,* 235–237.

Guilford, J. (1956). The structure of intellect. *Psychological Bulletin, 53,* 267–293.

Gurung, R. A. R., Weidert, J., & Jeske, A. (2010). Focusing on how students study. *Journal of the Scholarship of Teaching and Learning, 10,* 28–35.

Haigney, D., & Westerman, S. J. (2001). Mobile (cellular) phone use and driving: A critical review of research methodology. *Ergonomics, 44,* 132–143.

Hamann, S. B., Ely, T. D., Grafton, S. T., & Kilts, C. D. (1999). Amygdala activity related to enhanced memory for pleasant and aversive stimuli. *Nature Neuroscience, 2,* 289–293.

Hamilton, D. L. (1981). Illusory correlation as a basis for stereotyping. In D. L. Hamilton (Ed.), *Cognitive processes in stereotyping and intergroup behavior.* Hillsdale, NJ: Erlbaum.

Handford, M. (1997). *Where's Waldo?* Cambridge, MA: Candlewick Press.

Hardt, O., Nader, K., & Nadel, L. (2013). Decay happens: The role of active forgetting in memory. *Trends in Cognitive Sciences, 17,* 111–120.

Harrison, S. A., & Tong, F. (2009). Decoding reveals the contents of visual working memory in early visual areas. *Nature, 458,* 462–465.

Harvey, K., Kemps, E., & Tiggemann, M. (2005). The nature of imagery processes underlying food cravings. *British Journal of Health Psychology, 10,* 49–56.

Hassabis, D., Kumaran, D., Vann, S. D., & Maguire, E. A. (2007). Patients with hippocampal amnesia cannot imagine new experiences. *Proceedings of the National Academy of Sciences, 104,* 1726–1731.

Hauk, O., Johnsrude, I., & Pulvermüller, F. (2004). Somatotopic representation of action words in human motor and premotor cortex. *Neuron, 41,* 301–307.

Haviland, S. E., & Clark, H. H. (1974). What's new? Acquiring new information as a process in comprehension. *Journal of Verbal Learning and Verbal Behavior, 13,* 512–521.

Haxby, J. V., Hoffman, E. A., & Gobbini, M. I. (2000). The distributed human neural system for face perception. *Trends in Cognitive Science, 46,* 223–233.

Hayes, J. R. (1978). *Cognitive psychology.* Homewood, IL: Dorsey Press.

Hayhoe, M., & Ballard, C. (2005). Eye movements in natural behavior. *Trends in Cognitive Sciences, 9,* 188–194.

Hebb, D. O. (1948). *Organization of behavior.* New York: Wiley.

Hecaen, H., & Angelergues, R. (1962). Agnosia for faces (prosopagnosia). *Archives of Neurology, 7,* 92–100.

Hegarty, M. (2010). Visual imagery. In E. B. Goldstein (Ed.), *Sage encyclopedia of perception* (pp. 1081–1085). Thousand Oaks, CA: Sage.

Helmholtz, H. von. (1911). *Treatise on physiological optics* (J. P. Southall, Ed. & Trans.; 3rd ed., Vols. 2 & 3). Rochester, NY: Optical Society of America. (Original work published 1866)

Helson, H. (1933). The fundamental propositions of Gestalt psychology. *Psychological Review, 40,* 13–32.

Henderson, J. M., & Hollingworth, A. (2003). Global transsaccadic change blindness during scene perception. *Psychological Science, 14,* 493–497.

Henkel, L. A. (2004). Erroneous memories arising from repeated attempts to remember. *Journal of Memory and Language, 50,* 26–46.

Hetherington, M. M., & MacDiarmid, J. I. (1993). "Chocolate addiction": A preliminary study of its description and its relationship to problem eating. *Appetite, 21,* 233–246.

Hickok, G. (2009). Eight problems for the mirror neuron theory of action understanding in monkeys and humans. *Journal of Cognitive Neuroscience, 21,* 1229–1243.

Hillis, A. E., Rapp, B., Romani, C., & Caramazza, A. (1990). Selective impairment of semantics in lexical processing. *Cognitive Neuropsychology, 7,* 191–243.

Hinton, G. E., & Shallice, T. (1991). Lesioning an attractor network: Investigations of acquired dyslexia. *Psychological Review, 98,* 74–95.

Hirsh-Pasek, K., Reeves, L. M., & Golinkoff, R. (1993). Words and meaning: From primitives to complex organization. In J. B. Gleason & N. B. Ratner (Eds.), *Psycholinguistics* (p. 138). Fort Worth, TX: Harcourt Brace Jovanovich.

Hoffman, H. G., Doctor, J. N., Patterson, D. R., Carrougher, G. J., & Furness, T. A., III. (2000). Virtual reality as an adjunctive pain control during burn wound care in adolescent patients. *Pain, 85,* 305–309.

Hoffman, H. G., Patterson, D. R., Seibel, E., Soltani, M., Jewett-Leahy, L., & Sharar, S. R. (2008). Virtual reality pain control during burn wound debridement in the hydrotank. *Clinical Journal of Pain, 24,* 299–304.

Hoffman, P., & Lambon Ralph, M. A. (2013). Shapes, scenes and sounds: Quantifying the full multi-sensory basis of conceptual knowledge. *Neuropsychologia, 51,* 14–25.

Holmes, G., & Lister, W. T. (1916). Disturbances of vision from cerebral lesions, with special reference to the cortical representation of the macula. *Brain, 39,* 34–73.

Holyoak, K. J., & Koh, K. (1987). Surface and structural similarity in analogical transfer. *Memory & Cognition, 15,* 332–340.

Holyoak, K. J., & Thagard, P. (1995). Analogical mapping by constraint satisfaction. *Cognitive Science, 13,* 295–355.

Horstman, J. (2012). *The Scientific American healthy aging brain.* San Francisco: Jossey-Bass.

Hubel, D. H. (1982). Exploration of the primary visual cortex, 1955–1978. *Nature, 299,* 515–524.

Hubel, D. H., & Wiesel, T. N. (1959). Receptive fields of single neurons in the cat's striate cortex. *Journal of Physiology, 148,* 574–591.

Hubel, D. H., & Wiesel, T. N. (1961). Integrative action in the cat's lateral geniculate body. *Journal of Physiology, 155,* 385–398.

Hubel, D. H., & Wiesel, T. N. (1965). Receptive fields and functional architecture in two non-striate visual areas (18 and 19) of the cat. *Journal of Neurophysiology, 28,* 229–289.

Hupbach, A., Gomez, R., Hardt, O., & Nadel, L. (2007). Reconsolidation of episodic memories: A subtle reminder triggers integration of new information. *Learning and Memory, 14,* 47–53.

Huth, A. G., Nishimoto, S., Vo, A. T., & Gallant, J. L. (2012). A continuous semantic space describes the representation of thousands of object and action categories across the human brain. *Neuron, 76,* 1210–1224.

Hyman, I. E., Jr., Husband, T. H., & Billings, J. F. (1995). False memories of childhood experiences. *Applied Cognitive Psychology, 9,* 181–197.

Ikkai, A., & Curtis, C. E. (2011). Common neural mechanisms supporting spatial working memory, attention, and motor intention. *Neuropsychologia, 49,* 1428–1434.

Innocence Project. (2012). *250 Exonerated: Too many wrongfully convicted.* New York: Benjamin N. Cardozo School of Law, Yeshiva University.

Intons-Peterson, M. J. (1983). Imagery paradigms: How vulnerable are they to experimenters' expectations? *Journal of Experimental Psychology: Human Perception and Performance, 9,* 394–412.

Intons-Peterson, M. J. (1993). Imagery's role in creativity and discovery. In B. Roskos-Ewoldson, M. J. Intons-Peterson, & R. E. Anderson (Eds.), *Imagery, creativity, and discovery: A cognitive perspective* (pp. 1–37). New York: Elsevier.

Irish, M., Addis, D. R., Hodges, J. R., & Piguet, O. (2012). Exploring the content and quality of episodic future simulations in semantic dementia. *Neuropsychologia, 50,* 3488–3495.

Irish, M., & Piguet, O. (2013). The pivotal role of semantic memory in remembering the past and imagining the future. *Frontiers in Behavioral Neuroscience, 7,* 1–11.

Isaacs, E. A., & Clark, H. H. (1987). References in conversation between experts and novices. *Journal of Experimental Psychology: General, 116,* 26–37.

Ishai, A. (2008). Let's face it: It's a cortical network. *Neuroimage, 40,* 415–419.

Ishai, A., Pessoa, L., Bikle, P. C., & Ungerleider, L. G. (2004). Repetition suppression of faces is modulated by emotion. *Proceedings of the National Academy of Sciences, 101,* 9827–9832.

Itti, L., & Koch, C. (2000). A saliency-based search mechanism for overt and covert shifts of visual attention. *Vision Research, 40,* 1489–1506.

Izuma, K., & Adolphs, R. (2011). The brain's rose-colored glasses. *Nature Neuroscience, 14,* 1355–1356.

Jacoby, L. L., Kelley, C. M., Brown, J., & Jaseckko, J. (1989). Becoming famous overnight: Limits on the ability to avoid unconscious inferences of the past. *Journal of Personality and Social Psychology, 56,* 326–338.

James, W. (1890). *Principles of psychology.* New York: Holt.

Jansson, D. G., & Smith, S. M. (1991). Design fixation. *Design Studies, 12,* 3–11.

Jefferies, E. (2013). The neural basis of semantic cognition: Converging evidence from neuropsychology, neuroimaging and TMS. *Cortex, 49,* 611–645.

Jenkins, J. J., & Russell, W. A. (1952). Associative clustering during recall. *Journal of Abnormal and Social Psychology, 47,* 818–821.

Jobs, S. (2005). Stanford University commencement address.

Johnson, E. J., & Goldstein, D. (2003). Do defaults save lives? *Science, 302,* 1338–1339.

Johnson, E. J., Hershey, J., Meszaros, J., & Kunreuther, H. (1993). Framing, probability distortions, and insurance decisions. *Journal of Risk and Uncertainty, 7,* 35–51.

Johnson, K. E., & Mervis, C. B. (1997). Effects of varying levels of expertise on the basic level of categorization. *Journal of Experimental Psychology: General, 126,* 248–277.

Johnson, M. K. (2006). Memory and reality. *American Psychologist, 61,* 760–771.

Johnson, M. K., Foley, M. A., Suengas, A. G., & Raye, C. L. (1988). Phenomenal characteristics of memories for perceived and imagined autobiographical events. *Journal of Experimental Psychology: General, 117,* 371–376.

Johnson, M. K., Hashtroudi, S., & Lindsay, D. S. (1993). Source monitoring. *Psychological Bulletin, 114,* 3–28.

Johnson-Laird, P. N. (1983). *Mental models.* Cambridge, MA: Harvard University Press.

Johnson-Laird, P. N. (1995). Inference and mental models. In S. E. Newstead & J. St. B. T. Evans (Eds.), *Perspectives on thinking and reasoning: Essays in honour of Peter Wason.* Hove, UK: Erlbaum.

Johnson-Laird, P. N. (1999a). Deductive reasoning. *Annual Review of Psychology, 50,* 109–135.

Johnson-Laird, P. N. (1999b). Formal rules versus mental models in reasoning. In R. Sternberg (Ed.), *The nature of cognition* (pp. 587–624). Cambridge, MA: MIT Press.

Jonides, J., Lewis, R. L., Nee, D. E., Lustig, C. A., Berman, M. G., & Moore, K. S. (2008). The mind and brain of short-term memory. *Annual Review of Psychology, 59,* 193–224.

Joordens, S. (2011). *Memory and the human lifespan.* Chantilly, VA: The Teaching Company.

Kahneman, D. (2003). A perspective on judgment and choice. *American Psychologist, 58,* 697–720.

Kahneman, D. (2011). *Thinking fast and slow.* New York: Farrar, Straus and Giroux.

Kamitani, Y., & Tong, F. (2005). Decoding the visual and subjective contents of the human brain. *Nature Neuroscience, 8,* 679–685.

Kandel, E. R. (2001). A molecular biology of memory storage: A dialogue between genes and synapses. *Science, 294,* 1030–1038.

Kandel, E. R. (2006). *In search of memory.* New York: Norton.

Kane, M. J., & Engle, R. W. (2000). Working-memory capacity, proactive interference, and divided attention: Limits on long-term memory retrieval. *Journal of Experimental Psychology: Learning, Memory, and Cognition, 26,* 336–358.

Kanwisher, N. (2003). The ventral visual object pathway in humans: Evidence from fMRI. In L. M. Chalupa & J. S. Werner (Eds.), *The visual neurosciences* (pp. 1179–1190). Cambridge, MA: MIT Press.

Kanwisher, N., & Dilks, D. D. (2013). The functional organization of the ventral visual pathway in humans. In J. S. Werner & L. M. Chalupa (Eds.), *The new visual neurosciences* (pp. 733–746). Cambridge, MA: MIT Press.

Kanwisher, N., McDermott, J., & Chun, M. M. (1997). The fusiform face area: A module in human extrastriate cortex specialized for face perception. *Journal of Neuroscience, 17,* 4302–4311.

Kaplan, C. A., & Simon, H. A. (1990). In search of insight. *Cognitive Psychology, 22,* 374–419.

Karpicke, J. D. (2012). Retrieval-based learning: Active retrieval promotes meaningful learning. *Current Directions in Psychological Science, 21,* 157–163.

Karpicke, J. D., Butler, A. C., & Roediger, H. L. (2009). Metacognitive strategies in student learning: Do students practise retrieval when they study on their own? *Memory, 17,* 471–479.

Katzner, S., Busse, L., & Treue, S. (2009). Attention to the color of a moving stimulus modulates motion-signal processing in macaque area MT: Evidence for a unified attentional system. *Frontiers in Systems Neuroscience, 3,* 1–8.

Kaufman, J. C. (2009). *Creativity 101.* New York: Springer.

Kemps, E., & Tiggemann, M. (2007). Modality-specific imagery reduces cravings for food: An application of the elaborated intrusion theory of desire to food craving. *Journal of Experimental Psychology: Applied, 13,* 95–104.

Kemps, E., & Tiggemann, M. (2013). Hand-held dynamic visual noise reduces naturally occurring food cravings and craving-related consumption. *Appetite, 68,* 152–157.

Keppel, G., & Underwood, B. J. (1962). Proactive inhibition in short-term retention of single items. *Journal of Verbal Learning and Verbal Behavior, 1,* 153–161.

Keren, G., & Schul, Y. (2009). Two is not always better than one: A critical evaluation of two-system theories. *Perspectives on Psychological Science, 4,* 533–550.

Keri, S., Janka, Z., Benedek, G., Aszalos, P., Szatmary, B., Szirtes, G., et al. (2002). Categories, prototypes and memory systems in Alzheimer's disease. *Trends in Cognitive Sciences, 6,* 132–136.

Kermer, D. A., Driver-Linn, E., Wilson, T. D., & Gilbert, D. T. (2006). Loss aversion is an affective forecasting error. *Psychological Science, 17,* 649–653.

Kersten, D., Mamassian, P., & Yuille, A. (2004). Object perception as Bayesian inference. *Annual Review of Psychology, 55,* 271–304.

Kida, S., Josselyn, S. A., Peña de Oritz, S., Kogan, J. H., Chevere, I., Masushige, S., et al. (2002). CREB required for the stability of new and reactivated fear memories. *Nature Neuroscience, 5,* 348–355.

Kiefer, M., & Pulvermüller, F. (2012). Conceptual representation in mind and brain: Theoretical developments, current evidence and future directions. *Cortex, 48,* 805–825.

Kim, A., & Osterhout, L. (2005). The independence of combinatory semantic processing: Evidence from event-related potentials. *Journal of Memory and Language, 52,* 205–255.

Kindt, M., Soeter, M., & Vervliet, B. (2009). Beyond extinction: Erasing human fear responses and preventing the return of fear. *Nature Neuroscience, 12,* 256–258.

Kleffner, D. A., & Ramachandran, V. S. (1992). On the perception of shape from shading. *Perception and Psychophysics, 52,* 18–36.

Klein, S. B., Loftus, J., & Kihlstrom, J. (2002). Memory and temporal experience: The effects of episodic memory loss on an amnesic patient's ability to remember the past and imagine the future. *Social Cognition, 20,* 353–379.

Klein, S. B., Robertson, T. E., & Delton, A. W. (2011). The future-orientation of memory: Planning as a key component mediating the high levels of recall found with survival processing. *Memory, 19,* 121–139.

Kneller, W., Memon, A., & Stevenage, S. (2001). Simultaneous and sequential lineups: Decision processes of accurate and inaccurate eye witnesses. *Applied Cognitive Psychology, 15,* 659–671.

Koffka, K. (1935). *Principles of Gestalt psychology.* New York: Harcourt Brace.

Kohler, W. (1929). *Gestalt psychology.* New York: Liveright.

Körding, K. P., & Wolpert, D. M. (2006). Bayesian decision theory in sensorimotor control. *Trends in Cognitive Sciences, 10,* 319–326.

Kornell, N., & Son, L. K. (2009). Learners' choices and beliefs about self-testing. *Memory, 17,* 493–501.

Kosslyn, S. M. (1973). Scanning visual images: Some structural implications. *Perception & Psychophysics, 14,* 90–94.

Kosslyn, S. M. (1978). Measuring the visual angle of the mind's eye. *Cognitive Psychology, 10,* 356–389.

Kosslyn, S. M. (1980). *Image and mind.* Cambridge, MA: Harvard University Press.

Kosslyn, S. M. (1994). *Image and brain: The resolution of the imagery debate.* Cambridge, MA: MIT Press

Kosslyn, S. M. (1995). Mental imagery. In S. M. Kosslyn & D. N. Osherson (Eds.), *An invitation to cognitive science* (2nd ed., Vol. 2, pp. 267–296). Cambridge, MA: MIT Press.

Kosslyn, S. M., Ball, T., & Reiser, B. J. (1978). Visual images preserve metric spatial information: Evidence from studies of image scanning. *Journal of Experimental Psychology: Human Perception and Performance, 4*, 47–60.

Kosslyn, S. M., Pascual-Leone, A., Felician, O., Camposano, S., Keenan, J. P., Thompson, W. L., et al. (1999). The role of area 17 in visual imagery: Convergent evidence form PET and rTMS. *Science, 284*, 167–170.

Kosslyn, S. M., & Thompson, W. L. (2000). Shared mechanisms in visual imagery and visual perception: Insights from cognitive neuroscience. In M. Gazzanaga (Ed.), *The cognitive neurosciences* (2nd ed., pp. 975–985). Cambridge, MA: MIT Press.

Kosslyn, S., Thompson, W. L., & Ganis, G. (2006). *The case for mental imagery*. New York: Oxford University Press.

Kosslyn, S. M., Thompson, W. L., Kim, I. J., & Alpert, N. M. (1995). Topographical representations of mental images in primary visual cortex. *Nature, 378*, 496–498.

Kounios, J., Fleck, J. I., Green, D. L., Payne, L., Stevenson, J. L., Bowden, E. M., et al. (2008). The origins of insight in resting-state brain activity. *Neuropsychologia, 46*, 281–291.

Kreiman, G., Koch, C., & Fried, I. (2000). Imagery neurons in the human brain. *Nature, 408*, 357–361.

Kruglanski, A. W., & Gigerenzer, G. (2011). Intuitive and deliberative judgments are based on common principles. *Psychological Review, 118*, 97–109.

Kuhn, T. (1970). *The structure of scientific revolution* (2nd ed.). Chicago: University of Chicago Press.

Kuperberg, G. R. (2013). The proactive comprehender: What event-related potentials tell us about the dynamics of reading comprehension. In B. Miller, L. Cutting, & P. McCardle (Eds.), *Unraveling the behavioral, neurobiological, and genetic components of reading comprehension*. Baltimore: Paul Brookes.

Kyaga, S., Landen, M., Borman, M., Hultman, C. M., Langstrom, N., & Lichtenstein, P. (2013). Mental illness, suicide, and creativity: 40-year prospective total population study. *Journal of Psychiatric Research, 47*, 83–90.

LaBar, K. S., & Phelps, E. A. (1998). Arousal-mediated memory consolidation: Role of the medial temporal lobe in humans. *Psychological Science, 9*, 490–493.

Lafay, L., Thomas, F., Mennen, L., Charles, M. A., Eschwege, E., Borys, J., et al. (2001). Gender differences in the relation between food cravings and mood in an adult community: Results from the Fleurbaix Laventie Ville Santé study. *International Journal of Eating Disorders, 29*, 195–204.

Lakoff, G., & Turner, M. (1989). *More than cool reason: The power of poetic metaphor*. Chicago: Chicago University Press.

Lamble, D., Kauranen, T., Laakso, M., & Summala, H. (1999). Cognitive load and detection thresholds in car following situations: Safety implications for using mobile (cellular) telephones while driving. *Accident Analysis and Prevention, 31*, 617–623.

Lambon Ralph, M. A., Howard, D., Nightingale, G., & Ellis, A. W. (1998). Are living and non-living category-specific deficits causally linked to impaired perceptual or associative knowledge? Evidence from a category-specific double dissociation. *Neurocase, 4*, 311–338.

Lambon Ralph, M. A., Lowe, C., & Rogers, T. T. (2007). Neural basis of category-specific deficits for living things: Evidence from semantic dementia, HSVE, and a neural network model. *Brain, 130*, 1127–1137.

Land, M. F., & Hayhoe, M. (2001). In what ways do eye movements contribute to everyday activities? *Vision Research, 41*, 3559–3565.

Land, M. F., Mennie, N., & Rusted, J. (1999). The roles of vision and eye movements in the control of activities of daily living. *Perception, 28*, 1311–1328.

Lanska, D. J. (2009). Historical perspective: Neurological advances from studies of war injuries and illnesses. *Annals of Neurology, 66*, 444–459.

Larkin, J. H., McDermott, J., Simon, D. P., & Simon, H. A. (1980). Expert and novice performance in solving physics problems. *Science, 208*, 1335–1342.

Lavie, N. (2010). Attention, distraction, and cognitive control under load. *Current Directions in Psychological Science, 19*, 143–148.

Lavie, N., & Cox, S. (1997). On the efficiency of visual selective attention: Efficient visual search leads to inefficient distractor rejection. *Psychological Science, 8*, 395–398.

Lavie, N., & Driver, J. (1996). On the spatial extent of attention in object-based visual selection. *Perception & Psychophysics, 58*, 1238–1251.

Le Bihan, D., Turner, R., Zeffiro, T. A., Cuenod, A., Jezzard, P., & Bonnerdot, V. (1993). Activation of human primary visual cortex during visual recall: A magnetic resonance imaging study. *Proceedings of the National Academy of Sciences, USA, 90*, 11802–11805.

Lea, G. (1975). Chronometric analysis of the method of loci. *Journal of Experimental Psychology: Human Perception and Performance, 2*, 95–104.

Lee, D. (2006). Neural basis of quasi-rational decision making. *Current Opinion in Neurobiology, 16*, 191–198.

Lee, S.-H., Kravitz, D. J., & Baker, C. I. (2012). Disentangling visual imagery and perception of real-world objects. *Neuroimage, 59*, 4064–4073.

LePort, A. K. R., Mattfeld, A. T., Dickinson-Anson, H., Fallon, J. H., Stark, C. E. L., Kruggel, F., et al. (2012). Behavioral and neuroanatomical investigation of Highly Superior Autobiographical Memory (HSAM). *Neurobiology of Learning and Memory, 98*, 78–92.

Lerner, J. S., Small, D. A., & Lowenstein, G. (2004). Heart strings and purse strings: Effects of emotions on economic transactions. *Psychological Science, 15*, 337–341.

Lesgold, A. M. (1988). Problem solving. In R. J. Sternberg & E. E. Smith (Eds.), *The psychology of human thoughts*. New York: Cambridge University Press.

Levelt, W. J. M. (1999). *Producing spoken language: A blueprint of the speaker*. Oxford, UK: Oxford University Press.

Levelt, W. J. M. (2001). Spoken word production: A theory of lexical access. *Proceedings of the National Academy of Sciences, 98*, 13464–13471.

Levin, D., & Simons, D. (1997). Failure to detect changes to attended objects in motion pictures. *Psychonomic Bulletin and Review, 4*, 501–506.

Levine, B., Turner, G. R., Tisserand, D., Hevenor, S. J., Graham, S. J., & McIntosh, A. R. (2004). The functional neuroanatomy of episodic and semantic autobiographical remembering: A prospective functional MRI study. *Journal of Cognitive Neuroscience, 16*, 1633–1646.

Levy, I., & Glimcher, P. W. (2013). Neuroeconomics. In H. Pashler (Ed.), *Encyclopedia of the mind* (Vol. 14, pp. 565–569). Thousand Oaks, CA: Sage.

Li, F. F., VanRullen, R., Koch, C., & Perona, P. (2002). Rapid natural scene categorization in the near absence of attention. *Proceedings of the National Academy of Sciences, 99*, 9596–9601.

Lichtenstein, S., Slovic, P., Fischoff, B., Layman, M., & Combs, B. (1978). Judged frequency of lethal events. *Journal of Experimental Psychology: Human Learning and Memory, 4,* 551–578.

Lindsay, D. S. (1990). Misleading suggestions can impair eyewitnesses' ability to remember event details. *Journal of Experimental Psychology: Learning, Memory, and Cognition, 16,* 1077–1083.

Lindsay, D. S., Hagen, L., Read, J. D., Wade, K. A., & Garry, M. (2004). True photographs and false memories. *Psychological Science, 15,* 149–154.

Lindsay, R. C. L., & Wells, G. L. (1980). What price justice? Exploring the relationship of lineup fairness to identification accuracy. *Law and Human Behavior, 4,* 303–313.

Lindsay, R. C. L., & Wells, G. L. (1985). Improving eyewitness identifications from lineups: Simultaneous versus sequential lineup presentation. *Journal of Applied Psychology, 70,* 556–564.

Loewenstein, R. J. (1991). Psychogenic amnesia and psychogenic fugue: A comprehensive review. In A. Tasman & S. M. Goldfinger (Eds.), *American Psychiatric Press Review of Psychiatry* (Vol. 10, pp. 189–221). Washington, DC: American Psychiatric Press.

Loftus, E. F. (1979). *Eyewitness testimony.* Cambridge, MA: Harvard University Press.

Loftus, E. F. (1993a). Made in memory: Distortions in recollection after misleading information. In D. L. Medin (Ed.), *The psychology of learning and motivation: Advances in theory and research* (pp. 187–215). New York: Academic Press.

Loftus, E. F. (1993b). The reality of repressed memories. *American Psychologist, 38,* 518–537.

Loftus, E. F. (1998). Imaginary memories. In M. A. Conway, S. E. Gathercole, & C. Cornoldi (Eds.), *Theories of memory II* (pp. 135–145). Hove, UK: Psychology Press.

Loftus, E. F., Miller, D. G., & Burns, H. J. (1978). Semantic integration of verbal information into visual memory. *Journal of Experimental Psychology: Human Learning and Memory, 4,* 19–31.

Loftus, E. F., & Palmer, J. C. (1974). Reconstruction of an automobile destruction: An example of the interaction between language and memory. *Journal of Verbal Learning and Verbal Behavior, 13,* 585–589.

Lomber, S. G., & Malhotra, S. (2008). Double dissociation of "what" and "where" processing in auditory cortex. *Nature Neuroscience, 11,* 609–616.

Lorayne, H., & Lucas, J. (1996). *The memory book.* New York: Ballantine Books.

Lord, C. G., Ross, L., & Lepper, M. (1979). Biased assimilation and attitude polarization: The effects of prior theories on subsequently considered evidence. *Journal of Personality and Social Psychology, 46,* 1254–1266.

Lovatt, P., Avons, S. E., & Masterson, J. (2000). The word-length effect and disyllabic words. *Quarterly Journal of Experimental Psychology, 53A,* 1–22.

Lovatt, P., Avons, S. E., & Masterson, J. (2002). Output decay in immediate serial recall: Speech time revisited. *Journal of Memory and Language, 46,* 227–243.

Lovett, M. C. (2002). Problem solving. In D. L. Medin (Ed.), *Stevens' handbook of experimental psychology* (3rd ed., pp. 317–362). New York: Wiley.

Lowenstein, G., Rick, S., & Cohen D. (2008). Neuroeconomics. *Annual Review of Psychology, 59,* 647–672.

Lubart, T. I., & Mouchiroud, C. (2003). Creativity: A source of difficulty in problem solving. In J. E. Davidson & R. J. Sternberg (Eds.), *The psychology of problem solving* (pp. 127–148). New York: Cambridge University Press.

Luchins, A. S. (1942). Mechanization in problem solving—the effect of Einstellung. *Psychological Monographs, 54*(6), 195.

Luck, S. J., & Vogel, E. K. (1997). The capacity of visual working memory for features and conjunctions. *Nature, 390,* 279–281.

Luminet, O., & Curci, A. (Eds.). (2009). *Flashbulb memories: New issues and new perspectives.* Philadelphia: Psychology Press.

Luria, A. R. (1968). *The mind of a mnemonist* (L. Solotaroff, Trans.). New York: Basic Books.

Luus, C. A. E., & Wells, G. L. (1994). The malleability of eyewitness confidence: Cowitness and perseverance effects. *Journal of Applied Psychology, 79,* 714–724.

Mack, A., & Rock, I. (1998). *Inattentional blindness.* Cambridge, MA: MIT Press.

MacKay, D. G. (1973). Aspects of the theory of comprehension, memory and attention. *Quarterly Journal of Experimental Psychology, 25,* 22–40.

Mahon, B. Z., & Caramazza, A. (2009). Concepts and categories: A cognitive neuropsychological perspective. *Annual Review of Psychology, 60,* 27–51.

Mahon, B. Z., & Caramazza, A. (2011). What drives the organization of object knowledge in the brain? *Trends in Cognitive Sciences, 15,* 97–103.

Mahon, B. Z., Milleville, S. C., Negri, G. A. L., Rumiati, R. I., Caramazza, A., & Martin, A. (2007). Action-related properties shape object representations in the ventral stream. *Neuron, 55,* 507–520.

Maier, N. R. F. (1931). Reasoning in humans: II. The solution of a problem and its appearance in consciousness. *Journal of Comparative Psychology, 12,* 181–194.

Malpass, R. S., & Devine, P. G. (1981). Eyewitness identification: Lineup instructions and absence of the offender. *Journal of Applied Psychology, 66,* 482–489.

Malt, B. C. (1989). An on-line investigation of prototype and exemplar strategies in classification. *Journal of Experimental Psychology: Learning, Memory, and Cognition, 4,* 539–555.

Maner, J. K., & Schmidt, N. B. (2006). The role of risk avoidance in anxiety. *Behavior Theory, 37,* 181–189.

Manktelow, K. I. (1999). *Reasoning and thinking.* Hove, UK: Psychology Press.

Manktelow, K. I. (2012). *Thinking and reasoning.* New York: Psychology Press.

Manktelow, K. I., & Evans, J. St. B. T. (1979). Facilitation of reasoning by realism: Effect or non-effect? *British Journal of Psychology, 70,* 477–488.

Manktelow, K. I., & Over, D. E. (1990). Deontic thought and the selection task. In K. Gilhooly, M. Keane, R. Logie, & G. Erdos (Eds.), *Lines of thought: Reflections on the psychology of thinking* (Vol. 1). Chichester, UK: Wiley.

Mantyla, T. (1986). Optimizing cue effectiveness: Recall of 500 and 600 incidentally learned words. *Journal of Experimental Psychology: Learning Memory, and Cognition, 12,* 66–71.

Marino, A. C., & Scholl, B. (2005). The role of closure in defining the "objects" of object-based attention. *Perception & Psychophysics, 67,* 1140–1149.

Marsh, R., Cook, G., & Hicks, J. (2006). Gender and orientation stereotypes bias source-monitoring attributions. *Memory, 14,* 148–160.

Mast, F. W., & Kosslyn, S. (2002). Visual mental images can be ambiguous: Insights from individual differences in spatial transformation abilities. *Cognition, 86,* 57–70.

Mather, M., & Sutherland, M. R. (2011). Arousal-biased competition in perception and memory. *Perspectives on Psychological Science, 6*, 114–133.

McCarthy, J., Minsky, M. L., & Shannon, C. E. (1955). A proposal for the Dartmouth summer research project on artificial intelligence. Downloaded from http://www.formal.stanford.edu/jmc/history/dartmouth/dartmouth.html

McClelland, J. L., McNaughton, B. L., & O'Reilly, R. C. (1995). Why there are complementary learning systems in the hippocampus and neocortex: Insights from the successes and failures of connectionist models of learning and memory. *Psychological Review, 102*, 419–457.

McClelland, J. L., & Rogers, T. T. (2003). The parallel distributed processing approach to semantic cognition. *Nature Reviews Neuroscience, 4*, 310–322.

McClelland, J. L., & Rumelhart, D. E. (1986). *Parallel distributed processing: Explorations in the microstructure of cognition.* Cambridge, MA: MIT Press.

McDaniel, M. A., Anderson, J. L., Derbish, M. H., & Morrisette, N. (2007). Testing the testing effect in the classroom. *European Journal of Cognitive Psychology, 19*, 494–513.

McDermott, K. B., & Chan, J. C. K. (2006). Effects of repetition on memory for pragmatic inferences. *Memory & Cognition, 34*, 1273–1284.

McGaugh, J. L. (1983). Hormonal influences on memory. *Annual Review of Psychology, 34*, 297–323.

McKenzie, C. R. M. (2004). Hypothesis testing and evaluation. In D. J. Koehler & N. Harvey (Eds.), *Blackwell handbook of judgment and decision making* (pp. 200–219). Malden, MA: Blackwell.

McNeil, D. G. (2013, November 13). Car mechanic dreams up tool to ease births. *New York Times.*

McNeil, J. E., & Warrington, E. K. (1993). Prospoganosia: A face-specific disorder. *Quarterly Journal of Experimental Psychology, 46A*, 1–10.

Melzack, R., & Wall, P. D. (1965). Pain mechanisms: A new theory. *Science, 150*, 971–979.

Memon, A., Meissner, C. A., & Fraser, J. (2010). The cognitive interview: A meta-analytic review and study space analysis of the past 25 years. *Psychology, Public Policy, and Law, 16*, 340–372.

Mervis, C. B., Catlin, J., & Rosch, E. (1976). Relationships among goodness-of-example, category norms and word frequency. *Bulletin of the Psychonomic Society, 7*, 268–284.

Metcalfe, J., & Wiebe, D. (1987). Intuition in insight and noninsight problem solving. *Memory & Cognition, 15*, 238–246.

Metusalem, R., Kutas, M., Urbach, T. P., Hare, M., McRae, K., & Elman, J. (2012). Generalized event knowledge activation during online sentence comprehension. *Journal of Memory and Language, 66*, 545–567.

Meyer, D. E., & Schvaneveldt, R. W. (1971). Facilitation in recognizing pairs of words: Evidence of a dependence between retrieval operations. *Journal of Experimental Psychology, 90*, 227–234.

Miller, G. A. (1956). The magical number seven, plus or minus two: Some limits on our capacity for processing information. *Psychological Review, 63*, 81–97.

Miller, G. A. (1965). Some preliminaries to psycholinguistics. *American Psychologist, 20*, 15–20.

Miller, G. A. (2003). The cognitive revolution: A historical perspective. *Trends in Cognitive Sciences, 7*, 141–144.

Milner, A. D., & Goodale, M. A. (1995). *The visual brain in action.* New York: Oxford University Press.

Minda, J. P., & Smith, J. D. (2001). Prototypes in category learning: The effect of category size, category structure, and stimulus complexity. *Journal of Experimental Psychology: Learning, Memory, and Cognition, 27*, 775–799.

Mishkin, M., Ungerleider, L. G., & Macko, K. A. (1983). Object vision and spatial vision: Two central pathways. *Trends in Neuroscience, 6*, 414–417.

Misiak, H., & Sexton, V. (1966). *History of psychology: An overview.* New York: Grune & Stratton.

Mitchell, K. J., & Johnson, M. K. (2000). Source monitoring. In E. Tulving & F. I. M. Craik (Eds.), *The Oxford handbook of memory* (pp. 179–195). New York: Oxford University Press.

Moray, N. (1959). Attention in dichotic listening: Affective cues and the influence of instructions. *Quarterly Journal of Experimental Psychology, 11*, 56–60.

Morley, N. J., Evans, J. St. B. T., & Handley, S. J. (2004). Belief bias and figural bias in syllogistic reasoning. *Quarterly Journal of Experimental Psychology A, 57*, 666–692.

Morris, C. D., Bransford, J. D., & Franks, J. J. (1977). Levels of processing versus transfer appropriate processing. *Journal of Verbal Learning and Verbal Behavior, 16*, 519–533.

Moscovitch, M., Winocur, G., & Behrmann, M. (1997). What is special about face recognition? Nineteen experiments on a person with visual object agnosia and dyslexia but normal face recognition. *Journal of Cognitive Neuroscience, 9*, 555–604.

Mullen, B., Johnson, C., & Salas, E. (1991). Productivity loss in brainstorming groups: A meta-analytic integration. *Basic and Applied Social Psychology, 12*, 3–23.

Müller, G. E., & Pilzecker, A. (1900). Experimentelle Beitrage zur Lehr vom Gedachtniss. *Zeitschrift fur Psychologie, 1*, 1–300.

Mumford, M. D., Medeiros, K. E., & Partlow, P. J. (2012). Creative thinking: Processes, strategies, and knowledge. *Journal of Creative Behavior, 46*, 30–47.

Murdock, B. B., Jr. (1962). The serial position effect in free recall. *Journal of Experimental Psychology, 64*, 482–488.

Murphy, G. L., Hampton, J. A., & Milovanovic, G. S. (2012). Semantic memory redux: An experimental test of hierarchical category representation. *Journal of Memory and Language, 67*, 521–539.

Murphy, K. J., Racicot, C. I., & Goodale, M. A. (1996). The use of visuomotor cues as a strategy for making perceptual judgments in a patient with visual form agnosia. *Neuropsychology, 10*, 396–401.

Murray, D. J. (1968). Articulating and acoustic confusability in short-term memory. *Journal of Experimental Psychology, 78*, 679–684.

Nadel, L., & Moscovitch, M. (1997). Memory consolidation, retrograde amnesia and the hippocampal complex. *Current Opinion in Neurobiology, 7*, 217–227.

Nader, K., & Einarsson, E. O. (2010). Memory reconsolidation: An update. *Annals of the New York Academy of Sciences, 1191*, 27–41.

Nader, K., Schafe, G. E., & Le Doux, J. E. (2000a). Fear memories require protein synthesis in the amygdala for reconsolidation after retrieval. *Nature, 406*, 722–726.

Nader, K., Schafe, G. E., & Le Doux, J. E. (2000b). The labile nature of consolidation theory. *Nature, 1*, 216–219.

Nairne, J. S. (2010). Adaptive memory: Evolutionary constraints on remembering. *Psychology of Learning and Motivation, 53*, 1–32.

Nairne, J. S., Pandeirada, J. N. S., & Thompson, S. R. (2008). Adaptive memory. *Psychological Science, 19*, 176–180.

Nairne, J. S., Thompson, S. R., & Pandeirada, N. S. (2007). Adaptive memory: Survival processing enhances retention. *Journal of Experimental Psychology: Learning, Memory, and Cognition, 33*, 263–273.

Nash, R. A., & Wade, K. A. (2009). Innocent but proven guilty: Eliciting internalized false confessions using doctored-video evidence. *Applied Cognitive Psychology, 23*, 624–637.

Nash, R. A., Wade, K. A., & Lindsay, D. S. (2009). Digitally manipulating memory: Effects of doctored videos and imagination in distorting beliefs and memories. *Memory & Cognition, 37*, 414–424.

Nationwide Insurance. (2008, May). Driving while distracted: Public relations research. www.nationwide.com/pdf/dwd-2008-survey-results.pdf

Neisser, U. (1967). *Cognitive psychology*. New York: Appleton-Century-Crofts.

Neisser, U. (1988). New vistas in the study of memory. In U. Neisser & E. Winograd (Eds.), *Remembering reconsidered: Ecological and traditional approaches to the study of memory* (pp. 1–10). Cambridge, UK: Cambridge University Press.

Neisser, U., & Becklen, R. (1975). Selective looking: Attending to visually specified events. *Cognitive Psychology, 7*, 480–494.

Neisser, U., & Harsch, N. (1992). Phantom flashbulbs: False recollections of hearing the news about *Challenger*. In E. Winograd & U. Neisser (Eds.), *Affect and accuracy in recall: Studies of "flashbulb" memories* (pp. 9–31). New York: Cambridge University Press.

Neisser, U., Winograd, E., Bergman, E. T., Schreiber, C. A., Palmer, S. E., & Weldon, M. S. (1996). Remembering the earthquake: Direct experience vs. hearing the news. *Memory, 4*, 337–357.

Newell, A., & Simon, H. A. (1972). *Human problem solving*. Englewood Cliffs, NJ: Prentice-Hall.

Nichols, E. A., Kao, Y.-C., Verfaellie, M., & Gabrieli, J. D. E. (2006). Working memory and long-term memory for faces: Evidence from fMRI and global amnesia for involvement of the medial temporal lobes. *Hippocampus, 16*, 604–616.

Norman, D. (1968). Toward a theory of memory and attention. *Psychological Review, 75*, 522–536.

Noton, D., & Stark, L. W. (1971). Scanpaths in eye movements during pattern perception. *Science, 171*, 308–311.

Novick, J. M., Trueswell, J. C., & Thompson-Schill, S. L. (2005). Cognitive control and parsing: Reexamining the role of Broca's area in sentence comprehension. *Cognitive, Affective, and Behavioral Neuroscience, 5*, 263–281.

Nyberg, L., McIntosh, A. R., Cabeaa, R., Habib, R., Houle, S., & Tulving, E. (1996). General and specific brain regions involved in encoding and retrieval of events: What, where and when. *Proceedings of the National Academy of Sciences, USA, 93*, 11280–11285.

O'Craven, K. M., Downing, P. E., & Kanwisher, N. (1999). fMRI evidence for objects as the units of attentional selection. *Nature, 401*, 584–587.

O'Toole, A. J. (2007). Face recognition algorithms surpass humans matching faces over changes in illumination. *IEEE Transactions on Pattern Analysis and Machine Intelligence, 29*, 1642–1646.

O'Toole, A. J., Abdi, H., Jiang, F., & Phillips, P. J. (2007). Fusing face recognition algorithms and humans. *IEEE Transactions on Systems, Man and Cybernetics, 37*, 1149–1155.

Oliva, A., & Torralba, A. (2007). The role of context in object recognition. *Trends in Cognitive Sciences, 11*, 521–527.

Olshausen, B. A., & Field, D. J. (2004). Sparse coding of sensory inputs. *Current Opinion in Neurobiology, 14*, 481–487.

Olson, A. C., & Humphreys, G. W. (1997). Connectionist models of neuropsychological disorders. *Trends in Cognitive Sciences, 1*, 222–228.

Olson, R. L., Hanowski, R. J., Hickman, J. S., & Bocanegra, J. (2009). *Driver distraction in commercial vehicle operations*. U.S. Department of Transportation Report No. FMCSA-RRR-09-042.

Oosterhoff, N. N., Tipper, S. P., & Downing, P. E. (2013). Crossmodal and action specific: Neuroimaging the human mirror neuron system. *Trends in Cognitive Sciences, 17*, 311–318.

Orban, G. A., Vandenbussche, E., & Vogels, R. (1984). Human orientation discrimination tested with long stimuli. *Vision Research, 24*, 121–128.

Osborn, A. F. (1953). *Applied imagination*. New York: Scribner.

Osman, M. (2004). An evaluation of dual-process theories of reasoning. *Psychonomic Bulletin and Review, 108*, 291–310.

Ost, J., Vrij, A., Costall, A., & Bull, R. (2002). Crashing memories and reality monitoring: Distinguishing between perceptions, imaginations and "false memories." *Applied Cognitive Psychology, 16*, 125–134.

Osterhout, L., McLaughlin, J., & Bersick, M. (1997). Event-related brain potentials and human language. *Trends in Cognitive Sciences, 1*, 203–209.

Paczynski, M., & Kuperberg, G. R. (2012). Multiple influences of semantic memory on sentence processing: Distinct effects of semantic relatedness on violations of real-world event/state knowledge and animacy selection restrictions. *Journal of Memory and Language, 67*, 426–448.

Paivio, A. (1963). Learning of adjective-noun paired associates as a function of adjective-noun word order and noun abstractness. *Canadian Journal of Psychology, 17*, 370–379.

Paivio, A. (1965). Abstractness, imagery, and meaningfulness in paired-associate learning. *Journal of Verbal Learning and Verbal Behavior, 4*, 32–38.

Paivio, A. (2006). *Mind and its evolution: A dual coding theoretical approach*. Hillsdale, NJ: Erlbaum.

Palmer, S. E. (1975). The effects of contextual scenes on the identification of objects. *Memory & Cognition, 3*, 519–526.

Palmer, S. E. (1992). Common region: A new principle of perceptual grouping. *Cognitive Psychology, 24*, 436–447.

Palmer, S. E., & Rock, I. (1994). Rethinking perceptual organization: The role of uniform connectedness. *Psychonomic Bulletin and Review, 1*, 29–55.

Parker, E. S., Cahill, L., & McGaugh, J. L. (2006). A case of unusual autobiographical remembering. *Neurocase, 12*, 35–49.

Parkhi, O. M., Vedaldi, A., Zisserman, A., & Jawahar C. V. (2012). *Cats and dogs*. Computer Vision and Pattern Recognition Conference.

Parkhurst, D., Law, K., & Niebur, E. (2002). Modeling the role of salience in the allocation of overt visual attention. *Vision Research, 42*, 107–123.

Parkin, A. J. (1996). *Explorations in cognitive neuropsychology*. Oxford, UK: Blackwell.

Patterson, K., Nestor, P. J., & Rogers, T. T. (2007). Where do you know what you know? The representation of semantic knowledge in the human brain. *Nature Reviews Neuroscience, 8*, 976–987.

Paulus, M. P., & Yu, A. J. (2012). Emotion and decision-making: Affect-driven belief systems in anxiety and depression. *Trends in Cognitive Sciences, 16,* 476–483.

Pavlov, I. (1927). *Conditioned reflexes.* New York: Oxford University Press.

Payne, J. D., Chambers, A. M., & Kensinger, E. A. (2012). Sleep promotes lasting changes in selective memory for emotional scenes. *Frontiers in Integrative Neuroscience, 6,* 1–11.

Payne, J. D., Stickgold, R., Swanberg, K., & Kensinger, E. A. (2008). Sleep preferentially enhances memory for emotional components of scenes. *Psychological Science, 19,* 781–788.

Pearson, J., Clifford, C. W. G., & Tong, F. (2008). The functional impact of mental imagery on conscious perception. *Current Biology, 18,* 982–986.

Perfect, T. J., & Askew, C. (1994). Print adverts: Not remembered but memorable. *Applied Cognitive Psychology, 8,* 693–703.

Perky, C. W. (1910). An experimental study of imagination. *American Journal of Psychology, 21,* 422–442.

Perrett, D. I., Rolls, E. T., & Caan, W. (1982). Visual neurons responsive to faces in the monkey temporal cortex. *Experimental Brain Research, 7,* 329–342.

Peters, E., Vastfjall, D., Garling, T., & Slovic, P. (2006). Affect and decision making: A "hot" topic. *Journal of Behavioral Decision Making, 19,* 79–85.

Peters, J. (2004, November 26). "Hi, I'm your car. Don't let me distract you." *New York Times.*

Peterson, J. B., & Carson, S. H. (2000). Latent inhibition and openness to experience in a high-achieving student population. *Personality and Individual Differences, 28,* 323–332.

Peterson, L. R., & Peterson, M. J. (1959). Short-term retention of individual verbal items. *Journal of Experimental Psychology, 58,* 193–198.

Peterson, S. E. (1992). The cognitive functions of underlining as a study technique. *Reading Research and Instruction, 31,* 49–56.

Petrican, R., Gopie, N., Leach, L., Chow, T. W., Richards, B., & Moscovitch, M. (2010). Recollection and familiarity for public events in neurologically intact older adults and two brain-damaged patients. *Neuropsychologia, 48,* 945–960.

Phelps, E. A., & Sharot, T. (2008). How (and why) emotion enhances the subjective sense of recollection. *Current Directions in Psychological Science, 17,* 147–152.

Pickering, M. J., & Garrod, S. (2004). Toward a mechanistic psychology of dialogue. *Behavioral and Brain Sciences, 27,* 169–226.

Pillemer, D. B. (1998). *Momentous events, vivid memories.* Cambridge, MA: Harvard University Press.

Pillemer, D. B., Picariello, M. L., Law, A. B., & Reichman, J. S. (1996). Memories of college: The importance of specific educational episodes. In D. C. Rubin (Ed.), *Remembering our past: Studies in autobiographical memory* (pp. 318–337). Cambridge, UK: Cambridge University Press.

Plaut, D. C. (1996). Relearning after damage in connectionist networks: Toward a theory of rehabilitation. *Brain and Language, 52,* 25–82.

Pobric, G., Jefferies, E., & Lambon Ralph, M. A. (2010). Category-specific versus category-general semantic impairment induced by transcranial magnetic stimulation. *Current Biology, 20,* 964–968.

Pollack, I., & Pickett, J. M. (1964). Intelligibility of excerpts from fluent speech: Auditory vs. structural context. *Journal of Verbal Learning and Verbal Behavior, 3,* 79–84.

Porter, S., & Birt, A. R. (2001). Is traumatic memory *special?* A comparison of traumatic memory characteristics with memory for other emotional life experiences. *Applied Cognitive Psychology, 15,* S101–S117.

Posner, M. I., Nissen, M. J., & Ogden, W. C. (1978). Attended and unattended processing modes: The role of set for spatial location. In H. L. Pick & I. J. Saltzman (Eds.), *Modes of perceiving and processing information* (pp. 137–157). Hillsdale, NJ: Erlbaum.

Post, T., van den Assem, M. J., Baltussen, G., & Thaler, R. H. (2008). Deal or no deal? Decision making under risk in a large-payoff game show. *American Economic Review, 98,* 38–71.

Prentky, R. (1989). Creativity and psychopathology: Gamboling at the seat of madness. In J. A. Glover, R. R. Ronning, & C. R. Reynolds (Eds.), *A handbook of creativity* (pp. 243–270). New York: Plenum Press.

Pulvermüller, F. (2013). How neurons make meaning: Brain mechanisms for embodied and abstract-symbolic semantics. *Trends in Cognitive Sciences, 17,* 458–470.

Pylyshyn, Z. W. (1973). What the mind's eye tells the mind's brain: A critique of mental imagery. *Psychological Bulletin, 80,* 1–24.

Pylyshyn, Z. W. (2001). Is the imagery debate over? If so, what was it about? In E. Dupoux (Ed.), *Language, brain, and cognitive development* (pp. 59–83). Cambridge, MA: MIT Press.

Pylyshyn, Z. W. (2003). Return of the mental image: Are there really pictures in the brain? *Trends in Cognitive Sciences, 7,* 113–118.

Quillian, M. R. (1967). Word concepts: A theory and simulation of some basic semantic capabilities. *Behavioral Science, 12,* 410–430.

Quillian, M. R. (1969). The Teachable Language Comprehender: A simulation program and theory of language. *Communications of the ACM, 12,* 459–476.

Quinlivan, D. S., Wells, G. L., & Neuschatz, J. S. (2010). Is manipulative intent necessary to mitigate the eyewitness post-identification feedback effect? *Law and Human Behavior, 34,* 186–197.

Quiroga, R. Q., Reddy, L., Koch, C., & Fried, I. (2007). Decoding visual inputs from multiple neurons in the human temporal lobe. *Journal of Neurophysiology, 98,* 1997–2007.

Quiroga, R. Q., Reddy, L., Kreiman, G., Koch, C., & Fried, I. (2008). Sparse but not "grandmother-cell" coding in the medial temporal lobe. *Trends in Cognitive Sciences, 12,* 87–91.

Ramirez, G., & Beilock, S. L. (2011). Writing about testing worries boosts exam performance in the classroom. *Science, 331,* 211–213.

Ranganath, C., & Blumenfeld, R. S. (2005). Doubts about double dissociations between short- and long-term memory. *Trends in Cognitive Sciences, 9,* 374–380.

Ranganath, C., & D'Esposito, M. (2001). Medial temporal lobe activity associated with active maintenance of novel information. *Neuron, 31,* 865–873.

Raphael, B. (1976). *The thinking computer.* New York: Freeman.

Rathbone, C. J., Moulin, C. J. A., & Conway, M. A. (2008). Self-centered memories: The reminiscence bump and the self. *Memory & Cognition, 36,* 1403–1414.

Rauchs, G., Feyers, D., Landeau, B., Bastin, C., Luxen, A., Maquet, P., et al. (2011). Sleep contributes to the strengthening of some memories over others, depending on hippocampal activity at learning. *Journal of Neuroscience, 31,* 2563–2568.

Rayner, K., & Duffy, S. A. (1986). Lexical complexity and fixation times in reading: Effects of word frequency, verb complexity, and lexical ambiguity *Memory & Cognition, 14,* 191–201.

Rayner, K., & Frazier, L. (1989). Selection mechanisms in reading lexically ambiguous words. *Journal of Experimental Psychology: Learning, Memory, and Cognition, 15*, 779–790.

Rayner, K., Liersedge, S. P., White, S. J., & Vergilino-Perez, D. (2003). Reading disappearing text: Cognitive control of eye movements. *Psychological Science, 14*, 385–388.

Reber, A. S. (1995). *Penguin dictionary of psychology* (2nd ed.). New York: Penguin Books.

Reddy, L., Wilken, P., & Koch, C. (2004). Face-gender discrimination is possible in the near-absence of attention. *Journal of Vision, 4*(2), 106–117.

Redelmeier, D. A., & Shafir, E. (1995). Medical decision making in situations that offer multiple alternatives. *Medical Decision Making, 273*, 302–305.

Redelmeier, D. A., & Tibshirani, R. J. (1997). Association between cellular-telephone calls and motor vehicle crashes. *New England Journal of Medicine, 336*, 453–458.

Reder, L. M., & Anderson, J. R. (1982). Effects of spacing and embellishment for the main points of a text. *Memory & Cognition, 10*, 97–102.

Reicher, G. M. (1969). Perceptual recognition as a function of meaningfulness of stimulus material. *Journal of Experimental Psychology, 81*, 275–280.

Reitman, J. (1976). Skilled perception in Go: Deducing memory structures from inter-response times. *Cognitive Psychology, 8*, 336–356.

Renoult, L., Davidson, P. S. R., Palombo, D. J., Moscovitch, M., & Levine, B. (2012). Personal semantics: At the crossroads of semantic and episodic memory. *Trends in Cognitive Sciences, 16*, 550–558.

Rensink, R. A. (2002). Change detection. *Annual Review of Psychology, 53*, 245–277.

Rensink, R. A., O'Regan, J. K., & Clark, J. J. (1997). To see or not to see: The need for attention to perceive changes in scenes. *Psychological Science, 8*, 368–373.

Richards, R., Kinney, D. K., Benet, M., & Merzel, P. C. (1988). Assessing everyday creativity: Characteristics of the lifetime creativity scales and validation with three large samples. *Journal of Personality and Social Psychology, 54*, 476–485.

Richardson, A. (1994). *Individual differences in imaging: Their measurement, origins, and consequences.* Amityville, NY: Baywood.

Rimmele, U., Davachi, L., Petrov, R., Dougal, S., & Phelps, E. (2011). Emotion enhances the subjective feeling of remembering, despite lower accuracy for contextual details. *Emotion, 11*, 553–562.

Rips, L. J. (1995). Deduction and cognition. In E. Smith & D. N. Osherson (Eds.), *An invitation to cognitive science* (Vol. 2, pp. 297–343). Cambridge, MA: MIT Press.

Rips, L. J. (2002). Reasoning. In D. L. Medin (Ed.), *Stevens' handbook of experimental psychology* (3rd ed., pp. 363–411). New York: Wiley.

Rips, L. J., Shoben, E. J., & Smith, E. E. (1973). Semantic distance and the verification of semantic relations. *Journal of Verbal Learning and Verbal Behavior, 12*, 1–20.

Ritchey, M., Dolcos, F., & Cabeza, R. (2008). Role of amygdala connectivity in the persistence of emotional memories over time: An event-related fMRI investigation. *Cerebral Cortex, 18*, 2494–2504.

Rizzolatti, G., Fadiga, L., Gallese, V., & Forgassi, L., (1996). Premotor cortex and the recognition of motor actions. *Cognitive Brain Research, 3*, 131–141.

Rizzolatti, G., Forgassi, L., & Gallese, V. (2000). Cortical mechanisms subserving object grasping and action recognition: A new view on the cortical motor functions. In M. Gazzaniga (Ed.), *The new cognitive neurosciences* (pp. 539–552). Cambridge, MA: MIT Press.

Robbins, J. (2000, July 4). Virtual reality finds a real place. *New York Times.*

Roberson, D., Davies, I., & Davidoff, J. (2000). Color categories are not universal: Replications and new evidence from a stone-age culture. *Journal of Experimental Psychology: General, 129*, 369–398.

Robertson, L., Treisman, A., Freidman-Hill, S., & Grabowecky, M. (1997). The interaction of spatial and object pathways: Evidence from Balint's syndrome. *Journal of Cognitive Neuroscience, 9*, 295–317.

Roche-Miranda, C. (2011). Personal communication.

Rock, I. (1983). *The logic of perception.* Cambridge, MA: MIT Press.

Roediger, H. L. (1990). Implicit memory: Retention without remembering. *American Psychologist, 45*, 1043–1056.

Roediger, H. L., Guynn, M. J., & Jones, T. C. (1994). Implicit memory: A tutorial review. In G. d'Ydewalle, P. Eallen, & P. Bertelson (Eds.), *International perspectives on cognitive science* (Vol. 2, pp. 67–94). Hillsdale, NJ: Erlbaum.

Roediger, H. L., & Karpicke, J. D. (2006). Test-enhanced learning: Taking memory tests improves long-term retention. *Psychological Science, 17*, 249–255.

Roediger, H. L., & McDermott, K. B. (1995). Creating false memories: Remembering words not presented in lists. *Journal of Experimental Psychology: Learning, Memory, and Cognition, 21*, 803–814.

Rogers, T. B., Kuiper, N. A., & Kirker, W. S. (1977). Self-reference and the encoding of personal information. *Journal of Personality and Social Psychology, 35*, 677–688.

Rogers, T. T., & Cox, C. (in press). The neural basis of conceptual knowledge: Revisiting a Golden-Age hypothesis in the era of cognitive neuroscience. In A. Duarte, M. Barense, & D. R. Addis (Eds.), *The Wiley handbook of the cognitive neuroscience of memory.* Hoboken, NJ: Wiley.

Rogers, T. T., & McClelland, J. L. (2004). *Semantic cognition: A parallel distributed processing approach.* Cambridge, MA: MIT Press.

Rogin, M. P. (1987). *Ronald Reagan, the movie and other episodes in political demonology.* Berkeley: University of California Press.

Roland, D., Dick, F., & Elman, J. L. (2007). Frequency of basic English grammatical structures: A corpus analysis. *Journal of Memory and Language, 57*, 348–379.

Rolls, E. T. (1981). Responses of amygdaloid neurons in the primate. In Y. Ben-Ari (Ed.), *The amygdaloid complex* (pp. 383–393). Amsterdam: Elsevier.

Rolls, E. T., & Tovee, M. J. (1995). Sparseness of the neuronal representation of stimuli in the primate temporal visual cortex. *Journal of Neurophysiology, 73*, 713–726.

Roozendaal, B., & McGaugh, J. L. (2011). Memory modulation. *Behavioral Neuroscience, 125*, 797–824.

Rosch, E. H. (1973). On the internal structure of perceptual and semantic categories. In T. E. Moore (Ed.), *Cognitive development and the acquisition of language* (pp. 111–144). New York: Academic Press.

Rosch, E. H. (1975a). Cognitive representations of semantic categories. *Journal of Experimental Psychology: General, 104*, 192–233.

Rosch, E. H. (1975b). The nature of mental codes for color categories. *Journal of Experimental Psychology: Human Perception and Performance, 1*, 303–322.

Rosch, E. H., & Mervis, C. B. (1975). Family resemblances: Studies in the internal structures of categories. *Cognitive Psychology, 7,* 573–605.

Rosch, E. H., Mervis, C. B., Gray, W. D., Johnson, D. M., & Boyes-Braem, P. (1976). Basic objects in natural categories. *Cognitive Psychology, 8,* 382–439.

Rose, N. S., Olsen, R. K., Craik, F. I. M., & Rosenbaum, R. S. (2012). Working memory and amnesia: The role of stimulus novelty. *Neuropsychologia, 50,* 11–18.

Rosenbaum, R. S., Köhler, S., Schacter, D. L., Moscovitch, M., Westmacott, R., Black, S. E., et al. (2005). The case of K.C.: Contributions of a memory-impaired person to memory theory. *Neuropsychologia, 43,* 989–1021.

Ross, D. F., Ceci, S. J., Dunning, D., & Toglia, M. P. (1994). Unconscious transference and mistaken identity: When a witness misidentifies a familiar but innocent person. *Journal of Applied Psychology, 79,* 918–930.

Rubin, D. C., Rahhal, T. A., & Poon, L. W. (1998). Things learned in early adulthood are remembered best. *Memory & Cognition, 26,* 3–19.

Rumelhart, D. E., & McClelland, J. L. (1986). *Parallel distributed processing: Explorations in the microstructure of cognition.* Cambridge, MA: MIT Press.

Rundus, D. (1971). Analysis of rehearsal processes in free recall. *Journal of Experimental Psychology, 89,* 63–77.

Sacchi, D. L. M., Agnoli, F, & Loftus, E. F. (2007). Changing history: Doctored photographs affect memory for past public events. *Applied Cognitive Psychology, 21,* 1005–1022.

Sachs, J. (1967). Recognition memory for syntactic and semantic aspects of a connected discourse. *Perception & Psychophysics, 2,* 437–442.

Saffran, J. R., Aslin, R. N., & Newport, E. L. (1999). Statistical learning of tone sequences by human infants and adults. *Cognition, 70,* 27–52.

Saletin, J. M., Goldstein, A. N., & Walker, M. P. (2011). The role of sleep in directed forgetting and remembering of human memories. *Cerebral Cortex, 21,* 2534–2541.

Sanfey, A. G., Lowenstein, G., McClure, S. M., & Cohen, J. D. (2006). Neuroeconomics: Cross-currents in research on decision-making. *Trends in Cognitive Sciences, 10,* 106–116.

Sanfey, A. G., Rilling, J. K., Aronson, J. A., Nystrom, L. E., & Cohen, J. D. (2003). The neural basis of economic decision making in the Ultimatum Game. *Science, 300,* 1755–1758.

Schacter, D. L. (1987). Implicit memory: History and current status. *Journal of Experimental Psychology: Learning, Memory, and Cognition, 13,* 501–518.

Schacter, D. L. (2001). *The seven sins of memory.* New York: Houghton Mifflin.

Schacter, D. L. (2012). Adaptive constructive processes and the future of memory. *American Psychologist, 67,* 603–613.

Schacter, D. L., & Addis, D. R. (2007). The cognitive neuroscience of constructive memory: Remembering the past and imagining the future. *Philosophical Transactions of the Royal Society of London B, 362,* 773–786.

Schacter, D. L., & Addis, D. R. (2009). On the nature of medial temporal lobe contributions to the constructive simulation of future events. *Philosophical Transactions of the Royal Society of London B, 364,* 1245–1253.

Scheck, B., Neufeld, P., & Dwyer, J. (2000). *Actual innocence.* New York: Random House.

Schenkein, J. (1980). A taxonomy for repeating action sequences in natural conversation. In B. Butterworth (Ed.), *Language production* (Vol. 1, pp. 21–47). San Diego, CA: Academic Press.

Schiller, D., Monfils, M.-H., Raio, C. M., Johnson, D. C., LeDoux, J. E., & Phelps, E. A. (2010). Preventing the return of fear in humans using reconsolidation update mechanisms. *Nature, 463,* 49–54.

Schmolck, H., Buffalo, E. A., & Squire, L. R. (2000). Memory distortions develop over time: Recollections of the O. J. Simpson trial verdict after 15 and 32 months. *Psychological Science, 11,* 39–45.

Schneider, W., & Chein, J. (2003). Controlled and automatic processing: Behavioral and biological mechanisms. *Cognitive Science, 27,* 525–559.

Schneider, W., & Shiffrin, R. M. (1977). Controlled and automatic human information processing: I. Detection, search, and attention. *Psychological Review, 84,* 1–66.

Schrauf, R. W., & Rubin, D. C. (1998). Bilingual autobiographical memory in older adult immigrants: A test of cognitive explanations of the reminiscence bump and the linguistic encoding of memories. *Journal of Memory and Language, 39,* 437–457.

Schweickert, R., & Boruff, B. (1986). Short-term memory capacity: Magic number or magic spell? *Journal of Experimental Psychology: Learning, Memory, and Cognition, 12,* 419–425.

Scoville, W. B., & Milner, B. (1957). Loss of recent memory after bilateral hippocampal lesions. *Journal of Neurology, Neurosurgery, and Psychiatry, 20,* 11–21.

Segal, S. J., & Fusella, V. (1970). Influence of imaged pictures and sounds on detection of visual and auditory signals. *Journal of Experimental Psychology, 83,* 458–464.

Seidenberg, M. S., & Zevin, J. D. (2006). Connectionist models in developmental cognitive neuroscience: Critical periods and the paradox of success. In Y. Munakata & M. Johnson (Eds.), *Processes of change in brain and cognitive development: Attention and performance XXI.* Oxford, UK: Oxford University Press.

Shallice, T., & Warrington, E. K. (1970). Independent functioning of verbal memory stores: A neuropsychological study. *Quarterly Journal of Experimental Psychology, 22,* 261–273.

Sharot, T., Korn, C. W., & Dolan, R. J. (2011). How unrealistic optimism is maintained in the face of reality. *Nature Neuroscience, 14,* 1475–1479.

Shen, O., Rabinowitz, R., Geist, R. R., & Shafir, E. (2010). Effect of background case characteristics on decisions in the delivery room. *Medical Decision Making, 30,* 518–522.

Shepard, R. N., & Metzler, J. (1971). Mental rotation of three-dimensional objects. *Science, 171,* 701–703.

Shinoda, H., Hayhoe, M. M., & Shrivastava, A. (2001). What controls attention in natural environments? *Vision Research, 41,* 3535–3545.

Simons, D. J., & Chabris, C. F. (1999). Gorillas in our midst: Sustained inattentional blindness for dynamic events. *Perception, 28,* 1059–1074.

Simons, D. J., & Chabris, C. F. (2011). What people believe about how memory works: A representative survey of the U.S. population. *PLoS ONE, 6*(8), e22757.

Simonsohn, U. (2007). Clouds make nerds look good. *Journal of Behavioral Decision Making, 20,* 143–152.

Simonsohn, U. (2009). Weather to go to college. *Economic Journal, 20,* 1–11.

Simonton, D. K. (1984). Creative productivity and age: A mathematical model based on a two-step cognitive process. *Developmental Review, 4,* 77–111.

Simonyan, K., Aytar, Y., Vedaldi, A., & Zisserman, A. (2012). Presentation at Image Large Scale Visual Recognition Competition (ILSVRC2012).

Simonyan, K., Parkhi, O. M., Vedaldi, A., & Zisserman, A. (2013). *Fisher vector faces in the wild*. British Machine Vision Conference.

Singer, M., Andrusiak, P., Reisdorf, P., & Black, N. L. (1992). Individual differences in bridging inference processes. *Memory & Cognition, 20*, 539–548.

Sinha, P. (2002). Recognizing complex patterns. *Nature Neuroscience, 5*, 1093–1097.

Skinner, B. F. (1938). *The behavior of organisms*. New York: Appleton Century.

Skinner, B. F. (1957). *Verbal behavior*. New York: Appleton-Century-Crofts.

Slameka, N. J., & Graf, P. (1978). The generation effect: Delineation of a phenomenon. *Journal of Experimental Psychology: Human Learning and Memory, 4*, 592–604.

Slovic, P., Monahan, J., & MacGregor, D. G. (2000). Violence risk assessment and risk communication: The effects of using actual cases, providing instructions, and employing probability versus frequency formats. *Law and Human Behavior, 24*, 271–296.

Smith, C. N., Frascino, J. C., Kripke, D. L., McHugh, P. R., Tresiman, G. J., & Squire, L. R. (2010). Losing memories overnight: A unique form of human amnesia. *Neuropsychologia, 48*, 2833–2840.

Smith, C. N., & Squire, L. R. (2009). Medial temporal lobe activity during retrieval of semantic memory is related to the age of the memory. *Journal of Neuroscience, 29*, 930–938.

Smith, E. E. (1989). Concepts and induction. In M. L. Posner (Ed.), *Foundations of cognitive science* (pp. 501–526). Cambridge, MA: MIT Press.

Smith, E. E., Rips, L. J., & Shoben, E. J. (1974). Semantic memory and psychological semantics. In G. H. Bower (Ed.), *The psychology of learning and motivation* (Vol. 8, pp. 1–45). New York: Academic Press.

Smith, J. D., & Minda, J. P. (2000). Thirty categorization results in search of a model. *Journal of Experimental Psychology: Learning, Memory, and Cognition, 26*, 3–27.

Smith, S. M., Kerne, A., Koh, E., & Shah, J. (2009). The development and evaluation of tools for creativity. In A. B. Markman & K. L. Wood (Eds.), *Tools for innovation* (pp. 128–152). Oxford, UK: Oxford University Press.

Smith, S. M., & Rothkopf, E. Z. (1984). Contextual enhancement and distribution of practice in the classroom. *Cognition and Instruction, 1*, 341–358.

Smith, S. M., Ward, T. B., & Schumacher, J. S. (1993). Constraining effects of examples in a creative generation task. *Memory & Cognition, 21*, 837–845.

Snyder, A. (2009). Explaining and inducing savant skills: Privileged access to lower level, less-processed information. *Philosophical Transactions of the Royal Society B, 364*, 1399–1405.

Soderlund, H., Moscovitch, M., Kumar, N., Mandic, M., & Levine, B. (2012). As time goes by: Hippocampal connectivity changes with remoteness of autobiographical memory recall. *Hippocampus, 22*, 670–679.

Solomon, K. O., Medin, D. L., & Lynch, E. (1999). Concepts do more than categorize. *Trends in Cognitive Science, 3*, 99–105.

Spence, C., & Read, L. (2003). Speech shadowing while driving: On the difficulty of splitting attention between eye and ear. *Psychological Science, 14*, 251–256.

Sperling, G. (1960). The information available in brief visual presentations. *Psychological Monographs, 74*(11, Whole No. 498), 1–29.

Squire, L. R., & Bayley, P. J. (2007). The neuroscience of remote memory. *Current Opinion in Neurobiology, 17*, 185–196.

Squire, L. R., & Zola-Morgan, S. (1998). Episodic memory, semantic memory, and amnesia. *Hippocampus, 8*, 205–211.

Stanfield, R. A., & Zwaan, R. A. (2001). The effect of implied orientation derived from verbal content on picture recognition. *Psychological Science, 12*, 153–156.

Stanny, C. J., & Johnson, T. C. (2000). Effects of stress induced by a simulated shooting on recall by police and citizen witnesses. *American Journal of Psychology, 113*, 359–386.

Stanovich, K. E. (1999). *What is rational? Studies of individual differences in reasoning*. Mahwah, NJ: Erlbaum.

Stanovich, K. E. (2011). *Rationality and the reflective mind*. New York: Oxford University Press.

Stanovich, K. E., & West, R. F. (2000). Individual differences in reasoning: Implications for the rationality debate? *Behavioral and Brain Sciences, 23*, 645–726.

Stanovich, K. E., West, R. F., & Toplak, M. E. (2013). Myside bias, rational thinking, and intelligence. *Current Directions in Psychological Science, 22*, 259–264.

Steblay, N. K., Dysart, J. E., & Wells, G. L. (2011). Seventy-two tests of the sequential lineup superiority effect. *Psychology, Public Policy, and Law, 17*, 99–139.

Stevens, K. (2002, May 7). Out of the kitchen, and other getaways. *New York Times*.

Strayer, D. L., Cooper, J. M., Turrill, J., Coleman, J., Medeiros-Ward, N., & Biondi, F. (2013). *Measuring driver distraction in the automobile*. Washington, DC: AAA Foundation for Traffic Safety.

Strayer, D. L., & Johnston, W. A. (2001). Driven to distraction: Dual-task studies of simulated driving and conversing on a cellular telephone. *Psychological Science, 12*, 462–466.

Stroop, J. R. (1935). Studies of interference in serial verbal reactions. *Journal of Experimental Psychology, 18*, 643–662.

Suddendorf, T., Addis, D. R., & Corballis, M. C. (2009). Mental time travel and the shaping of the human mind. *Philosophical Transactions of the Royal Society of London B, 364*, 1317–1324.

Suri, G., Sheppes, G., Schwartz, C., & Gross, J. J. (2013). Patient inertia and the status quo bias: When an inferior option is preferred. *Psychological Science, 24*, 1763–1769.

Svoboda, E., & Levine, B. (2009). The effects of rehearsal on the functional neuroanatomy of episodic autobiographical and semantic remembering: A functional magnetic resonance imaging study. *Journal of Neuroscience, 29*, 3073–3082.

Taber, C. S., & Lodge, M. (2006). Motivated skepticism in the evaluation of political beliefs. *American Journal of Political Science, 50*, 755–769.

Talarico, J. M. (2009). Freshman flashbulbs: Memories of unique and first-time events in starting college. *Memory, 17*, 256–265.

Talarico, J. M., & Rubin, D. C. (2003). Confidence, not consistency, characterizes flashbulb memories. *Psychological Science, 14*, 455–461.

Talarico, J. M., & Rubin, D. C. (2009). Flashbulb memories result from ordinary memory processes and extraordinary event characteristics. In O. Luminet & A. Curci (Eds.), *Flashbulb memories: New issues and new perspectives*. Philadelphia: Psychology Press.

Tanaka, J. W., & Taylor, M. (1991). Object categories and expertise: Is the basic level in the eye of the beholder? *Cognitive Psychology, 23*, 457–482.

Tanenhaus, M. K., Spivey-Knowlton, M. J., Beerhard, K. M., & Sedivy, J. C. (1995). Integration of visual and linguistic information in spoken language comprehension. *Science, 268*, 1632–1634.

Tarkan, L. (2003, April 29). Brain surgery, without knife or blood, gains favor. *New York Times*, p. F5.

Tatler, B. W., Hayhoe, M. M., Land, M. F., & Ballard, D. H. (2011). Eye guidance in natural vision: Reinterpreting salience. *Journal of Vision, 11*(5), 1–23.

Tenenbaum, J. B., Kemp, C., Griffiths, T. L., & Goodman, N. D. (2011). How to grow a mind: Statistics, structure, and abstraction. *Science, 331*, 1279–1285.

Tiggemann, M., & Kemps, E. (2005). The phenomenology of food cravings: The role of mental imagery. *Appetite, 45*, 305–313.

Titcomb, A. L., & Reyna, V. F. (1995). Memory interference and misinformation effects. In F. N. Dempster & C. J. Brainerd (Eds.), *Interference and inhibition in cognition* (pp. 263–294). San Diego, CA: Academic Press.

Tolman, E. C. (1938). The determinants of behavior at a choice point. *Psychological Review, 45*, 1–41.

Tolman, E. C. (1948). Cognitive maps in rats and men. *Psychological Review, 55*, 189–208.

Tooley, V., Bringham, J. C., Maass, A., & Bothwell, R. K. (1987). Facial recognition: Weapon effect and attentional focus. *Journal of Applied Social Psychology, 17*, 845–859.

Torralba, A., Oliva, A. Castelhano, M. S., & Henderson, J. M. (2006). Contextual guidance of eye movements and attention in real-world scenes: The role of global features in object search. *Psychological Review, 113*, 766–786.

Traxler, M. J. (2012). *Introduction to psycholinguistics*. Oxford, UK: Wiley-Blackwell.

Treadeau, K. (1997). *Mega memory*. New York: William Morrow.

Treisman, A. M. (1964). Selective attention in man. *British Medical Bulletin, 20*, 12–16.

Treisman, A. M. (1986). Features and objects in visual processing. *Scientific American. 225*, 114–125.

Treisman, A. M. (1988). Features and objects: The fourteenth Bartlett memorial lecture. *Quarterly Journal of Experimental Psychology, 40A*, 207–237.

Treisman, A. M. (1999). Solutions to the binding problem: Progress through controversy and convergence. *Neuron, 24*, 105–110.

Treisman, A. M. (2005, February 4). *Attention and binding*. Presentation to the Cognitive Science Group, University of Arizona.

Treisman, A. M., & Schmidt, H. (1982). Illusory conjunctions in the perception of objects. *Cognitive Psychology, 14*, 107–141.

Tsao, D. Y., Freiwald, W. A., Tootell, R. B., & Livingstone, M. S. (2006). A cortical region consisting entirely of face-selective cells. *Science, 311*, 670–674.

Tulving, E. (1972). Episodic and semantic memory. In E. Tulving & W. Donaldson (Eds.), *Organization of memory* (pp. 381–403). New York: Academic Press.

Tulving, E. (1985). How many memory systems are there? *American Psychologist, 40*, 385–398.

Tulving, E., & Markowitsch, H. J. (1998). Episodic and declarative memory: Role of the hippocampus. *Hippocampus, 8*, 198–204.

Tulving, E., & Pearlstone, Z. (1966). Availability versus accessibility of information in memory for words. *Journal of Verbal Learning and Verbal Behavior, 5*, 381–391.

Tversky, A., & Kahneman, D. (1973). Availability: A heuristic for judging frequency and probability. *Cognitive Psychology, 5*, 207–232.

Tversky, A., & Kahneman, D. (1974). Judgment under uncertainty: Heuristics and biases. *Science, 185*, 1124–1131.

Tversky, A., & Kahneman, D. (1981). The framing of decisions and the psychology of choice. *Science, 211*, 453–458.

Tversky, A., & Kahneman, D. (1983). Extensional versus intuitive reasoning: The conjunction fallacy in probability judgment. *Psychological Review, 90*, 293–315.

Tversky, A., & Kahneman, D. (1991). Loss aversion in riskless choice. *Quarterly Journal of Economics, 106*, 1039–1061.

Ungerleider, L. G., & Mishkin, M. (1982). Two cortical visual systems. In D. J. Ingle, M. A. Goodale, & R. J. Mansfield (Eds.), *Analysis of visual behavior* (pp. 549–580). Cambridge, MA: MIT Press.

Van den Broek, P. (1994). Comprehension and memory of narrative texts. In M. A. Gernsbacher (Ed.), *Handbook of psycholinguistics* (pp. 539–588). San Diego, CA: Academic Press.

van Dongen, E. V., Thielen, J.-W., Takashima, A., Barth, M., & Fernandez, G. (2012). Sleep supports selective retention of associative memories based on relevance for future utilization. *PLoS ONE, 7*, e43426.

Van Petten, C., & Luka, B. J. (2006). Neural localization of semantic context effects in electromagnetic and hemodynamic studies. *Brain and Language, 97*, 279–293.

Venema, V. (2013, December 3). Odon childbirth device: Car mechanic uncorks a revolution. *BBC News Magazine*.

Violanti, J. M. (1998). Cellular phones and fatal traffic collisions. *Accident Analysis and Prevention, 28*, 265–270.

Viskontas, I. V., Carr, V. A., Engel, S. A., & Knowlton, B. J. (2009). The neural correlates of recollection: Hippocampal activation declines as episodic memory fades. *Hippocampus, 19*, 265–272.

Vo, M. L. H., & Henderson, J. M. (2009). Does gravity matter? Effects of semantic and syntactic inconsistencies on the allocation of attention during scene perception. *Journal of Vision, 9*(3), 1–15.

Vogel, E. K., McCollough, A. W., & Machizawa, M. G. (2005). Neural measures reveal individual differences in controlling access to working memory. *Nature, 438*, 500–503.

Voss, J. F., Greene, T. R., Post, T., & Penner, B. C. (1983). Problem-solving skill in the social sciences. In G. Bower (Ed.), *The psychology of learning and motivation*. New York: Academic Press.

Wade, K. A., Garry, M., Read, J. D., & Lindsay, S. D. (2002). A picture is worth a thousand lies: Using false photographs to create false childhood memories. *Psychonomic Bulletin & Review, 9*, 597–603.

Wagenaar, W. A. (1986). My memory: A study of autobiographical memory over six years. *Cognitive Psychology, 18*, 225–252.

Waldrop, M. M. (1988). A landmark in speech recognition. *Science, 240*, 1615.

Ward, T. B., Smith, S. M., & Vaid, J. (Eds.). (1997). *Creative thought: An investigation of conceptual structures and processes*. Washington, DC: American Psychological Association.

Warren, R. M. (1970). Perceptual restoration of missing speech sounds. *Science, 167*, 392–393.

Warrington, E. K., & McCarthy, R. A. (1987). Categories of knowledge. *Brain, 110*, 1273–1296.

Warrington, E. K., & Shallice, T. (1984). Category specific semantic impairments. *Brain, 107*, 829–854.

Wason, P. C. (1960). On the failure to eliminate hypotheses in a conceptual task. *Quarterly Journal of Experimental Psychology, 12*, 129–140.

Wason, P. C. (1966). Reasoning. In B. Foss (Ed.), *New horizons in psychology* (pp. 135–151). Harmondsworth, UK: Penguin Books.

Waters, A., Hill, A., & Waller, G. (2001). Internal and external antecedents of binge eating episodes in a group of women with bulimia nervosa. *International Journal of Eating Disorders, 29,* 17–22.

Watson, J. B. (1913). Psychology as the behaviorist views it. *Psychological Review, 20,* 158–177.

Watson, J. B. (1928). *The ways of behaviorism.* New York: Harper and Brothers.

Watson, J. B., & Rayner, R. (1920). Conditioned emotional reactions. *Journal of Experimental Psychology, 3,* 1–14.

Wearing, D. (2005). *Forever today.* London: Doubleday.

Weingarten, H. P., & Elston, D. (1990). The phenomenology of food cravings. *Appetite, 15,* 231–246.

Weisberg, R. W. (1995). Prolegomena to theories of insight in problem solving: A taxonomy of problems. In R. J. Sternberg & J. E. Davidson (Eds.), *The nature of insight* (pp. 157–196). Cambridge, MA: MIT Press.

Weisberg, R. W. (2009). On "out-of-the-box" thinking in creativity. In A. B. Markman & K. L. Wood (Eds.), *Tools for innovation* (pp. 23–47). Oxford, UK: Oxford University Press.

Weisberg, R. W., & Alba, J. W. (1981). An examination of the alleged role of "fixation" in the solution of several "insight" problems. *Journal of Experimental Psychology: General, 110,* 169–192.

Weisberg, R. W., & Alba, J. W. (1982). Problem solving is not like perception: More on Gestalt theory. *Journal of Experimental Psychology: General, 111,* 326–330.

Weisenberg, M. (1977). Pain and pain control. *Psychological Bulletin, 84,* 1008–1044.

Weissenberg, M. (1999). Cognitive aspects of pain. In P. D. Wall & R. Melzak (Eds.), *Textbook of pain* (4th ed., pp. 345–358). New York: Churchill Livingstone.

Wells, G. L., & Bradfield, A. L. (1998). "Good, you identified the suspect": Feedback to eyewitnesses distorts their reports of the witnessing experience. *Journal of Applied Psychology, 83,* 360–376.

Wells, G. L., & Quinlivan, D. S. (2009). Suggestive eyewitness identification procedures and the Supreme Court's reliability test in light of eyewitness science: 30 years later. *Law and Human Behavior, 33,* 1–24.

Wernicke, C. (1874) *Der aphasische Symptomenkomplex.* Breslau: Cohn.

Wertheimer, M. (1912). Experimentelle Studien über das Sehen von Beuegung. *Zeitchrift für Psychologie, 61,* 161–265.

Westmacott, R., & Moscovitch, M. (2003). The contribution of autobiographical significance to semantic memory. *Memory & Cognition, 31,* 761–774.

Wheeler, M. E., Stuss, D. T., & Tulving, E. (1997). Toward a theory of episodic memory: The frontal lobes and autonoetic consciousness. *Psychological Bulletin, 121,* 331–354.

Whorf, B. J. (1956). The relation of habitual thought and behavior to language. In J. B. Carroll (Ed.), *Language, thought and reality: Essays by B. L. Whorf* (pp. 35–270). Cambridge, MA: MIT Press.

Wickelgren, W. A. (1965). Acoustic similarity and retroactive interference in short-term memory. *Journal of Verbal Learning and Verbal Behavior, 4,* 53–61.

Wickens, D. D., Dalezman, R. E., & Eggemeier, F. T. (1976). Multiple encoding of word attributes in memory. *Memory & Cognition, 4,* 307–310.

Wiech, K., Ploner, M., & Tracey, I. (2008). Neurocognitive aspects of pain perception. *Trends in Cognitive Sciences, 12,* 306–313.

Wilding, J., & Valentine, E. R. (1997). *Superior memory.* Hove, UK: Psychology Press.

Wilhelm, I., Diekelmann, S., Molzow, I., Ayoub, A., Molle, M., & Born, J. (2011). Sleep selectively enhances memory expected to be of future relevance. *Journal of Neuroscience, 31,* 1563–1569.

Wilkes-Gibbs, D., & Clark, H. H. (1992). Coordinating beliefs in conversation. *Journal of Memory and Language, 31,* 183–194.

Wilmer, J. B., Germine, L., Chabris, C. F., Chatterjee, G., Williams, M., Loken, E., et al. (2010). Human face recognition ability is specific and highly heritable. *Proceedings of the National Academy of Sciences, 107,* 5238–5241.

Wilson, T. D., & Gilbert, D. T. (2003). Affective forecasting. In L. Berkowitz (Ed.), *Advances in experimental social psychology* (Vol. 35, pp. 345–411). San Diego, CA: Academic Press.

Winawer, J., Witthoft, N., Frank, M. C., Wu, L., Wade, A. R., & Bordoditsky, L. (2007). Russian blues reveal effects of language on color discrimination. *Proceedings of the National Academy of Sciences, 104,* 7780–7785.

Wiseman, S., & Neisser, U. (1974). Perceptual organization as a determinant of visual recognition memory. *American Journal of Psychology, 87,* 675–681.

Wissman, K. T., Rawson, K. A., & Pyc, M. A. (2012). How and when do students use flashcards? *Memory, 20,* 568–579.

Wittgenstein, L. (1953). *Philosophical investigations* (G. E. M. Anscombe, Trans.). Oxford, UK: Blackwell.

Wood, N., & Cowan, N. (1995). The cocktail party phenomenon revisited: How frequent are attention shifts to one's name in an irrelevant auditory channel? *Journal of Experimental Psychology: Human Perception and Performance, 21,* 255–260.

Yamauchi, T., & Markman, A. B. (2000). Inference using categories. *Journal of Experimental Psychology: Learning, Memory, and Cognition, 26,* 776–795.

Yang, M.-H. (2009). Face detection. In S. Z. Li (Ed.), *Encyclopedia of biometrics* (p. 308). New York: Springer.

Yang, S., Bo, L., Wang, J., & Shapiro, L. (2012). *Unsupervised template learning for fine-grained object recognition.* Neural Information Processing Systems Conference.

Yuille, A., & Kersten, D. (2006). Vision as Bayesian inference: Analysis by synthesis. *Trends in Cognitive Sciences, 10,* 301–308.

Zhang, W., & Luck, S. J. (2009). Sudden death and gradual decay in visual working memory. *Psychological Science, 20,* 423–428.

Zhu, Q., Song, Y., Hu, S., Li, X., Tian, M., Zhen, Z., et al. (2010). Heritability of the specific cognitive ability of face perception. *Current Biology, 20,* 137–142.

Zwaan, R. A. (1999). Situation models: The mental leap into imagined worlds. *Current Directions in Psychological Science, 8,* 15–18.

Zwaan, R. A., Stanfield, R. A., & Yaxley, R. H. (2002). Language comprehenders mentally represent the shapes of objects. *Psychological Science, 13,* 168–171.

Name Index

Chklovskii, D. B., 194
Chomsky, N., 12, 299
Christensen, B. T., 354
Chun, M. M., 141
Clare, L., 169
Clarey, C., 276
Clark, C., 231
Clark, H. H., 300, 322
Coley, J. D., 255, 256
Collins, A. M., 256–2
Colloca, L., 62
Conrad, C., 259
Conrad, R., 135, 159
Conway, M. A., 210
Coons, P. M., 173
Cooper, G. G., 73
Coppola, D. M., 67, 72
Corkin, S., 160
Cosmides, L., 395–39
Cotton, R., 231–232
Cowan, N., 89, 129, 13
Cox, C., 246, 267
Cox, J. R., 394
Craik, F. I. M., 180, 18
Craver-Lemley, C., 28
Cree, G. S., 267
Crick, F., 360
Crook, T. H., 292
Cunitz, A. R., 156
Curci, A., 217
Curtis, C. E., 141, 145
Curtis-Holmes, J., 39

D

Dale, A. M., 39
Damon, M., 107, 172
Daneman, M., 16
Danzinger, S., 383
D'Argembeau, A., 16(
Darwin, C. J., 126
Datta, R., 112, 113
Davidoff, J., 327
Davis, G., 173
DeCaro, M. S., 17
Deese, J., 225
DeGroot, A., 355
Dell, G. S., 300
Della Sala, S., 137, 159
Del Pero, L., 55, 56

Koh, K., 351, 352
Kohler, W., 337
Körding, K. P., 71
Kornell, N., 202
Kosslyn, S. M., 278–279, 280, 281, 282,
    283, 285, 286, 287, 288, 291
Kotovsky, K., 342, 345
Kounios, J., 337
Krause, J. A., 146
Kreiman, G., 38, 284, 285
Kruglanski, A. W., 398
Kuhn, T., 357
Kulik, J., 213–214
Kuperberg, G. R., 321
Kutas, M., 314
Kyaga, S., 363

L

LaBar, K. S., 212
Lafay, L., 292
Lakoff, G., 341
Lamble, D., 103
Lambon Ralph, M., 265, 266, 267
Land, M. F., 98
Lanska, D. J., 39
LaPaglia, J. A., 236
Larkin, J. H., 355
Lavie, N., 91, 92, 100, 105
Lea, G., 279
Le Bihan, D., 285
Lee, D., 385
Lee, S.-H., 287
LePort, A. K. R., 226
Lerner, J. S., 382
Lesgold, A. M., 357
Levelt, W. J. M., 299, 309
Levin, D. T., 107
Levine, B., 163, 164, 197
Levy, I., 386
Li, F. F., 108
Lichtenstein, S., 372, 373
Limber, J. E., 202
Lindsay, D. S., 229, 239, 395
Lindsay, R. C. L., 236, 237
Lister, W. T., 39
Lockhart, R. S., 180
Lodge, M., 376
Loewenstein, R. J., 173
Loftus, E. F., 227, 228, 231
Lomber, S. G., 79

Lomo, T., 194
Lorayne, H., 292
Lord, C. G., 376
Lovatt, P., 136
Lovett, M. C., 336
Lowenstein, G., 385, 386
Lubart, T. I., 358
Lucas, J., 292
Luchins, A. S., 340, 341
Luck, S. J., 129, 130, 131, 132
Luka, B. J., 310
Luminet, O., 217
Luria, A. R., 225
Luus, C. A. E., 235
Luzzatti, C., 288, 289

M

Macdiarmid, J. I., 293
Mack, A., 105
MacKay, D. G., 91
Mahon, B. Z., 265, 266
Maier, N. R. F., 339, 340
Makco, K. A., 77
Malhotra, S., 79
Malpass, R. S., 236
Malt, B. C., 253
Mandel, H., 379
Maner, J. K., 381
Manktelow, K. I., 378, 396
Mantyla, T., 189
Marino, A. C., 99, 100
Markman, A. B., 246
Markowitsch, H. J., 163
Marsh, R., 221, 222
Martin, A., 41
Mast, F. W., 291
Mather, M., 213
McAuliffe, C., 214
McCarthy, J., 13
McCarthy, R. A., 267
McClelland, J. L., 257, 260, 261,
    263, 264
McDaniel, M. A., 186
McDermott, K. B., 223, 225
McGaugh, J. L., 212, 226
McKenzie, C. R. M., 376
McNeil, D. G., 358
McNeil, J. E., 40
McRae, K., 267

Meltzer, J., 278
Melzack, R., 61, 62
Memon, A., 237
Mervis, C. B., 250, 251, 252, 255
Metcalfe, J., 190, 337, 338
Metusalem, R., 320, 321
Metzler, J., 136–137, 138
Meyer, D. E., 258–259
Miller, G. A., 14, 129, 130, 300
Milner, A. D., 77–78
Milner, B., 160
Milstein, V., 173
Minda, J. P., 253
Mishkin, M., 76, 77
Misiak, H., 14
Mitchell, K. J., 220
Molaison, H., 160
Moore, A. M., 146
Moray, N., 87, 88, 89
Morley, N. J., 389
Morris, C. D., 191, 192
Moscovitch, M., 40, 165, 196
Mouchiroud, C., 358
Mullen, B., 361
Müller, G. E., 193
Mumford, M. D., 359
Murdock, B. B., Jr., 154, 155
Murphy, G. L., 259
Murphy, K. J., 77
Murray, D. J., 136

N

Nadel, L., 196
Nader, K., 193, 199, 200
Nairne, J. S., 185
Nash, R. A., 238, 239
Neisser, U., 14, 106, 203, 214, 217
Newell, A., 14, 341, 343, 345
Nichols, E. A., 161
Nicklaus, J., 276
Nobre, A. C., 141
Norman, D. A., 91
Noton, D., 97
Novick, J. M., 39, 309
Nyberg, L., 145, 163

O

O'Craven, K. M., 113, 114
Odón, J., 358, 359, 360

Oliva, A., 59
Olshausen, B. A., 37
Olson, A. C., 264
Oosterhof, N. N., 268
Orban, G. A., 67
Osborn, A. F., 360
Osherson, D. N., 281, 286
Osman, M., 398
Ost, J., 217
Osterhout, L., 309, 310
O'Toole, A. J., 55, 56
Over, D. E., 396

P

Paczynski, M., 321
Paivio, A., 277, 278
Palmer, S. E., 66, 69, 228
Parker, E. S., 226
Parkhi, O. M., 55
Parkhurst, D., 96, 97
Parkin, A. J., 40
Patterson, K., 270
Pauling, L., 360
Paulus, M. P., 381
Pavlov, I., 10
Payne, J. D., 198
Pearce, G., 173
Pearl, M., 220
Pearlstone, Z., 188
Pearson, J., 283
Perfect, T. J., 171
Perky, C. W., 283
Perrett, D. I., 35
Peters, E., 382
Peters, J., 104
Peterson, J. B., 363
Peterson, L. R., 127, 128
Peterson, M. J., 127, 128
Peterson, S. E., 203
Petrican, R., 166
Phelps, E. A., 212, 213, 217
Pickering, M. J., 322
Pickett, J. M., 302
Piguet, O., 167
Pillemer, D. B., 209, 210, 212
Pilzecker, A., 193
Pinker, S., 281
Pitt, B., 107

Plaut, D. C., 264
Pobric, G., 271
Pokorny, J., 62
Pollack, I., 302
Porter, S., 173
Posner, M. I., 98, 99, 100
Post, T., 380
Prentky, R., 363
Pulvermüller, F., 246, 269, 271
Pylyshyn, Z. W., 279–280, 281, 287, 290

Q

Quillian, M. R., 256–258
Quinlivan, D. S., 231, 232, 235
Quiroga, R. Q., 37, 38

R

Racicot, C. I., 77
Ramachandran, V. S., 67
Ramirez, G., 146
Ranganath, C., 161
Raphael, B., 342
Rathbone, C. J., 210
Ratner, N. B., 300
Rauchs, G., 198
Rayner, K., 305, 306
Rayner, R., 10
Read, L., 103
Reagan, R., 220
Reber, A. S., 378
Reddy, L., 38, 109
Redelmeier, D. A., 103, 382
Reder, L. M., 203
Reeves, A., 283
Reicher, G. M., 303
Reisberg, D., 291
Reitman, J., 357
Rensink, R. A., 107
Reyna, V. F., 229
Richards, R., 363
Richardson, A., 277
Rimmele, U., 216, 217
Rips, L. J., 259, 391
Ritchey, M., 213
Rizzolatti, G., 268
Robbins, J., 62
Roberson, D., 327
Robertson, L. C., 111, 112

Rocha-Miranda, C. E., 35
Rock, I., 66, 105
Roediger, H. L., 171, 186, 225
Rogers, T. B., 182
Rogers, T. T., 246, 257, 261, 263, 264, 267
Rogin, M. P., 220
Roland, D., 304
Rolls, E. T., 35
Romona, G., 231
Roozendaal, B., 212
Rosch, E. H., 249, 250, 251, 252, 254–255
Rose, N. S., 161
Rosenbaum, R. S., 162
Ross, D. F., 233, 234
Rothkopf, E. Z., 203
Rubin, D. C., 209, 210, 211, 215, 216, 217
Rumelhart, D. E., 260
Rundus, D., 154–155
Russell, W. A., 183

S

Sacchi, D. L. M., 239
Sachs, J., 158
Saffran, J. R., 302
Saletin, J. M., 198
Sandler, A., 174
Sanfey, A. G., 385, 386
Sapir, E., 327
Schacter, D. L., 167, 171, 292
Scheck, B., 231
Schenkein, J., 324
Schiller, D., 201
Schmidt, H., 110, 111
Schmidt, N. B., 381
Schmolck, H., 215
Schneider, W., 101–102
Scholl, B., 99, 100
Schooler, L. J., 226
Schrauf, R. W., 210, 211
Schul, Y., 398
Schunn, C. D., 354
Schvaneveldt, R. W., 258–259
Schwartz, B. J., 357
Schwarzenegger, A., 173
Schweickert, R., 136
Scoville, W. B., 160
Segal, S. J., 283
Seidenberg, M. S., 264

Subject Index

A

Action
  courses of, 378
  perception and, 74–79
Action pathway, 78
Action potentials, 31–32
Advertisements, 171
Algebra problems, 338
Ambiguity
  in sentence comprehension, 91
  lexical, 305–307, 312, 316
  of image on the retina, 57–59, 63, 70
  temporary, 311
Ambiguity effect, 316
Ambiguous figure, 291
Amnesia
  anterograde, 195
  graded, 195
  implicit memory and, 168–169, 170
  retrograde, 195
Amygdala
  emotion and, 201, 212
  imagery and, 284
  memory and, 142, 160
  pain and, 19
Analogical encoding, 353–354
Analogical paradox, 354
Analogical problem solving, 348–355
  analogical encoding and, 353–354
  creative thinking and, 358
  in vivo research on, 354–355
  radiation problem and, 349–353
  transfer process in, 349
Analogical transfer, 349
Analogies, 348, 349
Analysis of problems, 357
Analytic introspection, 7
Anaphoric inference, 318
Animal communication, 298
Anisomycin, 199, 200
Anterior temporal lobe (ATL)
  hub and spoke model and, 270–271
  savant syndrome and, 364

Anterograde amnesia, 195
Apparent movement, 64
Articulatory rehearsal process, 134
Articulatory suppression, 136, 137
Artificial intelligence, 13–14
Association techniques, 202
Attention, 84–117
  attenuation model of, 90
  automatic processing and, 102
  binding problem and, 109
  brain activity related to, 112–114
  central executive and, 138–139
  cognitive factors and, 96–97
  coherence related to, 109–112
  covert, 94, 98–100
  definitions of, 86, 87
  distracted, 87
  divided, 87, 100–104
  early selection models of, 89–91
  eye movements and, 94, 95–98
  eyewitness testimony and, 232
  feature integration theory and, 109–112
  filter model of, 13, 87–89
  inattentional blindness and, 105–106
  late selection models of, 91
  load theory of, 92–94
  location-based, 98–99
  misinformation effect and, 236
  object-based, 100
  overt, 94, 95–98
  pain perception and, 61–62, 74
  perceptual load and, 91–92
  processing capacity and, 91–93
  research on the mind and, 13
  selective, 87
  task demands related to, 97–98
  visual perception and, 105–109
  William James quotation on, 8
  working memory and, 135, 138–141
Attentional capture, 87, 96
Attenuation model of attention, 90
Attenuator, 90
Auditory coding, 157, 159
Auditory imagery, 276, 293–294

Auditory stimuli
  coding of, 157, 159
  echoic memory of, 126
Autobiographical memory (AM), 164, 208–211
  definition of, 164, 208
  highly superior, 226
  life events and, 209–211
  multidimensional nature of, 208–209
Automatic processing, 102
Availability heuristic, 371–373, 377
Axons, 29–32, 35
  connectionism and, 260
  consolidation and, 193

B

Back propagation, 262
Balanced dominance, 305
Balint's syndrome, 111
Base rates, 374, 377
Basic level of categories, 254
Basis of Sensation, The (Adrian), 32
Bayesian inference, 70–71
Behaviorism, 9
  Skinner's operant conditioning and, 10
  Tolman's cognitive maps and, 11–12
  Watson's founding of, 9–10
Belief bias, 388–389, 397
Bias
  belief, 388–389, 397
  confirmation, 376
  lexical ambiguity and, 305–307
  memory and, 222
  myside, 376
  status quo, 383
Biased dominance, 305
Binding, 109, 111–112
Binding problem, 109
Blindness
  change, 107
  inattentional, 105–106
Bottleneck model, 89
Bottom-up processing, 59
  attention and, 96, 111

object perception and, 71

pain perception and, 61

visual perception and, 290

Bourne Identity, The (film), 172–173

Brain

attention and, 112–114

color processing in, 328–329

concepts represented in, 264–270

connectionist networks and, 264

consolidation of memories in, 193–201

decision making and, 385–386

distributed representation across, 44–45

early studies of, 28–29

experience-dependent plasticity of, 73–74

feature detectors in, 34

geography of, 46

imagery neurons in, 284–285

language processing in, 299, 308–310, 320

localization of function in, 39–41, 42–44

memory represented in, 160–161

microstructure of, 28–30

representation in, 33–38

syntax and semantics in, 308–310

visual imagery and, 284–291

working memory and, 138–139, 141–145

See also Mind; Neurons; Physiology

Brain ablation, 76

Brain damage

attention control and, 138–139

categorization and, 267

double dissociations and, 40

imagery problems and, 287–290

knowledge of concepts and, 270

language problems and, 308–309

localization demonstrated by, 39–40

memory impairment and, 47, 160, 162–163, 167, 209

savant syndrome and, 364

working memory and, 138–139, 142–143

Brain imaging, 41–45

attention and, 112–114

concept representation and, 269

embodied approach to categories and, 269

emotions and, 212

evidence for localization of function, 42–44

experience-dependent plasticity and, 73–74

fMRI method of, 41–42

memory and, 161, 163, 164, 167, 196, 209, 210

neural mind reading and, 145

visual imagery and, 285–287

working memory and, 144–145

Brainstorming, 360–362

Broca's aphasia, 308–309

Broca's area, 39, 308

C

Candle problem, 339

Categorical syllogisms, 387–391

Categories, 246

Categorization, 246, 247–259

brain representation of, 265–266

connectionist approach to, 260–264

definitional approach to, 247–249

embodied approach to, 268–269

exemplar approach to, 253

hierarchical organization and, 254

knowledge and, 255–256

levels related to, 254–256

multiple-factor approach to, 266–267

prototype approach to, 249–253

semantic category approach to, 265

semantic networks and, 256–259

sensory-functional hypothesis and, 265

usefulness of, 246

See also Concepts

Category-specific memory impairment, 265

Causal inference, 318

Cell body, 29

Cell phone use, and driving, 103–104, 109, 226

Central executive, 135, 138–139

Central vision, 96

Cerebral cortex, 39

Chain problem, 338

Challenger study, 214–215

Change blindness, 107

Change detection

attention and, 106–107

short-term memory and, 129–130

working memory and, 138–141

Cheating, and reasoning, 395

Choice reaction time, 6

Choking under pressure, 16–17, 146

Chunk, 130

Chunking, 130–131, 138, 203

Circle problem, 337

Circular reasoning, 181

Classical conditioning, 10, 172, 199–200

Cocktail party effect, 88

Coding, 157

auditory, 157, 159

long-term memory, 157, 158–160

semantic, 157–159

short-term memory, 157–158, 159–160

specificity, 35–36

visual, 157, 159

See also Encoding

Cognition

creative, 361–362

definition of, 5

evolutionary perspective on, 395–396

Cognitive economy, 257–258, 259

Cognitive hypothesis for reminiscence bump, 211

Cognitive interviews, 237

Cognitive maps, 11–12

Cognitive neuroscience, 25–48

Cognitive psychology

computers and, 12–13

definition of, 4

early work in, 5–9

first modern textbook on, 14

modern research in, 15–17

origin of term, 14

rebirth of, 12–15

role of models in, 17–20

timeline for development of, 15

Cognitive Psychology (Neisser), 14

Cognitive revolution, 12, 14, 277–278

Coherence, 318

Color perception, 326–329

Common ground, 323, 326

Computers

cognitive psychology and, 12–13

connectionist networks on, 260–264

flow diagrams for, 12–13

logic theorist program for, 14, 341

perception represented by, 57–59

semantic networks on, 256–259

vision systems based on, 55–57

Concepts

connectionist approach to, 260–264

definition of, 246

represented in the brain, 264–270

semantic networks and, 256–259

See also Categorization

Conceptual knowledge, 246

Conceptual peg hypothesis, 278

definition of, 298

development of, 12

effect of brain damage on, 308–309

event-related potential and, 309

knowledge and, 300

localization of function for, 39

predictions based on knowledge of, 315–316

sentences in, 308–317

speech segmentation and, 61, 302

study of, 299–300

text/story comprehension and, 317–321

universality of, 298–299

words in, 300–307

Language summary tables

perceiving phonemes, words, and letters, 303

understanding words, 306

understanding sentences, 316

understanding text and stories, 321

conversations, 326

Large numbers, law of, 375, 377

Late closure, principle of, 311

Latent inhibition (LI), 363, 364

Late selection models of attention, 91

Law of large numbers, 375, 377

Law of pragnanz, 65–66

"Leaky filter" model, 90

Learning

generalization of, 264

illusions of, 203

paired-associate, 181–182, 277–278

state-dependent, 190–191

study techniques and, 202–203

Letters, perception of, 303. *See also* Words

Levels of analysis, 27

Levels of categories, 254–256

Levels of processing theory, 180–181

Lexical ambiguity, 305–307

Lexical decision task, 259, 304

Lexical dominance, 305–307

Lexicon, 300

Lightbulb problem, 352–353

Light-from-above assumption, 67

Likelihood of the outcome, 70–71

Likelihood principle, 63, 67

Lineup procedures, 236–237

Listening, dichotic, 88

"Little Albert" experiment, 10

Load theory of attention, 92–94

Localization of function, 39–41

binding and, 109

brain imaging evidence for, 42–44

for categories, 43–44

of concepts, 264–265, 269

for face perception, 40, 42

neuropsychology demonstrating, 39–40

for places and bodies, 42–43

recording from neurons demonstrating, 40–41

for senses, 35, 39–40

for speech, 39, 308–309

Location-based attention, 98–99

Logical reasoning, 387

Logic theorist computer program, 14, 341

Long Kiss Goodnight, The (film), 173

Long-term memory (LTM), 19, 120, 121, 150–205

amnesia and, 168–169, 170

brain imaging and, 161

coding in, 157, 158–160

consolidation of, 193–201

definition of, 152

emotion linked to, 212–213

encoding process for, 180–187

episodic, 162–166

explicit, 168

future imagining and, 166–167

getting information into, 180–187

impairments of, 160, 168–169, 170, 195

implicit, 168–172

neuropsychology of, 160–161

procedural, 168–170

reconsolidation of, 198–201

retrieving information from, 180, 187–192

semantic, 162–166

serial position curve and, 154–156

short-term memory vs., 152–161

study methods and, 202–203

time passage and, 165–166

types of, 19–20, 164

working memory and, 141

Long-term potentiation (LTP), 194

Low-load tasks, 92

Low working memory capacity, 16–17

M

"Magical Number Seven, Plus or Minus Two, The" (Miller), 14

Magnetic resonance imaging (MRI), 41

Maintenance rehearsal, 180

Mapping analogical relationships, 351

Math performance, 146–147

Meaning

attention and, 89–91, 96–97

chunking and, 130–131

encoding based on, 191–192

language and, 300–321

lexical ambiguity and, 305–307

memory and, 141, 153, 157–159, 180–184, 191–192, 202–203

perception and, 59–62, 68–70

problem solving and, 355

semantics and, 312

speech segmentation and, 302

visual world paradigm and, 312–314

Meaning dominance, 305

Means–end analysis, 343

Media coverage of events, 217

Medial temporal lobe (MTL), 209

Memento (film), 173

Memory

amnesia and, 168–169, 170

autobiographical, 164, 208–211

brain damage and, 47, 160, 162–163, 167

brain imaging and, 161, 163, 164, 167, 209, 210

consolidation of, 193–201

constructive nature of, 218–227

definitions of, 120

Ebbinghaus's experiments on, 7–8

emotion linked to, 212–213

encoding process for, 180–187

episodic, 19, 46–47, 120

explicit, 168

extraordinary, 225–226

eyewitness testimony and, 231–238

false, 225, 230–231, 238–239

flashbulb, 213–217

future imagining and, 166–167

iconic and echoic, 126

impairments of, 47, 160, 162–163, 167, 168–169, 170, 195

implicit, 168–172

improving using imagery, 291–292

inferences and, 222–223

knowledge related to, 224

long-term, 19, 120, 121, 150–205

modal model of, 121–122, 123

perception and, 79–80

procedural, 20, 120, 168–170

process model of, 19–20

recognition, 158–159

reconsolidation of, 198–201

retrieving information from, 180, 187–192

Parallel distributed processing (PDP) models, 260
Parietal lobe, 40, 77, 78
Parsing, 310–316
  interactionist approach to, 312–316
  syntax-first approach to, 311–312
Partial report method, 125
Pegword technique, 292
Perception, 50–83
  action and, 74–79
  ambiguous objects and, 57
  attention and, 105–109
  Bayesian inference and, 70–71
  blurred objects and, 58
  bottom-up processing in, 59
  characteristics of, 52–53
  of colors, 326–329
  computers and, 55–59
  definition of, 52
  experience-dependent plasticity and, 73–74
  eyewitness testimony and, 232
  feature integration theory and, 109–112
  Gestalt approach to, 64–67, 71–72
  hidden objects and, 57–58
  of horizontals/verticals, 72–73
  imagery and, 278–291
  information for, 59–62
  language and, 326–329
  of letters in words, 303
  memory and, 79–80
  movement as facilitator of, 74–75
  nature of, 52–57
  neural representation and, 33–38
  object, 59–60, 63–72
  organization of elements in, 64–67
  pain, 19, 45–46, 61–62
  physiology of, 28, 59, 72–74, 76
  regularities in the environment and, 67–70, 72–73
  of scenes, 53–57
  of size and distance, 282–283, 288
  speech segmentation and, 61, 302
  top-down processing in, 59–62
  unconscious inference and, 63–64
  viewpoint invariance and, 58–59
  of words, 300–303
Perception pathway, 78
Perceptual load, 91–92
Perceptual organization, 64–67
Peripheral stimulus, 108
Peripheral task, 109

Peripheral vision, 96
Permission rules, 396
Permission schema, 394–395
Perseveration, 138–139
Persistence of vision, 123–124
Personal semantic memories, 164
Phonemes, 301
Phonemic restoration effect, 301, 303
Phonological loop, 134, 135–136, 293
Phonological similarity effect, 135
Phonological store, 134
Photographs
  flashbulb memories vs., 214–215
  own-photos vs. lab-photos, 209
  See also Pictures and memory
Physical regularities, 67–68, 72–73
Physiological approach to coding, 157
Physiology
  of the brain, 28–46
  of cognition, 27–28
  of imagery, 284–291
  of memory, 45, 194
  of perception, 28, 59, 72–74, 76
  See also Brain
Pictures and memory, 238–239
Placebo, 61–62
Placebo effect, 62
Population coding, 36, 37
Post-identification feedback effect, 235
Posttraumatic stress disorder (PTSD), 201
Pragmatic inference, 223
Pragnanz, law of, 65–66
Preattentive stage, 109–110
Precueing procedure, 98–100
Predictions
  based on neural responding, 287
  of behavior, 9
  emotion-related, 381–382
  environmental knowledge and, 314–315
  inductive reasoning and, 371
  language knowledge and, 304, 314–316
  neural mind reading and, 145
  situational knowledge and, 320–321
Prefrontal cortex (PFC)
  decision making and, 381, 386
  working memory and, 142–144
Preinventive forms, 361, 362
Premises, 387
Premotor cortex, 268
Primacy effect, 154–156
Primary receiving areas, 40

Priming, 170–171
  prototypicality and, 251–252
  repetition, 170
  syntactic, 324–326
Principle of good continuation, 65
Principle of good figure, 65–66
Principle of late closure, 311
Principle of neural representation, 33
Principle of similarity, 66
Principle of simplicity, 65–66
Principles of perceptual organization, 64–67
Principles of Psychology (James), 8
Prior probability, 70–71
Proactive interference
  release from, 158
  short-term memory and, 128–129, 157–158
Probability, prior, 70–71
Problems
  definition of, 336
  representing in the mind, 336–337
Problem solving, 334–367
  analogical, 348–355
  creative, 357–362
  expertise in, 355–357
  fixations and, 338–340, 362
  Gestalt approach to, 336–341
  idea generation and, 360–362
  insight and, 337–338
  knowledge and, 355–357
  mental sets and, 340–341
  modern research on, 341–348
  Newell and Simon's approach to, 341–345
  obstacles to, 338–341
  open mindedness and, 364
  problem statement and, 345–348
  process involved in, 359
  restructuring and, 337, 338
  solutions to sample problems, 367
  think-aloud protocol for, 347–348
Problem space, 343, 344
Procedural memory, 20, 120, 168–170
Processing capacity, 91–93
Process models, 19–20
Propaganda effect, 171
Propositional mechanisms, 279
Propositional representations, 280–281
Propranolol, 201
Prosopagnosia, 40
Prototype, 249
Prototype approach to categorization, 249–253